canadian edition

better
business

Michael R. Solomon
Contributing Editor

Mary Anne Poatsy

Kendall Martin

Kerri Shields
Centennial College

PEARSON

Toronto

Vice-President, Editorial Director: Gary Bennett
Editor-in-Chief: Nicole Lukach
Acquisitions Editor: Nick Durie
Marketing Manager: Leigh-Anne Graham
Developmental Editor: John Lewis
Project Manager: Richard di Santo
Manufacturing Manager: Susan Johnson
Production Editor: Rajni Pisharody, Cenveo Publisher Services
Copy Editor: Heather Sangster
Compositor: Cenveo Publisher Services
Permissions Researcher: Cheryl Freedman
Art Director: Julia Hall
Interior and Cover Designer: Miriam Blier
Cover Image: Gettyimages

10 9 8 7 6 5 4 3 2 1   CKV

Library and Archives Canada Cataloguing in Publication

Better business / Michael R. Solomon . . . [et al.]. — Canadian ed.

Includes index.
ISBN 978-0-13-272419-7

1. Industrial management. 2. Business. 3. Entrepreneurship. 4. Commerce. I. Solomon, Michael R.

HD31.B467 2012   658   C2011-907250-5

ISBN 978-0-13-272419-7

Brief Contents

Contents

How can you use *Better Business* as an effective learning tool?

Read Actively

Do you ever find that you need to reread a text many times before you fully understand it? Do you ever have trouble remembering what you read?

As a student, you are expected to read regularly. As an employee, reading to develop your skills and knowledge will likely be an important part of your job. Before you begin reading anything, you should determine your reading objective—what is it you want to gain from reading? When you read a newspaper or magazine, for example, you might simply skim over the material to discover the main points. But when you read a textbook, you must read carefully (that is, read every word), make notes, and question what you are reading.

You can use the SQ3R technique to improve your understanding of a text:[1]

- Survey (or skim),
- Question (ask yourself questions about what you are reading),
- Read,
- Recall (identify major points and answer questions from Q), and
- Review (review all sections).

When you are reading for a course, you need to make sure you're actively involved in the text. Active readers predict, make inferences, and draw conclusions; they ask questions while they read and stop often to check for understanding. Fortunately, *Better Business* provides in-text questions throughout every chapter, giving you built-in cues to make your study active, promote deeper thought, and engage your critical thinking skills. For example, instead of simply listing the tasks that managers perform, *Better Business* asks you, "What tasks do managers perform?" and gives you the information to answer that question.

If you think that active reading will take too much time, think again. Active reading saves time because it improves reading comprehension and retention—it helps you to understand and remember what you've read, meaning you won't have to reread material again and again. Reading actively takes only a little effort, but it produces big results.

Better Business strives to engage you in the material, pique your interest, drive your curiosity, and promote active reading. Active reading assists you in doing what you came to university or college to learn how to do—think deeply about issues of importance in our society. Ultimately, the process of active reading helps you to understand and retain what you read and assists you in mastering academic reading. This mastery leads to a successful educational experience and will also serve you well in your future profession.

Use the Learning Style that Works Best for You

Better Business provides you with multiple ways to learn. Each of us has a preferred learning "style"; some like to *watch* and learn (visual), others like to *do* and learn (kinesthetic), and still others like to *listen* and learn (auditory). So, while simply reading a textbook is a good start to learning, most of us will remember more and remember longer by learning in multiple ways. For auditory, visual, and kinesthetic learners, the MyBusinessLab online learning system is packed with videos, flashcards, audio chapter summaries, business case simulations, and much more.

You have likely completed a learning styles inventory in the past, but if you haven't, it would be beneficial for you to complete the "Multiple Pathways to Learning" activity on MyBusinessLab, which will help you to determine your preferred learning style. Knowing your learning style will help you compensate for your weaknesses and capitalize on your strengths. With the question-driven learning strategy implemented in the textbook and the wealth of learning resources at your disposal in MyBusinessLab, you will be well on your way to academic and career success.

What makes *Better Business* an effective teaching resource?

Question-Driven Learning

We all use questions to learn and to gain a better understanding of the knowledge that we need in our careers, our studies, and our lives. The importance of question-driven learning cannot be understated; the brain creates pathways to information in response to questions. Strong questions motivate and encourage students to achieve deeper understanding of any topic. *Better Business* applies the principles of question-driven learning by using in-text questions as the driving force for acquiring knowledge. The interactive writing style of this book makes it an easy-to-read, engaging text for students.

Multiple Levels of Thinking

Better Business reflects Benjamin Bloom's question-based philosophy by providing a suite of Discussion Questions, Application Exercises, and Critical Thinking Questions that may be used to teach and test not only students' knowledge, comprehension, and application of specific concepts, but also their higher level thinking skills (analysis, synthesis, and evaluation). Bloom's classification of educational objectives, popularly known as *Bloom's Taxonomy*, can help educators to better assess student learning and thinking skills. In the absence of such a classification system, educators may inadvertently emphasize memorization of facts instead of other (likely more important) learned capabilities. Questions in the Instructor's Manual and the electronic test bank are associated with specific levels of *Bloom's Taxonomy*. Instructors can select questions from *Better Business* and its online resources that reflect and reinforce each lesson plan's objective.

Multiple Modalities of Learning

Studies have shown that learning is more effective when it is multimodal. For example, using visuals alongside verbal or textual learning can yield significant benefits for the learner. A Metiri Group research study on multimodal learning recommended that instructors create multimodal and interactive or collaborative lessons in order to engage students' thinking in a variety of ways, using whatever media is best suited to the student and the material.[2] *Better Business* follows this approach with the inclusion of MyBusinessLab, Pearson's revolutionary online learning system. It gives professors and students easy access to a variety of media and activities that get students interacting with business and not just reading about it.

PEDAGOGICAL FEATURES

How do the *Better Business* chapters enhance teaching and learning?

Each chapter is packed with real, relevant, and timely examples that reinforce key concepts. A wealth of chapter-opening, in-chapter, and end-of-chapter features help students learn, link, and apply major concepts:

Opening Discussions   Each chapter begins with an engaging Opening Discussion that sets the stage for the chapter. These brief introductory case studies discuss real-world organizations and countries, introducing students to critical issues and business concepts. They include questions to inspire class discussion, prompt thinking, and generate interest in the chapter content.

CHAPTER

5

Entrepreneurship, Small Business, and New Venture Creation

LEARNING OBJECTIVES

After studying this chapter, you should be able to:

1. List the traits of an effective entrepreneur, and describe how these characteristics often lead to business success. (pp. 122–127)
2. Summarize the role of small business within the Canadian economy. (pp. 127–129)
3. Explain why a business plan is crucial to small business success, and describe the factors that lead to small business failure. (pp. 129–131)
4. Describe how resources—including government, banks, associations, business incubators, and advisory boards—provide assistance and guidance to small business owners. (pp. 131–133)
5. Summarize the potential benefits and drawbacks of each major source of small business financing. (pp. 133–134)
6. Outline the advantages and disadvantages of franchising within the context of entrepreneurship. (pp. 134–138)
7. List and explain the advantages and disadvantages of a sole proprietorship. (pp. 138–140)
8. Describe the advantages and disadvantages of a partnership and a partnership agreement. (pp. 140–142)
9. Explain how a corporation is formed, and how it compares with sole proprietorships and partnerships. (pp. 142–143)
10. Describe the characteristics of non-profit corporations and co-operatives. (pp. 143–145)
11. Summarize the different types of mergers and acquisitions and explain why they occur. (pp. 145–146)

OPENING DISCUSSION: STARTING A NEW BUSINESS

The WhyHire.me Innovation

As Facebook, LinkedIn, Twitter, and myriad other online social media become increasingly prevalent, more employers are scrutinizing these networking sites to screen potential employees. In a 2009 CareerBuilder survey, 45 percent of the 2,600 employers surveyed reported that they research job candidates through social media, which was a huge increase from the 22 percent reported in 2008.[1] Because of content found on social networking sites, 35 percent of employers reported that they chose *not to hire* candidates while 18 percent chose *to hire* candidates. Obviously, it is becoming imperative for job seekers to ensure their online image is not diminishing their job opportunities.

While teaching career positioning to a marketing class in 2008, Patti Church realized that students needed to start thinking about this topic sooner than later. At the same time, Andy Church and Robert Saric were discussing the value of having an established online personal brand when looking for employment

after noticing the tremendous positive impact it had on their own job search efforts. Patti brought to Robert's and Andy's attention the point that many university and college students did not realize how transparent they are on the Web. The three entrepreneurs formed a legal partnership and set out to develop a social media tool that would not only educate students about professional personal branding but also provide a venue whereby students could safely build an online career portfolio to showcase their skills, abilities, and knowledge; establish a positive online reputation; and proactively position themselves to get hired! It was time to start using digital tools for a digital generation.

Their efforts resulted in WhyHire.me, a career success platform where students can create a professional and unique online brand presence.[2] As head of curriculum design, Patti leads the development of learning materials and overall student learning experience. With his considerable experience in education technology 2.0, stakeholder management, and growing global

(continued)

On Target Boxes, Off the Mark Boxes, and Top 10 Lists Each chapter includes either an On Target or Off the Mark box. These boxed features illustrate positive and negative outcomes of business ventures related to chapter material. They are accompanied by questions to inspire classroom discussions and further understanding of the topics. These features, along with various Top 10 lists, help fuel in-class dialogue.

top10

World's Most Valuable Brands (2011)

Rank	Brand	Brand Value (US$mil)
1.	Apple	153,285
2.	Google	111,498
3.	IBM	100,849
4.	McDonald's	81,016
5.	Microsoft	78,243
6.	Coca-Cola	73,752
7.	AT&T	69,916
8.	Marlboro	67,522
9.	China Mobile	57,326
10.	GE (General Electric)	50,318

Source: MaryLou Costa, "The Most Valuable Brands in the World," *MarketingWeek* (online), May 12, 2011, http://www.marketingweek.co.uk/the-most-valuable-brands-in-the-

On **Target**

World Record for Kinect

The Microsoft Kinect device for the Xbox 360 made the 2011 Guinness World Records as the fastest-selling consumer electronics device. The controller-free gaming hardware sold an average of 133,333 units a day, for a total of eight million units in its first sixty days on the shelves. The sales figures beat both the iPhone and the iPad for the equivalent periods after launch.[8]

Microsoft developed the Kinect concept after the Nintendo Wii proved that gaming segments beyond the traditional young male do exist. Nintendo had released exercise programs and family games for which players used hand-held controllers to send body movement signals back to the processor to be emulated onscreen. Microsoft advanced the Wii idea by eliminating the controller altogether. Few companies would have the research depth to build something like Kinect. Researchers from a range of fields, including depth sensing, machine learning, speech recognition, gestural interface, computer vision, identity recognition, sound processing, and parallel computing, put their heads together to create Kinect.[9]

Discussion Questions

1. Using the PEST model for analysis (see Chapter 1), how might changes in the external business environment affect Kinect sales? Give an example.
2. What type of research would Microsoft have done before introducing Kinect regarding competitors and consumers? How might the research results affect Microsoft's development of the Kinect product?
3. Motion sensors and voice recognition have been available for several years in many devices we

Off the **Mark**

How Does China's Internet Censorship Affect Global Business?

While many parts of the world, notably the Middle East, are undergoing dramatic political and social changes because of Internet access, China has become more restrictive with what its net-izens are allowed to access.[26] Google and other tech companies have had difficulty doing business in China due to government censorship and regulations. Beijing's extensive censorship of online content—often called the "Great Firewall of China"—systematically removes material it deems harmful, including politically sensitive information, pornography, and violence.[27] As of 2011, Facebook, the world's largest online social media network, which had been blocked in China since 2009, was looking for ways to work within Chinese laws and with China's leading search engine and web conglomerate, Baidu. Meanwhile, Google declared war on censorship and decided not to censor its web searches in China any longer, so China started closing the doors on Google services, banning or highly restricting various services from the country. Microsoft, on the other hand, continued to comply with local regulations, including the censorship of some political material.

Some people are pushing the U.S. government to make Internet censorship a trade issue. The argument, which Google has made in congressional testimony, is that digital barriers to the free flow of information are equivalent to traditional trade barriers, which are illegal under World Trade Organization (WTO) rules. Google spokesperson Niki Fenwick says censorship is first a human right issue, then adds, "When a government blocks the Internet, it is the equivalent of a customs official stopping goods at the border."[29]

Under order of Pakistan's high court in 2010, the Pakistan Telecommunication Authority started to observe Google, MSN, YouTube, Yahoo, Hotmail, and other websites for any infringement of Muslim sentiments.[30] If the trend to block Internet access continues, what will happen to human rights and global trade? Where are we headed?

Discussion Questions

1. How do you feel about censorship? Is it a violation of human rights or does it protect citizens, government, or society? Do you think the Chinese government will be pressured into providing open Internet access for its citizens? Why or why not?
2. Do you think the Chinese government's censor-

BizChat Boxes *BizChat boxes* include questions that can spark thoughtful in-class discussions or virtual discussions via MyBusinessLab. BizChat boxes explore "hot topics" in business to help connect the chapter material to what's happening in business today.

BizChat

What Is Recruiting 2.0?

You're probably familiar with social networking sites such as Myspace and Facebook. The same concept is applied to the professional community through sites such as LinkedIn (www.linkedin.com), ZoomInfo (www.zoominfo.com), and Spoke (www.spoke.com). LinkedIn is an online network of more than 135 million experienced professionals worldwide whose connections are made through college and university, graduate school, or professional affiliations.[8] Most people would like to hire or work with someone they know, and LinkedIn can provide helpful colleague and customer recommendations. Additionally, LinkedIn may assist job seekers by providing insiders' information on companies and employees. If you've scheduled an interview, you might find a LinkedIn page for the person with whom you are meeting. This can give you some information on that person's professional background, including where he or she went to school, as well as information on hobbies. Knowing these details may provide for good conversation starters during the interview.

Discussion Questions

1. Do you think it is appropriate for an employer to view your Facebook page before an interview or before they hire you? Why or why not? If an employer viewed your Facebook page, do you think it would affect their decision to hire you? Why or why not?
2. Have you established an online "professional" image using a professional networking tool such as LinkedIn? If you don't have an online image now, do you think you should create one? What will it say about you? What can you do to ensure your online image is portraying you in a positive way to potential employers?
3. Some people say they don't care what others think of them. Should you care about what others think of your online image? Why or why not?

CHAPTER

13

Financial Management and Accounting

LEARNING OBJECTIVES

After studying this chapter, you should be able to:

1. Summarize the implications of financial management and how financial managers fulfill their responsibilities. (p. 369)

2. Describe how financial managers plan for financial needs. (pp. 369–372)

3. Describe the different options available for companies to finance their short-term business needs, including friends and family, credit cards, commercial banks and finance companies, trade credit, promissory note, factoring, and commercial paper. (pp. 372–375)

4. Summarize the pros and cons of debt and equity financing. (p. 375)

5. Outline the differences between each of the following types of

Learning Objectives, Key Terms, and Chapter Synopsis Tied directly to the synopsis at the end of the chapter and to the MyTest questions, each chapter's Learning Objectives preview the main points students should know after studying the chapter. Throughout the chapter, Key Terms are defined in marginal notes. At the end of each chapter, the Chapter Synopsis reminds students of the chapter's Learning Objectives and summarizes the main concepts discussed within the chapter.

CHAPTER SYNOPSIS

1. Summarize how marketing has evolved over the production concept era, sales concept era, marketing concept era, and customer relationship era. (pp. 300–302)

During the production concept era (from the Industrial Revolution until the 1920s), most companies focused solely on production. Demand was often greater than supply, and the prevailing mindset was that a good-quality product would simply sell itself.

During the sales concept era (from the mid-1920s through the early 1950s), technological advances meant that production increased more sharply than demand for goods and services. The use of heavy public advertising in all available forms of media

targeted customers. This blend is constrained by forces outside the firm's control that are found within the broader market environment.

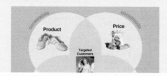

Primary data are raw data collected by the researcher. The data are frequently collected through observation, questionnaires, surveys (via mail, e-mail, or telephone), focus groups, interviews, customer feedback, samples, and controlled experiments.

A **focus group** is typically a group of eight to ten potential customers who are asked for feedback on a good or service, advertisement, idea, or packaging.

Secondary data are data that have already been collected and processed. An example of secondary data is census data.

Better Business, Better World Vignettes In Chapters 1 to 3 and 7 to 11, the Better Business, Better World vignettes illustrate how businesses are engaging in the solutions to sustainable development challenges, global citizenship and equity, and social responsibility. The vignettes contain discussion questions to enhance students' understanding of the topic and help initiate classroom discussion.

Critical Thinking Questions End-of-chapter Critical Thinking Questions are designed to get students to think about how the material they are studying applies to them as individuals, community members, and global citizens.

Better Business Better World

The Home Depot Canada Foundation[28]

Established in 2008, The Home Depot Canada Foundation expands "The Home Depot Canada's commitment to giving back to the communities it serves." As a private, Canadian charitable organization, the foundation brings together volunteerism, do-it-yourself expertise, product donation, and ~~monster~~ grants to meet community needs. It supports ~~development~~ of affordable housing built responsibly. healthy neighbourhoods by supporting local ~~such~~ as restoring and creating much-needed ~~green~~ spaces and other outdoor beautification ~~201~~, the foundation works with a number ~~community~~ partners, including Habitat for Humanity, Evergreen, Volunteer Canada, Boys & Girls ~~a~~, and Great Canadian Shoreline Cleanup.

to take a leadership role in their community by organizing and volunteering on projects with local and national partners. Annually, The Home Depot associates contribute more than 60,000 volunteer hours to community projects across Canada.

CRITICAL THINKING QUESTIONS

1. Contingency plans are important in any business. Discuss what kinds of plans your school might have in place. How would these plans differ, if at all, from those of a local business in your area? What are a few possible scenarios that would require contingency plans in your school or at a local business?

2. How do you rank leadership qualities? Rank the following qualities and compare your results with your classmates: honest, loyal, competent, caring, determined, ambitious, inspiring, forward-looking, self-confident, and imaginative. What are the top three qualities?

3. Analyze your own ability to be a manager. What already polished skills do you have now? What skills would you

need to improve? What skills would you still need to acquire? How could you go about acquiring or improving those skills you do not have?

4. What differences might you expect to find in the corporate cultures of Google and CIBC? Do you think there would be any similarities?

5. Perform a basic SWOT analysis for the school you are currently attending. Indentify at least five strengths, weaknesses, opportunities, and threats. Suggest several ways your school can take advantage of opportunities by using its strengths and several ways in which your school can protect itself from threats and overcome its weaknesses.

APPLICATION EXERCISES

1. **Ethical Decisions.** Locate a free ethics quiz online and test your ethical decision-making abilities. The following websites can help you to get started:
   a. ICMR—http://www.icmrindia.org/courseware/Business%20Ethics%20&%20Corporate%20Governance/Business%20ethics-quiz2.htm
   b. CareerBuilder—www.careerbuilder.com/Article/CB-1382-The-Workplace-Quiz-How-Ethical-Are-You/
   c. The Ethics Guy on CNN—http://youtu.be/Lhwhgf01Ozw
   d. Onveon—www.onveon.com/articles/how-ethical-are-you-quiz.htm
   Were there any dilemmas you found particularly challenging or surprising? Why?

2. **Volunteerism.** You don't have to wait until you graduate to start demonstrating your social responsibility. Volunteering

3. **Corporate Social Responsibility (CSR).** Visit the Canadian Business for Social Responsibility (CBSR), a non-profit organization, website at www.cbsr.ca and write a brief summary answering the following questions.
   a. What does the organization do? What is the CBSR model (under Approach)?
   b. Under CBSR Publications, what are some of the recent CSR trends?
   c. What are the upcoming CSR events?

4. **Corporate Ethics.** Visit two of the following three multinational company websites: Boeing, the world's leading aerospace company; Apple, Inc., the world's largest technology company; and Toyota Motor Corporation, the world's largest automobile manufacturer by sales. Compare and contrast the companies' code of ethics, mission, values, and code of conduct. Based solely on each company's ethical conduct,

Application Exercises End-of-chapter Application Exercises are designed to increase student involvement in the learning process through researching, completing tasks, and providing evidence either in or out of the classroom.

GLOBAL 500 RESEARCH PROJECT

INSTRUCTIONS
1. Choose a Global 500 company from *Fortune* magazine's annual rankings at http://money.cnn.com/magazines/fortune/global500/.
2. Research:
   a. What is the company name? Where is it located? Who is the CEO?
   b. How much revenue did the company generate last year?
   c. What products or services does the company offer?
   d. What industry is the company in?
   e. What is happening in the global or local economy currently that affects this company?
   f. What degree of competition is this company operating within (oligopoly, monopolistic competition, or perfect competition)?
   g. Use Porter's Five Forces analysis model to analyze the competitive environment this company is operating within. What strategies does this company employ to beat their competitors at the game of business? How does having competition actually help a company?
3. Prepare a report and submit to your professor.

Global 500 Research Project   The end-of-chapter Global 500 Research Project is designed so that students can work individually or in teams to research, explore, and make informed assumptions about an assigned Global 500 Company. The project may be assigned in one chapter only or may span many chapters.

Team Time Exercises   End-of-chapter Team Time Exercises have students work in teams to improve their collaboration and problem-solving skills.

TEAM TIME

Tobacco Wars
Divide into two even teams, one to represent each of the following:
a. tobacco company employees; pro-cigarette advertising in magazines
b. anti-tobacco advertising activists

SCENARIO
Does a company have a fundamental right to market its products wherever it wishes? Cigarette advertising in magazines has been a topic of great controversy. The large tobacco companies provide publications with a great deal of revenue by purchasing expensive advertising space, but many anti-smoking groups and some magazine publishers are questioning the ethical nature of this. Anti-smoking groups argue that these advertisements appeal to children and glamorize smoking. Tobacco companies

claim that they are merely making attractive advertisements with no intention of encouraging children to use their products. The European Union has banned tobacco advertisements from magazines entirely, and many U.S. publications have stopped selling ad space to tobacco companies. The Canadian government has taken bold steps to control tobacco marketing. Do tobacco companies have the right to advertise their products as they see fit? Is it morally wrong to advertise a product that is known to cause health problems?

PROCESS
Step 1. Collaborate with team members to discuss both sides of the issue, analyzing the arguments from each perspective.
Step 2. Prepare the most effective argument for your team's perspective, and think about counterpoints to arguments that the other team may raise.

ETHICS AND RESPONSIBILITY

Ethics in Teamwork
Being a member of a team means that you are accountable for your actions and the actions of your fellow teammates. Review the following scenario.

SCENARIO
Imagine you work at an advertising firm. You're on a team that is developing an ad campaign proposal for a chain of fitness centres. The firm has been struggling and needs your team to land this account. At a meeting, one of your teammates reveals that he has hacked into a competing firm's network and has a draft of its

proposal for the same account. Your teammate wants to steal the idea and use it in your team's proposal. Most of your teammates agree with this idea, but you think it is unethical.

DISCUSSION QUESTIONS
1. How would you handle this situation? Would you voice your objection or go along with the team?
2. If you decide to voice your objection, do you address the entire team or speak to members individually? Why?
3. How would you reconcile your role as a loyal employee and team player with your need to uphold ethical standards?

Ethics and Responsibility Exercises   End-of-chapter Ethics and Responsibility Exercises are designed to increase students' understanding of business ethics and corporate social responsibility.

Closing Cases   The Closing Case wraps up the chapter material by relating the experience of a company to the business topics discussed within the chapter.

CLOSING CASE

Competition, What Competition?
Apple sold close to one million units of the iPad 2 tablet computer during its launch weekend in March 2011. By comparison, the original iPad, launched in April 2010, reached the one million mark twenty-eight days after its debut.[24] By 2011, the original

iPad was the fastest-selling device of all time, measured in revenue (Microsoft's Kinect device holds the Guinness world record for fastest sold, measured by number of units). Apple released the iPod in 2001, the iPhone in 2007, and the iPad in 2010, and every one of these was an overwhelming success.

Study on the Go Barcodes

Study on the Go

At the end of each chapter you will find a unique barcode providing access to Study on the Go, an unprecedented mobile integration between text and online content. Students link to Pearson's Study on the Go content directly from their smartphones, allowing them to study whenever and wherever they wish! Visit one of the websites below to see how you can download an app to your smartphone for free. Once the app is installed, your phone will scan the code and link to a website containing Pearson's Study on the Go content, including the popular study tools Glossary Flashcards, Audio Summaries, and Quizzes, which can be accessed anytime.

ScanLife

http://getscanlife.com/

NeoReader

http://get.neoreader.com/

QuickMark

http://www.quickmark.com.tw/

The Moment You Know

Educators know it. Students know it. It's that inspired moment when something that was difficult to understand suddenly makes perfect sense. Our MyLab products have been designed and refined with a single purpose in mind—to help educators create that moment of understanding with their students.

MyBusinessLab delivers **proven results** in helping individual students succeed. It provides **engaging experiences** that personalize, stimulate, and measure learning for each student. And, it comes from a **trusted partner** with educational expertise and an eye on the future.

The textbook authors were deeply involved in the creation and adaptation of all *Better Business* MyBusinessLab media, ensuring that all online media is effective, relevant, and closely linked to the textbook content. The result is a seamless learning experience for students.

Students and instructors can make use of the following online resources:

Study Plan. MyBusinessLab offers chapter pre-tests that generate personalized Study Plans that show students exactly the topics that require additional practice. The Study Plan links to multiple learning aids, such as videos, eText, and flashcards. After students work through the learning aids, they can take a post-test to measure their improvement and demonstrate their mastery of the topics.

Audio Chapter Summaries help auditory learners review and understand key chapter concepts. They are also available in mobile format for on-the-go review.

Glossary Flashcards provide a targeted review of the Key Terms in each chapter. The Glossary Flashcards allow learners to select the specific terms and chapters that they would like to study. The cards can also be sorted by Key Term or by definition to give students greater flexibility when studying.

Pearson eText: MyBusinessLab also includes an eText version of *Better Business*, including a complete Glossary and Index. This dynamic, online version of the text is integrated throughout MyBusinessLab to create an enriched, interactive learning experience for business students. Users can create notes, highlight text in different colours, create bookmarks, zoom, and click hyperlinked words and phrases to view definitions. Pearson eText allows for quick navigation to key parts of the eText using a table of contents and provides full-text search.

✳ Explore on **MyBusinessLab** **BizChat Discussion Boards.** The BizChats from the text can be brought to life via discussion boards in MyBusinessLab.

🔵 **BizSkills Simulations.** BizSkills are real-world scenarios that invite students to assume the role of a decision maker at a company to apply the concepts they have just learned. Students are scored on the brief, five-minute simulation and then directed to the eText, quizzes, outlines, and other learning aids to help reinforce the concepts.

🔵 **BizSkills Simulation:** Ethics and Social Responsibility. Located in MyBusinessLab.

Decision-Making Mini-Simulation: Diversity. Located in MyBusinessLab.

Decision Making Mini-Simulations walk students through key business decision-making scenarios to help them understand how business decisions are made. Students are asked to make important decisions relating to core business concepts. At each point, students receive feedback to help them understand the implications of their choices in the business environment.

Document Makeovers. In Chapters 3, 5, 6, 7, 8, 9, 11, and 12, interactive Document Makeovers ask students to analyze and correct business documents such as e-mail messages, letters, memos, blogs, and resumés. Immediate feedback is provided.

Video Cases and Web Cases. Each chapter's Video and Web Case is available on MyBusinessLab.

Video Case:

To access the Chapter 3 Video Case: Patagonia: Ethics and Social Responsibility, see the Activities folder in the Assessment section of MyBusinessLab.

Web Case:

To access the Chapter 3 Web Case, see the Activities folder in the Assessment section of MyBusinessLab

Video Activities. MyBusinessLab also contains additional videos from Pearson's business resource library.

Business Plan Project. The simple, concise Business Plan Project is introduced in Chapter 5. The project and all necessary files can be accessed on MyBusinessLab.

Career Skills Modules. The online Career Skills modules are concise, engaging lessons that cover topics of interest and importance to students as they prepare for careers in the business world. Career Skills modules are available for chapters 1, 5, 6, 8, and 13, and cover such topics as academic success, effective business plans, business communication, finding a job, and personal finance.

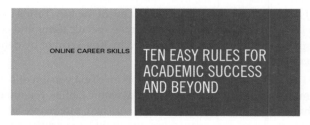

Appendix 13A: Securities and Investments. The online Appendix 13A contains an in-depth treatment of securities and investments, for those instructors who wish to teach this material. The Appendix includes Learning Objectives and a number of other pedagogical features.

All relevant MyBusinessLab resources are listed in the end-of-chapter "MyBusinessLab Chapter Resources."

MyBusinessLab can be used by itself or linked to any learning management system. To learn more about how MyBusinessLab combines proven learning applications with powerful assessment, visit www.pearsoned.ca/mybusinesslab.

MyBusinessLab—the moment you know.

INSTRUCTOR SUPPLEMENTS

Better Business includes an innovative supplement package for instructors. You can access the following resources from within MyBusinessLab or from the Instructor's Resource Centre at www.pearsoncanada.ca/highered/.

Instructor's Manual. This valuable resource includes chapter outlines, teaching tips, weblinks, supplemental activities, a chapter-video correlation guide, and answers to discussion and end-of-chapter questions. Each answer is tagged with the appropriate level of *Bloom's Taxonomy*.

PowerPoint® Slides. Each chapter presentation includes twenty-five to thirty high-quality slides. The PowerPoint Slides highlight key points from the text and are fully customizable.

MyTest and Test Item File. MyTest from Pearson Canada is a powerful online assessment-generation program that helps instructors easily create and print quizzes, tests, and exams, as well as homework or practice handouts. The *Better Business* MyTest contains multiple-choice, true/false, short answer, and essay questions—approximately 150 questions in total per chapter. Questions and tests can all be authored online, allowing instructors ultimate flexibility and the ability to efficiently manage assessments at any time, from anywhere. A Test Item File in Microsoft Word® is also available.

Personal Response System Questions. These slides are provided for instructors who wish to use a PRS to encourage class participation or facilitate in-class quizzes.

Image Library. The Image Library contains image files for all figures, photos, and tables from the textbook, online Appendix 13A, and the online Career Skills modules.

CBC Video Library. A selection of CBC videos are provided in MyBusinessLab and as a separate DVD (ISBN: 978-0-13-286322-3). These videos focus on Canadian companies and discuss business issues from a Canadian point of view.

Better Business is also available as a **CourseSmart** eTextbook. CourseSmart goes beyond traditional expectations—providing instant, online access to the textbook and course materials at a lower cost for students (average savings of 60 percent). With instant access from any computer and the ability to search the text, students will find the content they need quickly, no matter where they are. And with online tools such as highlighting and note-taking, students can save time and study efficiently.

Instructors can save time and avoid hassle with a digital eTextbook that allows them to search for the most relevant content at the very moment they need it. Whether it's evaluating textbooks or creating lecture notes to help students with difficult concepts, CourseSmart can make life a little easier. See all the benefits at www.coursesmart.com/instructors or www.coursesmart.com/students.

Pearson's **Technology Specialists** work with faculty and campus course designers to ensure that Pearson technology products, assessment tools, and online course materials are tailored to meet your specific needs. This highly qualified team is dedicated to helping schools take full advantage of a wide range of educational resources by assisting in the integration of a variety of instructional materials and media formats. Your local Pearson Canada sales representative can provide you with more details about this service program.

Pearson Custom Library

For enrolments of at least twenty-five students, you can create your own textbook by choosing the chapters that best suit your own course needs. To begin building your custom text, visit www.pearsoncustomlibrary.com. You may also work with a dedicated Pearson Custom editor to create your ideal text—publishing your own original content or mixing and matching Pearson content. Contact your local Pearson Representative to get started.

About the Authors

Michael Solomon

Michael R. Solomon, Ph.D. is Professor of Marketing and Director of the Center for Consumer Research in the Haub School of Business at Saint Joseph's University in Philadelphia. He also is Professor of Consumer Behaviour at the Manchester School of Business, The University of Manchester, U.K. Prof. Solomon's primary research and consulting interests include consumer behavior, branding, and marketing applications of virtual worlds. He has written several textbook and trade books; his *Consumer Behavior* text is the most widely-used in the world. Michael often speaks to business groups about new trends in consumer behavior and marketing strategy.

Mary Anne Poatsy, MBA, CFP

Mary Anne is a senior faculty member at Montgomery County Community College, teaching various computer application and concepts courses in face-to-face and online environments. She holds a BA in psychology and education from Mount Holyoke College and an MBA in finance from Northwestern University's Kellogg Graduate School of Management. Mary Anne has more than 11 years of educational experience, ranging from elementary and secondary education to Montgomery County Community College, Muhlenberg College, and Bucks County Community College, as well as training in the professional environment. Before teaching, she was a vice president at Shearson Lehman Hutton in the Municipal Bond Investment Banking Department.

mpoatsy@comcast.net

Kendall Martin, PhD

Kendall has been teaching since 1988 at a number of institutions, including Villanova University, DeSales University, Arcadia University, Ursinus College, County College of Morris, and Montgomery County Community College at both the undergraduate and graduate level. Kendall's education includes a BS in electrical engineering from the University of Rochester and an MS and a PhD in engineering from the University of Pennsylvania. She has industrial experience in research and development environments (AT&T Bell Laboratories) as well as experience with several start-up technology firms. At Ursinus College, Kendall developed a successful faculty training program for distance education instructors. She makes conference presentations throughout the year.

kmartin@mc3.edu

Kerri Shields

Kerri Shields is a college professor who enjoys learning as much as she enjoys teaching. Her education includes a Computer Programmer Diploma from Centennial College, a Bachelor of General Studies (Arts and Science) from Athabasca University and an MBA (Marketing and Finance) from Columbia Southern University. She has taught information systems, office administration, and business courses at Centennial College, St. Lawrence College Saint-Laurent, Seneca College, and Loyalist College both in the face-to-face and online learning environments. Before becoming a professor at Centennial College she worked as a consultant and project manager for a multinational workforce solutions provider where she held positions in training and development, information technology, management, recruitment and selection, sales and marketing, customer service, and quality control. The breadth of her work experiences and her ability to transfer learning and knowledge from one field to another is what makes her a unique and effective professor. As a result of student nominations, Kerri was selected from a prestigious group of contenders, as the recipient of the Government of Ontario's Leadership in Faculty Teaching (LIFT) Award and the Centennial College Board of Governors Teaching Excellence Award.

kerrishields@rogers.com

Acknowledgements

Thanks to:

Tammy Jones, Sales and Editorial Representative, for believing in me and taking the initiative to get the ball rolling.

Nick Durie, Acquisitions Editor, for his vision and ability to make the Canadian adaptation happen.

John Lewis, Developmental Editor, for putting forth 110 percent every day, staying on top of every task, and sharing his wonderful sense of humour.

Also, Richard di Santo, Project Manager; Rajni Pisharody, Production Editor; and Heather Sangster, copyeditor, for their hard work on this edition.

And a big "thank you" to each of the reviewers who provided invaluable feedback that helped shape the content of the textbook and the online resources that accompany it:

John Amendola, Seneca College
Laurentiu David, Centennial College
Dave Fleming, George Brown College
Gina Grandy, Mount Allison University
Patrick C.K. Hung, University of Ontario Institute of Technology
Drew Smylie, Centennial College
Peter Tingling, Simon Fraser University
Sandra Wellman, Seneca College

betterbusiness

Business Fundamentals

LEARNING OBJECTIVES

After studying this chapter, you should be able to:

1. Describe the roles the Canadian government plays in business. (pp. 4–6)

2. Define business and discuss the role of business in the economy. (p. 7)

3. Explain the difference between for-profit and non-profit organizational goals. (p. 7)

4. Explain the difference between private and public business sectors. (pp. 8–10)

5. Describe the factors of production. (pp. 10–12)

6. Identify the functional areas of most businesses. (pp. 12–13)

7. Describe the macro business environment and how managers use the PEST model to analyze external business opportunities and threats. (pp. 13–21)

OPENING DISCUSSION: EXTERNAL BUSINESS ENVIRONMENT

How Much Snooping Is Too Much Snooping?

Research In Motion (RIM), founded in 1984 and led by Mike Lazaridis and Jim Balsillie, is headquartered in Waterloo, Ontario, with offices throughout North America, Asia-Pacific, and Europe. RIM designs and manufactures the BlackBerry smartphone. The company also creates software for businesses and the operating system that allows the BlackBerry smartphone to provide mobile access to e-mail, instant messaging (IM), smartphone applications (apps), media files, and the Internet.

In the past couple of years, RIM has been facing challenges from the governments of India, United Arab Emirates, and Saudi Arabia. In the name of national security, these countries have been demanding access to the company's secure customer data, as they see such access as a necessary tool in their fight against terrorists. Each of these countries threatened to ban BlackBerry service unless RIM complied.

Concerned that terrorists may exploit the encryption in smartphones to plan illegal activity, the Indian government is urging telecommunications companies to devise solutions to meet its security needs. The government said it would ask RIM, Google Inc., Skype Technologies SA, and other service providers to establish local servers and authorize security agencies to monitor e-mail traffic. "They have to install servers in India," Home Secretary G.K. Pillai told reporters in New Delhi, adding, "This applies to all." He said notices would be sent to the companies for "lawful access" by India's security agencies.[1] Companies that do not comply could be banned.

For RIM, more than a million of its smartphone users would be affected by a ban, and the company would have to halt expansion into the world's second-biggest mobile phone market.[2] The company averted a ban in 2010 by giving government officials the ability to monitor its consumer messaging services, which

(continued)

include BlackBerry Messenger (BBM) and BlackBerry Internet Service (BIS) e-mail. But that access did not extend to the company's Enterprise Server (a virtual private network [VPN] for business customers). RIM states that it does not have encryption keys for the data flowing over its BlackBerry Enterprise Server because those keys are held by its corporate customers.

No business, including RIM, functions in a vacuum. They must continuously monitor the changing world in which they operate (the external macro-environment; see page 13). What happens outside the company could affect company operations, future processes, and decisions about future product offerings. Companies do not have much control over what happens in the macro-environment, but managers need to analyze trends and changes in this business environment to make informed decisions. Managers can categorize these external factors by using the PEST model (also see page 13–15). This classification distinguishes between:

- *Political-legal* factors. Government policy and political decisions can affect many vital areas for business. Factors may include ethical considerations, employment laws, competition laws, product regulations, consumer laws, sustainable environmental practices, and health and safety legislation.

- *Economic* factors. Changes in the local, national, or global economy can affect business operations. Factors may include interest rates, economic growth, industry changes, inflation and exchange rates, and taxation changes.

- *Socio-cultural* factors. Consumer behaviour and preferences will affect decisions about product offerings. Environmentally friendly business processes are affecting demand patterns and creating business opportunities. Other factors may include social trends, population, demographics, and ethical considerations.

- *Technological* factors. As technology changes, companies must adjust business practices to compete in the global business world. Factors include new technologies, online shopping, research and development, and global access.

Any business strategy needs to take into account all these factors so that opportunities and threats can be identified and the organization can create strategies for success by matching its internal strengths to external opportunities. Companies often use the PEST model to measure changes in their external environment that might affect the company's ability to prosper.

DISCUSSION QUESTIONS

1. Do you think it is an invasion of privacy for government to want to monitor digital communications? Is it the government's right to do so? Why or why not?

2. What political-legal and socio-cultural pressures is RIM dealing with?

3. What might happen to RIM's sales if they permit monitoring of digital communications? If the communications service provider does not oblige government, do you think the country would ban the service? Why or why not?

BUSINESS INTRODUCTION

A Glance at Canadian Business

Describe the roles the Canadian government plays in business.

How has business developed in Canada? During the sixteenth and seventeenth centuries, many adventurers came to Canada's east coast from Europe. They were drawn to Canada's rich land and natural resources. The area was first inhabited by First Nations peoples, who hunted and fished here for thousands of years. French adventurers were the first Europeans to settle permanently in Canada. Over time, they were joined by settlers from the British Isles and Germany. The settlers initially had to farm or starve. Eventually, they began working the land, excavating natural resources, and fur trading with First Nations peoples. Their home countries expected them to export raw materials, such as beaver pelts and lumber, back to Europe at low prices. The raw materials were then made into finished goods and sold back to the settlers in Canada at high prices. Attempts to develop industry in Canada were thwarted by England and France, who enjoyed large profits from these transactions (known as mercantilism). As a result, Canadian manufacturing was slow to develop.

From the mid-1700s to the mid-1800s, a new level of production—the **production concept**—was made possible by advances in technology and by the development of the factory system. Instead of many workers producing items one at a time from their homes, mass production took hold and huge factories were built, creating goods that were inexpensive and widely available. The production concept worked well at the time because companies produced what they could (largely basic necessities) most efficiently, which created a supply of low-cost products and a relatively high level of unfulfilled demand. In spite of British laws in North America against manufacturing and the export of technology, Canadian manufacturing operations existed and prospered. Toward the end of the 1800s, the government began passing laws to regulate business and protect consumers and workers, creating more balance in the economy.

In 1913, Henry Ford introduced the assembly line, which quickly became standard across major manufacturing industries. Managers were focused on efficiency, not on the customer. During the 1920s, the **sales concept** emerged and the emphasis turned to selling and advertising to persuade customers to buy the existing mass-produced goods. After the Great Depression in the 1930s and the Second World War, the balance of power shifted away from producers and toward customers. By this time, a variety of products was available and competition was making it imperative for companies to create products that customers wanted. Businesses tried to differentiate themselves from their competitors by developing brands, or distinctive identities. The marketing concept emerged, during which businesses recognized the need to be responsive to customers' needs. The **marketing concept** is a philosophy that businesses should analyze the needs of their customers and then make decisions to satisfy those needs better than the competition.

Canada has transformed from a largely rural economy into an industrial and urban one. Building on the marketing concept, businesses today look beyond each immediate transaction with a customer and aim to build long-term relationships. As technology advances, businesses find it easy to work more globally, and production and business operations move at an ever-increasing speed. Today, Canada is an affluent, high-tech industrial society in the trillion-dollar class. Canada resembles the United States in its market-oriented economic system, high living standards, and pattern of production.

What is the role of government in Canadian business?

Canada's system of government is based on the British parliamentary model and is quite distinct from the presidential system operating in the United States. Canada's legislative and executive jurisdiction is constitutionally divided between the federal government and the ten provincial governments (the three territories are subject to the federal government). Each government is separately elected; federal and provincial governments are often from different political parties. A business may be regulated at three levels: federal, provincial, and municipal. A business may also be affected by the policies and decisions of regulatory and administrative bodies and tribunals.

In the Canadian economy, government influences business activity through the many roles it plays:

- Government becomes a *regulator* when it regulates many aspects of business activity through administrative boards, tribunals, and commissions. Regulations promote competition between businesses, protect customers, achieve social goals, and protect the environment. For example, the Canadian Food Inspection Agency regulates dairy, egg, fish, and other food products.
- Government becomes a *provider of incentives* when it offers programs that help stimulate economic development. For example, the government offers funding for waste diversion initiatives, rebates for solar heating installations, and in some provinces, tax credits for employers who hire university and college students enrolled in co-operative education programs.
- Government becomes a *provider of essential services* when it supplies services that create the stability that encourages business activity, such as law enforcement (police) and health care (hospitals).

From the mid-1700s to the mid-1800s, the **production concept** emerged, in which mass production took hold and huge factories were built, creating goods that were inexpensive and widely available.

During the 1920s, **the sales concept** emerged and the emphasis turned to selling and advertising to persuade customers to buy the existing mass-produced goods.

The **marketing concept** is a philosophy that businesses should analyze the needs of their customers and then make decisions to satisfy those needs, better than the competition.

A **business** is any activity that provides goods or services in exchange for other goods and services or money, based on their perceived worth.

A **profit** is earned when a company's **revenue** is greater than its **expenses**.

■ Government becomes a *taxation agent* when taxes are imposed and collected by the three levels of government. For example, the federal government collects income tax through the Canada Revenue Agency (CRA), the provincial government collects sales tax and receives a share of income tax, and the municipal government collects property taxes.

■ Government becomes a *customer* when it buys from businesses. The Government of Canada buys many kinds of products and services, from aircraft to paper clips, from training services to scientific research.[3]

■ Government becomes a *competitor* when it competes with businesses through its Crown corporations, such as Canada Post, the Canadian Broadcasting Corporation (CBC), SaskTel, SaskEnergy, BC Hydro, and the Liquor Control Board of Ontario (LCBO).

Why conduct business in Canada? With its strong, stable, and dynamic economy, Canada is the ideal place to do business. From aerospace to software to life sciences, many of the world's most innovative and successful companies have a presence in Canada. Canada has many industry strengths:[4]

■ Canadian businesses are leaders in industries such as fibre optics, aerospace, and biopharmaceuticals.

■ Canada is the world's fourth-largest exporter of agricultural products.

■ After Japan and the United States, Canada is the third-largest exporter of automotive products.

■ Cutting-edge Canadian companies are converting energy crops and other agricultural residues into bio-fibres, bio-fuels, and bio-industrial oils.

■ Nine of the world's top ten chemical companies have Canadian production facilities.

■ The World Economic Forum ranks Canada's banks as number one globally.

■ Canada is the world's fourth fastest-growing market for pharmaceuticals.

■ Canada is the fourth-largest exporter of moulds in the world and the eighth-largest exporter of plastics processing machinery in the world.

■ Canada is a world leader in fields such as medical devices and digital gaming.

■ A low-cost, high-talent labour force; research and development (R&D) advantages; and smart regulations make Canada a lucrative location for enterprising investors.

Canada offers many advantages (based on 2010 comparisons) as a place to do business:

■ Canada has the lowest business costs (labour, facility, utility, and transportation) among the G7 established industrialized countries (France, Germany, Italy, United States, United Kingdom, Japan, and Canada), with business costs 5 percent below the United States.

■ Canada offers the lowest effective corporate income tax rate in corporate and IT services, manufacturing, and has the second lowest rate in research and development.[6]

■ Canada ranks eighth out of 125 countries and leads the G7 in effectiveness of market access, which combines factors—for example, border administration, transport, communications infrastructure, and business environment—to improve the efficient flow of goods over borders to their final receivers (World Economic Forum Global Enabling Trade Report 2010).

■ Canada ranks first among the G7 countries and second among OECD countries for providing the most efficient and cost-effective way to establish a new business.

■ Canada's overall economic competitiveness is ranked seventh in the world and second among the G7 countries.[7]

---

top10

Richest People in Canada (2010) (CDN$ billion)

Thomson family, Thomson Reuters, Woodbridge Co. Ltd. (media, information, distribution)	$23.36 (also ranked 20th richest in the world[5])
Galen Weston, George Weston Ltd., Loblaw Companies Ltd., Holt Renfrew (food, groceries, retail, real estate)	$8.5
Irving family, Irving Oil Ltd.(oil, forestry products, gas stations, media, transportation, real estate)	$7.46
Rogers family, Rogers Communications Inc. (Cable TV, communications, media, pro sports)	$6.02
James Pattison, Jim Pattison Group (auto sales, food, media, forestry products, entertainment, export services)	$5.53
Paul Desmarais, Power Corporation of Canada (financial services, media)	$4.28
Bernard Sherman, Apotex Group (pharmaceuticals)	$3.94
Jeff Skoll, eBay Inc. Participant Media (Internet, media)	$3.56
Saputo family, Saputo Inc. (food, real estate, transportation)	$3.52
Fred and Ron Mannix, Mancal Group (mining, energy, real estate)	$3.18

Source: "The Rich 100 (2010)," *Canadian Business*, http://dev.list.canadianbusiness.com/rankings/rich100/2010/Default.aspx?sp2=1&d1=a&sc1=0, Accessed September 5, 2011.

Business Benefits

Why is it important to the economy for businesses to earn a profit?

People establish businesses to perform economic activities. With some exceptions (such as co-operatives, non-profit organizations, and government institutions), businesses exist to produce profit. A **business** is any activity that provides goods or services in exchange for other goods and services or money, based on their perceived worth. Every business needs a sufficient number of customers to whom its output can consistently be sold at a profit. A **profit** is earned when a company's **revenue** (the total amount of money received for goods and services provided) is greater than its **expenses** (costs incurred while doing business). A **loss** occurs when a company's revenue is less than its expenses. More often than not, profit is the driving force behind a business' growth. As more profit is generated, a company is able to reward its employees, increase its productivity, or expand its business into new areas.

The proprietor of a business is not the only one who benefits from earned profits and business success. A successful business provides the goods and services people need and want, provides employment opportunities for members of the community, pays taxes, and generates income and spending in the economy. Socially responsible firms contribute even more by actively advocating for the well-being of the society that generates their success.

Successful businesses help to raise a country's standard of living and improve the quality of life. A country's **standard of living** is the level of wealth, comfort, material goods, and necessities available to its people. It is the ease by which people living in a time or place are able to satisfy their needs and wants. It is generally measured by standards such as income per person and poverty rate. Other measures are also used, such as access to and quality of health care, income-growth inequality, availability of employment, environmental quality, and educational standards. One measure of the standard of living is the Human Development Index (HDI), which was developed by the United Nations. High ratings for health care system, educational attainment, public safety, environmental sustainability, and social development in terms of gender equality helped Canada place eighth out of 169 countries on the 2010 HDI.[8]

The idea of a country's "standard" of living may be contrasted with the **quality of life**, which is more subjective and intangible. It takes into account not only the material standard of living, but also more intangible aspects that make up human life, such as freedom from slavery, torture, and discrimination; the right to rest and leisure, education, safety, choice of employment, and equal treatment; and freedom of religion and of thought. According to the OECD 2011 Better Life Initiative survey, Canada ranked second (after Australia) out of the 34 member countries in terms of having the best quality of life.[9]

2 Define business and discuss the role of business in the economy.

3 Explain the difference between for-profit and non-profit organizational goals.

Revenue is the total amount of money received for goods and services provided.

Expenses are costs incurred while doing business.

A **loss** occurs when a company's revenue is less than its expenses.

A country's **standard of living** is the level of wealth, comfort, material goods, and necessities available to its people. It is the ease by which people living in a time or place are able to satisfy their needs and wants. It is generally measured by standards such as income per person and poverty rate.

Quality of life is subjective and intangible. It takes into account not only the material standard of living, but also more intangible aspects that make up human life, such as freedom from slavery, torture, and discrimination; the right to rest and leisure, education, safety, choice of employment, and equal treatment; and freedom of religion and of thought.

Do all businesses operate to create a profit?

Not every organization that generates revenue and pays expenses is considered a for-profit business. They may operate like a business, but **non-profit organizations** do not go into business to pursue profits. Instead, a non-profit, also referred to as a not-for-profit, organization seeks to serve its community through social, educational, or political means. Organizations such as universities, hospitals, environmental groups, and charities are non-profit organizations (such as the Canadian Diabetes Association, Canadian Cancer Society, and Red Cross). Any excess revenue they generate is used to further their stated mission. Non-profit and voluntary organizations (discussed next) are an extension of the millions of Canadians who direct and support their activities, shaping the quality of our lives and our communities.

Manitobian Louise Yurchak is one of the many dedicated volunteers who support the non-profit Canadian Diabetes Association.

Business Sectors

4

Explain the difference between private and public business sectors.

What is the difference between the public and private business sectors?

Businesses are often categorized into specific groupings called sectors, which can be based on business activities, how profits are managed, or the industry in which the business operates.

The **public business sector** includes goods and services produced, delivered, and allocated by the government and public sector organizations (publicly controlled government business enterprises). The government sector includes all federal, provincial, municipal, and territorial government ministries and departments. It also includes public schools boards, public universities and colleges, and public health and social service institutions. Public sector organizations operate in the marketplace, often in competition with privately owned organizations. Government may have direct or indirect control over public sector organizations, which are also referred to as Crown corporations. The aim of the public sector is to provide services that benefit the public as a whole, either because it would be difficult to charge people for the goods and services concerned, or because people might not be able to afford to pay for them. The government can provide these goods and services at a lower price than if they were provided by a for-profit company. Examples include public utilities, such as water and sewage, electricity, and gas, and nationalized industries, such as coal and steel.

The **private business sector** includes goods and services produced and delivered by private individuals or groups as a means of enterprise for profit. The sector is not controlled by government. These businesses can be small firms owned by just one person, or large multinational businesses that operate globally. Large businesses may have many thousands of owners. A public (or publicly traded) company within the private business sector is not part of the public sector (government-provided services and government-owned organizations); it is a particular kind of private sector company that can offer its shares for sale to the general public (Microsoft, Apple, Procter & Gamble).

The **non-profit and voluntary sector** includes non-governmental, non-profit organizations that receive support from individual citizens, governments, and businesses. Non-profit organizations (NPOs) are also referred to as private voluntary organizations (PVOs); not-for-profit organizations (NFPOs); or non-profit making, non-governmental organizations (NGOs). In the global business world, there is inconsistency in how these terms are defined. A non-profit organization could be a not-for-profit corporation or an unincorporated association. A not-for-profit corporation is usually created with a specific purpose in mind and could be a foundation or charity or other type of non-profit organization. A private voluntary association is a group of volunteers who enter an agreement to form an organized body to accomplish a purpose. In this textbook, not-for-profit corporations, private voluntary organizations, and non-governmental organizations are classified in the non-profit and voluntary sector as non-profit organizations.

Non-profit organizations have the ability to respond to issues more quickly than government and are usually formed or expanded in reaction to a community need not being met by the government. The Canadian government recognizes the importance of the non-profit sector as a key partner in building a stronger Canada, and it supports the sector in a number of ways, such as partnering, streamlining funding practices and accountability, and developing knowledge on the non-profit sector.[10] The non-profit sector often relies heavily on the government for funding.[11]

Non-profit organizations operate in a variety of areas, including sports, religion, arts, culture, fundraising, and housing. The various organizations include hospitals, universities and colleges, education and research organizations, business and professional associations, and unions—CARE, Save the Children, Habitat for Humanity, Greenpeace, and World Vision are all non-profit organizations. Non-profit organizations experience problems with planning for the future, recruiting the types of volunteers needed by the organization, and obtaining board members and funding.[12] People who work in non-profit organizations may be paid employees or unpaid volunteers, which is why the sector is called the "non-profit and voluntary sector."

The **public business sector** includes goods and services produced, delivered, and allocated by the government and public sector organizations (publicly controlled government business enterprises).

The **private business sector** includes goods and services produced and delivered by private individuals or groups as a means of enterprise for profit.

The **non-profit and voluntary sector** includes non-governmental, non-profit organizations that receive support from individual Canadians, governments, and businesses.

Many people are confused as to which business sector certain organizations belong. Is a hospital in the public or private sector? Are all hospitals non-profit organizations? Is a private sector university a non-profit or for-profit organization? This confusion exists because some types of organizations typically thought of as belonging to the non-profit sector can cross sectors. For example, in Ontario there are four types of hospitals, including public, private, federal, and Cancer Care Ontario hospitals.[13] Public sector hospitals are owned by the government and receive government funding. Private sector hospitals are privately owned, often by a for-profit company or a non-profit organization, and are funded through patient payments, insurers, grants, donations, and foreign embassies. Private hospitals and health care clinics are classified as being in either the private, for-profit or private, non-profit sectors and are quite common in the United States and Australia. Canada's mix of public and private health care options leaves many people thinking that the hospitals in Canada belong to the public sector because hospital services are publicly delivered, funded, and governed, and hospitals are accountable to the public. In fact, hospital services in many provinces are delivered largely by private sector, non-profit organizations.[14]

Similarly, Canada has private sector, for-profit and private sector, non-profit colleges and universities in addition to its many public, non-profit universities and colleges. There are over 500 registered private career colleges in Ontario alone.[15] A private career college operating in Ontario must be registered and must have its programs approved by the Ministry of Training, Colleges, and Universities. Private universities and colleges are not operated by the government, although many receive public subsidies, and depending on the province in which they are located, private universities and colleges may be subject to government regulation. Some of the world's most renowned universities, such as Harvard University, Stanford University, and Massachusetts Institute of Technology (MIT), are private sector, non-profit universities.

In 2003, Statistics Canada conducted a national survey of non-profit and voluntary organizations. At that time, approximately 161 000 non-profit organizations were formally registered or incorporated in Canada, of which about 80 000 were registered charities. Charities registered with the federal government are exempt from a variety of taxes and enable donors to claim tax credits for the donations they make. Collectively, these charities reported annual revenues of $112 billion and employed more than two million people. With the exclusion of hospitals, universities, and colleges, the sector had $75 billion in revenues and 1.3 million employees.[16]

What are the different industries across the three business sectors?
Across these three sectors, businesses may be classified by industry, such as services-producing industries and goods-producing industries. The five economic sectors specified by the North American Industry Classification System (NAICS) as goods-producing industries are:[17]

- agriculture, forestry, fishing, and hunting
- mining, and oil and gas extraction
- utilities
- construction
- manufacturing

The fifteen economic sectors specified by NAICS as services-producing industries are:[18]

- wholesale trade
- retail trade
- transportation and warehousing
- information and cultural industries
- finance and insurance
- real estate, and rental and leasing
- professional, scientific, and technical services
- management of companies and enterprises
- administrative and support, waste management, and remediation services
- educational services
- health care and social assistance
- arts, entertainment, and recreation

- accommodation and food services
- other services, except public administration
- public administration

Do all businesses create a product? Whether a business is for-profit or non-profit, one of its goals is to provide some sort of product to its customer base. A product can be either a good or a service. **Goods** are any physical products offered by a business. A roast beef sandwich at Arby's, a forty-two-inch LCD television at Best Buy, and a Honda Civic at your local car dealer are all considered goods because they are tangible items. Conveyer belts, pumps, and sundries sold to other businesses are also goods, even though they are not sold directly to consumers. **Services** refer to intangible products that are bought or sold. Unlike a polo shirt on the rack at Old Navy, services cannot be physically handled. Services include products such as haircuts, health care, car insurance, and theatrical productions.

Some companies offer products that are both goods and services. Take, for example, an establishment like Montana's franchise of restaurants. When you order a stuffed chicken breast meal at the restaurant, you are paying for the good (a stuffed chicken breast meal) as well as the service of preparing, cooking, and serving the meal.

Goods are any physical products offered by a business.

Services refer to intangible products that are bought or sold.

⑤ Factors of Production

Describe the factors of production.

What resources are needed to produce goods or services?

To understand fully how a business operates, you must consider the **factors of production**, which are the resources (inputs) used to produce goods and services (outputs). For years, businesses focused on four traditional factors: labour, natural resources, capital, and entrepreneurial talent. However, in the economy of the twenty-first century, an additional factor has become increasingly important: technology.

The **factors of production** are the resources used to produce goods and services.

Labour is the human resource that refers to any physical or intellectual work people contribute to business production.

Natural resources are the raw materials provided by nature and used to produce goods and services.

- *Labour.* Businesses need people to get things produced. **Labour** is the human resource that refers to any physical or intellectual work people contribute to business production.
- *Natural resources.* Most workers who provide the labour to produce a good need something tangible to work with. **Natural resources** are the raw materials provided by nature and used to produce goods and services. Soil used in agricultural production; trees used for lumber to build houses; and coal, oil, and natural gas used to create energy are all examples of natural resources.

- *Capital.* There are two types of capital: real capital and financial capital. **Real capital** refers to the physical facilities used to produce goods and services. **Financial capital** is money used to facilitate a business enterprise. Financial capital can be acquired through business loans, from investors, or through other forms of fundraising, or even by tapping into personal savings.
- *Entrepreneurs.* An **entrepreneur** is someone who assumes the risk of creating, organizing, and operating a business and who directs all the business resources. Entrepreneurs are a human resource, just like labour, but what sets entrepreneurs apart from labour is their willingness to bear risks and their ability to manage an enterprise effectively. Successful entrepreneurs are rewarded with profits for bearing risks and for their managerial expertise.
- *Technology.* **Technology** includes human knowledge, work methods, physical

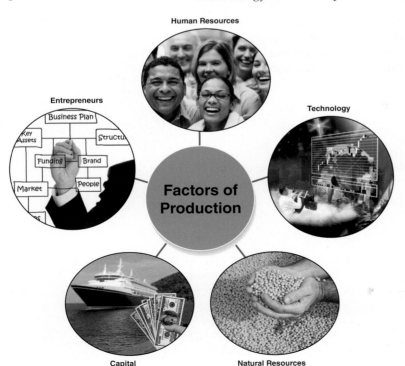

Human Resources

Entrepreneurs

Technology

Factors of Production

Capital

Natural Resources

On Target

Nantucket Nectars: Tom and Tom Partnership

Tom First and Tom Scott were college friends at Brown University who did not want to climb the traditional corporate ladder. After graduation, the friends moved to Nantucket, Massachusetts, and started a floating convenience store called Allserve. Based from Tom and Tom's red boat in Nantucket Harbor, the company provided delivery service of almost any item, from newspapers to laundry, to neighbouring boats. While Allserve proved to be a modest success, the pair soon had another idea. They decided to sell their own natural juice blend, and soon Nantucket Nectars was born. Popularity of the juice spread quickly in Nantucket, and Allserve purchased a distribution company to expand the reach of its products. While many national

chains are now carrying their products, Tom and Tom maintained their local roots by starting the Juice Guys Juice Bar in Nantucket.[19] This partnership is an example of how a successful business can be started by two eager and driven people. Tom and Tom have come a long way since their days as floating delivery boys in Nantucket Harbor, and they are now running a nationally recognized corporation.

Discussion Questions

1. Do you think the entrepreneurs' initial capital investment was large? Where do you think they got the money to start Allserve?
2. When the entrepreneurs had the new business idea for Nantucket Nectars, what factors of production do you think they required?
3. How do you think technology might help these entrepreneurs operate their juice business?

---

equipment, electronics and telecommunications, and various processing systems used to perform business activities. Technology refers to items and services such as smartphones, computer software, and digital broadcasting that make businesses more efficient and productive. Successful companies are able to keep pace with technological progresses and harness new knowledge, information, and strategies. Unsuccessful organizations typically fail because they have not kept pace with the latest technology and techniques.

Why are entrepreneurs so important? Entrepreneurs are the innovators who create business ideas and start businesses from those ideas. They attempt to make a profit by combining the factors of production (inputs) to create goods and services (outputs). The factors of production used to produce a pizza in a pizza restaurant would include:

- the land that the pizza restaurant is located on, the electricity used to run the store, and the wheat and other food products from which the pizza is made;
- the labourers who make the pizzas;
- the store and equipment used to make the pizza, and the money used to operate the business;
- the technology used to gather customer information, market to customers, deliver to customers, track inventory, and reorder supplies; and
- the entrepreneurship skills used to coordinate the other factors of production to initiate the production process.

Why is technology a key factor in production? Companies do not require technology for the sake of technology alone. Rather, technology has become a critical factor for obtaining and managing **information and knowledge**, which are quickly becoming the key factors of production as the new competitive business environment places a premium on these factors. Not only do companies need technology to obtain and manage information, they need human resources (knowledge workers) with the skills to manipulate the information and turn it into knowledge that the company can use for competitive advantage. Knowledge is a tricky thing to manage, but companies can translate their information

Real capital refers to the physical facilities used to produce goods and services.

Financial capital is money used to facilitate a business enterprise.

An **entrepreneur** is someone who assumes the risk of creating, organizing, and operating a business and who directs all the business resources.

Technology includes human knowledge, work methods, physical equipment, electronics and telecommunications, and various processing systems used to perform business activities.

Information and knowledge are quickly becoming the key factors of production as the new competitive business environment places a premium on these factors.

BizChat

What Do These Two Businesses Have in Common?

Let's take a look at two completely different businesses, YouTube and Chou's Chinese Restaurant.

In 2005 Steve Chen, Chad Hurley, and Jawed Karim, three twenty-something tech company employees, decided to pool their resources and expertise to launch the video-sharing website YouTube.[20] The three hatched the idea at a dinner party, and in less than a year, they developed a Silicon Valley company that became a huge phenomenon. Users anywhere in the world can post a YouTube video on the Internet for anyone to see.

Over three decades ago, the Chou family, immigrants from Hong Kong, set out to fulfill their goal of opening a Chinese restaurant. The Chous purchased the restaurant from an advertisement in the local newspaper. Although opening a restaurant was challenging, the Chous built a reputation for treating people like family, offering high-quality Chinese food, and having fair prices. They developed a loyal customer base.

What do these two businesses have in common? Their business models could not be more different. One is a new media portal that hosts hundreds of millions of videos, while the other is a family-run eatery. Although the products offered by these businesses vary considerably, the two businesses are similar because they were started by creative entrepreneurs determined to make a profit. For Steve Chen, Chad Hurley, and Jawed Karim, these profits came when YouTube was sold to Google for US$1.7 billion

in 2006.[21] For the Chou family, the profits are much more modest—they make a solid living, but are far from seeing a ten-figure profit. Nevertheless, the Chous, like the founders of YouTube, have realized a dream by starting a successful business.

Discussion Questions

1. Which business sector do you think YouTube operates within? Which business sector do you think the Chous' restaurant operates within? Are these businesses operating in the private, public, or non-profit sector?
2. One business is an eat-in restaurant, while the other is an online video-sharing website. How do the factors of production compare between these two businesses?
3. Considering the roles of government discussed earlier, what role do you think the government plays in relation to these two businesses?

---

assets into real value for the business by learning from past successes or failures, identifying opportunities to improve profitability, or simply enabling teams to become more productive. With increased mobility of information and the global workforce, information and knowledge can be transported around the world.

Identify the functional areas of most businesses.

Functional Areas of Business

What activities are needed to operate a business?   **Functional areas** in businesses are often separate departments where business activities are grouped by similar tasks or skills. Most large businesses consist of a number of different departments, each of which has a specific function. Smaller businesses must conduct the same business functions, but on a smaller scale. Therefore, they do not always have separate departments for each functional area. People are organized in different ways in different organizations, depending on factors such as the size of the organization, the culture of the organization, the nature of the industry, and the preferred structures of the managers. The main functional areas you will often see in businesses are sales and marketing; customer service; information technology and communications; accounting and finance; research

Functional areas in businesses are often separate departments where business activities are grouped by similar tasks or skills.

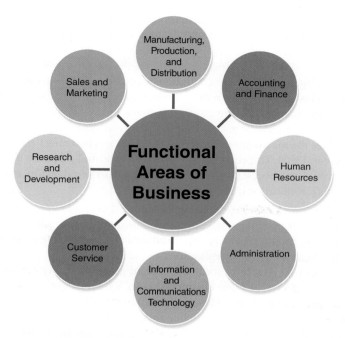

Figure 1.1 Functional Areas of Business

and development; manufacturing, production, and distribution; human resources; and administration (shown in **Figure 1.1**). Each of the functional areas of business will be discussed in more detail in subsequent chapters.

ENVIRONMENTS OF BUSINESS
Pest Model

What are the different business environments in which organizations operate? Organizations operate within several business environments that affect their potential for success:

1. The **internal environment** (what occurs within the organization) includes the five Ms: Management, Materials, Machinery (equipment), Money (wages, finance), and eMployees (internal customers). Companies have control over this environment and make changes to it according to strategic goals and conditions that occur outside the company.

2. The **external environment** (what occurs outside the organization) consists of micro and macro factors.

   a. The **micro-environment** may be defined as including groups and organizations that have a direct relationship with the business. For example, suppliers, distributors, competitors, and external customers deal with the firm regularly and have a direct interest in the activities of the company because they are clearly affected by its actions.

   b. The **macro-environment** is the external environment over which the organization can exert little influence. This environment is often referred to by the acronym PEST (political-legal, economic, socio-cultural, and technological). These factors create opportunities for and pose threats to the organization. For example,

The **internal environment** (what occurs within the organization) includes the five Ms: Management, Materials, Machinery (equipment), Money (wages, finance), and eMployees (internal customers).

The **external environment** (what occurs outside the organization) consists of micro and macro factors, including the micro-environment and the macro-environment.

The **micro-environment** may be defined as including groups and organizations that have a direct relationship with the business and have a direct interest in the activities of the company because they are clearly affected by its actions.

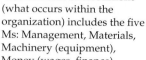

Describe the macro-environment of business and how managers use the PEST model to analyze external business opportunities and threats.

The **macro-environment** is the external environment over which the organization can exert little influence. This environment is often referred to by the acronym PEST (political-legal, economic, socio-cultural, and technological).

changes in government policy, fluctuations in the economy, social change, and new technologies can all have a significant effect on a company's success.

Why do organizations need to observe changes in the different business environments?

Organizations must continuously consider the environments within which they operate because changes in these environments feed all aspects of corporate planning. Measuring changes in business environments allows organizations to take actions to sustain the company or gain a competitive advantage.

To help analyze the macro-environment (external factors that affect an organization), managers use several analysis processes to gather, analyze, and dispense information for tactical or strategic purposes. One option is to analyze external factors using the **PEST model**. This classification distinguishes between:

The **PEST model** (Political-legal, Economic, Socio-cultural, and Technological) is used to measure changes in the external business environment that might affect the company's ability to prosper.

- *Political-legal* factors. Government policy and political decisions can affect many vital areas of business. Factors may include ethical considerations, employment laws, competition laws, product regulations, consumer laws, sustainable environmental practices, and health and safety legislation.
- *Economic* factors. Changes in the local, national, or global economy can affect business operations. Factors may include interest rates, economic growth, industry changes, inflation and exchange rates, and taxation changes.
- *Socio-cultural* factors. Consumer behaviour and preferences will affect decisions about product offerings. For example, environmentally friendly business processes affect demand patterns and create business opportunities. Other factors may include social trends, population, demographics, and ethical considerations.
- *Technological* factors. As technology changes, companies must adjust business practices to compete in the global business world. Factors include new technologies, online shopping, research and development, and global access.

Table 1.1   PEST Model for Analysis

Political-Legal	Economic	Socio-Cultural	Technological
Government type and stability	Levels of disposable income (after paying taxes) and income distribution	Cultural aspects, health consciousness, population growth rate, age, distribution	Maturity of technology, rate of obsolescence, and competing technologies
World trade agreements, regulations and restrictions	Interest rates, taxes, and inflation	Migration flows—labour mobility	Research and technological breakthroughs and improvements
Environmental regulations and protection	Overseas economic growth and emerging markets	Consumer demand for environmentally safe business practices	Government spending on research and development
Freedom of press, rule of law, and levels of bureaucracy and corruption	Current and projected economic growth	Lifestyle changes and trends	Industry focus on technology
Tax policies, and trade and tariff controls	Stage in the business cycle	Demographics: gender, age, family size, etc.	Energy use and costs
Consumer protection laws, employment laws, health and safety laws and regulations	Impact of technological changes on the economy	Living conditions, level of education, and earning capacity	Information technology, Internet, and mobile technology
Political stability	Government spending	Work–life balance attitudes	Global and local communications
Competition laws and regulations	Unemployment and supply of labour	Ethical and moral standards governing the practices of business—customer values, market values, stakeholder values	Technology access, licensing, intellectual property issues, and advances in manufacturing
Government organization and attitude	Labour costs and supply		Waste removal and recycling

There are several variations of the PEST model. Other forms you may encounter include SLEPT analysis (Social, Legal, Economic, Political, and Technological) or STEEPLE analysis (Social/demographic, Technological, Economic, Environmental (nature), Political, Legal, and Ethical), and sometimes PESTLE or PESTEL and PESTLIED (where the *I* represents International). The PEST model used above incorporates all these factors.

The PEST model (in any of its various forms) is used to measure changes in the external business environment that might affect the company's ability to prosper (see **Table 1.1**). Managers regularly analyze these changes on a local, national, and global scale so they can make informed decisions, set goals, and implement strategies to increase business revenue. These factors may include changes in government, popular opinion, fashion trends, weather, and new technology. Changes in one external environment can have an effect on the other external environments. PEST analysis is a useful tool for understanding market demand or decline, current business position, and potential opportunities or obstacles.

Another important tool that helps managers analyze the competitive environment is Porter's Five Forces analysis model. Developed by Michael Porter, this model is used to analyze the micro-environment for a strategic business unit. For example, Dell might analyze the market for business computers (one of its strategic business units). Porter's Five Forces will be discussed in more detail in Chapter 2.

There are also several other analysis tools managers use to measure changes in their business environments. A SWOT (Strengths, Weaknesses, Opportunities, and Threats) analysis is often completed after an external environmental analysis (PEST) and a competitive analysis (Porter's) have been done. The information gathered from a PEST analysis and a Porter's analysis feeds into the SWOT analysis. SWOT is a tool for auditing an organization and its environment. It is the first stage of planning and helps managers focus on key issues. Strengths and weaknesses are internal factors. Opportunities and threats are external factors. SWOT analysis will be discussed in more detail in Chapter 6.

Political-Legal Environment

How do politics affect an organization? The **political-legal environment** reflects the government's relationship with business. It is often a direct consequence of the political parties in power, which represent the popular opinion of the citizens of the region. Organizations hire lobbyists to influence legislation and run advocacy ads that state their point of view on public issues. Special interest groups have grown in number and power, putting more constraints on marketers. The public is placing high expectations on organizations to be ethical and responsible. Politicians work to get re-elected by listening to the concerns of their citizens. This can affect businesses in many ways. For example, if citizens protest having a new shopping mall built in their neighbourhood because they will lose a playground, the shopping mall may be forced to relocate.

The **political-legal environment** reflects the government's relationship with business.

Political decisions that affect the education of the workforce, the health of the nation, and the quality of an economy's infrastructure (such as roads and rail systems) can have an impact on many vital areas of a business. Here are three examples of how political decisions might affect a business:

1. If less of the workforce receives higher education because education fees rise, then qualified employees could be more difficult for businesses to find. Once found, these employees could demand higher wages, which would increase business costs.
2. If the cost of health care rises for individuals, then households will have less money to spend on the goods and services that they may have otherwise purchased from businesses, which would decrease business profits.
3. If roads and rail systems are not kept in good repair because government decides to spend tax money elsewhere, businesses may be forced to choose alternate transport methods or increase transport time by travelling a longer route, which would increase business costs.

Political stability is also an important consideration, especially for international firms. Many companies would not be willing to do business in a country where there is political unrest or where trade relationships are not defined and stable. Thus, Canadian firms are more likely to do business with the United States, Mexico, and England than with Afghanistan or Haiti.

How does the law affect an organization?   Laws pertaining to taxes, competition, consumers, products, and the environment (land, air, and water) are some of the laws about which organizations need to be aware. In Canada, there are strict regulations about advertising for alcohol and tobacco. Laws and regulations tell organizations what they can and cannot do, and companies that do not abide might be fined, have their managers imprisoned, or have their businesses closed for noncompliance with the law.

Economic Environment

The **economic environment** consists of factors that affect consumer purchasing power and spending patterns.

How does the economic environment affect an organization?   The **economic environment** consists of factors that affect consumer purchasing power and spending patterns. Such factors might include the changing value of the Canadian dollar, a skilled-labour shortage, and environmental sustainability. When there is a period of low sales, low employment, and low productivity (a recession), many people are out of work and household incomes are lower, thus consumer spending is lower. Less consumer spending means less revenue for businesses. Less revenue means businesses cannot afford to expand operations, hire additional employees, or spend money on researching and developing new products. When there is a period of high sales, high employment, and high productivity (business and therefore the economy are said to be booming), most people have jobs and make a good income, thus consumer spending rises. Economic change can also have a strong impact on a firm's behaviour. For example, higher interest rates can deter businesses from obtaining loans to expand their operations, a strong domestic currency might make exporting more difficult if it increases prices in terms of foreign currencies, and inflation might provoke higher wage demands from employees and increase operating costs.

Globalization makes it possible for German company Adidas Group to manufacture some of its products in China. These products later turn up on store shelves in Canada and other countries around the world.

Globalization is the movement toward a more interconnected and interdependent world economy.

A **socio-cultural environment** is an interconnected system of different demographic factors such as race, ethnicity, gender, age, income distribution, sexual orientation, and other characteristics.

How does globalization affect business?
Globalization is the movement toward a more interconnected and interdependent world economy. This means that economies around the world are merging as technology, goods and services, labour, and capital move back and forth across international borders. The effects of globalization on the business world vary, from economic transformation in India to the shutting down of major manufacturing plants in Canada. The Internet and modern technological advances are making it possible for a company of any size from anywhere in the world to compete globally. Competition between businesses consists of trying to get the customer to buy their product instead of the one offered by the competitor. They compete to see which has the greater market share (percentage of sales of a particular product or service in a given region) and thus is more successful. While Canada competes with its traditional economic partners and international allies, the United States and the United Kingdom, it must also compete with new emerging economies, such as China and India. To remain competitive in the global arena, Canada's competitiveness policies will have to strengthen the economic relationships with its traditional allies while at the same time developing sustainable and competitive economic relationships with emerging economies. The World Economic Forum uses the Growth Competitiveness Index (GCI) to measure and compare on an annual basis global competitiveness among the world's trading economies.

Socio-Cultural Environment

How does the socio-cultural environment affect an organization?   A **socio-cultural environment** is an interconnected system of different demographic factors such as race, ethnicity, gender, age, income distribution, sexual orientation, and other characteristics.

Better Business Better World

Be a Smart Consumer
Tips, Alerts and News
Posted Daily on our Blog

Do You Prefer To Do Business with Companies You Can Trust?

The Council of Better Business Bureaus (CBBB) is the North American umbrella organization for all Better Business Bureaus (BBB). Both the CBBB and BBB are dedicated to cultivating honest, responsive relationships between businesses and consumers, instilling consumer confidence, and contributing to a trustworthy marketplace. Founded in 1912, the BBB has grown to 128 bureaus serving communities across North America, evaluating and monitoring more than three million local and national businesses and charities.[22]

Financed by the private business sector, the BBB is a non-profit, unbiased public service organization that establishes and maintains high standards for fair and honest business behaviour. Businesses that earn BBB-accredited status contractually agree and adhere to the organization's high standards of ethical business behaviour. BBB accreditation does not mean that the business' products or services have been evaluated or endorsed by the BBB, or that the BBB has made a determination as to the business's product quality or competency in performing services. To be accredited by the BBB, a business or organization affirms that it meets and will abide by the following standards:[23]

- *Build trust:* establish and maintain a positive track record in the marketplace;
- *Advertise honestly:* adhere to established standards of advertising and selling;

- *Tell the truth:* honestly represent products and services, including clear and adequate disclosures of all material terms;
- *Be transparent:* openly identify the nature, location, and ownership of the business, and clearly disclose all policies, guarantees, and procedures that bear on a customer's decision to buy;
- *Honour promises:* abide by all written agreements and verbal representations;
- *Be responsive:* address marketplace disputes quickly, professionally, and in good faith;
- *Safeguard privacy:* protect any data collected against mishandling and fraud, collect personal information only as needed, and respect the preferences of customers regarding the use of their information; and
- *Embody integrity:* approach all business dealings, marketplace transactions, and commitments with integrity.

BBB **ACCREDITED BUSINESS**

The BBB provides objective advice, free Reliability Reports on businesses and Wise Giving reports on charities, and educational information on topics affecting marketplace trust. To further promote trust, the BBB also offers compliance- and dispute-resolution support for consumers and businesses when there is a difference in viewpoints.

Discussion Questions

1. Why is it important for businesses to build trust with consumers? Why is it important that consumers can trust the businesses they buy from?
2. Why would a business want to obtain BBB accreditation? Does this accreditation mean that consumers can trust the products the business sells to be high quality?
3. Have you ever been "scammed" by a business? What was the situation and what did you do about it? Did you go to the BBB for help? Why or why not?

Social, economic, and political movements and trends cause the social environment to change constantly; an influx of immigrants can change racial demographics, or an economic slump can change income distribution demographic. These changes affect where people live, what they buy, and how they choose to spend their money. To best serve employees, customers, and the community, businesses must consider shifts and changes in the social environment when making decisions.

How does an aging population affect business?

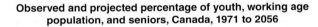 Changing demographics—age, gender, family size, income level, educational level—can change patterns in consumer demand. An aging population presents challenges as well as opportunities. Not only are older Canadians living longer, healthier lives, they are also better educated, wealthier, and have achieved a higher standard of living than previous generations. Baby boomers, the generation born between 1943 and 1960, represent the majority of the aging Canadian population. By 2020, they will be sixty to seventy-seven years old, and most of them will have begun their retirement. Over the past fifty years, the median age of Canadians has risen from 27.2 to 38.8 years, while the share of those aged 65 and older has increased from 7.7 to 13.2 percent. According to Statistics Canada, by 2026—when most baby boomers will have retired—the median age of Canadians will rise to 43.3 years and the share of seniors will be 21.2 percent. By 2051, these figures are estimated to rise to 46.8 years and 26.4 percent, respectively.[24]

Opportunities exist for businesses to market to baby boomers as they age. As boomers become empty-nesters, they will most likely move to smaller homes or condominiums closer to the cities, where they can be close to shopping, restaurants, and entertainment. Boomers are also tech-savvy and will continue to use the Internet, satellite connections, and other electronic devices. Many companies market specific product lines to boomers. For example, cosmetics company Revlon is targeting the aging population with an anti-aging beauty line aimed at baby boomer women. Revlon is hoping this product line will generate US$200 million in new sales.[25]

Although an aging population presents many opportunities for corporations, it also presents challenges for the Canadian economy. As the ratio of the non-working population to the working population increases, problems could occur, such as increased health care needs, higher taxes, and a reduction in government spending on pensions and health care.

According to Statistics Canada, by 2056 seniors will account for 25 to 30 percent of the Canadian population. While the senior segment is increasing, children and young people make up a decreasing segment of the Canadian population. As many older Canadians retire, relatively fewer young people are moving into the workforce to replace them, which means there will be a decreasing number of people available to provide social and economic support for seniors. In 2006 there were five working-age people (aged twenty to sixty-four) for every senior, down from seven in 1971. By 2056, it is estimated (medium-growth scenario) that there will be only two working-age people for every senior in Canada.[26] As shown in **Figure 1.2**, the result of such a trend could be a severe labour shortage for many years.

Despite these challenges, catering to the needs of an older population will ultimately present businesses with opportunities for growth—especially in the health care, pharmaceutical, and travel industries, as a bigger population translates to a larger market for these goods and services.

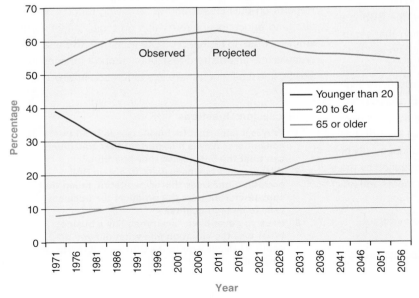

Observed and projected percentage of youth, working age population, and seniors, Canada, 1971 to 2056

Figure 1.2   Change in Age Demographics

Source: Data points from Statistics Canada, "Observed and Projected Percentage of Youth, Working Age Population, and Seniors, Canada, 1971 to 2056," http://www.statcan.gc.ca/pub/82-229-x/2009001/demo/desc/poc-desc1.2-eng.htm, Accessed February 10, 2011.

How does diversity affect business?   As Canada becomes more diverse, it is important for businesses to reflect that diversity in their workforce. By 2031, between 25 and 28 percent of the population could consist of people born outside of Canada. Between 29 and 32 percent of the population could belong to a visible minority group, as defined by the *Employment Equity Act*. By 2031, visible minority groups could comprise 63 percent of the population in Toronto, 59 percent in Vancouver, and 31 percent in Montreal.[27] This means that in some companies, visible minorities could account for the majority of the workforce. Royal Bank of Canada has more than 52 000 full-time employees in Canada, with 26 percent of employees being visible minorities. Boeing Canada has close to 1500 employees, with 26 percent of employees being visible minorities.[28]

However, in today's business climate, increasing and managing a company's diversity involves more than just employing an ethnically diverse workforce. Companies must develop a **diversity initiative**, which outlines their goals and objectives for managing, retaining, and promoting a diverse workforce. A diversity initiative might include a non-discrimination policy, minority network, or diversity education. According to Harvard sociology professor Frank Dobbin, "To increase diversity, executives must treat it like any other business goal."[29]

Although the inclusion and advancement of racial minorities in the workplace is an important step in establishing a diverse workforce, it is only part of the process. Today, the term *minority* applies to more than just people of different ethnicities. Some minority groups represent a person's gender, culture, religion, sexual orientation, or disability. Companies must include these minority groups in their diversity initiative to ensure that all minority employees are treated fairly by management and co-workers.

A focus on environmental issues is opening up markets such as wind turbines that will become increasingly important in the future.

A **diversity initiative** outlines a company's goals and objectives for managing, retaining, and promoting a diverse workforce. It might include a non-discrimination policy, minority network, or diversity education.

A **green economy** factors ecological concerns into its business decisions.

How does the "green movement" affect business?

In a 2007 United Nations study, many of the world's most respected environmental scientists reported that the threat of global warming and climate change is real.[30] As environmental anxieties become prevalent throughout society, it is important for businesses to get involved in a **green economy**—one that factors ecological concerns into business decisions. Businesses that manufacture products that contribute to higher emissions of carbon dioxide and consume inordinate amounts of fossil fuels must adapt to this new environmental awareness if they want to be relevant in a green economy. As an example, Toyota has seen its sales increase largely due to its Prius hybrid vehicles, which run on electricity as well as gasoline. Hybrid vehicles have not only become strong sellers, they have become part of our popular culture.[31]

A focus on environmental issues also creates a new market that will be increasingly important in the future. The demand for more green products presents new opportunities for entrepreneurs to meet those needs, and "green-collar" jobs could revitalize the currently decimated Canadian and U.S. manufacturing economies. Creating wind energy turbines, installing solar panels, and weatherproofing houses and office buildings are going to be necessary businesses of the twenty-first century.

How does the socio-cultural environment affect you?   As a prospective employee, any one of these social issues will probably affect the company for which you end up working. Since workers are increasingly retiring at later ages, competition for certain jobs and for career advancement might be fiercer than in previous years. However, the culture of business is constantly shifting to meet the ever-evolving needs of Canadian demographics. This means more opportunity for employees who can navigate a diverse environment.

In addition, jobs aimed at responding to the needs of the growing green economy will likely present new opportunities for job seekers. Entrepreneurial possibilities always exist for those who have the vision and desire to succeed and are willing to take risks.

Technological Environment

How do technological changes affect the business environment?

> The **technological environment** includes human knowledge, work methods, physical equipment, electronics and telecommunications, and various processing systems used to perform business activities.

The **technological environment** includes human knowledge, work methods, physical equipment, electronics and telecommunications, and various processing systems used to perform business activities. Over the past twenty years, advancements in information technology (IT) have been revolutionary. In today's business world, it is a necessity to stay on the cutting edge of technology to remain competitive. Regardless of the type of business, technology can be used to keep a company flexible, organized, and well connected—with either customers or employees.

Product and service technologies are used for creating products and services for customers. Organizations must constantly be watching for technological breakthroughs that might make their products or services better than those of their competitors. Organizations also have to be mindful of technologies that might make their products or services obsolete and thereby threaten their survival. For example, when DVDs hit the market, VHS sales dropped; now VHS is no longer on the market. For some companies (such as IBM, Apple, Microsoft, Rogers, and Dell), technology is the basis for competition, because these companies market themselves as being technological leaders.

Research and development technologies are being used to create new products, services, and processes. For example, SunChips uses solar energy at one of its eight manufacturing plants to produce snacks that are not only better for the consumer, but better for the planet as well. Technological improvements and innovation in general are important to the economic development of a country.

How expensive is it to keep up with technology?

There is no question that keeping up with the pace of technology is an expensive and time-consuming operation. The rapid pace of technological innovation means that computers are outdated after three years and obsolete after five years.[32] In addition, there is the cost of applicable software, training, and infrastructure, which often makes IT the largest expense in many companies.[33] However, cost is not the only aspect of technology to consider. In the same way that robotics completely revolutionized the automotive industry, advancements in computer and telecommunications technology are completely changing the foundation and focus of how many businesses are run.

Technology, when used and implemented effectively, can help streamline businesses; cut costs; increase productivity, security, and transparency; and improve communication with customers. Giving employees the technology they need to get their work done more efficiently and effectively is the simplest way to increase productivity. If employees can get more work done in a shorter time, productivity goes up. When employees are more productive, they are more valuable. This, in turn, makes the whole company more valuable. In addition, the right technology can help streamline a business' internal operations, so the business can be more effective, efficient, and productive.

Thirty years ago, businesses were often centrally located with all employees in one building. Today, this is less common. Technology is making it possible for employees to telecommute, or work from home or another location away from the office. The "virtual global workforce," or telecommuters who work on a global scale, expands the pool of potential employees, so that the right employee can be found for the job regardless of where he or she lives.[34] Teleconferencing (and video-conferencing) is keeping CEOs and other corporate representatives from having to travel constantly for meetings. It is also allowing companies to communicate more easily, regardless of distance. These advancements are saving money on what used to be necessary expenses. With less travel, there is less money spent on plane tickets, hotel rooms, and food, and with more employees telecommuting, many businesses can operate out of smaller offices, which are cheaper and easier to manage.

How has the Internet changed the way business is done?

While IT is the tool that is changing the function of business, the Internet is the tool that is changing the scope.

The Internet is a global data communications system. It offers a way for consumers and businesses to communicate with each other, as well as a way for businesses to communicate with other businesses and consumers to communicate with other consumers. Using the Internet to conduct online business is a concept known as e-commerce or e-business and will be discussed in more detail in Chapter 9. Although IT by itself would be extremely influential for the business world, the Internet makes it truly revolutionary. In 1995, the Internet was just starting to proliferate. Even though it had been commercially available for years at that point, the Internet had only recently become viable after the advent of the World Wide Web a few years before. Many people were intimidated by this new technology, and companies that operated solely on the Internet were not expected to do well. This changed in 1995, when both eBay.com and Amazon.com launched. These companies showed that Internet-based businesses were not only possible, but also potentially lucrative. Their high-profile success paved the way for today's e-business merchant.[35]

Many businesses that exist in the bricks-and-mortar (physical store) world of commerce are now finding they also need to have an Internet presence in order to compete for customer loyalty. Many new business start-ups begin as online stores, with no physical location where consumers can shop. Every year, conducting business over the Internet becomes a more significant element of the overall economy. As it becomes easier for consumers to find even the most obscure items at competitive prices, the sale of goods and services online will continue to be a driving force in our economy. As the Internet and its influence continue to grow, so will its economic importance and necessity for businesses. However, the prevalence of the Internet also presents dangers and concerns for business.

Technology makes it possible to work from virtually anywhere. Is that a good thing?

One important concern is privacy. E-mails, internal documents, and chat transcripts all contain private information not intended for public viewing. Nevertheless, many of these documents can be accessed online, because online storage has become a convenient alternative to hard drives. Web-based e-mail and documents are also becoming more common. Even gaining access to a work or home computer from a remote location is a simple process that is becoming more popular. With this universal access, it is increasingly difficult to ensure that information remains private. Web-based storage and services offer many benefits to business, yet privacy and security concerns cannot be overlooked. Over time, technology will continue to introduce challenges. Chapter 9 will discuss the benefits and challenges technology brings to businesses and how businesses and consumers use the Internet to buy and sell goods and services.

CHAPTER SYNOPSIS

❶ Describe the roles the Canadian government plays in business. *(pp. 4–6)*

Government influences business activity in the Canadian economy through its many roles:

- Government becomes a **regulator** when it regulates many aspects of business activity through administrative boards, tribunals, and commissions. Regulations promote competition between businesses, protect customers, achieve social goals, and protect the environment.
- Government becomes a **provider of incentives** when it offers programs that help stimulate economic development.

- Government becomes a **provider of essential services** when it supplies services that create the stability that encourages business activity.
- Government becomes a **taxation agent** when taxes are imposed and collected by the three levels of government.
- Government becomes a **customer** when buying from businesses.
- Government becomes a **competitor** when it competes with businesses through its Crown corporations, such as Canada Post, the Canadian Broadcasting Corporation, SaskTel, SaskEnergy, BC Hydro, and the Liquor Control Board of Ontario (LCBO).

❷ **Define business and discuss the role of business in the economy.** *(p. 7)*

Business is any activity that provides goods or services in exchange for other goods and services or money, based on their perceived worth. A **profit** is earned when a company's revenue (the total amount of money received for goods and services provided) is greater than its **expenses** (costs incurred while doing business). A **loss** occurs when revenue is less than its expenses.

Every business needs a sufficient number of customers to whom its output can consistently be sold at a profit. As more profit is generated, a company is able to reward its employees, increase productivity, or expand its business into new areas.

The proprietor of a business is not the only one who benefits from earned profits and business success. A successful business provides the goods and services people need and want, provides employment opportunities for members of the community, pays taxes, and generates income and spending in the economy. Socially responsible firms contribute even more by actively advocating for the well-being of the society that generates their success.

Successful businesses help to raise a country's standard of living and improve the quality of life. A country's **standard of living** is the level of wealth, comfort, material goods, and necessities available to its people.

❸ **Explain the difference between for-profit and non-profit organizational goals.** *(p. 7)*

People establish for-profit businesses to perform economic activities. With some exceptions (such as co-operatives, non-profit organizations, and government institutions), businesses exist to produce profit. A **non-profit organization** seeks to service its community through social, educational, or political means. Organizations such as universities, hospitals, environmental groups, and charities are non-profit organizations (such as the Canadian Diabetes Association, Canadian Cancer Society, and Red Cross). Any excess revenue they generate is used to further their stated mission.

❹ **Explain the difference between private and public business sectors.** *(pp. 8–10)*

The **public business sector** includes goods and services produced, delivered, and allocated by the government and non-profit entities created by public administrations.

The **private business sector** includes goods and services produced, delivered, and allocated by private individuals or groups, usually as a means of enterprise for profit. The sector is not controlled by government.

The **non-profit and voluntary sector** includes non-governmental, non-profit organizations that receive support from individual Canadians, governments, and businesses.

The aim of the public sector is to provide services that benefit the public as a whole, either because it would be difficult to charge people for the goods and services concerned, or because people might not be able to afford to pay for them. The government can provide these goods and services at a lower price than if they were provided by a for-profit company. The goal of businesses in the private sector is to make a profit.

❺ **Describe the factors of production.** *(pp. 10–12)*

The **factors of production are** the resources used to produce goods and services.

Labour is the human resource that refers to any physical or intellectual work people contribute to a business' production.

Natural resources are the raw materials provided by nature that are used to produce goods and services.

Real capital refers to the physical facilities used to produce goods and services. Financial capital is money used to facilitate a business enterprise.

An entrepreneur is someone who assumes the risk of creating, organizing, and operating a business and who directs all the business resources.

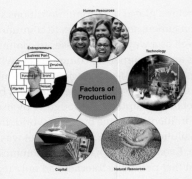

Technology refers to items and services such as smartphones, computer software, and digital broadcasting that make businesses more efficient and productive. Successful companies are able to keep pace with technological progresses and harness new knowledge, information, and strategies. **Information and knowledge** are quickly becoming the key factors of production as the new competitive business environment places a premium on these factors. Companies do not require technology for the sake of technology alone. They require technology to obtain and manage information, and they need human resources (knowledge workers) who have the skills to manipulate the information by turning it into knowledge that the company can use for competitive advantage. Knowledge is a tricky thing to manage, but companies can translate their information assets into real value for the business by learning from past successes or failures, identifying opportunities to improve profitability, or simply enabling teams to become more productive.

❻ **Identify the functional areas of most businesses.** *(pp. 12–13)*

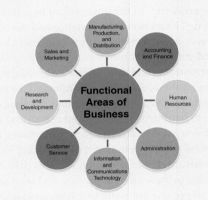

Functional Areas of Business

❼ **Describe the macro-business environment and how the PEST model is used by managers to analyze external business opportunities and threats.** *(pp. 13–21)*

The **macro-environment** (external factors that affect an organization) includes factors that create opportunities for and pose threats to the company. External factors include political-legal, economic, socio-cultural, and technological.

To help analyze the macro-environment, managers use several analysis processes to gather, analyze, and dispense information for tactical or strategic purposes. One option is to analyze external factors using the PEST model, which is a useful tool for understanding market demand or decline, current business position, and potential opportunities and obstacles. This classification distinguishes between:

■ *Political-legal* factors. Government policy and political decisions can affect many vital areas for business. Factors may include ethical considerations, employment laws, competition laws, product regulations, consumer laws, sustainable environmental practices, and health and safety legislation.

■ *Economic* factors. Changes in the local, national, or global economy can affect business operations. Factors may include interest rates, economic growth, industry changes, inflation and exchange rates, and taxation changes.

■ *Socio-cultural* factors. Consumer behaviour and preferences will affect decisions about product offerings. Environmentally friendly business processes are affecting demand patterns and creating business opportunities. Other factors may include social trends, population, demographics, and ethical considerations.

■ *Technological* factors. As technology changes, companies must adjust business practices to compete in the global business world. Factors include new technologies, online shopping, research and development, and global access.

KEY TERMS

business *(p. 7)*
diversity initiative *(p. 19)*
economic environment *(p. 16)*
entrepreneur *(p. 10)*
expenses *(p. 7)*
external environment *(p. 13)*
factors of production *(p. 10)*
financial capital *(p. 10)*
functional areas *(p. 12)*
globalization *(p. 16)*
goods *(p. 10)*

green economy *(p. 19)*
information and
    knowledge *(p. 11)*
internal environment *(p. 13)*
labour *(p. 10)*
loss *(p. 7)*
macro-environment *(p. 13)*
marketing concept *(p. 5)*
micro-environment *(p. 13)*
natural resources *(p. 10)*
non-profit organizations *(p. 7)*

non-profit and voluntary
    sector *(p. 8)*
PEST model *(p. 14)*
political-legal
    environment *(p. 15)*
private business sector *(p. 8)*
production concept *(p. 5)*
profit *(p. 7)*
public business sector *(p. 8)*
quality of life *(p. 7)*
real capital *(p. 10)*

revenue *(p. 7)*
sales concept *(p. 5)*
services *(p. 10)*
socio-cultural
    environment *(p. 16)*
standard of living *(p. 7)*
technology *(p. 10)*
technological
    environment *(p. 20)*

CRITICAL THINKING QUESTIONS

1. Consider all of the factors of production: labour, natural resources, capital, entrepreneurs, and technology. Is each of these resources a vital part of the school you attend or the company for which you work? Which factors do you believe are most important to the goods and services provided by your organization? Why?

2. Give examples of the ways in which each of the five factors of production can affect the business performance of McDonald's or Walmart.

3. It is not unusual to encounter businesses that have streamlined their activities to accommodate ecological factors. The text uses a change in auto sales as an example of how businesses are directly affected by the green movement. Can you think of other examples of businesses that might be forced to alter their business decisions based on ecological factors? How might these decisions affect their profits?

4. Most business owners agree that keeping up with the pace of technological change is a challenging task. Imagine you are the owner of a new restaurant business and must decide what technology would best suit your needs. From what types of technology would this business benefit? Consider the factors of production, organization, and communication in your decision.

5. Considering the rapid increase in e-commerce, it is likely that you have purchased or sold some sort of product online. If not, you have probably browsed the Web pages of eBay or your favourite clothing store. Can you list a few companies or organizations that do not offer their products or services online? How does their status and growth compare with similar companies who do offer goods and services online?

APPLICATION EXERCISES

1. **Demographics.** Imagine you are starting a new retail clothing business in the city where you attend school. To what demographic area would you market? Think about the following factors: race, ethnicity, gender, age, income, and sexual orientation. Visit www.statcan.gc.ca to locate reports on the demographic area in which you are interested. Do you believe your business can thrive in this area? If not, what area would be conducive to your obtaining future customers? Would you have to change your retail clothing products in any way for the demographic market?

2. **Languages of the Global Marketplace.** As globalization increases and the world markets become more intertwined, language barriers become important. Investigate online resources for automated translation tools. What happens if you want to read a Web page posted by a German firm? Can you make online purchases from a company based in Asia? What resources are there for translating telephone conversations in real time? Investigate Babelfish.com and personal interpreter services such as LanaguageLine.com.

3. **E-commerce.** Did you know there are websites dedicated to keeping businesses and consumers up-to-date on the latest e-commerce news and trends? Check out www.ecommercetimes.com and find a recent e-commerce trend, and write a brief summary.

4. **Political-legal Environment.** The political-legal macro-environment of business affects business operations in

many ways. For instance, the government has changed the consumer tax structure into a single federally administered tax, the Harmonized Sales Tax (HST). You will find information online at www.cra-arc.gc.ca and www.hstincanada.com. Previously, businesses applied a goods and services tax (GST) and a provincial sales tax (PST) to most sales transactions. How might this change affect business operations? Does HST apply to all provinces, all businesses, and all consumers?

5. **Socio-cultural Environment.** Public opinion has a huge bearing on how companies and the Canadian government

act. Conduct online research to find a recent news event that discusses consumers responding negatively to some business venture or change. For example, communities often respond negatively to garbage dumps and nuclear plants being placed in their neighbourhoods. They protest through rallies, writing letters to government, posting online discussions and opinions, word of mouth, meetings with company leaders, and e-mails. Share your findings with the class.

GLOBAL 500 RESEARCH PROJECT

INSTRUCTIONS

1. Choose a Global 500 company from *Fortune* magazine's annual rankings at http://money.cnn.com/magazines/fortune/global500/.

2. Research:
   a. What is the name and mission statement (or value/vision statements) of the company?
   b. Where does the company operate—locally, nationally, or globally?
   c. What does the company do—provide goods or services?
   d. How much revenue did the company generate last year? How much of that was profit?

   e. Perform a PEST analysis on the Global 500 company you chose. Use the PEST model given within the chapter as a guide to the questions you will seek answers to while completing an analysis of the macro-environment for this company. For example, how do legal and political regulations affect business operations? Has there been any recent news that demonstrates some aspect of the macro-environment factors? How does the macro-environment affect business operations locally, nationally, and globally?

3. Prepare a report and submit to your professor.

TEAM TIME

The Competitive Edge
Competition arises when two or more businesses contend to attract consumers and gain an advantage over one another. Divide into three groups: Company A, Company B, and Consumers.

SCENARIO

Company A and B: Collectively decide what type of business you want to represent (for example, sports apparel company, beauty salon, or pet care agency) then choose a product or service applicable to that type of business. (Both groups should choose the same type of business and product or service.)

PROCESS

Step 1. *Companies A and B:* Decide how you will present your product to your customers. Focus on the following factors: packaging/presentation, price/budget, quality. Consumers: Compile a list of what is important to you when choosing this product or service.
Step 2. *Companies A and B:* Provide a brief presentation to your competition and consumers. *Consumers:* Provide in-depth

feedback to both companies as to how they could improve; consider your initial list.
Step 3. *Companies A and B:* Use the consumer feedback to alter your product or service to gain advantage over your competition. *Consumers:* Discuss how the two companies compared to real-life companies offering similar products or services. Would you consider purchasing from either of these two companies? Why or why not?
Step 4. *Companies A and B:* Present your product again. Explain why your product or service surpasses that of your competition.
Step 5. *Consumers:* Discuss the changes made by both companies and consider how they accommodated your needs. Did each company effectively incorporate your feedback into its revised presentation? Choose one company that you think gained the competitive advantage.
Step 6. *Entire class:* Openly discuss the factors real companies must face in competition. Were these factors considered in the challenge?

ETHICS AND RESPONSIBILITY

Cultural Awareness: An Unwritten Law
There are many challenges facing multinational companies where diversity and cultural awareness are concerned.

Process
Step 1. Divide into six groups, each representing one of the following countries: China, France, Germany, Japan, Mexico, and the United States. Examine the cultural practices, customs, and values of the country you will represent. This may be done in class if you have Internet access, or as homework.
Step 2. Each group should pair together with a second group as follows: United States with Japan, Mexico with Germany, and China with France.

Step 3. Each group should produce one scenario of a business transaction that would be affected by cultural differences found in your research. Fabricate specific companies, characters, interactions, and resolutions.
Step 4. Answer these questions and discuss with the class: What were some challenges encountered in your business scenario and how did you overcome them? Why is it important for multinational companies to research a foreign country with which they intend to conduct business?

CLOSING CASE

GE's Imagination Is a Factor of Production

Traditionally, the name Thomas Edison is synonymous with the word *ingenious*. Similarly, his invention, the carbon filament incandescent lamp, or light bulb, is symbolic of all things innovative. This ingenuity and innovation created the building blocks for General Electric. GE is a business that started 130 years ago with a bright idea that developed into a world-changing product. The commercial light bulb not only had a profound impact on people's daily lives, it also gave birth to a business that would eventually grow into one of the world's largest corporations.

The roots of GE started to form in 1876, when Thomas A. Edison opened a laboratory to experiment with electricity and electric devices. These experiments resulted in the invention of the light bulb. By 1890, Edison had established the Edison General Electric Company. During this time, a competing business, The Thomas-Houston Company, was quickly becoming a leader in the field of electrical technology. Both Edison and Thomas-Houston's head, Charles A. Coffin, realized that with each organization's patents and technologies combined, they could create a successful and innovative company. So, in 1892, the two companies merged to create The General Electric Company.[36]

From that initial configuration, GE developed into a massive conglomerate that encompasses six different companies located in 160 countries with more than 300 000 employees worldwide. The company's multifaceted structure was formed by its ability to turn ideas into industry. In 1896, GE introduced the X-ray machine. It represented GE's ability to use important scientific discoveries in a practical manner. This product laid the groundwork for GE Healthcare. Likewise, the first electric fan, invented in 1902, was the first of many modern conveniences that helped develop GE Industrial. GE also formed the first national television network when its station, WRGB, became the first to relay a national broadcast from New York City. Each of these individual achievements produced the opportunity to develop new areas of business.[37]

Despite GE's years of successful growth, like any business, it must continue to ask itself, "Why are we here? What do we have to offer?" When GE was first established, its purpose was to bring electric energy and light to the masses through products such as dynamos and electric lamps. Today, GE has a somewhat broader purpose. The company says, "We exist to solve problems for our customers, our communities and societies, and ourselves."[38] GE considers imagination to be their greatest commodity. While imagination is not a good that you can box up and sell in a store or a service you can order online or over the phone, it is something that GE uses as a factor of production. An active imagination can conjure up innovative goods and services. GE hopes that these goods and services will fuel the global economy and improve people's lives.

Another benefit of imagination is that it has allowed GE to keep up with social and cultural changes. GE has developed high-tech imaging systems to detect cancer in the country's aging population, energy-efficient appliances to combat global warming and save money, and large-scale infrastructures to help developing countries. Staying in touch with the wants and needs of the market has made GE a successful business for 130 years. Since its inception, GE has tailored its imagination to produce innovative products that are useful to the world. "Anything that won't sell, I don't want to invent. Its sale is proof of utility, and utility is success," stated Thomas A. Edison. That philosophy is what has allowed GE to turn its imagination into industry, and industry into profits.

DISCUSSION QUESTIONS

1. How important do you think it is for a business to be innovative? Is the newest idea always the best idea? Do you think GE would still be a successful company today if it continued to focus solely on electrical technologies?
2. Why did Edison Electric Company and The Thomas-Houston Company merge? What challenges might each company have encountered if they had remained competitors? Why is it beneficial for businesses, particularly technology-based businesses, to merge?
3. Thomas Edison is often credited with being the inventor of the light bulb because he created the first light bulb that was appropriate for use in a person's home. Is it important for a business to create products that are practical? Why or why not?

MyBusinessLab CHAPTER RESOURCES

MyBusinessLab in an online learning and testing environment that features the perfect study tools to help you master the concepts covered in this chapter. Log in to MyBusinessLab at www.pearsoned.ca/mybusinesslab to test your knowledge of key chapter concepts, participate in simulations modelled on real-world business situations, and explore the following additional practice tools:

- Study Plan
- Audio Chapter Summaries
- Glossary Flashcards
- eText
- BizChat Discussion Boards

Video Case:

To access the Chapter 1 Video Case: Helping Business Do Business, see the Activities folder in the Assessment section of MyBusinessLab.

Web Case:

To access the Chapter 1 Web Case, see the Activities folder in the Assessment section of MyBusinessLab

Career Skills:

Visit the Career Skills module "Ten Easy Rules for Academic Success and Beyond" on MyBusinessLab, where you will gain insight on how to become an academic all-star. You will learn how to get the most out of all the resources your school provides and how to build transferrable skills that you can apply to your academic and professional careers.

2

Economics and Banking

LEARNING OBJECTIVES

After studying this chapter, you should be able to:

1. Define economics and describe the different types of economic systems. (pp. 28–31)

2. Describe the law of supply and demand and how supply and demand affect price. (pp. 32–37)

3. Summarize the four degrees of competition and describe how competition affects demand. (pp 38–44)

4. Identify how economic indicators such as the gross domestic product (GDP), price indexes, the unemployment rate, and productivity reflect economic health. (pp. 44–48)

5. List and describe the four stages of the business cycle. (p. 48)

6. Summarize how the government uses both fiscal policy and monetary policy to control changes in the business cycle. (pp. 48–52)

Countries and Consumers
TOP 10 BIGGEST ECONOMIES: 2010 VS 2020

EUROMONITOR INTERNATIONAL

GDP 2020
PPP in I$

GDP in 2020
I$ bn
- 1000 +
- 100–1000
- 10–100
- 0–10
- Not Illustrated

Rank Shift in GDP
2010 vs 2020; PPP in I$

Rank	2010	2020
1	United States	China
2	China	United States
3	Japan	India
4	India	Japan
5	Germany	Russia
6	Russia	Germany
7	United Kingdom	Brazil
8	France	United Kingdom
9	Brazil	France
10	Italy	Mexico
11	Mexico	South Korea
12	South Korea	Indonesia
13	Spain	Italy
14	Canada	Canada
15	Indonesia	Spain

OPENING DISCUSSION: EMERGING ECONOMIES

Which Emerging Economies Are Gaining Global Economic Power?

To strengthen international co-operation, country leaders have established several forums as mechanisms to bring together developed and emerging economies in informal discussions to achieve stable and sustainable world growth that benefits all. The G7 is a forum of the world's leading countries—Canada, the United States, France, Germany, Italy, Japan, and the United Kingdom—that meet periodically to achieve a co-operative effort on international economic and monetary issues. This powerful group of nations does not include any developing nations. The G8, which adds Russia to the G7 countries, holds an annual meeting of heads of government to discuss issues such as the global economic outlook and macro-economic management, international trade, energy, climate change, political-security issues, and relations with developing countries. Since 2005, the G8 has been conducting dialogues with the major emerging economies of Brazil, China, India, Mexico, and South Africa.[1] The G20 is an informal forum that advocates open, constructive discussion between industrial and emerging-market countries on key issues in the global economy (e.g., energy, economic development, and trade).

In recent years, there has been a shift in global economic power away from the developed G7 economies toward the developing world. The emerging countries, known as the E7 countries, include the BRIC (Brazil, Russia, India, and People's Republic of China), Mexico, Indonesia, and Turkey. Despite lagging behind the other members in terms of economic growth, China formally invited South Africa to join the BRIC in 2010 (and so the acronym changed to the BRICS).

(continued)

By 2020, the E7's combined wealth will overtake the G7's combined wealth, and China is on course to succeed the United States as the world's largest economy, according to accounting firm PriceWaterhouseCoopers.[2]

"India's growth may accelerate to 9.5 percent between 2011 to 2015," Morgan Stanley economist Chetan Ahya recently said in an interview. "India's gross domestic product has expanded at an average 7.1 percent over the decade through the third quarter of 2009, compared with 9.1 percent in China, which surpassed Japan as the second-largest economy last quarter."[3]

John Hawksworth, chief economist at PriceWaterhouseCoopers, said, "In many ways, the renewed dominance by 2050 of China and India, with their much larger populations, is a return to the historical norm prior to the Industrial Revolution of the late eighteenth and nineteenth centuries that caused a shift in global economic power from Asia to Western Europe and the United States—this temporary shift in power is now going into reverse. This changing world order poses challenges and opportunities for businesses in the current advanced economies."[4]

Rising international economic integration, or globalization as it is commonly known, offers many opportunities. However, the public often associates globalization with job losses and downward pressures on wages and working conditions.

DISCUSSION QUESTIONS

1. Why do you think people in Canada might associate globalization with job loss and lower wages?
2. What opportunities and challenges might arise for Canadian businesses (consider small and large firms)?
3. Will a global marketplace change the way we work, business laws, or the technology required to do business? If so, how?

BASICS OF ECONOMICS

Economics Defined

Define economics and describe the different types of economic systems.

Economics is the study of how individuals, businesses, and government make decisions about how to allocate limited (scarce) resources to best satisfy people's wants, needs, and desires.

What is economics?   Do you ever wonder what makes the price of oil rise, why unemployment climbs, or why you should care about inflation? Do you wonder why some jobs pay more than others, why tuition fees keep rising, or why rent is higher in different parts of the city or country? Studying economics can help you answer these questions. **Economics** is the study of how individuals, businesses, and government make decisions about how to allocate limited (scarce) resources to best satisfy people's wants, needs, and desires. It is about businesses making goods (such as books, pizza, or computers) or supplying services (such as giving haircuts, painting houses, or installing home entertainment networks) that people want or need to buy. The resources—labour, capital, natural resources (i.e., land), entrepreneurship, and technology—are known as the factors of production (as discussed in Chapter 1) because they are the required inputs that help businesses produce outputs (goods and services).

Because resources are scarce and businesses do not have enough tools, money, or products to provide all the books, pizza, or haircuts that we want, businesses must decide what and how much to make. Not everyone will be able to have what he or she wants because of the limited resources (such as money, space, or time) and supplies—this is the fundamental economic problem known as scarcity. Therefore, economists look at how resources are distributed in the marketplace and how equitably and efficiently those resources are disbursed. Economics examines capitalism versus socialism, management of inflation and unemployment, economic development of poor countries, pollution and global warming, energy policies, national defence, international trade and finance, old age security, and many specific government policies (such as minimum wage, agricultural price supports, and rent control).

How do government, businesses, and households interact?

Households provide businesses with inputs to production: labour (as workers), land and buildings (as landlords), entrepreneurs, and capital (as investors). Businesses use those inputs to produce goods and services (outputs), which they provide to government and households. Government and households buy those goods and services, which provides businesses with revenue. The revenue obtained by businesses is then used to buy additional resources. Businesses and households provide government with tax payments. Government uses the tax money to provide businesses and households with incentives, services, and programs (e.g., health care, roads, and community programs). This cycle is known as the **circular flow of Canada's economy** (see Figure 2.1).

Figure 2.1 Circular Flow of Canada's Economy

Why is it important to study economics?

There are many reasons to study economics, but one of the most important is to learn about how people get the goods and services they need and want. Economics helps us understand the impact government decisions have on firms, industries, and nations. It helps us understand the effect international trade has on a global and national level. It helps us recognize secondary effects of decisions—for example, if the government creates a tax to pay for some needed social program, the secondary effect might be that people, now paying higher taxes, spend less money shopping, causing economic growth to slow. Studying economics is important as it allows us to learn from our mistakes; understand business cycles, investments, and standards of living; solve problems; and make better decisions. There are two basic studies of economics: *microeconomics* and *macroeconomics*.

What is microeconomics?

Microeconomics is the study of how individual businesses, households, and consumers make decisions to allocate their limited resources in the exchange of goods and services. When a real estate sales executive tries to determine how a change in prices could help generate sales or analyzes the number of existing houses that are already for sale in the local market, he or she is using the microeconomic principles of supply and demand.

What is macroeconomics?

Macroeconomics looks at the bigger picture. It is the study of the behaviour of the overall economy. Economy-wide occurrences, such as changes in unemployment, interest rates, inflation, and prices, are all part of the study of macroeconomics. For example, macroeconomics examines how a change in interest rates affects the demand for housing, or how a change in the housing market affects the overall economy. The government and individuals in a society also affect how resources are allocated and define the economic system in which goods and services are allocated.

The circular flow of Canada's economy is an economic cycle in which businesses and households provide government with tax payments generated from revenue and wages, and government uses the tax money to provide businesses and households with incentives, programs, and services.

Microeconomics is the study of how individual businesses, households, and consumers make decisions to allocate their limited resources in the exchange of goods and services.

Macroeconomics is the study of the behaviour of the overall economy. Economy-wide occurrences, such as changes in unemployment, interest rates, inflation, and prices, are all part of the study of macroeconomics.

Types of Economic Systems

What are the different types of economic systems?

Economists have created several economic models to categorize the world's many economic systems. These economic models include:

- traditional economies
- planned (or controlled) economies
- market economies
- mixed economies

Traditional economies were found in earlier agrarian communities, which were primitive in nature and based on a strong social network. Very few traditional economies exist today. Most economies today represent some form of a mixed economic system or a market economic system. **Table 2.1** summarizes the features of the three most common basic economic models.

What is a planned economy?

In a **planned economic system**, the government plays a greater role in determining the goods and services provided and how they are produced and distributed. Both communism and socialism are planned economic systems.

Communism is an economic system in which government makes all economic decisions and controls all the social services and many of the major resources required for production of goods and services. Karl Marx, the originator of communist principles in his book *The Communist Manifesto*, envisioned the workers themselves eventually taking over the government's responsibilities to provide the services. No communist country has achieved this level of Marx's vision. Existing communist states, including North Korea and Cuba, are failing economically. Problems that have arisen with communist systems include shortages of goods and services. In fact, in the later years of the twentieth century, most former Soviet republic states and Eastern European countries, as well as China, turned from a communism-based economy to a market economy to combat these problems.

Socialism provides that the government plans and controls the economy. Government owns or controls many basic businesses and services, while individuals own and operate less crucial industries. It is similar to communism but allows for some capitalism (individual ownership). In socialist economic systems, governments traditionally run some of the social services, such as education, health care, retirement, and unemployment, as well as other necessary businesses, such as utility companies (telephone, electric, water, sewer). The government charges high tax rates to pay for the services it provides.

In a **planned economic system**, the government plays a greater role in determining the goods and services provided and how they are produced and distributed. Both communism and socialism are planned economic systems.

Communism is an economic system in which government makes all economic decisions and controls all the social services and many of the major resources required for production of goods and services.

Socialism provides that the government plans and controls the economy. Government owns or controls many basic businesses and services, while individuals own and operate less crucial industries.

Table 2.1 World Economic Models

Type of Economy	What to Produce	How to Produce	For Whom to Produce
Planned (Controlled)	Government or other centralized group determines what to produce.	Government or other centralized group determines and controls the resources and means of production.	Government or other centralized group determines wages and sets prices. Resources and products are distributed to common group.
Market	Individuals and private firms make decisions based on consumer needs and wants.	Individuals and private firms determine the production methods. The focus is on efficiency and profitability.	Individual income ultimately controls purchasing decisions.
Mixed	Individuals determine what to produce with some level of government involvement.	Individuals and government control resources and determine production methods.	Government distributes some goods and services through selected social programs. Individual income determines purchasing decisions for other goods and services.

For example, the people of Denmark are regularly voted to be the happiest people in the world, while income tax rates range from 38 to 59 percent.[5] In comparison, Canada's income tax rate is 15 to 29 percent.[6] Although citizens of socialist countries pay higher tax rates, they benefit from social programs that tax proceeds are used to fund. Many Western European countries, such as France and Sweden, have adopted a socialist planned economy. Generally, workers in socialist economies work fewer hours, have longer vacations, and receive more health, education, and childcare benefits than do workers in purely capitalist economies.

Although many feel government-controlled and government-supplied social services provide a fair and equitable distribution of such services, a concern with true socialism is a diminishing motivation for workers. In a true socialist system, workers turn over their earnings and profits to the state rather than keep their own earnings, thus reducing the incentive to work hard. Therefore, it is difficult to find purely socialist economies. Many socialist and communist countries are beginning to change to market-based economies through the practice of **privatization**—the conversion of government-owned production and services to privately owned, profit-seeking enterprises.

Privatization is the conversion of government-owned production and services to privately owned, profit-seeking enterprises.

What is a market economy?   In a market economy, individuals are able to make their own economic decisions. For example, there may be several pizza parlours in your town, and each one may sell slices of pizza at different prices—no one is restricting the number of pizza parlours, nor is anyone controlling what price they can charge. Similarly, people are free to choose any pizza they would like to buy. This freedom of choice for both the buyer and seller defines a free market economy. The United Kingdom, United States, and Japan are examples of market economies.

Capitalism, also known as a market economy, free market, or free enterprise, is the economic system that allows such freedom of choice and encourages private ownership of the resources required to make and provide goods and services. Capitalism has become a major influence in the Western world's economic system. In a capitalist economy, the production and pricing of goods and services are determined through the operation of a market—the mechanism by which buyers and sellers exchange goods and services.

Capitalism, also called a market economy, free market, or free enterprise, allows freedom of choice and encourages private ownership of the resources required to make and provide goods and services consumers enjoy.

What is a mixed economy?   Today, most economic systems are **mixed economies**, meaning a blend of market and planned economies. Most Western European countries, for example, operate with a mixed economy of privately owned businesses and government control of selected social programs, such as health care. Although the United States is closest to a market economy, there is still some government intervention. Although Canada's system is largely a free market, some aspects of it have socialist characteristics. For example, Canada Post, the Canadian Broadcasting Corporation (CBC), and the Royal Canadian Mint are examples of **Crown corporations**—businesses owned by the federal government that provide important services to Canadians. By collecting taxes, Canada's government is able to provide Canadians with employment insurance, health insurance, and pension benefits. Because the government controls important aspects of the economy, Canada is considered a mixed economy. China was once a communist country but is now more of a patchwork of public and private businesses.

Mixed economies are a blend of market and planned economies with a mixed economy of privately owned businesses and government control of selected social programs, such as health care.

Crown corporations are businesses owned by the federal government that provide important services to Canadians, including Canada Post, the Canadian Broadcasting Corporation (CBC), and the Royal Canadian Mint.

One way to think about the various mixed economies and how they relate to either a market or planned economic system is to place them on a continuum, as shown in **Figure 2.2**.

Figure 2.2   Continuum of Economic Systems: Degree of Government Control

Source: Adapted from David O'Connor and Christopher Faille, *Basic Economic Principles*. Westport, CT: Greenwood Press, 2000.

BUSINESS AND ECONOMICS

Supply and Demand

BizSkills Simulation:
Supply and Demand.
Located in MyBusinessLab.

2

Describe the law of supply and demand and how supply and demand affect price.

The act of **bartering** involves people trading goods or services without an exchange of money. The "price" of something is determined by the needs of each person in the bartering exchange and what they are willing to trade.

Currency, a unit of exchange for the transfer of goods and services, provides a consistent and equitable standard, the value of which is based on an underlying commodity, such as gold.

Supply and demand is a complicated process involving multiple factors, such as income levels, tastes, and the amount of competition in the market. The need for an item is **demand**, and the availability of that item is **supply**.

Why do business managers need to be concerned with economics?
Business managers and owners must understand the principles of economics because the nature of business is to provide items or services for purchase in exchange for something, generally money. Businesses need to know how much of their products to produce or how many services to offer, as well as how much to charge for these products and services. For example, as the demand for new housing begins to dwindle, a real estate company needs to make decisions that affect other areas of the business, such as land acquisitions and staffing.

Business managers also need to be aware of the potential impact that government decisions (such as changing interest rates) and the decisions of collective businesses (such as the general level of unemployment) can have on their individual business or industry. Understanding economics, how prices are determined, the relationship of supply and demand, and the involvement of government is instrumental to operating a successful business.

How do supply and demand affect business?
In the days of **bartering**, when people traded goods or services without an exchange of money, the "price" of something was determined by the needs of each person in the bartering exchange and what they were willing to trade. For example, if you wanted milk and had no cow, but you did have chickens, you were willing to give up eggs for some milk. You would look for someone who wanted to trade his or her milk for your eggs. At the end of the trade, everyone was happy—you got the milk you needed and the other person got the eggs he or she needed.

However, there were problems with this exchange system. Bartering can be inefficient and inconsistent. What if the person who had the cow did not need eggs, or what if the owner of the cow thought the milk was worth a chicken, but you thought it was worth only a dozen eggs? To offset some of the difficulties of bartering, the concept of currency, or money, was developed. **Currency**, a unit of exchange for the transfer of goods and services, provides a consistent and equitable standard, the value of which is based on an underlying commodity, such as gold.

In a system using currency, items such as milk, eggs, and chickens are assigned a price, or a value, based on how much the item is worth against the standard. Today, although we do have currency, ultimately the price for a product or service is determined by two fundamental economic concepts: supply and demand.

Supply and demand is actually a very complicated process because many factors are involved, such as income levels, tastes, and the amount of competition in the market. However, if we ignore those factors for the moment (and economists do this all the time—it's called "all else held constant") and just examine the fundamentals, we find that the market price for a product or service is the price at which everyone who wants the item can get it without anyone wanting more or without any of the item being left over. The need for an item is demand, and the availability of that item is supply.

The closest real-world example of determining a market price that is based on pure supply and demand is the auction process, like that found on eBay. In an auction process, bidders state the price they are willing to pay for a particular item. The price increases depending on the demand: the greater the demand, the higher the price the bidders are willing to pay. Supply also affects price: if similar or identical items are available for auction, the price is kept lower. When a unique item is auctioned, prices tend to be higher because demand is higher and supply is lower. Eventually, the winning bid establishes the market price.

What does supply refer to?　**Supply** refers to how much of a product or service is available for purchase at any given time. It is dependent on the resources required to produce the product or offer the service, such as land, labour, and capital (buildings and machinery), and the quantity of similar products that can easily be substituted for the product and that are competing for the consumer's attention. However, if all of these factors are ignored or held constant, then supply is directly affected by price (selling price).

Supply is derived from a producer's desire to maximize profits. The more money a business can get for its good or service, the more of its product it is willing to supply. In economic terms, the **law of supply** states that the amount supplied will increase as the price increases; if the price is lower, less of the product is supplied.

Here is an example: If Eddie opens a coffee kiosk in the middle of a college campus, he will want to supply more cups of coffee at the price of $2.00 per cup than at the price of $0.50 per cup, because he will have a greater incentive to supply coffee at the higher price. To illustrate this point, let's assume the cost for Eddie to make a cup of coffee is $0.30, factoring in the cost of labour, supplies, equipment, and rent. Selling a cup of coffee at $0.50 means Eddie makes $0.20 profit, but selling a cup of coffee at $2.00 means Eddie makes $1.70 profit—that's a big incentive when you multiple that profit by the hundreds of cups per day Eddie would sell. Notice in **Table 2.2** that Eddie supplies only ten cups of coffee at $0.50 per cup. However, if Eddie can charge $1.25, he has a greater incentive to supply more cups of coffee and produces seventy cups. At the price of $2.00, Eddie wants to supply even more cups of coffee, and his supply increases to 115. The more he can charge, the more he will want to supply, or sell. This relationship between supply and price can be illustrated in a graph, which economists call a supply curve, like the one shown in **Figure 2.3**. However, the demand for coffee has a very different reaction to price.

What does demand refer to?　**Demand** refers to how much of a product or a service people want to buy at any given time. People are willing to buy as much as they need, but they have limited resources (money). Therefore, the **law of demand** states that people will buy more of an item at a lower price than at a higher price. In our coffee example, as shown in **Table 2.3**, students buy twelve cups of coffee when Eddie charges $2.00 a cup, but they buy 120 cups of coffee from Eddie at $0.50 a cup. In other words, as price decreases, demand increases. Economists illustrate the

---

Imagine you are a chef and have just realized your dream of opening your own gourmet Italian food restaurant. Do you know enough about supply and demand? You can test yourself by taking the following **quiz**.

1. You purchase a pasta machine that makes pasta three times faster than your current process. Your supply of fresh pasta will go:

   A. up

   B. down

2. The price of flour skyrockets. Your supply of pasta will go:

   A. up

   B. down

3. Te A highly publicized scientific study claims that low-carb diets help people lose weight faster than any other type of diet. The demand for your fresh pasta will go:

   A. up

   B. down

4. A highly publicized scientific study claims that low-carb diets help people lose weight faster than any other type of diet. The demand for your fresh pasta will go:

   A. up

   B. down

Answers: 1. A; 2. B; 3. B; 4. A

If you got . . .

0 or 1 answer(s) correct: You're not supply-and-demand savvy yet. This section will help.

2 or 3 answers correct: You're semi-savvy in the fundamentals of supply and demand. Read this section carefully to build on your knowledge base.

4 answers correct: You're supply and demand savvy. Read this section to learn even more.

> **Supply** refers to how much of a product or service is available for purchase at any given time.

Table 2.2　The Relationship between Price and Supply

Price ($)	Coffee Supplied (cups)
0.50	10
0.75	30
1.00	50
1.25	70
1.50	85
1.75	100
2.00	115

> The **law of supply** states that the amount supplied will increase as the price increases; if the price is lower, less of the product is supplied.

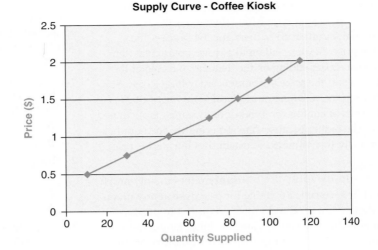

Figure 2.3
Supply Curve

The supply curve illustrates the incentive to supply more of an item as prices increase.

Table 2.3   The Relationship between Price and Demand

Price ($)	Coffee Demand (cups)
0.50	120
0.75	95
1.00	72
1.25	55
1.50	38
1.75	23
2.00	12

Demand refers to how much of a product or a service people want to buy at any given time.

The **law of demand** states that people will buy more of an item at a lower price than at a higher price.

A **surplus** occurs when sellers supply more of a product than buyers are willing to purchase.

relationship between demand and price with a graph that they call a demand curve, as shown in **Figure 2.4**.

What factors determine price?   As shown in the example of Eddie's Coffee Kiosk, there is an obvious conflict when setting a price. The higher the price, the more the product is likely to be supplied, but the lower the price, the more customers will likely purchase, or demand. If these two concepts of pricing are at odds with each other, then what determines the final price? Holding all other factors constant, prices are set at a point where supply equals demand. The supply-demand relationship is one of the fundamental concepts of economics. At Eddie's Coffee Kiosk, for example, at some point, supply and demand balance each other out. Although Eddie would love to sell coffee at $2.00 a cup (or even more), he realizes that not too many students are willing to buy coffee at that price. At the price of $2.00 a cup, Eddie would not use up his entire supply, creating a **surplus**, which occurs when sellers supply more of a product than buyers are willing to purchase.

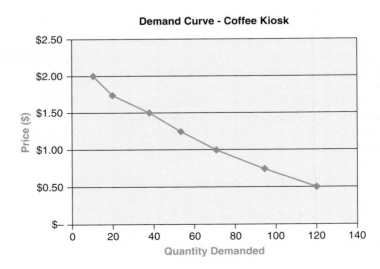

Figure 2.4   Demand Curve

The demand curve illustrates that demand increases as prices decrease.

As Eddie begins to lower his price, he finds that more students are willing to buy his coffee. However, if Eddie lowers his price too much—to $0.50 a cup, for example—then the demand would be so great that Eddie would run out before he was able to satisfy all the students who wanted coffee. This would create a **shortage**, which occurs when sellers do not produce enough of a product to satisfy demand.

Ideally, Eddie would strive to determine a price at which he is willing to sell (supply) the coffee and at which students are willing to buy (demand) the coffee without anyone wanting more or without any coffee being left over. The price at which supply equals demand is the equilibrium price, or market price. The equilibrium price is illustrated in a supply-and-demand curve, as shown in **Figure 2.5**. In this case, sixty cups of coffee is equally demanded and supplied at a price of $1.15.

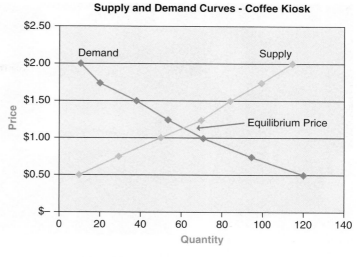

Figure 2.5 Equilibrium Price

The equilibrium or market price is the price at which supply equals demand.

What factors affect supply?
Imagine you are the owner of a retail specialty shop specializing in unique or hard-to-find items, such as handmade rugs or homemade jams. What would happen if your supplier of handmade rugs just increased the price they charge you to buy their rugs? What would happen if your supplier of homemade jams opened up a factory to make the same jam products faster and in more abundance? Both of these occurrences would affect your supply. Many factors can create a change in supply. These factors, known as the determinants of supply, are:

A **shortage** occurs when sellers do not produce enough of a product to satisfy demand.

- technology changes
- changes in resource prices
- price expectations
- number of suppliers
- the price of substitute goods

Changes in any of these factors can shift the supply curve to the left (have a negative effect on supply) or to the right (have a positive effect on supply). **Table 2.4** summarizes the key determinants of supply.

Let's examine each key determinant in more detail.

Technology Changes Improvements in technology enable suppliers to produce their goods or services more efficiently and with fewer costs. A baker who purchases a larger oven is able to make more fresh breads and rolls in less time.

Table 2.4 Examples of Determinants of Supply

Determinant of Supply	Example
Technology changes	Continuing improvements in technology result in lower costs of production and create a higher level of productivity, which increases quantity and lowers price.
Changes in resource prices	Decrease in the cost of lumber increases the number of new homes built.
Price expectations	An anticipated lowering of interest rates may indicate a future increase in new housing contracts.
Number of suppliers	An increase in homebuilders increases the supply of new homes and decreases the cost of new homes.
Price of substitute goods	Construction of apartment buildings is an alternate construction project to building new single-family residences.

Changes in Resource Prices   The price of the resources used to produce a good or service affects the cost of production. An increase in resource prices increases the cost of production and reduces profits, which lowers the incentive to supply a product. An increase in the cost of flour would raise the price of fresh baked goods.

Price Expectations   Price expectations reflect the producer's best guess at the future price of a good. Current supply may be increased or decreased depending on expectations of future prices. If prices are expected to increase in the future, the supplier may reduce supply now to supply more later at higher prices. If prices are expected to decrease in the future, the supplier may make every attempt to deplete supplies now at the higher price.

Number of Suppliers   The supply of a product or service increases as the number of competitors increases. It makes sense that the number of suppliers often increases in more profitable industries. For example, although Starbucks remains the leader in the retail coffee market, many companies, such as Tim Hortons and McDonald's, are marketing to coffee drinkers because of Starbucks' success, thus increasing the supply of coffee. Similarly, as an industry becomes less popular, maybe due to a change in technology, the number of suppliers decreases. When the digital camera became popular, the number of suppliers of film cameras decreased.

Price of Substitute Goods   The price of comparable substitute goods also affects the supply of a product. If there are other equally comparable goods available at a lower price, the supply of the higher-priced goods will be affected. For example, if margarine, a substitute for butter, is priced lower than butter, then the supply of butter could be affected by consumers switching from butter to margarine.

Assuming that everything else is held constant, a change in any of these determinants of supply will affect the supply of a product and shift the demand curve. If the change is a positive effect, thereby increasing supply, the supply curve shifts to the right. Negative changes decrease supply and shift the supply curve to the left.

What factors affect demand?   Just as there are factors that affect supply, there are also factors that affect demand for a product. These factors, known as the determinants of demand, are:

- changes in income levels
- population changes
- consumer preferences
- complementary goods
- substitute goods

A positive change in any of these determinants of demand shifts the demand curve to the right, and negative changes shift the demand curve to the left. **Table 2.5** summarizes the determinants of demand.

Let's examine each of these key determinants in more detail.

Changes in Income Levels   When income levels rise, people are able to buy more products. Conversely, when income levels fall, most people cut back on spending and buy fewer products. Therefore, when the economy enters a recession and people begin to lose their jobs, the demand for some goods and services decreases. An improving economy will bring an increase in spending as more people find jobs and create an increase in demand for some goods and services. Change in income levels is one factor that affects the housing market, for example. With an increase in income, people can afford to buy a home for the first time or can afford to upgrade to a bigger, more expensive home if they already own.

Table 2.5 Determinants of Demand

Determinants of Demand	Example
Changes in income levels	Job loss will reduce discretionary income and decrease the amount of coffee one buys. A promotion may allow a homeowner to buy a larger house or a house in a better neighbourhood.
Population changes	An increase in young, working professionals in a neighbourhood may increase the demand for coffee shops and single-family homes.
Consumer preferences	Needs and wants change based on fads and often manipulation by advertisers. A health alert concerning the negative effects of caffeine might reduce the demand for coffee.
Complementary goods	If the construction of new houses is in demand, complementary goods such as appliances and other home goods are also in demand. A reduction in new housing would negatively affect these other industries.
Substitute goods	Products or services that can be used in place of another. In the housing industry, modular housing or trailers can be substituted for building a new home from scratch.

Population Changes   Vacation rentals in resort communities experience demand shifts when populations fluctuate due to seasonal changes. Increases in population create greater demand for utilities (telephone, electricity, sewer, and water services) and public and consumer services (banks, drugstores, and grocery stores).

Consumer Preferences   Demand for a product can change based on what is "cool" or "popular" at any given moment. Tickle Me Elmo dolls, Xbox 360 gaming machines, and the Apple iPhone are all products that had high initial demand. As the demand for these items increases, there is a shift in the demand curve to the right. As demand begins to decrease, the demand curve shifts to the left.

For example, there has been an explosion in high-definition television (HDTV) sales over the last few years. Consumer demand for flat-panel TVs came from the developed TV markets, such as North America, Japan, and Western Europe, as well as from emerging markets. Because more manufacturers and retailers have entered the HDTV market, prices for sets continue to decrease. Prices have continued to decline but at the expense of profitability for many in the supply chain, especially at the brand and reseller level; however, increased sales usually mean additional customers and market share. Because of consumer demand, it is expected that Internet connectivity will rapidly become a standard feature on all but the lowest-priced TV models, just as 120 Hz has become standard for most LCD HDTV models. About 25 percent of new TVs sold in 2010 were able to connect to the Internet, and this number is forecasted to reach 76 percent by 2015.[7]

Complementary Goods   Products or services that complement each other and are consumed together, such as the iPod and iTunes, are considered complementary goods. The demand for iTunes is great as long as consumers are buying and using iPods. If a new technology renders the iPod obsolete, the demand for iTunes will decrease, shifting the demand curve for iTunes to the left.

Substitute Goods   Goods that can be used in place of other goods, such as Coca-Cola for Pepsi or a McDonald's Quarter Pounder for a Burger King Whopper, are substitute goods. Suppose, for example, someone reported getting violently ill after eating a McDonald's Quarter Pounder. The demand for the Burger King Whopper might increase, shifting the Whopper's demand curve to the right.

Imagine you are the owner of a bakery. How would you determine prices for your goods? At this point in the chapter, you should be able to answer this question. Your prices are a factor of supply and demand. A higher price provides you with an incentive to supply more baked goods. Conversely, a lower price will increase demand for these goods. The simple solution is to set prices at a point at which supply equals demand. Ideally, you would determine a price at which you are willing to supply various baked goods and at which customers are willing to purchase the goods without creating either a surplus or a shortage.

◎ On Target

World Record for Kinect

The Microsoft Kinect device for the Xbox 360 made the 2011 Guinness World Records as the fastest-selling consumer electronics device. The controller-free gaming hardware sold an average of 133 333 units a day, for a total of eight million units in its first sixty days on the shelves. The sales figures beat both the iPhone and the iPad for the equivalent periods after launch.[8]

Kinect comes with interfaces that accept body movements as inputs. At the time of release, it was recognized as one of the most advanced gaming devices on the market.

Microsoft developed the Kinect concept after the Nintendo Wii proved that gaming segments beyond the traditional young male do exist. Nintendo had released exercise programs and family games for which players used hand-held controllers to send body movement signals back to the processor to be emulated onscreen. Microsoft advanced the Wii idea by eliminating the controller altogether. Few companies would have the research depth to build something like Kinect. Researchers from a range of fields, including depth sensing, machine learning, speech recognition, gestural interface, computer vision, identity recognition, sound processing, and parallel computing, put their heads together to create Kinect.[9]

Discussion Questions

1. Using the PEST model for analysis (see Chapter 1), how might changes in the external business environment affect Kinect sales? Give an example.
2. What type of research would Microsoft have done before introducing Kinect regarding competitors and consumers? How might the research results affect Microsoft's development of the Kinect product?
3. Motion sensors and voice recognition have been available for several years in many devices we use every day. Can you think of such devices? Microsoft has taken motion-sensing technology to another level. Use the Internet to research other industries (besides gaming) in which this type of enhanced motion-sensing technology might be used. What did you discover?

 Business and Competition

Summarize the four degrees of competition and describe how competition affects demand.

How does competition influence business? In a market-based economy, such as those of the United States and Canada, there is an emphasis on individual economic freedom and a limit on governmental intervention—although Canada's government interacts with business and the economy to a greater degree than the U.S. government does. In a market economy, competition is a fundamental force. **Competition** arises when two or more businesses (local, national, or global) contend with one another to attract customers and gain an advantage. Canada's private-enterprise system is based on the belief that competition benefits consumers by motivating businesses to produce a greater variety of better and cheaper goods and services. Competition is good for consumers, good for the economy, and can be good for businesses. For example, 7UP created a new market because of extremely fierce competition in the cola industry. It positioned itself as the "un-cola," and with the launch of Cherry 7UP and Diet Cherry 7UP, the company secured its third-place spot in the soft drink industry in early 1987. The two new "light, refreshing" drinks seized 1.4 percent of the more than US\$40 billion total soft drink market in

Competition arises when two or more businesses contend with one another to attract customers and gain an advantage.

their first year and boosted 7UP's total share to 6.2 percent.[10]

Competition varies within industries and has a big influence on how companies operate. Through competing for a finite number of consumers, less efficient companies and less desirable products are usually eliminated from the marketplace. Because profit is the ultimate goal, it is the job of a successful business to convince customers that its product is either better or less expensive than that of its competitors. For example, there is currently competition between cable TV services (such as Rogers), satellite TV services (such as DirecTV), and Internet TV services (such as Netflix). How serious a threat is streaming content over the Internet? WitsView, a market-tracking company, predicts that by 2015, sales of Internet-connected TVs could hit 200 million units, or about two out of every three televisions sold. This does not take into consideration all the Internet-connecting Blu-ray DVD players, video game consoles, and network media players. The idea is that with Internet TV, consumers can pay for the services they want without all the other packaged services, offering consumers a low-cost and focused option. Are satellite and cable companies going to offer the same option? Can satellite and cable companies continue if consumers don't want to pay for a multitude of channels they don't watch?[11] It will be interesting to see what happens.

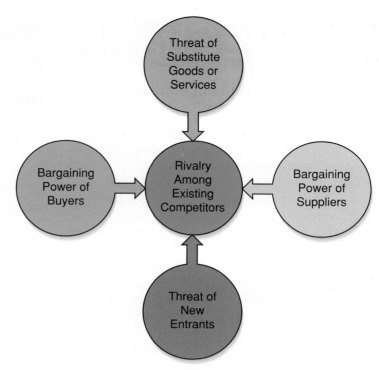

Figure 2.6   Michael Porter's Five Forces Model: The Five Forces That Shape Industry Competition

Source: Adapted from www.valuebasedmanagement.net/methods_porter_five_forces.html, Accessed January 13, 2010.

One of the most important external factors that affects most companies is the degree of industry competition—how fiercely businesses compete for the same customers, the same resources, or with products or services similar to what they sell. The intensity of the competition within an industry has a big influence on how a company operates. To be effective, managers must understand the company's competitive situation and then develop competitive strategies to take advantage of opportunities and combat threats in the industry. One tool used by managers to analyze competitive situations is **Porter's Five Forces analysis model,** which depicts the five forces that affect industry competition (see **Figure 2.6**).

Let's examine these five forces in more detail.

> **Porter's Five Forces analysis model** depicts the five forces that affect industry competition: threat of new entrants, threat of substitutes, bargaining power of buyers, bargaining power of suppliers, and rivalry among existing competitors. The intensity of the competition within an industry has a big influence on how a company operates.

1. *Threat of new entrants.* How easy or difficult is it for new entrants to start competing? Some industries, such as automotive manufacturing, require much investment (capital) and therefore are difficult to enter. Other industries, such as home cleaning or lawn care, require very little capital and therefore are relatively easy to enter. Government regulations may restrict entrance until certain criteria are met. The threat of entry of new competitors is high when brand names are not well known, capital investment is low, government regulation is not restrictive, and there is little differentiation between products.

2. *Threat of substitutes.* How easily can a product or service be substituted or made more inexpensively? If there are many substitutes available, the industry is more competitive and the profit potential for the firms in the industry is decreased. To combat the threat of substitutes, companies try to differentiate their products and services in many ways, some of which may include price (Walmart's lowest-price guarantee), quality (Maytag says you'll never need to call the repairman), service (Saturn is known for superior service), or image (the now iconic "hip Mac" versus "stuffy PC" commercials.). The threat of substitutes is high if consumers can easily switch to another comparable product that is cheaper, can find a substitute that has better quality or performance, or can switch at a low personal cost.

Apple: Taking a Bite out of Microsoft?

Apple and Microsoft have a history of bitter rivalry revolving around the desire to dominate the personal computer market. The main point of contention between these companies is the Graphical User Interface (GUI), which is the user interface for the main program that runs personal computers. Apple released the first GUI to include folders and long file names in 1983. When Microsoft released Windows 2.0 in 1988, Apple took Microsoft to court, complaining that the "look and feel" of the Windows interface was stolen from the Apple interface. This suit continued until 1992, when Apple finally lost. Microsoft led the competition in the early 1990s. It became industry standard to have Windows operating systems pre-installed on most PCs, which were dominating the personal computer market at the time. The ten-year battle finally ended when Apple announced an official alliance with Microsoft in 1997. Microsoft and Apple agreed to a five-year deal in which Microsoft would continue to develop Office software for Apple computers, and Apple agreed to bundle Microsoft's Internet Explorer in all its operating systems.[12] The computer industry went through some tough times around the turn of the century, but Apple and Microsoft remained two of the most successful companies in the world. The element of competition between these companies drove them to succeed, and perhaps led to the production of higher-quality operating software.

Discussion Questions

1. **Some people say that Microsoft imitated Apple's "look and feel" in their user interface. Why might they do that?**
2. **You've likely seen the TV commercials that pit the cool Mac guy against the awkward PC nerd. Are these ads effective in illustrating the competition between the two companies? Why or why not?**
3. **Are you a Mac or PC person? How do you think you developed this preference?**

3. *Bargaining power of buyers.* How strong is the position of buyers? Can they order large volumes to push the cost down? When there are only a few buyers and many suppliers the buyers have a great deal of bargaining power, but when there are only a few suppliers and many buyers the buyers have little bargaining power. The bargaining power of buyers is high when buyers purchase products in high volume, buyer switching costs are low, and substitutes are available.
4. *Bargaining power of suppliers.* Do many potential suppliers exist or only a few? If there are many suppliers from which a company can order its supplies, then the suppliers do not have much bargaining power (the company has the power). When there are only a few suppliers from which a company can order the supplies it needs to do business, then the suppliers have a great deal of bargaining power. The bargaining power of suppliers is high when the product is highly differentiated, or substitutes are unavailable.
5. *Rivalry among existing competitors.* Does a strong competition between the existing players exist? Is one player very dominant, or are they mostly equal in strength and size? Companies are always trying to increase market share (more sales and more customers). To do this, they must devise creative marketing strategies, cut costs, and improve customer service and product quality. Some companies focus on quality, image, or service (such as BMW), while others focus on lower prices (such as Walmart). The intensity of rivalry is high when there are many competitors, competitors have equal size or market share, there is little differentiation between products, or consumers have no preference for a particular brand.

What are the degrees (levels) of competition?   Some products or services have no substitutes, whereas others share the market with many similar products. Various industries experience different degrees of competition, ranging from many competitors to few or no competitors. The number of substitutes for a certain product or service determines the degree (level) of competition. Economists have identified **four degrees of competition:**

The **four degrees of competition** are monopoly, oligopoly, monopolistic competition, and perfect competition.

- monopoly
- oligopoly
- monopolistic competition
- perfect competition

These degrees of competition are four points on a scale, not absolute measures. For example, many industries fall somewhere between monopolistic competition and oligopoly.

Is there any competition if there is only one seller?

If one Internet company were the sole provider of Internet services, that company would be considered a monopoly. Likewise, if Eddie's Coffee Kiosk is the only place students can buy coffee on campus, then Eddie has a monopoly. A **monopoly** occurs when there is only one provider of a service or product and no substitutes for the product exist. In Canada, as well as in other countries, large monopolies are rarely allowed. In fact, Canada's Competition Bureau reviews all mergers in all sectors to determine whether they will likely result in substantial lessening or prevention of competition. Petro-Canada and Suncor Energy Inc. merged following approval from the Competition Bureau. Rogers Communications Inc. acquired Atria Networks LP following approval from the Competition Bureau. Canada's Competition Bureau denied Interac Association's request to become a for-profit organization,[13] and has challenged the Canadian Real Estate Association over rules they say limit consumer choices.[14]

Natural monopolies include public utilities, such as those that sell gas or water. These organizations require huge investments, and it would be inefficient to duplicate the products they provide; therefore, they may be permitted to hold monopolies in an effort to conserve natural resources. However, the government regulates the prices for these goods and services. **Legal monopolies** occur when a company receives a patent giving it exclusive use of an invented product or process. Polaroid held a patent on instant photography technology for a number of years (patents exist for a predetermined amount of time). During this time, Polaroid benefited from having no competition and was able to recover the high costs of bringing the new technology to the market. Without competition, the company enjoyed a monopolistic position with regard to pricing.

What happens when another seller enters a monopoly?

An oligopoly may be formed when another company enters a monopoly. An **oligopoly** is a form of competition in which only a few sellers exist. In the example of Eddie's Coffee Kiosk, a bookstore on campus might open a café, offering coffee to the students. Students now have a choice to buy coffee either at the bookstore or at Eddie's Coffee Kiosk. The situation has now changed from a monopoly to an oligopoly. When there are few sellers in a given market,

A **monopoly** occurs when there is only one provider of a service or product and no substitutes for the product exist.

Natural monopolies include public utilities, such as those that sell gas or water. These organizations require huge investments, and it would be inefficient to duplicate the products they provide.

Legal monopolies occur when a company receives a patent giving it exclusive use of an invented product or process.

An **oligopoly** is a form of competition in which only a few sellers exist.

Utility companies, such as those that sell gas, water, or electricity, may hold monopolies, but the government regulates the prices for these goods and services to protect consumers.

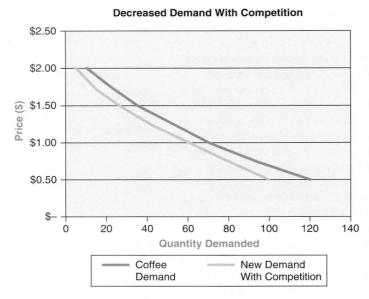

Figure 2.7 Demand and Competition

Increased competition negatively changes coffee demand and moves the demand curve to the left.

Monopolistic competition occurs when there are many buyers and sellers and little differentiation between the products, but there is a perceived difference among consumers, who therefore favour one product offering over another.

Perfect competition occurs when many buyers and sellers of products are virtually identical, and any seller can easily enter and exit the market.

each seller has a fairly large share of the market. Typically, oligopolies occur in industries in which there is a high investment to enter, so oligopolies are often major corporations in the airline, pharmaceutical, high-tech, automobile, and tobacco industries.

Because there is little differentiation between products, competition is strong in an oligopoly, and prices differ only slightly, if at all, between the few suppliers. If one company cuts prices, its action is usually matched quickly by the competition. Therefore, competition in an oligopoly is centred on product differentiation (making one product stand out from another) more than on price.

What if there are many sellers with little difference between their products, but buyers perceive them as different? **Monopolistic competition** occurs when there are many buyers and sellers and little differentiation between the products, but there is a perceived difference among consumers, who therefore favour one product offering over another. As an example, assume that the campus cafeteria begins to offer Tim Hortons brand coffee. Also assume that the perception among students is that Tim Hortons coffee is superior to Eddie's and the bookstore's. The added choice of a perceived superior product creates monopolistic competition. Eddie's Coffee Kiosk faces new competition that is perceived to be better than his product, and demand for his coffee decreases, as shown in **Figure 2.7**.

Monopolistic competition is everywhere. It exists in the shoe industry among Nike, Adidas, Reebok, and others; in the coffee industry among Tim Hortons, Starbucks, Country Time, and others; and in the ice cream industry among Breyers, Häagen-Dazs, and Ben & Jerry's, to name a few. These are traditional monopolistic competitive businesses because there are many buyers and sellers and the products are similar, but not identical. Is there a shoe, coffee, or ice cream you prefer? Why?

What if there are many sellers and each seller's products are almost identical? **Perfect competition** occurs when many buyers and sellers of products are virtually identical and any seller can easily enter and exit the market. When these conditions exist, no single supplier can influence the price. In reality, there are very few, if any, examples of perfect competition. However, agricultural products, such as grains, fruits, and vegetables, come close.

Competition encourages businesses to make creative decisions and gives customers options. Because of this need for competition, the Canadian government keeps a close watch on monopolies, and ensures that no single seller drastically influences the price of a certain service or product.

How has globalization affected business competition? Multinational enterprises are companies that have operations in more than one country, such as Nike, McDonald's, and Coca-Cola. They are among the leaders of globalization, which is the movement toward a more interconnected and interdependent world economy. This means that economies around the world are merging as technology, goods and services, labour, and capital move back and forth across international borders. For example, FedEx, the world's largest express shipping company, conducts business in more than 220 countries and territories around the world. Although the concept of globalization is essential for corporations such as FedEx, it is still a highly controversial subject for many people. Globalization has sparked fierce debates among politicians, business people, and the public for the past few decades.

The effects of globalization on the business world vary, from economic transformation in India to the shutting down of major manufacturing plants in Canada. The Internet and modern technological advances are making it possible for a company of any size from anywhere in the world to compete globally. Lower tariffs and other trade restrictions give Canadian companies the option to export or import goods to and from other countries or to conduct their business overseas. Instead of building their products at Canadian plants, a growing number of companies are choosing to relocate their production facilities overseas or subcontract at least some components of their products to foreign companies around the world at low costs. This is called off-shoring (discussed in more detail in Chapter 4). The low labour costs in countries such as China and India make these countries ideal locations for multinational companies seeking technology services and manufactured products at a low cost.

Globalization presents both benefits and risks to the Canadian economy. For example, lowered production costs allow prices on consumer products to go down, meaning the consumer benefits by purchasing goods at lower prices. Yet concerns remain about the workers in Canada who lose their jobs to foreign workers. Increased competition

Better Business **Better World**

Building a Stronger, Cleaner, Fairer World

The Organisation for Economic Co-operation and Development (OECD) was formed in 1960 when members from eighteen European countries, the United States, and Canada joined to create an organization dedicated to global development. Today, the OECD comprises thirty-four member countries from many of the world's developed countries as well as emerging countries such as Chile, Mexico, and Turkey.

The OECD works closely with non-member emerging giants such as China, India, and Brazil and other developing economies to build a stronger, cleaner, fairer world by helping governments and society reap the full benefits of globalization while tackling the economic, social, and governance challenges that can accompany it.

The complex and often lengthy accession procedure involves a series of assessments of a country's ability to meet OECD standards across a range of policy areas, which makes it difficult to add more than a small number of new members at once. In 2010, after completing the necessary formalities (including parliamentary approval), Chile, Slovenia, Israel, and Estonia became OECD members.[15]

OECD specialized committees comprise representatives from the various countries. There are about 250 committees and about 40 000 senior officials from national administrations that meet each year to review progress in specific policy areas. Once officials return home, they can continue to exchange information through a special network.

The OECD supports policies that will improve the social and economic well-being of people around the globe.

It provides a forum in which governments can collaborate to seek solutions to common problems and understand what drives economic, social, and environmental change. It measures productivity and international flows of trade and investment, analyzes and compares data to forecast future trends, and sets the global standards on issues ranging from the safety of chemicals and nuclear plants to the quality of cucumbers.

Canada—a founding member of the OECD—views the OECD as a key forum to discuss domestic and international economic and social issues and to collectively define policy and guidelines designed to improve economic growth, stability, and standards of living. Canada obtains useful peer recommendations (from other member countries) on Canadian policies to improve performance in a range of areas. Recent peer reviews include the Canadian economy, a rural policy review of Quebec, the Canadian energy policy, and jobs for youth.[16]

Discussion Questions

1. **What are the benefits of OECD membership? How does co-operation between countries lead to higher standards of living?**
2. **Why might a country not meet the standard admission criteria for accession to OECD? Do you think that, eventually, all countries will be eligible to join? Why or why not?**
3. **Visit the OECD website (www.oecd.org) and read about the Key Issues. What is being said about our economic outlook? What issues are discussed pertaining to education, health, corporate governance, or trade affairs?**

from international companies, fluctuations in the value of the Canadian dollar, security and patent protection concerns, and unstable political climates in foreign countries are additional risks that globalization has created for Canadian companies.

Benefits and risks aside, globalization is here to stay. To stay competitive in the global market, companies must work to enhance quality and develop and implement innovative strategies for the long term. The increasingly global nature of business increases the demand for workers who can communicate with international business partners, have up-to-date technological talents, can demonstrate excellent communication and creative problem-solving skills, and possess leadership skills.

How do competitive challenges affect prospective employees?   In a competitive environment, it is essential for a company to empower workers to feel free to deal with customer needs. This means employers seek workers who have interpersonal, communication, and decision-making skills. Companies today need to be more reactive to customers' needs to retain their competitive advantage. Therefore, more companies are placing greater decision-making responsibilities with employees, rather than having decisions trickle down through layers of management. This also means greater employee satisfaction and more career advancement opportunities. For example, Calgary-based WestJet Airlines has a positive corporate culture and has empowered its front-line employees to do what they feel is right for customers. Employees are also part-owners in the company. If you were a part-owner in the company you worked for, do you think your performance would improve? WestJet believes if employees are happy, then the customers will be too, and happy customers mean return on investment for investors.[17]

ECONOMIC INDICATORS

Economic Growth

Identify how economic indicators like the gross domestic product (GDP), price indexes, the unemployment rate, and productivity reflect economic health.

How do we determine whether the economy is growing?   Businesses must monitor changes in the economy so they can plan accordingly. Let's look at an example: Greg Johnson's lumber company. Greg needs to decide how much inventory to purchase for his lumber company. He has seen new housing starts decline over the past several months, but he knows that if certain conditions change, he could be supplying lumber for another housing boom. His staffing needs can change as quickly as his inventory supply. Not knowing if demand will increase, how can Greg decide how much inventory to hold or how many staff to keep or let go? As a business owner, Greg knows that the economy plays a big part in business. In Greg's situation, the economy is affecting new housing starts, which in turn affect his business. Which aspects of the economy should Greg watch to help him make his business decisions? How can he tell how well or how poorly the economy is doing?

In the previous section, you learned about several factors that affect supply and demand. The overall state of the economy also affects supply and demand. In a good economy, demand for most consumer goods and business expansion will be high. In a bad economy, the opposite will be the case. The economy is an indicator of how well or poorly businesses are doing in general. Because changes in the economy can affect a business, managers need to be aware of a number of key economic indicators and how they relate to business. Economists primarily use the following three **economic indicators** to determine how well businesses are performing overall:

Economic indicators such as gross domestic product (GDP), consumer and producer price indexes, and the unemployment rate are used by economists to determine how well businesses are performing overall.

The **gross domestic product (GDP)** measures economic activity—the overall market value of final goods and services produced in a country in a year.

Nominal GDP includes all of the changes that have occurred in market prices during the year due to inflation and deflation.

Real GDP takes inflation into account, allowing for comparisons against other historical periods.

- gross domestic product (GDP)
- consumer and producer price indexes
- unemployment rate

We'll look at these economic indicators, as well as productivity, in this section.

All the world's economies share three main goals: economic growth, price stability, and full employment. The broadest measure of the health of any country's economy is the **gross domestic product (GDP)**. The GDP measures economic activity—the overall market value of final goods and services produced in a country in a year. This

nominal GDP includes all of the changes that have occurred in market prices during the year due to inflation and deflation. **Real GDP** takes inflation into account, allowing for comparisons against other historical periods.

Only goods actually produced in the country are counted in the country's GDP (which is where the term "domestic" in gross domestic product comes from). When comparing GDP between countries to determine standards of living, calculations are based on **purchasing power parity (PPP)**. PPP takes into account the relative cost of living and the inflation rates of the countries, rather than just exchange rates, which might distort the real differences in income.

The **gross national product (GNP)** attributes earnings to the country where a firm was owned, not where a product was manufactured. GDP can be contrasted with GNP in that GDP defines its scope according to location, while GNP defines its scope according to ownership. For example, the Canadian-based aircraft manufacturer Bombardier has significant presence in China, Japan, India, Russia, Europe, and the Middle East. The market value (selling price) of all products produced at all of Bombardier's locations is included in Canada's GNP. The market value of all products produced at Bombardier in China is included in China's GDP, but not in Canada's GDP. So the GNP measures the Canadian income resulting from production, whereas the GDP measures production in Canada, regardless of country of ownership. Canada was ranked fifteenth in GDP in 2010 with a GDP of US$ 1 330 000 million.[18]

How does the GDP act as an economic indicator of growth?

When the GDP goes up, the indication is that the economy is in a positive state. Goods and services are being produced and businesses are doing well. A downward-moving GDP indicates problems with the economy because fewer goods are being produced, fewer services are being sold, and businesses are not doing well and may have to lay off employees or shut their doors altogether. Therefore, business owners use GDP data to forecast sales and adjust production and investment in inventory. GDP is an aggregate figure and does not account for differing sizes of nations; therefore, GDP can be stated as **GDP per capita** (per person), in which total GDP is divided by a country's population.

How does producing more goods and services result in lower costs?

In its broadest terms, **productivity** measures the quantity of goods and services that human and physical resources can produce in a given time. Many factors go into measuring productivity. For example, comparing output to the amount of labour used is one popular measure.

However it is measured, productivity is an indicator of a business' health. An increase in productivity indicates that existing resources are producing more goods or services in the same amount of time. Therefore, higher productivity often results in lower costs and lower prices, which generates more income and more profitability. Companies can reinvest the economic benefits of productivity growth by increasing wages and improving working conditions, reducing prices for customers, increasing shareholder value, and increasing tax revenue to the government, thus improving GDP. Therefore, overall productivity is an important economic indicator of the economy's health.

Inflation

How is price stability measured?

There are two price indexes used as economic indicators: the consumer price index and the producer price index. You may not hear about these indicators often, but you've probably heard of inflation and deflation. A consistent increase in either indicator indicates **inflation**, which is a rise in the general level of prices over time. A decrease in the rate of inflation is **disinflation**, and a continuous decrease in prices over time is **deflation**. The government also uses these indicators to make monetary policy decisions to control inflation and deflation (which is discussed later in this chapter).

Countries by GDP (2010)

Country	U.S. Millions of dollars (PPP)
1. European Union	14 820 000
2. United States	14 660 000
3. China	10 090 000
4. Japan	4 310 000
5. India	4 060 000
6. Germany	2 940 000
7. Russia	2 223 000
8. United Kingdom	2 173 000
9. Brazil	2 172 000
10. France	2 145 000

Source: Central Intelligence Agency, *The World Factbook*, https://www.cia.gov/library/publications/the-world-factbook/rankorder/2001rank.html?countryName=Canada&countryCode=ca&regionCode=noa&rank=15#ca, Accessed January 4, 2012.

When comparing GDP between countries to determine living standards, calculations are based on **purchasing power parity (PPP)**. PPP takes into account the relative cost of living and the inflation rates of the countries, rather than just exchange rates, which might distort the real differences in income.

The **gross national product (GNP)** attributes earnings to the country where the firm was owned, not where the product was manufactured.

GDP per capita (per person) measures the country's total GDP divided by a country's population.

Productivity measures the quantity of goods and services that human and physical resources can produce in a given time.

Inflation is a rise in the general level of prices over time.

Disinflation is a decrease in the rate of inflation.

Deflation is a continuous decrease in prices over time.

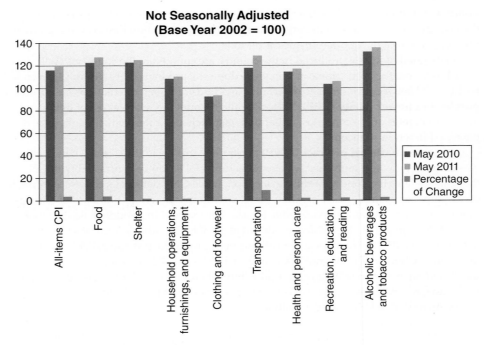

Figure 2.8   CPI Changes from May 2010 to May 2011

Source: Data points from Statistics Canada, "Consumer Price Index and Major Components, Canada," www.statcan.gc.ca/daily-quotidien/110629/t110629a1-eng.htm, Accessed August 17, 2011.

The **consumer price index (CPI)** is a benchmark used to track changes in prices over time. The CPI measures price changes by creating a "market basket" of a specified set of goods and services (including taxes) that represent the average buying pattern of urban households.

The **cost of living** is the average monetary cost of the goods and services required to maintain a particular standard of living. It is closely related to the CPI.

The **producer price index (PPI)** tracks the average change in prices at the wholesale level (from the seller's perspective). Therefore, it tracks prices of goods sellers use to create their products or services, such as raw materials, product components that require further processing, and finished goods sold to retailers. The PPI excludes energy prices and prices for services.

How are changes in the price of consumer goods measured?   The **consumer price index (CPI)** is a benchmark used to track changes in prices over time. The CPI measures price changes by creating a "market basket" of a specified set of goods and services (including taxes) that represent the average buying pattern of urban households. Through the monthly CPI, Statistics Canada tracks the retail price of a representative shopping basket of about 600 goods and services from an average household's expenditures: food, housing, transportation, furniture, clothing, and recreation. The basket of goods and services is evaluated by the Canadian government to ensure that it reflects current consumer buying habits. The value of this market basket is determined by the combined prices of these goods and services, which is then compared to its value in a previous period (generally a month), and the change is noted. Monthly CPI figures track the changes in prices of goods and services purchased by households (see **Figure 2.8**). The **cost of living** is the average monetary cost of the goods and services required to maintain a particular standard of living. It is closely related to the CPI. Statistics Canada uses 2002 as a base year to measure CPI changes, so in 2002 the CPI was equal to 100. This means that the basket of goods in 2002 cost Canadians $100. The CPI in May 2011 was measured at 120.6, meaning that the same basket of goods that cost $100 in 2002 cost $120.60 in May 2011.[19] Canada Pension Plan (CPP) rate increases are calculated once per year using the CPI **All-Items Index**. Increases come into effect each January, and the *Canada Pension Plan Act* dictates that benefits keep up with the cost of living.

Does the CPI measure changes in all prices?   The CPI measures changes in prices of consumer goods only. It does not measure changes in prices of goods used to create consumer goods, such as capital and resource expenditures. The **producer price index (PPI)** tracks the average change in prices at the wholesale level (from the seller's perspective). Therefore, it tracks prices of goods sellers use to create their products or services, such as raw materials, product components that require further processing, and finished goods sold to retailers. The PPI excludes energy prices and prices for services.

Why are price indexes important? A change in prices is an important economic indicator. It is a measurement of purchasing power, and it triggers certain business decisions. During periods of increasing prices as reflected by the CPI, the purchasing power of a dollar decreases, meaning that less is bought with a dollar today than could have been bought with the same dollar yesterday. To compensate for such price increases, wages eventually need to be increased. In turn, businesses must eventually increase prices to compensate for the higher cost of labour. Similarly, if the price to produce goods or services increases, businesses will need to pass on those cost increases in the form of higher prices, again decreasing the consumer's purchasing power. Therefore, business leaders watch the CPI and PPI to determine the rate at which consumer and wholesale prices change, respectively.

Unemployment

What other indicators are used to measure the economy? The **unemployment rate** measures the number of people who are at least fifteen years old, are seeking work, and are currently unemployed.[20] Because there are different reasons that people are not working, there are several different measurements of unemployment:

- Frictional unemployment measures temporary unemployment in which workers move between jobs, careers, and locations.
- Structural unemployment measures permanent unemployment that happens when an industry changes in such a way that jobs are terminated completely. Many steel workers and miners lost jobs due to declines in those industries. More recently, many bank tellers have been replaced by automated teller machines (ATMs). These workers can learn new skills or receive additional training in an effort to keep their jobs or find new ones.
- Cyclical unemployment measures unemployment caused by a result of businesses not having enough demand for labour to employ those who want to work. This generally follows the economy. Companies must cut back their workforce when there is a downturn in the business cycle. Once the demand for goods and services increases, companies begin to hire again. When economic output falls, as measured by the gross domestic product (GDP), the business cycle is low and cyclical unemployment will rise.
- Seasonal unemployment measures those out of work during the off-season, such as people employed in snow- or beach-related industries, agriculture, or tourism activities.

Why is unemployment an important economic measure? Businesses, as well as government policy-makers, pay close attention to unemployment rates. High unemployment results in an increase in unemployment benefits and government spending on social programs, such as welfare and health care. High unemployment can also result in increases in mental stresses and physical illnesses and can bring on increases in crime. It is costly for businesses to lay off workers, and then hire and train new workers as the economy eventually improves. In a declining economy, businesses prefer to reduce their workforce through retirement and natural attrition, which takes planning. However, if the unemployment rate drops too low, the concern is that more workers have increased buying power and spend more, which ultimately causes prices to increase, resulting in a higher inflation rate. Therefore, the challenge is to keep both inflation and unemployment low—a difficult task since they seem to have an inverse relationship.

How do economic indicators help businesses make decisions? Earlier in this chapter, we looked at the example of Greg Johnson's lumber company. After ensuring there is inventory to fill current needs, Greg keeps a close eye on all economic indicators, especially the CPI and unemployment rate, to help guide his future buying decisions. He knows that movements in the CPI determine the trend of current prices. Such trends can help Greg determine whether it is better to stock up now at lower prices or wait to buy later if prices are expected to fall.

The **unemployment rate** measures the number of people who are at least fifteen years old, are seeking work, and are currently unemployed.

The **business cycle** describes how the economy fluctuates over time, going through periods of increased growth (expansion) and decreased growth (contraction).

Equally important is the unemployment rate. Greg's business is tied closely to the new housing industry. Unfortunately, Greg is feeling the pressures of a sagging housing industry and a declining economy. Because there is less for his employees to do, he has already laid off workers. A continued downturn in the housing industry will increase the unemployment rate, an indicator for Greg that his inventory might not move quickly. Although no economic indicator can guide Greg's decision precisely, watching the indicators over time allows him to get a feel for future expectations and helps him make better business decisions.

 **BizSkills Simulation:** Adapting to the Economic Environment. Located in MyBusinessLab.

List and describe the four stages of the business cycle.

Summarize how the government uses both fiscal policy and monetary policy to control changes in the business cycle.

A **recession** is a decline in the GDP for two or more successive quarters of a year.

A **depression** is a severe or long recession.

A **fiscal policy**, in which the government determines the appropriate level of taxes and spending, and a **monetary policy**, in which the government manages the supply of money, are applied by governments to smooth out the fluctuations in the business cycle.

GOVERNMENT AND THE ECONOMY
Controlling Fluctuations in the Economy

What are fluctuations in the economy?   As the cost of the consumer basket of goods (CPI) rises, the annual rate of inflation rises. Canada's annual rate of inflation, which reached a high of 12.5 percent, has averaged 2 percent since 1991.[21] Over time, the economy naturally fluctuates, which means it goes through periods of increased growth (expansion) and decreased growth (contraction). Economists refer to these increases and decreases as the **business cycle**.

There are four stages of the business cycle, as illustrated in **Figure 2.9**.

- *Peak:* This stage occurs when the economy is at its most robust point. The peak occurs when an expansion ends and a recession begins.
- *Recession:* By definition, a **recession** is a decline in the GDP for two or more successive quarters of a year. In recessionary times, corporate profits decline, unemployment increases, and the stock market reacts with large selling sessions that result in decreasing stock prices. A severe or long recession is a **depression**. Depressions are usually associated with falling prices (deflation). After the onset of the Great Depression of 1929, the government used policies to control the economy to avoid another such depression.
- *Trough:* A trough occurs when the recession hits bottom and the economy begins to expand again.
- *Expansion or recovery:* Eventually, after a recession, or even a depression, the economy hits a trough and begins to grow again. It enters into an expansionary or recovery phase. Eventually, the recovery will hit a peak, and the cycle begins again.

How does the government control fluctuations in the economy?   Ideally, the economy could stay near its peak all the time. But left to its own forces and in reaction to external actions on the economic system, such as wars and weather variations, the economy will inevitably cycle through peaks and troughs. To smooth out the fluctuations in the business cycle, the government influences the economy through its **fiscal policy**, in which the government determines the appropriate level of taxes and spending, and through its **monetary policy**, in which the government manages the supply of money.

Why does the government increase taxes?   The government increases taxes in an attempt to offset rising inflation. Higher taxes translate into lower consumer spending. This slows the growth of businesses, and slows down the economy by reducing the amount of money in the system. Decreasing taxes does not have quite the opposite effect on the economy as increasing taxes. It would seem that if increasing taxes would slow down an economy, a tax cut would help stimulate the economy. Although that is partially true, the amount of

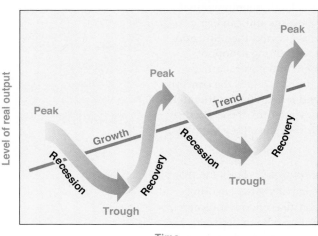

Figure 2.9   Business Cycle

Security features of the $20 bill include:
1. Metallic stripe (holographic stripe)
2. Ghost image (watermark)
3. Dashes (security thread)
4. See-through number
5. Raised ink (intaglio)
6. UV (fluorescence)

money entering the system depends on how much of the tax reduction consumers spend and how much they save. Money put into savings does not help stimulate the economy immediately. **Contractionary measures** include raising taxes and decreasing government spending in an attempt to slow the economy.

How does government spending help stimulate the economy?   Increasing government spending is a fiscal policy tactic that the government uses to help fuel a lagging economy. The government spends money on a variety of projects, such as infrastructure improvements and projects that benefit the military, education, and health care. Government spending increases cash flow to the economy faster than decreasing taxes, because it provides an immediate injection of funds into the system. Often, government spending creates additional jobs, which also helps stimulate the economy. During periods of high economic growth, the government may decrease its spending, potentially affecting interest rates. **Expansionary measures** include decreasing taxes and increasing government spending to boost the market and put money back into the hands of businesses and consumers, encouraging businesses to expand and consumers to buy more goods and services.

Money Supply

Besides changes to fiscal policy, what else can be done to control the economy?   The **Bank of Canada** acts as the federal government's financial advisor and is responsible for promoting the economic and financial well-being of Canada. The Bank of Canada manages the country's money supply through its monetary policy to control inflation. In addition to setting monetary policy, the Bank of Canada provides banking services to member banks and to the federal government. It is headed by a board of directors and has the power to increase or decrease the money supply and raise or lower short-term interest rates, making it harder or easier to borrow money. When inflation is seen as a problem, the Bank of Canada will take contractionary measures to decrease the money supply and raise interest rates (causing people to borrow less and save more, which reduces the amount of money in the economy). To counter a recession, the Bank of Canada will take expansionary measures to increase the supply of money and lower interest rates on borrowing money (causing people to save less and borrow more, which increases the amount of money in the economy).

What is a budget surplus?   Every year the government creates a budget, a financial plan that outlines expected revenues from taxes and fees and expected spending. If the money the government takes in (through taxes and fees) exceeds the money the

Contractionary measures include raising taxes and decreasing government spending in an attempt to slow the economy.

Expansionary measures include decreasing taxes and increasing government spending to boost the market and put money back into the hands of businesses and consumers, encouraging businesses to expand and consumers to buy more goods and services.

The **Bank of Canada** acts as the federal government's financial advisor and is responsible for promoting the economic and financial well-being of Canada. The Bank of Canada manages the country's money supply through its monetary policy to control inflation.

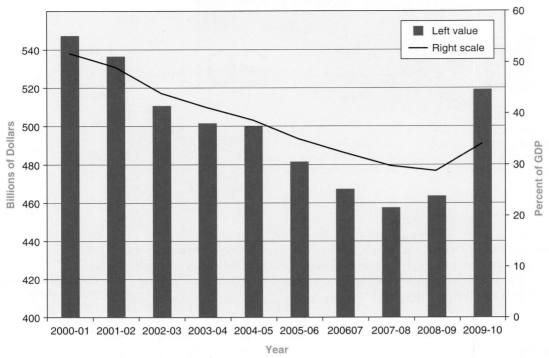

Canada's National Debt (Accumulated Deficit)

Figure 2.10 Canada's National Debt (Accumulated Deficit)

Source: Data points from the Department of Finance Canada, "Annual Financial Report of the Government of Canada Fiscal Year 2009–2010," *2010 Publications*, www.fin.gc.ca/pub/annual-annuelle/2010-eng.asp, Accessed August 18, 2011.

A **budget surplus** occurs when the money coming into the government exceeds the money being spent by government.

A **budget deficit** occurs when the money being spent by government exceeds the money coming into government.

National debt is the accumulated total yearly deficits.

government spends (for things such as social services, defence, and transportation), the result is a **budget surplus**. If the money being spent by government exceeds the money coming into government, there is a **budget deficit**. Historically, budget deficits occur more often than surpluses, and the yearly deficits (or surpluses) are totalled, resulting in an accumulated **national debt** (see **Figure 2.10**).

What is the money supply? When determining the amount of money in our system, it is natural to think of all the coins and bills held by people, businesses, and banks. However, that would only represent a portion of the money supply. Money supply is the combined amount of money available within the economy, but there are different ways to measure it. The standard measures usually include currency in circulation and demand deposits (depositors' easily accessed assets on the books of financial institutions). Some of the other measures are called monetary aggregates (see **Table 2.6**). In 2010, Canada's money supply was $565 768 million gross M1, $993 262 million M2, and $1 369 445 M3.[22]

Why is controlling the money supply important? Money has a direct effect on the economy, because the more money consumers have, the more they tend to spend. When consumers spend more, businesses do better. Demand for resources, labour, and capital increases due to the stimulated business activity, and, in general, the economy improves. However, there can be too much of a good thing. When the money supply continues to expand, eventually there might not be enough goods and services to satisfy demand, and when demand is high, prices will rise. (Remember the demand curve? It shifts to the right.) Inflation results from an increase in overall prices. Economists

Table 2.6   Bank of Canada Measures of Money

M1+ (gross)	Currency outside the banks plus all chequable deposits held at chartered banks, trust and mortgage loan companies, credit unions, and caisses populaires (excluding deposits of these institutions); plus continuity adjustments. Coins, bills, travellers' cheques, and chequing accounts constitute the narrowest measure of our money supply. These assets are the most liquid in that they are already in the form of cash or are the easiest to change into cash.
M1++ (gross)	M1+ (gross) plus all non-chequable deposits (other than fixed-term deposits) held at chartered banks, trust and mortgage loan companies, credit unions, and caisses populaires; less interbank deposits; plus continuity adjustments.
M2 (gross)	Currency outside banks plus bank personal deposits, bank non-personal demand and notice deposits; less interbank deposits; plus continuity adjustments.
M3 (gross)	M2 (gross) plus bank non-personal term deposits and foreign-currency deposits of residents; less interbank deposits; plus continuity adjustments.
M2+ (gross)	M2 (gross) plus deposits at trust and mortgage loan companies and at government savings institutions; deposits and shares at credit unions and caisses populaires; life insurance company individual annuities; money market mutual funds; plus continuity adjustments and other adjustments.
M2++ (gross)	M2+ (gross) plus Canada Savings Bonds and other retail debt instruments; plus non-money market mutual funds.

Source: Bank of Canada/Banque du Canada, "Canada's Money Supply," www.bank-banque-canada.ca/en/backgrounders/bg-m2.html, Accessed March 20, 2011.

carefully watch the CPI to monitor inflation, because they don't want inflation to go too high.

The opposite can also happen when the supply of money becomes limited following a decrease in economic activity. When the economy begins to slow down due to decreased spending, either disinflation or deflation results. The Bank of Canada uses monetary policy to help keep inflation within the inflation-control target range of 1 to 3 percent. To help avoid the economic extremes of inflation or deflation, the Bank of Canada uses two tools (see **Table 2.7**) to affect money supply: open market operations and the overnight rate.

What are open market operations?   One of the main tools the Bank of Canada uses in its monetary policy is open market operations, which is the buying and selling of government securities (bonds and Treasury bills, or other financial instruments). Monetary

Table 2.7   Bank of Canada's Monetary Tools and Their Effects

Tool	Action	Measure	Effect on Money Supply	Effect on Interest Rates	Effect on Economic Activity
Open Market Operations	Buy government securities	Expansionary (money is put into circulation)	Increases	Lowers	Increases
	Sell government securities	Contractionary (money is taken out of circulation)	Decreases	Raises	Decreases
Overnight Rate	Raise overnight rate	Contractionary (interest rates go up, dollar goes up)	Decreases	Raises	Decreases
	Lower overnight rate	Expansionary (interest rates go down, dollar goes down)	Increases	Lowers	Increases

targets such as inflation, interest rates, or exchange rates are used to guide these transactions. The Bank of Canada does not place transactions with any particular security dealer; rather, the securities dealers compete in an open market. When the Bank of Canada buys or sells Canadian securities, it is changing the level of reserves in the banking system. When it buys securities, it adds reserves to the system, money is said to be "easy," and interest rates drop. Lower interest rates help stimulate the economy by decreasing the desire to save and increasing the demand for loans such as home mortgages. Since new homebuyers would benefit by getting a mortgage with the lowest interest rate possible, they should watch for reports that would indicate what the Bank of Canada intends to do with its open market operations.

What is the overnight rate?

The Bank of Canada carries out monetary policy by influencing short-term interest rates. The overnight rate is the interest rate at which major financial institutions borrow and lend one-day (or "overnight") funds among themselves; the Bank of Canada sets a target level for that rate. The bank rate is the rate of interest that the Bank of Canada charges on short-term loans to financial institutions. It is adjusted in accordance with changes to the overnight rate and is used to administer monetary policy.[23] To help ensure that inflation remains low for sustained economic growth and job creation, the bank rate is adjusted from time to time. Banks usually increase the rate they charge their customers, the prime rate, whenever the Bank of Canada raises the overnight rate. Changes to the overnight rate not only influence interest rates that customers pay on loans and mortgages, but it might also affect interest rates consumers receive on investments.

By lowering the overnight rate, commercial banks are encouraged to borrow funds from the Bank of Canada. The commercial banks then lend money to businesses, thereby stimulating the economy by putting funds into the economic system. When prime rates are low, demand increases for more expensive items, such as housing, furniture, automobiles, and appliances, because businesses and households can borrow money at lower interest rates. When interest rates are low, businesses and households also tend to spend more and save (or invest) less, because they are not receiving a big return on their invested money.

If the economy is too robust, the Bank of Canada can increase the overnight rate, which discourages banks from borrowing additional funds. Businesses are then discouraged from borrowing because of the higher interest rates.

As demand for goods and services and spending increase, the Canadian dollar appreciates, which increases the cost of Canadian products relative to foreign ones, thus leading to adjustments in spending. Specifically, the demand by foreign consumers for Canadian products decreases (fewer exports) and the demand by Canadians for foreign products increases (more imports).

When you deposit money into a bank, the money does not sit in a vault waiting for the time when you want to withdraw it. Instead, banks use your deposited money to make loans to others: people, small businesses, corporations, and other banks. Banks make money by the interest charged on those loans. However, the bank must be able to give you back your money when you demand it. Therefore, banks do not lend out the entire balance of deposits, but instead they retain a portion of it, a reserve, that is sufficient to cover any demands by customers for funds on any given day. This includes trips to ATM machines, use of debit cards, requests for loans, and payment of cheques that customers write. If the banks do not have enough funds to cover daily demands, customers might get nervous that the bank will lose their money, and might withdraw all their funds.

It is important to be aware of the overall state of the economy when making decisions on large investments. Because the government's actions affect the economy, it is also important to know what these actions are and what effect they will have. For example, in making a decision about whether to buy a home, you should observe whether the Bank of Canada is buying or selling securities. If the Bank of Canada buys securities, it is putting money back into the economy in an attempt to stimulate or boost the economy (expansionary measure); therefore, it is likely that interest rates for mortgage loans will decrease (expansionary measure).

CHAPTER SYNOPSIS

❶ Define economics and describe the different types of economic systems. *(pp. 28–31)*

Economics is the study of how individuals, businesses, and government make decisions about how to allocate limited (scarce) resources to best satisfy the wants, needs, and desires of people.

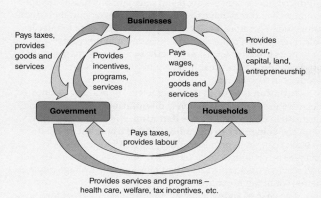

Circular Flow of Canada's Economy

Microeconomics is the study of how individual businesses, households, and consumers make decisions to allocate their limited resources in the exchange of goods and services.

Macroeconomics is the study of the behaviour of the overall economy. Economy-wide occurrences, such as changes in unemployment, interest rates, inflation, and price levels, are all part of the study of macroeconomics.

In a **planned economic system**, the government plays a greater role in determining the goods and services provided and how they are produced and distributed. Both communism and socialism are planned economic systems.

Communism is an economic system in which government makes all economic decisions and controls all the social services and many of the major resources required for production of goods and services.

Socialism provides that the government plans and controls the economy. Government owns or controls many basic businesses and services, while individuals own and operate less crucial industries.

Capitalism, also called a market economy, free market, or free enterprise, is the economic system that allows freedom of choice and encourages private ownership of the resources required to make and provide the goods and services consumers enjoy.

Today, most countries use a **mixed economy**, which is a blend of market and planned economies. Most Western European countries, for example, operate with a mixed economy of privately owned businesses and government control of selected social programs, such as health care.

❷ Describe the law of supply and demand and how supply and demand affect price. *(pp. 32–37)*

Supply and demand is a very complicated process because many factors are involved, such as income levels, tastes, and the amount of competition in the market. The need for an item is demand, and the availability of that item is supply.

Supply refers to how much of a product or service is available for purchase at any given time.

In economic terms, the **law of supply** states that the amount supplied will increase as the price increases; if the price is lower, less of the product is supplied.

Demand refers to how much of a product or a service people want to buy at any given time.

Therefore, the **law of demand states** that people will buy more of an item at a lower price than at a higher price.

When sellers supply more of a product than buyers are willing to purchase there is a **surplus**.

When sellers do not produce enough of a product to satisfy demand there is **a shortage**.

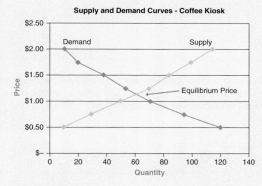

Equilibrium Price

Table 2.1   World Economic Models

Type of Economy	What to Produce	How to Produce	For Whom to Produce
Planned (Controlled)	Government or other centralized group determines what to produce.	Government or other centralized group determines and controls the resources and means of production.	Government or other centralized group determines wages and sets prices. Resources and products are distributed to common group.
Market	Individuals and private firms make decisions based on consumer needs and wants.	Individuals and private firms determine the production methods. The focus is on efficiency and profitability.	Individual income ultimately controls purchasing decisions.
Mixed	Individuals determine what to produce with some level of government involvement.	Individuals and government control resources and determine production methods.	Government distributes some goods and services through selected social programs. Individual income determines purchasing decisions for other goods and services.

Factors or determinants of supply include:
- technology changes
- changes in resource prices
- price expectations
- number of suppliers
- the price of substitute goods

Factors or determinants of demand include:

- changes in income levels
- population changes
- consumer preferences
- complementary goods
- substitute goods

❸ Summarize the four degrees of competition and describe how competition affects demand.   *(pp. 38–44)*

Competition arises when two or more businesses contend with one another to attract customers and gain an advantage.

Porter's Five Forces analysis model depicts the five forces that affect industry competition. The intensity of the competition within an industry has a big influence on how a company operates.

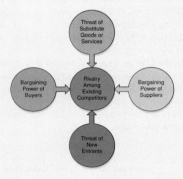

Michael Porter's Five Forces Model: The Five Forces that Shape Industry Competition

The amount of substitutes for a certain product or service determines the degree (level) of competition. Economists have **identified four degrees of competition:**
- monopoly
- oligopoly
- monopolistic competition
- perfect competition

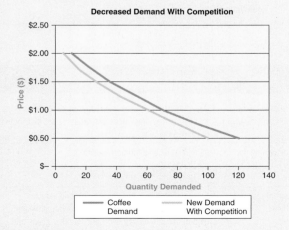

Demand and Competition

❹ Identify how economic indicators such as the gross domestic product (GDP), price indexes, the unemployment rate, and productivity reflect economic health.   *(pp. 44–48)*

Economists primarily use the following three **economic indicators** to determine how well businesses are performing overall: gross domestic product (GDP), consumer and producer price indexes, and the unemployment rate.

When the **GDP** goes up, the indication is that the economy is in a positive state. Goods and services are being produced and businesses are doing well. A downward-moving GDP indicates problems with the economy because fewer goods are being produced, fewer services are being sold, and businesses are not doing well and may have to lay off employees or shut their doors altogether. Therefore, business owners use GDP data to forecast sales and adjust production and investment in inventory.

In its broadest terms, **productivity** measures the quantity of goods and services that human and physical resources can produce in a given time.

Inflation is a rise in the general level of prices over time. A decrease in the rate of inflation is **disinflation**, and a continuous decrease in prices over time is **deflation**.

The **consumer price index (CPI)** is a benchmark used to track changes in prices over time. The CPI measures price changes by creating a "market basket" of a specified set of goods and services (including taxes) that represent the average buying pattern of urban households.

The **cost of living** is the average monetary cost of the goods and services required to maintain a particular standard of living. It is closely related to the CPI.

❺ List and describe the four stages of the business cycle.   *(p. 48)*

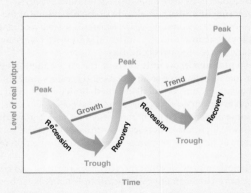

Business Cycle

❻ Summarize how the government uses both fiscal policy and monetary policy to control changes in the business cycle.   *(pp. 48–52)*

To smooth out the fluctuations in the business cycle, the government influences the economy through its **fiscal policy**, in which the government determines the appropriate level of taxes and spending, and through its **monetary policy**, in which the government manages the supply of money.

Contractionary measures include both raising taxes and decreasing government spending in an attempt to slow the economy.

Expansionary measures include both decreasing taxes and increasing government spending to boost the market and put money back into the hands of businesses and consumers, encouraging businesses to expand and consumers to buy more goods and services.

KEY TERMS

Bank of Canada (p. 49)
bartering (p. 32)
budget deficit (p. 50)
budget surplus (p. 50)
business cycle (the) (p. 48)
capitalism (p. 31)
circular flow of Canada's
economy (p. 29)
communism (p. 30)
competition (p. 38)
consumer price index
(CPI) (p. 46)
contractionary
measures (p. 49)
cost of living (p. 46)
Crown corporations (p. 31)
currency (p. 32)

deflation (p. 45)
demand (p. 33)
depression (p. 48)
disinflation (p. 45)
economic indicators (p. 44)
economics (p. 28)
expansionary
measures (p. 49)
fiscal policy (p. 48)
four degrees of
competition (p. 40)
GDP per capita (p. 45)
gross domestic product
(GDP) (p. 44)
gross national product
(GNP) (p. 45)
inflation (p. 45)

law of demand (p. 33)
law of supply (p. 33)
legal monopolies (p. 41)
macroeconomics (p. 29)
microeconomics (p. 29)
mixed economies (p. 31)
monetary policy (p. 48)
monopolistic
competition (p. 42)
monopoly (p. 41)
national debt (p. 50)
natural monopolies (p. 41)
nominal GDP (p. 45)
oligopoly (p. 41)
perfect competition (p. 42)
planned economic
system (p. 30)

Porter's Five Forces analysis
model (p. 39)
privatization (p. 31)
producer price index
(PPI) (p. 46)
productivity (p. 45)
purchasing power parity
(PPP) (p. 45)
real GDP (p. 45)
recession (p. 48)
shortage (p. 35)
socialism (p. 30)
supply (p. 33)
supply and demand (p. 32)
surplus (p. 34)
unemployment rate (p. 47)

CRITICAL THINKING QUESTIONS

1. What might happen if the government did not attempt to control inflation? Inflation can be both a good thing and a bad thing. Explain.
2. The text discusses unemployment rate as a measure of economic performance. Another way to gauge economic performance is to count the number of people employed in the economy. Is it possible for the unemployment rate to rise and the number of people employed to rise at the same time? Is either measurement better than the other?
3. Look in the newspaper or on the Internet to find the most current economic indicators, such as GDP, unemployment rate, and CPI. What forces are working to improve or worsen the economy?
4. What are the advantages of capitalism? What are the advantages of socialism? What are the disadvantages of these two

economic systems? How does this information relate to your everyday life?
5. The text defines the GDP as the measurement of economic activity—the market value of products and services produced in a country in a year. Think about other things that might "help" the GDP that are really not good for our society in general, such as the economic activity required to clean up oil spills or increases in consumer debt to buy more goods. Other situations could also "hurt" the GDP by limiting expenditures on items, but help the overall good of society, such as reusing plastic bags or installing solar water heaters (thus limiting spending on oil, gas, and electricity). Does the definition of GDP need to be revised?

APPLICATION EXERCISES

1. **Getting Acquainted with Canadian Banks.** What bank branch is nearest your home or school? Go to the website of your local bank and determine what the current interest rates are for various types of investments. What are the latest policies? What other kinds of information does the website give you?
2. **Competitive Analysis.** Use Porter's Five Forces analysis model to analyze the competitive positions of any one of the following companies: Toyota, Walmart, First Choice HairCutters, Canadian Tire, or Cara (Cara Foods). Describe the five forces and how they affect the company's operation and strategies.
3. **Pro Sports and the Economy.** How do professional sports and the economy interact? Play Peanuts and Crackerjacks (http:// www.bos.frb.org/peanuts/indexnosound.htm), and test your knowledge of basic economic principles in the context of professional sports. Write a brief summary of your experience. What did you learn from playing the game?

4. **Learning More about Supply and Demand.** Go to www.lemonadestandgame.com and play a round or two. Using information you learned from this chapter, write a brief paper about your experience. How much money did you make each time you played the game? What are the important variables? How does this game illustrate the effects of supply and demand?
5. **Monetary Policy: You're in Control.** How would it feel to be in control of the monetary policy for a country? Play MoPoS (the Monetary Policy Simulation Game, at http://www.snb.ch/en/ifor/research/id/research_mopos). Once you download this game, you act out the role of a fictitious central bank by implementing monetary policy in a simple virtual economy so you can get a feel for the options and limitations of monetary policy. Write a brief summary of your experience. What did you learn from playing the game?

GLOBAL 500 RESEARCH PROJECT

INSTRUCTIONS

1. Choose a Global 500 company from *Fortune* magazine's annual rankings at http://money.cnn.com/magazines/fortune/global500/.
2. Research:
   a. What is the company name? Where is it located? Who is the CEO?
   b. How much revenue did the company generate last year?
   c. What products or services does the company offer?
   d. What industry is the company in?
   e. What is happening in the global or local economy currently that affects this company?
   f. What degree of competition is this company operating within (oligopoly, monopolistic competition, or perfect competition)?
   g. Use Porter's Five Forces analysis model to analyze the competitive environment this company is operating within. What strategies does this company employ to beat their competitors at the game of business? How does having competition actually help a company?
3. Prepare a report and submit to your professor.

TEAM TIME

The Great Debate

Your instructor will divide the class into three groups and assign each group one of the following debate topics. Once in your group, divide the group into two smaller groups to prepare stances on your assigned debate issues.

DEBATE TOPICS

1. Walmart is interested in creating an industrial loan bank in Utah. What are the implications of having a retail giant enter the banking industry? Should this be allowed?
2. What impact does increasing the minimum wage have on unemployment? Does increasing the minimum wage benefit the worker, or does it ultimately result in higher unemployment?
3. Taxation and tax cuts cause volatile debate among political leaders. Many propose that tax cuts help strengthen the economy by freeing money to increase spending. Others propose that past tax cuts have not had a positive effect on the economy and have only caused greater stress on the government budget

and reduced the government's ability to spend on important public needs. Do tax cuts benefit the economy?

PROCESS

Step 1. After dividing your group into two debate sides, meet separately to discuss the issues of the debate.
Step 2. Group members should then individually prepare their responses to their side of the debate issue.
Step 3. Gather your smaller groups and go over the responses provided by each group member. Develop a single list of responses.
Step 4. Determine who will be the group's primary spokesperson for the debate.
Step 5. Each group will be given five minutes to present its side of the issue. After each group has presented its argument, each team will be given five minutes to prepare a rebuttal and then three minutes to present the rebuttal.
Step 6. Repeat this process with the other groups.

ETHICS AND RESPONSIBILITY

Economic Inequality

Economic inequality refers to the differences of assets and income between groups. It has long been the subject for great discussion and can refer to the inequality between individuals, city versus rural areas, countries, or economic structures. As a class or on an individual basis, discuss the following:

1. How do you define economic equality? For example, is economic equality simply making sure everyone has equal income, or is it enough to provide all equal opportunity to earn income?
2. Is economic equality feasible? Would other problems result from economic equality?
3. One method used to measure differences in national income equality around the world is the national Gini coefficient. Research the Gini coefficient. Which countries have the most equality? Which have greater inequality?
4. What other methods could be used to measure economic equality?

CLOSING CASE

Competition, What Competition?

Apple sold close to one million units of the iPad 2 tablet computer during its launch weekend in March 2011. By comparison, the original iPad, launched in April 2010, reached the one million mark twenty-eight days after its debut.[24] By 2011, the original

iPad was the fastest-selling device of all time, measured in revenue (Microsoft's Kinect device holds the Guinness world record for fastest sold, measured by number of units). Apple released the iPod in 2001, the iPhone in 2007, and the iPad in 2010, and every one of these was an overwhelming success.

Steve Jobs, the late co-founder and chair of Apple, predicted that 2011 would be the year of the iPad 2.[25] The next-generation model is one-third thinner and a little lighter than the original iPad, with the improved performance of iOS 4.3, video-mirroring (picture projection), rear- and front-facing cameras, video conferencing, and video/audio streaming between compatible devices. Around the time of the iPad release, competitors had introduced tablets based on Android and WebOS that included more memory, more processing power, and had cameras, yet their sales figures were not impressive. Jobs noted that many competitors were looking at tablets like PCs, just emphasizing parts and speeds. His comments were that these tablets are post-PCs, and they have to be seamless and user-friendly. In a post-PC world, consumers have a more intimate relationship with their devices. They use them on the couch, in the park, and they show them to other people. Fostering that desire is a smart way to differentiate your piece of glass from other pieces of glass that perform essentially the same functions.

The iPad 2 addressed many of the criticisms regarding the first-generation iPad, particularly its lack of cameras, video recording, and web conferencing. Apple took a couple of apps they were already selling to Mac OS X users, GarageBand and iMovie, and made a tablet-optimized version of each, which sold for $5 in the App Store. The availability of the apps that are unique to media tablets, and that differentiate the experience of using one compared with a PC or smartphone, is crucial for driving consumer demand. As tablets evolve beyond a nice-to-have device into a need-to-have device for many consumers, sales will rise even more. Through marketing the iPad 2, Jobs made sure to let consumers know that this device was more than a toy. It was something they could use for real work.[26] Apple also was the only vendor selling a case made to fit the iPad 2 just right, which gave the company a few weeks without competition to rake in profits on the $40 to $70 Smart Cover before third-party case manufacturers created other variations of protective accessories for the iPad 2.

When the iPad 2 first launched, Apple set a two-per-household limit on sales, yet buyers were lining up multiple times to purchase additional units. Many were paying others up to US$900 for their spot in line to purchase iPad 2s, or paying others to purchase an extra one on their behalf. Many iPad 2 customers were apparently dominating lines outside the Apple Stores, buying as many iPad 2s as they could then sending them overseas to sell at a profit (known as a grey market). For those in the United States and abroad, the biggest grey market is eBay, where iPad 2s were selling for as much as US$4000.

Seventy percent of iPad 2 buyers were novice iPad users, and the split between Mac (51 percent) and PC (49 percent) owners was almost even.[27] Apple worked hard to get the iPad 2 out to every customer who wanted one as quickly as possible. Many existing customers found improvements in the iPad 2 over the original iPad and upgraded. Apple's strategy was to expand its base of iPad users, which was critical to maintaining its early lead in the growing tablet market. As the user base grew, Apple's lead widened, and the company enjoyed a competitor-free market for a while. Soon after the iPad 2 hit the market, competitors such as Samsung, Research In Motion, HP, Cisco, and Toshiba quickly developed and began marketing devices that would compete with the iPad 2 for consumer dollars. While Apple is a tough competitor to beat because consumers are very loyal to the brand, demand for the iPad 2 may dwindle as other similar, cheaper devices become available. Apple's competitors will surely stay on top of the inventory situation because if Apple were to purchase many of the critical parts required to build additional iPad 2s, it could cause a ripple effect in the supply chain (a shortage of raw inventories), thereby affecting other companies building new smartphones and other tablet products.

DISCUSSION QUESTIONS

1. Why do you think demand was so high for the iPad or iPad 2 to begin with? What did Apple do to increase demand for their product? When will demand drop? What factors might affect demand?

2. What degree of competition is Apple operating in (monopoly, oligopoly, monopolistic competition, perfect competition)? How did Apple corner the post-PC, tablet market so quickly?

3. Using Porter's Competitive Forces model, analyze Apple's competitive situation where the iPad 2 is concerned. Rivalry among existing competitors? What about new competitors? Availability of suppliers? Substitute products? Bargaining power of buyers?

MyBusinessLab CHAPTER RESOURCES

MyBusinessLab in an online learning and testing environment that features the perfect study tools to help you master the concepts covered in this chapter. Log in to MyBusinessLab at www.pearsoned.ca/mybusinesslab to test your knowledge of key chapter concepts, participate in simulations modelled on real-world business situations, and explore the following additional practice tools:

- Study Plan
- Audio Chapter Summaries
- Glossary Flashcards
- eText
- BizChat Discussion Boards
- BizSkills Simulations: Supply and Demand; Adapting to the Economic Environment

Video Case:

To access the Chapter 2 Video Case: Black October—The Crash of 2008, see the Activities folder in the Assessment section of MyBusinessLab.

Web Case:

To access the Chapter 2 Web Case, see the Activities folder in the Assessment section of MyBusinessLab.

3

Legal, Ethical, and Responsible Business

LEARNING OBJECTIVES

After studying this chapter, you should be able to:

1. Define ethics and describe different ethical systems. (pp. 60–61)

2. Summarize how to create a personal code of ethics. (pp. 61–64)

3. Explain how personal ethics can play a role in the workplace. (pp. 64–66)

4. Evaluate a company's ethical code using available resources such as a mission statement. (pp. 66–67)

5. Describe how a company's policies and decisions affect its achievement of corporate social responsibility (CSR). (pp. 67–73)

6. Identify some challenges a company faces in balancing the demands of social responsibility with successful business practices. (pp. 73–74)

7. Define legal compliance and explain how it can affect ethical conduct. (pp. 74–79)

8. List some strategies a company can use to recover from ethical lapses. (pp. 79–81)

9. Describe the approaches a company can use to develop and maintain an ethical environment. (pp. 81–83)

10. Summarize how companies can apply ethical standards to create new business opportunities. (pp. 83–85)

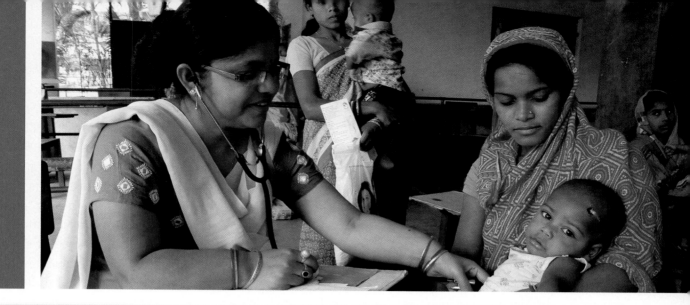

OPENING DISCUSSION: RESPONSIBLE BUSINESS

IKEA's Never-Ending List

Within six decades, IKEA has grown from a single home furnishings store in a small town in southern Sweden into a major retail experience in forty countries around the world. IKEA not only sells home furnishings worldwide, but it also engages in various socially responsible activities to help improve the international communities in which it conducts business. "We know this continuous improvement is a never-ending job," states IKEA's website, "and that we are sometimes part of the problem. But we work hard to be part of the solution."[1]

IKEA posted "The Never Ending List" on its website as a pledge to work diligently toward sustaining the environment, the Earth's resources, and the world's people. Some of the biggest projects IKEA manages are in South Asia, especially India, where the needs of children are great and where IKEA has been doing business for many years. In co-operation with UNICEF, the IKEA Group operates a broad community program in northern India to address the root causes of child

labour, and the IKEA Way on Preventing Child Labour specifies that its suppliers and their subcontractors use no child labour. The IKEA Foundation supports health, human rights, and educational programs that improve the lives of children in need around the world, providing, for example, immunizations, deworming medicines, vitamin supplements, and mosquito nets to protect against malaria.

The IKEA Way on Purchasing Home Furnishing Products (IWAY) defines what suppliers can expect from IKEA and specifies what IKEA expects from its suppliers in terms of legal requirements, working conditions, active prevention of child labour, external environment, and forestry management. IKEA maintains a strict sourcing policy for its suppliers of wood products, refusing to accept illegally felled wood or wood from intact natural forests. The policy requires all suppliers to document the origin of their wood, and supports this policy with in-house forestry specialists who monitor and work closely with suppliers and forestry

(continued)

companies.[2] As well, for more than ten years, IKEA Canada has partnered with Tree Canada in an annual tree-planting event: "Pick a Tree, Plant a Tree." With the help of IKEA co-workers, volunteers, and Tree Canada experts, saplings, trees, and shrubs are planted in community parks, schools, and riverside areas across Canada.

Even the coffee IKEA sells in its restaurants is UTZ Certified, indicating that the product has met stringent sustainability requirements. UTZ-approved growers must provide workers with health, safety training, access to proper health care, affordable housing, and schools for children. Coffee producers who work with UTZ must reduce the environmental impact of their operations—preventing soil erosion and using less energy, water, fertilizer, and pesticides.

IKEA has a long tradition of co-operating with different non-government organizations (NGOs), such as Greenpeace. Over the years, IKEA has phased out the use of bleach for printed materials, the use of PVC in products, as well as working toward protecting natural intact forests. The company regularly conducts environmental audits to ensure its stores maintain and improve their internal efforts to recycle, reduce waste, and save energy. Canadian stores include recycling depots where customers can drop off used compact fluorescent light bulbs (which contain low levels of mercury), halogen bulbs, and batteries free of charge. Two GREEN parking spaces at every Canadian store—located near the front entrance directly after the handicapped and family parking—are reserved for customers driving hybrid or fuel-efficient vehicles, a reward for driving "green." It's easy to see why IKEA Canada Limited Partnership was selected as one of Canada's Greenest Employers for 2010.[3] The company also partnered with the Make-A-Wish Foundation of Canada for its local charitable initiatives, helping grant room makeover wishes to children living with life-threatening medical conditions in local communities.

IKEA believes it can accomplish so much more on social and environmental improvements by working with experienced partners rather than working alone, so it cooperates with the World Wildlife Fund (WWF), Save the Children, UNICEF, and many other such organizations. Since no single action or product can bring about the change that's needed in the world, IKEA aims to make the most out of every step along the way.

DISCUSSION QUESTIONS

1. Do you think more companies will be prompted to follow IKEA's example and become more socially responsible? Why or why not?

2. Is IKEA simply following the law with its initiatives or is it going beyond the law? What benefits does the company gain by spending money on these initiatives?

3. Think about how a company affects its community, investors, employees, and the world at large. What types of project, actions, or initiatives do you think would be included under the umbrella of corporate social responsibility (CSR)? How can you help with such initiatives?

ETHICS: THE BASICS

Ethics Defined

Define ethics and describe different ethical systems.

Ethics are moral principles and values that govern human conduct, with respect to the rightness and wrongness of the choices humans make.

Ethical behaviour (moral behaviour) is behaviour that conforms to a set of approved standards of social or professional behaviour.

So what exactly are ethics?   **Ethics** are moral principles and values that govern human conduct, with respect to the rightness and wrongness of the choices humans make. In effect, ethics are the guidelines you use to make decisions each day. **Ethical behaviour** (moral behaviour) is behaviour that conforms to a set of approved standards of social or professional behaviour. But not all people share the same ethics. Many systems of ethical conduct exist. Some are based on religious systems, some are cultural or national, and some have been passed from generation to generation within a specific ethnic group.

What are the different systems of ethical conduct?   One ethical system is **moral relativism**, which maintains that there is no universal moral truth but instead only people's individual beliefs, perspectives, and values. This means that no single view is more valid than any other; therefore, no single standard exists to assess ethical truth. According to moral relativists, each person has his or her own ideas of right and wrong, so who are you to judge anyone else? Imagine trying to organize any group of people—a family, a company, or a country—according to this ethical system.

Another ethical system is **situational ethics**, in which people make decisions based on a specific situation instead of universal laws. Joseph Fletcher, a Harvard Divinity School professor, developed situational ethics because he believed that applying the Golden Rule—treating others as you would like to be treated—was more important in making ethical decisions than applying complex sets of moral rules.

Many other ethical systems exist, some of which are defined by religious traditions. Judeo-Christian ethics refer to the common set of basic values shared across both Jewish and Christian religions, which include respecting property and relationships, respecting one's parents, and being kind to others. According to Buddhist teachings, ethical and moral principles are governed by examining whether a person's action is likely to be harmful to oneself or others and if so to avoid that action. Hindu ethics are related to expressing reciprocity, as one may end up in someone else's shoes in their next incarnation. Selfless action for the benefit of others without thought for oneself is an important rule in Hinduism. Kindness and hospitality are key Hindu values.

But don't some people behave without regard for ethics?   It is true that sometimes people act in a manner that violates the beliefs they hold or the beliefs of the ethical system they say they follow. **Unethical behaviour** (immoral behaviour) is behaviour that does not conform to a set of approved standards of social or professional behaviour. This is different from **amoral behaviour**, in which a person has no sense of right and wrong and no interest in the moral consequences of his or her actions.

Personal Ethics

What are personal ethics?   Every day you have thoughts that lead you to say and do certain things. As you choose your words and actions, you're following a **personal code of ethics**, a set of principles that guide the decisions you make in your life with respect to what is right or wrong. Sometimes, people have a very clear, well-defined set of principles they follow. Other times, a person's ethics are inconsistent or are not applied the same way in every situation. Still other times, people have not taken the time to clarify what they value most.

Sometimes, it seems clear that making an unethical decision will produce an immediate benefit. This is when it is most challenging to adhere to your own ethical system. Consider this example: when applying for her dream job, a college senior exaggerates on her résumé about her experiences and responsibilities during an internship to seem more qualified. Is this lying or is the behaviour justified?

Now consider how you treat property. Say you bring home a few pads of paper, some pens, and a stack of blank CDs from the supply closet at work. Is this stealing? What if it was just one piece of paper you brought home? Some would say it depends on whether you use the material to do work at home. What if you used some of it on work projects and some on personal projects? And what if it wasn't you who was taking office supplies but someone you work with? It's often easy to have one view when you're taking the supplies and another when it's the person you like the least in the office.

Have you ever examined your personal code of ethics?   Although it takes time and effort, if you have a clear idea of what values are most important to you, it may be easier to handle situations in your professional life that require you to make complex ethical decisions. Refer to **Table 3.1**, which outlines one way to analyze your ethical system, as you answer the following questions. Be sure to summarize what you've written in a list. Later, you'll see that businesses follow a similar plan when creating their own statements of values. Why is this important? It will be easier for you to align your personal

Moral relativism maintains that there is no universal moral truth but instead only people's individual beliefs, perspectives, and values.

Situational ethics maintain that people make decisions based on a specific situation instead of universal laws.

Unethical behaviour (immoral behaviour) is behaviour that does not conform to a set of approved standards of social or professional behaviour.

Amoral behaviour occurs when a person has no sense of right and wrong and no interest in the moral consequences of his or her actions.

Summarize how to create a personal code of ethics.

A **personal code of ethics** is a set of principles that guide the decisions you make in your life with respect to what is right or wrong.

Table 3.1   Determining Your Personal Code of Ethics

	Question	Examples
Base Character	What characteristics would others use to describe you?	Honest, reliable, kind, self-centred, aggressive
Beliefs	What are the most important beliefs you hold and use to make decisions in your life?	"Nice guys finish last." "Hard work always pays off."
Behaviour	How do your relationships reflect your character and beliefs?	I have mostly shallow relationships because I tend not to follow through on my commitments. I have many deep, long-lasting friendships because I value friendship and work to retain my friends.
Why	Where did your beliefs and your view of your character come from?	Family, religion, movies, personal experiences, and so on.

ethics with that of the workplace, making it easier for you to choose businesses to work for, and with, in the future. Most employees feel greater job satisfaction when their personal values are in align with the company's values.

Answer these questions to help you determine your personal code of ethics:

1. Write down what kind of person you are—what is your *character*? Would a friend describe you as helpful and kind? Ambitious and greedy? Be honest in your assessment of yourself.
2. Make a list of the *beliefs* that influence your decision making. For example, would you feel comfortable working in a lab that uses animals for medical research purposes? Think about whether your answers are "flexible"—that is, how committed are you to adhering strictly to your ethical positions?
3. Consider your *behaviour* regarding the places where you work and live and how you relate to the people around you. Would you like to change anything about your behaviour? For example, do you ever find yourself gossiping or speaking in a way that creates a more divisive workplace? You may feel justified in the comments you're making, but is your ethical position on gossiping creating the kind of environment you ultimately want?
4. Now that you have your beliefs written down, think about *why* you believe them. Have you accepted these beliefs without investigation, or do they stand up to the test of real-world experiences in your life? Would it be worth making a short-term sacrifice to uphold these values?

How do your ethics develop?   Life experiences offer us opportunities to develop our personal ethics. We also need to decide whether the behaviour we see around us makes sense within the ethical systems that we learned from our family, our place of worship, or our first-grade teacher. Sometimes, our experiences lead us to abandon some ethical rules and to adopt others. And for some of us, our ethical rules are modified depending on what is at stake.

How can an ethical life get you ahead?   Ethics can feel like an abstract ideal, ideas that would be nice in a utopian world but that don't have any real impact on your life in the here and now. But there are some clear benefits from living ethically.

First, society has established its own set of rules of conduct as *laws*. It's no surprise that ignoring or being inconsistent in following these principles can have an immediate impact on your life. Whether complying with a law about the way you run your business or following laws that affect your personal life, decision-making principles that work within society's legal boundaries can make your life much simpler. Ethics and legality are two very different things. Laws do not make people honest, reliable, or truthful. Following the law is an important first step for any individual or organization, but ethical behaviour requires more than that. Ethical behaviour is accepted by society as right versus wrong. Many people have few moral absolutes because most decisions in life are complicated and do not often have a simple yes or no answer. Morals and ethics develop differently in different cultural groups, countries, and religions. However, among many sources from different times and places—such as the Bible, Aristotle's *Ethics*, the Qur'an,

Explore on MyBusinessLab

Can Living Ethically Make You Happy?

Research suggests that happiness itself is a result of living ethically, based on a new area of psychology known as *positive psychology*. Dr. Martin Seligman of the University of Pennsylvania[5] pioneered this field to discover the causes of happiness instead of treating mental dysfunctions only with medication. Seligman's research has shown that by identifying your personal strengths and values, as shown in **Table 3.2**, and aligning your life so you can apply your personal strengths and values every day, you will see an increase in happiness (and a decrease in depression) equivalent to the effects of antidepressant medication and

therapy. Finding a way to identify and then apply your ethics and values to your daily life does indeed have an impact on your happiness.

Discussion Questions

1. **Do you think there is a connection between living ethically and being happy? Why or why not?**
2. **According to research, about 50 percent of a person's happiness is based on his or her genes. What do you think accounts for the other 50 percent?**
3. **Dr. Martin Seligman lists six virtues and strengths for authentic happiness in Table 3.2. Is the list complete, or do you think any factors are missing?**

Table 3.2   Virtues and Strengths for Authentic Happiness

Virtue	Definition	Character Strength
Wisdom	The acquisition and use of knowledge	Creativity, curiosity, open-mindedness
Courage	The will to accomplish goals in the face of opposition	Authenticity, bravery, persistence, zest
Humanity	Tending to and befriending others	Kindness, love, social intelligence, empathy
Justice	Just behaviour or treatment	Fairness, leadership, teamwork
Temperance	Strengths that protect against excess	Forgiveness, modesty, prudence, self-regulation
Transcendence	Forging connections to the larger universe	Gratitude, hope, humour, appreciation of beauty

Adapted from M.E.P. Seligman, T. Steen, N. Park, and C. Peterson, "Positive Psychology Progress: Empirical Validation of Interventions," *American Psychologist, Vol. 60, No. 5, July 2005.*

and Confucius—you'll find many similar basic moral values. Almost all organized religions have a version of the Golden Rule: Do unto others as you would have them do unto you (also known as "Ethics of Reciprocity").[4]

Living ethically may even be good for your health. When your day-to-day decisions are in conflict with the values you consider most important, you often feel stressed and angry. In situations in which there is constant conflict between what you value and what actions you're forced to take, a variety of mental and physical damages may follow.

For example, Renate Schulster was vice-president of human resources in a financial services firm.[6] She was asked to investigate an employee's allegation of sexual harassment. Schulster's investigation led her to believe that the chief executive officer (CEO) of the corporation was guilty of the offence. Her personal ethics dictated following-through with the employee's claim, which put her at odds with the company. As the pressure from the conflict between her own values and those of the company's CEO grew, she sought psychological counselling for the emotional impact of the stress. She was eventually able to recover her medical and legal expenses from the employer and left the position. Renate held on to her integrity; however, the battle was not an easy one.

As you probably discovered when analyzing your own ethical system at the beginning of the chapter, personal ethics are a large part of how people define themselves, their roles in society, and their business conduct. Have you ever cheated on a test? How did you feel about yourself afterward? Have you seen others cheat on assignments or tests? How did this make you feel? Students use many reasons to rationalize such behaviour— "I didn't have enough time to study" or "everyone else is doing it" or "just this one time since the content is too hard to remember." Many colleges and universities combat cheating and plagiarism with clearly visible policies—such as a "Code of Conduct" or "Academic Honesty Policy"—in place. One anti-plagiarism tool gaining popularity in academic institutions is Turnitin.com, which scans and compares students' papers against a database of document information and determines the percentage of possible plagiarized content. Because students have been observed gathering information from cellphones or instant-messaging others during tests, many schools have policies that ban cellphones, smartphones, and electronic dictionaries and allow only specific calculators during exams. Researchers have conducted studies to determine whether a relationship exists between academic dishonesty among undergraduate students and dishonesty later when the same students are in the workforce—it appears that it does, and those who cheat in school often are dishonest in the workplace.[7] Students need to realize that by cheating on tests they are cheating themselves of the knowledge they need to perform well in the workplace, and once hired, they may soon be fired for not having the skills and knowledge their diploma states they do. This not only makes the student look bad in the employer's eyes, but it also makes the educational institution appear to have low standards for graduating students.

By investing careful thought into your personal ethical standards, you can be clearer on what you must do when facing an ethical conflict in the workplace. What exactly you will do may be a little more difficult. Nonetheless, a personal analysis such as the one you completed earlier will help guide you through the challenge.

PERSONAL ETHICS MEETS BUSINESS ETHICS

You As a Person and As an Employee

Explain how personal ethics can play a role in the workplace.

Decision-Making Mini-Simulation:
Ethics. Located in MyBusinessLab.

An **ethical decision** entails making a right-versus-wrong decision—one in which there is a right (ethical) choice and a wrong (unethical or possibly illegal) choice.

An **ethical lapse** is an error in judgement that produces a harmful outcome but does not show a complete lack of integrity.

An **ethical dilemma** is a morally problematic situation in which guiding moral principles cannot determine which course of action is right or wrong.

What is an ethical dilemma?   An **ethical decision** entails making a right-versus-wrong decision—one in which there is a right (ethical) choice and a wrong (unethical or possibly illegal) choice. An **ethical lapse** is an error in judgement that produces a harmful outcome but does not show a complete lack of integrity. Routinely producing harmful results is not considered a "lapse," it is simply unethical. Ethical lapses, even small ones, harm the perception of a values-driven corporate culture. Questionable behaviour by one employee can demotivate others and detracts from productivity and job satisfaction. Time spent on personal e-mails wastes hours per day, which isn't a big ethical lapse but may demotivate other employees and cause a decrease in productivity. An **ethical dilemma** is a morally problematic situation in which guiding moral principles cannot determine which course of action is right or wrong. A classic ethical dilemma in business is whether tobacco companies should be allowed to advertise. Allowing them to do so encourages unhealthy behaviour, but not allowing them to do so violates their freedoms and hinders their ability to do business. Consider this: your corporation is having financial difficulty, and knowing that your corporation has obligations to both shareholders and employees, would you reduce dividends to shareholders or reduce wages to employees to improve its financial well-being? Some moral dilemmas result from uncertainty about the kind of actions one should take to achieve the best outcome, possibly because future outcomes are unknowable. For example, employees have a right to privacy, but employers have a right to expect safe, competent behaviour from employees. Should employers be allowed to administer drug tests to their employees? What about in jobs where employees operate heavy machinery or trucks? What about in jobs where employees are manufacturing pharmaceuticals that will be sold to the public or are administering medicine to patients? If employers knew that the tests would result in "clean" employees, then they would not need to administer tests, but they do not know and must ensure safety in the workplace.

Randy Marks faced an ethical dilemma when he had to decide whether to continue making tiles that polluted the environment. "It was a beautiful glaze," Randy says with a sigh. His modest pottery shop, Oak Hills Tile, depends on orders from individuals and small architecture firms who are looking for authentic custom pieces of tile to adorn their kitchens, floors, or fountains. "I used copper and a special firing method to give the glaze a stunning crimson colour," Randy explains. "It was our best-selling item." However, part of the production process called for additional copper to be introduced during firing, and a thick black smoke laced with toxic copper was produced. As orders increased, more often than not the kiln in the back of the workshop was spewing this smoke into the air, in contrast to the clean white smoke produced by normal glazes. But Randy had been part of environmental groups in his community for years, so he knew how detrimental this process was to the environment. How could he find a way to stay true to his ethical standards and still be mindful of his responsibilities to his employees and customers?

We often find ourselves torn between several choices, and finding a path that works for both you and the company you work for can be challenging. In some settings, the line between right and wrong can be difficult to see. Other times, when your own personal values just won't align with the company's, you may wish you had understood more about the company's sense of ethical culture early in your career there, before you had invested your time and effort. Let's look at some examples, resources, and techniques to help you navigate ethical conflict in the workplace.

What role do personal ethics have in a business environment?
Our personal ideas of right and wrong influence our actions, words, and thoughts. But how does that carry over into the workplace? After all, at work our employer is purchasing our time and energy. As employees, our responsibility is to follow the ethics that the owner or director has established for the business. However, a business owner has no control over or even input into your conduct outside the office.

But is this really true? Perhaps at one time this model applied to life in Canada, but the modern workplace is more complex. Now, behaviour, integrity, and honesty off the job relate to on-the-job performance. For example, today's workers telecommute, working from home using technologies to connect electronically to office systems, materials, and meetings. In this newly expanded workplace, an employer may indeed care if an employee drinks at home during the workday or experiments with drugs recreationally after hours. The business environment is a changing landscape, and the lines of privacy laws are becoming blurred. Do employers really have a say over employees' behaviour outside the office if that behaviour may affect the company for which he or she works?

Likewise, stockholders (people who own stock in the company) and employees sometimes have a say over the behaviour of management outside the office. In 2004, Boeing was recovering from a set of scandals involving how it obtained military contracts. The aerospace leader fired its current CEO and hired a former Boeing employee, Harry C. Stonecipher, to lead the company back to stability. Fifteen months later, Stonecipher, who was married, was discovered to be having an affair with a female employee.[8] The very same code of conduct Stonecipher had created and pointed to as a sign of the return of ethical conduct at Boeing was used to force his resignation. There were no charges of sexual harassment, and the woman did not work directly for Stonecipher. He never showed her any favoured treatment within Boeing. But there still was a conflict between his personal ethics and his role in the business. It took a great toll on him personally as well as the company he was working to restore.

What if you are asked to do something outside your understanding of ethical behaviour?
It can be challenging to decide whose ethics to follow—yours or your company's. Each path has legal and moral consequences. For example, Andrea Malone was ordered by the president of her company to fire an employee who had a brain tumour because the tumour had lowered the employee's productivity.[9] Andrea knew it was a violation of federal law to fire the employee under these conditions.

In 2004, Boeing fired its CEO, Harry Stonecipher, for unethical conduct. Ironically, Stonecipher had been hired to lead Boeing back to stability after a number of scandals had rocked the aerospace company.

However, her company insisted she fire the employee and say that it was for other reasons, not the tumour. Andrea chose to leave the company rather than fire the person unfairly, but she has since had difficulty finding other employment. Andrea held to her personal ethics but was not properly prepared for the short-term consequences.

And what if you find you are taking part in unethical activity without having known that you were doing so? Before Bruce Forest accepted a job offer to be a human resources director, he asked the firm about rumours that they hired undocumented immigrants.[10] He was assured that was no longer the case, but soon after Bruce started to work for the company, reports began arriving that such illegal hiring was a continuing practice. His boss ordered Bruce to stop investigating the situation, saying that the company would prefer the risk of being fined. The fine the company would have to pay was "an acceptable business expense," according to Bruce's boss. So now Bruce was complicit in this activity and had to make some tough decisions. Should he move his family, take a pay cut, and lose his promised bonus, or stay knowing that he was now a party to this deception?

Price fixing occurs when a group of companies agree among themselves to set the products' prices, independent of market demand or supply.

To stumble unknowingly into unethical and even illegal activity brings consideration of our own ethics to the forefront. Both inside and outside the office, people can find themselves involved in difficult ethical situations, but it is especially difficult when your job is on the line. Consider Mark Whitacre, a senior executive with the agricultural giant Archer Daniels Midland (ADM).[11] ADM was involved for years in a multinational price-fixing scheme. **Price fixing** occurs when a group of companies agree among themselves to set the products' prices, independent of market demand or supply. Based on such price fixing, ADM stole millions of dollars from its customers by agreeing with its own competitors to set a product's price. Whitacre was a participant in all illegal activities and was set to rise to the very top of the organization. His wife, however, became increasingly conflicted with what was happening at ADM and with her own ethical values. She finally threatened to divorce Whitacre unless he found a way to end his involvement. Whitacre then went to the FBI and agreed to tape secret meetings at ADM, ultimately recording more than 250 hours of incriminating audio and video tape. Although some people decide they will be flexible with their own ethical standards at the workplace, it can often take a toll on their mental state, relationships, and physical health.

ADM was at the centre of an international price-fixing scandal, meeting with its own competitors to set the price and amount of product it sold. This huge conspiracy was uncovered because ADM employee Marc Whitacre became an FBI informant for two years.

What did Randy Marks, the owner of Oak Hills Tile, decide to do when his personal ethics and business ethics collided with the production of the special pottery glaze? No one was "watching"—there was no censure from any environmental authority, and no laws were being broken. But the conflict for Randy was too much. "I had campaigned against factory emissions of air pollution for years," Randy said. "The ethical conflict was too great; I had to stop making the glaze." Randy's decision led to difficult times for the shop. Orders dwindled and the workers were frustrated. They loved producing such interesting, beautiful pieces, and the new orders meant extra hours and extra earnings. Their shop was so small, they argued, how could a little smoke possibly matter in the big scheme of things? Randy had to be firm, explaining repeatedly that his personal ethics had to be consistent with his workplace ethics, and that he was sure that in the end, Oak Hills Tile would benefit from his decision.

Business ethics is the application of ethical behaviour in a business context. It deals with internal values that are part of corporate culture and shapes decisions and actions concerning social responsibility.

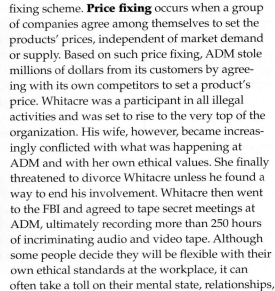

④ Identifying a Company's Ethics

Evaluate a company's ethical code using available resources such as a mission statement.

How do you examine a company's ethics?   **Business ethics** is the application of ethical behaviour in a business context. It deals with internal values that are part of corporate culture and shapes decisions and actions concerning social responsibility.

Acting ethically in business means more than just abiding by laws and regulations; it means doing what is right, fair, and just, which is not always easy. It means being honest, considering the interests of all people involved, and doing what is right even when it is difficult or personally disadvantageous.

Some companies may have a written **corporate code of ethics**, which is a formal statement of the organization's commitment to certain values regarding ethics and social issues. Additionally, many companies have a public mission statement (sometimes called a *corporate vision*) that defines the core purpose of the organization—why it exists—and often describes its values, goals, and aspirations. Consider the following mission statement of Fetzer Vineyards:

> We are an environmentally and socially conscious grower, producer, and marketer of wines of the highest quality and value. Working in harmony and with respect for the human spirit, we are committed to sharing information about the enjoyment of food and wine in a lifestyle of moderation and responsibility. We are dedicated to the continuous growth and development of our people and business.[12]

This mission statement has led to 100 percent organic wine production, awards for conservancy of energy, and a company-wide English as a Second Language training program offered as part of its education package to employees. Paul Dolan, president of Fetzer Vineyards, states, "When the first words of your mission statement are *environmentally and socially conscious*, it opens up new perspectives on how to operate the entire business."[13]

Smaller firms, such as Randy's Oak Hills Tile, often benefit from the same kind of focus on key principles. Although Oak Hills Tile does not have a formal written mission statement, Randy's behaviour and willingness to discuss his decision behind discontinuing the popular glaze let each employee see clearly the priorities Randy holds for the business. Even though the employees did not easily accept his decision, they felt the larger mission of the business was well defined and respected.

How can I find out the best and worst aspects of a company's ethical conduct?

In addition to a company's code of ethics and mission statement, other resources allow you to evaluate the acts of responsibility of, and legal violations by, any given company. Websites such as Canada Legal Information Institute (www.canlii.org) or the U.S. Law-Crawler (www.lawcrawler.com) can help you find relevant cases or lawsuits filed by or against many corporations.

Checking to see whether a company has been audited, rated, or certified by a governing body or association is a good way to find out more about a company's commitment to ethical conduct and social responsibility. For instance, the International Standards Organization has a certification for environmentally sustainable practices in its ISO 14 000 certification. The Ethics Practitioners' Association of Canada (EPAC) supports ethics officers, consultants, educators, students, and others interested in applying ethics within organizations. The Dow Jones Sustainability Index measures companies' sustainability initiatives. To get onto the Dow Jones Sustainability Index, companies are assessed and selected based on their long-term economic, social, and environmental asset management plans. The FTSE4Good Index Series has been designed to measure objectively the performance of companies that meet globally recognized corporate responsibility standards. KLD Indexes are accepted as the standard for defining strategies and benchmarking investments that integrate environmental, social, and governance factors. The Walt Disney Company, for example, is a member of the Dow Jones Sustainability North America Index, KLD Indexes, and a constituent of the FTSE4Good Index Series.

CORPORATE SOCIAL RESPONSIBILITY (CSR)

Five Pillars of CSR

What is corporate social responsibility (CSR)?

Corporate decisions reflect a company's desire to fulfill a sense of corporate social responsibility. Every day, large companies such as Gap, Disney, and Shell, as well as medium-sized firms and small local

---

top10

Ten of the World's Most Ethical Companies (2011)

1. Encana (Energy/Utilities, Canada)
2. Thomson Reuters (Media, Canada)
3. eBay
4. Ford Motor
5. General Electric
6. General Mills
7. Microsoft
8. PepsiCo
9. Singapore Telecom
10. Starbucks Coffee

Source: Jacquelyn Smith, "The World's Most Ethical Companies," *Forbes.com*, March 15 2011, www.forbes.com/2011/03/15/most-ethical-companies-leadership-responsibility-ethisphere.html, Accessed April 12, 2011.

A **corporate code of ethics** is a formal statement of the organization's commitment to certain values regarding ethics and social issues.

Describe how a company's policies and decisions affect its achievement of corporate social responsibility (CSR).

BizSkills Simulation: Ethics and Social Responsibility. Located in MyBusinessLab.

businesses, must make decisions regarding corporate social responsibility. Let's look at what it means, who it affects, and how companies can achieve it.

■ Gap Inc., a major clothing retailer with factories around the world, launches a program called P.A.C.E.—Personal Advancement, Career Enhancement—in India and Cambodia, with plans for expansion to other countries. The program aims to help women in developing countries by providing them with education and leadership training.[14]

■ The Walt Disney Company bans cigarettes from its family films.[15]

■ Shell Oil works toward reducing emissions of nitrous oxide and sulfur dioxide—both of which contribute to smog and acid rain—from its facilities.[16]

Think about what these actions have in common. Why did Gap, Disney, and Shell make these decisions? What do you think was their motivation, or goal? What kind of effects have these decisions likely had?

Corporate social responsibility (CSR) is a company's obligation to conduct its activities with the aim of achieving social, environmental, and economic development. Like ethics, CSR means distinguishing right from wrong and doing the right thing. It means being a good corporate citizen by making choices and taking actions that will contribute to the welfare and interests of society as well as the organization. Archie B. Carroll suggests that the following four kinds of social responsibility constitute total CSR and can be depicted as a pyramid (see **Figure 3.1**).[17]

> **Corporate social responsibility (CSR)** can be defined as a company's obligation to conduct its activities with the aim of achieving social, environmental, and economic development.

1. Companies must make money to stay in business. They have an *economic responsibility* to perform in a manner consistent with maximizing profits.

2. Companies have *legal responsibilities* as well. They must perform in a manner consistent with the expectations of government and the law. They must fulfill their legal obligations to produce goods and services in a manner that at least meets minimal legal requirements.

3. Once companies have met their economic and legal responsibilities, they can then fulfill their *ethical responsibilities*. Companies are expected to perform in a manner

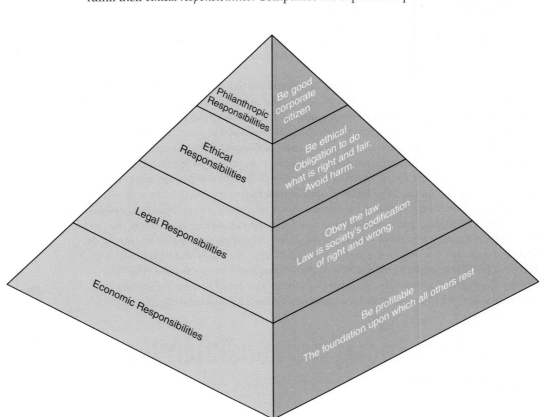

Figure 3.1 Pyramid of Corporate Social Responsibility (CSR)

consistent with societal morals and ethical norms, and not compromise ethics in order to achieve corporate goals. They are expected to recognize that corporate integrity and ethical behaviour go beyond mere compliance with laws and regulations. Society expects companies to do what is right, fair, and just, and assert ethical leadership.

4. Once companies have met their economic, legal, and ethical responsibilities, they may then choose to satisfy their *philanthropic responsibilities*. Philanthropic actions are discretionary, but if a company has the means then it is in their best interest to participate in philanthropy because society desires companies to be good corporate citizens. They are expected to participate in voluntary and charitable activities within their local communities. They are expected to provide assistance to education, culture and arts, health services, non-profit organizations that do "good" for society, and assist in projects that enhance society's "quality of life."

All business organizations, regardless of their size, have a corporate responsibility. Companies have responsibility to their stakeholders. **Stakeholders** are individuals or groups to whom a business has a responsibility: employees, customers, investors, suppliers, government, community, and society overall (which includes environmental responsibility). Multinational corporations often must balance conflicting interests of stakeholders when making decisions regarding social responsibilities, especially in the area of human rights. By being socially responsible, a company makes decisions in five major areas (see **Figure 3.2**):[18]

1. Human rights and employment standards in the workplace
2. Ethical sourcing and procurement

Stakeholders are individuals or groups to whom a business has a responsibility: employees, customers, investors, suppliers, government, community, and society overall (which includes environmental responsibility).

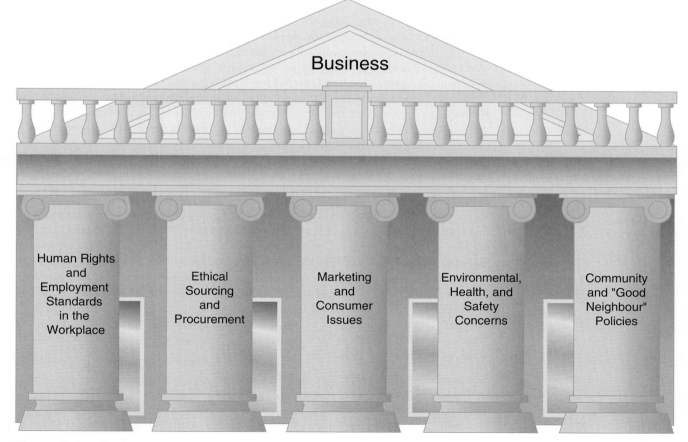

Figure 3.2   Five Pillars of CSR

Corporate social responsibility is the collection of policies covering five major areas and can be the foundation of a business.

3. Marketing and consumer issues
4. Environmental, health, and safety concerns
5. Community and "good neighbour" policies.

Let's examine each of these areas in more detail.

Human Rights and Employment Standards in the Workplace   CSR concerns affect the world outside the office in both the local and global communities. For example, employment standards—how a company respects and cares for its employees—are reflected locally in the policies a company sets and the impact the company has on the community. As a business interacts more with the global marketplace, the company will have to make decisions about working with companies with different ethical standards on tough issues such as child labour, pollution, fair wages, and human rights. Consider the case of the Vedanta Resources, a mining and aluminum refining company based in the United Kingdom. When Vedanta came into the Indian community of Orissa, it promised improved quality of life for its employees and the entire region. The quality of life has not improved, and due to the refining company's practices, the air is hard to breathe. Meanwhile, the river, the main source of drinking water, is so polluted that bathing in it causes rashes and blisters.[19] What responsibility does Vedanta have to its employees, the people of the area, and company stockholders?

Ethical Sourcing and Procurement   Finding a source for raw materials and making agreements with suppliers is an aspect of many businesses. In today's global marketplace, many companies find themselves working with international suppliers. Once a business has to consider purchasing materials from a supplier in a different country or even a different region of the country, they are tied to environmental and social concerns in that area. Consider a company that has an assembly plant in a different country. That company is now tied to the social conditions there. To keep its supplier operating or to keep an assembly plant running smoothly, the company has a stake in the quality of the schools in that area so that the local workforce is educated.

The banana supplier Chiquita, for example, has a vested interest in other parts of the world where it gets its produce—bananas. Chiquita has had a decades-long reputation of allowing dangerous conditions for its farm workers, contaminating water, and clear-cutting tropical forests. With the threat of these environmental and workers' rights issues endangering the brand, Chiquita began to improve conditions. It constructed housing and schools for employees' families, and now all of Chiquita's farms are certified by the environmental group Rainforest Alliance.[20] A commitment to CSR means that companies must be aware of the ethical impact of their behaviour—both at home and in communities far from their shores.

Marketing and Consumer Issues   Marketing can often present ethical challenges. In addition to issues regarding truth in advertising, marketers must consider messages that may be manipulative even if they are not outright lies. For example, *Brigitte*, a leading German fashion magazine, recently announced it will no longer accept advertising featuring professional "zero-sized" models.[21] Medical authorities have linked the viewing of these images with eating disorders. The magazine publishers were faced with an ethical decision and decided to begin using "real" women in place of professional models to connect better with their readers. Companies must confront and respond to many consumer and marketing issues if they are to behave in a socially responsible manner. Do you think magazines that use professional models are socially irresponsible? Who determines what irresponsible behaviour is?

Environmental, Health, and Safety Concerns   Many industries, and even small companies, make decisions every day that affect the environment and the safety of their workers or their neighbours. From multinational manufacturing giants to the local auto body shop, any industry involved with processes that produce toxic waste must make decisions that directly affect the environment. Meanwhile, the production of toxic materials is moving at a far faster pace than the growth of proper storage facilities and recycling techniques, so disposal becomes more and more expensive. One of the most serious cases of water supply contamination in Canadian history, the poisoning of Walkerton, Ontario, exposed an alarming, unstable waterworks system that made more than two thousand people ill and killed seven.[22] What are the short- and long-term costs of ignoring these concerns? Companies that have a CSR focus concentrate on ways to make decisions in a socially sound way.

Community and "Good Neighbour" Policies   Finally, CSR is concerned with how the company affects the community, particularly the surrounding neighbourhood. Consider the Nestlé Waters Canada "good neighbour" policy:*

> What does it mean to be a good neighbour? It means:
> - Demonstrating integrity and accountability
> - Working collaboratively and sharing our passion for a clean planet
> - Supporting community development projects with product and financial donations, employment opportunities and participation in volunteer programs
> - Helping in times of need
>
> It means saying what we mean and doing what we say. These are our commitments and you can hold us to them. To us, this is what it means to be a good neighbour.[23]

It's in a company's best interest to be a good neighbour. What do you think might happen if a company wasn't?

What are the benefits of CSR?

Having a strong and clear ethical policy helps a business in a number of ways:[24]

- The company develops a positive reputation in the marketplace with consumers as well as with its suppliers and vendors.
- The company enjoys strong recruitment and retention of the best available talent.
- Efficiency increases when companies use materials efficiently and minimize waste.
- Sales increase through new product innovations and environmentally and ethically conscious labelling.

Although businesses reap benefits while being socially responsible, high-level management who set strategic goals need to have a common vision of how the interests of the business can be supported by an effective CSR policy.

Is it possible to measure a company's level of CSR?

It may seem impossible to measure something as complex as CSR, but certain reports present a useful picture of the overall strength of a company's CSR effort.

Social Audits   A **social audit** is a study of how well a company is doing at meeting its social responsibilities. It is an internal systematic examination measuring and monitoring what goals the company has set, what progress it has made, and how resources such as funding and labour have been applied to the goals of CSR.

Ratings and Rankings   In addition to social audits, companies such as The Boston College Center for Corporate Citizenship (North America–based companies), CSRHub (global companies), Calvert Investment Company (U.S. companies), and Jantzi (Canadian companies) assess corporate responsibility and publish their findings. As mentioned earlier, several indexes measure sustainability initiatives, such as the Dow Jones Sustainability Index, the FTSE4Good Index Series, and KLD Indexes.

A number of magazines, such as *Fortune*, also publish lists of admired companies each year. Other organizations award businesses for superior CSR. For example, the WorldBlu List of Most Democratic Workplaces 2011 included the following Canadian companies: 1-800-GOT-JUNK?, Axiom News, Chaordix, I Love Rewards, LEARN, Rypple, TakingITGlobal, and Total Debt Freedom.[25] Razor Suleman, CEO and founder of I Love Rewards, says that the company practises transparent, two-way communication that empowers employees to play a larger role within the organization and have a voice in shaping its future, and that this generates innovation, excellence, and growth.[26]

Self-Reporting   Self-reporting by companies of their own efforts in addressing ethically complex issues and issues of social responsibility is also becoming more prevalent. For example, Time Warner's CSR report addresses a wide range of topics, including

Decision-Making Mini-Simulation: Diversity. Located in MyBusinessLab.

A **social audit** is a study of how well a company is doing at meeting its social responsibilities.

*Reprinted courtesy of Nestle Waters Canada

diversity (workforce, suppliers, and content), journalistic integrity, content accessibility, ethics, environmental sustainability, governance, and philanthropy.[27]

CSR reporting in Canada has evolved from relatively simple environmental statements to comprehensive triple-bottom reports supported by web reporting. **Triple-bottom-line** (also referred to as TBL, 3BL, or "People, Planet, Profit") reporting is used as a framework for measuring and reporting corporate performance against economic, social, and environmental parameters. PricewaterhouseCoopers (professional services company) has established sustainability reporters' roundtables in Toronto, Calgary, and Vancouver, where twice per year, representatives from companies involved in CSR reporting meet to share ideas and perspectives.

Triple-bottom-line (also referred to as TBL, 3BL, or "People, Planet, Profit") reporting is used as a framework for measuring and reporting corporate performance against economic, social, and environmental parameters.

Corporate philanthropy occurs when companies donate some of their profits or resources to charitable organizations.

Corporate Philanthropy   Many companies participate in **corporate philanthropy**, donating some of their profits or resources to charitable organizations. Often companies view such charitable activity as a marketing investment that builds a stronger relationship with the community and with their own employees. For example, the Bill and Melinda Gates Foundation was started by Microsoft chair Bill Gates. The foundation has an endowment of US$33 billion and has tackled issues such as global infant survival rates, has begun an initiative for a malaria vaccine, and is working to upgrade public access to technology. Even though the foundation is not directly associated with Microsoft, it has had a positive impact on the public perception of Microsoft.[28]

How does CSR affect society as a whole?   Business does not operate separately from society as a whole, so CSR affects us all in many ways.

Environmental Effects   Environmentally, how businesses operate has both local and global effects. For example, people living in the Silicon Valley area around San Francisco rely on groundwater for their main supply of water. This leaves the entire Silicon Valley area dependent on proper industry practices by the many semiconductor manufacturers in the area. If these companies allow chemical contaminants to enter the groundwater system, the entire region suffers.

Businesses raise troubling environmental questions on a global scale as well. Some say that allowing free trade—in which countries produce and sell products anywhere in the world—will produce an "export" of pollution to less-developed countries. Would companies move "dirty industries," those that have a high risk of pollution, danger to workers, or toxic damage of the environment, to a country where environmental regulations are lacking? It's increasingly important for industry leaders to have some structured ethical system to make such complex, long-reaching decisions.

Economic Effects   As an individual, CSR affects you as well. Financially, the long-term consequences of businesses implementing a strong CSR plan have an impact on the prices you pay for products, the availability of products, as well as the quality of these products. Both your short-term savings and long-term investments also rely on interest rates related to the perception of how stable your business is. Industries that act in ways that jeopardize their own long-term sustainability can create economic ripples that affect your bottom line.

Effects on Employee Morale   Think of your own career. Your potential for advancement, your day-to-day work environment, and your overall sense of purpose and value are affected by the degree to which the company you work for practices sound CSR. Even from the initial interview, aspects of a company's CSR plan may be apparent. Some companies find that personality testing of job candidates helps them find employees who match their own corporate values. Tools such as the Hogan Personality Inventory assess a candidate in areas such as interpersonal sensitivity, stress tolerance, and learning approach. As a job seeker, you'll want to decide whether you value a company for using these tools or if their use violates your sense of appropriate business/personal privacy boundaries.

How can you affect whether a business operates ethically?   As an individual, you can use many ways to work toward a more ethical world filled with more ethical businesses. In addition to contributing by means of your own personal conduct, both at the workplace and outside it, your choices about how to spend your money greatly influence corporate behaviour. Companies survive only because consumers buy their products or use their services. If you don't believe in a company's ethics, you can take your business elsewhere.

Meanwhile, if you choose to invest money in mutual funds and the stock market, you have another opportunity to make a statement about corporate ethics. **Socially responsible investing (SRI)** is investing only in companies that have met a certain standard of corporate social responsibility. This means funds managers look at the social and environmental behaviour of companies to decide which companies to include and exclude from the investment fund portfolio. As a shareholder, you can also use your voice to encourage a company to improve or maintain a high standard of ethics.

Finally, when you choose an employer, you're making a clear statement on ethical conduct by offering the company your valuable time and energy. By agreeing to work for a company, you're saying that you agree with its mission and ethics.

> **Socially responsible investing (SRI)** is investing only in companies that have met a certain standard of corporate social responsibility.

Challenges of CSR

Can a corporation really be socially responsible?   Nobel Prize–winning economist Milton Friedman said, "Asking a corporation to be socially responsible makes no more sense than asking a building to be."[29] He argued that an abstract construct, such as a corporation, cannot perform human functions, such as meeting responsibilities. There has long been debate around these ideas. A company does have a unique responsibility to its stockholders: they expect a profit at the end of the year. It is difficult to measure whether that responsibility outweighs a long-term responsibility to the community or the planet. Conflict can occur between the company's need to produce profit for its shareholders and the demands of quality in the product it delivers to its customers. With so many competing interests, companies must carefully analyze the idea of appropriate social and corporate responsibility.

> **6**
> Identify some challenges a company faces in balancing the demands of social responsibility with successful business practices.

What challenges does CSR pose?   It's clear that the many conflicting demands facing businesses today pose numerous ethical challenges. Consider the dilemma facing companies that produce unique products, such as pharmaceutical companies developing medications to treat AIDS. What is their exact moral and ethical obligation regarding the AIDS pandemic in Sub-Saharan Africa? AIDS killed 1.3 million people in Africa in 2009.[30] Tuberculosis kills approximately 2 million people each year,[31] and at least 1 million people die from malaria each year, mostly children.[32] Meanwhile, 70 percent of the population exists on less than two dollars a day and is unable to pay for the medications at a price point that would reimburse pharmaceutical companies for their research investment. It is a challenge for modern business leaders to balance their need to respond to investors and produce a profit with their desire to alleviate human suffering. No fixed training can equip business decision makers to navigate such difficult decisions.

Some corporations do manage to balance the demands of social responsibility and successful business practices consistently. For example, Intel scores high as an industry leader in the commitment to the practices of strong CSR. Environmentally, it has decreased the emissions from

The Bill and Melinda Gates Foundation commits more than US$1.5 billion a year in grants to global health and development projects such as funding the search for a vaccine to prevent malaria.

its operations over the past four years, mitigating its impact on global warming. It has shown a strong commitment to its employees by providing benefits for domestic partners as well as carefully monitoring workers for exposure to hazardous chemicals. The company also has human rights policies in place in all the countries in which it operates, and it donates computer equipment to many organizations, supports many charitable organizations through monetary donations, and is responsive to community needs.

Corporate social responsibility is a complex idea that requires companies and consumers to examine the ethical implications of their actions. Review the examples at the beginning of this section. Which of the "five pillars" are Gap, Disney, and Shell addressing with their actions? Do you agree with the ethical implications of their actions? Are they making a real difference? Why or why not?

DANGERS OF A WEAK ETHICAL FOCUS
Legal Regulations, Compliance, and Consequences

 Define legal compliance and explain how it can affect ethical conduct.

Is it illegal to be unethical? "To me, it was stealing, and bottom line: stealing is wrong." The software company that Lana Phillips worked for had finished developing a program to deliver movie content on-demand to home cable subscribers. Before the company could break into the market, however, it needed to test its product and make appearances at big electronics trade shows. To test the program, it needed data—that is, DVD movies. But DVD movies are copyrighted and protected with specific software encoding schemes so they cannot be copied onto a computer hard drive. As the testing phase approached, the word came down from management: purchase some DVDs, break the encoding scheme, and rip them to hard drives to use as testing. After all, the managers reasoned, the company was not going to make money off violating the DVD copyrights—it was just using it to test its software. And if it worked well, it would then run demos for clients and at trade shows using those DVDs. What was the harm?

The company consulted its attorneys and half felt the use of the DVDs might be illegal and half felt it could be defended. Lana suggested some other solutions: the company could use Hollywood films that were older and not covered by copyright protection, or it could use public domain documentaries, which were freely available for public use. Company managers worried what the impact on business would be. Would a product shown running a thirty-year-old movie or an unknown documentary grab the attention of buyers on a busy Vegas tradeshow floor? The danger on the other side was that a successful product launch by the company might not save it from facing legal action years down the line for copyright infringement. How could Lana and her boss resolve the issue when it wasn't even clear what the correct legal path was?

Depending on the industry, there may be significant legal consequences to business behaviour that ignores agreed-upon ethical standards. Acting ethically and following the law can be two different things or one in the same (see **Table 3.3**). Most societies

Table 3.3   Legal versus Ethical Comparison

Legal and Unethical	Legal and Ethical
■ Paying below the cost of living wages to workers in developing countries ■ Producing low-quality products that will not last ■ Promoting R-rated movies to young teens	■ Producing high-quality products that will last ■ Treating employees fairly in wages, benefits, and other perks ■ Contributing to the community ■ Respecting the environment
Illegal and Unethical	**Illegal and Ethical**
■ Engaging in sexual harassment ■ Embezzling money ■ Colluding with competitor companies ■ Fraudulent accounting practices	■ Colluding with medical suppliers to guarantee low prices in low-income countries ■ Providing the lowest prices only to distributors in underserved areas

also have legal rules that govern behaviour, but **ethical norms** are standards in moral behaviour and tend to be broader and more informal than laws. Most companies strive to both follow the law and conduct business ethically. Legality should be the floor—not the ceiling—for how to behave in both your personal and business actions. Companies are responsible for following complex sets of laws, and if they violate them, even unknowingly, their business may be in jeopardy. Violating the law deliberately can be the result of a lapse in emphasis and understanding of ethics and will have a serious impact on the future of the people inside the company and on the entire business community.

How is a company regulated legally?   **Business law** refers to rules, statutes, codes, and regulations established to provide a legal framework within which business may be conducted. Legal regulations are the specific laws governing the products or processes of a specific industry. When enough people think that a particular ethical standard is important, it eventually becomes law. Businesses must comply with business laws, which are enforceable by the Canadian court system and pertain to many business functions and processes. **Legal compliance** refers to conducting a business within the boundaries of all the legal regulations of that industry. The Department of Justice Canada's website (www.laws.justice.gc.ca) is a comprehensive source of Canada's myriad consolidated acts and regulations. Legislation governing business practice includes the following:

- *Income Tax Act, Excise Tax Act*
- *Bankruptcy and Insolvency Act, Companies' Creditors Arrangement Act*
- *Consumer Protection Act, Consumer Packaging and Labelling Act, Food and Drug Act, Weights and Measures Act, Textile Labelling Act, Hazardous Product Act, Motor Vehicle Safety Act, Aeronautics Act, Consumer Product Safety Act*
- Contract law (governed by common law in all provinces and territories except Quebec, which is governed by civil law)
- *Employment Standards Act, Workplace Health and Safety, Canada Labour Code*
- *Sale of Goods Act*
- Intellectual property law (i.e., patents, copyrights, plagiarism, property, and trademarks)
- *Personal Information Protection and Electronic Documents Act* (PIPEDA)
- *Competition Act, Canadian Code of Advertising Standards*
- *Canadian Business Corporations Act* (i.e., incorporation)

Let's discuss a few of these laws in more detail, specifically how they change or affect business practices.

What laws protect individuals' rights and freedoms in Canada?   *The Canadian Charter of Rights and Freedoms* guarantees certain political rights to Canadian citizens and civil rights to everyone in Canada. The Charter forms the first part of Canada's *Constitution Act, 1982*, which is made up of acts of the British and Canadian Parliaments as well as legislation, judicial decisions, and agreements between the federal and provincial governments.[33] The Charter indicates the rights of each citizen in relationship to each other and to the government. It is considered the supreme law of Canada. It works together with our system of laws to make up the rules of the country and allocates powers to different levels of government, such as federal, provincial, and municipal.

The *Canadian Charter of Rights and Freedoms* is a binding legal document that protects the basic human rights of all Canadians, such as fundamental freedoms, democratic rights, mobility rights, legal rights, equality rights, and language rights. The Charter is often cited in legal cases pertaining to human rights issues.

Under the Charter, everyone has the following fundamental freedoms:[34]

a. freedom of conscience and religion
b. freedom of thought, belief, opinion, and expression, including freedom of the press and other media of communication
c. freedom of peaceful assembly
d. freedom of association

While the Charter allows all Canadians to express their thoughts and opinions freely, it also protects everyone's right to be treated fairly, without discrimination. We all expect

---

Ethical norms are standards in moral behaviour and tend to be broader and more informal than laws.

Business law refers to rules, statutes, codes, and regulations established to provide a legal framework within which business may be conducted.

Legal compliance refers to conducting a business within the boundaries of all the legal regulations of that industry.

The Canadian Charter of Rights and Freedoms is a binding legal document that protects the basic human rights of all Canadians, such as fundamental freedoms, democratic rights, mobility rights, legal rights, equality rights, and language rights.

3

life to be reasonably fair. You expect your exams to be fair, the grading to be fair, and your wages to be fair based on the type of work being done.

The Canadian Constitution and legal system affect the governance and function of businesses. Individuals and businesses are subject to fines or imprisonment for violating laws. Laws govern business hiring practices, health and safety, importing/exporting, marketing, advertising, product safety, consumer rights, environmental sustainability, information privacy, and a number of other business functions.

Which laws pertain to how employers treat employees?   Canadian employers should be familiar with the following types of **employment-related legislation**:

Employment-related legislation covers the following subjects: employment standards legislation, human rights legislation, federal and provincial privacy legislation, occupational health and safety legislation, workers' compensation legislation, and labour relations legislation.

- employment standards legislation
- human rights legislation
- federal and provincial privacy legislation
- occupational health and safety legislation
- workers' compensation legislation
- labour relations legislation

Federally regulated organizations must comply with the *Canada Labour Code*, while other organizations are subject to the *Employment Standards and Labour Codes* of the individual provinces and territories. Enforcement and administration of the *Canada Labour Code* comes under the responsibility of the Labour Program of Human Resources and Skills Development Canada in partnership with Transport Canada and the National Energy Board.[35] Subjects treated include:

- duties of employers
- duties of employees
- workplace health and safety committees
- policy health and safety committees
- health and safety representatives
- Canada occupational health and safety regulations
- three basic rights: right to know, right to participate, right to refuse
- internal complaint resolution process
- health and safety officer
- offences and punishment
- monthly inspection

What does it mean that individuals should have an "equal opportunity"?

The Canadian Human Rights Act extends the law to ensure equal opportunity to individuals who may be victims of discriminatory practices based on a set of prohibited grounds (e.g., gender, disability, or religion).

The Canadian Human Rights Act extends the law to ensure equal opportunity to individuals who may be victims of discriminatory practices based on a set of prohibited grounds (e.g., gender, disability, or religion). It applies to all federally regulated activities, but each province and territory has its own anti-discrimination laws that apply to non-federally regulated activities. According to the *Canadian Human Rights Act*, all individuals should have an equal opportunity to create a life for themselves without being hindered by discriminatory practices based on race, colour, religion, national or ethnic origin, age, sex, sexual orientation, marital status, family status, disability, or conviction for an offence for which a pardon has been granted.[36] The Canadian Human Rights Commission administers the *Canadian Human Rights Act*, it investigates claims of discrimination, and the Canadian Human Rights Tribunal judges the cases.

The **Employment Equity Act** states that no person shall be denied employment opportunities or benefits for reasons unrelated to ability. It seeks to improve the employment conditions experienced by women, Aboriginal peoples, persons with disabilities, and members of visible minorities.[37] It applies to federally regulated employers with one hundred or more employees. It requires employers to develop and implement employment equity plans and programs, and to report annually to the Labour Program of Human Resources and Skills Development Canada (HRSDC) on their progress in achieving a representative workforce. The Canadian Human Rights Commission administers the *Employment Equity Act*. Since the act is federal legislation it applies only to

The **Employment Equity Act** states that no person shall be denied employment opportunities or benefits for reasons unrelated to ability. It seeks to improve the employment conditions experienced by women, Aboriginal peoples, persons with disabilities, and members of visible minorities.

certain industries that are federally regulated under the Canadian Constitution, namely chartered banks, airlines, federal departments, agencies and Crown corporations (companies where the federal government owns the majority of shares), television and radio stations, interprovincial communications and telephone companies, buses and railways that travel between provinces, and certain mining operations. The vast majority of employers, including nearly all retailers and manufacturing companies, fall outside its jurisdiction, although some provinces use the term *employment equity* in conjunction with their enforcement of provincial-level human rights legislation.

What rights do consumers have when buying from a company?   **Consumerism** is a social movement that seeks to increase and strengthen the rights and powers of buyers in relation to sellers. In his 1962 speech to U.S. Congress, President John F. Kennedy outlined four basic consumer rights, which later became known as the Consumer Bill of Rights. In 1985, the United Nations expanded upon the Bill of Rights to cover eight consumer rights. Consumer protection can only survive in highly industrialized countries because of the resources needed to finance consumer interests. The Consumers' Association of Canada wants consumers to know their rights and seeks to uphold these rights, which are:[38]

- the right to choice—choose what they want to buy, open competition among companies
- the right to be informed—about all relevant aspects of a product, food ingredients, clothing, labels, and so on
- the right to safety—safe products, safe foods, and so on
- the right to be heard—questions, complaints, returns, and so on
- the right to redress—satisfaction for wrong or injury, justice, reparation
- the right to consumer education—prescription drugs now come with detailed information
- the right to participate in marketplace decision making
- the right to have access to basic service
- the right to a sustainable environment

Consumer protection laws regulate many marketing activities both federally and provincially. The Consumer Protection Act governs most common consumer transactions in Ontario.

How is competition between companies regulated?   According to the Competition Bureau Canada website (www.competitionbureau.gc.ca), the **Competition Act** is a federal law regulating most business conduct in Canada. Its criminal and civil provisions are aimed at preventing anti-competitive practices in the marketplace. The Competition Bureau administers and enforces the *Competition Act, Consumer Packaging and Labelling Act, Textile Labelling Act*, and *Precious Metals Marking Act*.[39] It maintains and encourages competition in Canada in order to:

- promote an efficient and adaptable Canadian economy
- expand Canada's participation in world markets while recognizing the role of foreign competition in Canada
- ensure that small and medium-sized business have equal opportunities to participate in the Canadian economy
- provide consumers with competitive prices and product choices

The *Consumer Packaging and Labelling Act* is a criminal statute governing the packaging, labelling, sale, importation, and advertising of pre-packaged and certain other products. To help consumers make informed purchasing decisions, it specifies mandatory label information and requires that pre-packaged consumer products bear accurate and meaningful labelling information.

Businesses may need to become large to achieve lower production costs or to compete against foreign and domestic competitors. However, when a company becomes so large that it uses its market power to harm competitors or lessen competition, the *Competition Act* may come into play.

Consumerism is a social movement that seeks to increase and strengthen the rights and powers of buyers in relation to sellers.

The **Competition Act** is a federal law regulating most business conduct in Canada. Its criminal and civil provisions are aimed at preventing anti-competitive practices in the marketplace.

3

The Charities Directorate of the Canada Revenue Agency (CRA) registers qualifying organizations as charities, provides information to donors, and handles audit and compliance activities.

Tax law is the system of laws that describe government levies on economic transactions.

The *Federal Accountability Act* (Fed AA) helps strengthen accountability and increases transparency and oversight in government operations.

Does the Canada Revenue Agency (CRA) administer tax law?   The **Charities Directorate of the Canada Revenue Agency** (CRA) registers qualifying organizations as charities, provides information to donors, and handles audit and compliance activities.[40] The CRA is also responsible for administering tax law for most provinces and territories as well as various incentive and economic benefit programs delivered through the tax system. **Tax law** is the system of laws that describe government levies on economic transactions. Businesses pay taxes on revenues, payroll, and some types of supplies and must keep precise records of operations.

Do companies influence changes in the law?   A company does not generally influence changes in the law (although it is accepted that they could lobby or be part of a trade organization). In 2006, the *Federal Accountability Act* (Fed AA) was implemented to help strengthen accountability and increase transparency and oversight in government operations. This Fed AA created the *Conflict of Interest Act*, which set out clear conflict of interest and post-employment rules applicable to public office holders (e.g., ministerial staff, heads of agencies and Crown corporations, members of federal boards and tribunals).

What happens if a company breaks the law?   Violations of governing laws can damage a company severely. Companies that have broken the law have been fined, closed, or have had certain involved employees imprisoned. They often receive a bad reputation with the public and business partners, which negatively affects sales and future productivity. Business law sets a foundation for a code of ethical conduct but certainly does not encompass all that is ethical. Many companies enact policies and create boards to govern legal compliance and help the company uphold a good reputation with customers, authorities, the public, and other stakeholders. We mentioned earlier how Archer Daniel Midlands, the agriculture giant, was involved in a large price fixing scheme in which it bilked its own customers out of millions of dollars. The company was later fined US$100 million for its role in the price fixing. Likewise, Bernard L. Madoff's US$65 billion scam bankrupted thousands of individual investors, closed several charities, and ruined countless lives and fortunes. Six months after his arrest, Madoff—who pleaded guilty—received the maximum sentence of 150 years in prison, and 8800 people have filed claims (thus far) for restitution.[41] Due to Alberta-born Bernie Ebbers's US$11 billion fraud scandal, thousands of investors lost money and about 20 000 WorldCom employees lost their jobs. Ebbers received a twenty-five-year prison term and is serving time in a U.S. prison.[42] Both Madoff and Ebbers have made the list of infamy for the biggest cons of all time (see www.thehallofinfamy.org). Obviously, crime doesn't pay!

Don't companies often break the law and still make money?   Plenty of companies have broken the law and seemed to benefit for a time. Take the case of Enron. With twenty-one thousand staff members in more than forty countries, Enron had grown to become America's seventh-largest company. The company was lauded by *Fortune* magazine as the Most Innovative Company in America many times and was in the top 25 of *Fortune*'s 100 Best Companies to Work For. Enron had published its social and environmental positions, noting that the company made decisions based on the values of:[43]

- *Respect:* mutual respect with communities and stakeholders affected by the company's operations
- *Integrity:* examining the impacts, positive and negative, of the business on the environment and on society, and integrating human health, social and environmental considerations into the company's management and value system
- *Excellence:* continuing to improve performance and encouraging business partners and suppliers to adhere to the same standards.

But by October 2001, a series of scandals began to emerge when it was found that Enron's success had been largely based on fraudulent activities. The company had hidden debts totalling more than US$1 billion to inflate its own stock price, had manipulated the Texas and California power markets, causing enormous hardship, and had bribed foreign governments to win contracts abroad. A few months later, the company dissolved in bankruptcy, and founder Kenneth Lay was convicted on ten counts of fraud and conspiracy. He later died while awaiting sentencing. CEO Jeffrey Skilling was convicted of eighteen counts of fraud and faces a sentence of twenty-four years in prison.

Even the accounting auditor that Enron had hired, the famous firm Arthur Andersen, collapsed because of its involvement. Andersen was convicted of obstruction of justice for destroying thousands of documents relating to its work with Enron and its knowledge of the criminal fraud taking place there. For Enron and Arthur Anderson, the flagrant violations of ethical conduct led to outside agencies levying huge penalties. It also led to the internal collapse of the company, with the loss of the company's management and many of the employees within the firm. Most sadly, it led to the loss of the pensions of thousands of employees who had dedicated their lives to the company, not knowing management was participating in such illegal activities.

To avoid future occurrences such as these, the *Sarbanes-Oxley Act* of 2002 was passed. Under this act, CEOs are required to verify their companies' financial statements and vouch for their accuracy with the U.S. Securities and Exchange Commission (SEC). Canadian securities regulation is managed through laws and agencies established by Canada's thirteen provincial and territorial governments. The largest of the provincial regulators is the Ontario Securities Commission (OSC). The provincial and territorial regulators work together to coordinate and harmonize regulation of the Canadian capital markets through the Canadian Securities Administrators (CSA).

Recovering from Weak Ethical Conduct

What if your company is breaking the law and you want it to stop?   Some people risk their positions and future careers to stop corporate abuse when they see it in the workplace. A **whistleblower** is an employee who reports misconduct, most often to an authority outside the firm. In 2008, Bob Gale, a former commissioner of the Niagara Parks Commission, exposed that his employer had secretly extended a twenty-five-year lease with the current operator of the *Maid of the Mist* boat tours. Other potential operators were shut out of the opportunity for the lease, worth hundreds of millions of dollars, even though they were offering more favourable terms. After an eight-month investigation, the Ontario Ministry of Tourism overruled the commission and ordered it to conduct an open competitive tender process for the lease.[44]

Whistleblower protection has become a prominent topic in corporate governance in the wake of numerous high-profile corporate fraud scandals. Employees often play an important role in revealing corporate misdeeds. Canada's Bill C-11 (2005) provides whistleblowers with protection from reprisal by their employer by establishing a procedure for the disclosure of wrongdoings in the public sector, including the protection of persons who disclose the wrongdoings. It applies to the public sector, and suggestions have been made to include private-sector workers who, in their dealings with the federal government, have seen wrongdoings they wish to disclose. Additional federal and provincial statutes also contain provisions designed to protect whistleblowers; however, these are limited in scope and target particular types of offences related to the specific purpose of legislation (such as the *Employment Standards Act*). It is now a criminal offence for an employer to take action or to threaten the employee with disciplinary action (such as demotion, termination of employment, or to adversely affect the employee's employment) in order to force the employee to refrain from providing information to law enforcement officials about wrongdoing within the organization.[45] The Public Sector Integrity Office (Canada) is an office for the protection of whistleblowers who speak up against abuses in government.

The United States has both state and federal laws that prevent whistleblowers working for government or corporations from being harassed or fired. Both Australia and the U.K. also have strong laws to ensure that people aren't unfairly punished for speaking out. Whistleblowers keep our institutions honest. From Enron, to Walkerton, to the intelligence failures around 9/11, whistleblowers have made a huge contribution to informing the public and fighting corruption and incompetence.

Can a company really recover from an ethical lapse?   Companies seeking to recover from publicized ethical lapses often face long battles once customer loyalty and

List some strategies a company can use to recover from ethical lapses.

A **whistleblower** is an employee who reports misconduct, most often to an authority outside the firm.

the company's reputation have been lost. Recovery almost certainly requires pervasive change, and usually people who were not involved in the wrongdoing are involved in the efforts to forge a new image.

Companies attempting to recover from scandal often follow some common strategies:

1. They work to find a leader who will set an example of the new ethical image of the company.
2. They restructure their internal operation to empower all employees to consider ethical implications of decisions and to feel free to speak up when they spot a concern.
3. They redesign internal rewards—for example, restructuring the incentive package for a sales department so that there is a financial reward for building an ongoing relationship with a client rather than just closing a sale one time.

Better Business Better World

Transparency and Anti-Corruption

Transparency International (TI), a global organization fighting against corruption, raises awareness and diminishes apathy and tolerance of corruption while implementing feasible actions to address it. For example, TI's national chapters fight corruption by bringing together relevant players from society, business, government, and the media to promote transparency in public administration, procurement, business, and elections.[46] TI uses advocacy campaigns to lobby governments to implement anti-corruption reforms; it does not undertake investigations of alleged corruption or expose individual cases but at times will work with organizations that do. TI describes corruption and its impact on the world as follows:

Corruption is the abuse of entrusted power for private gain. It hurts everyone whose life, livelihood, or happiness depends on the integrity of people in a position of authority.

Why does fighting corruption matter?

Corruption hurts everyone, and it harms the poor the most. Sometimes its devastating impact is obvious:

■ A father who must do without shoes because his meagre wages are used to pay a bribe to get his child into a supposedly free school.

■ The unsuspecting sick person who buys useless counterfeit drugs, putting his or her health in grave danger.

Other times corruption's impact is less visible:

■ The prosperous multinational corporation that secured a contract by buying an unfair advantage in a competitive market through illegal kickbacks to corrupt government officials, at the expense of the honest companies who didn't.

■ Post-disaster donations provided by compassionate people, directly or through their governments, that never reach the victims, callously diverted instead into the bank accounts of criminals.

■ The faulty buildings—built to lower safety standards because a bribe passed under the table in the construction process—that collapse in an earthquake or hurricane.

Corruption has dire global consequences, trapping millions in poverty and misery and breeding social, economic, and political unrest. Corruption is both a cause of poverty, and a barrier to overcoming it. Human rights are denied where corruption is rife, because a fair trial comes with a hefty price tag where courts are corrupted. Corruption undermines democracy and the rule of law. Corruption distorts national and international trade. Corruption jeopardises sound governance and ethics in the private sector. Corruption threatens domestic and international security and the sustainability of natural resources.

The conclusion—Corruption hurts everyone.[47]

Discussion Questions

1. Which countries do you think are the most corrupt? Why? What is meant by transparency and why is transparency important? Visit <http://transparency.org/policy_research/surveys_indices/cpi> to review the most recent Corruption Perceptions Index (CPI) that will reveal the most, and least, corrupt countries in the world.
2. Do you think it matters if a Canadian multinational company establishes manufacturing operations in a less-developed country simply to take advantage of a less-restrictive pollution law? Who does this harm? How can we help?
3. How does bribery hurt anyone? It's not that big a deal, right? Is it legal? When a company pays an auditor with a bribe to overlook certain issues not up to standard, who does this hurt? Give an example of a situation where this may occur and who the victims might be.

Source: Copyright Transparency International: the global coalition against corruption. Used with permission. For more information, visit http://www.transparency.org

By using creative thinking and adhering to clearly stated ethical principles, a company can actually turn a scandal into something good. For example, in 2004, many shoppers boycotted Target because the chain had a policy of not allowing solicitors to collect money outside its doors, including volunteers collecting for the Salvation Army. In fact, the Salvation Army claimed the ban cost them more than US$9 million in possible donations.[48] Target could have responded with a defensive attack on the Salvation Army. Instead, the company chose to work with the charity, first donating the lost $9 million directly and then by creating an online "Wish List" that shoppers could use to donate toys, clothes, and household items to needy families during the holiday season. By acting together with the Salvation Army in new ways, Target was able to turn a negative situation into something beneficial for both Target and the community.

HOW CAN A BUSINESS DEVELOP ETHICAL PRACTICES

Ethical Focus: Day One and Beyond

How can a business improve its own culture of ethical and responsible conduct?   Almost every business wants to promote an ethical environment, but sometimes managers find it difficult to know how to implement this successfully. Let's look at some different approaches being used by businesses to help their employees' decision-making processes become attuned to an emphasis on ethical conduct. Businesses can take a number of steps to ensure that employees get off to an ethical start:

9 Describe the approaches a company can use to develop and maintain an ethical environment.

1. Managers can ensure that a meaningful and current mission statement and code of ethics are in place and that this information is clearly communicated throughout the many levels of the business. The mission statement and code of ethics should be posted throughout the workplace.
2. Managers can focus on ethics themselves, setting clear examples for the standards of behaviour expected at all levels of the organization. Managers can show they are ethical individuals by treating people fairly, being honest, having integrity, and inspiring trust.
3. The company can offer orientation programs to new employees to inform them of the ethical standards in place and the conduct expected of them right from the beginning of their careers.

How can a business maintain its policy of ethical conduct in the workplace?   When employees are faced with unethical situations daily, adhering to a company's code of ethics can be very difficult. Business leaders must take steps to ensure that all employees are making ethical decisions. Most organizational leaders implement the following strategies to ensure ethical business conduct:

■ Develop a corporate code of ethics.
- Check sporadically to make sure the code is being followed. Create an ethics committee and assign a chief ethics officer. Help shape the corporate culture through policies such as codes of conduct, codes of ethics, value statements, mission statements, and vision statements.

Zhang Yue, chief executive of Broad Air Conditioning, has emerged as one of China's most outspoken tycoons on environmental issues. Broad Air Conditioning manufactures energy-efficient units sold to thirty countries worldwide and has developed the first solar air-conditioning unit. The factory employs three thousand people, most of whom live in factory dorms and eat organic food grown on the grounds.

■ Be a role model and lead by example.
  • Communicate regularly about acceptable and unacceptable business practices, uphold ethical organizational values, and administer swift discipline for unethical behaviour in a fair and consistent manner. Reward ethical behaviour.
■ Create a way for employees to report violations of the ethics code anonymously.
  • Ensure allegations are investigated. Also, ensure that whistleblowers are not retaliated against for identifying infractions.
■ Employ ongoing ethics training programs designed to boost the awareness of ethical issues.
  • Such training occurs at all levels of the organization. From top management that makes strategic and far-reaching decisions, to front-line managers who use their decision-making skills to put out fires, to salespeople who work with vendors and must navigate ethical questions, to lower-level employees who make decisions regarding whether to follow the advice of their leaders, all levels of employees require training on ethical decision making.

Of course, private sector businesses are not alone in wanting ethics training programs for their employees. Government organizations face similar challenges. Many law enforcement agencies have ethics training programs to help officers deal with cases in which there may be no clear response.[49] For example, when a police officer responds to a domestic disturbance call but decides no crime has been committed, does he or she have a responsibility to try to prevent a potential escalation into a future criminal incident? By discussing, role-playing, and writing about these scenarios, the officers are more prepared for the ethical dilemmas facing them on the job. The code of ethics established by the Canadian Medical Association demonstrates that the medical field is also concerned with ethics as it pertains to physician-patient relationships, reproductive technology and interventions, death and dying, and research and experimentation upon human beings.[50]

Are there other tools besides ethics training that can help you make ethical decisions?

Several prominent scholars in the field of business ethics have developed various models for use in difficult situations. One such mode for resolving ethical dilemmas, the **Three Questions Model**, states that people faced with ethical dilemmas should ask themselves three questions before making a decision: 1) Is it legal? If it's not legal, you should not proceed. 2) Is it balanced? Look at the situation from all participants' viewpoints; you may have the upper hand this time, but you may not have it in the future, so play fair. 3) How does it make me feel? Examine how comfortable you are with the decision. If it doesn't feel right, it probably isn't.

Another simple ethical model is the **Front-Page-of-the-Newspaper Test**, which simply asks you to envision how a reporter would describe your decision on the front page of the newspaper the next day. How will this news affect your company? How will it affect you? Condensing conduct into a headline often gives a harsh dose of reality and an indication of consequences. For example, consider the headlines "Coca-Cola 'Misleading' Investors over Water Use in India"[51] or "AT&T Blocks PlayBook Tethering to BlackBerry Devices."[52]

The **Hidden Video Test** is a good measure of whether your actions are ethical. Ask yourself how you would feel about what you are doing if you found a video of yourself on YouTube the next day. Would you feel proud or ashamed if your family saw the video? If you need to hide your actions, or if you would feel ashamed of what you've done, then you most probably should not be doing it.

Another technique is to **Put-Yourself-in-the-Other-Person's-Shoes**. By asking yourself how you would feel if the other person (or company) was doing this to you, you may discover that what you are doing does not feel right. For instance, if you are about to accept credit for a report you did not write, ask yourself how you would feel if someone else in the company took credit for your work.

Developing an ethical environment involves a number of components and often requires a concentrated investment of time and resources; however, it remains a priority for most businesses.

The **Three Questions Model** states that people faced with ethical dilemmas should ask themselves three questions before making a decision: 1) Is it legal? 2) Is it balanced? 3) How does it make me feel?

The **Front-Page-of-the-Newspaper Test** asks you to envision how a reporter would describe your decision on the front page of the newspaper the next day.

The **Hidden Video Test** allows you to measure how you would feel about what you are doing if you found a video of yourself on YouTube the next day.

Put-Yourself-in-the-Other-Person's-Shoes. By asking yourself how you would feel if the other person (or company) was doing this to you, you may discover that what you are doing does not feel right.

On Target

Playing the Ethics Game

A unique approach to ethics training is used by Cadbury Schweppes. The international confectionery and beverage company has created a board game called "Ethical Risk" that its employees play to help bridge the gap between the values the company wants to achieve and the day-to-day decision making and practices of its managers.[53] Scenarios are presented to teams, who are asked not to compete but to work together to rank the possible answers from most to least preferred. This approach promotes a stronger dialogue within the company and builds insight into the practical ways to address the complex issues of corporate ethics and social responsibility.

Discussion Questions

1. Do you think using games to teach ethics is a good idea? Wouldn't employees just think that learning ethics is not a serious need?
2. What are the disadvantages of playing on teams? What are the advantages of playing on teams?
3. Do you think this would be an engaging way to learn? Do you think participants will remember what they learn? Why or why not?

Increasing Profits through an Ethical Focus

How can firms generate business by acting ethically? By examining the world with an eye toward social responsibility, many firms have created opportunities with new types of products and services. There are opportunities and the potential for gain by understanding and applying ethical standards to a business. Some companies focus on creating new markets with an ethical focus. Others redesign their business so that they no longer have a negative impact on the environment. Still others use ethical challenges as a tool to unite and empower employees.

10 Summarize how companies can apply ethical standards to create new business opportunities.

Offering Clean Fuel Canadian-based Topia Energy has opened the first chain of "alternative fuel" stations, named GreenStop, which offer only renewable fuel blends, such as gasoline combined with corn ethanol. The gasoline products can be used in regular cars, and the stations themselves are constructed from renewable, chemical-free products. Inside you won't see the same lineup of cigarettes and candy, but you will have your choice of organic veggie wraps and coffee roasted using solar energy.[54]

Creating Medical Vaccines Other companies have created business opportunities by addressing the world's most serious medical needs. Malaria is the leading cause of death in children worldwide, mostly in Africa. The disease is transmitted very easily, whereas the drugs currently used to treat it are becoming increasingly ineffective. Many businesses haven't found a way to balance the tremendous cost of research for creating a malaria vaccine with the anticipated meagre profits. Enter Sanaria, a new pharmaceutical company founded by scientist Dr. Stephen Hoffman, whose mission is to create a malaria vaccine. Hoffman remarks, "I haven't spent

Earth-friendly Topia GreenStop gas stations are popping up in Canada and the United States.

25 years working on diseases of the most disadvantaged and neglected people in the world to start a company that's just here to make money."[55] The company has received several multimillion-dollar grants from the Bill and Melinda Gates Foundation and the U.S. government.[56]

Fighting Censorship   Still other companies are creating business opportunities by fighting censorship. The Chinese government maintains a tight rein on the flow of information to its citizens, including controlling the accessibility of certain Internet sites. This policy of censorship garnered the attention of the international business community when in 2010, after four years of complying with China's system of censorship so that search results were edited before being presented to users, Google did an about-face and announced it would no longer censor search results for China.[57]

This censorship left Dynamic Internet Technology (DIT) company founder Bill Xia with a very skewed view of the world when he arrived in the United States from China. "I was a believer of the propaganda," he says.[58] Now DIT and similar companies provide a service to their clients in an effort to counteract the impact of censorship. When a site is placed onto the list of censored sites by the Chinese government, DIT quickly creates a new, uncensored Web address that points users to the same material. A list of the new accessible sites is then e-mailed to Web surfers who want full Internet access. Chinese censors often stamp out the new site within a few days, at which point DIT starts the process again, determined to override censorship through its business. DIT and other companies are showing there are ways to tackle difficult ethical issues and create business opportunities at the same time.

How can businesses benefit by "going green"?   While some businesses are tackling ethical issues and offering consumers more ethical choices through their businesses, others are attempting to reduce the affect they have on the environment. Take Interface Inc., the world's largest commercial carpet manufacturer. The company was careful to follow all laws and regulations relating to its industry in its first twenty-one years of business, but it made no special commitment to stewardship of the environment beyond that. "It was like a spear in the chest," said CEO Ray Anderson when he first read Paul Hawkens's book *The Ecology of Commerce*.[59] He was so inspired by the book's message that he began reorganizing his US$1.4 billion company using the principles of sustainability—the process of working to improve the quality of life in ways that simultaneously protect and enhance Earth's life support systems.[60] Interface has a mission statement, nicknamed Mission Zero, which reads: "Our promise is to eliminate any negative impact our company may have on the environment by the year 2020."[61]

Interface is considering all aspects of its business in its goal to operate without having a negative effect on the planet. The **ecological footprint** is a measure of human demand on Earth's ecosystems based on consumption and pollution. It compares the human demand with the planet's capacity to regenerate. Since the 1970s, humanity has been in ecological overshoot with annual demand on resources exceeding what Earth can regenerate each year.[62] The ecological footprint is now in wide use by scientists, businesses, governments, individuals, and institutions working to monitor ecological resource use and advance sustainable development. Interface helps to reduce its ecological footprint by eliminating waste and toxic substances from its products, using renewable energy, and finding how to route its trucks for more efficient transportation routes.

Cool Carpet is considered one of Interface's more revolutionary sustainable innovations. The "cool" part of Cool Carpet is that it allows customers to affect global warming. Interface ensures that all the carbon dioxide emissions over the full life cycle of a Cool Carpet—from its manufacture through to its delivery—are offset. Actions such as purchasing energy from wind farms and choosing ecologically friendly suppliers balance out the necessary carbon dioxide produced in other stages of carpet production. Anderson recognizes that the choices Interface makes today will ultimately affect future generations and hopes his customers see the value in these choices and go green themselves.

Many companies today are making green claims. Consumers need to be aware of companies that are "**greenwashing**," however; making claims about their environmental

---

Ten of Canada's 100 Greenest Employers (2010)

1. Hewlett-Packard (Canada) Co.
2. IKEA Canada Limited Partnership
3. KPMG LLP
4. Loblaw Companies Limited
5. Mountain Equipment Co-op
6. Research In Motion Limited
7. Royal Bank of Canada
8. SAS Institute Canada, Inc.
9. State Farm Insurance
10. The Home Depot Canada

Source: Canada's Top 100 Employers, "Canada's Greenest Employers 2010," www.canadastop100.com/environmental/, Accessed April 20, 2011.

The **ecological footprint** is a measure of human demand on Earth's ecosystems based on consumption and pollution. It compares the human demand with the planet's capacity to regenerate.

Greenwashing occurs when a company makes claims about its environmental record that aren't supported by its actions.

record that aren't supported by their actions. Sustainable business is about doing business according to financial, environmental, and social returns (triple-bottom-line). Interface implements several strategies to disclose, verify, and share information on its progress toward Mission Zero.

Another large international company that has worked for more than a decade to reduce its environmental footprint is coffeehouse giant Starbucks. Its corporate Shared Planet progress plan sets clear objectives for the company in recycling, energy and water usage, building, and climate change.[63] In 2009, it convened a summit with local governments, cup manufacturers, and recyclers to identify the steps required to make its cups recyclable. Stores are being redesigned to include recycling locations in front, and customers receive a 10-cent discount when they use a reusable container. In 2009, 26.3 million beverages were served in reusable serverware or tumblers in Canada, the U.S., and the U.K. combined, which totalled 1.5 percent of all beverages served. Starbucks' goal is to serve 25 percent of beverages made in their stores in reusable serverware or tumblers by 2015.[64]

Companies can create opportunities based on ethical challenges in a number of different ways. New businesses are appearing, focused on addressing the ethical issues of our times. Other businesses redesign their business so that they leave no negative impact on the environment. Some respond to ethical needs in ways that both benefit the environment and boost employee morale. As many of today's most successful innovative companies have demonstrated, upholding ethical standards need not be a burden to businesses; it can instead be a portal to great opportunities.

Starbucks discounts coffee if customers bring their own reusable serverware or tumblers and has a goal to serve 25 percent of all beverages this way by 2015.

CHAPTER SYNOPSIS

❶ Define ethics and describe different ethical systems.
(pp. 60–61)

Ethics are moral principles and values that govern human conduct, with respect to the rightness and wrongness of the choices humans make.

    Moral relativism maintains that there is no universal moral truth but instead only people's individual beliefs, perspectives, and values.

    Situational ethics maintain that people make decisions based on a specific situation instead of universal laws.

❷ Summarize how to create a personal code of ethics.
(pp. 61–64)

A **personal code of ethics** is the set of principles that guide the decisions you make in your life with respect to what is right or wrong.

    Life experiences offer us opportunities to develop our personal ethics. We also need to decide whether the behaviour we see around us makes sense within the ethical systems that we learned from our family, our place of worship, or our first-grade teacher. Sometimes, our experiences lead us to abandon some ethical rules and to adopt others. And for some of us, our ethical rules are modified depending on what is at stake.

❸ Explain how personal ethics can play a role in the workplace.   *(pp. 64–66)*

We often find ourselves torn between several choices, and finding a path that works for both you and the company you work for can be challenging. In some settings, the line between right and wrong can be difficult to see. Other times, when your own personal values just won't align with the company's, you may wish you had understood more about the company's sense of ethical culture early in your career there, before you invested your time and effort. At work, our employer is purchasing our time and energy. As employees, our responsibility is to follow the ethics that the owner or director has established for the business.

❹ Evaluate a company's ethical code using available resources such as a mission statement.   *(pp. 66–67)*

Some companies may have a written code of ethics or a statement of their commitment to certain ethical practices. Additionally, many companies have a public mission statement (sometimes called a corporate vision) that defines the core purpose of the organization—why it exists—and often describes its values, goals, and aspirations.

    Other resources allow you to evaluate the acts of responsibility of, and legal violations by, any given company. For example, websites

your lower-level employees are struggling with these issues. What do you do?

Do you know how you'd handle each situation? Do you have ideas for ways to avoid these situations in the future?

3. Where are the boundaries between personal ethics and business ethics? Are there rules to indicate where one begins and the other ends? Should there be?

4. How does a corporation's responsibility to shareholders to produce a profit interact with its social responsibility? Name several areas of possible conflict and analyze them from both a short-term and long-term view.

5. What is your college's or university's code of conduct? Does your school have an academic honesty policy? If not these codes, what policies are in place that set expectations for behaviour, and attempt to create a fair and ethical environment? Do you feel that most students and most employees follow these policies? What behaviour violates academic integrity? What happens if you are accused of violating policy?

APPLICATION EXERCISES

1. **Ethical Decisions.** Locate a free ethics quiz online and test your ethical decision-making abilities. The following websites can help you to get started:
   a. ICMR—http://www.icmrindia.org/courseware/ Business%20Ethics%20&%20Corporate%20Governance/ Business%20ethics-quiz2.htm
   b. CareerBuilder—www.careerbuilder.com/Article/ CB-1382-The-Workplace-Quiz-How-Ethical-Are-You/
   c. The Ethics Guy on CNN—http://youtu.be/ Lhwhgf01Ozw
   d. Onveon—www.onveon.com/articles/ how-ethical-are-you-quiz.htm
   Were there any dilemmas you found particularly challenging or surprising? Why?

2. **Volunteerism.** You don't have to wait until you graduate to start demonstrating your social responsibility. Volunteering in your community or at your school is a great way to gain experience, make contacts, and do something good. It also looks great on your résumé. Go to www.volunteer.ca and find an organization in your area looking for volunteers. What opportunities are there for volunteers? What are the current hot issues? What is the Canadian Code of Volunteer Involvement? List a couple organizations in your province or territory that have adopted the code.

3. **Corporate Social Responsibility (CSR).** Visit the Canadian Business for Social Responsibility (CBSR), a non-profit organization, website at www.cbsr.ca and write a brief summary answering the following questions.
   a. What does the organization do? What is the CBSR model (under Approach)?
   b. Under CBSR Publications, what are some of the recent CSR trends?
   c. What are the upcoming CSR events?

4. **Corporate Ethics.** Visit two of the following three multinational company websites: Boeing, the world's leading aerospace company; Apple, Inc., the world's largest technology company; and Toyota Motor Corporation, the world's largest automobile manufacturer by sales. Compare and contrast the companies' code of ethics, mission, values, and code of conduct. Based solely on each company's ethical conduct, mission, and values, which company would you rather work for? Why?

5. **Stakeholder Responsibility.** Non-profit organizations, such as your college or university, have social responsibilities to their stakeholders. Identify the stakeholders at your school and for each category of stakeholder indicate the ways your school is socially responsible to that group.

GLOBAL 500 RESEARCH PROJECT

INSTRUCTIONS

1. Choose a Global 500 company from *Fortune* magazine's annual rankings at http://money.cnn.com/magazines/ fortune/global500/.

2. Research:
   a. Has this company been in a news scandal? If so, what was it about?
   b. Has this company had an ethical lapse? If so, what was it about and how did the company recover its lost good image?
   c. Does this company have a code of ethics? Does its mission statement mention ethical values or morals? What does it say?

   d. Does this company's vision or values statement discuss the environment or treatment of people? If so, what do they say?
   e. How does this company set an ethical culture within?
   f. Does this company engage in philanthropy? If so, what does it do?
   g. Does anything in the news or in public opinion contradict what this company portrays itself to be?
   h. Is this company a good corporate citizen? What is it doing toward the "green" movement?
   i. How do you feel about this company? Would you work there? Would you shop there? Why or why not?

3. Prepare a report and submit it to your instructor.

TEAM TIME

One Issue, Three Sides

Divide into three teams, one to represent each of the following:
   a. pharmaceutical company executives
   b. people with a catastrophic but treatable illness
   c. people identified as having "unique" DNA

SCENARIO

Are there some things that can't be owned? Leukemia patient John Moore would answer yes. After Moore had his cancerous spleen removed at the University of California, the university kept the spleen and was eventually granted a patent for DNA removed from the organ. The value of the DNA was estimated to be more than US$1 billion. When Moore demanded that his cells be returned, the California Supreme Court ruled against him, saying that he had no right to his own cells after they had been removed from his body. Pharmaceutical researchers, such as those at the University of California, often hope to later license the DNA patterns or sell them to other companies so they may use them to develop drugs or tests for the presence of disease. Does the person or group of people who have that specific, perhaps unique, gene have ownership? Do they deserve

payment? Do they have a right to a voice in the use of their genetic material?

PROCESS

Step 1. Record your ideas and opinions about the issue presented in the scenario above. Be sure to consider the issue from your assigned perspective.

Step 2. Meet as a team and review the issue from the multiple perspectives. Discuss together what one best policy could be developed to address the concerns of all three groups.

ETHICS AND RESPONSIBILITY

Personal and Business Ethics

As you've learned, sometimes a person's personal code of ethics does not fall in with the code of ethics used in his or her profession. What is your personal code of ethics? What profession do you hope to have in the future? How does your personal code of ethics match the code of ethics used in that profession? Would you be willing to ignore your personal ethical code for business?

Process

Step 1. Draft your personal code of ethics. Use the steps for analyzing one's own ethical system that is outlined at the beginning of this chapter.

Step 2. Think about a profession that you'd like to have in the future. Visit http://ethics.iit.edu/codes/codes_index.html to find the code of ethics employed in this profession.

Step 3. Compare your personal code of ethics to the profession's code of ethics. Then, write a paragraph explaining how the two codes compare.

CLOSING CASE

The Ethics of BP'S Oil Spill*

Eleven people died and others were injured in the explosion of the Deepwater Horizon oil rig April 20, 2010. The explosion led to oil spilling into the Gulf of Mexico for three months, which killed many birds, turtles, dolphins, and other wildlife and had a devastating effect on the Gulf's ecosystem that will be felt long-term. Many communities rely on the Gulf economically, specifically for fishing and tourism, and the spill destroyed their means of livelihood. BP was forced to dole out millions of dollars to Gulf communities in reparation for the damage done to their economies and billions more in cleanup costs. Situations such as these cost huge amounts of money to rectify, and depending on BP's response to the social and environmental accountabilities arising from the spill, the company's public image will be defined by it for years to come. The public called for greater accountability from government and BP and for stricter regulations and oversight of operations. Debates revolved around who was responsible and how such industrial catastrophes could be avoided in the future. Although legal liabilities could have arisen from taking immediate action to reduce further damage from the oil spill, BP thought it was the right thing to do and quickly tried to contain the spill. BP's actions were consistent with the principles of "product stewardship"—the belief that producers and manufacturers are responsible for the life cycle management of their products as well as the damage and benefits that their products bring to consumers and society at large.

The ethical issues are fourfold: Who was responsible for the deaths from the explosion and the resulting oil spill? Who is responsible for the cleanup of our global commons? Who is going to compensate the thousands of land based people whose livelihoods are likely to be destroyed? And what should be the overall responsibility of a corporation when it has significant negative externalities associated with its operations?"[65]

The U.S. government has asserted that the cost of the cleanup must be borne by BP. But who restores the damaged ecosystem?

When the consequences of business, intended or otherwise, cause people to lose their lives or livelihoods, then financial compensation is due to those affected. Many lawsuits were filed against BP.

There is an added ethical dimension to this, as was played out the in the past, in how long it can take to pay that compensation. In the case of Exxon Valdez, the last similar oil spill catastrophe which happened back in 1989, the cost of the cleanup, fines and compensation was put at $3.5 billion, but the punitive damages were originally set at $5 billion to compensate the fishermen who lost their businesses in a $12 million a year herring industry which eventually collapsed. The case was dragged through the courts for 19 years until the US Supreme Court determined that the damages were excessive and reduced them by 50%. One of the considerations the court took into account was that no one was killed. Twenty years after the disaster, the money had still to be paid . . . Exxon remains one of the least trusted companies in the world.[66]

The oil spill that was thought to bring economic ruin to the Gulf Coast has instead brought some people rich monetary rewards. For example, local governments collected more retail tax because businesses had an increase in sales for products and services used to cleanup the oil spill. In taking responsibility for the cleanup (including the health and safety of Gulf residents and the people who helped respond to the spill) and swiftly compensating people affected by the accident, BP has spent US$17.7 billion (as of December 31, 2010).[67] In trying to do right, however, it seemed BP had made another wrong. BP had established an Immediate Action Claims Team in an attempt to cut through paperwork and expedite payments, but in doing so BP's fairness and manner in which the company was paying claims became

*Reprinted courtesy of Managing Values

a controversial issue. As BP purchased goods and services for cleanup and paid compensation for damage and loss, some businesses and individuals were thought to be gouging BP by charging prices that were up to twenty times the going rates (e.g., for boats, lumber, bottles of water, hotel rooms) and reporting losses higher than actually incurred.[68]

After seventeen months of investigations, the U.S. Coast Guard and the Bureau of Ocean Energy Management, Regulation and Enforcement issued a detailed report concluding that BP was not solely responsible for the accident. Their findings showed that fault was to be shared by BP, Halliburton (the company that worked on sealing the well), Cameron (the company that supplied the blowout preventer), and Transocean (the owner and operator of the Deepwater Horizon drilling rig, who then issued their own report placing blame solely on BP). The report included thirty-six recommendations for new regulations and safety procedures.[69]

DISCUSSION QUESTIONS

Research the answers to the following questions on the Internet and provide a report of your findings. Provide your sources of information.

1. How did BP respond to this accident? Do you think BP is responding in an ethical manner? Why or why not? Do you think BP should be expected to clean up this mess alone? Why or why not?
2. What are the devastating effects of this catastrophe? Who has been hurt by this oil spill? Discuss at least three ethical situations, conflicts, or dilemmas this oil spill has caused. It might help to think about these questions: How does this affect you? How does this affect the environment? How does this affect the citizens closest to the spill as well as citizens of the world? How has this affect government, legislation, the oil drilling industry, the supply of oil, and BP company?
3. Who is profiting from the oil spill? What is meant by "spillionaires"? Discuss at least three groups, companies, or individuals that you feel have profited from the oil spill in an unethical manner.

MyBusinessLab CHAPTER RESOURCES

MyBusinessLab in an online learning and testing environment that features the perfect study tools to help you master the concepts covered in this chapter. Log in to MyBusinessLab at www .pearsoned.ca/mybusinesslab to test your knowledge of key chapter concepts, participate in simulations modelled on real-world business situations, and explore the following additional practice tools:

- Study Plan
- Audio Chapter Summaries
- Glossary Flashcards
- eText
- BizChat Discussion Boards
- BizSkills Simulation: Ethics and Social Responsibility
- Decision Making Mini-Simulations: Ethics; Diversity
- Document Makeovers: Letter from Paradigm, Building Access

Video Case:

To access the Chapter 3 Video Case: Patagonia: Ethics and Social Responsibility, see the Activities folder in the Assessment section of MyBusinessLab.

Web Case:

To access the Chapter 3 Web Case, see the Activities folder in the Assessment section of MyBusinessLab

OPENING DISCUSSION: GLOBAL TRADE

Japan's Disaster Affects Imports, Exports, and Productivity around the Globe

On March 11, 2011, an 8.9-magnitude earthquake off the northeast coast of Japan's main island unleashed a seven-metre (twenty-three-foot) tsunami and generated more than fifty aftershocks, causing widespread ruin. In particular, these natural disasters damaged a nuclear power plant in Fukushima, triggering the worst nuclear crisis since Chernobyl in Ukraine. Most tragic of course was the heavy loss of human life and devastation of livelihoods in the affected regions. Authorities said more than 20 000 people were confirmed dead or missing in the weeks after the disaster. Countries around the world offered their sympathy for Japan's loss and took action by sending aid to the traumatized nation.

It is evident that Japan has been severely incapacitated and will need some time to clean up, rebuild, and re-establish a comfortable livelihood for its residents. Let's take a closer look at Japan's crisis and consider how it affects multinational and global business operations.

- Many organizations, businesses, and governments rushed to Japan's aid, donating time, people, and money to help the disaster victims. For example, the BMO Financial Group, among others, donated $100 000 to the Red Cross to support disaster relief efforts.[1] The Salvation Army provided hot drinks and packed meals to the many people whose homes were destroyed or left without power. Doctors Without Borders had teams working throughout the country while World Vision focused on easing the emotional and psychological stress that children faced during this crisis. The Canadian government sent medical, biological, chemical, radiological, and nuclear expertise, supplies, and equipment.[2]

- Manufacturers across Japan shut down production lines or cut back on output because of damage, power shortages, and supply chain problems. The country's production of parts used by manufacturers around the world suffered major disruptions, with global car and technology industries particularly affected.[3]

(continued)

- Japan accounts for some 60 percent of the global silicon wafer supply, and some of the biggest silicon manufacturing units in Japan were damaged in the disaster. Since silicon wafers are used in micro devices and a wide range of electronic equipment, a shortfall in their supply has a negative effect on global manufacturers.[4]

- Due to business closures, disruptions to ports, and slowed shipments from Japan, Western companies such as Molycorp Inc. and Avalon Rare Metals were struggling to restart idle rare earth metal mines. Rare earth metals are used in everything from computers and cellphones to armoured vehicles and wind turbines.[5]

- After the nuclear leak, the demand for anti-radiation drugs, specifically potassium iodine (KI) tablets, skyrocketed not only in Japan, but also in the United States and Canada, where "radiated" rain and ocean water was feared.[6] Iodine tablets can prevent the body from absorbing radioactive iodine.[7] Cancer is a key long-term risk from radiation exposure, and officials will undoubtedly be monitoring the health outcomes of the population around Fukushima for many years. The radiation leak will have a psychological impact on people who live with the fear of radiation contamination as well as the stress of being displaced from their homes.

- Food shortages occurred in Japan when radioactive matter was found in food sources, thus creating an increased demand for imported foods and a decreased demand for exported foods. Fishing ports and vessels were damaged, and both aquaculture and wild seedbeds for key products such as scallops and oysters were washed away. Contamination of seawater caused Japanese consumers to avoid fresh local seafood and choose canned or imported products.[8] Japan allocated 700 million yen (more than CA$9 million) to help pay for exporters' radiation screening costs.[9] Bans on importing food from Japan were imposed by Russia, China, Hong Kong, India, the United States, Taiwan, and Singapore. Seoul insisted that Japan provide safety certificates for food products from the radiated areas.[10] Restaurant owners in Mumbai and New Delhi assured customers that the restrictions wouldn't take sushi off the menu immediately. Restaurants noticed an increase in supplier prices when ordering substitute goods from Thailand, Vietnam, or China, and imported seafood from Scotland.[11]

- Japan is bound to suffer tremendously from a decline in tourism. As well, most Japanese people feel a sense of responsibility toward their country after such a national crisis and will choose not to travel outside the country for the short term. This will reduce tourism, at least temporarily, around the world.[12] Japanese tourists are among the top international visitors to the United States, comprising almost 20 percent of the visitors to Hawaii alone. Hawaii projected a possible US$2 billion decline in tourism from Japan for 2011.[13] Australia, Nepal, and Indonesia predicted lower tourism numbers to and from Japan.[14] Japan supplies 3 to 4 percent of the globe's jet fuel, including exports to Asia, and damage to fuel infrastructure facilities in Japan could push jet fuel prices higher.[15]

What other changes have occurred or may occur due to lessons learned from Japan's crisis? Think about regulations (nuclear risk), cooperation among nations, insurance companies (life, home, disaster, etc.), national debt, and increased government spending on roads and building repairs. While the insurance industry can handle many claims, the Japanese government may have to set up a compensation fund to help deal with the vast number of people affected by the disaster. Japan's recovery will also be complicated by financial questions: how it will manage to pay the bills?

DISCUSSION QUESTIONS

1. How do these events increase business opportunities for the Japanese? How do these events increase business opportunities for foreigners?

2. How do these events decrease business opportunities for Japan with other countries? How do these events decrease business operations for businesses located in foreign countries?

3. Do you think foreign countries were justified in banning imported food from Japan was justified? Why or why not? How does such a ban affect global supply and demand for these food products? How does such a ban affect the productivity, employment rates, and gross domestic product (GDP) in Japan? Besides banning imported food from Japan, what other measures could foreign countries take? Would you feel safe buying food exported from Japan? Why or why not?

GLOBALIZATION: WHAT'S IT ALL ABOUT?
International Business

How does doing business globally affect you? In recent years, the rise of globalization has made a dramatic influence on the lives of people around the world. Canadians to Taiwanese to Argentinians are all connected and dependent on one another for a variety of goods and services. Canada and other nations are increasingly **importing**, or buying products from other countries, and **exporting**, or selling domestically produced products to other countries. This trend is why you'll notice that many products you own were made in countries other than Canada. Not only has globalization affected individual lives, it has also affected the way companies conduct business around the world.

Studying international business will make you a better employee, business owner, person, and citizen. It will broaden your horizons, requiring you to think outside your own domestic economic, social, and political box. Because the world is truly a global village, studying international business can also help you understand and appreciate the complex nature of the global economy, the rich diversity of world cultures, and the intricacies of international politics. At the very least, studying international business will give you the tools to answer questions inherent in many of today's headline-grabbing issues. For example, what can people do to enhance their country's ability to compete in the global economy? What can a country do to provide good-paying jobs for its citizens? How can Canadian companies increase their profitability in the face of foreign competition at home or enhance their market share overseas? When Canada's dollar is stronger or weaker than other countries' currencies, how does it affect business in Canada? After studying this chapter, you'll be able to answer these and other questions.

Let's perform a fact-finding exercise. Check the labels on the following items to determine where in the world they were manufactured:

- shoes
- shirt
- pants
- purse or backpack
- technological device (cellphone, laptop computer, digital camera, MP3 player, etc.)

Calculate the number of countries, other than Canada, that are represented. If your personal belongings represent . . . 0 countries, then they are homegrown; 1-2 countries, then they have an international flair; and 3 or more countries, then they truly reflect the growing trend in globalization.

What is globalization? The old sayings "No man is an island" and "It's a small world after all" both describe globalization. **Globalization**, the movement toward a more interconnected and interdependent world economy, may be one of the most profound factors affecting people around the globe.[16] Globalization has resulted in the concept of a worldwide consumer. Changes in the Canadian economy can affect other countries as changes in foreign countries' economies can produce a ripple effect on Canadian consumers, businesses, and workers.

One example of globalization can be seen in the booming economies of India and China, whose growth is a major reason for the increasing global demand for energy. Increased energy demand is a significant cause of the world's rising oil prices, which have created higher prices at the gas pump. As a result, people have less money to spend on other things, such as eating out. Local restaurants and other local businesses feel the pinch, and their sales decrease. In response to lower demand, businesses curtail production and lay off employees. Higher energy prices can also drive up production costs, which, in turn, can drive up the prices businesses must charge consumers.

As you can see, globalization means that the behaviour of each country influences other countries. Of course, markets have not only become more interconnected but also more reliant on one another. If you inspect the packaging of items you buy, you'll see that many products consumed in Canada today, such as laptop computers and cars, are made from parts manufactured in countries halfway around the world.

Outline the implications of the globalization of markets and the globalization of production.

Importing is the act of buying products from other countries.

Exporting is the act of selling domestically produced products to other countries.

BizSkills Simulation: Going Global. Located in MyBusinessLab.

4

Globalization, the movement toward a more interconnected and interdependent world economy, may be one of the most profound factors affecting people around the globe.

The **globalization of markets** is the movement away from thinking of the market as being only local or national to including the entire world.

Decision-Making Mini-Simulation:
Global Marketing. Located in MyBusinessLab.

How does globalization offer more marketing opportunities to businesses?

Globalization has two main components: the globalization of markets and the globalization of production.[17] The **globalization of markets** is the movement away from thinking of the market as being only local or national to including the entire world. Although what sells in one country may not sell in another because of different consumer tastes, to some extent consumer preferences in different nations are beginning to converge, thereby helping to create a global market. Companies such as Research In Motion, IKEA, General Electric, Dell, and Toyota are not just selling to customers in domestic markets, they are selling to customers all over the globe. Even some relatively small companies find it profitable to sell their products abroad.

The globalization of markets has become so widespread that more and more businesses must "think globally and act locally." Companies often need to adjust their products or marketing campaigns to suit the unique preferences of their local customers, wherever they may be. For example, Coca-Cola often has to tweak its recipes to appeal to the tastes of consumers in different parts of the world. In India, Coca-Cola adapted its Minute Maid orange soda recipe to suit the taste of the majority Indian population, who prefer a sweeter version of the drink than is sold in North America.[18] Similarly, many foreign-owned companies advertise or adapt their products for sale in Canada to attract consumers. For example, when Walmart first entered Canada in 1994 it had to change the product mix it carried for Canadians: hockey equipment was prominently featured in stores across the country and halal foods were sold to meet the requirements of the Muslim market in Toronto.[19] As a result of such variations, it can be difficult to determine whether a company is Canadian owned.

How does globalization make it easier to manufacture products?

The **globalization of production** is the trend of individual firms moving production to different locations around the globe to take advantage of lower costs or to enhance quality.

The **globalization of production**, the other facet of globalization, is the trend of individual firms moving production to different locations around the globe to take advantage of lower costs or to enhance quality. When faced with intense foreign competition, firms may be forced to relocate at least some of their production to another country to realize lower costs so they can offer customers lower prices.

Globalization of markets and production is certainly nothing new. In fact, countries have been trading with one another since ancient times. What has raised so many eyebrows in the last several decades is the rapid pace at which globalization has been accelerating. Globalization of markets and production has resulted in some international firms becoming so large that they generate more revenue than the gross domestic product (GDP) of some nations. According to Fortune's Global 500 list for 2010, if Walmart were a nation, it would rank as the twenty-sixth largest country in the world in terms of the total revenue it generates (Royal Dutch/Shell would rank thirty-fourth, ExxonMobil thirty-fifth, British Petroleum thirty-seventh, and Toyota forty-sixth).[20]

Reasons for the Rise in Globalization

Explain why globalization has accelerated so rapidly.

Why has globalization accelerated so rapidly?

Two main factors seem to underlie the trend toward greater globalization: technological innovations and the dramatic decline in trade and investment barriers among countries since the end of the Second World War.[21] For example, the North American Free Trade Agreement (NAFTA) of 1994 (discussed later in this chapter) made it easier for North American companies to shift work between Canada, the United States, and Mexico and opened the door to offshore expansion.

How do innovations in technology accelerate globalization?

When you consider the dramatic advances in communications, transportation, and information technology, it is easy to see how technological innovations have made it possible to manage the global production and marketing of products. People are able to communicate and share information more rapidly and cheaply than ever before. Using teleconferencing, a business manager in Vancouver can meet with contacts at a firm's European or

Asian operations without ever leaving the office. If a restaurant needs to purchase fresh Norwegian salmon, it can have the product flown in. Recent technological advancements have been the great equalizer for small companies, enabling them to access customers worldwide through their websites at negligible expense so they can more effectively compete with huge global corporations.

Technology is changing where businesses are located, what goods are produced, how goods and services are marketed, and what will be expected of employees in the new global marketplace. One result of technology has been the increase in **offshoring**, a practice in which work is shifted from its original domestic location to other foreign locations. In the past, this practice was employed primarily for production and manufacturing. As technology provided secure and simple means to transmit data files, white-collar offshoring increased. Workers in many economic sectors who had been insulated from foreign competition began to see change. In considering international offshoring, two trends stand out: 1) Many American and Canadian firms are offshoring to China because it is quickly becoming the world's cheapest manufacturer, and 2) An increasing number of traded services, involving advanced, high-tech processes and employing well-paid white-collar workers, are being offshored. In the past, it was thought unlikely that low-cost countries such as India could export high-value-added services.[22] Now it is common to find Indian software programmers customizing sophisticated software applications for businesses worldwide. In addition, the financial services industry—retail banking, investment banking, and insurance—has been very aggressive in moving call centre jobs and clerical jobs offshore.

Location has become much less important, and countries with educated, English-speaking citizens can bid for work that has previously taken place in Canada or the United States. With a population of more than one billion, India graduates many more engineers each year than either Canada or the United States does. This outpouring has fuelled ten years of double-digit increases in salary in India for many technology workers, as Canadian and American firms send a variety of programming and support positions to Indian companies. Although the income of Indian workers has risen, the economic advantage of offshoring to India is fading. Now China is beginning to show it has the necessary infrastructure and pool of talent to become an offshoring destination for knowledge work.

Although countries in Asia are seeing the most offshoring activity, some North American companies like to keep their business a little closer to home. **Near-shoring** is a form of off-shoring in which a company moves jobs to a foreign location geographically close or linguistically and culturally similar to its own country. Sending work from Canada to countries such as the United States, the United Kingdom, and Australia could be considered near-shoring. Canadian lawyers are quietly starting to outsource legal work to India, where they can pay substantially less per hour and enjoy a faster turnaround time than they would by paying junior lawyers in Canada. The United States outsources work to Canada because the culture, geography, and language are so similar. As such, despite the stronger numbers of outsourcing firms and employees in offshore locations such as India and the Far East, Canada is holding its own against overseas competitors, especially in high-end project areas. Google, Yahoo!, and Hewlett-Packard all have offices in Dublin, where they send a portion of their IT work. Although labour in these countries may not be as low cost as labour in some Asian countries, similarities in geography, language, and culture make it easier to integrate foreign workers into the daily operations of the original location.

Offshoring is a practice in which work is shifted from its original domestic location to other foreign locations.

Near-shoring is a form of offshoring in which a company moves jobs to a foreign location geographically close or linguistically and culturally similar to its own country.

Companies such as GE Capital employ people in Delhi, Bangalore, and other cities in India to answer calls from credit card customers, perform accounting tasks, and manage computer systems.[23]

What changes might offshoring bring for Canadian companies and employees?

The drastic difference in wages between offshore countries and Canada is the key ingredient in making offshoring profitable for a business. As the international pool of technical talent becomes the new marketplace, Canadian workers can expect to see a slowing of wage growth. It will be important for Canadian workers to have increased language skills and to shift their view of their careers and opportunities toward the reality of a global economy.

It is also useful to point out that Canadian workers will see benefits from offshoring. As middle-class jobs appear in India and other developing countries, the middle class in those countries will expand. Companies and workers in Canada will benefit in the long run when more countries are politically stable and the demand for Canadian products and services increases. Another benefit comes from time zone differences. For example, there is almost an eleven-hour time difference between India and Canada. As the workday ends in Toronto, people begin to wake up and head to work in Bangalore and Hyderabad. By using teams of workers divided between both locations, companies can conduct business almost twenty-four hours a day.

Outsourcing occurs when a company contracts with an outside firm to handle a specific part of its business activities.

What is the difference between outsourcing and offshoring?　**Outsourcing**

occurs when a company contracts with an outside firm to handle a specific part of its business activities. For example, the college or university you currently attend most probably outsources various functions such as security, maintenance, bookstore, and food services to outside organizations operating within the same city as your school. Another example of outsourcing would include a real estate company hiring a graphic design firm to create a special layout for a sales brochure (the graphic design firm might be located anywhere in the world). Most companies outsource work to outside firms that can do a job or project better, faster, or cheaper than the company could do on its own. Outsourcing to a foreign country is often referred to as offshore (outside the country) outsourcing. Some people use the term *offshoring* to refer distinctly to the relocation of part of a business to a lower-cost location, typically a foreign country, and not simply as contracting work outside the country's borders.

Trade and investment barriers are government barriers that prevent the flow of goods, services, and financial capital across national boundaries.

How does the decline in trade and investment barriers accelerate globalization?

Trade and investment barriers are government barriers that prevent the flow of goods, services, and financial capital across national boundaries. The lowering of trade barriers makes global business much cheaper and easier. It also allows international firms to move their production facilities to the least-cost location for that activity. A firm might design its products in one country, produce component parts in two or three other countries, assemble the product in yet another country, and then export it around the world.

INTERNATIONAL TRADE

International Competition

3 Explain the meaning of *comparative advantage* and absolute advantage as it compares with international competition.

What is the theory of comparative advantage?　Many theories apply to international trade. The most popular theory is the *theory of comparative advantage*, which states that specialization and trade between countries benefit all who are involved. The theory of comparative advantage suggests that a country should sell to other countries the goods that it manufactures most efficiently and effectively, and buy from other countries the goods it cannot manufacture as efficiently or effectively. If this method is practised, each nation will have a greater quantity and variety of higher-quality products to consume at lower prices.

For this mutually beneficial system to work, each country must specialize in the production of those products for which it possesses a comparative advantage. To possess a **comparative advantage** means that a country can produce a good or service relatively more efficiently than any other country. A comparative advantage should not be confused with an **absolute advantage**, which is a country's ability to produce *more* of a good or service than any other country. Just because a large country can produce more of a good than a small country doesn't necessarily mean it is relatively more efficient at producing that good. What matters is relative efficiency, or comparative advantage—not absolute advantage.

A **comparative advantage** is a country's ability to produce a good or service relatively more efficiently than any other country.

An **absolute advantage** is a country's ability to produce more of a good or service than any other country.

When all countries focus on producing those products for which they have a comparative advantage, collectively they all have more production to share. This, in turn, creates higher standards of living for these countries. As you've probably guessed, countries export those products for which they have a comparative advantage and import those products for which they do not have a comparative advantage.

What can a country do to get ahead in world markets?

In many nations, governments focus on improving the nation's resources—natural resources, labour, capital (plant, equipment, and infrastructure), technology, and innovation and entrepreneurialism—to improve competitiveness.

Governments can't do much to improve a nation's natural resources; they have to work with what they have. Nations with abundant natural resources will likely have a comparative advantage in the production of goods that require these raw materials. For example, if Brazilians can grow coffee more easily than they can produce dairy products, and Canadians can produce dairy products more easily than they can grow coffee, we would say that Canadians have a comparative advantage in producing dairy products, and Brazilians have a comparative advantage in coffee production. Trading Canadian dairy products for Brazilian coffee would clearly benefit both groups.

However, governments can and do invest in health, education, and training designed to increase the productivity of their labour forces. All international businesses are constantly looking for good workers, and each country wants to attract businesses to enhance employment opportunities for its citizens.

Many governments try to create incentives for private company investments in capital (plant and equipment). For example, governments may try to keep interest rates low so private companies will invest in the latest state-of-the art equipment, thereby giving them an edge over foreign competition. Governments also invest in *public capital*, which is sometimes called *infrastructure*. Infrastructure includes roads, bridges, dams, electric grid lines, and telecommunications satellites that enhance productivity. Governments also try to promote technological advances to give their nations a competitive edge. This can include investments in basic and applied research at government-funded higher educational institutions. Finally, governments might also promote innovation and entrepreneurialism.

What can businesses do to be more competitive?

Can a business create a competitive or comparative advantage? The ingredients for national competitiveness are the same for business competitiveness. That is, successful firms try to gain access to cheap raw materials, invest in their workers' training, and purchase state-of-the-art capital (plant and equipment). Successful companies also invest in cutting-edge technology in their research and development (R&D) departments. Finally, they promote innovativeness throughout their organizations. Conversely, if a company, an entire industry, or even a nation has lost its comparative (or competitive) advantage, then it probably failed in one or more of these areas. It is the joint job of government and private business to determine where to focus improvements in order to compete more effectively. Remember, comparative advantage is really a relative advantage—relative to the competition.

Global 500 Largest Corporations in the World (2010)

Company	Sales (US$ Millions)
1. Walmart Stores (United States)	$408 214
2. Royal Dutch/Shell (Netherlands)	$285 129
3. Exxon Mobil (United States)	$284 129
4. BP (British Petroleum) (Britain)	$246 138
5. Toyota Motor (Japan)	$204 106
6. Japan Post Holdings (Japan)	$202 196
7. Sinopec (China)	$187 518
8. State Grid (China)	$184 496
9. AXA (France)	$175 257
10. China National Petroleum (China)	$165 496

Source: CNNMoney.com, "Global 500 (2010)," http://money.cnn.com/magazines/fortune/global500/2010/full_list/, Accessed April 27, 2011.

When foreign imports arrive in Canada, they increase the supply of the product, pushing its price down. Consumers welcome the competition and the lower prices, but domestic competitors are displeased.

4

Describe the benefits and costs of international trade.

Benefits and Costs of International Trade

What are the benefits of international trade? The theory of comparative advantage indicates that countries participating in international trade will experience higher standards of living because of the greater quantity and variety of higher-quality products offered at lower prices. These results stem from the increased competition associated with more open trade. But these benefits are not without their costs.

What are the costs of international trade? The costs of international trade are borne by those businesses and their workers whose livelihoods are threatened by foreign competition. Some domestic businesses may lose market share to foreign companies, stunting their profitability and ability to create jobs. Other firms may not be able to compete and will be driven out of business entirely.

Do the benefits of international trade outweigh the costs? This is a difficult question to answer. The answer depends on the timing of the benefits and the costs, and the extent to which they are felt within any given period. The critics point out the costs—including lost jobs to foreign competitors—but the advocates point out the benefits—greater quantity and variety of higher-quality products available for purchase. However, the benefits may not be easily traced to increased international trade because they are often slow and subtle. People benefit from lower-priced products, although the price reductions may only save people a nickel here and a dime there. But the sum of these lower prices for the public at large can be dramatic—especially over time.

Although international trade happens all the time in today's society, companies still have to abide by certain rules and regulations. Governments often impose restrictions on the quantity and types of goods that can cross national borders.

5

Summarize the different types of trade barriers.

Free trade is the unencumbered flow of goods and services across national borders.

A **tariff** is a tax that governments impose on an imported good or service, such as French wine. Governments prefer to impose tariffs because they raise tax revenues.

A **subsidy** is a payment that governments make to domestic producers.

A **quota** is a limitation on the amount of an import allowed to enter a country.

An **embargo** is a total restriction on an import (or an export).

Administrative trade barriers are government rules designed to limit imports.

Local content requirement is a requirement that some portion of a good be produced domestically.

Trade Barriers and Protectionism

What is free trade? **Free trade** is the unencumbered flow of goods and services across national borders. That is, free trade is free from government intervention or other impediments that can block the flow of goods across borders. Virtually all economists are free-trade advocates because they argue that over time the benefits far outweigh the costs for the nation as a whole.

Still, even if virtually all economists are free-trade advocates, all real-world governments do have trade barriers in place to protect selected domestic industries from foreign competition.

What trade barriers can governments put in place? There are three types of trade barriers:

1. *Tariffs and subsidies.* The most common trade barrier is the **tariff**, a tax imposed on an imported good or service, such as French wine. Governments prefer to impose tariffs because they raise tax revenues. The opposite of a tariff is a **subsidy**; governments make payments to domestic producers. A subsidy can take many forms. It can be a direct cash grant or a payment in-kind that could include tax concessions or a low-interest loan.

2. *Quotas and embargoes.* A **quota** is a limitation on the amount of an import allowed to enter a country. For example, a quota on French wine might limit the quantity to 10 000 cases per day. The most heavy-handed government trade barrier is an **embargo**, a total restriction on an import (or an export). Since the 1960s, for example, the United States has imposed an embargo on most goods traded with Cuba. Embargoes may be used to achieve a political goal. In the case of Cuba, the American embargo has been used to apply pressure for change toward a more democratic system.[24]

3. *Administrative trade barriers.* Several other types of trade barriers can be lumped under the heading of **administrative trade barriers**—government rules designed to limit imports. One example is a **local content requirement**, which is a requirement that some portion of a good be produced domestically. This usually drives up the cost of the import. Administrative trade barriers may also require an import to

meet some technical standard or bureaucratic rule (for instance, customer regulations that are different from generally accepted international standards), effectively shutting the import out of the domestic market. The European Union (EU) does not accept beef products that have been pro duced with growth hormones. Much of the American and Canadian beef could not be sold in the EU. In 2010, Canada won some duty-free access (a quota) to the EU market; therefore, if Canadian producers chose to produce this type of beef, despite the higher costs of doing so, at least they see that a market does exist.[25] Although administrative trade barriers can be legitimate, they may be designed purely to protect domestic producers from international competition.

Who benefits and who suffers from protectionist trade barriers?   Without a doubt, trade barriers benefit domestic producers and their workers, and they hurt domestic consumers. How does this occur? Trade barriers increase costs to foreign companies or restrict the supply of imports, driving up their prices and reducing their sales in the domestic market. As a result, the higher-priced imports increase the demand for domestically produced substitute goods or services. This higher demand also increases the domestically produced product's price, although it simultaneously increases domestic sales. And this is exactly what the trade barriers are designed to do—restrict sales of imports while stimulating sales for domestic firms. Because the domestic firms are selling more at higher prices, they are more profitable. This profitability also creates more job security for their employees. The undesirable outcome, however, is that both the imports and the domestically produced substitute products are now more expensive. Domestic consumers lose while domestic producers and their workers gain. Trade barriers also hurt consumers because the overall quantity, variety, and quality of products are lower because of curtailing foreign competition. **Table 4.1** summarizes the economic benefits and costs of free trade and protectionism for a nation.

What are common arguments in favour of protectionist trade barriers?   Four main arguments exist for implementing protectionist trade barriers:

1. *National security.* The national security argument states that certain industries critical to national security should be protected from foreign competition. For example, Canada wouldn't want to become dependent on another nation for a critical component of national defence. However, rarely have protected industries using this argument proven critical to national defence.
2. *Infant industry.* The infant industry argument states that an undeveloped domestic industry needs time to grow and develop in order to acquire a comparative advantage in the global economy. The protected time to grow allows opportunities for the industry to make the investments needed to become innovative. Once the comparative advantage is captured, then protection from foreign competition will no longer be necessary. However, in practice, it can be very difficult to determine whether an industry legitimately holds promise of developing a comparative advantage. In addition, rarely do infant industries ever grow up, and the government protection can become addictive.

Table 4.1   Economic Benefits and Costs of Free Trade and Protectionism for a Nation

	Free Trade	Protectionism
Economic Benefits	A greater quantity and variety of higher quality products at lower prices	Increased sales at higher prices improves the profitability of the protected domestic companies, creating greater job security for their workers
Economic Costs	Reduced sales and lower prices for domestic firms that find it difficult to compete internationally, which reduces their profitability and lowers job security for their workers	Lower quantity and variety of lower-quality products at higher prices

Off the **Mark**

How Does China's Internet Censorship Affect Global Business?

While many parts of the world, notably the Middle East, are undergoing dramatic political and social changes because of Internet access, China has become more restrictive with what its net-izens are allowed to access.[26] Google and other tech companies have had difficulty doing business in China due to government censorship and regulations. Beijing's extensive censorship of online content—often called the "Great Firewall of China"—systematically removes material it deems harmful, including politically sensitive information, pornography, and violence.[27] As of 2011, Facebook, the world's largest online social media network, which had been blocked in China since 2009, was looking for ways to work within Chinese laws and with China's leading search engine and web conglomerate, Baidu. Meanwhile, Google declared war on censorship and decided not to censor its web searches in China any longer, so China started closing the doors on Google services, banning or highly restricting various services from the country. Microsoft, on the other hand, continued to comply with local regulations, including the censorship of some political material.

In 2011, one of China's largest social networks, Renren, was looking to raise US$500 million on the New York Stock Exchange. It may seem unusual that while a Chinese social network can tap U.S. capital markets, American social networks, especially Facebook, cannot tap Chinese consumer markets. If Facebook grew rice or manufactured textiles, it could be argued that China was putting up trade barriers, but that has yet to happen because China's Internet censorship is considered a human rights issue and not a trade problem.[28]

Some people are pushing the U.S. government to make Internet censorship a trade issue. The argument, which Google has made in congressional testimony, is that digital barriers to the free flow of information are equivalent to traditional trade barriers, which are illegal under World Trade Organization (WTO) rules. Google spokesperson Niki Fenwick says censorship is first a human right issue, then adds, "When a government blocks the Internet, it is the equivalent of a customs official stopping goods at the border."[29]

Under order of Pakistan's high court in 2010, the Pakistan Telecommunication Authority started to observe Google, MSN, YouTube, Yahoo, Hotmail, and other websites for any infringement of Muslim sentiments.[30] If the trend to block Internet access continues, what will happen to human rights and global trade? Where are we headed?

Discussion Questions

1. How do you feel about censorship? Is it a violation of human rights or does it protect citizens, government, or society? Do you think the Chinese government will be pressured into providing open Internet access for its citizens? Why or why not?
2. Do you think the Chinese government's censorship is an attempt to control Internet usage in favour of its own domestic Baidu search engine and other domestic social media companies (a form of protectionism)? What if other countries did the same? Could censorship become more prevalent?
3. How does Internet censorship affect global business? As more countries move toward market economies, do you think there will be a decline in Internet censorship by government? Should the Internet be kept "open" for all world citizens?

3. *Cheap foreign labour.* The cheap foreign labour argument centres on the sometimes significantly lower wages paid to workers of foreign companies. How can domestic companies compete with these low wages? Sometimes they can't, but trying to protect these jobs creates still higher costs for the nation in the form of higher prices and a reduced quantity, quality, and variety of products from which to choose. Note also that what is relevant for costs of production is not just wages but productivity in relation to wages. A company's costs of production can be lower even when it pays its workers twice as much if the productivity of workers is at least twice as high. It's no surprise that if a country wants to maintain high wages in a global marketplace, it needs to find a way to increase the productivity of its labour force.

4. *Threat of retaliation.* The threat of retaliation (or the bargaining chip) argument says that if a trading partner increases its trade barriers on your exports, or fails to reduce

trade barriers as you reduce yours, then an uneven, unfair playing field is created. Domestic companies may also be put at a disadvantage if a foreign firm is dumping its product. **Dumping** is selling a product at a price below the price charged in the producing country; it is illegal but can be difficult to prove. The intent of dumping is to dominate an industry and then control it. The threat of higher trade barriers can be a bargaining chip in retaliation for dumping or for negotiating lower trade barriers for exports. However, the threat of trade barriers can be a risky policy. If it fails, the result can be a trade war—nations would implement higher trade barriers and leave everyone at a disadvantage.

Dumping is selling a product at a price below the price charged in the producing country; it is illegal but can be difficult to prove.

How do economists feel about protectionist trade barriers? As noted earlier, most economists are free trade advocates because they believe that the economic benefits of free trade outweigh the economic costs. Economists insist that the best way to address the concerns of those industries and their workers whose livelihoods are threatened by foreign competition is *not* to impose protectionist trade barriers. Instead, these displaced individuals need to be equipped with the education, training, and skills necessary to smooth their transition into a line of business or work in which the nation has a comparative advantage and demand is rising. Although all governments have protectionist trade barriers in place, they have been working to reduce them because they believe the economic benefits of doing so generally outweigh the costs. This political position explains the recent trend toward reduced trade and investment barriers that have fuelled globalization.

International Organizations Promoting Free Trade

What are some international organizations that promote free trade? Countries realize that unilaterally reducing their trade barriers puts their businesses at an unfair disadvantage. The key for realizing the mutual benefits of international trade is to get all countries to lower their trade barriers simultaneously, which was the reason for creating organizations such as GATT and the WTO.

6 Describe the organizations that aid trade and attempt to eliminate trade barriers.

The **General Agreement on Tariffs and Trade (GATT)** was created in 1948 with twenty-three member nations to provide rules for world trade; its membership grew to 123 countries by 1994. Although GATT was not an organization with any real enforcement powers, its eight rounds of negotiated agreements, or treaties, were very successful in reducing tariffs and other obstacles to free trade on goods. This, in turn, spurred significant world economic growth.[31] However, GATT was not as successful in reducing trade barriers on services, protecting intellectual property rights, or enforcing agreements among member nations. As a result, the WTO replaced GATT in 1995 during the eighth and final round of negotiations (called the Uruguay Round because it was launched in Punta del Este, Uruguay).

The **General Agreement on Tariffs and Trade (GATT)** was created in 1948 with twenty-three member nations to provide rules for world trade; its membership grew to 123 countries by 1994.

The **World Trade Organization (WTO)** has strengthened the world trading system by extending GATT rules to services, increasing protection for intellectual property rights, and perhaps most significantly, taking on the responsibility for arbitrating trade disputes and monitoring the trade policies of member countries (see **Figure 4.1**).[32] The WTO operates as GATT did—on the basis of consensus—in the area of dispute settlement. However, unlike GATT, the WTO doesn't allow losing parties to ignore their arbitration reports. The WTO has the power to enforce decisions, which gives the WTO something that the GATT never had: teeth.

Replacing the GATT in 1995, the **World Trade Organization (WTO)** strengthened the world trading system by extending GATT rules to services, increasing protection for intellectual property rights, and, perhaps most significantly, taking on the responsibility for arbitrating trade disputes and monitoring the trade policies of member countries.

Two international financial organizations are instrumental in fostering global trade: the World Bank and the International Monetary Fund (IMF). Founded in 1944, the **World Bank** offers low-interest loans, advice, and information to developing countries. To receive loans, countries must agree to lower trade barriers and aid private enterprise. Founded one year after the World Bank, the **International Monetary Fund (IMF)** promotes trade through financial cooperation. The IMF makes short-term emergency loans to member nations and operates as a lender of last resort for troubled nations. In return for these emergency funds, borrowers must make significant commitments to address the problems that lead to the crises in the first place.

The **World Bank** offers low-interest loans, advice, and information to developing countries.

The **International Monetary Fund (IMF)** promotes trade through financial cooperation.

WTO members and observers

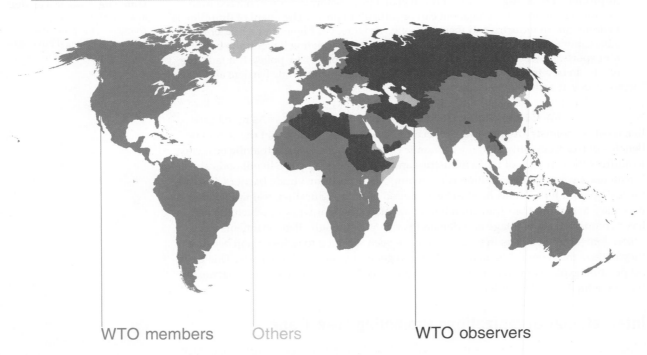

WTO members   Others   WTO observers

Figure 4.1   Countries in the WTO

What more can be done to promote free trade?   Advocates of free trade argue that much remains to be done to reduce trade barriers in the global economy. The first round of WTO talks was launched in Seattle in 1999, but anti-globalization protestors disrupted and derailed these talks. The meetings were relaunched in 2001 in Doha, Qatar, in the Persian Gulf, with an agenda to curtail dumping, reduce protectionist trade barriers, protect intellectual property rights, and reduce government barriers on foreign direct investment.[33] The Doha Round was slated to last three years, but had not yet concluded by fall 2011.

Critics argue that exploitation of workers can contribute to the gap between the rich and poor. Environmentalists have also expressed a growing concern that expanded international trade encourages companies to move production to countries in which they are freer to pollute and degrade the environment, which contributes to global climate change and all the problems that may stem from global warming. These concerns highlight the fact that the economic perspective on the benefits and costs of free trade is not the only perspective. Important social, ethical, political, and environmental concerns are also important.

Regional Free Trade Agreements

What is a free trade agreement?   Many nations have been so eager to achieve the higher standards of living associated with free trade that they have struck out on their own by creating **free trade areas or agreements (FTA)** to abolish trade barriers among member countries. Although all current free trade areas still have some obstacles to free trade among their members, many have made considerable headway in reducing these barriers.

Free trade areas or agreements (FTA) abolish trade barriers among member countries.

The **European Union (EU)**, with twenty-seven member nations, is the oldest and largest free trade area.

What is the largest free trade area in the world?   The greatest free trade area exists among member nations of the **European Union (EU)**, which is the oldest and largest free trade area. The EU can trace its roots to 1957, with the creation of the European

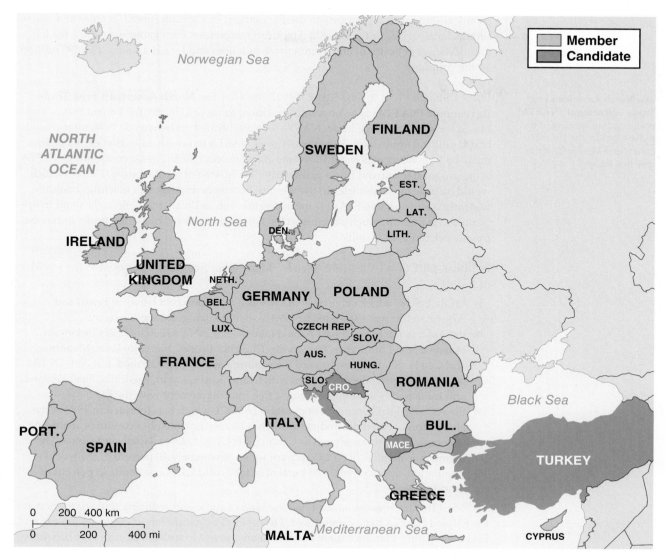

Figure 4.2 The Twenty-Seven Member Countries of the European Union

Economic Community (or Common Market), which consisted of the six founding countries of Belgium, France, Germany, Italy, Luxembourg, and the Netherlands. Although many obstacles had to be overcome, like the concern over the potential loss of national sovereignty, the EU has grown to its current membership of twenty-seven countries, as shown in **Figure 4.2**. The EU's success is due, in large part, to its demonstrated commitment to the free flow of goods, services, capital, and people across borders in Europe.

The EU is currently the world's largest single market, surpassing the United States. It accounts for approximately one-third of the world's total production. The EU is the largest exporter in the world and the second largest importer.[34] In 1999, the EU also surpassed all other free trade areas with respect to economic integration by adopting a common currency—the euro. The euro is currently used by twenty-three of the twenty-seven member countries and has become a major currency in global financial markets.[35] The EU has a population of nearly 500 million people and is likely to continue to grow as many other countries—such as Croatia, the former Yugoslav Republic of Macedonia, and Turkey—apply to join.

The European Union's economic power and political clout has a huge influence on international businesses worldwide. For example, some international businesses have been motivated to invest in production facilities within the EU to hedge against any potential trade barriers. The EU has also established many legal, regulatory, and technical standards for imports to the EU market. In addition, the EU's anti-trust rulings have significantly affected American businesses. For example, in 2004, the EU found Microsoft guilty of anti-competitive practices and levied a fine of US$690 million on the company.[36]

The **North American Free Trade Agreement (NAFTA)** is an ongoing agreement to move Canada, the United States, and Mexico closer to true free trade.

Does Canada have a free trade agreement?   The **North American Free Trade Agreement (NAFTA)** is an ongoing agreement to move Canada, the United States, and Mexico closer to true free trade. NAFTA was established on January 1, 1994, after considerable political opposition. The experience of NAFTA so far indicates that earlier claims made by both advocates and critics were exaggerated. One big issue confronting NAFTA is the proposal to expand into a greater Free Trade Area of the Americas (FTAA), which would include most countries in the western hemisphere. Although meetings continue to strategize a workable FTAA, some countries such as Brazil and Venezuela stand in opposition. As a result, much progress in the near future toward more free trade within the framework of FTAA is unlikely.

Is China part of a free trade area?   Many other free trade areas exist in the world, including:

- MERCOSUR, which originated in 1988 as a free trade pact between Brazil and Argentina but was expanded in 1990 to include Paraguay and Uruguay.
- the Association of Southeast Asian Nations (ASEAN), which includes Indonesia, Malaysia, the Philippines, Singapore, Thailand, Brunei, Vietnam, Laos, Myanmar, and Cambodia. Progress toward integration has been very limited, but ASEAN has negotiated free trade agreements with China, Korea, Japan, Australia, New Zealand, and India and is working to create a free trade agreement with the EU.
- the Asia-Pacific Economic Cooperation (APEC), which was founded in 1989 at the suggestion of Australia and currently has twenty-one member countries, including economic powerhouses such as Canada, the United States, Japan, and China. The member economies of APEC account for approximately 40 percent of the world's population, approximately 54 percent of the world GDP, and about 43 percent of world trade.[37]

Most free trade areas haven't had the kind of success in reducing trade barriers that the EU and NAFTA have experienced. However, it's clear that most countries are eager to come together to reduce trade barriers in an attempt to realize the economic benefits of greater free trade.

CONDUCTING BUSINESS ACROSS BORDERS

Strategies for International Business

7 Distinguish the three basic strategies of international business.

What types of strategies can an international business follow?   All business is undertaken within an economic, socio-cultural, political, and legal environment wherever it operates. When doing purely domestic business, keeping up with environmental forces can be a huge challenge for even the savviest manager. However, managing an international business is even more complex because additional and different economic, social, and political environments must be considered. Two major factors determine an international firm's strategy. The first factor involves how important it is for a business to keep its costs down and, therefore, its prices low. The second factor is how necessary it is for a company to customize or differentiate its product to adapt to different customer tastes and preferences around the globe. Three basic strategies for international business are global, multi-domestic, and transnational.

Can companies compete with low prices?

One basic strategy of international business is the **global strategy**, which involves competing primarily based on price while selling a standardized (or homogenous) product. Standardized products are basic products that meet universal needs. Examples of standardized products include agricultural products, oil, and raw material commodities. These goods are essentially the same from company to company—they are homogenous—because they are universally recognized and appeal to consumers across many cultures. When selling standardized products, firms compete aggressively based on price. Firms pursuing a global strategy face strong cost pressures to keep their prices low because they are selling a standardized product. The company with the lowest price captures most market share. Sony and Boeing are companies that pursue a global strategy.

A **global strategy** involves competing primarily based on price while selling a standardized (or homogenous) product.

Can companies compete by customizing products?

A second basic strategy of international business is the **multi-domestic strategy**, which involves competing primarily by customizing or differentiating the product to meet unique local needs, tastes, or preferences. Firms pursuing a multi-domestic strategy face relatively low pressures for cost reduction because the price is often of secondary concern to buyers. Instead, what is important to customers is whether the product meets their needs or is distinct from the product of competitors. Companies that pursue a multi-domestic strategy, such as Procter & Gamble and General Foods, all work to make their respective products appeal to different customers around the globe.

A **multi-domestic strategy** involves competing primarily by customizing or differentiating the product to meet unique local needs, tastes, or preferences.

Are companies able to compete with low prices and still customize products?

A third basic strategy of international business is the **transnational strategy**, which involves competing by offering a customized product while simultaneously selling at the lowest possible price. The strong cost pressures and strong pressures for differentiation that motivate this type of strategy are typically at odds. Therefore, the successful pursuit of this type of strategy is extremely difficult in practice. Frito-Lay, American Express, and British Airways all pursue a transnational strategy.

A **transnational strategy** involves competing by offering a customized product while simultaneously selling at the lowest possible price.

Entering Foreign Markets

How do international firms enter foreign markets?

In addition to determining a business strategy, international businesses must decide how they will serve foreign customers. Companies may undertake one of six strategies to enter foreign markets:

8
Outline the ways international firms can successfully enter foreign markets.

1. Export their product.
2. Implement a turnkey project.
3. Undertake franchising.
4. Enter into a licensing agreement, a joint venture, or a strategic alliance.
5. Undertake contract manufacturing.
6. Establish a wholly-owned subsidiary.

Let's look briefly at these options.

Exporting   As noted earlier, exporting is the sale of a domestically produced good in a foreign market. Most businesses typically begin serving a foreign market by exporting and only later switch to another mode to expand sales abroad. Exporting has two advantages. First, exporting is relatively easy and inexpensive compared with establishing a physical presence in a foreign market. Second, exporting may help a firm realize lower costs because companies can move production to an inexpensive location and then export its product from that location around the world. Exporting also has a few disadvantages. It is not economical for heavy or bulky products with high transportation costs. Exporting may also become uneconomical if foreign trade barriers are unexpectedly imposed.

Turnkey Projects   When firms export their technological expertise in exchange for a fee, they have implemented a **turnkey project**. Turnkey projects are common in the production of sophisticated and complex manufacturing facilities such as those involved in petroleum refining, steel, and hydroelectric energy production.

A **turnkey project** is implemented when firms export their technological expertise in exchange for a fee.

Once the facility is up and running, the locals are trained, then the keys are turned over to the new foreign owners. Black & Veatch, an engineering firm in Kansas City, has built power plants in China as turnkey projects. Turnkey projects allow firms with specialized knowledge, like Black & Veatch, to earn higher profits from their technical expertise. The drawback is that the firm may create a viable competitor if their technological expertise is easily accessible.

Franchising involves selling a well-known brand name or a proven method of doing business to an investor in exchange for a fee and a percentage of sales or profits. The seller is the **franchisor**, and the buyer is the **franchisee**.

Franchising   **Franchising** involves selling a well-known brand name or a proven method of doing business to an investor in exchange for a fee and a percentage of sales or profits. The seller is the **franchisor**, and the buyer is the **franchisee**. Franchising, which will be discussed in depth in Chapter 5, is popular both domestically and internationally. Examples of franchising abound in the fast-food and entertainment industries. McDonald's and KFC restaurants are now found all over the world. Walt Disney has recently franchised 150 stores in India.[38] Domino's Pizza has 500 stores in Mexico, 300 in the United Kingdom, 300 in Australia, 300 in South Korea, 200 in Canada, and many other stores around the world.[39] Undoubtedly, all of these franchises must be careful to adapt their goods and services to appeal to their different global customers.

The main advantage of franchising is that the franchisor shifts to the franchisee the costs and risks of opening a foreign market. Disadvantages include the enforcement of franchise contracts that ensure quality control over distant franchisees and ensuring that the product is properly adapted to appeal to customers.

Licensing is an agreement in which the licensor's intangible property—patents, trademarks, service marks, copyrights, trade secrets, or other intellectual property—may be sold or made available to a licensee in exchange for a royalty fee.

Licensing   **Licensing** is an agreement in which the licensor's intangible property—patents, trademarks, service marks, copyrights, trade secrets, or other intellectual property—may be sold or made available to a licensee in exchange for a royalty fee. The advantage of licensing is the speed with which the licensor can enter a foreign market and the assumption of risks and costs by the licensee. The disadvantage is the loss of technological expertise to the licensee and the creation of a potential competitor. SRI International is a company that licenses its vast array of intellectual property around the world. Its technological specialty is patents in the biosciences, computing, and chemistry-related materials and structural areas.[40]

Joint ventures involve shared ownership in a subsidiary firm. International joint venture partners involve an international business teaming up with a local partner in order to enter a foreign market.

Joint Ventures   **Joint ventures** involve shared ownership in a subsidiary firm. International joint venture partners involve an international business teaming up with a local partner in order to enter a foreign market. The advantages of a joint venture include gaining local knowledge of the economic, social, and political landscape while sharing the costs and risks of accessing a foreign market. For example, due to many restrictions on shopkeeper business in India, Walmart must enter India through a joint venture in order to sell to consumers there. Through its joint venture with Bharti Enterprises, it has launched two stores and plans twelve more over the next few years.[41]

Entering a joint venture, like entering into a marriage, requires considerable thought in the selection of a complementary partner. The disadvantage of joint ventures is losing control over the company because compromise with the partner is inevitable. The risk of losing proprietary technology in the event of dissolution or divorce of the joint venture is also a major drawback.

International franchising abounds in the fast-food industry.

Strategic Alliances **Strategic alliances** are cooperative arrangements between actual or potential competitors. Unlike a joint venture, each partner retains its business independence. Strategic alliances are typically agreements for a specific period or for only the duration of a particular project. The advantages of strategic alliances include the pooling of unique talents and expertise and the sharing of the costs and risks of a project for mutual benefit. The disadvantages include loss of technology and initial difficulty in finding a compatible partner.

Strategic alliances are cooperative arrangements between actual or potential competitors. Unlike a joint venture, each partner retains its business independence.

Contract Manufacturing **Contract manufacturing** occurs when a firm subcontracts part or all of its goods to an outside firm as an alternative to owning and operating its own production facility. When doing international business, the subcontractor is a foreign firm. Therefore, contract manufacturing is really a form of offshore outsourcing. Contract manufacturing allows international business to enter a foreign market by placing its label on the good and selling it in the foreign market where it was produced. Contract manufacturing also enables a firm to test market its product in a foreign market with very little expense compared with the high start-up costs of building its own facility. The disadvantage centres on the lack of quality control over the subcontractor.

Contract manufacturing occurs when a firm subcontracts part or all of its goods to an outside firm as an alternative to owning and operating its own production facility.

Wholly-Owned Subsidiaries A **wholly-owned subsidiary** involves establishing a foreign facility that is owned entirely by the investing firm. For example, as its sixth expansion into foreign markets, South Korean automotive manufacturer Hyundai entered the Russian market with Hyundai Motor Manufacturing Russia, a wholly-owned subsidiary of Hyundai.[42] The advantages of this entry choice include total control over foreign operations and technological expertise. The disadvantage is that the parent company must bear all of the costs and risks of entering a foreign market.

A **wholly-owned subsidiary** involves establishing a foreign facility that is owned entirely by the investing firm.

Which mode of entering foreign markets is optimal? The optimal entry mode depends on many factors, including the firm's strategy. Companies must weigh the advantages and disadvantages of each when making a decision. **Table 4.2** summarizes the advantages and disadvantages of the various entry modes.

Table 4.2 Advantages and Disadvantages of the Various Entry Modes

	Advantages	Disadvantages
Exporting	• Speed of entry • Production site in lowest-cost location	• High transport costs • Threat of trade barriers such as tariffs • Lack of access to local information
Turnkey project	• Increased profits for high-tech firms	• Loss of technical know-how to potential competitors
Franchising	• Costs and risks of opening the foreign market fall on the franchisee	• Difficulty in maintaining quality control over distant franchises
Licensing	• Speed of entry	• Licensee may become competitor • Loss of knowledge to potential competitor
Joint venture	• High potential for learning • Benefit of combined resources	• Shared control of business • Risk of losing specialized technology to partner
Strategic alliance	• Pooled talents and expertise • Shared costs and risks	• Risk of losing specialized technology to partner • Difficulty in finding a compatible partner
Contract manufacturing	• Speed of entry • Low test-marketing costs	• Lack of quality control over distant subcontractor
Wholly-owned subsidiary	• Total control over all operations • Preservation of proprietary technology	• Risks and costs of entering a foreign market

INTERNATIONAL BUSINESS: ECONOMIC FACTORS AND CHALLENGES

The Effect of Exchange Rates

 Define exchange rates and explain how they affect international business.

 List the economic factors and challenges that play a role in conducting business on a global scale.

Exchange rates are the rates at which currencies are converted into another currency.

Currency appreciation, an increase in the exchange rate value of a nation's currency, causes the relative price of imports to fall as the relative price of exports rises.

Currency depreciation, a decrease in the exchange rate value of a nation's currency, has the opposite effect on the relative prices of exports and imports. A weak currency causes exports to become cheaper and imports to become more expensive.

The **balance of trade** is the difference between the value of a country's exports and the value of its imports during a specific time.

A **trade deficit**, or unfavourable balance of trade, exists when the value of a country's imports exceeds the value of its exports.

A **trade surplus**, or favourable balance of trade, occurs when the value of a country's exports exceeds the value of its imports.

The **balance of payments** is a summary of a country's international financial transactions.

What are exchange rates?   Foreign exchange markets determine **exchange rates**, the rates at which currencies are converted into another currency. Depending on a firm's perspective, it may prefer a strong or weak dollar. Canadian exporters prefer a weak dollar because their products will be more affordable to foreigners. However, Canadian importers prefer a strong dollar because the cost of importing foreign goods is cheaper. If goods are imported cheaply, then those savings can be either passed on to the consumer or kept as higher profits.

Businesses are affected by fluctuating exchange rates every day. Transactions between international companies not only have to specify what each side will be paid but also in which currency. In addition, multinational enterprises use foreign currency to pay foreign workers or to invest spare cash in other nations where interest rates may be more attractive.

How do exchange rates affect international business?   Changes in exchange rates can have important implications for international businesses. Suppose that the value of the Canadian dollar rises or gets stronger against the Chinese yuan. What effect will this have on Canadian and Chinese business? Goods exported from Canada will become more expensive because the Chinese will now have to come up with more yuan to purchase each dollar. This means, for example, the cost of a $40 pair of jeans made in Canada will increase in price for the Chinese consumer. Chinese consumers will buy fewer Canadian goods, such as jeans, and exports to China will fall. Canadian businesses selling to China will be hurt through no fault of their own. At the same time, this stronger dollar will cause a decline in the relative price of goods from China for Canadian consumers because fewer dollars are required to purchase each yuan. Thus, due to the currency exchange rate change, Canada will import more goods from China and Canadian businesses will lose market share to Chinese companies. This example illustrates that **currency appreciation**, an increase in the exchange rate value of a nation's currency, causes the relative price of imports to fall as the relative price of exports rises. When currency appreciates, the currency becomes stronger. **Currency depreciation**, a decrease in the exchange rate value of a nation's currency, has the opposite effect on the relative prices of exports and imports. A weak currency causes exports to become cheaper and imports to become more expensive.

Changes in exchange rates create other challenges for international business. In fact, rapid changes in exchange rates can create huge losses for some businesses. In the 1980s, Japan Airlines purchased several 747 jumbo jets from Boeing and agreed to pay in U.S. dollars. In the interim period between signing the contract and the delivery of the jets for payment, the value of the dollar rose dramatically. Japan Airlines had to pay a lot more money than anticipated for the jets, and it almost went bankrupt. This story illustrates a currency exchange rule: unanticipated exchange rate changes can pose huge risks for international businesses.

Changing exchange rates also affect multinational firms in other ways. Many companies, such as General Electric, feel competitive pressure to shift production to countries with weak or low-valued currencies to take advantage of lower costs of production. For example, a weak Chinese currency reduces labour costs in China. If a firm doesn't shift more of its production to China and its competitors do, then its costs will be higher and the company will lose global market share.

Trade Deficit and Trade Surplus   The **balance of trade** is the difference between the value of a country's exports and the value of its imports during a specific time. A **trade deficit**, or unfavourable balance of trade, exists when the value of a country's imports exceeds the value of its exports. A strong Canadian dollar may cause a trade deficit because a strong dollar can cause export prices to rise and import prices fall.

Which Is Better—A Strong Dollar or a Weak Dollar?

The answer to this question depends on the type of business a firm undertakes. Companies that do a lot of exporting—such as auto companies, chemical manufacturers, and farmers—prefer a weak dollar because their product's price is lower in the global marketplace so their sales and profits will be higher. On the other hand, companies that import components or finished goods for resale in the domestic market prefer a strong dollar because the relative price of their imports is lower.

From a consumer's perspective, a strong dollar is typically preferred because import prices are lower, which has a tendency to keep domestic competitors' prices low as well. As an employee, if you work for a company that exports much of its product, you would prefer a weak dollar to stimulate sales and ensure your job security.

The benefits of a strong dollar for a nation as a whole are lower priced imports (such as oil), lower prices, and a lower inflation rate in general. However, a strong dollar creates a trade deficit. A weak dollar, on the other hand, is good for domestic international businesses because it stimulates employment and raises standards of living. The drawback of a weak dollar is the higher costs of energy and other imports that create higher rates of inflation. So, which is better—a strong dollar or a weak dollar? Like most real-world issues, the answer depends on your perspective.

Discussion Questions

1. As a person living in Canada, would you prefer a strong Canadian dollar or a weak dollar? Why?
2. If you were an importer in China, would you prefer a strong Canadian dollar or a weak one? Why?
3. Use the Internet to find a currency exchange converter and compare the value of the Canadian dollar to: the Chinese yuan, Japanese yen, Indian rupee, Mexican peso, German euro, and U.S. dollar. Based on your findings, which country would you most like to import goods from? How many Canadian dollars would it cost you to buy a Big Mac in each of these countries?

A **trade surplus**, or favourable balance of trade, occurs when the value of a country's exports exceeds the value of its imports. Each year of the ten years preceding 2009, Canada's total export and import values had resulted in a trade surplus. However, in 2010, Canada recorded a trade deficit of $3.9 billion, up from a deficit of $5.3 billion in 2009.[43] The advantage of a trade deficit for a nation is that it enables the country to consume more than it produces. However, the disadvantage is that domestic assets such as real estate or stocks and bonds must be sold to foreigners to pay for the trade deficit. This is similar to an individual who spends more money than he or she makes. The individual will go into debt and eventually have to sell off assets to continue to live beyond his or her means.

Another measure of international trade is the **balance of payments**, which is a summary of a country's international financial transactions. The balance of payments includes: imports and exports (balance of trade), government loans to and from other countries, long-term investments in overseas business operations, gifts and foreign aid, military expenditures made to other countries, and money transfers into and out of foreign banks. The balance of payments shows the difference between the country's total payments to and the total receipts from other countries.

Fixed and Freely Floating Exchange Rate Systems Exchange rates can be manipulated or fixed by governments. For example, China has fixed its currency to a rate that is weak compared to the dollar. This means Chinese exports to Canada are cheap, and Chinese imports from Canada are expensive. As a result, China's products are artificially cheap, which has a variety of negative effects on the rest of the world. This is one reason why manufacturing has been leaving North America and going to China. Several countries are now calling upon the Chinese to allow their currency to "float," or to change in response to changing market conditions. Indeed, most

Canada's Top Export Destinations (2010)

Country	Exports (CA$ Billions)
1. United States	299.1
2. United Kingdom	16.4
3. China	13.2
4. Japan	9.2
5. Mexico	5.0
6. Germany	3.9
7. South Korea	3.7
8. Netherlands	3.2
9. Brazil	2.6
10. Norway	2.5

Source: Industry Canada, "International Trade Canadian Economy (NAICS 11-91)," http://www.ic.gc.ca/eic/site/cis-sic.nsf/eng/h_00029.html#it1, Accessed May 1, 2011.

A **freely floating (or flexible) exchange rate system** uses the global supply and demand for currencies to determine exchange rates.

countries use a **freely floating (or flexible) exchange rate system**, which uses the global supply and demand for currencies to determine exchange rates. Many specific factors affect the demand and supply of a nation's currency, such as changing interest rates, tax rates, and inflation rates. But generally, changes in exchange rates in a freely floating exchange rate system reflect the country's current economic health and its outlook for growth and investment potential. The problems with floating exchange rates are that they can create relative price changes outside the control of international businesses, as well as engender risks of losses due to rapid and unexpected changes in exchange rates.

A **nonconvertible currency** is a currency that can't be converted into another currency in the foreign exchange market.

Capital flight is the transfer of domestic funds into foreign currency held outside the country.

Countertrade is a form of international barter, the swapping of goods and services for other goods and services.

Nonconvertible Currency and Countertrade   Governments also reserve the right to restrict the convertibility of their currency. For example, many developing countries have a **nonconvertible currency**, a currency that can't be converted into another currency in the foreign exchange market. These governments often fear that allowing convertibility will result in **capital flight**, the transfer of domestic funds into foreign currency held outside the country. Capital flight would deprive the nation of much-needed funds for investment and development.

Global companies can still do business with countries that have nonconvertible currencies by using countertrade. **Countertrade** is a form of international barter, the swapping of goods and services for other goods and services. Currently, countertrade may account for as much as 10 to 15 percent of total world trade. Companies engage in countertrade because of necessity and profitability. Examples of companies that have undertaken countertrade include General Foods, Goodyear, General Electric, Westinghouse, 3M, General Motors, Ford Motor Company, Coca-Cola, and PepsiCo.[44]

Other Economic Challenges to Conducting International Business

What challenges does rapid growth of a nation pose to international businesses?   Changing exchange rates and nonconvertible currencies are not the only economic challenges to conducting international business. Companies must also consider how to adapt their products for sale in developing nations, how certain government policies might affect their business, and how the socio-economic factors of an area influence the types of products they sell.

Many developing countries are experiencing more rapid growth than advanced economies are, and they have hundreds of millions of eager new customers ready to put their money into the global market. It is also true that many developing countries still lack the basic infrastructure necessary for effective transportation of goods and/or lack access to dependable electricity. They may also be lacking in modern communications systems. The implications are obvious. For example, the types of food products offered for sale would have to be altered and packaged differently. Makers of electric can openers would need to produce manual can openers for sale. The modes of advertising would shift from television to radio, and marketing a product via the Internet wouldn't be effective because few customers would own a computer. It would be important for a business entering India, for example, to know the explosive growth there is not as much toward computer ownership as it is toward mobile phone ownership. Advertising delivered via mobile phones would be critical.

How does government intervention in the markets pose a challenge to international business?   The degree to which markets are allowed to operate free from government intervention is another important economic consideration. International businesses prefer free market economies to state-run or socialized economies because the bureaucratic hassles associated with government intervention drive costs up. Other economic factors include the debt load of a nation, its unemployment and inflation rates, and its fiscal and monetary policies. Unit labour cost—a measure that divides a worker's wages by the average productivity of that worker—is also important. Global companies are concerned with labour costs when looking for lowest-cost locations to establish production facilities. In addition, the degree of competition that exists in a nation is important because it's more attractive to relocate to places with fewer competitors.

How do socio-economic factors affect doing business internationally?   Several socio-economic factors also need to be taken into account, such as the demographics of population density and age distribution. The birthrates of many developing countries are high and offer exciting opportunities to toy manufacturers such as Mattel. Other socio-economic factors that firms must consider include income distribution, ethnicity, and the cultural behaviours of a community.

Socio-Cultural, Political, Legal, and Ethical Challenges

What is culture?   **Culture** is the complex set of values, behaviours, lifestyles, arts, beliefs, and institutions of a population that are passed on from generation to generation. Culture affects all aspects of business, from managing workers and production techniques to marketing and beyond. When a business expands into an international market and lacks cross-cultural and political awareness, it is destined to fail. The role of government involvement in business is not universal, so knowing how specific government policies govern business activity is critical for business success. And because there is no global court to settle differences and disputes, businesses need to study thoroughly what is acceptable legally and ethically.

Why is the study of culture important for international business?   Most international businesses that fail do so because they suffer from a lack of cross-cultural awareness. Attitudes toward time and work, aesthetics, religion, language, political systems, legal systems, and ethical ideals vary from country to country. **Cross-cultural awareness** is an understanding, appreciation, and sensitivity to foreign culture. **Ethnocentrism**, a belief that one's own culture is superior to all other cultures, is a guaranteed recipe for disaster when undertaking international business.

Why do aesthetics matter when it comes to international business?   *Aesthetics* is what is considered beautiful or in good taste and includes etiquette, customs, and protocol. Few things are more embarrassing than violating a sense of good taste. For example, a company selling eyeglasses in Thailand used ads featuring various cute animals wearing glasses. But because animals are considered a low form of life in Thailand and no Thai would wear anything worn by animals, the ads were a poor choice. Another example involves an American oil rig supervisor in Indonesia who yelled at an employee to take a boat to shore. Since it is considered rude to berate a worker in front of others, outraged workers brandishing axes chased the supervisor.[45]

How do different attitudes toward time and work affect international business?   *Attitudes toward time* vary considerably around the world. Time is paramount to those in the Canada and the United States, where people in general expect promptness and often insist on getting down to business. Some cultures view this as pushy and impersonal—a cultural turnoff. In addition, the Canadian time horizon differs markedly from the Japanese perspective. A Canadian may consider a long-term view to be four to seven years into the future, while the Japanese may be preparing for decades in advance. *Attitudes toward work* also vary. In Spain, business hours are generally from 9 a.m. to 2 p.m. and from 5 p.m. to 8 p.m., with an afternoon siesta (sleep or slowdown) in between. Sunday is still considered a holiday in Spain so the majority of businesses are closed.[46] Of course, restaurants are open from 1 p.m. to 4 p.m. and after 8 p.m., when people are off work. A business person from Canada should not expect to hold a business meeting during siesta time. Business meetings in Germany should be scheduled two to three weeks in advance and are usually held between 11 a.m. and 1 p.m. and 3 p.m. and 5 p.m. Meetings on Friday afternoons or during the holiday months of July, August, and December are avoided.[47]

⑪ Summarize the socio-cultural, political, legal, and ethical challenges to conducting business in a global marketplace.

4

Culture is the complex set of values, behaviours, lifestyles, arts, beliefs, and institutions of a population that are passed on from generation to generation.

Cross-cultural awareness is an understanding, appreciation, and sensitivity to foreign culture.

Ethnocentrism is a belief that one's own culture is superior to all other cultures

How do different religious beliefs affect international business?   *Religion* plays a profound role in shaping a culture. International businesses are therefore well advised to educate themselves on varying religious value systems, customs, and practices if they don't wish to offend customers in marketing campaigns. For example, when Arabs interpreted a soft drink with a label that had six-pointed stars on it as pro-Israeli they refused to buy it.[48]

Can inaccurate language translation cost a company money?   *Language*, both spoken and unspoken, is also extremely important. Consider a few more examples of international business blunders due to a lack of cross-cultural awareness. In Italy, Schweppes Tonic Water was translated as "Schweppes Toilet Water," and in Sweden, Kellogg had to rename its Bran Buds cereal when it discovered that the name roughly translated to "burned farmer."[49]

Unspoken language, or body language, also differs significantly around the world. Shaking your head side-to-side means "no" in Canada but "yes" in Bulgaria. In Asian cultures, it is considered rude to look someone in the eyes, yet in North American and other cultures, not looking at someone while speaking with them may be interpreted as disinterest, disrespect, or a sign that the person should not be trusted.

Although the world is getting smaller and a global culture is emerging, profound and significant cultural differences still exist. Cross-cultural awareness is a prerequisite to successful international business.

Should you bow or shake hands when you visit a Japanese client in Japan?

Cultural IQ Quiz

Answer the following questions to determine your cultural IQ.

1. Between 1 and 4 p.m., business people in Spain are more likely to
   a. attend a lunch meeting with clients.
   b. return home for a family lunch and nap.

2. In Venezuela, it's common for business associates to
   a. maintain at least three feet of personal space.
   b. offer a handshake and pat on the shoulder upon greeting.

3. If you receive a business card from a Japanese business acquaintance, you should
   a. put it in your pocket without looking at it.
   b. receive the card with both hands and examine the information.

4. During a lunch meeting with a Muslim partner, you should avoid ordering
   a. lamb.
   b. pork.

5. If an Indian business acquaintance offers you a gift, you should
   a. politely decline the offer.
   b. open the present after your acquaintance has left.

If your answers are . . .
Mostly As—It is time to brush up on your cultural awareness.
Mostly Bs—Congratulations! With your high cultural IQ, you'll need to get your passport ready for global business encounters.

What are the political challenges to conducting international business?   International businesses look for nations that have a stable government, a well-established educational system, and a well-maintained infrastructure. Political changes can create disruptive environments that affect business concerns. The political differences among nations can also pose a challenge when conducting international business.

Although companies are better equipped (and therefore prefer) to pursue their self-interests in market-based or capitalist economies, global companies often do business in government-controlled socialist economies such as China, Cuba, and North Korea. The differences between political systems can cause tensions. However, even in market economies, governments must address *market failures*, or shortcomings associated with free markets. The extent to which government is involved in addressing market failures can vary dramatically from country to country, which can have very important implications for international businesses. Many products that pollute the environment are deemed undesirable and have been regulated in one form or another by most governments around the world. The differences in these regulatory standards can impose big differences in costs of production for global businesses. There are also growing pressures on governments to address global climate change issues that will affect international business. **Table 4.3** summarizes the failures of markets and government attempts to address these shortcomings.

Table 4.3 Failures of Markets and Government Interventions

Market Failures	Government Interventions
Growth of monopoly power	Government enforces anti-trust laws
Undesirable and desirable social side effects from production and consumption	Government curtails the production and consumption of undesirable goods and promotes desirable products
Lack of public goods and services	Government provides them
Unfair distribution of income	Government redistributes income
Macroeconomic instability	Government uses fiscal and monetary policies to stabilize the business cycle

Just because governments intervene doesn't mean they succeed in improving market outcomes. Indeed, *government failure*—government intervention that fails to improve a market outcome—exists around the world. Government failure stems from corruption, ignorance, or pressure that special-interest groups place on politicians. International businesses prefer politically stable democracies because the probability of government failure is lower than for nondemocratic and unstable regimes.

What are the legal challenges to conducting international business? Laws, regulatory standards, and access to unbiased judicial systems based on a rule of law differ considerably around the world. No universal laws, regulatory standards, or global courts exist to settle disputes in the global economy. The different laws governing contracts, product safety and liability standards, and property rights are of particular importance when conducting global business. Property rights violations, including violations of patents and copyrights in the software, music, and publishing business, have cost businesses billions of dollars a year. Without adequate protection of intellectual property, technological developments would be too expensive and risky for companies to continue to fund long-term research and development (R&D).

Different laws also govern the use of bribery throughout the world. In Canada and the United States, offering bribes to foreign officials to gain contracts or other favours as a part of doing business in not only frowned upon, it is illegal. The Canadian government has concerns that Canadian businesses are at a disadvantage with many foreign companies that routinely pay bribes and are even able to deduct the cost of bribes from their taxes as legitimate business expenses. The Organisation for Economic Co-operation and Development (OECD), which currently consists of thirty member nations, is committed to combating bribery. In many places in the world, however, bribes are not uncommon and may even be necessary to do business.[50]

What are some ethical challenges to conducting international business?
Bribery is just one of the many ethical dilemmas surrounding global business. But even when something isn't illegal, it doesn't mean it isn't unethical. Unique differences in economic conditions and cultural values give rise to many ethical dilemmas surrounding global business. For example, should a firm conform to its home country's environmental, workplace, and product safety standards—even though it is not legally required to do so—while operating in another country? Should a company do business with a repressive totalitarian regime? When conducting international business, companies must decide whether they're willing to defy their ethical codes to make a larger profit or even to survive.

Think back to the quiz that you took at the beginning of this section. It is truly important is to realize that you can't assume that people will behave in similar ways in different cultures. Understanding and respecting these differences will help you in life, whether you're hoping to work for a large international company or planning to visit foreign countries as a tourist.

CHAPTER SYNOPSIS

❶ Outline the implications of the globalization of markets and the globalization of production.   *(pp. 95–96)*

The **globalization of markets** is thinking of the market as being the entire world rather than a local or national one. Companies often need to adjust their products or marketing campaigns to suit the unique tastes and preferences of their customers, wherever they may be.

The **globalization of production** occurs when companies move production to different locations around the globe (through outsourcing or offshoring) to take advantage of lower costs or to enhance quality. When faced with intense foreign competition, companies may be forced to relocate at least some of their production to another country to realize lower costs so they can offer customers lower prices.

The globalization of markets and production has resulted in some international firms becoming so large that they generate more revenue than the gross domestic product (GDP) of some nations.

❷ Explain why globalization has accelerated so rapidly. *(pp. 96–98)*

Two main factors increase globalization: technological innovations and the dramatic decline in trade and investment barriers among countries since the end of the Second World War. For example, the North American Free Trade Agreement (NAFTA) of 1994 made it easier for companies to shift work between Canada, the United States, and Mexico and opened the door to expanding offshoring.

❸ Explain the meaning of *comparative advantage* and *absolute advantage* in international competition. *(pp. 98–100)*

A country has a **comparative advantage** when it can produce a good or service relatively more efficiently compared with other countries. An **absolute advantage** is a country's ability to produce *more* of a good or service than any other country. Just because a large country can produce more of a good than a small country doesn't necessarily mean it is relatively more efficient at producing that good. What matters is relative efficiency, or comparative advantage—not absolute advantage.

❹ Describe the benefits and costs of international trade. *(p. 100)*

The theory of comparative advantage indicates that countries participating in international trade will experience higher standards of living because of the greater quantity and variety of higher-quality products offered at lower prices. These results stem from the increased competition associated with more open trade.

The costs of international trade are borne by those businesses and their workers whose livelihoods are threatened by foreign competition. Some domestic businesses may lose market share to foreign companies, stunting their profitability and ability to create jobs. Other firms may not be able to compete with the foreign competition and be driven out of business entirely.

❺ Summarize the different types of trade barriers. *(pp. 100–103)*

A **tariff** is a tax on an imported good or service such as French wine. Governments prefer to impose tariffs because they raise tax revenues. The opposite of a tariff is a **subsidy**, in which governments make payments to domestic producers.

A **quota** is a limitation on the amount of an import allowed to enter a country. The most heavy-handed government trade barrier is an **embargo**, a total restriction on an import (or export).

Administrative trade barriers are government rules designed to limit imports. A **local content requirement** demands that some portion of a good be produced domestically, which usually drives up the cost of the import. Administrative trade barriers may also require an import to meet some technical standard or bureaucratic rule (for instance, customer regulations that are different from generally accepted international standards), effectively shutting the import out of the domestic market.

❻ Describe the organizations that aid trade and attempt to eliminate trade barriers.   *(pp. 103–106)*

The **World Trade Organization (WTO)** has strengthened the world trading system by extending GATT rules to services, increasing protection for intellectual property rights, and, perhaps most significantly, arbitrating trade disputes and monitoring the trade policies of member countries. The **World Bank** offers low-interest loans, advice, and information to developing countries. The **International Monetary Fund (IMF)** promotes trade through financial cooperation.

❼ Distinguish the three basic strategies of international business.   *(pp. 106–107)*

The **global strategy** involves competing primarily based on price while selling a standardized (or homogenous) product. The **multi-domestic strategy** involves competing primarily by customizing or differentiating the product to meet unique local needs, tastes, or preferences. Firms pursuing a multi-domestic strategy face relatively low pressures for cost reduction because the price is often of secondary concern to buyers. The **transnational strategy** involves competing by offering a customized product while simultaneously selling at the lowest possible price. The strong cost pressures and strong pressures for differentiation that motivate this type of strategy are typically at odds.

❽ Outline the ways international firms can successfully enter foreign markets.   *(pp. 107–109)*

Companies may undertake one of six strategies to enter foreign markets:
1. Export their product.
2. Implement a turnkey project.
3. Undertake franchising.
4. Enter into a licensing agreement, a joint venture, or a strategic alliance.
5. Undertake contract manufacturing.
6. Establish a wholly-owned subsidiary.

❾ Define exchange rates and explain how they affect international business.   *(pp. 110)*

Businesses are affected by fluctuating exchange rates, the rates at which currencies are converted into another currency, every day. Transactions between international companies not only have to specify what each side will be paid but also in which currency. **Currency appreciation**, an increase in the exchange rate value of a nation's currency, causes the relative price of imports to fall as the relative price of exports rises. **Currency depreciation**, a decrease in the exchange rate value of a nation's currency, has the opposite effect on the relative prices of exports and imports. A weak currency causes exports to become cheaper and imports to become more expensive.

⑩ **List the economic factors and challenges that play a role in conducting business on a global scale.** *(pp. 110–113)*

A **trade deficit**, or unfavourable balance of trade, exists when the value of a country's imports exceeds the value of its exports. A strong Canadian dollar may cause a trade deficit because a strong dollar can cause export prices to rise and import prices fall. A **trade surplus**, or favourable balance of trade, occurs when the value of a country's exports exceeds the value of its imports.

Most countries operate under a **freely floating (or flexible) exchange rate system**, a system in which the global supply and demand for currencies determine exchange rates.

Many developing countries have a **nonconvertible currency**, a currency that can't be converted into another currency in the foreign exchange market.

Companies must also consider how to adapt their products for sale in developing nations, how certain government policies might affect their business, and how the socio-economic factors of an area influence the types of products they sell.

⑪ **Summarize the socio-cultural, political, legal, and ethical challenges to conducting business in a global marketplace.** *(pp. 113–115)*

Culture—the complex set of values, behaviours, lifestyles, arts, beliefs, and institutions of a population passed on from generation to generation—culture affects all aspects of business, from managing workers and production techniques to marketing and beyond. Attitudes toward time and work, aesthetics, religion, language, political systems, legal systems, and ethical ideals vary from country to country. **Cross-cultural awareness** is an understanding, appreciation, and sensitivity to foreign culture. Most international businesses fail because they suffer from a lack of cross-cultural awareness.

KEY TERMS

absolute advantage   *(p. 98)*
administrative trade
   barriers   *(p. 100)*
balance of payments   *(p. 110)*
balance of trade   *(p. 110)*
capital flight   *(p. 112)*
comparative advantage   *(p. 98)*
contract manufacturing   *(p. 109)*
countertrade   *(p. 112)*
cross-cultural
   awareness   *(p. 113)*
culture   *(p. 113)*
currency appreciation   *(p. 110)*
currency depreciation   *(p. 110)*
dumping   *(p. 103)*
embargo   *(p. 100)*
ethnocentrism   *(p. 113)*

European Union (EU)   *(p. 104)*
exchange rates   *(p. 110)*
exporting   *(p. 95)*
franchisee   *(p. 108)*
franchising   *(p. 108)*
franchisor   *(p. 108)*
free trade   *(p. 100)*
free trade areas or agreements
   (FTA)   *(p. 104)*
freely floating (or flexible)
   exchange rate
   system   *(p. 112)*
General Agreement on Tariffs
   and Trade (GATT)   *(p. 103)*
global strategy   *(p. 107)*
globalization   *(p. 95)*
globalization of markets   *(p. 96)*

globalization of
   production   *(p. 96)*
importing   *(p. 95)*
International Monetary Fund
   (IMF)   *(p. 103)*
joint ventures   *(p. 108)*
licensing   *(p. 108)*
local content
   requirement   *(p. 100)*
multi-domestic
   strategy   *(p. 107)*
near-shoring   *(p. 97)*
nonconvertible
   currency   *(p. 112)*
North American Free Trade
   Agreement (NAFTA)   *(p. 106)*
offshoring   *(p. 97)*

outsourcing   *(p. 98)*
quota   *(p. 100)*
strategic alliances   *(p. 109)*
subsidy   *(p. 100)*
tariff   *(p. 100)*
trade and investment
   barriers   *(p. 98)*
trade deficit   *(p. 110)*
trade surplus   *(p. 110)*
transnational strategy   *(p. 107)*
turnkey project   *(p. 107)*
wholly-owned
   subsidiary   *(p. 109)*
World Bank   *(p. 103)*
World Trade Organization
   (WTO)   *(p. 103)*

CRITICAL THINKING QUESTIONS

1. The text explains that sometimes an international business needs to modify its product to adjust to the specific needs or tastes of the local market. How would a company such as Hewlett-Packard adjust its laptop computers in order to market them to families in developing nations such as India?
2. Think about the technological advancements the world has embraced over the last ten years. The World Wide Web, cellphones, and wireless Internet connections have allowed businesspeople to have mobile offices. How does this technology reduce cultural distance and decrease business costs?
3. What are the advantages of increased competition in the global market? What are the disadvantages? Is foreign competition *always* good for the consumer? Is foreign competition *always* bad for the local business?
4. Review the three basic strategies of international business. Discuss the type of companies that would most likely pursue a global strategy, a multi-domestic strategy, and a transnational strategy.
5. Imagine you own a furniture store in Canada that specializes in handcrafted dining room tables and chairs. You would like to sell your product to countries in Western Europe. What would be a good mode of entering the foreign market for your company?

APPLICATION EXERCISES

1. **Go Shopping.** Select two different luxury cars—one very exclusive and high performance and the other very energy conscious and environmentally friendly. For each car and each manufacturer, investigate where the car is designed, assembled, and where the component parts are manufactured. Submit a summary of your findings.
2. **Check out Foreign Websites.** Go to the website of an international company such as Swedish furniture maker IKEA (www.ikea.com). Under the "select a location" option, choose Canada. Review the site and note the products and the design of the page. Then go back to the home page and choose a different country from Europe, Asia, Caribbean, or the Middle East. Look for differences in the appearance of the website and the products offered. Why do you think these sites are different for each county?
3. **Learning More about Foreign Trade.** Go to www.wto.org to learn more about foreign trade. Click on "Trade Topics" and choose a topic that interests you. Write a paper about the issues surrounding this topic.

4. **Cultural Guidelines.** Knowing how to behave in a variety of countries is critical with increased globalization. Using the materials at <www.kwintessential.co.uk/etiquette/doing-business-in>, select two different countries from very different regions of the world. Review the "Doing Business in . . ." guides for each country. Create a pamphlet for business travellers on the business do's and don'ts for each country.

5. **You're the Trader.** Imagine you're in charge of trading goods for a country. Would you focus on building wealth by selling commodities? Or on developing an industry by purchasing raw materials? Visit <www.imf.org/external/np/exr/center/students/trade/index.htm> and become the trader. Measure your success on the global economics conditions scale.

GLOBAL 500 RESEARCH PROJECT

INSTRUCTIONS

1. Choose a Global 500 company from *Fortune* magazine's annual rankings at http://money.cnn.com/magazines/fortune/global500/.
2. Research:
   a. Obviously, this company is a global organization, so list three countries in which this company has a physical headquarters or manufacturing plant or other facility.
   b. How much revenue did this company generate last year? You may find this not only at the *Fortune* website, but also in a company annual report.
   c. What was its rank in the Global 500 list? In which country did it make the most money? Why?
   d. Has this company had any sort of obstacles it had to overcome when entering a foreign market? Has the company ever made a cross-cultural blunder?
   e. Did this company have to customize or modify its products or services in order to appeal to a specific country's citizens?
   f. Which international business strategy does this company use?
   g. How did this company enter a foreign market: by exporting, franchising, or forming a strategic alliance?
3. Prepare a report and submit it to your instructor.

TEAM TIME

The Devil's Advocate

Read the following Discussion Questions. Which side of the issue do you believe is correct? Form a group with other students in the class who share your belief. As a group, play devil's advocate by creating a case for the opposing side of the issue. Now that you've considered both sides, you're ready to debate the opposition.

DISCUSSION QUESTIONS

1. In the recent wave of globalization, developing countries have become the focus for many international businesses. Is this process of globalization the best way to strengthen developing countries and establish a level playing field or does it keep them under the control of wealthy industries and drive income inequality?
2. Free trade versus protectionism is a heated debate in today's fragile economy. Which is better for the health of the Canadian economy over the next ten years: free trade or protectionism?
3. What types of ethical concerns might a Canadian company be faced with when outsourcing work to foreign countries?

What about child labour, fair wages, or safety in food and drugs? Is there need to be concerned? What is being done?

PROCESS

Step 1. Meet as a group to discuss the issue. Remember that you must build a case for the side you chose. Look for problems with your own personal beliefs to develop a case for your side.
Step 2. Prepare an individual response that supports your side of the issue.
Step 3. Share your response with your group. Think of possible rebuttals for each response. Then alter any responses that can produce a strong rebuttal.
Step 4. Determine who will be the group's primary spokesperson for the debate.
Step 5. Each group will be given five minutes to present its side of the issue. After each group has presented their argument, each team will be given five minutes to prepare a rebuttal and then three minutes to present the rebuttal.
Step 6. Repeat with other groups.
Step 7. After each group has debated, discuss whether anyone's personal view has changed after this assignment.

ETHICS AND RESPONSIBILITY

Outsourcing

Workers in Canada often view outsourcing in a negative light. Many people believe that this practice is a way for companies to make more money by eliminating Canadian jobs. However, outsourcing is sometimes necessary for the survival of a company. Review the following scenario.

SCENARIO

You are the owner of a company that makes industrial sewing machines. Currently, your company's profits are decreasing because your competitors have lower prices. You cannot lower the price of your machines without losing a significant amount of money. The majority of your costs come from labour. You have 2000 employees in your factory, and your company is a primary employer in the region. You could sell your product for one-third of the price if you outsourced half your production to a foreign country. However, this would eliminate one thousand jobs and devastate a community. Also, the country that you would be outsourcing to has a reputation for unsafe working conditions and practices. If you don't outsource some of your production, over time, your company may be unable to compete and you will have to shut down your company.

DISCUSSION QUESTIONS

1. As a business owner, what are the costs and benefits of moving half your production overseas?
2. Do the benefits of outsourcing outweigh the costs? Why or why not?
3. Are there any possible alternatives to consider? What other decision could you make so that each side (domestic and international) benefits?

CLOSING CASE

GE's Company-to-Country Strategy

When Jeffery R. Immelt stepped into the position of CEO of General Electric, he recognized that with the combination of growth in emerging countries with raw material inflation and changes in government, many opportunities were looming. By focusing on these emerging markets, Immelt and GE put themselves in a good position to provide this infrastructure and, eventually, other consumer needs.

While globalization is not a new concept for GE, the company-to-country strategy that Immelt implemented changed the way GE approached the global market. The goal of the company-to-country strategy is to form close business relationships with foreign governments and consumers and tailor products to their needs. GE's company-to-country strategy was exemplified by their involvement in the Beijing 2008 Olympic Games. GE provides a wide range of innovative products and services that are integral to successful Olympic Games. The company has an Olympic partnership, launched in 2005, that continues through the London 2012 Olympic Games. Immelt thought the Games would be a great way to combine the presence of GE's global entertainment franchise (NBC) with the value of its infrastructure technology.[51] GE works closely with host countries to provide infrastructure solutions for Olympic venues, including power, lighting, water treatment, transportation, and security.[52] Immelt commented, "GE's leadership position in the Olympics will create $2 billion of revenues in 2008 and decades of goodwill in China."[53] GE hopes this goodwill will translate into big dollars when it comes to providing for China's increasing growth.

GE has focused a majority of its company-to-country efforts in China. As a country that has seen a significant increase in the population of urban areas, China has an extreme demand for new infrastructure. The company states on its website: "China is a market of tremendous opportunity for GE—particularly for our infrastructure businesses."[54] A growing China will also need more energy, water, security, and health care. GE hopes to build a relationship with China that will allow the company to be a one-stop-shop for all of the country's needs.

GE is not only looking to globalize its market, it also wants to globalize its products. GE's goal is to create products in China for China. Instead of modifying existing products, GE has established a research centre in Shanghai to create innovative products that meet the most pressing needs of the emerging Chinese consumer. This method has been successfully utilized in GE's health care division. Now, GE can provide much-needed equipment such as mobile screening technology and low-cost diagnostic imaging tools to China and other major emerging markets.

GE's traditional customers, such as hospitals that buy defibrillators or car companies that buy lighting systems, cannot provide the type of double-digit growth that Immelt would like to see. By becoming a "familiar face" to consumers in emerging markets, GE is well positioned to become the go-to company for future ventures such as consumer finance. If and when the wealth in developing countries moves down to the working class, these people may look to GE to get financial products and services such as credit cards, loans, and financial advising. To GE, globalization isn't just about reaching more customers; it's about creating more opportunity.

DISCUSSION QUESTIONS

1. Why does GE feel that investing in emerging markets is a good idea? Do you agree with this approach? What problems could GE face by entering emerging markets?
2. What is unique about the company-to-country philosophy? How is it different from just selling GE products to emerging countries?
3. Consider what you've learned about market failure in this chapter. Do you think it is wise for GE to focus on infrastructure in emerging countries as opposed to, say, health care?

MyBusinessLab CHAPTER RESOURCES

MyBusinessLab in an online learning and testing environment that features the perfect study tools to help you master the concepts covered in this chapter. Log in to MyBusinessLab at www.pearsoned.ca/mybusinesslab to test your knowledge of key chapter concepts, participate in simulations modelled on real-world business situations, and explore the following additional practice tools:

- Study Plan
- Audio Chapter Summaries
- Glossary Flashcards
- eText
- BizChat Discussion Boards
- BizSkills Simulation: Going Global
- Decision-Making Mini-Simulation: Global Marketing

Video Case:

To access the Chapter 4 Video Case: Gawker Media: Business in a Global Economy, see the Activities folder in the Assessment section of MyBusinessLab.

Web Case:

To access the Chapter 4 Web Case, see the Activities folder in the Assessment section of MyBusinessLab

5

Entrepreneurship, Small Business, and New Venture Creation

LEARNING OBJECTIVES

After studying this chapter, you should be able to:

1. List the traits of an effective entrepreneur, and describe how these characteristics often lead to business success. (pp. 122–127)

2. Summarize the role of small business within the Canadian economy. (pp. 127–129)

3. Explain why a business plan is crucial to small business success, and describe the factors that lead to small business failure. (pp. 129–131)

4. Describe how resources—including government, banks, associations, business incubators, and advisory boards—provide assistance and guidance to small business owners. (pp. 131–133)

5. Summarize the potential benefits and drawbacks of each major source of small business financing. (pp. 133–134)

6. Outline the advantages and disadvantages of franchising within the context of entrepreneurship. (pp. 134–138)

7. List and explain the advantages and disadvantages of a sole proprietorship. (pp. 138–140)

8. Describe the advantages and disadvantages of a partnership and a partnership agreement. (pp. 140–142)

9. Explain how a corporation is formed, and how it compares with sole proprietorships and partnerships. (pp. 142–143)

10. Describe the characteristics of non-profit corporations and co-operatives. (pp. 143–145)

11. Summarize the different types of mergers and acquisitions and explain why they occur. (pp. 145–146)

whyhire.me

OPENING DISCUSSION: STARTING A NEW BUSINESS

The WhyHire.me Innovation

As Facebook, LinkedIn, Twitter, and myriad other online social media become increasingly prevalent, more employers are scrutinizing these networking sites to screen potential employees. In a 2009 CareerBuilder survey, 45 percent of the 2600 employers surveyed reported that they research job candidates through social media, which was a huge increase from the 22 percent reported in 2008.[1] Because of content found on social networking sites, 35 percent of employers reported that they chose *not to hire* candidates while 18 percent chose *to hire* candidates. Obviously, it is becoming imperative for job seekers to ensure their online image is not diminishing their job opportunities.

While teaching career positioning to a marketing class in 2008, Patti Church realized that students needed to start thinking about this topic sooner than later. At the same time, Andy Church and Robert Saric were discussing the value of having an established online personal brand when looking for employment after noticing the tremendous positive impact it had on their own job search efforts. Patti brought to Robert's and Andy's attention the point that many university and college students did not realize how transparent they are on the Web. The three entrepreneurs formed a legal partnership and set out to develop a social media tool that would not only educate students about professional personal branding but also provide a venue whereby students could safely build an online career portfolio to showcase their skills, abilities, and knowledge; establish a positive online reputation; and proactively position themselves to get hired! It was time to start using digital tools for a digital generation.

Their efforts resulted in WhyHire.me, a career success platform where students can create a professional and unique online brand presence.[2] As head of curriculum design, Patti leads the development of learning materials and overall student learning experience. With his considerable experience in education technology 2.0, stakeholder management, and growing global

(continued)

brands for publishers, Andy is responsible for the development of product requirements and go-to-market planning. Robert—a right-brained engineer and head of digital—is responsible for the strategy and development of all online career success services and solutions.

Additional WhyHire.me Facts (as of 2011):

- WhyHire.me has more than 2700 registered students and is being used by Algonquin College (Ottawa), Memorial University (St. John's), Centennial College (Toronto), and Carleton University (Ottawa).
- The entrepreneurial team funded the new venture from personal capital, up-front money paid by their first client in support of developing the prototype, and government grants.
- WhyHire.me's mission statement is "To create a safe learning space for post-secondary students to experiment and learn about the power of social media as a personal marketing tool."[3]
- The ongoing development process will never stop. The team is constantly applying user feedback to consider possible system enhancements, developments, and new features offered by the open-source community.
- Each entrepreneurial team member is working two jobs. At different times, each of them has a different emphasis on WhyHire.me and their other contract work. It is a delicate balancing act when self-financing your own business.

- The entire back-end infrastructure is leased on a monthly basis. Open-source tools, methods, and technologies are leveraged. Currently, there is no patent or copyright.
- Sales and marketing are done by all three team members, but contractors are used for various functions, including accounting, legal, graphic design, specialty programming, and sales lead generation.
- The entrepreneurial team is not being paid because all revenue goes toward programming and other contracting costs.
- Social media (i.e., Twitter, blogging, social channels) and personal selling have been the entrepreneurial team's primary marketing tools and have opened the doors to the clients they currently have.

Patti Church says, "It's very hard to stay ahead of the competition especially when there are free tools in the marketplace which people often compare us to. Understanding our positioning is key and being able to clearly communicate it is important also."[4]

DISCUSSION QUESTIONS

1. Visit the WhyHire.me website and compare this social media tool to others. Perform a PEST analysis for WhyHire.me (see Chapter 1). Do you think this was a good business idea? What are the risks?

2. Do you think WhyHire.me could become as popular as LinkedIn or Facebook? Why or why not? What can these partners do to grow their business?

3. What types of issues or problems do you think these entrepreneurs have had to deal with or will have to deal with?

ENTREPRENEURSHIP: WHAT'S IN IT FOR ME?

The Traits of Successful Entrepreneurs

List the traits of an effective entrepreneur, and describe how these characteristics often lead to business success.

Entrepreneurs are people who assume the risk of creating, organizing, and operating a business.

An **opportunity niche** is a need in the marketplace that is not being adequately fulfilled.

What is an entrepreneur? We've all heard of Starbucks, Nike, and Microsoft, but you probably don't associate these big-name companies with small business. But at one point, each of these companies was a small business started by **entrepreneurs**—people who assume the risk of creating, organizing, and operating a business. Not all small businesses are entrepreneurial. What makes a new venture entrepreneurial is that the idea behind the business is innovative or change-oriented. Entrepreneurs most often start a business to satisfy an **opportunity niche**—a need in the marketplace that is not being adequately fulfilled.

The brothers who started McDonald's spotted an opportunity niche. Realizing that the hamburger was the bestseller in their California restaurant, they created an assembly line that allowed them to produce burgers quickly and inexpensively, and business boomed. It expanded even more when Ray Kroc, who was selling milkshake machines in California, convinced the brothers not only to use his milkshake machines but also to let him open another McDonald's restaurant in Chicago. Seeing the opportunity niche in fast food, Kroc later bought the McDonald's restaurants from the McDonald brothers.

The company now operates more than 32 000 restaurants in 117 countries, generating more than US$20 billion in revenue annually.[5]

What are the traits of successful entrepreneurs?   Wayne

Huizenga started Waste Management Inc., now a leader in the waste and environmental services industry, by buying a single garbage truck in 1968. He expanded the company by buying other trash collection services, and by 1983, the company had grown into the largest of its kind in the United States. But Huizenga didn't stop there. He also started Blockbuster Video, the nation's largest video rental company, as well as AutoNation, the behemoth automotive dealer.[6] How can some entrepreneurs such as Huizenga begin successful businesses while others have a difficult time getting their ideas off the ground? How do successful entrepreneurs see an opportunity niche and know exactly what they need to do to seize the opportunity and succeed?

Although luck and timing play a large role in entrepreneurial success, research has also shown that successful entrepreneurs:

- are innovative
- take risks
- are motivated to succeed
- are flexible and self-directed
- work well with others and possess good leadership skills
- are "system thinkers," seeing the whole process rather than just individual pieces of it

How are entrepreneurs innovative?   Successful entrepreneurs see problems to be

solved or opportunities that aren't being addressed in the marketplace—they recognize opportunity niches. They also make improvements to existing products or systems, or they introduce something new and make profitable solutions out of problems. Renowned management and business thinker Peter Drucker noted that successful entrepreneurs "exploit change as an opportunity for a different business or a different service."[7] For example, Henry Ford turned his knowledge of engines into the first "horseless carriage," which he later improved to become the Model T.[8] His improvement was not only in creating a new machine but also in developing an assembly line process by which his company could make multiple automobiles more efficiently. Ford's innovative assembly process became the standard for efficient manufacturing. Think about other entrepreneurs and the innovation behind their success. Ben Cohen and Jerry Greenfield of Ben & Jerry's Ice Cream didn't invent ice cream; rather, they capitalized on people's growing desire for high-quality food products and used the best and biggest chunks of nuts, fruits, candy, and cookies in their ice cream.[9] The McDonald brothers learned how to produce good hamburgers quickly and cost-effectively. **Figure 5.1** lists some other important innovations by entrepreneurs in the twentieth century.[10]

FM radio	Polaroid camera	Supercomputer	Portable computer	Digital X-ray	Portable MP3 player
1933	1947	1958	1981	1983	1998

Figure 5.1   20th-Century Entrepreneurial Innovations

How do entrepreneurs take risks?

Being an entrepreneur involves risk, encompassing the risk of failure, the risk of losing one's career, and, of course, financial risks. Because entrepreneurs are often creating new and innovative products, the processes they develop are also often untried and therefore involve risk. Successful entrepreneurs are aware of these risks, recognize that they can influence events but do not have complete control over them, and are willing to accept the knowledge that they may fail. Successful entrepreneurs therefore take calculated risks—that is, they consider the likelihood of success before deciding whether to take a particular risk.

> "If you take risks, you may still fail; but if you do not take risks, you will surely fail. The greatest risk of all is to do nothing.[11]"
>
> —*Roberto Goizueta, CEO of Coca-Cola (1980–1997)*

What makes entrepreneurs motivated to succeed?

Entrepreneurs are motivated by many different factors. Some entrepreneurs are motivated to provide for themselves or their families. These individuals may be driven to pursue multiple ventures before uncovering a successful idea. Other entrepreneurs are motivated to succeed by the personal fulfillment they feel upon successfully launching a business.

Entrepreneurs' keen desire to succeed has led one entrepreneur, Ted Kennedy, to start a company rooted in this notion. Kennedy noticed that many participants in the Ironman Triathlon Challenge were corporate executives. He also noticed that these executive triathletes sought above-average accommodations prior to and during their competition. So he formed CEO Challenges, a company that organizes luxury sports experiences for corporate executives. CEO Challenges provides luxury accommodations the night before a race, ensures family members and friends are positioned alongside the race to have the perfect view of their racer, and offers other amenities an executive might want when competing in physical challenges. Although Kennedy began his company focusing on triathlons, he has since expanded it to offer golf, sailing, tennis, and other competitive adventures to executives.[12]

Why do successful entrepreneurs need to be flexible and self-directed?

Because entrepreneurial ventures are subject to uncertainty and risk, entrepreneurs need to be able to react quickly to new and unexpected situations. And because entrepreneurs are their own bosses, they need to be able to make their own decisions. An entrepreneur must be able to wear many hats, acting as not only the executive but also as the sales manager, financial director, administrative assistant, and mailroom clerk.

Why are people skills and leadership skills important to entrepreneurs?

They may come up with the initial idea behind their business, but entrepreneurs rarely work by themselves. As much as they have

---

Becoming a successful entrepreneur involves a complex blend of skill, savvy, and luck. Before embarking on such an endeavour, however, you'll need to familiarize yourself with a few concepts. Test your entrepreneurial vocabulary with the following **quiz**.

1. "It's all about fulfilling an opportunity niche!" Liza, a budding entrepreneur, exclaims. Liza is likely referring to
   a. a need in the market.
   b. a storage nook.
   c. a sense of belonging.

2. A system thinker is someone who
   a. contemplates the technological side of a business.
   b. focuses on the entire process of turning an idea into a reality.
   c. designs methods of doing things.

3. Micropreneurs are likely to
   a. be petite.
   b. hire thousands of employees.
   c. enjoy running a small business.

4. When you hear the word *gazelle*, you think
   a. antelope.
   b. fast-growing business.
   c. graceful.

Are you confident in your understanding of entrepreneurial lingo? Or do you need a primer in the use of these terms? Whatever the case, read on for in-depth information on entrepreneur basics, types of entrepreneurs, and what it takes to be an entrepreneur.

the capacity to wear many hats, at some point most entrepreneurs need other people with complementary skills to join them in their venture. If their business expands, they must hire employees and other managers to help them run it. Leadership and communication skills are therefore important traits of successful entrepreneurs who must motivate others to feel as passionately about the entrepreneurial enterprise as they do.

What does it mean for entrepreneurs to be "system" thinkers?   Although entrepreneurs develop companies from an idea, they must focus on the entire process of turning their idea into a business in order to succeed. Successful entrepreneurs are able to see the whole picture when they set up their businesses. They determine how to resolve a problem or to capitalize on an opportunity by developing a solid plan, including the production, financing, marketing, and distribution of the service or product. For example, Pete Slosberg, founder of Pete's Brewing Company, recognized the rise in popularity of microbreweries and brewpubs around the country. Slosberg saw the opportunity and began the process of creating his company not with just an idea but with a system: create a "great beer, a great name, and an interesting label. Have the name and the label to get people to try it for the first time, and a great beer so they keep coming back."[13] In 1998, Pete's Brewing Company had $19 million in sales before being sold to the Gambrinus Company.

Types of Entrepreneurs

Are there different types of entrepreneurs?   Beyond the traditional entrepreneurs described in the previous sections, other entrepreneurial categories have begun to crop up, including:

- lifestyle entrepreneurs
- micropreneurs
- growth entrepreneurs
- intrapreneurs

What are lifestyle entrepreneurs?   **Lifestyle entrepreneurs** look for more than profit potential when they begin their business. Some lifestyle entrepreneurs are looking for freedom from corporate bureaucracy or the opportunity to work at home or in a location other than an office. Others are looking for more flexibility in work hours or travel schedules.

What are micropreneurs?   **Micropreneurs** start their own business but are satisfied with keeping the business small in an effort to achieve a balanced lifestyle. For example, a micropreneur might open a single restaurant and be satisfied with running only that one restaurant, instead of expanding as Ray Kroc did with the McDonald brothers' restaurant. Micropreneurs, or small-business people, have no aspirations of growing large and/or thiring hundreds or thousands of employees. Businesses such as dog-walking services, painters, and special-occasion cake bakers would all be considered micropreneurial opportunities.

What are growth entrepreneurs?   **Growth entrepreneurs** strive to create fast-growing businesses and look forward to expansion. The companies that these types of entrepreneurs create are known as gazelles. Typically, a gazelle business has at least 20 percent sales growth every year for five years, starting with a base of at least $100 000.[14] It is hard to recognize a gazelle business during its rapidly growing period, though companies such as eBay and Google can clearly be identified in retrospect as having been gazelles in their early years.

What are intrapreneurs?   You don't necessarily have to leave your company to have an entrepreneurial experience. Some companies are fostering **intrapreneurs**—employees who work in an entrepreneurial way within the organizational environment. At the home appliance company Whirlpool, for example, developing intrapreneurs is an important part of corporate success. The company's success depends on producing creative solutions to household problems. Instead of relying solely on the traditional research and development (R&D) process, Whirlpool management is tapping the creative juices of

top10

Canada's Top Entrepreneurial Cities (2010)

1. Grande Prairie (AB)
2. Lloydminster (AB/SK)
3. Saskatoon (SK)
4. Prince Albert (SK)
5. Kelowna (BC)
6. Edmonton (AB)
7. Red Deer (AB)
8. Parksville (BC)
9. Saint-Georges (QC)
10. Wood Buffalo (AB)

Source: Ted Mallett and Queenie Wong, "Communities in Boom: Canada's Top Entrepreneurial Cities," Canadian Federation of Independent Business, http://www.cfi b-fcei.ca/cfi b-documents/rr3206. pdf, Accessed May 3, 2011.

Lifestyle entrepreneurs look for more than profit potential when they begin their business.

Micropreneurs start their own business but are satisfied with keeping the business small in an effort to achieve a balanced lifestyle.

Growth entrepreneurs strive to create fast-growing businesses and look forward to expansion.

Intrapreneurs are employees who work in an entrepreneurial way within the organizational environment.

On Target

Facebook's Mark Zuckerberg

When Mark Zuckerberg, a Harvard student, came up with the idea for Facebook, he didn't realize that he was spearheading a billion-dollar organization. The idea behind "The Facebook," as it was originally called, was to provide a forum for students on the Harvard campus to network and display pictures of themselves and their friends. The site was launched February 4, 2004, and within a month, half of

the undergraduates on the Harvard campus were users of the site. Expansion came quickly, as Dustin Moskovitz and Chris Hughes joined Zuckerberg to help promote the site. Within two months, the entire Ivy League was included in the Facebook network. In September 2005, these entrepreneurs decided to allow high schools to join the network. Finally, on September 11, 2006, the public was allowed to join Facebook, so long as all potential members had a valid e-mail address and were at least thirteen years old.

Zuckerberg's brainchild has become so successful that he reportedly turned down a US$750 million offer to purchase Facebook. Media giants such as Google and Yahoo! have been attempting to outbid each other for ownership of Facebook, but Zuckerberg claims that he is not interested in parting with his creation. And why should he be? The site has more than 70 million active users worldwide and is constantly expanding![15]

Discussion Questions

1. Why do you think Facebook is so popular? Is it without problems?
2. How was Facebook able to grow so quickly? What marketing strategy was used?
3. Research Mark Zuckerberg on the Internet and read about the history of Facebook. What characteristics does Mark have that relate to those of entrepreneurs?

their employees by encouraging them to generate ideas that will enhance the company's existing products. Although employees are not separately compensated for their ideas, they are pleased that the company asks for their ideas and have responded enthusiastically. By the end of the first year of the program, sixty ideas were in the prototype stage and 190 were close to entering the marketplace.[16,17]

BizSkills Simulation: Small Business and the Entrepreneur. Located in MyBusinessLab.

What It Takes To Be an Entrepreneur

How do I know if I would be a good entrepreneur? Look at the list of entrepreneurial traits described earlier in this section. Do you have these traits? If so, you may have what it takes to be an entrepreneur. However, if you don't possess all these traits, it doesn't preclude you from starting your own business and becoming a successful entrepreneur. If you have an idea and really want to make it happen, you might want to think about assembling an entrepreneurial team.

An **entrepreneurial team** is a group of qualified individuals with varied experiences and skills that come together to form a new venture.

What is an entrepreneurial team? An **entrepreneurial team** is a group of qualified individuals with varied experiences and skills that come together to form a new venture. The skills of the entrepreneurial team members complement one another so that as a group the team has the necessary skills and traits to manage a successful project.

Entrepreneurial teams are also great for those who want to run their own business but perhaps lack the personal experience. For example, many university, college, and business school students form entrepreneurial teams to get their first project launched. There are several examples of people who met in school and began to work on projects together that turned out to be successful businesses. Students from Stanford University have come together to create well-known companies such as Google, Hewlett-Packard, Cisco, Imagen, and Yahoo!.

Perhaps you're part of an entrepreneurial team, an employee in an intrapreneurial company, or prefer to go it alone. Maybe you want to keep your business small or expand it like McDonald's. Entrepreneurial opportunities exist if you're up to the challenge.

Look back at the quiz at the beginning of the section. How did you do? As you've learned, opportunity niches, system thinking, micropreneurship, and gazelle businesses are just a few of the concepts that budding entrepreneurs must consider before starting their businesses. Which of these business ideas appeals to you most?

SMALL BUSINESS, THE RISKS, AND WHERE TO GET SUPPORT

Small Business and the Economy

What role do small businesses play in the economy? Although starting your own small business might not be the answer to all your problems, it can mean independence, control, and flexibility. For many people seeking a new opportunity, it's a promising and attractive option. In addition, many new small businesses today are founded to solve a unique problem with an innovative solution and ultimately to provide a specialized service to other corporations. Small businesses often fill a niche that large companies cannot.

As a whole, small and medium-sized businesses in Canada play a major role in the economy. The **Canadian Federation of Independent Business (CFIB)** is an advocacy organization representing more than 108 000 small and medium-sized enterprises. The CFIB's criteria when identifying a **small or medium-sized enterprise (SME)** is that an SME is a business that is independently owned and operated and has fewer than 500 employees.[18] The size of a business can be defined in many ways, such as by the value of its annual sales or shipments, its annual gross or net revenue, the size of its assets, or by the number of employees. Industry Canada defines small business as a company with fewer than 100 employees if operating in the goods-producing sector and fewer than 50 employees if operating as a service-producing firm. If a company employs 50 to 499 people, it is considered medium-sized. Businesses with less than five employees are considered micro-sized.[19] Institutions define small businesses differently depending on their needs; for example, Export Development Canada defines small business as companies that export less than CDN$1 million, and the Canadian Bankers Association defines small business as companies that qualify for loans of less than CDN$250 000. Small and mid-sized enterprises are essential to Canadian society and its economy. SMEs play a role in shaping local communities, creating new jobs, and serving consumers. As of 2009, 98 percent of Canadian businesses had fewer than 100 employees, small businesses employed approximately 48 percent of the total labour force in the private sector, and roughly 25 percent of all Canadian small businesses were in the goods-producing industry while the remaining 75 percent were in the service industry.[20]

How do small businesses foster innovation? Small companies often introduce new products or procedures that many large businesses do not have the flexibility, time, resources, or inclination to offer. Smaller companies are also often better poised to take risks, more flexible to explore innovative techniques, and better equipped to push through inventions than larger firms.

The impact of small business innovations is well known in the computer, information science, and communications industries. For example, Michael Dell shook up the computer retail industry by marketing computers directly to customers via the Internet

5

2 Summarize the role of the small business within the Canadian economy.

The **Canadian Federation of Independent Business (CFIB)** is an advocacy organization representing more than 108 000 small and medium-sized enterprises.

A **small or medium-sized enterprise (SME)** is independently owned and operated and has fewer than 500 employees.

rather than through retail stores. By taking direct orders from customers, Dell was able to order parts directly from suppliers on an as-needed basis, freeing his company from carrying large inventories of parts that could become outdated by the next technological innovation. Michael Dell's process improvement gave Dell an advantage over its competitors and helped Dell Computers, then a fledgling start-up company, take the lead in the personal computer retail market. The market responded favourably, and the competition responded in kind. Today, Dell's competitors—Hewlett-Packard, Toshiba, and Sony—all have online customized shopping options.

Other industries have also benefited from the innovative contributions of small businesses. For example, in the biotechnology industry, many small businesses have found innovative solutions to medical issues. One such company is the Insulet Corporation, which recently received an innovation award from the Smaller Business Association of New England for developing the OmniPod. This tiny instrument, weighing a little more than an ounce, sticks to the skin and delivers insulin at a constant rate based on instructions programmed into its wireless companion.[21] The flexibility inherent in small businesses such as these allows them to react more quickly than larger companies to changing market trends and needs. As such, small businesses play an important role in maintaining a healthy economy.

How do small businesses help bigger companies?

Small businesses often operate in co-operative relationships with bigger businesses. In the automotive industry, for example, small businesses are important because they make or supply parts required in large manufacturing processes. In fact, 70 percent of the 15 000 parts that go into a single automobile, such as seats, engine blocks, and bumpers, are provided by independent suppliers.[22] Using small businesses to provide the small and specialized parts not only helps large manufacturers such as GM reduce their costs but also helps with product design and innovation. Many of the latest features in cars, such as heated seats, were first developed by small companies and later sold to large automotive manufacturers.

How do small businesses help consumers?

Small businesses directly provide us with many of the specialized products and services we use every day. Service businesses such as hair salons, landscapers, and dry cleaners, as well as local restaurants, auto repair, and many other "mom and pop" stores provide the services and products larger businesses can't or don't want to provide.

The Impact of Technology on Small Businesses

How has technology affected small business?

Entrepreneurial success stories such as YouTube, MySpace, and eBay illustrate the vast opportunities that technology creates for new business start-ups. In addition to creating entirely new business opportunities, the personal computer and the Internet have made starting a new business much easier. Small businesses can flourish with an Internet connection, a modest website for marketing and communication, and a computer for financial, database, and research needs. Entrepreneur Nick Swinmurn, for example, went on a search for a new pair of his favourite boots one fateful day in 1999 and had a complete lack of success. He decided to form an Internet shoe store, www.shoestore.com. The site started small, but after Swinmurn realized the potential for advancement, he expanded the selection and shipping capacity of the site. The name of the site is now zappos.com, from the Spanish word for shoes, *zapatas*. Swinmurn's small Internet shoe store is now a successful enterprise. More than 80 percent of small businesses have a home page, and nearly 25 percent take sales and orders online. Almost 45 percent of small businesses promote their products on a company website, and one-third of small businesses promote their products through e-mail marketing.[23]

In addition, sites such as alibaba.com and elance.com help with locating product designers, manufacturers, and freelance professionals. New advancements in technology such as blogs, social networks, video hosting sites, smartphone apps, and podcasts offer an inexpensive way for small businesses to market themselves.

Starting Your Own Business

Why would you want to start your own business?
The CFIB conducted a survey of 900 small business owners about the benefits and challenges of owning a small business. Some of the most common reasons most entrepreneurs start a business are as follows:[24]

3

Explain why a business plan is crucial to small business success, and describe the factors that lead to small business failure.

1. *Be Your Own Boss.* Many people starting their own business state that they want to take more control of business decisions than their current position allows. Others know that they wouldn't be satisfied working for someone else.
2. *Fits with Lifestyle.* Many small business owners appreciate the work/life balance that owning their own business affords, and many say running their own business allows them the flexibility to adjust their work to their particular situations.
3. *Make Better Use of Skills.* Some small business owners are motivated by the chance to apply their skills and knowledge better.
4. *Financial Freedom.* Many begin a small business because they want financial independence. Still, most small businesses don't start out as profitable ventures. Traditionally, it takes three to five years for new businesses to become profitable.

5. *Had a Great Idea.* An idea for a new company often starts when someone envisions a product or a service that isn't being offered yet or creates an opportunity from their own obstacles. For example, a father frustrated at watching his autistic child try to communicate with others founded Animated Speech Corporation, a company that develops software-based conversational language learning systems to help autistic children communicate.
6. *Unemployment.* Whereas most individuals start their own business for the reasons mentioned previously, some are pushed into starting their own businesses because they have no other employment opportunities. "Life begins when you get fired," muses Bruce Freeman, owner of ProLine Communications Inc. Three months after being fired, he couldn't think of what to do next. Then, encouraged by a friend, Bruce started his own business. His first client was a company he worked with in his previous job. Now, more than ten years later, he's making more money than he ever could have in his old job.[25]

What are the advantages and disadvantages of starting a new business?
Starting a business is a lot of hard work and comes with no guarantee for success. Small business survival rates in Canada decline over time. About 96 percent of small businesses (1–99 employees) that enter the marketplace survive for one full year, 85 percent survive for three years, and 70 percent survive for five years.[26]

Substantial benefits await the successful entrepreneur, including financial rewards (profit), social rewards (pride, making a difference, worthwhile cause), and independence rewards (work for yourself, at your own pace). With these rewards come potential risks, including:[27]

- *Financial risk.* Substantial financial loss for the entrepreneur (and other stakeholders) and even bankruptcy are possible results of business failure. Business owners also have to take taxes and insurance costs into consideration, such as a health insurance plan to cover employees. They also need liability insurance, which will protect the company in the event of stolen or damaged property or if an employee is injured on the job. For example, if a local jewellery store is broken into and inventory is stolen, liability insurance will cover the cost of the broken window and the stolen property. If the jewellery store is not insured, the business could go bankrupt if the owner can't afford to cover the loss anddamages.
- *Social risk.* Due to the excessive amount of time an entrepreneur has to devote to a new business venture, he or she has less time for family, friends, and social events, so the potential for losing a friend or even a marriage is very real.
- *Career risk.* Entrepreneurs usually quit their jobs to pursue their own start-up, but if things go wrong in the new business venture, it may be difficult to resume a career.

■ *Psychological risk.* Owning your own business can be rather stressful. There is a difference between good stress (eustress), which gives a person enough adrenalin to handle difficult situations in a positive way, and bad stress (distress), which can hurt the entrepreneur and the business. Some factors that may cause distress are having too much worry, working too hard for long periods, and having no one to turn to for help when feeling over-stressed.

While many entrepreneurs feel that the rewards of owning their own business are worth the risks, it's important to be aware of why businesses fail. These reasons include:

■ accumulating too much debt
■ inexperienced management
■ poor planning
■ unanticipated personal sacrifices

Let's look at each of these reasons for failure in more detail.

What causes excessive debt accumulation?
One reason many new businesses fail is that they accumulate too much debt. Most begin a new business borrowing funds. Regardless of whether the loan comes from a bank, an outside investor, or a credit-card company, if the new business does not generate returns quickly enough to begin to pay back the initial loan, there is temptation to take on more loans to keep the business running. Interest on loans can accumulate too, causing an owner to become further entrenched in a potentially unrecoverable situation. What's worse is that some business owners borrow against their personal assets, putting them at risk of personal bankruptcy.

How does inexperienced management lead to failure?
Although entrepreneurs and small business owners are good at coming up with ideas, they may not be great at managing the books and their employees. Many businesses fail due to high levels of debt, which can be a sign of poor financial and business management. It's important that financial statements and budgets are created and adhered to honestly and accurately each month, and that accounts receivable are religiously collected and accounts payable are aggressively managed.

For some businesses, the challenge of managing growth has driven them under when they find that they cannot handle the increase in sales. This was a large part of many dot-com busts in the late 1990s. Many successful e-commerce businesses did not plan for rapid growth and therefore did not have sufficient inventory to fulfill orders when they came in. They also didn't take into consideration the subsequent impact this would have on dealers and retailers who were a part of their distribution channel.

Many business owners ignore the signs of a business beginning to fail or attribute the failure to the wrong reasons. In addition, although owners need to build a team, they can't hand over all control. Good management stays on top of all aspects of the business and makes the tough decisions when necessary. As Nina Riley, CEO and founder of Water Sensations, a company that makes clear-liquid flavour enhancers for water, says, "When things go bad—at the first indication—you gotta nip it in the bud, wrestle it to the ground to fix it. You just can't let it go. If this is your own company, you have to strive to be perfect."[28]

How important is planning to business success?
Accumulating debt and poor business management happen after the business has developed. One of the biggest reasons businesses fail is that there was no formal plan in place to begin with. Planning is sometimes harder than doing because it takes time, brainwork, and requires delaying your personal gratification, but the old adage is true:"businesses that fail to plan, plan to fail." The good news is that poor planning is completely avoidable once you know what kinds of planning you should do before you start your small business, it is just a matter of educating yourself and getting it done

Figure 5.2 A Business Plan Outlines a Company's Goals and Strategies

Many budding business owners, in the excitement of starting something new, neglect to take the "boring" but necessary steps of building an effective business plan.

A **business plan** is a formal document that states the goals of the business as well as the plan for reaching those goals. A business plan should tell the story of your business concept, it is a blueprint for the company, and it is an indispensable tool in attracting investors or obtaining loans. Preparing a business plan takes a lot of time, but it is time well spent because your business plan is an ongoing guide. You use it to acquire start-up capital as well as to assess your company's progress, remembering to update it periodically. A realistic business plan forces you to think critically about your proposed business and reduces your risk of failure. Business plan templates are available online, and the Royal Bank of Canada (RBC) has a very useful site (www.rbcroyalbank.com/sme/) for entrepreneurs starting a business, which includes sample business plans and templates. Business plans vary in format and number of sections. The main components in most business plans are shown in **Figure 5.2** and include the company's mission statement, history, and the qualifications of the owners and management team and any resources they might have to contribute to the business. It also includes a marketing plan, an operational plan, a financial plan, a risk analysis, and identifies the competition and highlights opportunities for success.

> A **business plan** is a formal document that states the goals of the business as well as the plan for reaching those goals.

How important is anticipating personal sacrifices to business success? New businesses also may fail when owners do not adequately anticipate the many personal sacrifices—financial and otherwise—that new business owners are forced to make. For example, the cost of insurance, payroll deductions, and income tax falls solely on the shoulders of the new business owner. Additionally, the amount of time and effort owners must invest in the business, as well as the necessity to take on multiple responsibilities, makes running your own business not for the faint of heart.

Small Business Support

Where do small business owners go for help? There are several sources of help that a small business owner can turn to.

Government of Canada, Canada Business This government resource (www.canadabusiness.ca/eng) offers start-up services for entrepreneurs, including developing

4
Describe how resources—including government, banks, associations, business incubators, and advisory boards—provide assistance and guidance to small business owners.

Bizskills Simulation: Getting Your Business off the Ground. Located in MyBusinessLab.

a business plan, naming and registering a business, buying a business, and financing a business.

Ontario Ministry of Economic Development and Trade, Small and Medium Enterprise Centres   The Small Business Enterprise Centres (SBECs) across Canada provide entrepreneurs with all the necessary start-up and development tools. Each centre can help entrepreneurs determine what they need to do before, during, and after launching their business. Business support exists for specific groups, such as Aboriginal entrepreneurs, women entrepreneurs, and young entrepreneurs (see http://www.ontariocanada.com/ontcan/1medt/smallbiz/en/sb_sbec_en.jsp).

Industry Canada, Businesses   The business section of Industry Canada's website (www.ic.gc.ca/eic/site/ic1.nsf/eng/h_00140.html) offers business owners many resources (i.e., financing program, internship program) and information (i.e., statistics, research, and regulations).

Small Business Association of Canada (SBA-Canada)   A non-profit organization, SBA-Canada (http://vkoopia.com/SBA-Canada) provides growth and development opportunities to small businesses through networking, mentorship, collaboration, self-development, and education.

Entrepreneurs' Organization (EO)   EO (www.eonetwork.org/) provides individual mentoring by connecting business owners with experts in their industry. Although EO is for those who are currently in a viable operation (its requirements are that you must be a founder, co-founder, owner, or controlling shareholder of a business with a minimum of CDN$1 million in annual gross sales and younger than fifty years old), such mentoring services can be helpful to second-stage small business owners.

What kind of training is appropriate for small business owners?   Before jumping into any endeavour, it's always good to have some experience or training. In addition to formal classroom training, you can gain hands-on experience by interning, volunteering, or working part-time for a company in a related field. If opportunities don't exist in a related field, working for a small company in any field will give you first-hand experience in business operations. If you are currently in university or college, look for internship, placement, or co-op opportunities in your industry of interest. Many companies are beginning to realize that hiring interns can be a cost-effective way to get some help.

Business incubators are organizations that support start-up businesses by offering resources such as administrative services, technical support, business networking, and sources of financing that a group of start-up companies share.

One of the biggest overhead costs for many new businesses is the support services required to run the business. **Business incubators** are organizations that support start-up businesses by offering resources such as administrative services, technical support, business networking, and sources of financing that a group of start-up companies share. There are several benefits to incubation beyond sharing a receptionist and copy machine. Business incubators are often run by two- and four-year colleges, universities, and technical schools, and many are sponsored by economic development organizations, cities, or countries. The Canadian Association of Business Incubation (CABI) is a vital national body of organizations dedicated to supporting the growth of new and emerging businesses.

What other support options exist for small business advice and assistance?   As noted earlier, starting up a small business requires owners to take on multiple roles, acting as not only the chief executive officer (CEO) but also as the chief operations officer (COO), chief financial officer (CFO), and any other position that may need to be filled. Many owners quickly realize that their strengths lie in only one or a few of these areas and therefore seek assistance from others. One option is to team up with partners who offer the company strengths that the new owner does not possess and in turn share in its profits and liabilities. Forming an advisory board is another option. An **advisory board** is a group of individuals who offer guidance to the new business owner. Such boards are similar to boards of directors in publicly held companies, except that they generally do not have the authority to make decisions.

An **advisory board** is a group of individuals who offer guidance to the new business owner.

Unfortunately, many business owners don't look for outside help when they start their companies. Thinking that they couldn't afford professional advice, they rely on their own efforts, advice from friends and family, and trial and error. Often, they find that it takes more than a good idea and hard work to make a business successful. Knowing all the resources available to fledgling businesses can help entrepreneurs avoid making the mistakes that eventually lead to the demise of their business. Careful financial decision-making, savvy management, meticulous planning, and the willingness to make significant personal sacrifices all play key roles in a successful business. Knowing when, where, and how to ask for help is also a factor critical to success.

FINANCING CONSIDERATIONS

Cash and Credit

How should business owners finance their ventures?   Drain their personal savings accounts? Beg their family and friends for money? Max out their credit cards? All or none of the above? The options, as well as the potential pitfalls, involved in choosing how to finance a business are numerous. Let's look at the many sources of funding available to small business owners, and discuss the problems associated with some of them.

Where can I get the money to start a business?   Most new ventures need some capital to purchase inventory, secure a physical location, and begin some modest marketing efforts. Most business owners tap into their own personal savings when they initially invest in their business. Friends and family are generally secondary sources of cash. Such contacts are often good sources for financing because, unlike banks or other lending institutions, they often do not require a high rate of return or demand to see the business turn a quick profit. However, it's important when borrowing from friends and family that you treat them as professionally as possible. Make sure you give them a document with an indication of how you intend to pay them back and some sort of a contingency plan if things go wrong. In addition, they should be kept informed of any risks of the venture—upfront and ongoing.

Can I use credit cards to finance my business?   Credit cards offer a convenient way to obtain funds quickly, especially with some of the zero percent financing available. If used wisely, credit cards are a convenient means of acquiring short-term cash, and nearly 50 percent of small business owners use personal credit cards as a source of financing for their small business. However, credit cards should be used only if you can pay the balance completely every month. The risk associated with using credit cards for your initial business financing is the high rate of interest charged on unpaid balances.

Loans and Grants

What if I need more money than I can provide myself?   For larger amounts, new business owners sometimes obtain a loan, borrowing against their own assets, such as the equity in their house or against their retirement account, but the consequences of the business failing are very severe. If you're purchasing an existing business or a franchise, banks and other financial institutions often provide funding. In fact, roughly half of all small businesses use bank loans and lines of credit as part of their financing strategy (discussed in more detail in Chapter 13). These institutions offer start-up loans and lines of credit to help businesses make payroll during slower periods as well as capital loans to buy equipment or machinery. The Business Development Bank of Canada (BDC)

⑤
Summarize the potential benefits and drawbacks of each major source of small business financing.

5

- -

Which of the following is a *do* and which is a *don't*?

When financing a business . . .

1. Do or Don't: Give friends and family who you borrow from a document indicating how and when you intend to pay them back.
2. Do or Don't: Rely heavily on credit cards if you can't pay the balance completely every month.
3. Do or Don't: Borrow against your own assets without fully understanding the potentially severe personal consequences of business failure.
4. Do or Don't: Consider applying for a start-up loan or line of credit from your bank.
5. Do or Don't: Seek financing from a venture capitalist if the idea of relinquishing any control over your business does not appeal to you.

Answers: 1. Do; 2. Don't; 3. Don't; 4. Do; 5. Don't

promotes entrepreneurship by providing highly tailored financing, venture capital, and consulting services to entrepreneurs.

Grants are financial awards usually offered by federal and provincial governments and some private organizations.

Can I apply for grants to help start a business?   **Grants** are financial awards usually offered by federal and provincial governments and some private organizations. The Canadian government realizes that small business is a significant part of our economic growth; therefore, the government's Small Business Finance Centre (www.grants-loans .org/small-business-grants.php) provides the necessary financial resources to facilitate this. The government set aside more than CDN$21 billion in 2011 for small businesses in grants (non-repayable), low or no-interest loans (repayable), tax refunds or credits, guaranteed purchases, financial insurance against business risks, and repayable contributions.[29]

Venture Capital and Other Forms of Financing

What if I need additional sources of funds through investors?   There are other sources of funding for your business, such as venture capital, angel investors, or small business investment companies (SBIC).

Venture capitalists contribute money to your business in return for some form of equity—a piece of ownership.

- *Venture Capitalists.* Unlike banks, where there is a contractual agreement to pay back the money, **venture capitalists** contribute money to your business in return for some form of equity—a piece of ownership. Venture capitalists are very picky about the projects in which they invest. They look for the potential of a public stock offering; therefore, such financing is generally only available to those businesses that have been operating for several years and that have the potential to become larger regional or national companies. To protect their investment, venture capitalists sometimes require that they play an active role in the management of the company, so business owners must be open to the idea of relinquishing control when they seek venture capital funding.

Angel Investors are wealthy individuals who are willing to put up their own money in hopes of a profit return later on.

- *Angel Investors.* **Angel investors** are wealthy individuals who are willing to put up their own money in hopes of a profit return later on. Angel capital fills the gap in start-up financing between "friends and family" who help provide you with start-up money and venture capital. Angel investors are often retired entrepreneurs or executives who may be interested in angel investing for reasons that go beyond purely monetary returns.

Small Business Investment Companies (SBIC) are private venture capital firms that make equity capital or long-term loans available to small companies.

- *SBIC Program.* If venture capital is not available or suitable, an alternative is the **Small Business Investment Company (SBIC) program**. SBICs are private venture capital firms that make equity capital or long-term loans available to small companies. Canada's Venture Capital and Private Equity Association (CVCA) represents the majority of private equity companies in Canada, with more than 1800 members.

Keep in mind that, to protect their investments, outside investors often are looking for some controlling or managerial role in the business. Funding a business is a task fraught with challenges and difficult decisions. When a great deal of money is on the line, the stakes—personal, professional, and financial—are quite high. Thorough research and careful planning are essential to navigating these tricky issues. By understanding the available options and being prepared to deal with financial predicaments, business owners give themselves the best chance at success.

A **franchise** is a method of doing business whereby the business (the **franchisor**) grants the buyer (the **franchisee**) the right to use its brand name and to sell its goods and services for a specified time.

BUYING A FRANCHISE OR AN EXISTING BUSINESS

Buying A Franchise

Outline the advantages and disadvantages of franchising within the context of entrepreneurship.

What is a franchise?   A **franchise** is a method of doing business whereby the business (the **franchisor**) grants the purchaser (the **franchisee**) the right to use its brand name and to sell its goods and services for a specified time. In return, the franchisee provides a share of the income back to the franchisor. Franchising is one of the more popular business venture concepts within Canada. According to the Canadian Franchise Association (CFA)—which promotes excellence in franchising and educates Canadians about franchising, specific franchise opportunities, and proper due diligence—in April 2011, there were 78 000

Table 5.1 Helpful Websites for Potential Franchisees

www.betheboss.ca	BeTheBoss.ca is an information and resource directory for buying a franchise in Canada.
www.cfa.ca	The Canadian Franchise Association (CFA) educates Canadians about franchising, specific franchise opportunities, and proper due diligence.
www.canadabusiness.ca/eng	Canada Business offers government services for entrepreneurs, information about grants and loans, and links to many other resources.
www.entrepreneur.com/franchises/index.html	Entrepreneur.com's Franchise Zone allows users to search a directory of franchising opportunities and provides tips on buying a franchise. This site also ranks the top franchises in terms of growth, cost, global appeal, and other aspects.
www.franchise.org	The International Franchise Association provides answers to frequently asked questions about franchising and resources for potential and current franchisees. This site also hosts a directory of franchising opportunities in various industries.
www.franchiseinfo.ca	*Canadian Business Franchise Magazine* (online edition) offers a unique, behind-the-scenes look at those entrepreneurs who have embraced the franchise lifestyle.

Failproof Canadian Franchises (2011)

Name	Initial Investment
1. Tim Hortons	$430 000–$480 000
2. McDonald's	$300 000
3. Canadian Tire	$125 000, plus 25% of inventory value
4. Subway	$80 001–$240 000
5. Sports Experts	$600 000
6. Second Cup	$300 001–$450 000
7. M&M Meat Shops	$350 000
8. Harvey's	$500 000
9. Shoppers Drug Mart/ Pharmaprix	$0
10. Pizza Pizza	$30 000–$350 000

Source: Ryan Barnett, "Top 10: Failproof Canadian Franchises," *AskMen.com*, http://ca.askmen.com/top_10/entertainment/top-10-failproof-canadian-franchises_1.html, Accessed May 4, 2011.

franchises (units) in Canada[30] and nearly 1100 registered franchise opportunities (franchise systems).[31] The CFA has more than 500 franchise systems in membership, which represent some of Canada's best known brands, including McDonald's, Tim Hortons, Pizza Pizza, and Canadian Tire.[32] The average term of a franchise agreement in Canada is five years, although, franchise agreements come in several fixed periods, including ten and twenty years. Additionally, franchising provides a great opportunity to do business internationally. **Table 5.1** lists some helpful websites for potential franchisees.

What are the advantages of franchising? For many, franchising is an easier, less risky means of starting a business. Since the franchisor provides much of the marketing and financial tools needed to run the business, all the franchisee is expected to bring to the table is management and marketing skills, time, and money. In addition to a recognized brand name, there are many other advantages of owning a franchise.

- *It is a proven system of operation.* Instead of wading through the muddy waters of new business ownership by themselves, franchisees benefit from the collective experience of the franchise company. The franchisor has determined, through trial and error, the best system of daily operations for the established business. New franchisees can therefore avoid many of the common start-up mistakes made by new business owners since they will be working with standardized products, systems, and financial and accounting systems.

- *There is strength in numbers.* You are not alone when you buy a franchise. Because as a franchisee you belong to a group, you might benefit from economies of scale achieved by purchasing materials, supplies, and services at discounted group rates. In addition, it is often easier to get approval for business loans when running a franchise, as the lending institution views less risk associated with a franchise.

- *Initial training is part of the deal.* The beauty of franchising is that you're in business for yourself but not by yourself. The franchisor offers initial training to ensure a successful store opening and might offer ongoing training if new products or services are being incorporated into the franchise line.

■ *Marketing support is provided.* As a franchisee, you are often given marketing materials generated at the corporate level and have the benefit of any national advertising programs that are created. Although you are expected to run your own local marketing efforts, you have the support of other franchisees in the area to help you in your efforts.

■ *Market research is often provided.* Good franchisors do considerable market research and can generally conclude whether there is demand for the product or service in the area before selling the franchisee a franchise. The franchisor should also help to identify the competition and offer strategies to differentiate the franchise from them.

What are the disadvantages of franchising?   Although buying a franchise provides the franchisee with many benefits, there are some disadvantages too.

■ *Lack of control.* There is not much opportunity to contribute creatively to the franchise since the franchisor often controls the look of the store and the product or service. The franchisee, however, is expected to bring the necessary drive and spirit to make the franchise a success.

■ *Start-up costs.* More than 70 percent of all franchises require more than $50 000 to start. In addition, franchisees must pay a monthly royalty fee to the franchisor. The royalty fees are due regardless of how the business is doing, and can be a huge overhead expense. Other costs the franchisee might incur include real estate purchase or rental, equipment purchase or rental, extra signage, and opening inventory. For example, a Tim Hortons franchise in Canada costs $430 000 to $480 000, with at least $144 000 of this being liquid or cash assets. In addition, a franchisee must have at least $50 000 in start-up cash. Royalty fees of 4.5 percent on gross sales are paid each week, advertising fees of 4 percent on gross sales are paid each month, and rental fees of 8.5 percent of gross sales are paid each month.[33]

■ *Workload.* As with any new business owner, new franchisees shouldn't expect easy hours. However, because you can hire employees to run the day-to-day operations, your time can be spent more on the business development and management of the business.

■ *Competition.* Some franchises do not restrict the location or number of their franchise locations. In those instances, franchisees could experience serious competition not only from another company but also from other franchisees in the same franchise organization. In addition, some frantchises do not offer geographic or demographic studies of the best location to open a new store and instead may expect the franchisee to have completed a good market analysis and be familiar with the surrounding competition.

■ *Share common problems.* If the franchisor or another franchisee is having problems, all franchisees will feel its pain. For example, when a Wendy's restaurant was falsely accused of serving chilli with a human thumb mixed in, business in all Wendy's restaurants plummeted.

What are things to watch out for when considering buying a franchise?   The most common piece of advice offered to anyone interested in buying a franchise is to do homework up front. Although a lot of the start-up process is done for you, you are still buying a business that will require your time and money and is not guaranteed to succeed. **Table 5.2** shows suggested questions to ask the company that you are buying the franchise from (franchisor) and other people who have bought franchises from the company (franchisees) before you take the plunge.

Buying an Existing Business

What are the advantages of buying an existing business?   While buying a franchise is a popular way to begin a business without starting from scratch, another way is to buy a pre-existing business. The decision to get into any form of business ownership must be well thought out. Just as with buying a franchise, buying an existing business has certain advantages.

■ *Ease of start-up.* It's often simpler to buy an existing business than to start one from scratch. For example, there is a reduction in start-up time and energy when you purchase an operational business with no serious problems. This means that

Table 5.2 Questions to Ask before Buying a Franchise

	Questions to Ask the Franchisor	Questions to Ask Other Franchisees
Competition	• What is the competitive advantage of the product/service? • What makes the business more attractive to an owner and more attractive to a customer?	• How is your system better than competitors'? • How does your business match up? • Who are competitors?
Franchise System	• How time tested and standardized is the franchise system? • What franchise system is used and how does it work? • How long has the franchise been in business and what improvements has it made recently?	• How long have you been in business? • Does your location meet your customers' needs? • Who selected the site?
Support and Training	• How much support does the franchisor give the franchisee? • What is the initial and ongoing training? • Are there toll-free help lines, field support, annual meetings, local meetings, purchasing programs, and marketing promotion?	• How is the relationship with franchisor? • How was the initial training, ongoing training, and ongoing support? • How are the marketing, advertising, and promotional programs handled?
Financial Strength	• What is the financial strength of the company and the experience of management? • How much revenue comes from franchise fees and how much revenue comes from royalties? • How has the stock performed?	• Are you pleased with earnings? • Is volume growing?
Franchise Relationships	• How important is the franchisee to the franchise? • How can they describe the relationship with the franchisor? • Have there been lawsuits/arbitration? • If so, how have they been resolved?	• Do you have second thoughts (would you do this again)? • Would you own more units?

Source: Based on "A Checklist of Questions to Answer Before You Buy a Franchise," PowerHomeBiz.com, http://www.powerhomebiz.com/vol2/franchisechecklist.htm.

suppliers, existing staff and management, and equipment and inventory are all in place to help facilitate the transition.

■ *Existing customer base.* An existing business may have a satisfied customer base already in place. If no significant changes are made to drive away current customers, the business can continue to run and provide immediate cash flow.

■ *Financing opportunities.* If the business has had a positive track record, it might be easier to obtain financing to purchase the existing business.

What are the disadvantages of buying an existing business? There are also disadvantages to buying an existing business.

■ *High purchase price.* Because you may need to buy the owner out of the business, the initial purchase price may be high. This can be more than the immediate up-front costs associated with a start-up, but not necessarily any different from a franchise. Although you can easily determine the value of the physical business and its assets, it is more difficult to determine the true value of the previous owner's goodwill—the intangible assets represented by the business's name, customer service, employee morale, and other factors—that might be lost with a change in ownership. Often the intangible assets are overvalued, making the business cost more than it is worth.

Table 5.3   Things to Consider before Buying a Business

Initial Questions to Ask
Why is the business for sale?
What do current customers say?
How much time does the current owner put into the business?
Are there opportunities for growth?
Who is the competition?

Due Diligence Checklist
Get an independent valuation of inventory and equipment.
Have an accountant go over financial statements for the past three years.
Have a lawyer analyze pertinent business documents—property leases, employment contracts, etc.
Talk to suppliers to see if they will continue to supply the business when ownership changes hands.
Check for lingering or festering hazardous waste problems. They'll become your responsibility as the new owner.

- *Inheriting the previous owner's mistakes.* If the previous owner had made some poor choices, you may have to deal with the ramifications. For instance, you might inherit dissatisfied customers, bad debt, and unhappy distributors or purchasing agents. You'll need to work to change the minds of people who have had a bad experience with the previous ownership.
- *Unknown in transition.* There is no guarantee that existing employees, management, customers, suppliers, or distributors will continue to work with the business once new ownership takes over. If staff does stay, you might be inheriting unanticipated problems.

What do you need to check before you buy a business?   Existing businesses are sold for many reasons. Before buying an existing business, make sure you perform **due diligence**—research and analysis of the business to uncover any hidden problems associated with it. You want to avoid buying a company with a dissatisfied customer base or with a large amount of unpaid bills. **Table 5.3** provides a brief checklist of things you should look into before buying a business. Not all businesses for sale have problems. For example, some family-run businesses run out of family members to pass the business on to, the owners, at that point, might be left with no choice but to sell the business. Whether you buy an existing business or franchise or begin a business of your own, you'll be joining a large group of small business owners who make a significant contribution to the Canadian economy.

FORMS OF BUSINESS OWNERSHIP

Sole Proprietorships

List and explain the advantages and disadvantages of a sole proprietorship.

What is it called when one person owns a business?   Whether they intend to run large factories, small retail stores, or e-businesses, entrepreneurs must decide which form of legal ownership best suits their goals: sole proprietorship, partnership, corporation, or co-operative.

A **sole proprietorship** is a business that is owned by one person. A sole proprietorship does not need to register with the government and it is not legally separated from the owner. This means the company's debts are the responsibility of the owner, and the owner pays personal income tax on his or her profits rather than corporate taxes. A sole proprietorship is simpler to operate and is under less government regulation than other businesses, but there is also more risk involved. If the company is sued, the owner is liable. If the company owes a debt that the business can't afford to pay, the creditors can legally collect personal assets, such as funds from the owner's retirement accounts,

Due diligence involves research and analysis of the business to uncover any hidden problems associated with it.

A **sole proprietorship** is a business owned by one person and not protected by limited liability.

BizChat

Explore on MyBusinessLab

What's in a Name?

Naming a business should be fun, but it can be stressful, especially if you make some of the more common mistakes:

Mistake 1 | Involving friends, family, employees, or clients in the naming decision. You want to make the name communicate the key elements of your business, not the combined efforts of your friends and family.

Mistake 2 | Description + Product = Name. Although it seems catchy at the time, the result of company names that try to marry description with product is forced and often trite. A service franchise named QualiServe or a day spa named TranquiSpa ultimately aren't the right choices.

Mistake 3 | Using generic names. Gone are the days when General Electric or ACME Foods work as corporate names. In such highly competitive times when new products or services are fighting for attention, it is best to choose a unique name.

Mistake 4 | Making up a name. While using generic names may not be good, be careful to avoid names that are obscure, hard to pronounce, or hard to spell unless there is solid market research behind it.

Mistake 5 | Using geographic names. Unless you plan to stay local, including a specific geographic name may imply that you won't go beyond that regional territory.

TIP: You might need to hire a company to create a name for you. Acura, Flixx, and Compac are all names that were created by experts.

Discussion Questions

1. Can you think of a company name that you are not fond of? Do you shop there? Do you wonder why the owner gave it that name?
2. Can you think of a company name that is difficult for you to pronounce? Do you think this causes a loss of business for the company?
3. Why do you think some business owners name their companies starting with an "A" or an "AA" or sometimes even an "AAA"? Does this make it easy for customers to remember? Can it be confusing for customers?

---

property, or cars. A sole proprietorship is not protected by *limited liability*, which would require owners to be responsible only for losses up to the amount they invested. **Limited liability** safeguards personal assets from being seized as payment for debts or claims.

> **Limited liability** safeguards personal assets from being seized as payment for debts or claims.

How do I start a sole proprietorship? The minute you begin doing business by yourself—that is, collecting income as a result of performing a service or creating a product—you are operating as a sole proprietor. There are no special forms to fill out, nor any special filing requirements with the federal or provincial government. At a minimum, you might need to obtain local licensing or permits, or you might have to ensure that you're operating in an area zoned for such business activity.

What are the advantages of being a sole proprietor? There are several advantages to forming your business as a sole proprietorship, the first of which is ease of formation. With only one person making all the decisions and no need to consult other owners or interested parties, sole proprietors have greater control and more flexibility to act quickly. Another advantage is that there are no specific corporate records to keep or reports to file, including tax reporting. Since there is no legal distinction between the owner and the business, no separate tax return is required. As a result, the income and expenses of a sole proprietorship flow through the owner's personal tax return. For example, imagine you run a landscaping business during the summer in addition to your regular job. If the lawn mower breaks down and needs to be replaced, that expense could be more than all the earnings you collected, generating a loss for your lawn mowing business. You can subtract that loss from the income earned from your regular job, reducing your income tax obligation.

What are the disadvantages of being a sole proprietor? If the type of business you're running has the potential for someone to sue you because of errors on your part, you may not want to operate as a sole proprietorship. A sole proprietor is personally responsible for all the debts and liabilities of the business. A **liability** is the obligation to

> A **liability** is the obligation to pay a debt such as an account payable or a loan.

pay a debt such as an account payable or a loan. A sole proprietor may also incur a liability if he or she becomes responsible for paying for any damages or personal injuries the owner's employees cause. While there may be an unlimited number of employees in a sole proprietorship, there is also unlimited liability for their actions. **Unlimited liability** means that if business assets aren't enough to pay business debts, then personal assets, such as the sole proprietor's house, personal investments, or retirement plans, can be used to pay the balance. In other words, the proprietor can lose an unlimited amount of money.

Imagine that you're running a catering business, and while you're preparing food in someone's house, the oven catches fire because you forgot to take the egg rolls off the paper tray. You are personally responsible, or liable, for paying for any damages if your business assets are not sufficient to cover the damages. If the damages are severe enough—perhaps your client's entire house burns down—you could lose all your assets, including your own home and savings.

Another drawback of a sole proprietorship is the potential difficulty in borrowing money to help your business grow. Banks will be lending to you personally, not to your business, so they will be more reluctant to lend large amounts, and the loan will be limited to the amount of your personal assets. Other business structures, which will be discussed later in the chapter, are more helpful should you need to raise large amounts of additional money.

> **Unlimited liability** means that if business assets aren't enough to pay business debts, then personal assets, such as the sole proprietor's house, personal investments, or retirement plans, can be used to pay the balance.

❽ Partnerships

> Describe the advantages and disadvantages of a partnership and a partnership agreement.

What are the advantages of bringing in a partner?

Sometimes, running a business by oneself can be a daunting task, and adding one or more owners can help share the responsibilities. A **partnership** is a type of business entity in which two or more owners (or partners) share the ownership and the profits and losses of the business. There are several reasons why joining with someone else in starting a business makes sense. More owners help contribute to both the starting and ongoing capital of the business. Multiple people are involved in partnerships, so there is more time available to increase sales, market the business, and generate income. Sharing the financial responsibility brings on more people who are interested in the company's overall profitability and are as highly motivated as you are to make the business succeed. Therefore, additional owners, unlike employees, are more likely to be willing to work long hours and go the extra mile.

> A **partnership** is a type of business entity in which two or more owners (or partners) share the ownership and the profits and losses of the business.

Adding partners to help share the workload also allows for coverage for vacations, illness, or personal issues. Moreover, if partners have complementary skills, they create a collaboration that can be quite advantageous. Partners can help discuss ideas and projects as well as make the big decisions. For example, if you're great at numbers but hate to make sales calls, bringing in a partner who loves to knock on doors would be beneficial for your business.

> A **general partnership** is similar to the sole proprietorship in that all the (general) partners are jointly liable for the obligations of the business.

The two most common partnership forms include general partnerships and limited partnerships. A **general partnership** is similar to the sole proprietorship in that all the (general) partners are jointly liable for the obligations of the business. The **general partners** are full owners of the business, are responsible for all the day-to-day business decisions, and remain liable for all the debts and obligations of the business. Sometimes, a business can bring on additional "limited" partners, mostly to provide capital and earn a share in the profits, but not to operate the business. **Limited partners** don't participate actively in the business, and their liability is limited to the amount they invested in the partnership. **Limited partnerships** consist of at least one general partner (who has unlimited liability) and one or more limited partners who cannot participate in the day-to-day activities of the business or they will risk the loss of their limited liability status. Limited partnerships can be very complex to form, so it may be worth exploring other business structures before deciding on this strategy.

> The **general partners** are full owners of the business, are responsible for all the day-to-day business decisions, and remain liable for all the debts and obligations of the business.

> **Limited partners** don't participate actively in the business, and their liability is limited to the amount they invested in the partnership.

> **Limited partnerships** consist of at least one general partner (who has unlimited liability) and one or more limited partners who cannot participate in the day-to-day activities of the business or they will risk the loss of their limited liability status.

What are the disadvantages to adding partners?

For every advantage a partner can bring, adding the wrong partner can be equally problematic. Obviously, adding partners means sharing profits and control. A potential partner may have different work habits and styles from you, and if the partner's style isn't complementary, the differences can prove challenging. In addition, as the business begins to grow and change, your partner might want to take the business in a different direction than you do. Like entering into marriage, you want to consider carefully the person(s) with whom you will be sharing your business.

As a form of business ownership, how does a partnership compare to a sole proprietorship?

Partnerships and sole proprietorships are very similar; in fact, the biggest difference between the two is the number of people contributing resources and sharing the profits and the liabilities. It's just as easy to form a partnership as a sole proprietorship. The government does not require any special forms or reports—although some local restrictions may apply for licenses and permits. For example, if you and your brother-in-law form a small partnership called "All in the Family Electricians," before you are able to do business you might have to apply for a license, but you do not need any special papers to create the partnership itself. Also, like a sole proprietorship, partnerships do not file a separate tax return. All profits and losses of the partnership flow directly through each partner's own tax return.

What goes into a partnership agreement?
Although no formal documentation is required to create a partnership, it's a good idea to draw up an agreement. A partnership can begin with a handshake, and many of them do, but it is best for all involved parties that a written document, called a partnership agreement, formalizes the relationship between business partners. Think of a partnership agreement as a business prenuptial agreement. It helps to settle conflicts when they arise and may discourage small misunderstandings from erupting into larger disagreements. Many points can be included in a partnership agreement; however, the following items should always be included in the agreement:

1. *Capital Contributions*. The amount of **capital**, or investments in the form of money, equipment, supplies, computers, and any other tangible thing of value, that each partner contributes to begin the business should be noted in the partnership agreement. In addition, the agreement should also address how additional capital can be added to the business—who will contribute it and whether there will be a limit to a partner's overall capital contribution.
2. *Responsibilities of Each Partner*. To avoid the possibility of one partner doing more or less work than others, or a conflict arising over one partner assuming a more controlling role than others, it's best to outline the responsibilities of each partner from the beginning. Unless otherwise specified, any partner can bind the partnership to any debt or contract without the consent of the other partners. Therefore, it's especially important to spell out the policy regarding who assumes responsibility for entering into key financial or contractual arrangements.
3. *Decision-Making Process*. It is important to consider how decisions will be made. Knowing whether decisions will be the result of mutual consent of all or several partners, or whether just one or two partners will make the key decisions is essential to help partners avoid disagreements. What constitutes a "key" decision should also be defined in the agreement. In a partnership of two, where the possibility of a deadlock is likely, some partnerships provide for a trusted associate to act as a third partner whose sole responsibility is to act as the tiebreaker.
4. *Shares of Profits or Losses*. Not only should the agreement specify how to divide profits and losses between the partners, but it should also specify how frequently this will be done. One partnership agreement might stipulate that the profits and losses will be proportional to each partner's initial contribution to the partnership, whereas another partnership agreement might just split the profits evenly. It's also important to detail how adjustments to the distributions will be made—if any at all—as the partnership matures and changes.
5. *Departure of Partners*. Eventually, the composition of partners will change; original partners will leave and new partners will come aboard. The partnership agreement should have rules for a partner's exit, whether it's voluntary, involuntary, or due to

Capital is investments in the form of money, equipment, supplies, computers, and any other tangible thing of value.

death or divorce. Provisions to remove a partner's ownership interest are necessary so the business does not need to liquidate. The agreement should include how to determine the amount of ownership interest and to whom the departing partner is permitted to transfer his or her interest. It's important to consider whether a partner can transfer his or her ownership solely to the remaining partners or whether individuals outside the existing partnership can buy the departing partner's share.

6. Addition of Partners. The partnership agreement also helps spell out the requirements for new partners entering the partnership. How the profits will be allocated and whether there will be a "junior partner" period during which the new partner can prove him or herself before obtaining full partner status should also be included.

9 Explain how a corporation is formed, and how it compares with sole proprietorships and partnerships.

Corporations

What is a corporation?   When you think of corporations, you might think of large companies such as Canadian Tire, Research In Motion, or Air Canada, but any-sized company can incorporate. A **corporation** is a specific form of business organization that

is a separate legal entity, that is liable for its own debts, and whose owners' liability is limited to their investment in the company. Because a corporation is considered a separate entity apart from its owners, it has legal rights like an individual, so a corporation can own property, assume liability, pay taxes, enter into contracts, and can sue and be sued—just like any other individual. Unlike partnerships and sole proprietorships, *corporations* provide business owners with better protection of their personal assets.

How do corporations raise capital?

Sole proprietorships and partnerships, by their nature, are dependent on their founding owners. When an owner dies or otherwise leaves, the partnership or sole

A **corporation** is a specific form of business organization that is a separate legal entity, that is liable for its own debts, and whose owners' liability is limited to their investment in the company.

Public corporations are companies whose shares of stock are widely held and available for sale to the public.

Private corporations are companies whose shares of stock are held by only a few people and not generally available for sale.

Articles of incorporation lay out the general nature of the corporation, the name of the corporation and its directors, the type and number of shares to be issued, and location of the company's operations.

proprietorship is usually terminated. On the other hand, shareholders own a corporation, so its existence doesn't depend on its founding members. Shares of ownership are easily exchanged, so the corporation will continue to exist should the owner die or wish to sell his or her interest in the business. A corporation is capable of continuing forever, in theory.

Incorporating offers a business greater flexibility when raising money. Banks and venture capitalists are more likely to lend money to a business that is incorporated. In times when greater sources of funds are needed than venture capital or bank loans can raise, a corporation can extend its ownership by "going public"—selling shares of ownership in the corporation to the public on the stock exchange. A stock certificate is tangible evidence of investment and for some investors that is very important. Corporations are said to be **public corporations** when shares of stock are widely held and available for sale to the public—such as Bombardier and Petro-Canada. The stock of a **private corporation** is held by only a few people and not generally available for sale—such as Cirque du Soleil and Pattison.

How is a corporation formed?   If a company intends to do business in more than one province, it must incorporate under the federal Canada Business Corporations Act. If a company intends to do business in only one province, it may incorporate under that province's corporation act. Generally, a corporation files **articles of incorporation** with the government, laying out the general nature of the corporation, the name of the corporation and its directors, the type and number of shares to be issued, and location of the company's operations. Once the articles are approved, the

Figure 5.3 Steps in Forming a Corporation

corporation's directors meet to create bylaws that govern the internal functions of the corporation (see **Figure 5.3**). Specific duties of the board of directors and individual board members, committees, and officers are set by the corporate bylaws. The **bylaws** are the rules of a corporation, established by the board of directors during the process of starting a corporation. All corporations must attach the word "Incorporated" (Inc.), "Limited" (Ltd./Ltée), or "Corporation" (Corp.) to the company name.

Bylaws are the rules of a corporation, established by the board of directors during the process of starting a corporation.

How is a corporation structured?

Shareholders—investors who buy shares of ownership in the form of stock—are the real owners of a corporation. Dividends are payments made by a corporation to its shareholders (discussed in more detail in Chapter 13). When a corporation earns a profit, it can either reinvest that profit in the business (called retained earnings) or it can be paid to the shareholders as a dividend. Many corporations retain a portion of earnings and pay the remainder in dividends. A dividend is allocated as a fixed amount per share; therefore, a shareholder receives dividends in proportion to their shareholdings (the more shares, the more dividends). Shareholders can attend annual meetings, elect a board of directors, and vote on matters that affect the corporation, in accordance with its charter and bylaws. Each share or stock generally carries only one vote. The shareholders elect a **board of directors** to govern and handle the overall management of the corporation. A corporate board has great power and great responsibility: the board must act with the corporation's best interest in mind. The directors set corporate goals and policies, hire corporate officers (e.g., president, vice-president, CEO, CFO, COO, CIO), and oversee the firm's operations and finances.

Shareholders are investors in a corporation who buy shares of ownership in the form of stock.

A **board of directors** is elected by shareholders to govern and handle the overall management of the corporation.

What are the advantages of incorporation?

Aside from the obvious, biggest advantage of the corporate structure of limited liability, continuity is another advantage. In theory, a corporation could continue forever because shares of stock may be sold or passed on the heirs. As mentioned above, they also have an advantage when raising money.

What are the disadvantages of incorporation?

It is costly to incorporate and there are many government regulations. Because a corporation is a separate legal entity, many requirements must be fulfilled in order to maintain the corporate status. For example, all companies must file an annual report and maintain written minutes of annual and other periodic board of director and shareholder meetings. Double taxation is considered a disadvantage of incorporation. **Double taxation** means that the corporation must pay income taxes on its profits and the shareholders must pay personal income taxes on the dividends they receive from the corporation.

Double taxation means that the corporation must pay income taxes on its profits and the shareholders must pay personal income taxes on the dividends they receive from the corporation.

Non-Profit Corporations

Must a non-profit corporation be legally incorporated?

Some businesses don't fit the mould of sole proprietorship, partnership, or corporation. When this occurs, business owners might form non-profit organizations or co-operatives. Legally, a non-profit corporation is an incorporated business that does not seek a net profit and instead utilizes revenue available after normal operating expenses for the corporation's declared social or educational goals (as discussed in Chapter 1). Incorporation is not necessary, but to receive limited liability protection, a non-profit organization must file incorporation papers and become established as a separate legal entity.

 Describe the characteristics of non-profit corporations and co-operatives.

Similar to a for-profit corporation, a non-profit corporation is required to hold board of director meetings and to keep complete books and records. The greatest difference from a for-profit corporation is that a non-profit organization cannot be organized for any person's private gain. Non-profit organizations do not issue shares of stock, and their members may not receive personal financial benefit from the organization's profits (other than salary as an employee). However, some non-profit organizations do provide employee benefits such as health insurance. In addition, should the not-for-profit dissolve, the organization's assets must go to a similar non-profit group.

Do non-profit corporations generate profits?   Non-profit corporations are not in business to generate a profit, unlike for-profit organizations; however, they still need to generate even a modest profit to survive. Non-profit organizations generate their revenue primarily through fundraising and donations. To maintain their tax-exempt status, non-profit organizations must demonstrate that a substantial portion of their income or revenue is spent on services to achieve their goals. Non-profit corporations must apply for charitable status to benefit from tax-exempt status and to issue tax-deductible receipts to donors. The Canada Customs and Revenue Agency (CCRA) (formerly Revenue Canada) is the government department responsible for granting organizations charitable tax status.

What are the benefits of being tax-exempt?   As a corporation that has received tax-exempt status, the donations that are the organization's primary source of revenue are tax-deductible to the donor, which encourages funding. Other benefits of tax-exempt status are that the non-profit is exempt from paying most federal and/or provincial corporate income taxes and may be exempt from provincial sales and property taxes. Such organizations are able to apply for grants and other public or private distributions, as well as discounts on postal rates and other services.

Co-Operatives

How do co-operatives differ from the other forms of business ownership?

A **co-operative** is a business owned and governed by members who use its products or services, not by outside investors.

Co-operatives differ from other forms of business because they have a different purpose, control structure, and allocation of profit. A **co-operative** is a business owned and governed by members who use its products or services, not by outside investors. The primary purpose of co-operatives is to meet the common needs of their members. For instance, Mountain Equipment Co-op is Canada's largest retailer co-operative, which sells outdoor gear, clothing, and offers services to its members. Co-operatives exist in virtually every sector of the economy, from agriculture, retail, and financial services to housing, child care, funeral services, and renewable energy. The Canadian Co-operative Association provides leadership to promote, develop, and unite co-operatives in Canada and around the world. See **Table 5.4** for a comparison of the forms of business ownership.

How are co-operatives structured?   Co-operatives depend on their members to volunteer for projects supported by the co-op and serve on boards and committees. The control structure in a co-operative differs from that of a corporation in that each member

Table 5.4   Comparison of Forms of Business Ownership

Characteristic	Sole Proprietorship	Partnership	Corporation	Co-operative
Ease of formation	High	High	Medium	Medium
Continuity	Low	Low	High	High
Protection against liability	Low	Low	High	High
Tax advantages	High	High	Low	High
Ease of raising money	Low	Medium	High	High
Government regulation	Low	Low	High	Medium

receives one vote, not one-vote-per-share. This helps co-operatives serve the common need rather than the individual need. Profits are shared among the members based on how much they use the co-op, not on how many shares they hold. Some people may consider the democratic voting arrangement and dividends based purely on patronage a disadvantage and may be discouraged from forming or joining a co-operative.

Business Combinations: Mergers and Acquisitions

What are mergers and acquisitions?   Sometimes, in the evolution of a business or in response to market forces, companies seek opportunities to expand by adding new product lines, spreading out into different geographic areas, or growing the company to increase their competitive advantage. Often product or market expansion is done gradually by slowly adding new product lines or penetrating new areas. However, it takes time and investment to research and develop new products or to locate and build in new areas. Often, especially to remain competitive, expansion needs to happen more quickly. In that case, it's easier to integrate another established business through the process of mergers or acquisitions.

A **merger** occurs when two or more firms combine to form one new company, which often takes on a new corporate identity. Generally, a merger implies that the two companies involved are about the same size and have mutually agreed to form a new combined company. When a "merger of equals" happens, both merging companies cease to exist and one new company takes over. For example, in 2009, Suncor Energy merged with Petro-Canada, stating that by merging, the two oil companies would create Canada's largest energy company, which would provide protection against potential foreign buyouts.[34] Under the *Competition Act*, mergers of all sizes and in all sectors of Canada's economy are subject to review by the Competition Bureau to determine whether they will likely result in a substantial lessening or prevention of competition. For instance, when TD Bank wanted to acquire Canada Trust in 2000, the Competition Bureau concluded that the merger would likely lessen competition and affect consumers negatively. To remedy the bureau's concerns, TD Bank proposed to sell the branches in the identified problematic markets and either convert its Visa credit card portfolio to MasterCard or sell the Canada Trust MasterCard credit portfolio. The bureau announced that the government had approved the Canada Trust acquisition contingent upon the proposed remedies being fully implemented.[35]

An **acquisition**, on the other hand, occurs when one company or investor group buys a corporation and the identity of the acquired company might be lost. Often the purchased company ceases to exist, and it operates and trades under the buying company's name. A company can also acquire divisions or subsidiaries of another firm. When the acquisition is supported by the target company's management and board of directors, it is called a **friendly takeover**, but if the takeover goes against the wishes of the target company's management and board of directors, it is called a **hostile takeover**. Hostile takeovers are usually accomplished through a *proxy fight*, whereby the acquiring company quietly purchases enough stock on the open market to gain a controlling interest in the company and affect a change in management. Another method used in hostile acquisition occurs through a *tender offer*, where the acquiring firm offers to buy the target company's stock at a price higher than its current value, which is meant to induce shareholders into selling.

Why do mergers and acquisitions occur?   *Synergy* is the business buzzword often used to justify a merger or an acquisition. **Synergy** is the achieved effect when two companies combine and the result is better than each company could achieve individually. Synergistic value is created when the new company can realize operating or financial economies of scale (the cost advantage that a business obtains due to expansion). Combined firms often lower costs by trimming redundancies in staff, sharing resources, and obtaining discounts accessible only to a larger firm. Often, companies join to gain a greater competitive advantage or become the dominant force in their market.

Are there different types of mergers?   The rationale and strategy behind every merger is different, but, as illustrated in **Figure 5.4**, there are some consistencies, distinguished by the relationship between the two companies that are merging:

11
Summarize the different types of mergers and acquisitions and explain why they occur.

5

A **merger** occurs when two or more firms combine to form one new company, which often takes on a new corporate identity.

An **acquisition** occurs when one company or investor group buys a corporation and the identity of the acquired company might be lost.

A **friendly takeover** occurs when the target company's management and board of directors support the acquisition.

A **hostile takeover** occurs when the takeover goes against the wishes of the target company's management and board of directors.

Synergy is the achieved effect when two companies combine and the result is better than each company could achieve individually.

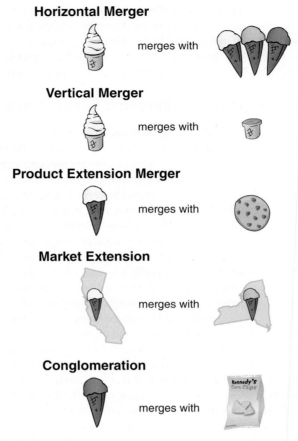

Figure 5.4 Different Types of Mergers

Companies merge for different strategic reasons. Sometimes companies merge to enter new markets, whereas others want to expand into new fields and save costs.

- *Horizontal merger:* two companies that share the same product lines and markets and are in direct competition with each other, such as a soft drink company and a mineral water company.
- *Vertical merger:* two companies that have a company/customer relationship or a company/supplier relationship, such as Walt Disney and Pixar or eBay and PayPal.
- *Product extension merger:* two companies selling different but related products in the same market, such as the 2005 merger between Adobe and Macromedia.
- *Market extension merger:* two companies that sell the same products in different markets, such as Morrison and Safeway supermarkets. Although both companies are in the United Kingdom, Morrison is mainly in Great Britain and Safeway is mainly in Scotland.
- *Conglomeration:* two companies that have no common business areas merge to obtain diversification, such as Citicorp, a banking services firm, and Travelers Group Inc., an insurance underwriting company, which combined to form one of the world's largest financial services group, Citigroup Inc.

Are there disadvantages with mergers?   Although cost-cutting may be the initial primary focus of some mergers, revenues and profits ultimately suffer because day-to-day activities are neglected. Additionally, corporate cultures may clash, and communications may break down if the new division of responsibilities is vague. Conflicts may also arise due to divided loyalties, hidden agendas, or power struggles within the newly combined management team. Employees may be nervous because most mergers result in the elimination of jobs and some may actually leave the company, feeling their jobs are in jeopardy, seeking a more stable environment.

CHAPTER SYNOPSIS

❶ List the traits of an effective entrepreneur, and describe how these characteristics often lead to business success. *(pp. 122–127)*

Successful entrepreneurs:
- are innovative
- take risks
- are motivated to succeed
- are flexible and self-directed
- work well with others and possess good leadership skills
- are "system thinkers," seeing the whole process rather than just individual pieces of it

Successful entrepreneurs see problems to be solved or opportunities that aren't being addressed in the marketplace—they recognize **opportunity niches**. They also make improvements to existing products or systems, or they introduce something new and make profitable solutions out of problems.

❷ Summarize the role of small business within the Canadian economy. *(pp. 127–129)*

Small and medium-sized enterprises (SMEs) in Canada play a major role in the economy: in shaping local communities, creating new jobs, and serving consumers. As of 2009, 98 percent of Canadian businesses had fewer than 100 employees; small businesses employed approximately 48 percent of the total labour force in the private sector; and roughly 25 percent of all Canadian small businesses were in the goods-producing industry while the remaining 75 percent were in the service industry.

Small companies often introduce new products or procedures that many large businesses do not have the flexibility, time, resources, or inclination to offer. Smaller companies are also often better poised to take risks, more flexible to explore innovative techniques, and better equipped to push through inventions than larger firms. Small businesses directly provide us with many of the specialized products and services we use every day.

❸ Explain why a business plan is crucial to small business success, and describe the factors that lead to small business failure. *(pp. 129–131)*

A **business plan** is a formal document that states the goals of the business as well as the plan for reaching those goals. A business plan should tell the story of your business concept, it is a blueprint for the company, and it is an indispensable tool in attracting investors or obtaining loans. Preparing a business plan takes a lot of time, but it is time well spent because your business plan is an ongoing guide. You use it to acquire start-up capital as well as to assess your company's progress, remembering to update it periodically. A realistic business plan forces you to think critically about your proposed business and reduces your risk of failure.

Businesses fail because of the following reasons:
- accumulating too much debt
- inexperienced management
- poor planning
- unanticipated personal sacrifices

❹ Describe how resources—including government, banks, associations, business incubators, and advisory boards—provide assistance and guidance to small business owners. *(pp. 131–133)*

Government of Canada, Canada Business

This government resource (www.canadabusiness.ca/eng) offers start-up services for entrepreneurs, including developing a business plan, naming and registering a business, buying a business, and financing a business.

Ontario Ministry of Economic Development and Trade, Small Business Enterprise Centres (SBECs)

The SBECs across Canada provide entrepreneurs with all the necessary start-up and development tools. Each centre can help entrepreneurs determine what they need to do before, during, and after launching their business. Business support exists for specific groups, such as Aboriginal entrepreneurs, women entrepreneurs, and young entrepreneurs (see http://www.ontariocanada.com/ontcan/1medt/smallbiz/en/sb_sbec_en.jsp).

Industry Canada, Businesses

The business section of Industry Canada's website (www.ic.gc.ca/eic/site/ic1.nsf/eng/h_00140.html) offers business owners many resources (i.e., financing program, internship program) and information (i.e., statistics, research, and regulations).

Small Business Association of Canada (SBA-Canada)

A non-profit organization, SBA-Canada (http://vkoopia.com/SBA-Canada) provides growth and development opportunities to small businesses through networking, mentorship, collaboration, self-development, and education.

Business incubators support start-up businesses by offering resources such as administrative services, technical support, business networking, and sources of financing that a group of start-up companies share. Business incubators are often run by two- and four-year colleges, universities, and technical schools, and many are sponsored by economic development organizations, cities, or countries. The Canadian Association of Business Incubation (CABI) is a vital national body of organizations dedicated to supporting the growth of new and emerging businesses.

An **advisory board** is a group of individuals who offer guidance to the new business owner. Such boards are similar to boards of directors in publicly held companies, except that they generally do not have the authority to make decisions.

Careful financial decision-making, savvy management, meticulous planning, and the willingness to make significant personal sacrifices all play key roles in a successful business. Knowing when, where, and how to ask for help is also a factor critical to success.

❺ Summarize the potential benefits and drawbacks of each major source of small business financing. *(pp. 133–134)*

For larger amounts, new business owners sometimes obtain a loan, borrowing against their own assets, such as the equity in their house or against their retirement account, but the consequences of the business failing are very severe. **Grants** are financial awards that are usually offered by federal and provincial governments and some private organizations. Venture capitalists are another source of funding. Unlike banks, where there is a contractual agreement to pay back the money, **venture capitalists** contribute money to your business in return for some form of equity—a piece of ownership. **Angel investors** are wealthy individuals willing to put up their own money in hopes of a profit return later on.

Often outside investors are looking for some controlling or managerial role in the business. When a great deal of money is on the line, the stakes—personal, professional, and financial—are quite high. By understanding the available options and being prepared to deal with financial predicaments, business owners give themselves the best chance at success.

⑥ Outline the advantages and disadvantages of franchising within the context of entrepreneurship.   *(pp. 134–138)*

For many, franchising is an easier, less risky means of starting a business. Since the franchisor provides much of the marketing and financial tools needed to run the business, all the franchisee is expected to bring to the table is management and marketing skills, time, and money. In addition to a recognized brand name, other advantages include a proven system of operation, strength in numbers, initial training, marketing support, and market research is often provided.

Although buying a franchise provides the franchisee with many benefits, other disadvantages include lack of control, heavy workload, competition, shared common problems, high start-up costs, and franchisees must pay a monthly royalty fee to the franchisor. Other costs the franchisee might incur include real estate purchase or rental, equipment purchase or rental, extra signage, and opening inventory.

⑦ List and explain the advantages and disadvantages of a sole proprietorship.   *(pp. 138–140)*

There are several advantages to forming your business as a sole proprietorship, the first of which is ease of formation. With only one person making all the decisions and no need to consult other owners or interested parties, sole proprietors have greater control and more flexibility to act quickly. Another advantage is that there are no specific corporate records to keep or reports to file, including tax reporting. Since there is no legal distinction between the owner and the business, no separate tax return is required. As a result, the income and expenses of a sole proprietorship flow through the owner's personal tax return.

A sole proprietor is personally responsible for all the debts and liabilities of the business. **Unlimited liability** means that if business assets aren't enough to pay business debts, then personal assets, such as the sole proprietor's house, personal investments, or retirement plans, can be used to pay the balance. Another drawback of a sole proprietorship is the potential difficulty in borrowing money to help your business grow.

⑧ Describe the advantages and disadvantages of a partnership and a partnership agreement.   *(pp. 140–142)*

With more owners, there are more available contributions to both the starting and ongoing capital of the business. Sharing the financial responsibility means the owners are interested in the company's overall profitability and are as highly motivated as you are to make the business succeed. Therefore, additional owners, unlike employees, are more likely to be willing to work long hours and go the extra mile.

Adding partners to help share the workload also allows for coverage for vacations, illness, or personal issues. Moreover, if partners have complementary skills, they create a collaboration that can be quite advantageous. Partners can help discuss ideas and projects as well as make the big decisions. Partners can help in sales and marketing to generate income.

For every advantage a partner can bring, adding the wrong partner can be equally problematic. Obviously, adding partners means sharing profits and control. A potential partner may have different work habits and styles from you, and if the partner's style isn't complementary, the differences can prove challenging. In addition, as the business begins to grow and change, your partner might want to take the business in a different direction than you do.

⑨ Explain how a corporation is formed, and how it compares with sole proprietorships and partnerships.   *(pp. 142–143)*

A **corporation,** as a specific form of business organization, is a separate legal entity, liable for its own debts, and whose owners' liability is limited to their investment in the company. Because a corporation is considered a separate entity apart from its owners, it has legal rights like an individual, so a corporation can own property, assume liability, pay taxes, enter into contracts, and can sue and be sued—just like any other individual. Unlike partnerships and sole proprietorships, corporations provide business owners with better protection of their personal assets.

If a company intends to do business in more than one province, it must incorporate under the federal *Canada Business Corporations Act*. If a company intends to do business in only one province, it may incorporate under that province's corporation act.

⑩ Describe the characteristics of non-profit corporations and cooperatives.   *(pp. 143–145)*

Legally, a non-profit corporation is an incorporated business that does not seek a net profit and instead utilizes revenue available after normal operating expenses for the corporation's declared social or educational goals.

Co-operatives differ from other forms of business because they have a different purpose, control structure, and allocation of profit. A co-operative is a business owned and governed by members who use its products or services, not by outside investors. The primary purpose of co-operatives is to meet the common needs of their members

⑪ Summarize the different types of mergers and acquisitions and explain why they occur.   *(pp. 145–146)*

Sometimes, in the evolution of a business or in response to market forces, companies seek opportunities to expand by adding new product lines, spreading out into different geographic areas, or growing the company to increase their competitive advantage. Often product or market expansion is done gradually by slowly adding new product lines or penetrating new areas. However, it takes time and investment to research and develop new products or to locate and build in new areas. Often, especially to remain competitive, expansion needs to happen more quickly. In that case, it's easier to integrate another established business through the process of mergers or acquisitions.

■ Horizontal merger: two companies that share the same product lines and markets and are in direct competition with each other, such as a soft drink company and a mineral water company

■ Vertical merger: two companies that have a company/customer relationship or a company/supplier relationship, such as Walt Disney and Pixar or eBay and PayPal

■ Product extension merger: two companies selling different but related products in the same market, such as the 2005 merger between Adobe and Macromedia

■ Market extension merger: two companies that sell the same products in different markets. For example, Morrison supermarket and Safeway. Although both are in the United Kingdom, Morrison is mainly in Great Britain and Safeway is mainly in Scotland.

■ Conglomeration: two companies that have no common business areas merge to obtain diversification, such as Citicorp, a banking services firm, and Travelers Group Inc., an insurance underwriting company, combining to form one of the world's largest financial services group, Citigroup Inc.

KEY TERMS

acquisition (p. 145)
advisory board (p. 132)
angel investors (p. 134)
articles of incorporation
 (p. 142)
board of directors (p. 143)
business incubators (p. 132)
business plan (p. 131)
bylaws (p. 143)
Canadian Federation of
 Independent Business
 (CFIB) (p. 127)
Canadian Franchise
 Association (CFA) (p. 134)

capital (p. 141)
co-operative (p. 144)
corporation (p. 142)
double taxation (p. 143)
due diligence (p. 138)
entrepreneurial team (p. 126)
entrepreneurs (p. 122)
franchise (p. 134)
franchisee (p. 134)
franchisor (p. 134)
friendly takeover (p. 145)
general partners (p. 140)
general partnership (p. 140)
grants (p. 134)

growth entrepreneurs (p. 125)
hostile takeover (p. 145)
intrapreneurs (p. 125)
liability (p. 139)
lifestyle entrepreneurs
 (p. 125)
limited liability (p. 139)
limited partners (p. 141)
limited partnerships (p. 141)
merger (p. 145)
micropreneurs (p. 125)
opportunity niche (p. 122)
partnership (p. 140)
private corporation (p. 142)

public corporation (p. 142)
shareholders (p. 143)
Small Business Investment
 Company (SBIC) program
 (p. 134)
small or medium-sized
 enterprise (SME) (p. 127)
sole proprietorship (p. 138)
synergy (p. 145)
unlimited liability (p. 140)
venture capitalists (p. 134)

CRITICAL THINKING QUESTIONS

1. Bill Gates, Donald Trump, and Oprah Winfrey are some well-known successful entrepreneurs. What common traits do these individuals possess that have led to their success?
2. Compare the different sources of funding available to small business owners. Which sources of funding seem best when a business is just starting? Which sources of funding seem best once the business is established and is looking to expand?
3. How has technology affected small businesses? If you opened your own business, give examples of two ways in which you would use technology in your company that you feel are critical to small business success in today's world. Explain.

4. Discuss the different risks facing someone creating a new business on their own and someone buying an existing small business. What risks will both new business owners face? Compare the advantages and disadvantages of each option. Which would you rather do and why?
5. Businesses, especially small businesses, often compete for customers through customer experience—customer service, quality of the experience, or exceeding the customer expectations. Imagine that you open your own business. Identify how you could build a competitive advantage by offering a better customer experience. Be specific. What would your business offer customers that would entice them to buy from you instead of your competitors?

APPLICATION EXERCISES

1. **A Closer Look at Franchising.** Using the Internet, research a franchise that you think would be a viable investment opportunity for you. Put together a brief report that outlines the following information about your chosen franchise: fees (initial and ongoing), location/site assistance, training and ongoing support, marketing assistance, competition (both from other businesses and additional franchises within the organization), and the pros and cons of starting a business with this franchise.
2. **Micro-Financing: A Little $ Can Go a Long Way.** Visit www.kiva.org and click on the "Lend" tab to view the list of entrepreneurs. Use the drop-down menus in the "Find Loans" search bar to locate an entrepreneur or entrepreneurial team to whom you would consider lending. In a brief report, discuss the entrepreneur or group you chose, including information on the loan amount requested, the percentage of funds raised, the entrepreneur's country of origin, and a summary of the entrepreneur's business venture. In your report, explain your reasons for choosing to loan to this particular entrepreneur.
3. **Do You Have What It Takes to Be an Entrepreneur?** Visit the Business Development Bank of Canada's (BDC) website at www.bdc.ca/en/. Go to the Advice Centre, Tools, and complete the Entrepreneurial self-assessment. What aspects of your personality make you a good candidate to be an entrepreneur? What is holding you back?
4. **Business Combinations.** Look on the Internet for a current example of a business merger, takeover, or

acquisition. Explain the circumstances of the event. What companies are involved? Was the event friendly or hostile? What are the reasons given for the combination? What is your opinion of this business combination? Do you think it is a good business decision? Why or why not?
5. **Small Business Owners.** In the results of the 2006 Census, Barrie, Ontario, was named the fastest-growing community in Canada. Imagine that you want to start a catering business in Barrie (or another fast-growing community). You see that a catering business is for sale in Barrie for $150 000. The company specializes in catering business events. The owner, currently operating the business from home, is moving to another country and wants to sell. You will need outside investors to help you purchase the business. Develop questions to ask the owner about the business. What other types of information would you need before making a decision to buy this company? Either you will purchase this existing business or start a catering business of your own, therefore you should investigate the feasibility of each option. Once you've gathered the necessary information, visit Sample Business Plans (www.bplans.com) and search for a sample catering business plan and review it. Visit www.inc.com's Tools page and download the Business Plan Executive Summary Template or re-create it in a document, and complete the business plan executive summary for your catering business proposal.

GLOBAL 500 RESEARCH PROJECT

INSTRUCTIONS

1. Choose a Global 500 company from Fortune magazine's annual rankings at http://money.cnn.com/magazines/fortune/global500/.
2. Research:
   a. Who was the entrepreneur(s) that started this company? How long has it been in business? Where was the first location? Does it offer a franchise option?
   b. What does the company sell? In which countries?
   c. Name three strengths this company has—reputation, price, quality, etc.? Has it always been this way?
   d. Search online for this company's annual report. Use the annual report (along with other information you gather) to create a short Business Plan Executive Summary. Visit www.inc.com's Tools page and download the Business Plan Executive Summary Template or re-create it in a document, and complete the business plan executive summary for this company.
   e. If this company were to go out of business, who would it affect, and how?
3. Prepare a report and submit to your professor.

TEAM TIME

Starting a Business: Brainstorming

Assemble into groups of four or five.
1. Before meeting as a group, think about what you are passionate about and whether there is a potential market involving your interests. Develop one or two ideas for potential businesses based on your passions. Do not consider any idea impossible at this stage.
   a. Consider if there is something missing in the current market. For example, are you passionate about locally grown organic vegetables but are frustrated that there isn't a place nearby to purchase these items? If so, you've developed an idea for a local farmers market.
   b. Consider combining two ideas together. When school has a half or full day off, consider having high-school students form a daytime child care service for elementary students.
   c. Consider business ideas that have potential but aren't doing very well now. Are there ways to make them better?
2. Gather your group and go over each other's ideas. Refine the list to two or three ideas.
3. Have each group member refine an idea even further, identifying the target market and outlining the business goals and objectives.
4. Meet as a team one more time to pick one business idea.
5. If time permits, the group can develop this idea further by using the Business Plan project template. See the Career Skills module in MyBusinessLab for more information.

ETHICS AND RESPONSIBILITY

Social Responsibility: Forming a Plan of Action

Milton Hershey, founder of Hershey Chocolate Company, dedicated himself to caring about his customers, his employees, and his community at large. Hershey felt that giving back to the community was not only his moral obligation but also a crucial part of his success.

Step 1 Imagine that you operate a business in your community (choose from a restaurant, a landscaping service, or a beauty salon).

Step 2 As a class or in smaller groups, discuss the ways in which your business can contribute to customers, employees, and the community in socially responsible ways. Write down a list of ideas that your group came up with.

Step 3 Create a social responsibility plan for your company. In the document, describe your business and the ways in which your business can contribute to specific organizations in your community. Be as specific with your plan as possible. Your instructor may ask you to submit your work or discuss it with the class.

CLOSING CASE

The Fish That Pulled Him Under

Born in Europe, avid angler Kevin Hengeveld immigrated to Canada in the early 1980s. In the 1990s, Hengeveld started an import/export wholesale business in Ontario whereby he would import products not currently sold in the Canadian market and sell them to fishing stores all over Ontario. There was a big demand for this type of equipment, especially from Canadians of European descent. He dealt with many fishing storeowners and learned much about how the retail fishing industry worked.

Hengeveld created an online store called Fish in the Net where he could sell his imported goods directly to customers, acquiring many loyal customers. He was very knowledgeable about many types of fishing (i.e., float fishing, carp fishing, sport fishing, ice fishing) and published a fishing magazine in two languages.

During the second year of business, Hengeveld noticed that many stores were not paying on time, but the products were selling well. For many years, Hengeveld had thought about opening his own fishing equipment store. Recreational fishing/angling was a passion of his since he was a small child, so when a retail space became available in 2003 in a wealthy area of town, Hengeveld decided to rent it and start his own brick-and-mortar retail business. The store specialized in European-style fishing and float fishing and sold equipment and bait. Hengeveld continued his wholesale operations, but focused on his new venture. He held seminars at the store and provided information to customers regarding new and current fishing techniques. The business was established as a sole proprietorship, and Hengeveld initially financed the start-up of the business through personal savings of $20 000 and a $25 000 line of credit. Later he obtained another $75 000 line of credit. He never did have enough time to write his business plan fully.

The live bait the store sold generated a big percentage of the income, but it also generated a big percentage of the expenses.

Not only were storage tanks, refrigerated tanks, and fridges needed, but the government had many regulations pertaining to the type of bait a store could sell and the reporting that must be done. Due to the hours anglers would go fishing, the store had to be open very early in the mornings and twenty-four hours on the weekends. Staff had to be trained on how to handle live bait. There was a 40 percent loss in bait product, and suppliers insisted on cash on delivery payments with no returns.

The bookkeeping and reporting was extensive. Provincial sales tax (PST) and goods and services Tax (GST) had to be reported quarterly, and income tax was done once per year as a sole proprietorship structure. The store sold fishing licences, which required monthly reporting to the Ministry of Natural Resources (MNR) but also attracted customers. A yearly live bait sales report was also required by the MNR, which was very time-consuming because it detailed the number of fish sold. The business was audited once by Canada Revenue Agency and it went well because Hengeveld had hired an accountant to be sure all payroll deductions, special reporting, and income tax calculations were accurate and complete.

There was not a lot of competition in the area, just a few small, family-operated stores. Hengeveld's wife helped with the bookkeeping and the purchases and reporting processes when she could, but she also had a full-time career. Hengeveld soon was doing enough business that he actually purchased a second store, taking over his main competitor of the family-operated stores. Hengeveld was doing so well in this second store location that he decided to close the first store, as he was feeling a bit stretched running between the two stores and trying to be a good husband and father. He felt the original store's business was only about half that of the second store so it was best to focus his efforts on the second store, even though the second store was not in as good a neighbourhood and the operating costs were somewhat higher. The property owner had Hengeveld sign a lease that included a clause stating that the leaser was responsible for all repairs and for paying the hydro bills for both the store space as well as the apartment upstairs. To Hengeveld's dismay, the store space was dilapidated, and he found out later that he was responsible for many more repairs than he initially thought.

Hengeveld hired a programmer to update the business website since this was his primary marketing tool, and soon it became the first of its kind for sports anglers in Canada. Customers could order online, use message boards, chat with each other, and arrange to meet at the store and go fishing together. The site offered an interactive experience for customers and brought many new customers not only from Canada but also from the United States.

He installed a security system in his store, and had an alarm system in place because the store was open twenty-four hours on weekends. Hengeveld had a difficult time finding qualified staff that he could rely on to show up for work and not steal from the store. He had a couple of employees who did not deal with customers well and customers had complained about them to Hengeveld. Part-time staff consisted of mostly college students taking a break from their studies; while most had good customer service skills, they proved unreliable in other ways.

In 2005, a major outdoors store, Bass Pro, opened within a twenty-kilometre range, and Hengeveld estimated that he lost around 25 percent of his revenue after the mega store moved in. Business started to slow in 2007 just before the recession hit in 2008. In the beginning, Hengeveld's business was not making a profit, but he was able to cover expenses and repay creditors. During the last few years, the store was losing money. In the end, Hengeveld decided to close his brick-and-mortar store but continue to operate his online store as more of a part-time pursuit.

DISCUSSION QUESTIONS

1. What entrepreneurial traits does Hengeveld have? What made him want to start his own business?
2. Analyze the situation. What do you think went wrong? Did Hengeveld make mistakes? If so, what were they?
3. What might Hengeveld had done differently in order to continue his business success? Search for one or more sample business plans for a retail fishing store (you should find at least one at www.bplans.com). Review it. What stands out in your mind about the plan? Do you think Hengeveld could have done better with his business if he had a business plan to start with? Why or why not?

MyBusinessLab CHAPTER RESOURCES

MyBusinessLab in an online learning and testing environment that features the perfect study tools to help you master the concepts covered in this chapter. Log in to MyBusinessLab at www.pearsoned.ca/mybusinesslab to test your knowledge of key chapter concepts, participate in simulations modelled on real-world business situations, and explore the following additional practice tools:

- Study Plan
- Audio Chapter Summaries
- Glossary Flashcards
- eText
- BizChat Discussion Boards
- BizSkills Simulations: Small Business and the Entrepreneur; Getting Your Business Off the Ground
- Document Makeovers: Outline of CEO's Speech; Interview Questions for Owner of a Small Business
- Video Activities: AZ Teen Magazine; HomestarRunner.com; Entrepreneurship; Boston Boxing and Fitness; Nom Nom; Our Labour of Love; Kaneva

Video Cases:
To access the Chapter 5 Video Cases: Joie D'Vivre: Small Business and Entrepreneurship; Amy's Ice Cream: Doing Business

Privately, see the Activities folder in the Assessment section of MyBusinessLab.

Web Case:
To access the Chapter 5 Web Case, see the Activities folder in the Assessment section of MyBusinessLab

Career Skills:
Visit the Career Skills module "Constructing an Effective Business Plan" on MyBusinessLab, where you'll learn that writing a formal business plan is a crucial part of a successful business. You'll gain insight on how to write an effective business plan and learn how to use your well-developed business plan to help obtain financing for your new business venture.

6

Business Management and Organization

LEARNING OBJECTIVES

After studying this chapter, you should be able to:

1. Summarize the ways managers apply technical, interpersonal, decision-making, conceptual, and time management skills to business. (pp. 154–157)

2. Outline the strategies managers use to establish the corporate vision and mission statement and keep the company on task. (pp. 157–161)

3. Describe the implications of tactical plans, operational plans, and contingency plans within the context of management. (pp. 161–162)

4. Explain the significance of organizing and how most management is organized. (p. 163)

5. Distinguish vertical organizations, horizontal organizations, and network organizations. (pp. 163–166)

6. Describe what makes a good leader and the various styles of leadership. (pp. 166–169)

7. Evaluate the implications of control within a business. (pp. 170–171)

OPENING DISCUSSION: EFFECTIVE MANAGEMENT

What Makes PepsiCo's CEO Such an Effective Manager?

PepsiCo Inc. CEO Indra K. Nooyi has used her management skills to rise to the top of a multibillion-dollar corporation. PepsiCo is the second-largest food and beverage business in the world (after Nestlé) and the largest in North America, with net revenues of approximately US$60 billion and almost 300 000 employees.[1] The corporation owns some of the world's most popular brands, including Pepsi-Cola, Mountain Dew, Tropicana, Lay's, Doritos, Diet Pepsi, Quaker, and Gatorade. PepsiCo includes four major divisions: PepsiCo Americas Foods, PepsiCo Americas Beverages, PepsiCo Europe, and PepsiCo Middle East and Africa, which generated combined estimated worldwide (more than 200 countries) retail sales of US$119 billion in 2010.[2]

Nooyi joined PepsiCo in 1994 and was named president and CFO in 2001. In 2006, she was named president and CEO, and in 2007, she assumed the role of chairman, making her the fifth CEO in the company's forty-four-year history.[3] Since becoming CEO, Nooyi has restructured the organization to further its globalization (and lessen its preoccupation with the U.S. market), expanded the power structure by doubling her executive team to twenty-nine, and increased PepsiCo's focus on health-conscious snacks and beverages.[4] She has been a key player in the 1997 divestiture of PepsiCo's restaurants (Taco Bell, Pizza Hut, and KFC) into Tricon, now known as Yum! Brands; the acquisition of Tropicana in 1998; the merger with Quaker Oats Company that brought Gatorade to PepsiCo in 2001; and the mergers with the Pepsi Bottling Group Inc. (PBG) and PepsiAmericas (PepsiCo's bottlers) in 2010.[5] It was expected that the PBG deal would provide the companies with US$300 million in annual savings. Each of these moves has certainly paid off.

In 2007, Nooyi spent US$1.3 billion acquiring companies such as Naked Juice, a soy drink and organic juice maker from California.[6] She's trying to balance the profit motive with producing healthier products, aiming for a net-zero impact on the environment, and supporting her workforce. Nooyi states,

"Companies today are bigger than many economies. We are little republics. We are engines of efficiency. If companies don't do [responsible] things, who is going to?"[7] By producing and promoting whole-grain snacks and vitamin-enhanced water, Nooyi says that PepsiCo can lead the industry's push toward better nutrition, which would benefit not just consumers but investors too.[8]

Nooyi shifted a US$20 million chunk of PepsiCo's US$616 million annual advertising budget from traditional media to social media to start a worldwide campaign in 2010—Pepsi Refresh. Applying the idea that great ideas can come from anywhere, Pepsi Refresh invites anyone to submit a grant proposal to a website, then encourages online voters to choose the winners (amounts ranging from US$5000 to US$250 000). "It blurs the line between philanthropy and advertising. Brands have to speak to millenniums; young people want to make a difference," says Nooyi.[9]

Nooyi holds a master's degree in business from the Indian Institute of Management in Calcutta, India, and a master's degree in public and private management from the Yale School of Management. She worked for Boston Consulting Group and later held corporate strategy positions at Motorola Inc. and what is now ABB Group.[10] She is married and has two daughters.[11] She is known for being an innovative thinker, brilliant business strategist, and powerful and persuasive speaker.

She has been named as one of the world's most powerful women in business by *Fortune* magazine five years running (2005–2010).[12] In 2009, the Global Supply Chain Leaders Group chose her as CEO of the Year for making the most significant contributions to sustainable, responsible business practices in global operations.[13] She's a well-educated, strategic thinker who has wide-ranging and cosmopolitan views—she defines management. Her multi-year strategy, "Performance with Purpose," is designed to balance making profits and expanding market share with giving back to communities worldwide. It encapsulates the "triple bottom line"—people, planet, profit—and has become the motto for the way PepsiCo does business.

DISCUSSION QUESTIONS

1. What are some of the skills needed by a CEO such as Nooyi to implement decisions such as new acquisitions, restructuring moves, and marketing strategies?

2. Why do you think Nooyi wants PepsiCo to offer healthier products?

3. What do you think Nooyi means when she says, ". . . it blurs the lines between philanthropy and advertising"? How do PepsiCo's philanthropic actions help the company? The investors? The consumers? Others?

SKILLS OF SUCCESSFUL MANAGERS

Working with People and Resources

Summarize the ways managers apply technical, interpersonal, decision-making, conceptual, and time management skills to business.

Management is the process of working with people and resources to accomplish the goals of the organization.

Who are managers?   Have you ever been in a team situation in which one person has been instrumental in making the group work more effectively? That person could have been a peer or a superior, but somehow he or she knew exactly what had to be accomplished, assessed the resources available to achieve the goal, and organized and led other group members in such a way to accomplish the goal. If so, you've seen management in action.

Management is the process of working with people and resources to accomplish the goals of the organization. The organization can be a simple working group, a corporate department, or a multibillion-dollar company. The size of the group doesn't matter, but the skills of a manager and the process a manager goes through are similar across all management levels (low-level or first-line managers, middle-level managers, and top-level managers—discussed later in this chapter).

What skills do managers need?   Since managerial tasks are so varied, a successful manager needs to possess a variety of skills, including *technical, interpersonal, conceptual,* *decision-making*, and *time management skills*. It is a rare person who is master of all these skills. Moreover, because they are responsible for a variety of jobs, and because these jobs can change quite rapidly, managers must assess the skills required in any given situation. Managers must also be willing to acquire these skills quickly if necessary.

Technical Skills   Every job has a specific set of technical skills that are important for managers to possess. **Technical skills** include the abilities and knowledge that enable an employee to carry out the specific tasks required of a discipline or department, such as drafting skills for an architect, programming skills for a software developer, or market analysis skills for a marketing manager. Technical skills may also include how to operate certain machinery. Managers must be comfortable with technology and possess good analytical skills to interpret a variety of data. In addition to having the skills pertinent to their own jobs, managers must also know how to perform, or at least have a good understanding of, the skills required of the employees they supervise.

Interpersonal Skills   Managers achieve goals working with people both inside and outside the organization, so it's important that they possess good interpersonal or human relations skills. **Interpersonal skills** enable a manager to interact with other people in order to motivate them. It's important that a manager develop trust and loyalty with the people he or she interacts with often and that the manager can motivate and encourage employees to work together.

Interpersonal skills are important skills at any management level. Top managers must be able to communicate with the board of directors, investors, and other leaders in the business community. They must also communicate with middle managers in order to understand clearly the goals and strategies of the organization. Middle managers must communicate with all levels of management and act as liaisons among groups. Lower-level managers must be able to motivate employees, build morale, and train and support those who perform the daily tasks of the organization. As workforce and business relationships continue to be more diverse, it is becoming increasingly important for managers to take into consideration the needs, backgrounds, and experiences of many different people when communicating with individuals and groups in an organization.

Decision-Making Skills   It is critical that a manager has good problem-solving and **decision-making skills**—the ability to identify and analyze a problem, examine the alternatives, choose and implement the best plan of action, and evaluate the results. When making important decisions, managers often go through a formal decision-making process similar to that shown in **Figure 6.1**. The steps in such a process are as follows:

1. In analyzing any situation or case, managers *identify problems* or opportunities by analyzing data and searching for trends. Such problems may include poor growth in sales, an increase in customer dissatisfaction, or excess inventory buildup. The same situations may also be opportunities in disguise. For instance, excess inventory may offer an opportunity to offer a special sale to customers.
2. Once a problem is defined, managers then *generate alternative solutions*.
3. One they have identified several alternatives, managers *evaluate the alternatives* based on various criteria, such as cost, feasibility, time, resources needed, market acceptance, and compatibility with the company's mission, values, and goals. Managers often rank the evaluated alternatives by various criteria. This evaluation process can be tedious, but identifying and evaluating alternatives is critical to making a good decision. Many times the best routes are not taken because management has not taken the time to explore all alternatives thoroughly.

Technical skills include the abilities and knowledge that enable an employee to carry out the specific tasks required of a discipline or department.

Interpersonal skills enable a manager to interact with other people in order to motivate them.

Decision-making skills involve the ability to identify and analyze a problem, examine the alternatives, choose and implement the best plan of action, and evaluate the results.

 Decision-Making Mini-Simulation: Decision Making. Located in MyBusinessLab.

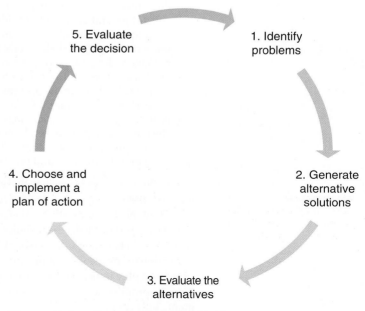

Figure 6.1   Stages of Decision Making

5. Evaluate the decision
1. Identify problems
2. Generate alternative solutions
3. Evaluate the alternatives
4. Choose and implement a plan of action

4. Once managers have evaluated all alternatives, they *choose the best plan of action*. As a final check, management may seek customer or market opinion on the chosen plan of action before completely committing to this choice. In some instances, if the market or customer feedback is not positive, management will look to pursue another alternative. When the final choice has been made, plans are put in place to *implement the plan of action*.

5. Managers also *evaluate the decision* to ensure it is carried out correctly and meets the goals of the organization. If the goals are not being met, the decision-making process may possibly become cyclical, beginning again with *identifying problems*.

Conceptual skills involve the ability to think abstractly in order to picture the organization as a whole and to understand its relationship to the rest of the business community.

Conceptual Skills   To make good decisions, a good manager must also have **conceptual skills**—the ability to think abstractly in order to picture the organization as a whole and to understand its relationship to the rest of the business community. Such skills also include understanding the relationships between the parts of the organization itself. Whenever new market opportunities or potential threats arise, managers rely on their conceptual skills to help them analyze the impending outcomes of their decisions. Conceptual skills are extremely important for top-level managers and are often developed with time and experience.

Time management skills involve the ability to achieve the maximum amount of productivity in a set amount of time.

Time Management Skills   **Time management skills** refer to the ability to achieve the maximum amount of productivity in a set amount of time. A manager may possess all the skills discussed above, but that may not be enough to manage a successful business. For example, say that the manager of a small deli built his business from humble beginnings; he had a vision and expanded from there. His knowledge of business logistics is superb, and every day he makes important decisions. He spends hours each day talking with his employees and has gained their respect. Taking all of this into consideration, you would think that his deli would be successful. But this is not the case.

Although this manager has the vision, knowledge, and interpersonal skills, he does not make efficient use of his time. For example, instead of socializing with his employees on Friday, he could manage a workshop to help them sharpen their customer service skills. Time management requires that managers have the ability to recognize specific ways in which they can make every task or situation productive. The following steps are crucial to effective time management for almost any manager:

1. *Determine the level of urgency of paperwork.* Some paperwork, such as billing, may be more important than others, such as a quarterly report due in three months. Managers must therefore separate paperwork according to due dates and clearly label each pile. Keeping a schedule—either electronically or on a calendar—and crossing off each task when completed are important time management skills.

2. *Create folders for e-mail.* Managers receive plenty of e-mail, which can be a tremendous time drain. To manage e-mail effectively, managers should filter spam to a specific folder and create other folders based on subject, such as "advertising samples," "employee requests," and so on. Effective managers leave the messages requiring an immediate reply in their in-box and address urgent messages right away. Otherwise, managers designate a time each day that they will address all other messages.

3. *Designate a time for telephone calls.* Of course, as in the case with e-mail, there may be urgent calls that a manager must take immediately. However, effective managers have an office assistant take messages and allocate a specific time to return calls.

4. *Identify clear agendas for meetings.* Time can be easily wasted if a meeting agenda is not clear and goals are not set. Effective managers distribute an agenda to all attendees before a meeting that specifies the goals the meeting must achieve. An agenda helps everyone stay on task and end the meeting on time.

By following steps such as these, managers find that their productivity levels increase and more time is freed for completing other tasks required of the job.

Think back to Indra K. Nooyi (see "Opening Discussion"). How might her education have equipped her with the technical skills she uses to achieve success? Do you think her success reflects strong interpersonal skills? What do the changes she has made at PepsiCo say about her decision-making and conceptual skills? How might time management skills come into play in her ability to manage three divisions of a giant corporation? Clearly, Nooyi's prominence and success in business demonstrate that a combination of management skills is vital.

What tasks do managers perform? Administration can be defined as the universal process of organizing people and resources efficiently to direct activities toward common goals and objectives. In some organizations, management is seen as a subset of administration. In business, administration consists of the management of business operations. It includes making major decisions such as setting long-term goals for the organization, determining which products or services the organization will produce, deciding how employees will be organized, and developing strategies for effective, efficient, and successful business operations. Administrators, or managers, engage in a common set of functions to meet the organization's goals. These include planning, organizing, leading (directing), and controlling.

FUNCTIONS OF MANAGEMENT
Planning

Why do managers need to plan? As illustrated in **Figure 6.2**, management involves four primary functions: planning, organizing, leading, and controlling. These functions integrate all of the company's resources, including human, financial, and technological.

In today's busy world, it's easy to get distracted. Goals and plans help to keep you on task. **Planning** is the process of establishing goals and objectives and determining the best ways to accomplish them. **Goals** are broad, long-term accomplishments an organization wants to achieve within a certain period—in most companies, this is about five years. **Objectives** are the short-term targets designed to help achieve these goals.

Both goals and objectives are best set with deadlines and quantifiable measures. Managers should keep the acronym SMARTER in mind when designing and wording goals and objectives. Goals should be Specific, Measurable, Acceptable (to those working to achieve the goals), Realistic, Timely, Extending (the capabilities of those working to achieve the goals), and Rewarding.[14]

What types of plans do managers make? Planning happens at all levels of an organization. A **strategic plan** is the main course of action created by top-level managers that sets the approach for achieving the long-term goals and objectives of the organization. A strategic plan serves as a framework for decisions and assists in setting corporate benchmarks. Simply put, a strategic plan points the organization to where it wants to be in the future and identifies how it's going to get there. It helps answer questions such as "Where are we going?" "What do we want to focus on?" and "What is the best means to get there?" A strategic plan is realistic and obtainable and looks at the big picture. Although individual goals sometimes contribute to the plan, the overall strategic plan is focused on the entire

2 Outline the strategies managers use to establish the corporate vision and mission statement and keep the company on task.

BizSkills Simulation: Plan for Success. Located in MyBusinessLab.

6

Planning is the process of establishing goals and objectives and determining the best ways to accomplish them.

Goals are broad, long-term accomplishments an organization wants to achieve within a certain period.

Objectives are the short-term targets designed to help achieve these goals.

A **strategic plan** is the main course of action created by top-level managers that sets the approach for achieving the long-term goals and objectives of the organization.

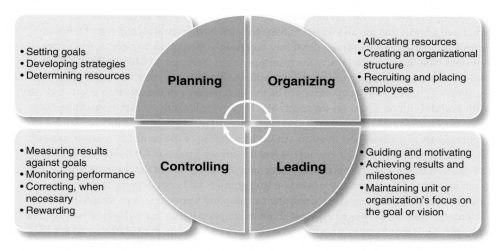

- Setting goals
- Developing strategies
- Determining resources

Planning

Organizing

- Allocating resources
- Creating an organizational structure
- Recruiting and placing employees

- Measuring results against goals
- Monitoring performance
- Correcting, when necessary
- Rewarding

Controlling

Leading

- Guiding and motivating
- Achieving results and milestones
- Maintaining unit or organization's focus on the goal or vision

Figure 6.2 The Four Functions of Management

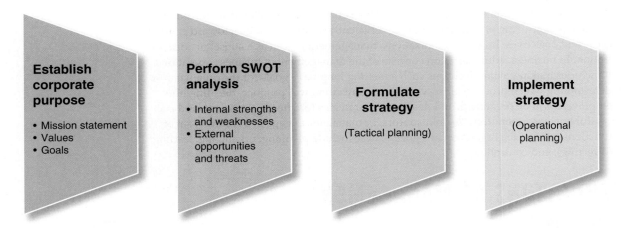

Figure 6.3   The Strategic Planning Process

organization or an entire department. Those making strategic plans must pay attention to the capabilities and resources of the organization, as well as changes in the environment.

How is a strategic plan developed?   A good strategic plan reflects what is going on inside and outside the organization and how those conditions and changes will affect the organization in the future. Management takes several steps while developing a strategic plan, as shown in **Figure 6.3**.

How do managers ensure their decisions match the overall objectives of the company?   As managers carry out the strategic plan, it's important that they ensure their decisions continue to match the overall objectives of the organization. The first step in creating a strategic plan is to establish a corporate purpose through a *vision* and a *mission statement*. A **vision** identifies what the business wants to be in the future. For example, the vision statement for Domino's Pizza is "Exceptional people on a mission to be the best pizza delivery company in the world!"[15] Often times a company will not have one set statement defining its vision, but rather the vision may be a series of goals and plans. The vision should be made clear to all employees and people investing in the company.

People often confuse the vision of a company with the mission statement. The **mission statement** is a description of the organization's purpose, basic goals, and philosophies. A mission statement not only helps management remain focused but also lets employees understand the core values of the company for which they work. Because mission statements reflect the personality of a company, they can be very different in design and content. For example, Nike's mission statement is directed toward a large target audience— "if you have a body, you are an athlete."[16] Nike refrains from technical jargon and relies on simplicity to inspire the average consumer and not the stereotypical athlete. You might envision Nike being worn by anyone from a physical therapist, to a high-school basketball player, to an Olympic gold medallist. Adidas's mission statement targets a sporting lifestyle—"The Adidas Group strives to be the global leader in the sporting goods industry with brands built on a passion for sports and a sporting lifestyle."[17] But these differences don't necessarily make one mission statement more effective than the other. Both statements clearly articulate their mission. An understanding of the company mission can help fuel employee enthusiasm. If employees feel the owner's passion for the business through the mission statement, their goals and objectives as employees of the business are incorporated into their daily work and passed on to customers and suppliers through their words and actions. This clarity tends to strengthen a company's position. Even simple mission statements have the power to say a lot about a company if they are written effectively. For example, McDonald's mission is to "be our customers' favorite place and way to eat."[18]

Non-profit organizations also have mission statement, but because these organizations are not centred on investor return, their mission statements focus their outreach on

A **vision** identifies what the business wants to be in the future.

The **mission statement** is a description of the organization's purpose, basic goals, and philosophies.

the community or a specific public service. For example, the Canadian Cancer Society's mission statement states, "The Canadian Cancer Society is a national, community-based organization of volunteers whose mission is the eradication of cancer and the enhancement of the quality of life of people with cancer."[19] This statement reflects the organization's commitment to serving the community.

Both the vision and mission statement are usually posted on an organization's website. However, because the mission statement is directed toward customers—unlike the vision, which is directed toward employees—it is often used alone on advertising materials or on the actual product. A mission statement describes the true essence of what the company does, while a vision is what the company wants to do in the future. A vision challenges a company to grow. The vision and mission statement are critically important as they help keep management on track, inspire employees working for an organization, and indicate to investors or consumers what type of organization they are investing in. They also provide a guide for management as they evaluate alternative plans and strategies to ensure they are consistent with the organization's current and future direction.

How do managers define a company's values?

As you have learned, management creates a mission statement and vision to keep them focused on corporate strategy and objectives. The mission statement and vision also help create the "feel" or workplace environment, also known as the corporate culture. The **corporate culture** is a collection of values, norms, and behaviour shared by management and workers that defines the character of the organization. Google, for example, has a unique culture, set by a corporate philosophy that includes statements such as "You can make money without doing evil" and "You can be serious without a suit."[20]

In a corporation in which the culture is not well defined or, even worse, it supports questionable behaviour, problems result. This was the case for the natural-gas giant Enron, which eventually went bankrupt because of significant lack of control and poor ethical behaviour from top management. On the other hand, when the corporate culture is strong, and all employees accept the culture as their own, they are motivated to maintain it and monitor their own behaviour.

After defining a mission and vision statement, companies often define core values or principles. **Core values**—the fundamental beliefs about what is important and appropriate when conducting company activities—affect a company's overall planning processes and operations. For the mission and vision statements to be enacted upon, they must reflect the values of the company. They serve as guidelines for conduct and behaviour as a company works toward its vision. Values may be embedded in a company's code of conduct, code of ethics, code of business conduct, or other such document.

Here are a few examples of core values that help define workplace culture:

- Coca-Cola: "Our inclusive culture is defined by our seven core values: leadership, passion, integrity, collaboration, diversity, quality, and accountability."[21]
- Volvo Cars: "Cars are driven by people. Therefore the guiding principle behind everything we make at Volvo is—and must remain—safety."[22]
- Cara Foods: The strength of Cara is built on five core values. "They are the essence of Cara, cherished by all teammates. People, Self-responsibility, Integrity, Passion for Winning, Quality."[23]
- Canadian Tire: "Integrity, honesty and respect are core values at Canadian Tire."[24] These values are embedded into the company's code of business conduct, and Canadian Tire expects all employees to abide by the code's principles and expectations when conducting business on behalf of the company.

How do managers determine if the company has the means to fulfill its mission?

Once the company's vision and mission statement have been articulated, management must assess the company's own strengths and weaknesses as well as its position among its competitors. In addition, management must assess what changes are anticipated to occur and determine whether the company is poised appropriately to respond to such changes. This situational analysis of strengths, weaknesses, and anticipated changes is called a **SWOT analysis** and helps determine the strategic fit between

The **corporate culture** is a collection of values, norms, and behaviour shared by management and workers that defines the character of the organization.

Decision-Making Mini-Simulation: Organizational Culture. Located In Mybusinesslab.

Core values—the fundamental beliefs about what is important and appropriate when conducting company activities—affect a company's overall planning processes and operations.

SWOT (Strengths, Weaknesses, Opportunities, and Threats) analysis is a situational analysis of strengths, weaknesses, and anticipated changes that helps determine the strategic fit between an organization's internal, distinctive capabilities, and external possibilities relative to the business and economic environments.

an organization's internal, distinctive capabilities, and external possibilities relative to the business and economic environments.

SWOT stands for Strengths, Weaknesses, Opportunities, and Threats (see **Table 6.1**). In evaluating the company's strengths and weaknesses, management must analyze the company's internal resources, including finances, human resources, marketing, operations, and technological resources. A company's strength might be its strong marketing department, but the company's weakness might be an unfavourable location. To evaluate the company's business threats and opportunities, management needs to assess external

Table 6.1   SWOT Analysis

Internal Analysis	External Analysis
Strengths	**Opportunities**
Potential assets that give a company a competitive advantage, such as:	Foreseeable changes that could favourably affect a company's competitive capability, such as:
• Price, value, quality	• Developing markets (other countries, Internet)
• Patents, strong brand names	• Niche target markets
• Quality processes, capabilities, systems	• Technology development and innovation
• Resources, assets, people	• Competitors' vulnerabilities
• Experience, knowledge, data	• Loosening of government regulations
• Good reputation among customers	• Industry or lifestyle trends
• Financial reserves, likely returns	• Global influences, removal of international trade barriers
• Marketing reach, distribution, expertise	• Information and research
• Location of your business	• Local events
• Management	• Partnerships, joint ventures, strategic alliances
• Accreditations, qualifications, certifications	• Seasonal, weather, fashion influences
• IT, communications	
• Cultural, attitudinal, behavioural	
• Philosophy and values	
Weaknesses	**Threats**
Lack of capability or expertise compared to competition, such as:	Conditions that could negatively affect a company's competitive capability, such as:
• Poor reputation, weak brand name	• Political and legal changes, new regulations, new taxation of your product or service
• Undifferentiated products or service (i.e., in relation to your competitors)	• Economy (local and global)
• Poor marketing reach, distribution, expertise	• Environmental changes
• Poor financials, bad debt or cash-flow problems	• IT developments
• Poor processes and systems	• Increase in cost of supplies
• Lack of competitive strength, size	• New competitors, emergence of substitute products or services
• Vulnerabilities	• Market demand
• Deadlines and pressures	• Bad debt or cash-flow problems
• Distractions	• Available suppliers
• Morale, commitment, leadership	• Seasonal, weather effects
• Lack of accreditations, certifications	• Vital partners and contracts
• IT, innovation, communications	• Obstacles faced
	• Limited human resources

elements, such as the competitive environment and the political, economic, socio-cultural, and technological factors that could affect the company and industry. For example, a recession could threaten an alternative energy company, whereas increasing awareness of global warming may provide greater opportunity for market growth.

Managers at all levels within an organization use several tools to measure changes within the environments they operate. As you discovered in Chapter 1, a PEST analysis measures a business according to external factors: Political, Economic, Social, and Technological. It is often helpful to complete a PEST analysis prior to completing a SWOT analysis because similar factors would appear in each. As you discovered in Chapter 2, another important analysis tool is Michael Porter's Five Forces Analysis Model, which helps managers analyze the micro-external competitive environment. It is helpful to complete a competitive environment analysis prior to a SWOT because through understanding external forces, a company can take advantage of its strengths, improve its weaknesses, and avoid taking wrong steps where opportunities and threats are concerned. An external analysis such as PEST and a competitor analysis such as Porter's Five Forces assess a market from the standpoint of a particular proposition or business. It is important to identify the subject of a SWOT analysis clearly because a SWOT analysis is a perspective of one thing, be it a company (yours or a competitors), a product, a proposal, a method, a potential partner, a change in supplier, an investment opportunity, and so on. Strategic planning is not a precise science—no tool is mandatory—but it's a matter of pragmatic choice as to what helps best to identify and explain the issues.

To develop strategies that take into account the SWOT profile, managers might develop a matrix of these factors. The SWOT matrix (also known as a TOWS matrix) is shown in **Table 6.2**. The SWOT matrix is a relatively simple tool for generating strategic options. Managers use it to look intelligently at how they can best take advantage of the opportunities open to their company while minimizing the impact of weaknesses and protecting the company against threats.

What other types of plans do managers make?
Once the strategic planning process is complete and long-term goals and objectives have been determined, middle management generates *tactical plans* to carry out the goals determined by the strategic plan. **Tactical plans** specifically determine the resources and the actions required to implement particular aspects of the strategic plan. Whereas strategic plans have a long-term focus, tactical plans are made with a one- to three-year horizon in mind. Determining the company's annual budget, for example, is one function of a tactical plan. Say the strategic plan of a paper supply company is to sell more products to large offices on the East Coast. One part of this company's tactical plan might be to determine how much money should be allocated to advertising in that area.

The specifics of carrying out tactical plans are *operational plans*. In **operational plans**, first-line managers precisely determine the process by which tactical plans can be achieved. Operational plans depend on daily or weekly schedules and focus on specific departments or employees. For example, once the paper supply company determines how much of its budget can be allocated to advertising, specific department managers might have to decide which employees will travel to advertise the product.

Tactical and operational planning are two methods that companies use to carry out plans, assuming there are no external factors affecting the business. But, sometimes, extreme circumstances occur that force the company to find alternative means to survive.

BizSkills Simulation: Conducting a SWOT Analysis. Located in MyBusinessLab.

Decision-Making Mini-Simulation: Change. Located In Mybusinesslab.

3
Describe the implications of tactical plans, operational plans, and contingency plans within the context of management.

Tactical plans specifically determine the resources and the actions required to implement particular aspects of the strategic plan.

Operational plans determine the process by which tactical plans can be achieved.

Table 6.2 SWOT Matrix

	Strengths	Weaknesses
Opportunities	S-O strategies are used by the company to pursue opportunities by using the firm's strengths.	W-O strategies are used by the company to overcome weaknesses to pursue opportunities.
Threats	S-T strategies are used by the company to identify ways that the firm can use its strengths to reduce its vulnerability to external threats	W-T strategies are used by the company to establish a defensive plan to prevent the firm's weaknesses from making it highly susceptible to external threats—mainly used by firms that are not in a good or stable position.

How do managers plan for the unexpected?

We have seen all too frequently the effects that natural disasters (i.e., hurricanes, floods, and earthquakes) can have on businesses—job loss, physical damage, and indirect losses because of physical destruction slowing or halting operations. We have also seen companies quickly fall into disfavour due to unexpected failures in product quality, such as the lead paint found on Mattel toys that resulted in millions of toys being recalled. All the best corporate strategies can be negated swiftly if an unexpected crisis occurs and a plan is not in place to deal with it adequately. What happens if a company suddenly has more sales than production can handle, or if the best-selling product is recalled due to a defect? Who would run the company upon the unexpected death of the CEO or company owner? How should a company fight off an unpredictable takeover threat from a competitor or a rapidly spreading computer virus that threatens to shut down all internal and external lines of communication?

These are the sorts of questions answered through contingency planning. **Contingency planning** is a set of plans that ensures that the organization will run as smoothly as possible during an unexpected disruption. Such planning encompasses how management will communicate, both internally and externally. Internally, management must inform its employees how they should continue to do their jobs. Externally, an organization must have a plan in place to deal with requests for information from either employees, the families of employees, or even the media. Contingency planning involves determining what departments within the company are vital to the immediate needs of the organization when an unexpected crisis occurs. The particulars of each plan differ depending on the size and function of the company and the magnitude of crisis for which the plan is needed.

The Vanguard Group, a U.S. investment management company, has in place specific, formal business contingency plans to respond to a range of incidents—from worst-case scenarios such as the loss of a data centre, buildings, or staff to more common occurrences such as power outages.[25] As important as it is to have plans in place, it's just as important to ensure the plans are tested and key individuals know exactly what is expected of them. Like fire drills in school, companies should periodically review and rehearse their plans. Vanguard officials put their contingency plans through rigorous testing, including full-scale practice drills in which the company closes a building and works from a remote location. The company also conducts mock disaster drills together with local, state, and federal authorities. Since Vanguard's business would be affected significantly should a disruption in any of its technical systems occur, it also conducts tests to determine how quickly its information technology systems can become operational in the event of a disruption. **Table 6.3** summarizes the types of plans that companies such as Vanguard use to carry out their goals.

Contingency planning is a set of plans that ensures that the organization will run as smoothly as possible during an unexpected disruption.

Table 6.3 The Four Types of Management Plans

Strategic Plan	Tactical Plan
• Sets the approach for achieving an organization's long-term goals and objectives • Acts as a framework for decisions • Assists in setting corporate benchmarks	• Determines resources and actions necessary to implement strategic plan • Made with a one- to three-year horizon in mind
Operational Plan	**Contingency Plan**
• Involves planning the execution of the tactical plan • Depends on daily or weekly schedules • Focuses on specific departments or employees	• Keeps an organization running in the event of a disruption • Details internal and external communication procedures for such an event • Determines which departments are most vital to an organization during a crisis

Organizing

How are plans put into action?

Once goals have been finalized and plans have been made, the next step in the management process is to put those plans into action. **Organizing** is the process of structuring the capital, personnel, raw materials, and other resources to carry out the plans in a way that best matches the nature of the work. Part of organizing is to establish an organizational structure. Organizational structure depends on a variety of factors, such as the number of employees in the organization, the speed at which decisions need to be made, the subjectivity of the business to rapid change, and the collaborative nature of the work. Planning and organizing are two of a manager's most important responsibilities. How a manager goes about accomplishing these tasks has a tremendous effect on every aspect of the company. Every company, regardless of its size or specialty, needs a solid organizational structure. Without one, employees may have trouble making decisions and assigning responsibility.

Are most companies organized in the same way?

Not all corporations are organized in the same way. The traditional way of organizing management falls into a vertical, hierarchical structure. **Figure 6.4** shows a traditional vertically structured managerial pyramid.

At the peak of the pyramid, **top-level managers** are the corporate officers responsible for the organization as a whole. Most established corporations determine the corporate officers, especially the chief executive officer (CEO), or president. Depending on the size and organizational complexity of the company, top management can also include

Explain the significance of organizing and how most management is organized.

Distinguish vertical organizations, horizontal organizations, and network organizations.

Organizing is the process of structuring the capital, personnel, raw materials, and other resources to carry out the plans in a way that best matches the nature of the work.

Top-level managers are the corporate officers responsible for the organization as a whole.

6

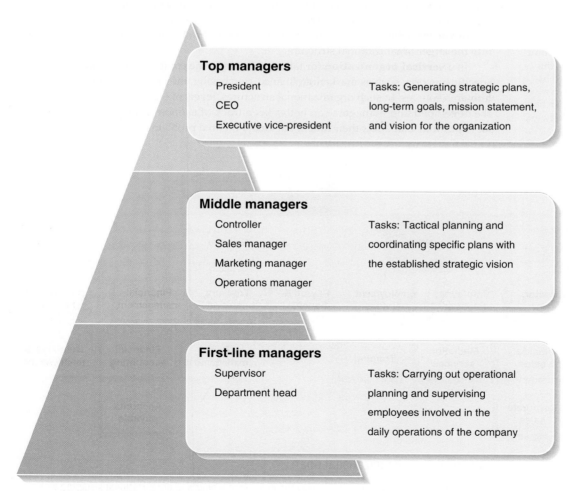

Top managers

President
CEO
Executive vice-president

Tasks: Generating strategic plans, long-term goals, mission statement, and vision for the organization

Middle managers

Controller
Sales manager
Marketing manager
Operations manager

Tasks: Tactical planning and coordinating specific plans with the established strategic vision

First-line managers

Supervisor
Department head

Tasks: Carrying out operational planning and supervising employees involved in the daily operations of the company

Figure 6.4 The Managerial Pyramid

Decision-Making Mini-Simulation: Communication. Located in MyBusinessLab.

the chief financial officer (CFO), chief operations officer (COO), and chief information officer (CIO). Top managers generate the strategic plans, long-term goals, mission statement, and vision for the organization. They establish the culture of the organization and inspire employees to adopt senior management's vision of the organization. In smaller corporations, especially small start-up companies, top managers may also be responsible for planning and carrying out the day-to-day tasks of the company. But as the business grows, such companies will need to add more employees and divide the work into smaller tasks and areas of specialty.

Middle-level managers can be thought of as top managers for only one division or a part of an organization. As such, middle-level managers are responsible for tactical planning and for creating more specific plans that coordinate with the strategic vision set by the top managers. Included in this management layer are positions such as division managers (finance, marketing, sales, operations, and IT) or team leaders who are not arranged by function but are responsible for a group of employees who must carry out specific tasks for the organization.

Middle-level managers are top managers for only one division or a part of an organization.

The bottom of the managerial pyramid includes **first-line managers,** who carry out operational planning. These managers fill a supervisory role over those employees who carry out the day-to-day operations of the company.

First-line managers carry out operational planning.

Not all companies have all three layers of management—some have more, and some have fewer. Typically, you'll find the "extra" layers are middle managers. However, the organizational pattern of a vertically structured business generally can be represented by the managerial pyramid.

Smaller companies that have relatively few employees tend to be organized differently than large corporations. Small companies tend to have much simpler structures compared with large companies. Regardless, to accomplish many tasks at the same time, organizations must have some division of labour and allocate work into smaller tasks. An **organizational chart**, such as the one in **Figure 6.5**, shows how groups of employees fit into the larger organizational structure.

An **organizational chart** shows how groups of employees fit into the larger organizational structure.

In a **vertical organization** (or tall organization), the company is organized by specific function, such as marketing, finance, purchasing, information technology, and human resources.

In a **vertical organization** (or tall organization), the company is organized by specific function, such as marketing, finance, purchasing, information technology, and human resources. In such organizational structures, levels of expertise within functions are developed and managers can better keep track of economic and environmental conditions that affect their functional area. Potential problems may arise, however,

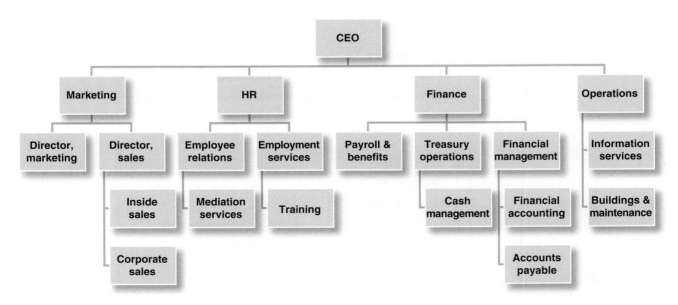

Figure 6.5 Organizational Chart

An organizational chart is used to display the division of labour and organizational structure within a company.

because integration between functions and divisions is not always easy. Vertical organization usually calls for long lines of communication and "reporting up." This makes it difficult for a company to respond quickly to changes in a market or to provide innovation because keeping each division updated means spending time doing so.

What are the differences between a vertical and horizontal organizational structure?

Vertical organization has been the primary structure of business since the Industrial Revolution. Although such traditional pyramidal management has its benefits, in the early 1990s, vertical organizational structures were criticized as being overspecialized, fragmented, and inflexible. Some businesses, such as Ford Motor Company, Xerox Corp., Motorola, and Barclay's Bank, found that they were more successful when they organized in a horizontal structure and formed management groups around areas of specific production or product units.[26] In a **horizontal organization** (or flat organization), the traditional managerial pyramid is flattened and the management layers are collapsed. A horizontally structured organization still has some of the pyramidal aspects, including a CEO and perhaps another layer of middle management, but then the organization concentrates the majority of the remaining employees into working teams or groups. **Figure 6.6** illustrates the basic differences in organizational charts of a vertically structured organization and a horizontally structured organization.

The benefit of a horizontal organization is that each team has more responsibility for the outcome of its work. There are fewer layers of management, so fewer reporting issues arise, and, if needed, the bosses' approval can be sought and received much faster. The company can be more responsive since individuals in a horizontal organization are more empowered to make decisions. Horizontal structures have been deemed the "model for the knowledge age." They are suitable for industries that require rapid responses to quick changes.

Occasionally, when companies have grown so large that the variety of product lines, geographic regions, or manufacturing processes can be difficult to manage, they restructure from a vertical organization to a horizontal one. In these circumstances, managers

> In a **horizontal organization** (or flat organization), the traditional managerial pyramid is flattened, and the management layers are collapsed.

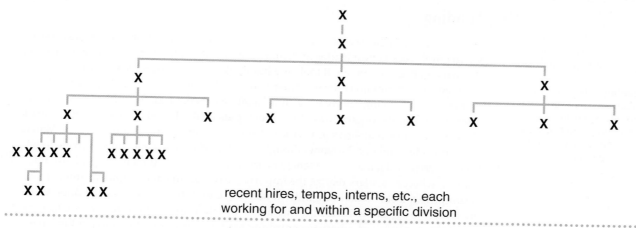

Vertical organization (five levels)

recent hires, temps, interns, etc., each working for and within a specific division

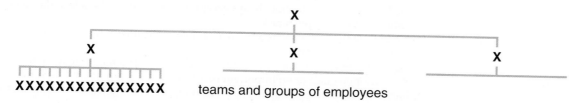

Horizontal organization (three levels)

teams and groups of employees

Figure 6.6 Vertically and Horizontally Structured Organizations

often try to streamline functions to make management easier. For example, they might structure the organization into divisions of employees who work on just one product line. Or they might divide the company into teams in which each team specializes in just one geographic region or works through just one manufacturing process. In essence, these divisions work like separate mini-companies. Each division has its own set of functional expertise, so separate managers are in charge of finance, marketing, human resources, informational technology, and so on. The groups work autonomously and are highly differentiated—so much so that they create barriers to coordination across functions. In today's business environment, there are fewer and fewer organizations structured vertically by function.

Decision-Making Mini-Simulation: Organizational Structure. Located in MyBusinessLab.

Network organizations are collections of independent, mostly single-function firms that collaborate on a product or service.

What other types of organizational structures are there?   Although the majority of companies are structured with the more traditional vertical structure or the group-oriented horizontal structure, a new business structure is emerging. Instead of the customary means of producing a product or service in which one company is responsible for all functions, **network organizations** are collections of independent, mostly single-function firms that collaborate on a product or service. For example, Boeing recently completed production of its latest airplane, the Boeing 787. In the past, airplanes were assembled in one hangar. This time, however, Boeing relied on the expertise of hundreds of manufacturers worldwide to independently manufacture the components of the plane and ship the individual pieces for assembly in its main plant. The wings and landing gear are assembled in Italy, and the nose and cockpit are assembled in Wichita, Kansas. Individual or combined elements are then shipped to Everett, Washington, where they are finally assembled into a single 787 plane.

In addition to Boeing, other companies are using a network arrangement, including Nike, which only owns one manufacturing plant, and Reebok, which only designs and markets but does not produce any of its products. A network structure is not suitable for every company, but it may be successful for those companies that need

- to be as flexible and innovative as possible
- to respond quickly to threats and opportunities
- to save time
- to reduce costs and risk

⑥ Leading

Describe what makes a good leader and the various styles of leadership.

Leading is the process of influencing, motivating, and enabling others to contribute to the success and effectiveness of the organization by achieving its goals.

Why does an organization need leaders?   An organization is often successful when employees have a leader to demonstrate what it takes for a company to achieve its goals. In this section, we'll look at what it takes to be a strong leader and how managers can maintain control of their teams and their companies. **Leading** is the process of influencing, motivating, and enabling others to contribute to the success and effectiveness of the organization by achieving its goals. Therefore, the quality of leadership exhibited by managers is a critical determinant of organizational success. Managers and leaders are not the same, though it is important for a manager to strive to be both a leader and a manager. Managers are task-oriented and focus on process and control, whereas leaders realize the importance of guiding and inspiring others to help accomplish a task. Sometimes, individuals prove that they can get the job done and are therefore considered effective managers. But they are not necessarily true leaders if they have not inspired others to contribute to the process. As illustrated in **Figure 6.7**, the best leaders are defined as those who:

1. *Challenge the process* by not always accepting conventional beliefs and practices as the only way to accomplish tasks.
2. *Model the way* by serving as a living example of the ideals in which they are asking their employees to share.
3. *Inspire a shared vision* and appeal to people's values and motivate them to care about the corporate goals or an important mission.
4. *Encourage the heart* by showing appreciation, providing rewards, and so on, to motivate people in positive ways.

5. *Enable others to act* by giving people the access to information and empowering them to perform to their fullest potential.[27]

What are the traits of a good leader?

In addition to these five means of effective leadership, most leadership analysts agree that good leaders share several traits.

- *Determination.* Leaders need to achieve and are constantly striving for improvement. They have a high energy level and are ambitious and persistent in the face of obstacles. Leaders don't give up easily. True leadership drive, however, does not come at the expense of others; therefore, leaders delegate authority and responsibility to others to promote their success also. They are the catalysts for positive action.
- *Inspiration.* Leaders influence in a positive and moral way (rather than in a selfish and destructive way) and garner trust, respect, and commitment to their vision. They can communicate a vision throughout the organization and inspire others to adopt the same vision and work toward common goals.
- *Flexibility and empathy.* Leaders are good listeners, can perceive the need for a change in tactics, and, if necessary, can adjust their leadership style to fit the current environment, people, and situation. Leaders must take into account the overall well-being of others and be mindful of their values and feelings.
- *Innovativeness.* Leaders set goals and have a vision of the future that may be different from the norm. Leaders are not afraid to alter their methods, plans, or even thinking if the situation calls for change. In addition, leaders exemplify resourcefulness as they continually brainstorm for solutions to problems and more effective ways of reaching goals.
- *Honesty.* Leaders are honest and credible. Employees can trust that the leader will deal with them in a fair and equitable manner.
- *Self-confidence.* Leaders have the confidence to overcome inevitable obstacles and to make tough decisions despite uncertainty. A leader's confidence promotes calm in stressful situations.
- *Knowledge and competence.* Leaders have a good handle on their business and industry. They are willing to admit mistakes and constantly seek more information to make informed and reasoned decisions. Good leaders base their decisions on facts. They are well-organized and detail-oriented.

These traits are essential to effective leadership and are common to most good leaders.

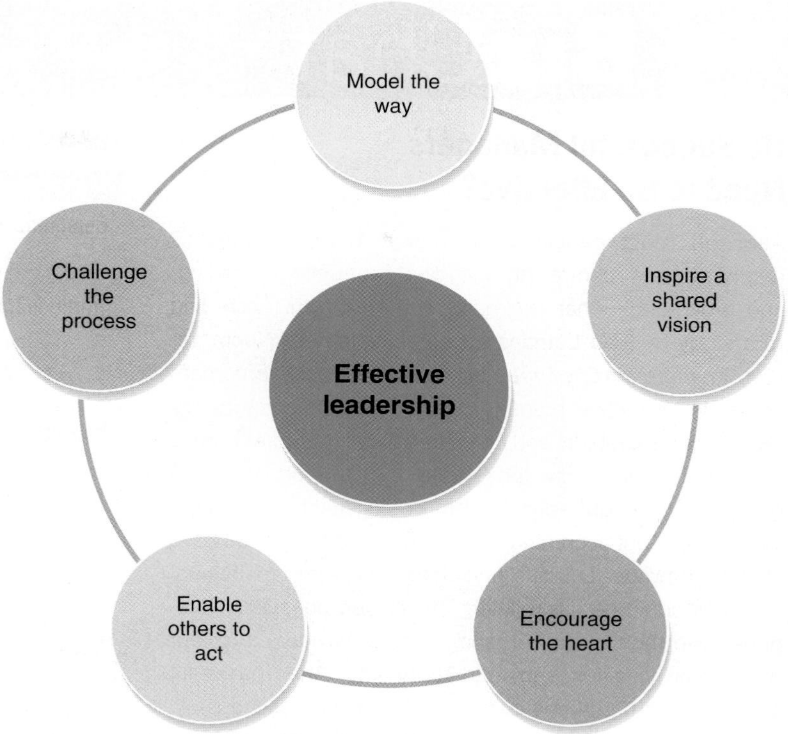

Figure 6.7   Traits of Effective Leadership

When it comes to the concepts of leadership and control within the business context, myths abound. Can you separate the facts from the fiction? Test your knowledge with the **quiz** below.

1. Fact or Fiction: All managers are good leaders.
2. Fact or Fiction: There is a difference between a successful manager and an effective manager.
3. Fact or Fiction: Good leaders don't challenge conventional beliefs because that would undermine their authority.
4. Fact or Fiction: Autocratic leadership—making decisions without consulting others—is never a good idea.
5. Fact or Fiction: Lack of controlling can cause companies to implode.
6. Fact or Fiction: Bureaucratic reporting tools have no real purpose.
7. Fact or Fiction: Corporate culture has a big impact on control.

Answers: 1. Fiction; 2. Fact; 3. Fiction; 4. Fiction; 5. Fact; 6. Fiction; 7. Fact

How did you do? Do you have your facts straight? Read on to learn the truth about leadership and control.

•—[Explore on MyBusinessLab

Do Successful Managers Need to Be Effective?

Although most people would agree that a manager's responsibilities centre on planning, controlling, leading, and organizing, what do managers really do? According to a study by Fred Luthans at the University of Nebraska-Lincoln, there are two types of managers: successful managers and effective managers. Successful managers are those who are rapidly and consistently promoted, whereas effective managers are those who "get the job done and do it right." It might seem that to be successful, you must be effective, but according to the study, the two types have little in common. Luthans first determined that managers' activities could be assimilated into eleven behaviour categories. He then further organized the behaviours into four managerial activities, shown in **Table 6.4**.[28] After four years of observation, Luthans determined that the "successful" managers—those who were promoted relatively quickly—spent most of their time networking, whereas the "effective" managers—those who have satisfied subordinates and high-performing units—spent most of their time performing communication and human resources management activities. Interestingly, of the nearly 400 managers tracked, no more than 10 percent of the group fell into both "successful" and "effective" categories.

Table 6.4   The Activities of Managers

Management Activities	Descriptive Categories
Communication	Exchanging information
	Paperwork
Traditional management	Planning
	Decision making
	Controlling
Networking	Interacting with outsiders
	Socializing/politicking
Human resources management	Motivating/reinforcing
	Disciplining/punishing
	Managing conflict
	Staffing

Discussion Questions

1. **How might this idea of "success" in management affect a company?**
2. **What's the difference between an effective manager and an efficient manager? Can a manager be effective without being efficient or vice versa?**
3. **Why do you think only 10 percent of the managers surveyed fell into both "successful" and "effective" categories? Why wouldn't a higher percentage be both successful and effective?**

French chef Alain Ducasse (centre) prepares the wedding menu for Prince Albert II of Monaco in the Hotel de Paris Louis XV restaurant. Chefs like Ducasse use a variety of leadership styles, depending on the situation.

What are the different leadership styles?

Henry Chang runs the kitchen of a five-star restaurant. While preparing for lunch and dinner, Henry allows his staff to offer opinions as he develops the menu. Prepping for the day's meals, the staff members can choose what area in which they want to work. He also lets them experiment with different recipes and food presentations and features their work on the main menu when possible. The kitchen staff members love working with Henry because he allows them to be creative and innovative. He also encourages them to cultivate the skills they need to run their own restaurant some day. Henry's restaurant often attracts important political dignitaries and famous entertainers, and sometimes the restaurant becomes unexpectedly busy. In these circumstances, Henry doesn't leave anything to chance and dictates exactly what needs to be done and who should do it. Henry knows he might hurt someone's feelings, but, ultimately, his staff trusts him to make the right decisions to obtain the best results for the restaurant.

For the most part, Henry is a democratic leader. A **democratic leader** delegates authority and involves employees in decision-making. Because Henry knows that by involving his employees they become more invested in the process, he feels the ultimate output is better. The trade-off, Henry recognizes, is that his democratic style of leadership requires more time and advanced planning. When such time is not available, Henry must take complete charge. In those instances, he becomes an autocratic leader. An **autocratic leader** makes decisions without consulting others. A good leader knows that autocratic leadership can be an effective style in certain circumstances when quick decisions need to be made or when it seems like the group cannot come to a consensus.

Some leaders take a more hands-off approach to management and act more as consultants rather than participants. **Laissez-faire leaders (or free-reign leaders)** are more advisory in style, encouraging employees to contribute ideas rather than specifically directing their tasks. This style of leadership is often best used with groups and teams. However, it is possible for the laissez-faire leader to lose too much involvement in the group's processes. Both employees and leaders should take caution to avoid this and to make sure that all goals are aligned. If the group or team members feel that management is virtually absent, team members may choose actions and strategies that are easy but inappropriate or unethical. Laissez-faire leadership implemented properly can give employees a sense of challenge, commitment, and renewed energy as they are left to handle tasks on their own. As businesses continue to reduce the layers of management, laissez-faire and democratic styles are becoming the leadership styles of choice.

As in the case with Henry and his restaurant, no one style of leadership will work in every situation. In reality, managers recognize that they need to be flexible and use whatever style works best for the particular situation. You can think of this adaptive style of leadership as **contingency leadership**. Contingency leadership places a range of leadership styles on a continuum, such as the one in **Figure 6.8**. Those who opt for contingency

top10

North America's Best Companies for Cultivating Leadership Skills (2010)

1. IBM (information technology)
2. Procter & Gamble (consumer products)
3. General Mills (food consumer products)
4. McKinsey (consulting)
5. McDonald's (food services)
6. General Electric (diversified financials)
7. Colgate-Palmolive (consumer products)
8. Deere (industrial and farm equipment)
9. Whirlpool (appliances)
10. 3M (diversified manufacturer)

Source: Beth Kowitt and Kim Thai, "25 Top Companies for Leaders," Fortune (online), November 20, 2009, http://money.cnn.com/2009/11/19/news/companies/top_leadership_companies.fortune/index.htm, Accessed March 31, 2011.

A **democratic leader** delegates authority and involves employees in decision-making.

An **autocratic leader** makes decisions without consulting others.

Laissez-faire leaders (or free-reign leaders) encourage employees to contribute ideas rather than specifically directing their tasks.

Contingency leadership is a more adaptive style of leadership in which managers recognize that they need to be flexible and use whatever style works best for the particular situation.

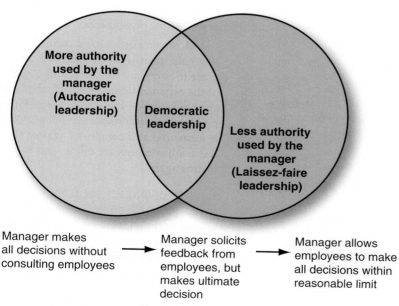

Figure 6.8 Continuum of Leadership Behaviour

leadership recognize that forces in today's business environment change, and management may need to respond to different situations in different ways. Leadership will be discussed in more detail in Chapter 7.

Evaluate the implications of control within a business.

Controlling

Why does a company need good controls? *Leadership* and *control*—they're both slippery terms that leave ample room for misinterpretation. And yet how managers apply these concepts plays a vital role in the success or failure of a business. As managers form the plans and strategies to carry out the goals of the organization, they must also determine whether their plans and strategies are adequate to generate the desired results. **Controlling** ensures that the plans and strategies set in place by management are properly carried out. Controlling helps to identify and correct weaknesses and errors in the system. Such weaknesses and errors, left uncorrected, can hurt an organization and have caused large companies to implode with illegal or immoral behaviours. Chapter 3 discussed the importance of running an ethical organization. Making sure that people are doing what they should and acting appropriately is a primary rationale for instituting control functions in an organization. Controls also pick up errors in the system, so if a plan is not meeting its goals, it can be modified.

Controlling ensures that the plans and strategies set in place by management are properly carried out.

There are three broad control strategies that managers use either individually or in combination to achieve organizational control: bureaucratic control, market control, and clan control.[29] Each control strategy serves a different purpose:

- **Bureaucratic control** uses rules, regulations, and formal authority to guide performance. Budgets, statistical reports, and performance appraisals are all part of bureaucratic control.
- **Market control** involves evaluating workers on their attainment of specific objectives. Performance goals are set at various levels, and periodic reviews determine whether the goals have been achieved. Rewards (pay raises and promotions) are tied to goal attainment.
- **Clan control** assumes that employees and management have common goals and values and therefore will measure and monitor one another without the need for more formal external controls. Clan control is based on the concept that employees trust each other and, if invested in the same goals and values, will act for the best benefit of themselves, as well as the organization.

Most companies have control systems that help measure the plans they set in place to carry out the goals and objectives of the organization. In general, the control system forms a cycle, as shown in **Figure 6.9**: performance standards are set, performance is measured and compared against the standard, adjustments are made, and the cycle begins again.

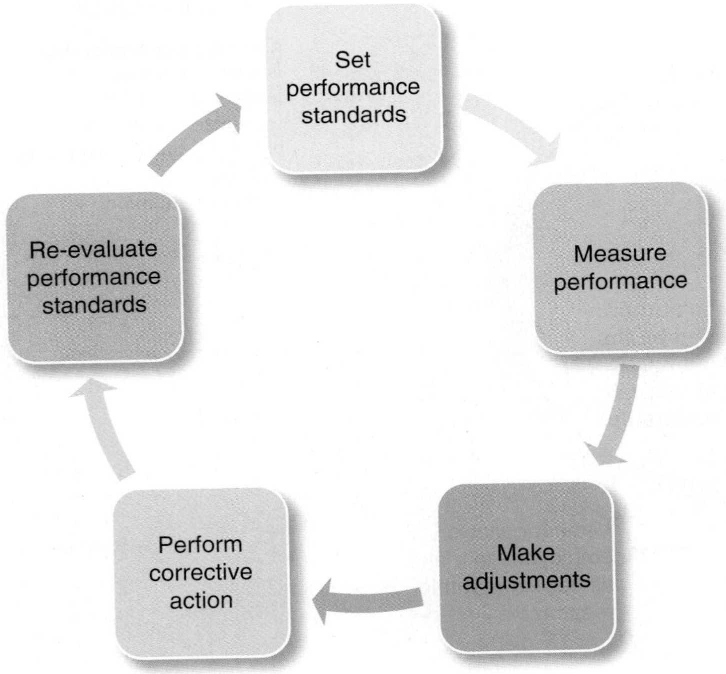

How do managers measure performance? To manage a business and ensure that the goals are being met, managers measure performance in a variety of ways. Bureaucratic reporting tools such as financial statements and sales reports are used to measure performance. These reports help determine whether the products are competitive, are using capital wisely, and are being produced as efficiently as possible.

Set performance standards

Measure performance

Make adjustments

Perform corrective action

Re-evaluate performance standards

Figure 6.9 The Control Cycle

On Target

Loblaw's Restructuring[30]

Craig Hutchinson is the easygoing senior vice-president of marketing at Loblaw Companies Limited, and as such, he's responsible for all marketing activities at Canada's largest food distributor and leading provider of general merchandise products, drugstore, and financial products and services. Loblaw's more than 139 000 full-time and part-time employees execute its strategy, which is developed under three core themes: simplify, innovate, and grow. The company has more than 1000 corporate and franchised stores across Canada and is one of Canada's largest private sector employers. Loblaw's strives to be consumer-focused, community focused, cost-effective, proactive in corporate citizenship, and agile with the goal of achieving long-term growth for its many stakeholders.[31] In 2007, however, experiencing infrastructure challenges and increased competition, Loblaw Companies reported its first annual loss in more than twenty years. Coupled with management changes in 2008, the company suffered in the media and the eyes of shareholders. Loblaw countered Walmart's entry into the fresh food business by building larger stores that carried more general merchandise, but the strategy did not help Loblaw compete against the low-price giant, particularly in Ontario, and Loblaw stopped building Superstores in Ontario until they could get the format right.[32]

In 2008, Hutchison stepped in to provide a central marketing voice and restructured the company into five teams: the Joe Fresh and PC Home team, brands, events, the retail team, and a dedicated flyer team. "During the 18 months I was trying to get these people in place I probably had 50 of the 80 people reporting directly to me at one point or another," he says. "So it gave me an opportunity to get to know the team intimately, to know what their strengths were, where they want to grow.

A little challenging having 21 direct reports, but it was really a great experience." Hutchison considers the reorganization his greatest accomplishment during that time.

Hutchinson's management style is very hands-on and part of the restructuring included a delayering of the organization. "[From] the first person in marketing up to me there are only three layers, so it's a very flat organization and one where ideas are shared very seamlessly."

To ensure that seamlessness, Hutchison visits stores every Wednesday, engaging with consumers and employees and tackling issues. On the executive level, he reviews weekly sales numbers with senior management every Monday to generate timely responses to consumer behaviour fluctuations. "I've always been a very quick marketer, but to be able to see that attention to detail, especially during this economic situation, allowed us to develop much faster insights and put our Spidey radar up early."

David Rosenberg, whose Toronto-based advertising agency, Bensimon Byrne, has worked with Loblaw since 2002, says Hutchison has brought a sharper focus to the brand. "Loblaw is a complex, multifaceted organization that often has to turn on a dime," he says. "To get the whole organization aligned behind a direction is a pretty gargantuan task, and he seems to be able to manage that very difficult task unbelievably well."

Discussion Questions

1. Does Hutchison's leadership style seem to lean toward autocratic, democratic, or laissez-faire?
2. What are the advantages of flattening the layers?
3. Does it seem that Hutchison is acting in conjunction with the three core themes of Loblaw's? Why or why not?

Source: Toan, Carey, (December 2009) Strategy, Overall Winner - Loblaw's Craig Hutchinson: Back to the Future.

In addition to meeting financial, production, and sales measures, another measure of performance is quality so that the products or services the company provides meet or exceed customer requirements. Many managers use **total quality management**, an integrated approach focusing on quality from the beginning of the production process up through managerial involvement to detect and correct problems. Another quality initiative that is receiving much attention is **Six Sigma**, a statistically based, proactive, long-term process designed to look at the overall business process to prevent problems. To achieve the Six Sigma standard, a business must not allow more than 3.4 defects per million opportunities.

Total quality management is an integrated approach focusing on quality from the beginning of the production process up through managerial involvement to detect and correct problems.

Six Sigma is a statistically based, proactive, long-term process designed to look at the overall business process to prevent problems.

7

Motivation, Leadership, and Teamwork

LEARNING OBJECTIVES

After studying this chapter, you should be able to:

1 Explain how motivation and work environment encourage "flow." (pp. 179–181)

2 Describe the intricacies of Maslow's hierarchy of needs, McClelland's "three needs" theory, and Herzberg's motivator-hygiene theory. (pp. 181–183)

3 Distinguish the factors between extrinsic and intrinsic motivators. (pp. 183–184)

4 Summarize the implications of Theory X, Theory Y, Theory Z, and the Vroom models. (pp. 184–187)

5 Explain how motivational theories and industrial psychology have changed the work environment since the early twentieth century. (pp. 187–188)

6 List the various identifiable leadership styles and personality traits, and explain how they affect business leadership. (pp. 188–197)

7 Outline the best ways to create, manage, and participate in teams, taking into account factors such as technology, group flow, Belbin's nine team roles, and Covey's Seven Habits model. (pp. 197–200)

OPENING DISCUSSION: INVESTING IN TALENT

General Electric (GE) Ranked No. 1 for Leadership

"We have always believed that building strong leaders is a strategic imperative. When times are easy, leadership can be taken for granted. When the world is turbulent, you appreciate great people."[1]—Jeff Immelt, GE chairman and CEO

Jeff Immelt, GE's chair and CEO, is a rather impressive person. Since he took the helm at GE, he's been named one of the "World's Best CEOs" by *Barron's* magazine three times and General Electric was named "America's Most Admired Company" in a *Fortune* magazine poll as well as one of "The World's Most Respected Companies" in polls by *Barron's* and the *Financial Times*.[2] Immelt says his company trains the best leaders in the world.[3] He meets one-on-one with each of his 185 officers to discuss their "fit" in the organization, their strengths and weaknesses, and their careers. He also explores new ideas about how to develop and measure GE's leaders.

GE refers to its executive team—men and women at the forefront of GE's diversified portfolio of business—as "growth leaders," who encourage professional development and employee integrity. Each of their 191 most-senior executives has spent at least twelve months in training and professional development programs during their first fifteen years with GE,[4] and more than 9000 candidates fly in from around the world every year to participate in GE leadership programs.[5] While many corporations view training somewhere between a burdensome cost to a competitive advantage, GE spends US$1 billion a year on training and devotes weeks, even months, of each year to evaluating talent. By investing in human assets, GE develops employee skills and traits, creating a stronger workforce and producing the leaders it requires to grow GE business.

Immelt has sought management input from a wide variety of sources—including China's Communist Party[6]—and sends GE's rising young stars to study an array of organizations, from Google to West Point.

(continued)

What can managers from the 132-year-old industrial giant learn from Google? A corporate mindset that values "constant entrepreneurship," says Immelt.[7] Such self-scrutiny of its leadership style may seem unusual because GE's reputation remains unmatched year after year, with the world considering it a gold standard for talent. In a recent Hay Group global survey of the best companies for leadership, GE topped the list.[8] But one of the reasons GE's leadership is so admired worldwide comes from the company's determination to keep the development and measurement of talent at the forefront of its strategy discussions.[9]

Immelt's broadest responsibility at GE is to "drive change and develop people." Any executive who wants to change things, he says, should be guided by "a point of view about what's going on in the world, and you invest around that point of view."[10] According to advisers and colleagues, Immelt's approach is a mix of analysis, encouragement, cajoling, and sometimes orders by decree. Immelt says, "I think that if you run a big company, you've got to four or five times a year, just say, 'Hey team, look, here's where we're going.' If you do it 10 times, nobody wants to work for you. If you do it zero times, you have anarchy."[11]

DISCUSSION QUESTIONS

1. GE thinks that having its senior executives spend at least twelve months during their first fifteen years in training is a gain. How might it be a loss?

2. When a CEO of Immelt's stature puts his company under the microscope, his own management style inevitably comes under scrutiny. Why would he do this?

3. Visit the GE website to discover what GE is doing for its employees, the community, volunteerism, and worldwide citizenship. Does GE sound like a place you'd like to work? Do your values and beliefs seem to be aligned with those of GE?

MOTIVATION: THE BASICS

Personal Motivation

Personal motivation is what drives us internally and externally to succeed in whatever we want to succeed in.

What drives you to do your personal best?   Feeling driven and inspired to complete a task—this is what it means to be motivated. Do you ever feel this way? **Personal motivation** is what drives us internally and externally to succeed in whatever we want to succeed in. Understanding personal motivation, recognizing the role of motivation in the workplace, and examining theories that explain it are important parts of business. Even when pursuing personal goals, each of us retains and loses our motivation for very singular reasons. Think of times that you have pushed to be your best, whether at school, in sports, or in other activities. Is it easier for you to build enthusiasm for tasks that you're sure you can accomplish? Or do you set difficult goals and draw energy from the challenge of attaining them? Some people need immediate gratification or success in order to stay motivated. Others are able to postpone short-term success in pursuit of long-term gains. Do you need to be rewarded immediately for what you do or are you more motivated by long-term benefits?

Now think about how hard you work when you receive a lot of positive feedback (either financial or emotional). Is getting praise or money for a job important to you? Or are you driven more by the values of the place where you work, your beliefs, or in doing a job well? For some people, being part of the accomplishments of a team is what motivates them. You may not be sure what exactly motivates you. If so, you can take tests to determine your own motivational style.

How can you improve your motivation?   Some people may be naturally more motivated than others because they have been brought up in environments where self-motivation is encouraged and fostered. Personal motivation is fundamental to your success in business and in life in general. Think of what you could achieve if you were more motivated to succeed, had more energy, and more determination on a daily basis. Here are a few ways to improve your motivation:

- *Avoid negative experiences and people.* Emotionally draining situations, pessimistic people, and interpersonal conflicts are unnecessary setbacks that cause you to lose focus on your pursuits and productivity. Instead, find other motivated, positive people to affiliate with.
- *Become passionate about your mission.* Enthusiasm can be a powerful personal motivator because it keeps you energized, so if you are not enthusiastic about the work you are currently doing, find ways to incorporate aspects of what you enjoy doing into your daily life. Sometimes this may mean changing your point of view or attitude toward something so that you look for ways to make tasks you'd rather not do (but which must be done) interesting, rewarding, meaningful, and maybe a little fun.
- *Feel good about yourself.* Personal motivation is not something that happens overnight; you may have to work at it and you might need outside help. Listening to self-help CDs, reading material on the subject, or meeting with a counsellor or life coach might be just what you need to start a successful life.
- *Give yourself a reward.* Personal motivation comes from within, and no one can give you the motivation you need to start, work on, or complete a project. The motivation itself depends on the reward and whether it satisfies your needs or wants. Set goals, or milestones (mini-targets), for you to reach each day or along the way during a long-term project, and then reward yourself as you reach each milestone. For many, this may be a tangible reward, such as money, but for others this may be an intangible, intrinsic reward, such as self-satisfaction of a job well done or mastery of a skill.

Feeling motivated often involves the achievement of an intangible yet valuable state called *flow*. Are you a flow-starter? Or does the flow state float right past you? Take this **quiz** to find out.

1. When completing a task, I feel completely involved and focused on what I'm doing.
   a. Always
   b. Sometimes
   c. Never
2. I lose track of time when I'm working on a project or assignment.
   a. Always
   b. Sometimes
   c. Never
3. I feel like tasks are challenging yet doable.
   a. Always
   b. Sometimes
   c. Never
4. I feel like work isn't really "work"; it seems natural and effortless.
   a. Always
   b. Sometimes
   c. Never
5. I feel in control and content when tackling a project.
   a. Always
   b. Sometimes
   c. Never

Answers: If you answered . . .
Mostly a's . . . You are a flow-starter of the highest degree.
Mostly b's . . . You foray into flow state on occasion.
Mostly c's . . . Your familiarity with flow state is almost nonexistent.

Motivation, Engagement, and Flow

Does time fly by when you are engaged in your work?   Have you ever been working on a project and you were so immersed in what you were doing that when you looked at your watch, four hours had gone by? Psychologist Mihaly Csikszentmihalyi refers to this state of captivated attention as flow.[12] A **flow state** happens when you are completely involved and focused on what you are doing. Often people produce their best work, make the best use of their skills, and feel the most pleasure when they are in such a flow state. They are engaged in an activity when they feel a strong match between their own abilities and the challenge of a task—it is neither too difficult, which can lead to frustration, nor too simple, which can lead to boredom. They report a sense of control over what is happening and a feeling of effortlessness in their working. Creating a workplace that fosters the kind of motivation required to engage employees in their work and help get them to into a state of "flow" is the subject of **organizational psychology**—the study of how to create a workplace that fosters motivation and productivity among employees.

How many employees are in a "flow" state?   In 2007–2008, Towers Watson (formerly Towers Perrin), a professional services firm, conducted a Global Workforce Study, the largest of its kind, to identify the drivers of attraction, retention, and engagement through the eyes of employees at midsize to large organizations worldwide.[13] An **engaged employee** is one who is fully involved in, and enthusiastic about their work and thus will act to further their organization's interests. The study measured employees'

Explain how motivation and work environment encourage "flow."

A **flow state** happens when you are completely involved and focused on what you are doing. Often people produce their best work, make the best use of their skills, and feel the most pleasure when they are in such a flow state.

Organizational psychology studies how to create a workplace that fosters motivation and productivity among employees.

An **engaged employee** is one who is fully involved in, and enthusiastic about, their work, and thus will act in a way that furthers their organization's interests.

Table 7.1   Top Five Engagement Drivers across the Generations in the Workplace

Rank	Global Overall	Ages 18 to 24	Ages 25 to 34	Ages 35 to 44	Ages 45 to 54	Ages 55 and older
1	Senior management sincerely interested in employee well-being	Organization develops leaders at all levels	Have excellent career advancement opportunities	Senior management sincerely interested in employee well-being	Senior management sincerely interested in employee well-being	Senior management sincerely interested in employee well-being
2	Improved my skills and capabilities over the last year	Organization quickly resolves customer concerns	Senior management acts to ensure organization's long-term success	Improved my skills and capabilities over the last year	Improved my skills and capabilities over the last year	Organization's reputation for social responsibility
3	Organization's reputation for social responsibility	Senior management sincerely interested in employee well-being	Organization's reputation for social responsibility	Organization's reputation for social responsibility	Organization's reputation for social responsibility	Improved my skills and capabilities over the last year
4	Input into decision making in my department	Seek opportunities to develop new knowledge/skills	Input into decision making in my department	Input into decision making in my department	Appropriate amount of decision-making authority to do my job well	Input into decision making in my department
5	Organization quickly resolves customer concerns	Improved my skills and capabilities over the last yea	Set high professional standards	Organization quickly resolves customer concerns	Enjoy challenging work assignments that broaden skills	Set high personal standards

Source: Towers Watson, Closing the Engagement Gap: A Road Map for Driving Superior Business Performance, Towers Perrin Global Workforce Study 2007-2008, Reprinted with permission.

rational, emotional, and motivational connections to their companies and jobs to calculate their level of engagement and better understand how engagement affects behaviour and performance. The study also explored employees' views about a broad array of workplace factors, including the actions and behaviour of senior leadership and direct managers, company culture, and so on. The study's results showed that employee engagement rises when employees experience a combination of effective and caring leadership, interesting work, appealing development opportunities, and both tangible and intangible rewards (see **Table 7.1**).[14] Of the 90 000 respondents in eighteen countries, only 21 percent were fully engaged (giving full effort, willing to go that extra mile to help their companies succeed) in their work, 41 percent were enrolled (partly engaged), 30 percent were disenchanted (partially disengaged), and 8 percent were fully disengaged (disconnected rationally, emotionally, and motivationally from their workplace). According to Towers Perrin managing director Julie Gebauer, the employees who fall into the middle (either disenchanted or enrolled) category (71 percent) "pose the biggest opportunity, and the biggest threat, to employers. These are the employees who could go either way on the engagement continuum—either becoming more engaged and contributing more to the company, or becoming more disengaged and contributing nothing or, worse, actively disrupting the efforts of others in the work environment."[15] Gebauer suggests that placing employees on the engagement continuum with precision helps a company to identify the most effective strategies to improve engagement or find other ways to deal with those who can't or won't engage. The study also found that companies with the highest levels of employee engagement achieve better financial results and are more successful in retaining their most valued employees than companies with lower levels of engagement.[16]

Three of the study's key insights were: 1) Employees are eager to invest more of themselves to help the company succeed but want to understand what's in it for them; 2) Senior leaders need to make the leap to a more inspirational and engaging style of leadership to help drive higher engagement; and 3) Companies need to understand their employees as well as they understand their customers to design a work environment and experience that will drive higher engagement and performance.[17] The survey showed that senior leadership has a significant impact on engagement. The top engagement driver is employees' belief that senior management has their best interests at heart. Yet, only about four out of ten respondents believed this was true in their organizations. The challenge for senior management is to recognize the value of employees' untapped potential and to channel it in ways that yield real improvements in business performance. These results make it clear that encouraging flow in the workplace is a challenge.

The Towers Watson's 2010 Global Workforce Study covers more than 20 000 full-time employees in twenty-two markets around the world and is the most comprehensive analysis of the post-recession employee mindset available today. The recession has changed employees' attitudes and given them new priorities, with job security rising to the top (see www.towerswatson.com/global-workforce-study for more details).[18]

Canadian companies that topped the charts of Hewitt Associates' 2010 Best Employers in Canada list were: PCL Constructors Inc., EllisDon Corporation, Cisco Canada, Bennett Jones LLP, CIMA + Partners in Excellence, and WestJet for their commitment to employee engagement and corporate social responsibility.[19] Through mentorships, open communication, rewarding and challenging work, professional and career development opportunities, flexible employment practices, and recognition, these companies prove that they care about their employees. They strive to create work environments in which cash compensation is not the driving determinant of employee satisfaction. They engage their employees in meaningful ways.

What are the benefits of keeping employees motivated? Both employer and employee benefit from a motivated workforce. Employers find workers are more productive, more creative, and have much better retention levels when care is taken to provide a motivating environment and tasks. Employees often spend the majority of their waking day at their jobs, and their quality of life and overall happiness are enhanced when they feel excited about the work they contribute. The Global Workforce Study (mentioned above) found that firms with the highest percentage of engaged employees collectively increased operating income by 19 percent and earnings per share by 28 percent year to year.[20] If there were 100 employees averaging 70 percent engagement, it would take 116 employees averaging 60 percent engagement to achieve the same results as those 100 employees at 70 percent.[21] The cost of 16 employees working 37.5 hours per week at approximately $14.50 per hour is $8700, so the price of 10 percent disengagement per annum is $452 400! If those employees were senior employees or managers and were receiving a much higher pay level, the cost of disengagement could potentially put a company out of business. Not only does employee disengagement hurt companies financially, but it also may lead to poor company reputation, poor customer service, and lower quality output.

Early Theories of Motivation

Do basic needs for food or shelter motivate us to certain actions?
Several theories explain how and why people are motivated. One of the most popular theories was created by an early researcher in the area of human motivation, Abraham Maslow (1908–1970), who published the book *The Hierarchy of Needs* in 1954. **Maslow's hierarchy of needs** suggests that our primary needs are met first before our higher-level needs are addressed (see **Figure 7.1**). Maslow suggested that different people find themselves at different places in the hierarchy and so their motivations may be different. While an offer of overtime pay may be a successful motivator for a person concerned with safety needs, it might be the opposite of what someone working to satisfy their need for self-actualization finds motivating.

- *Physiological Needs.* The first needs to be met are inborn, basic needs—termed *physiological needs*—such as the need for water, food, sleep, and shelter. This means that

2

Describe the intricacies of Maslow's hierarchy of needs, McClelland's "three needs" theory, and Herzberg's motivator-hygiene theory.

Maslow's hierarchy of needs suggests that our primary needs are met first before our higher-level needs are addressed.

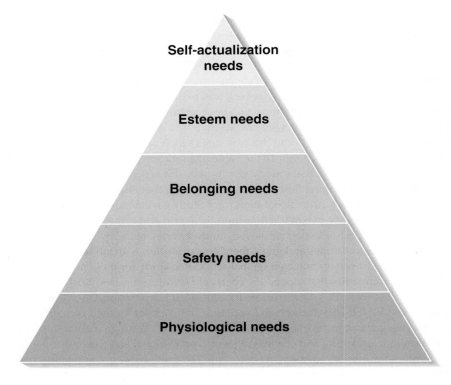

Figure 7.1   Maslow's Hierarchy of Needs

before we can think about anything else in our lives, we must ensure that these basic physiological needs are met. Physiological motivation in the workplace may include lunch breaks and paying salaries that enable workers to buy life's essentials.

■ *Safety Needs.* Once our physiological needs have been met, Maslow's theory holds that we strive to satisfy safety needs, including establishing safe and stable places to live and work (medical insurance, financial savings, relative job security, non-bullying workplace, or living in a safe area).

■ *Social Needs.* Once both physiological and safety needs have been met, we can consider social or belonging needs. This includes the need to belong to a group and to feel accepted by others. Social motivators in the workplace may include a culture of acceptance, belonging, and community.

■ *Esteem Needs.* The next level in Maslow's hierarchy includes esteem needs, which are satisfied by the mastery of a skill and by the attention and recognition of others. Some examples of esteem needs are recognition (external motivator), social status (external motivator), accomplishment (internal motivator), and self-respect (internal motivator).

■ *Self-actualization Needs.* Finally, at the top of the hierarchy are self-actualization needs that cannot be addressed unless and until the lower-level needs have been adequately met. These needs include the desire to maximize our own potential through education, self-fulfillment, as well as experiences of beauty and spirituality. Self-actualized people tend to have motivators such as truth, justice, wisdom, and meaning. Challenging and meaningful work assignments that enable innovation and creativity would motivate someone in the self-actualization level of Maslow's hierarchy of needs.

Do we need to form close personal relationships in the workplace?   Other researchers have proposed different models to map human needs to motivation. Psychologist **David McClelland's** (1917–1998) **"three needs" theory** suggests there are three main motivators.

McClelland's "three needs" theory suggests there are three main motivators: 1) the need for achievement (to accomplish something difficult on your own); 2) the need for affiliation (to form close personal relationships); and 3) the need for power (to be able to control the behaviour of others).

1. *the need for achievement*—to accomplish something difficult on your own
2. *the need for affiliation*—to form close personal relationships
3. *the need for power*—to be able to control the behaviour of others

According to McClelland, which need we try to satisfy depends on a variety of complex factors, including our cultural background. Although an individual may have multiple needs, McClelland suggests that one tends to be dominant over the others. In a workplace, this theory could account for differences in motivation among co-workers. For example, a person whose main need is for affiliation may have little motivation to perform a solitary task, whereas a person with a high need for achievement may be highly motivated to perform a difficult task alone. This theory is easy to understand and it gives managers critical insights about human nature so they can improve the impact of their motivational efforts. It is easy to apply because successful leaders are naturally skilled at determining the three-needs profile of their employees.

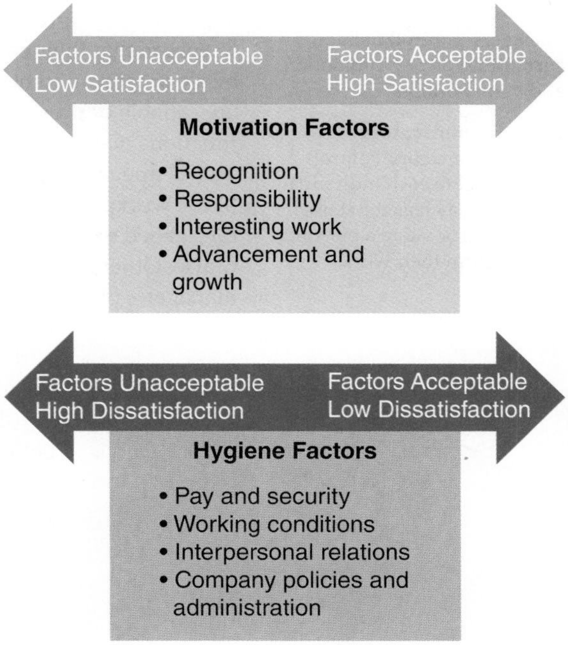

Do we need a safe work environment? Psychologist Frederick Herzberg's (1923–2000) **motivator-hygiene theory** (or **two-factor theory**), developed in 1959, suggests that two factors influence a person's motivation—hygiene factors (cause job dissatisfaction) and motivation factors (cause job satisfaction) (see **Figure 7.2**). Hygiene factors include a safe working environment, proper pay and benefits, and positive relationships with co-workers. People rarely notice hygiene factors if they are present. However, if hygiene factors are absent or inadequate, people tend to be dissatisfied. Consider basic working conditions, benefits, or other company policies. If there suddenly is no heat in the place where you work or if your pay is cut, you may be motivated to find a way to meet these needs. But if these are already in place, they are taken for granted and may not serve to motivate you.

The second set of factors in Herzberg's theory are motivator factors, which include a sense of responsibility, recognition, promotion, and job growth. Consider the self-actualization needs from Maslow's hierarchy. If there is no path for growth in your job or little recognition of your achievements, you probably would not immediately quit, but it would create a set of conditions that fail to motivate you.

Review the flow state quiz you took at the beginning of the chapter. Do you understand now what a flow state is and why it is important? What are the benefits of flow state in the workplace? And how can the different theories of motivation account for your achievement, or lack thereof, of flow state?

Factors Unacceptable Low Satisfaction | Factors Acceptable High Satisfaction

Motivation Factors

- Recognition
- Responsibility
- Interesting work
- Advancement and growth

Factors Unacceptable High Dissatisfaction | Factors Acceptable Low Dissatisfaction

Hygiene Factors

- Pay and security
- Working conditions
- Interpersonal relations
- Company policies and administration

Figure 7.2 Herzberg's Motivator-Hygiene Theory

Herzberg's motivator-hygiene (two-factor) theory suggests that two factors influence a person's motivation—hygiene factors (cause job dissatisfaction) and motivation factors (cause job satisfaction).

MOTIVATION: BUSINESS APPLICATIONS
The Complexity of Motivation

Do managers actually use theories of motivation? Theories of motivation can be very abstract. How can a manager of an assembly line at an automotive plant or a team leader of a software development company take what researchers know about human behaviour and use it to increase productivity and the satisfaction of the employees? The theories of human motivation you have just read about have given rise to a number of different approaches to organize and motivate people in the workplace. Using motivational theories to address the practical matters of motivation in the workplace is no easy task. Finding a way to inspire employees often requires patience and persistence. Fortunately, motivational theories that specifically take into account the dynamics of the business environment abound, giving managers many options from which to choose.

3 Distinguish the factors between extrinsic and intrinsic motivators.

 Decision-Making Mini-Simunlation: Motivation. Located in MyBusinessLab.

Extrinsic motivators (within managers' control) include such things as pay, promotion, and verbal praise.

Intrinsic motivators (outside managers' control) are internal to each individual employee, such as the sense of purpose or value a person derives from their work.

What could a manager do to enhance employee motivation?   Managers need to ensure that their employees are productive and eager to do the best job possible. Yet every organization has employees who simply do not produce work in the quality they are capable of providing, which can create costly problems for managers. Of all the functions managers perform, motivating employees is probably the most complex. This is due, in part, to the fact that what employees are motivated by changes constantly. In the workplace, managers can control some external motivating factors. These motivators, called **extrinsic motivators**, include such things as pay, promotion, and verbal praise. Other factors, called **intrinsic motivators**, are outside the set of factors under a manager's control because they are internal to each individual employee. These motivating influences are based on a person's actual interest in his or her work and stem from the sense of purpose or value a person derives from their work.

In 2006, an educational study in England showed the differences between these two types of motivators.[22] Children from a boys' school and a girls' school were asked to make a poster about their lives. One group was told its poster would decorate a local hospital for sick children. The other group was told it would be paid for its work. Which group of children would produce the better work—those who perceived the task as being worthwhile or those who were promised payment? In this case, much more sophisticated and detailed work came from the group that was working for free. The children were motivated more by the knowledge that they would be helping sick children than by financial reward.

Different people have different balances between intrinsic and extrinsic motivators. So how can business managers best motivate all their employees? An individual motivated intrinsically is working for his or her own satisfaction and may value challenging work he or she perceives as meaningful to the company more than extrinsic factors such as pay. Intrinsic motivators also tend to be higher on Maslow's hierarchy. So, for example, a boss who offers unsatisfying work, even though he or she offers bonuses and promotions, will have difficulty motivating an intrinsically motivated worker.

When you are first entering the workforce, money may motivate you as you save for a new car, house, or other things you'd like to buy. As you gain work experience and seniority in your job, money may not motivate you to do *more* in your job, but it may help motivate you *not* to do less. At this career point, you may be better motivated by recognition, promotions, interesting work projects, authority, health benefits, time away from work to spend with family, or other non-monetary incentives. Some workers are motivated by an increase in pay, while others are motivated by a flexible work schedule (e.g., a compressed workweek or the opportunity to work from home), and still others might be motivated by rewards the employer has not yet offered. Employees are often motivated by work that engages them: they need to like what they are doing and be inspired by their work. Other factors, such as a good work–life balance, also play a role in motivating or de-motivating employees, affecting quality of work, productivity, and customer relations. Managers need to ask employees what they want, then find a cost-effective way to offer it to them while at the same time increase company productivity.

 Motivational Models Used in Business

Summarize the implications of Theory X, Theory Y, Theory Z, and the Vroom models.

Besides early theories of motivation, what other models are there?   In addition to the theories proposed by Maslow, McClelland, and Herzberg, several models (in detail below) provide theoretical explanations of what motivates employees specifically in a business or workplace context.

McGregor's Theory X suggests that people inherently dislike work and want to avoid it.

Do most people dislike work?   In 1960, social psychologist Douglas McGregor proposed the Theory X and Theory Y models (see **Table 7.2**). **McGregor's Theory X** suggests that people inherently dislike work and want to avoid it. Because of this view,

Table 7.2   Comparison of Theory X and Theory Y

Theory X		Theory Y
Not motivated: People naturally dislike working and avoid it when given the opportunity.	*Motivation*	**Naturally motivated:** People see work as a natural part of life.
Authoritarian: Managers must use heavy controls to get people to work efficiently.	*Management*	**Democratic:** Managers need not use heavy controls. Managers allow employees to create their own motivation.
Followers: Employees would prefer to follow the direction of management than solve problems on their own.	*Leadership*	**Leaders:** People are creative problem-solvers whose ideas can be used in the workplace.
Avoiders: People do not want responsibility and avoid it when possible.	*Responsibility*	**Seekers:** People inherently seek responsibility and are willing to accept it when asked.
Security: People are not complex and mainly want security in their jobs.	*Needs*	**Creativity:** People need to be intellectually stimulated and feel their ideas are utilized.

Theory X management proposes that employees have to be coerced and controlled by management in order to be productive. This leads to an authoritarian, hard-line management style. In contrast, **McGregor's Theory Y** suggests that people view work as being as natural as playing and resting. People are naturally motivated and will direct themselves to work for the aims of the organization if they are satisfied with their jobs. **Theory Y management** assumes that, on average, people will accept and seek out responsibility. Such managers have a softer style of management that involves the participation of many.

Clearly, Theories X and Y would not work equally well in any given situation. Theory X–style management—which is authoritarian and hard line—is often seen in large-scale operations such as mass manufacturing. In the knowledge industry, in which there is a mix of professionals working together to solve complex problems, Theory Y is more likely to be seen with a participative, gentler management style.

Do most people like to be included in decision making?   In 1981, William Ouchi put forward a **Theory Z**, based on a Japanese management style that relied heavily on collaborative decision making. In many corporations in Japan in the 1980s, one person might be responsible for many different aspects of a single project. Employees tended to become generalists rather than specialists, who were trained in a very narrow set of tasks. **Theory Z management** is a combination of American and Japanese management philosophies characterized by long-term employment security, consensual decision making, and slow evaluation and promotion procedures, with an emphasis on individual responsibility within a group context. Workers tend to show a desire to co-operate and be loyal to the organization. As a result, companies that apply Theory Z management often reap the benefits of low turnover, high productivity, and strong morale among the workforce. Morale, a sense of purpose and enthusiasm toward one's work, is an important factor in an employee's level of motivation.

Does working hard result in a better outcome for the employee?   Although Maslow's hierarchy and other theories describe human motivation, they do so in terms of an overall model for all employees. In 1964, Victor Vroom proposed his expectancy theory, which has been developed by other researchers since. **Vroom's Expectancy theory** suggests an individual's motivation in any given situation can be described by the relationship among three psychological forces, illustrated in the formula:

Motivation = Expectancy ∗ Instrumentality ∗ Valence

Expectancy theory suggests that people are motivated to work toward rewards they want and which they believe they have a reasonable chance—or expectancy—of obtaining.[23] A reward that seems out of reach, for example, is not likely to be a motivator.

Theory X management proposes that employees have to be coerced and controlled by management in order to be productive. This leads to an authoritarian, hard-line management style.

McGregor's Theory Y suggests that people view work as being as natural as playing and resting.

Theory Y management assumes that, on average, people will accept and seek out responsibility. Such managers have a softer style of management that involves the participation of many.

Theory Z is based on a Japanese management style that relied heavily on collaborative decision making.

Theory Z management is a combination of American and Japanese management philosophies characterized by long-term employment security, consensual decision making, and slow evaluation and promotion procedures, with an emphasis on individual responsibility within a group context.

Vroom's Expectancy theory suggests an individual's motivation in any given situation can be described by the relationship among three psychological forces, illustrated in the formula: Motivation = Expectancy ∗ Instrumentality ∗ Valence.

Expectancy is the idea that a person's effort has an appreciable effect on a situation's result, whether it is a success or failure. Does working harder lead to a more positive outcome for the employee and/or the company? Or does it not make a difference? This is what expectancy measures. *Instrumentality* refers to the idea that the outcome of a situation is related to rewards or punishment. For those who are extrinsically motivated, instrumentality answers the question "What are the chances I'm going to be rewarded if I do a good job?" Expectancy theory helps to explain why some people do not work as hard as they can when their salaries are based purely on seniority. For those who are intrinsically motivated, instrumentality answers the question "How good will I feel if I can accomplish this task?" *Valence* is the importance that the individual places on the expected outcome of a situation. It answers questions such as "How great a reward will there be if my performance is exemplary?" and "How serious a punishment do I expect if I underperform?" Put simply, Vroom's formulas for high and low motivations read as follows:

High Motivation = (My work actually affects the outcome) * (There's a good chance I'll get a reward if this works out) * (If it works out, it'll be a really big reward!)

Low Motivation = (Nothing I do is going to impact this situation) * (Even if it does go well, I probably won't see any benefit) * (The only reward from this is incredibly small)

The Vroom formula can be used to analyze factors including how satisfied employees are at their jobs, how likely it is they will remain at their jobs, and how hard they will work at their jobs. In addition, unlike Maslow's and McClelland's models, which address typical needs across large groups of people, Vroom's model, with its three independent variables measuring the specific levels of expectancy, instrumentality, and valence, can generate a much more specialized result, attuned to the mental state of a specific individual.

Equity theory focuses on social comparisons—people evaluating their treatment by the organization relative to the treatment of others.

How can employees' perception of fair treatment affect motivation?   **Equity theory** focuses on social comparisons—people evaluating their treatment by the organization relative to the treatment of others. Employees begin to analyze what they contribute to the company (experience, skills, effort, time, education, and so forth) relative to what they get in return (salary, benefits, security, friendly work culture, recognition, power, and so forth). The result is a ratio of contribution to return. Employees then compare their own ratios to the ratios they have calculated for other employees. If they feel there is an inequity, such that they contribute more than someone else does yet are paid less, then they try to restore fairness. They may ask for a pay raise, reduce their level of work effort, or complain more about work and begin to become disengaged. They may try to rationalize their situation by finding another person to compare ratios with or, simply, they may quit.

Participative management and empowerment involves encouraging employees to become engaged in their jobs and loyal to the company by inspiring them to be self-motivated and giving them responsibility with the power (empowerment) to make decisions.

How can employers encourage workers to be self-motivated?   **Participative management and empowerment** involves encouraging employees to become engaged in their jobs and loyal to the company by inspiring them to be self-motivated and giving them responsibility with the power (empowerment) to make decisions. The 2010 World-Blu List of Most Democratic Workplaces comprises forty-four organizations from various industries and several countries. Canada had a few companies make the list, including Chaordix (Calgary), Axiom News Services (Peterborough), I Love Rewards (Toronto), La Siembra Co-operative International (Ottawa), TakingITGlobal (Toronto), and Rypple (Toronto).[24] Many other Canadian companies embrace empowerment and participative management. At WestJet, for example, call centre agents booking flights can override fees and extend special discounts if the customer has a compelling reason (personal tragedy), and ticket agents can immediately reroute passengers without supervisory intervention.[25] The philosophy is to produce satisfied customers; by not having to wait for supervisory approval, customer service is expedited. Employees feel they are important to the company and their decisions affect customers directly.

Management by objectives (MBO) is a performance goal–setting method in which management and employees work together to set goals and evaluate performance.

How can employers motivate employees through goal setting?   One of the most popular methods for setting performance goals is called **management by objectives (MBO)**, in which management and employees work together to set goals and evaluate

performance. This gives employees a clear understanding of their roles and responsibilities within the organization and how their activities relate to the achievement of overall organizational goals. Employees feel that they are important and empowered, resulting in improved motivation, job satisfaction, and commitment. The use of MBO must be carefully aligned with the culture of the organization. While MBO programs have not been as popular as they were in the late 1980s and early 1990s, it still has its place in management today.

Should management invest in employee skills development? Management often works to help employees improve skills in areas in which they are weak. But is this the best investment of resources for a corporation? **Strength-based management** is a system based on the belief that, rather than improve weak skills, the best way to help employees develop is to determine their strengths and build on them.[26] This system is supported by research that shows that people can learn the most about areas in which they already have a strong foundation. Strength-based programs identify employees' current talents and skills and then provide additional training and support to develop them into areas of excellence. When people are not operating (at work) from their strengths, they usually dislike going to work and talk negatively about the company they work for, interact more negatively than positively with co-workers, deal with customers/clients poorly, and accomplish less on a daily basis.[27]

Evolution of Motivational Theories in Business

How have motivational theories changed? In the early twentieth century, as the Industrial Age saw the creation of large corporations, issues of efficiency and labour costs became critical. Researchers such as Frederick Taylor (1856–1950) began to study how to manage people optimally. In 1911, Taylor published his findings in *The Principles of Scientific Management*, proposing ways that managers could increase productivity. He encouraged managers to use scientific study to determine the best methods to complete tasks and then to train employees in these methods. Many of his ideas were implemented in factories. Taylor's theory became known as **scientific management,** which comprised methods aimed at determining the one best way for a job to be done.[28] By the 1920s and 1930s, a field of academic study called **industrial psychology** was created to further study scientifically how to manage employees and work optimally. Other researchers, such as Frank and Lillian Gilbreath, used photography to study employee work patterns and then analyzed these patterns to increase productivity. For example, they used time-motion studies to analyze factory jobs and then train workers in the precise sequence of steps that would make them most productive. As scientific management theory spread widely, plant managers were hiring time-motion experts to perform the first "scientific" studies that attempted to break jobs down into easily repeated components and to devise more efficient tools and machines for performing them.

Another famous study of the period was Harvard professor Elton Mayo's work at the Hawthorne plant of the Western Electric Company in Illinois. Between 1927 and 1932, Mayo examined physical influences on the workplace (such as lighting and humidity) as well as psychological aspects (such as group pressure and working hours). The major finding, known as the Hawthorne effect, was that *regardless of the experimental changes made*, the production of the workers improved. Researchers concluded that the increase in productivity was based on the attention the workers were receiving. Because they knew they were being studied, the employees felt special and produced more, regardless of the conditions Hawthorne studied. Now, the **Hawthorne effect** is used to describe the increase in productivity caused by workers being given special attention. The results of the Hawthorne study launched the radically new Human Relations Movement, in which researchers studied more complicated motivation theories and the emotional world of the worker.[29] After World War II, the direction of research in management theory shifted from management of an individual worker toward management of the entire organization, its structure, and policies.

How do these theories apply to the modern workplace? The fields of organizational psychology and industrial psychology are still very active, and new theories of

Strength-based management is a system based on the belief that, rather than improve weak skills, the best way to help employees develop is to determine their strengths and build on them.

Scientific management comprises methods aimed at determining the one best way for a job to be done.

Industrial psychology studies scientifically how to manage employees and work optimally.

 Explain how motivational theories and industrial psychology have changed the work environment since the early twentieth century.

The **Hawthorne effect** describes the increase in productivity caused by workers being given special attention.

Best Companies to Work For (2011)

(Fast-growing Canadian companies that offer tremendous career advancement opportunities together with leading-edge employee perks and benefits)

1. Cameco Corporation
2. Digital Extremes
3. IMP Group Limited
4. Ledcor Group of Companies
5. Molson Coors Canada
6. Nexen Inc.
7. Research In Motion Limited
8. Stantec Inc.
9. TD Bank Financial Group
10. Toyota Motor Manufacturing Canada Inc.

Source: Canada's Top 100 Employers, "*Financial Post's* Ten Best Companies to Work For" 2010, http://www.canadastop100.com/fp10/, Accessed April 2, 2011.

Uncertainty management theory suggests that when people face increased uncertainty, fairness becomes more important to them.

Sociocracy is a system of organization and management in which the interests of everyone are served equally.

management practices continue to develop. These theories aim to better describe and understand the challenges in managing a modern, globalized, knowledge-based economy. One recent theory is the **uncertainty management theory**, which suggests that when people face increased uncertainty, fairness becomes more important to them. They have very strong reactions to actions and situations they judge to be unfair, which in turn influences their job satisfaction and performance.[30]

Another theory for motivating and organizing a modern workplace is based on the idea of sociocracy. **Sociocracy** is a system of organization and management in which the interests of everyone are served equally. In a sociocracy, all members of the organization are involved in decision making, and the final decision must be acceptable to all.[31] This doesn't mean everyone has to love the decision, but the goal is that no one finds the decision impossible to live with. Companies adopting a system of sociocracy find that workers feel they are treated fairly, are appreciated, and are respected. Proponents of sociocracy claim the system naturally fosters innovation, creativity, and a sense of belongingness among employees.

❻ List the various identifiable leadership styles and personality traits, and explain how they affect business leadership.

 Decision-Making Mini-Simulation: Leadership. Located in MyBusinessLab.

Leadership is the processes and behaviours used by managers to motivate, inspire, and influence subordinates to work toward certain goals.

Great leaders are able to be both managers and leaders: they define a vision, foster agreement across the company, and then implement the strategy.

LEADERSHIP
Leadership in Business

Is being a manager the same thing as being a leader?
Famed management researcher and author Peter Drucker once noted, "Management is doing things right; leadership is doing the right things."[32] Both leaders and managers strive to motivate people, but they have different scopes. Typically, managers spend their time making sure that specific tasks are done well and are completed on time. The leadership of the company, on the other hand, is focused on setting the long-term vision and strategies the company will need to survive and flourish. **Leadership** is the processes and behaviours used by managers to motivate, inspire, and influence subordinates to work toward certain goals. Truly **great leaders** are able to be both managers and leaders: they define a vision, foster agreement across the company, and then implement the strategy (also see "Leading" in Chapter 6).

How do business leaders inspire?
Naturally, many different leadership styles exist. Which style leaders employ depends on a complex mix of their own personality, the corporate culture, the type of company, the employees they manage, and the given situation. A successful leader knows how to shift between these styles as different situations present themselves.

1. *Transformational leaders* are able to create valuable, positive change in individuals and social systems. Transformational leaders enhance the morale, motivation, and performance of their employees because they are concerned and involved not only in project processes but also with helping team members.
2. *Charismatic leaders* use personality and charm, rather than any form of external power or authority, to motivate employees. They show great confidence in their employees and can be very persuasive. The charismatic leader and transformational leader have many similarities, in that transformational leaders may be charismatic. The main difference is that transformational leaders focus on transforming the organization and, possibly, their employees, while the charismatic leader may not want to change anything. The charismatic leader, despite all outward displays, may be more concerned with him- or herself than anyone else. If the charismatic leader is well intentioned toward others, he or she might evolve into a transformational leader and could very well transform an entire company.
3. *Transactional leaders* use the reward system to motivate employees. They set clear expectations and goals for subordinates and expect employees to work toward these goals and meet these expectations; when employees succeed, they are rewarded, but when they fail, they are sanctioned. This type of leadership assumes people are motivated by reward and punishment.

CEOs with Good Reputations in the Financial Community

1. the late Steve Jobs, Apple (1955–2011)
2. Jeffrey Immelt, General Electric
3. Warren Buffett, Berkshire Hathaway
4. Satoru Iwata, Nintendo
5. Jong-Yong Yun, Samsung Electronics
6. Terry Leahy, Tesco
7. A.G. Lafley, Procter & Gamble
8. Henning Kagermann, SAP AG
9. Jim Sinegal, Costco Wholesale
10. Lakshmi Mittal, Arcelor Mittal

Source: Barron's Magazine, "The World's Best CEOs," http://articles. moneycentral.msn.com/Investing/ Extra/TheWorldsBestCEOs.aspx, Accessed April 3, 2011.

Another way of examining leadership is to consider the idea of *resonance*, a term used repeatedly in Don Goleman et al.'s book *Primal Leadership*.[33] An experience resonates with you when it causes a distinctive emotional reaction and thus makes a lasting impression.

Table 7.3 Styles of Leadership

	Visionary	Coaching	Affiliative	Democratic	Pacesetting	Commanding
Leader characteristics	Inspires, believes in own vision, is empathetic, explains how and why people's efforts contribute to the "dream"	Listens, helps people identify their own strengths and weaknesses, acts as a counsellor, encourages, delegates	Promotes harmony, is empathetic, boosts morale, solves conflicts	Is a superb listener, team worker, collaborator, influencer	Has strong drive to achieve, has high standards and initiative, has low empathy and collaboration, is impatient, micromanaging, numbers-driven	Is commanding, "do it because I say so," threatening, tight control, monitoring studiously, creating dissonance, contaminates everyone's mood, drives away talent
How style builds resonance	Moves people toward shared dreams	Connects what a person wants with the organization's goals	Creates harmony by connecting people to one another	Values people's input and gets commitment through participation	Meets challenging and exciting goals	Soothes fear by giving clear direction in an emergency
When style is appropriate	When changes require a new vision or when a clear direction is needed; radical change	To help competent, motivated employees improve performance by building long-term capabilities	To heal rifts in a team, motivate during stressful times, or strengthen connections	To build buy-in or consensus, or to get valuable input from employees	To get high-quality results from a motivated and competent team; sales	In a crisis, to kick-start an urgent turnaround, or with problem employees; traditional military

A **resonant leader** is highly aware of others' emotional states and skilled at inspiring people to feel more positive. A resonant leader also connects with others by being honest and open about their own ideals, concerns, and goals. In working with these types of leaders, people tend to feel secure and free to explore and share their creative ideas. Resonant leaders usually possess a high degree of **emotional intelligence**—a skills set (including self-awareness, self-management, social awareness, and relationship management) that enables one to understand both one's own and others' emotions. Resonance can be created through six leadership styles (see **Table 7.3**). Typically, the most effective leaders are able to switch skilfully between the six styles as various situations dictate.

A **resonant leader** is highly aware of others' emotional states and skilled at inspiring people to feel more positive.

Emotional intelligence involves a skills set (including self-awareness, self-management, social awareness, and relationship management) that enables one to understand both one's own and others' emotions.

Which corporate leaders exemplify the styles of leadership? Visionary leaders are able to inspire others, believe in their own vision, and move people toward a shared dream. Other managers use different styles of leadership, with varying results. For example, Robert L. Nardelli, named CEO of Home Depot in 2000, is known for his commanding leadership style.[34] Nardelli required that all aspects of store performance be measured carefully, and he held executives responsible for meeting strict goals. He also implemented major cost-cutting measures, replacing thousands of full-time workers with part-time employees. Financially, Nardelli's style seemed a boon for the company; Home Depot sales rose from US$46 billion in 2000 to US$81.5 billion in 2005, an average annual growth rate of 12 percent. However, the strong numbers could not make up for an authoritarian leadership style that many experts say alienated both employees and customers. In January 2007, facing pressure from the board of directors, Nardelli resigned from the company.

In stark contrast to Nardelli is Jon Huntsman of the Huntsman, Corp., who uses coaching and affiliative styles of

Leaders employ different leadership styles. Former Home Depot CEO Robert Nardelli is known for his commanding leadership style.

Better Business **Better World**

Japan Relief

Corporate leaders set the goals, mission, vision, and core values for their companies. Their decisions and actions create a corporate culture and move the company in specific directions. Most people seek employment with, and many consumers prefer to make purchases from, companies that have similar values to their own personal values. The decision leaders make for a company shape how the public views the company, the employees' job satisfaction and their ability to identify with the company, and the company's ability to be successful in the future.

In March 2011, more than fifty nations offered aid, both monetary and non-monetary, to Japan after the 9.0-magnitude earthquake, the seven-metre tsunami it spawned, and the displacement caused by troubles at a nuclear power plant left Japan's people devastated. Not only did many nations' governments provide assistance, but many corporations offered their support as well. For example:

Coca-Cola	Donated US$31 million (2.5 billion yen), with US$7.3 million in cash, toward relief and rebuilding efforts (over three years). The company also donated beverages such as water, ice tea, and juice to government and disaster relief centres, as well as other venues. Muhtar Kent, chair and CEO of The Coca-Cola Company, said, "We have been deeply moved by what we have seen and heard, and impressed by the hard work and tenacity of those involved in the relief efforts. Given our nearly 60-year proud presence in Japan and our strong relationship with its people, we want to do everything we can to contribute to the rebuilding effort as we shift our focus from immediate efforts to reconstruction and infrastructure rebuilding in the coming weeks and months."[35]
Aflac	Donated US$1.2 million (100 million yen) to the International Red Cross to help disaster relief efforts. Aflac chair and CEO Dan Amos said, "Our thoughts and prayers go out to the Japanese people during this very difficult time. We stand ready to assist in the healing process and are pledging these funds to ensure the basic needs are cared for during this crisis."[36]
Molson Coors	Donated US$50 000 to the Japan relief efforts being coordinated by the International Red Cross. Bart Alexander, chief corporate responsibility officer for Molson Coors, said, "We are very grateful that all our employees in Japan are safe and accounted for. We know the current relief efforts will be followed by a long period of recovery and reconstruction, and we wanted to express our solidarity with our Japanese team with a concrete demonstration of support. In addition to our corporate donation, we have worked with the Red Cross to set up a microsite that will make it easier for Molson Coors employees to donate individually as well. We hope these efforts, in conjunction with those of other companies, will facilitate a faster recovery in Japan."[37]
Kraft Foods Foundation	Donated US$200 000 to the Red Cross for relief efforts. Foundation vice-president Nicole Robinson said, "We are grateful that our Japanese colleagues are unharmed, and deeply saddened by the devastation these natural disasters have caused. As the world's second-largest food company, it is our responsibility to give back in time of crisis. We are proud to partner with the Red Cross as they support all the people of Japan in rescue, rebuilding and relief efforts."[38] Food and funds will be donated for Japan's long-term recovery, and all donations to the Red Cross made by Kraft Foods employees in the United States and Japan will be matched by the foundation.

Discussion Questions

1. Do you think it is important for global businesses to offer this type of support? Is it not enough for governments to offer this support? Why or why not?
2. What type of public image is each of the companies above creating? Will this help them gain new customers? Why or why not?
3. How might their actions help or hurt their business? Will investors like this? Will their generosity be reciprocated? Should it be?

leadership. Huntsman started his petrochemical and plastics company in 1970, and by 2000, it had worldwide revenue of US$8.5 billion. But in January 2001, the market saw some dramatic changes, and every adviser advocated that the company file Chapter 11 bankruptcy. Huntsman refused, and the company rebounded. By early 2005, when the company went public, its annual revenues were more than US$12 billion. Huntsman outlines the pillars of his innovative leadership style in his 2005 book, *Winners Never Cheat*:

- Compete fiercely and fairly, but do not cut in line.
- Set the example for handling risk, handling responsibility, and demonstrating reliability.
- Revenge is unproductive—learn to move on.
- Operate businesses and organizations as if they are family-owned.[39]

Huntsman also emphasizes the importance of being ethical, respectful, and charitable in both business dealings and in life. And Huntsman practises what he preaches: the Huntsman Cancer Institute in Salt Lake City, which he founded in 1995, has received more than US$225 million from the company.

Personality Traits

Can we measure someone's personality?
Personality assessment tools can help employers determine whether a candidate will "fit" the corporate culture and work well with the team. Personality assessments can help leaders determine their personality tendencies; once identified, they can consciously adjust their leadership style as the situation dictates. Personality assessments do measure specific metrics in people's personality, quantify them, categorize them, and indicate which traits make up an individual's personality. There are various personality models in use today, and while no one model is recognized as the perfect tool, all of these personality assessments or type indicators produce reports that may give us a better understanding of the personality traits required to be successful in a variety of roles, including leadership.

How can we categorize human personality traits?
The **Big Five**, also referred to as the Five Factor Model, is one of the most widely accepted models of personality.[40] The model categorizes most human personality traits into five broad dimensions and then assigns people a score for each dimension (see **Table 7.4**).

When the Big Five test is scored for individual feedback, it is usually presented in a percentile form. For example, if a person scores in the 30th percentile for extraversion, they most likely tend to shy away from social situations. A person scoring in the 80th percentile for conscientiousness most likely has a strong sense of responsibility and orderliness.

What are the implications of the Big Five model in the workplace?[41]
People with a high degree of openness perform well in situations that require require learning new skills and they often hold unconventional beliefs. In the workplace, they adjust quickly to new jobs and adapt well to change because they seek information and feedback. People with lower scores in openness tend to have more conventional, traditional interests and prefer the straightforward and obvious over the complex and ambiguous. Knowing the degree to which someone is open can give a manager some insight to creating interesting and engaging work for the employee. It also helps those hiring determine how well the individual might fit into the corporate culture and work environment.

Conscientious people are less likely to quit the job or be absent from work and are more likely to have high performance levels and work in a safe manner. Businesses started by highly conscientious people have longer survival rates compared to those who are not as conscientious. People with high scores of conscientiousness prefer planned rather than spontaneous behaviour and have a tendency to act dutifully and measure their performance against external expectations.

Extraverts tend to thrive in jobs involving sales or marketing and are effective as managers, demonstrating inspirational leadership behaviours. They enjoy being with people and are often perceived as having lots of energy. They do well in job interviews and have an easier time than introverts when settling in to a new job. In jobs without social interaction, however, extraverts do not necessarily perform well. They tend to be

The **Big Five**, also referred to as the Five Factor Model, is one of the most widely accepted models of personality. The model categorizes most human personality traits into five broad dimensions and then assigns people a score for each dimension: openness, conscientiousness, extraversion, agreeableness, and neuroticism (emotional stability).

Table 7.4 Big Five Personality Traits

Trait	High Degree	Low Degree
Openness	• Curious • Intellectual • Creative • Open to new ideas	• Consistent • Cautious
Conscientiousness	• Organized • Responsible • Systematic • Self-disciplined • Thorough • Dependable	• Easygoing • Careless • Spontaneous • Not self-disciplined
Extraversion	• Sociable • Talkative • Assertive • Open to new relationships	• Reserved • Quiet time alone • Need less social stimulation
Agreeableness	• Tolerant • Co-operative • Understanding • Trusting • Sensitive to the needs of others	• Cold • Unkind • Suspicious • Antagonistic
Neuroticism (Degree of Emotional Stability)	• Irritable • Moody • Anxious • Experience unpleasant emotions easily	• Secure • Confident • Emotionally Stable

absent from work more often, potentially because they may miss a workday to attend to the needs of their friends.

People who are high in *agreeableness* are likeable and get along well with others. They are valuable team members who may be effective leaders because they create a fair environment when they are in a leadership role. They lean toward compassion and co-operation rather than suspicion and antagonism toward others. Agreeable people have an optimistic view of human nature (Theory X), but they are less likely to engage in constructive, change-oriented communication because disagreeing with the status quo may create conflict, which, in most instances, they'd rather not do. Conflict creates change in many cases, however, and changes may bring improvements (unions, government regulations, etc.), so not-so-agreeable personality types are needed in society and in the workplace as well. When hiring a lawyer, what degree of agreeableness would you prefer them to have?

People very high in *neuroticism* experience a number of problems at work, such as relationship difficulties (not getting along with others). They tend to be unhappy in their jobs and have lower levels of career success. If they do achieve managerial jobs, they tend to create an unfair working environment. Those scoring highu in neuroticism are vulnerable to stress and they often interpret ordinary situations as threatening. People scoring low in this trait tend to be less emotionally reactive and free from persistent negative feelings (although being free from negative feelings does not conclude that they experience many positive feelings).

Generally, there is a significant link between the Big Five personality traits and job performance in many jobs. Not all five traits predict job performance in all types of jobs, however. Conscientiousness and extraversion are the two Big Five aspects that always correspond to positive job performance, although conscientiousness is more positively linked.[42] Extraversion is negatively associated when it appears to inspire more absenteeism or when combined with low levels of conscientiousness. Much of the current research is on sales and other occupations in which interacting with people is required, so perhaps researching individuals in jobs that require little human interaction would yield different results.

Do we have a consistent and constant underlying personality? According to the **Cattell 16 personality factors (16 PF)**, another widely used model of personality, each of us has a consistent and constant underlying personality. However, the way we see ourselves is influenced by our intelligence, upbringing, and education. These influences may have taught us to suppress or emphasize certain aspects of our personality. If we can understand our basic personality type, this model suggests, we can make better use of our natural strengths and weaknesses. The 16 PF is often used in hiring or in promotion recommendations as well as to improve relationships. Some sample reports that the 16 PF can produce are shown in **Figure 7.3**.[43] Would this person, report (a), be your choice for

The **Cattell 16 personality factors (16 PF)** suggest that each of us has a consistent and constant underlying personality.

16PF Profile

(a)

Sten	Factor	Left meaning	Low 1 2 3	Average 4 5 6 7	High 8 9 10	Right meaning
4	Warmth (A)	Reserved				Warm
1	Reasoning (B)	Concrete				Abstract
5	Emotional stability (C)	Reactive				Emotionally stable
2	Dominance (E)	Deferential				Dominant
5	Liveliness (F)	Serious				Lively
5	Rule-consciousness (G)	Expedient				Rule-conscious
4	Social boldness (H)	Shy				Socially bold
5	Sensitivity (I)	Utilitarian				Sensitive
3	Vigilance (L)	Trusting				Vigilant
6	Abstractedness (M)	Grounded				Abstracted
6	Privateness (N)	Forthright				Private
5	Apprehension (O)	Self-assured				Apprehensive
4	Openness to change (Q1)	Traditional				Open to change
6	Self-reliance (Q2)	Group-oriented				Self-reliant
5	Perfectionism (Q3)	Tolerates disorder				Perfectionistic
5	Tension (Q4)	Relaxed				Tense

16PF Profile

(b)

Client 1	Client 2	Factor	Left meaning	Low 1 2 3	Average 4 5 6 7	High 8 9 10	Right meaning
4	4	Warmth (A)	Reserved				Warm
1	6	Reasoning (B)	Concrete				Abstract
5	4	Emotional stability (C)	Reactive				Emotionally stable
2	4	Dominance (E)	Deferential				Dominant
5	5	Liveliness (F)	Serious				Lively
5	2	Rule-consciousness (G)	Expedient				Rule-conscious
4	5	Social boldness (H)	Shy				Socially bold
5	5	Sensitivity (I)	Utilitarian				Sensitive
3	4	Vigilance (L)	Trusting				Vigilant
6	7	Abstractedness (M)	Grounded				Abstracted
6	5	Privateness (N)	Forthright				Private
5	6	Apprehension (O)	Self-assured				Apprehensive
4	4	Openness to change (Q1)	Traditional				Open to change
6	5	Self-reliance (Q2)	Group-oriented				Self-reliant
5	7	Perfectionism (Q3)	Tolerates disorder				Perfectionistic
5	4	Tension (Q4)	Relaxed				Tense

Figure 7.3 Sample 16 PF Personality Reports

Legend: ◆ = Client 1, ◇ = Client 2

a position in the human resources department or in the sales department? The 16 PF can also help with analyzing relationships. Would these two people, report (b), work well on a team? Where might there be conflicts?

The **Thematic Apperception Test (TAT)** presents a person with a series of images and interprets his or her responses.

How can describing pictures give insight to our personality?   The **Thematic Apperception Test (TAT)**, developed by Morgan and Murray of Harvard University in the 1930s, is another personality test. Similar to the well-known Rorschach, or inkblot, test, the TAT presents a person with a series of images and interprets his or her responses. However, instead of ambiguous blots of ink, the TAT shows a subject pictures of persons participating in various activities, such as riding a bike or playing a guitar. The subject is asked to make up a story about the individuals in the pictures to explain why the pictured persons are engaged in particular acts. These stories are supposed to reveal the subject's needs. If the subject explains that the woman riding a bike is trying to get exercise, that subject might carry a need for physical activity. Another subject may suggest that the woman is riding the bike to save money on gasoline. That subject might carry a need for financial stability.

What is the perfect personality tool?   While no one model is recognized as the perfect tool, all these personality tests can help to give us a better understanding of the traits that form the foundation of successful leadership.

TEAMWORK

Advantages of Teams in the Workplace

What is the value of using teams in the workplace?   Have you ever seen a Motorola Razr cellphone? If so, you've seen the product of true teamwork in action. At the start of the project, Motorola began with a modest goal: to design a phone that

Explore on MyBusinessLab

Do You Have to Be Tall to Be a Leader?

What does height have to do with successful leadership in business? A lot, according to many industry experts and observers. Lara Tiedens, an organizational behaviour professor at the Stanford University Graduate School of Business, cites height—or in some cases, the illusion of height—as a tool business leaders use to appear powerful. Several studies have also found positive correlations between height and salary.[44] Some people believe that height, voice quality, and stance used in an assertive, dominant manner help people get noticed, listened to, and promoted. This theory resembles that of the animal kingdom's "survival of the fittest," the strongest live the longest and the weakest are eaten up by the others. Some people believe that height, voice quality, and stance do not make the grade without substance. Linda Sawyer, CEO of Deutsch advertising agency,

says, "Survival of the fittest has become survival of the brightest."[45] What do you think? How much does appearance affect success in business and, more specifically, as a leader?

Discussion Questions

1. **What would you be thinking if you observed co-workers complaining to your boss about a situation at work and your boss did not make eye contact with your co-workers, nor did he or she stand confidently or speak in a confident tone?**
2. **Do you think that your height rather than your skills and talents can determine your leadership opportunities? Why or why not?**
3. **Do top CEOs tend to be taller than average? Do good-looking people make more money than others? Is there a specific look for a leader? Is our society that shallow that we make decisions about people based on their looks? Research these questions on the Internet to find out.**

celebrities would be happy to show off during the Academy Awards, generating a lot of publicity and buzz for Motorola products. A special team of twenty engineers was formed and given the task of creating the thinnest phone ever released. Would they be able to do it?

For almost a year, the team met daily, often for hours at a time, to work on the top-secret project. The team struggled to come up with a practical yet innovative design, often engaging in spirited debate over such matters. Despite the many challenges, the hard work paid off. The Razr team not only created one of the best-selling technology products of all time but also contributed to creating a new Motorola.[46] In fact, Motorola reported that in 2006, its Razr cellphone even outsold the popular Apple iPod.

Teams that function well produce great results.

A **team** comprises a group of people linked in a common purpose. Teams are especially appropriate for conducting tasks high in complexity with many interdependent subtasks. A group in itself does not necessarily constitute a team. While different personalities have the potential to create conflict within a team, they can also create unique ideas. Teams normally have members with complementary skills and generate synergy through a coordinated effort that allows each member to maximize their strengths and minimize their weaknesses. Teamwork can bring about great success in business, as was the case with the development of the Motorola Razr. But effective teams must be created and managed thoughtfully in order for businesses to reap the benefits. How can managers accomplish this?

A **team** comprises a group of people linked in a common purpose.

In good working teams, there's agreement on the objectives at hand and on the best approach to solve the problem.[47] Teammates depend on one another's ideas and efforts to successfully complete tasks. There is a sense of accountability, and members are committed to one another's success. From 1987 to 1997, MasterCard implemented five different advertising campaigns, yet was still eclipsed by rival company Visa.[48] In an attempt to change this pattern, MasterCard commissioned advertising agency McCann Erikson to come up with a new campaign. The agency enlisted the skills and talents of a seasoned creative team to tackle the project. After much brainstorming and debate, the team came up with a new tag line: "There are some things money can't buy. For everything else, there's MasterCard." The team then worked on developing ideas for commercials based on the tag line. By combining their creative talents, the team members came up with a "priceless" idea. Their commercials started by listing the prices of ordinary items, such as popcorn or soda. Then, they ended by mentioning an item that is priceless, such as spending time with your family. The "priceless campaign" was a great lead in to MasterCard's new tag line. Since then, commercials based on this theme have been shown in 105 countries and translated into forty-eight languages. Most importantly for MasterCard, it has issued U.S. credit cards at nearly twice the rate Visa has since 1997.

What are the challenges teams face in the workplace?

Some people suggest that teamwork does not always lead to more creative output. A 2006 study conducted by Barry Staw at University of Berkeley found that when college students were asked to think of business

Not every team performs at its best.

Off the **Mark**

Dream Team or Nightmare?

If we look at Michael Eisner, the former Disney chief executive officer (CEO), we see that for his first ten years at Disney (Research), he and chief operating officer (COO) Frank Wells were a great team. Under their guidance, Disney revived its famous animation tradition and the movie business prospered. Eisner and Wells not only saved a legendary company, but they also made shareholders rich. When Wells died, Eisner then formed one of the most famously ill-fated teams in recent history.[49]

In 1995, Michael Ovitz—one of Hollywood's most powerful talent agents and the founder of Creative Artists Agency—was brought on as Disney president under CEO and board chair Michael Eisner. Ovitz quickly grew frustrated with his role and vague definition of duties.[50] After a tumultuous fourteen months as Disney's second-in-command, he was dismissed by Eisner. Disney shareholders later sued Eisner and Disney's board of directors for awarding Ovitz roughly US$140 million in severance. The 2005 trial lasted three months, with the judge ruling that Eisner and the other directors properly carried out their fiduciary duties. Although Disney won, the case aired some embarrassing testimony about the "Machiavellian atmosphere inside the Magic Kingdom."[51] Eisner stepped down as CEO that same year.

In analyzing what went wrong, the overriding answer is conflicting business and personal agendas. Ovitz wanted to put big money into projects that Eisner dismissed as "off-strategy," such as buying a National Football League franchise. Eisner also did not approve of Ovitz spending US$2 million renovating his own office. This team failure cost Disney enormously—in both money and reputation.[52]

Discussion Questions

1 What steps can companies take to ensure they don't hire someone who won't work with the team?
2 Does thinking differently mean two people won't get along? Why or why not?
3 How much time and money did Disney lose over this situation?

BizSkills Simulation: Team Management. Located in MyBusinessLab.

Groupthink is a type of narrow-mindedness that can emerge in a group situation if team members have not been carefully selected for a range of skills and attributes.

ideas either individually or in teams, the individuals came up with more ideas than did the teams. In addition, the individual's ideas were voted as more creative than were the teams' concepts. Staw concluded that collective thinking does not lead to increased creativity and can, in fact, hamper it. One possible reason, Staw proposes, is that team members often want to "fit in" rather than "stand out," and true creativity and original thinking is largely dependent on one's willingness to stand out and take risks.[53]

Selecting teams for optimal performance is another challenge. If a team is not carefully selected for a range of skills and attributes, a type of narrow-mindedness can emerge. This is the phenomenon referred to as **groupthink**. People who are from similar backgrounds and from similar sectors of the company tend to have a set of familiar ideas and work with the same set of unspoken assumptions. These may lead to rejecting different ideas without fair examination. The impact of groupthink can be chilling to the creative output of a team, although this challenge can be minimized with thoughtful design of the team membership.

In the twenty-first century, another challenge to successful workplace teams is that a wide mix of generations is in the workforce (see **Table 7.5**). In fact, it is possible for three or even four generations to be assigned to a single team. People from separate generations have grown up with social and educational experiences that are so different that they take on distinct styles in the workplace.

In their book *Millennials Rising*, researchers William Strauss and Neil Howe discuss the three dominant generations in the workplace today: the baby boomers (those born between 1943 and 1960); the Gen-Xers (those born between 1961 and 1981); and the Millennials (those born between 1982 and 2002).[54] The baby boomers are the veterans in

Table 7.5   Four Generations in the Workplace

Generation	Birth Years	Famous Man	Famous Woman
Silent	1925–1942	Colin Powell	Barbara Walters
Boomer	1943–1960	Steven Spielberg	Oprah Winfrey
Gen-X	1961–1981	Matt Damon	Jennifer Lopez
Millennial	1982–2002	LeBron James	Miley Cyrus

Sources: William Strauss and Neil Howe, Generations: The History of America's Future, 1584 to 2069 *(New York: William Morrow & Co., 1991).*

the workforce, and many have been with the same company for more than thirty years. Gen-Xers, who are known for their independent thinking and hankering for change, are the first generation of workers to value family life over work life. Like Gen-Xers, Millennials want their jobs to accommodate their personal lives, but they also have very high expectations for achievement in their careers. Millennials, who are now entering university and college campuses and the workforce, believe in their self-worth and value, whether deserved or not.[55] They feel they have the capability to change the company they work for and the world. According to Strauss and Howe, members of this generation expect to make their greatest marks in society by using technology to empower the community. Also important to note is that this generation is the focus of marketing efforts because they are the biggest youth spenders in history, most often in "co-purchases" with their parents. Teamwork, good behaviour, and citizenship are much more important to Millennials than to earlier generations, and they see equality between different races and genders. How will this affect business? Strauss predicts, "Young workers will demand that employers adjust to the needs of workers who wish to build careers and families at the same time and to lead lower-stress lives than their parents did. Older employees will admire their skills, confidence, and team spirit, but will question their creativity and toughness."[56]

Best Practices For Teams

How do you create an environment for achieving the best team performance?

Psychologist Mihaly Csikszentmihalyi has extended his idea of flow into the team setting. **Group flow** occurs when a group knows how to work together so that each individual member can achieve flow.

The characteristics of such a setting include:

- *Creative spatial arrangements:* Pinning ideas on the walls and using large charts to combine ideas from the entire group tend to lead to open consideration of ideas. Tables are used less since working while standing and moving promotes more discussion and interaction.
- *Playground design:* This begins with creating a "safe space," agreeing it is safe to bring out ideas that normally one might just keep to him- or herself. Often a large number of charts display information inputs, graphs, and the project summary. Wall space can be used to collect results and lists of open topics.
- *Constant focus* on the target group for the product.
- *Heavy use of visualization* and prototyping to construct early models. These are then refined to make models more efficient.

The environment itself can also be fine-tuned to help promote the success of the team. Management must also be sure to praise team accomplishments. The Razr team, for example, was asked to come to company headquarters for a meeting of top executives. What was the purpose of the meeting? The company's top executives wanted to thank the team members; they did so by giving them a standing ovation as well as stock options.[57]

7

Outline the best ways to create, manage, and participate in teams, taking into account factors such as group flow, Belbin's nine team roles, technology, and Covey's Seven Habits model.

Group flow occurs when a group knows how to work together so that each individual member can achieve flow.

How can managers form the best teams?   Some important aspects a manager should consider in forming a team include the following:

- ■ *Size.* A team that is too large may struggle with cohesiveness. At the same time, a large group can offer the benefit of diverse perspectives.
- ■ *Time.* Some teams may be formulated to work on a specific problem or project within a short time frame, while others may work together for longer periods on everyday tasks.
- ■ *Status.* A team formally created by a company may be required to provide progress reports and updates, and it often has access to company resources. Less formal teams may need to take initiative in maintaining lines of communication.

Effective teams are made up of people with diverse skills, talents, and points of view. Team members' attributes should complement one another in order for the team to perform at the optimal level.

According to business writer and theorist R.M. Belbin, **effective teams** are made up of people with diverse skills, talents, and points of view. Team members' respective attributes should complement one another in order for the team to perform at the optimal level. For example, what might happen if everyone on a team was extremely creative yet inexperienced in effective time management? Or if five of six team members were all aggressive leaders? Clearly, a balance of people who embody different "team roles" is key to the success of a team.

Belbin's model of nine team roles is outlined in **Table 7.6**. Considering both these roles and the personality traits of potential members can be helpful when designing teams.

How can leaders encourage collective action?   Getting team members into a cohesive unit is no easy task, especially if the members have never worked on a team before. Being the manager of a team requires strong leadership qualities to coordinate and manage others' abilities to the fullest. Team members are more productive when encouraged and supported. Leaders need to communicate the project goals clearly, assign tasks to members, establish performance expectations, set communication guidelines, require members to be accountable for their performance, encourage input and idea-sharing, aid the team in monitoring and measuring its progress toward project goals, offer timely feedback, and offer support and assistance when required. Leaders should avoid micromanaging the team or giving feedback in a non-constructive manner.

A **virtual team** comprises members located in different physical locations but working together to achieve a goal.

How might technology affect the design of teams?   In a **virtual team**, members are located in different physical locations but work together to achieve a goal. The need for virtual teams grows out of the increased globalization of business. Familiar tools such as conference calls and e-mail have evolved to include video conferencing and live broadcasting of key meetings and events over the Web. Webcasts can now support interactive participation of the viewing audience. In real time, audience members can ask

Table 7.6   Belbin's Nine Team Roles

Role	Personality Traits
Plant	Creative and imaginative
Resource investigator	Extroverted and communicative
Coordinator	Mature and confident
Shaper	Challenging and dynamic
Monitor evaluator	Serious and strategic
Teamworker	Cooperative and diplomatic
Implementer	Disciplined and reliable
Completer finisher	Painstaking and conscientious
Specialist	Dedicated and self-starting

Source: Belbin Team-Role Summary Sheet, http://www.belbin.com/content/page/731/Belbin_Team_Role_Descriptions.pdf, Accessed December 8, 2011

questions, exchange their own electronic files with the group, and record the presentation for repeated viewing. Web conferencing software such as WebEx and Microsoft Office Live allow participants in any geographic location to brainstorm together in real time on a common "virtual whiteboard," to watch demos and presentations live, and to record and annotate these discussions for later playback.

The promise of much higher-speed Internet transfer is also being explored. Many colleges and universities are using virtual teams for student competitions whereby teams are created across the globe and communicate and compete in the virtual world. In 2011, new technology made it possible for Queen's University in Kingston, Ontario, to welcome its first virtual class of executive MBA students from across Canada and Bermuda, delivering Canada's most respected MBA program directly to their desktops.[58] Loyalist College in Belleville, Ontario, has been using Second Life (an online virtual world in which users interact through avatars) to meet and teach students in the virtual world. Students taking their customs and immigration diploma experience working as a border guard virtually because security issues have hampered their placement options.[59] This process helps students learn early on that distance does not have to keep people from communicating and working well together. The potential to connect students and workers from many parts of the world may lead to exciting new possibilities for synergy.

The best practices for creating strong virtual teams are emerging as virtual teams become a more accepted and useful teaming solution.[60] Most successful virtual teams include some face-to-face meeting time periodically. Very few virtual teams are 100 percent virtual.

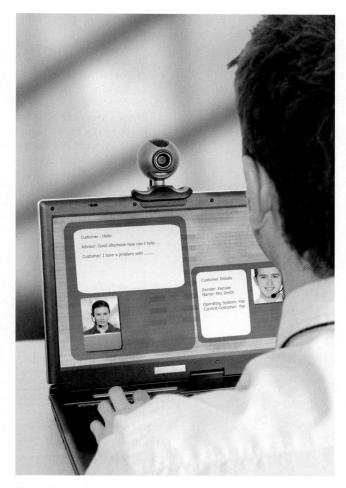

Using Web conferencing software, teams with people in various countries can work together seamlessly.

Although technology allows teams to communicate without ever meeting face to face, it is still important to have the group occasionally meet with one another in the same space to build social connections. Keeping the team connected is a key priority to a virtual team, and it can be difficult to keep contacts strong from a distance. There can be communication delays from working across time zones or using e-mail as a primary mode of communication. Establishing team rules, such as agreeing to respond to e-mail messages within a certain window of time or initiating global office hours, can minimize these problems. Managing a virtual team means managing the whole spectrum of communication strategies and project management techniques as well as human and social processes in ways that support the team.

How can you be a valued team player? It is important to begin now to build the skills that will make you successful in team settings. As we have seen, the best teams are carefully planned and selected and can be the place where some of the most exciting and innovative work in the company is happening. Preparing yourself to contribute in a team setting may be the most important thing you can do to increase your value to an organization, no matter what position you hold.

There are many skills that you can build to enhance your success as a member of a team. One way to organize these skills is the **Seven Habits model** developed by famed management author Stephen Covey.[61] He has found that successful people exhibit the following seven habits of behaviour:

Stephen Covey developed the **Seven Habits model** which lists the seven habits that successful people exhibit.

1. *Be proactive.* This is the ability to control your environment rather than have it control you. Proactive team members are constantly looking "down the road" in terms of

their time management, work, and possible obstacles that may impede the success of the project.

2. *Begin with the end in mind.* This means that you are able to see the desired outcome and concentrate on activities that help in achieving it. Staying focused on the ultimate goal allows you to avoid taking the team in directions that will cause divisiveness and will waste resources and energy.

3. *Put first things first.* This skill works together with habit #2 in pushing you toward success in your team role. Manage your time and energy so that the required tasks are prioritized. Covey thinks of habit #2 as a mental creation and habit #3 as a physical creation.

4. *Think win-win.* This is the most important aspect of interpersonal leadership because most achievements are based on co-operative effort; therefore, the aim needs to be win-win solutions for all.

5. *Seek first to understand and then to be understood.* In communicating with other members of the team, it is critical to develop and maintain positive relationships. This style of communication recommends listening and working to let your teammates know they have been heard as key to your own success in being understood and contributing.

6. *Synergize.* This is the habit of creative co-operation—the principle that collaboration often achieves more than could be achieved by individuals working independently toward attaining a purpose.

7. *Sharpen the saw.* This catchphrase comes from the metaphor of chopping down a tree. If you are constantly sawing and never take time to stop and sharpen the saw, you'll feel that you're investing tremendous energy but the results will not be what they could be if you just stopped to sharpen the saw first. Strong team contributors avoid the work mode of continually reacting to crisis. Instead, they take time to step back and develop skills and to analyze the task at hand so that they can work more efficiently.

Work to develop and use these habits in your role on teams and you will find that your teams become more successful—and that you are in demand for the next team. Effective teamwork involves a complex blend of personalities, skills, and actions. Achieving this blend in the business environment can be a great challenge. As the Motorola Razr team demonstrated, however, it can be done. Its success is the kind to which all managers and team members aspire.

CHAPTER SYNOPSIS

❶ Explain how motivation and work environment encourage "flow." *(pp. 179–181)*

A **flow state** happens when you are completely involved and focused on what you are doing. Often people produce their best work, make the best use of their skills, and feel the most pleasure when they are in such a flow state. They are engaged in an activity when they feel a strong match between their own abilities and the challenge of a task—it is neither too difficult, which can lead to frustration, nor too simple, which can lead to boredom. They report a sense of control over what is happening and a feeling of effortlessness in their working. Creating a workplace that fosters the kind of motivation required to engage employees in their work and help get them to into a state of "flow" is the subject of organizational psychology—the study of how to create a workplace that fosters motivation and productivity among employees.

❷ Describe the intricacies of Maslow's hierarchy of needs, McClelland's "three needs" theory, and Herzberg's motivator-hygiene theory. *(pp. 181–183)*

Maslow's hierarchy of needs suggests that our primary needs are met first before our higher-l evel needs are addressed (see **Figure 7.1**).

Maslow's Hierarchy of Needs

McClelland's "three needs" theory suggests there are three main motivators: 1) the need for achievement (to accomplish something difficult on your own); 2) the need for affiliation (to form close personal relationships); and 3) the need for power (to be able to control the behaviour of others).

Herzberg's motivator-hygiene (two-factor) theory suggests that two factors influence a person's motivation—hygiene factors (cause job dissatisfaction) and motivation factors (cause job satisfaction).

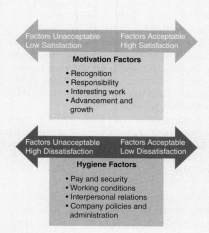

Herzberg's Motivator-Hygiene Theory

❸ Distinguish the factors between extrinsic and intrinsic motivators. *(pp. 183–184)*

In the workplace, managers can control some external motivating factors. These motivators, called **extrinsic motivators,** include such things as pay, promotion, and verbal praise. Other factors, called **intrinsic motivators**, are outside the set of factors under a manager's control because they are internal to each individual employee.

❹ Summarize the implications of Theory X, Theory Y, Theory Z, and the Vroom model. *(pp. 184–187)*

McGregor's Theory X suggests that people inherently dislike work and want to avoid it. **Theory X management** proposes that employees have to be coerced and controlled by management in order to be productive. This leads to an authoritarian, hard-line management style.

In contrast, **McGregor's Theory Y** suggests that people view work as being as natural as playing and resting. People are naturally motivated and will direct themselves to work for the aims of the organization if they are satisfied with their jobs. **Theory Y management** assumes that, on average, people will accept and seek out responsibility. Such managers have a softer style of management that involves the participation of many.

Theory Z management is a combination of American and Japanese management philosophies characterized by long-term employment security, consensual decision making, and slow evaluation and promotion procedures, with an emphasis on individual responsibility within a group context.

Vroom's Expectancy theory suggests an individual's motivation in any given situation can be described by the relationship among three psychological forces, illustrated in the following formula:

Motivation = Expectancy * Instrumentality * Valence

The Vroom formula can be used to analyze factors including how satisfied employees are at their jobs, how likely it is they will remain at their jobs, and how hard they will work at their jobs.

❺ Explain how motivational theories and industrial psychology have changed the work environment since the early twentieth century. *(pp. 187–188)*

In 1911, Frederick Taylor developed the theory of **scientific management,** which comprised methods aimed at determining the one best way for a job to be done. He encouraged manager s to use scientific study to determine the optimal methods to complete tasks and then to train employees in these methods. By the 1920s and 1930s, a field of academic study called **industrial psychology** was created to further study scientifically how to manage employees and work optimally.

The **Hawthorne effect** describes the increase in productivity caused by workers being given special attention. The results of the Hawthorne study (1927–1932) launched the radically new Human Relations Movement, in which researchers studied more complicated motivation theories and the emotional world of the worker. After World War II, the direction of research in management theory shifted from management of an individual worker toward management of the entire organization, its structure, and policies.

Table 7.3   Styles of Leadership

	Visionary	Coaching	Affiliative	Democratic	Pacesetting	Commanding
Leader characteristics	Inspires, believes in own vision, is empathetic, explains how and why people's efforts contribute to the "dream"	Listens, helps people identify their own strengths and weaknesses, acts as a counsellor, encourages, delegates	Promotes harmony, is empathetic, boosts morale, solves conflicts	Is a superb listener, team worker, collaborator, influencer	Has strong drive to achieve, has high standards and initiative, has low empathy and collaboration, is impatient, micro- managing, numbers-driven	Is commanding, "do it because I say so," threatening, tight control, monitoring studiously, creating dissonance, contaminates everyone's mood, drives away talent
How style builds resonance	Moves people toward shared dreams	Connects what a person wants with the organization's goals	Creates harmony by connecting people to one another	Values people's input and gets commitment through participation	Meets challenging and exciting goals	Soothes fear by giving clear direction in an emergency
When style is appropriate	When changes require a new vision or when a clear direction is needed; radical change	To help competent, motivated employees improve performance by building long-term capabilities	To heal rifts in a team, motivate during stressful times, or strengthen connections	To build buy-in or consensus, or to get valuable input from employees	To get high-quality results from a motivated and competent team; sales	In a crisis, to kick-start an urgent turnaround, or with problem employees; traditional military

The fields of organizational psychology and industrial psychology are still very active, and new theories of management practices continue to appear, such as **uncertainty management theory** (when people face increased uncertainty, fairness becomes more important to them) and **sociocracy** (a system of organization and management in which the interests of everyone are served equally).

Which style leaders employ depends on a complex mix of their own personality, the corporate culture, the type of company, the employees they manage, and the given situation. Often a recognized leader knows how to shift between these styles as different situations present themselves.

❻ List the various identifiable leadership styles and personality traits, and explain how they affect business leadership. *(pp. 188–197)*

See Table 7.3 on previous page.

❼ Outline the best ways to create, manage, and participate in teams, taking into account factors such as group flow, Belbin's nine team roles, technology, and Covey's Seven Habits model. *(pp. 197–200)*

Group flow occurs when a group knows how to work together so that each individual member can achieve flow.

Table 7.6 Belbin's Nine Team Roles

Role	Personality Traits
Plant	Creative and imaginative
Resource investigator	Extroverted and communicative
Coordinator	Mature and confident
Shaper	Challenging and dynamic
Monitor evaluator	Serious and strategic
Teamworker	Cooperative and diplomatic
Implementer	Disciplined and reliable
Completer finisher	Painstaking and conscientious
Specialist	Dedicated and self-starting

Source: Belbin Team-Role Summary Sheet, http://www.belbin.com/content/page/ 731/Belbin_Team_Role_Descriptions.pdf, Accessed December 8, 2011

Effective teams are made up of people with diverse skills, talents, and points of view. Team members' respective attributes should complement one another in order for the team to perform at the optimal level.

Increased globalization of business demands the need for **virtual teams,** in which members are located in different physical locations but work together to achieve a goal using technological tools such as conference calls, e-mail, video conferencing, and live broadcasting of key meetings and events over the Web. Web conferencing software such as WebEx and Microsoft Office Live allow participants in any geographic location to brainstorm together in real time on a common "virtual whiteboard," to watch demos and presentations live, and to record and annotate these discussions for later playback.

There are many skills that you can build to enhance your success as a member of a team. One way to organize these skills is the **Seven Habits model** developed by famed management author Stephen Covey. He has found that successful people exhibit the following seven habits of behaviour:
1. Be proactive.
2. Begin with the end in mind.
3. Put first things first.
4. Think win-win.
5. Seek first to understand and then to be understood.
6. Synergize.
7. Sharpen the saw.

Work to develop and use these habits in your role on teams and you will find that your teams become more successful—and that you are in demand for the next team.

Being the manager of a team requires strong leadership qualities to coordinate and manage others' abilities to the fullest. Team members are more productive when encouraged and supported. Managing a virtual team means managing the whole spectrum of communication strategies and project management techniques as well as human and social processes in ways that support the team.

KEY TERMS

CRITICAL THINKING QUESTIONS

1. Consider the responsibilities and risks of a management position in a national firm. What do you feel is a reasonable salary ratio between the highest paid manager of a company and the lowest paid employee? Does it depend on the industry?
2. Is it better for a business to respond to a changing climate by hiring a different style of leader or to expect the current leadership to adapt its style to what is required?
3. What factors are the most important to creating a team that works efficiently together? What problems have you seen in your own academic career when working in group settings, and how could they be prevented?
4. Are there personality differences between genders? Between generations? Explain your answers.
5. Stephen Covey's Seven Habits model is focused on making you a more successful, efficient person. What impact would these seven habits have on your relationships with your friends and family?

APPLICATION EXERCISES

1. **Testing 1, 2, 3 . . .** Find and complete three online leadership, team roles, and/or personality assessment tools. See www.psychtests.com/tests/alltests.html for examples. How consistent are the results in describing your personality or tendencies? How accurate would you rate the results?
2. **Great Leaders.** Locate information about two Canadian and two American managers who you think also qualify as great leaders. You may find www.hbs.edu/leadership/database/index.html, Great American Leaders a good place to start. Select one leader of your gender, one leader of the same ethnicity, and two additional people profiled from different industries. What similarities and differences do you see in this group of four great leaders?
3. **Running the Family Business.** Locate two Web resources that offer an analysis of the special challenges and rewards of a family-run business. Validate the sites with additional references for statements made.
4. **Your Emotional IQ.** Review your strengths in areas of emotional intelligence by taking an online emotional IQ quiz. What roles in a business would take advantage of your emotional IQ strengths? Which role on a team would be best fit for you?
5. **Evaluating Leadership Styles.** Using the Internet, research a person heading a national business that exhibits three of the six leadership styles presented in **Table 7.3**. What evidence can you locate to decide whether that style is effective in his or her business setting?

GLOBAL 500 RESEARCH PROJECT

INSTRUCTIONS:
1. Choose a Global 500 company from *Fortune* Magazine's annual rankings at http://money.cnn.com/magazines/fortune/global500/
2. Research:
   a. Who is the CEO?
   b. How much money did the CEO make last year?
   c. Where did they work before this? How long have they been here?
   d. What management style does this CEO seem to have? Explain your answer.
   e. How does this company motivate its employees—reward programs, benefits, training, meaningful work?
   f. What have the leaders of this company done lately to increase company profits? Locate one news article and summarize. Cite the sources you use to obtain your information.
3. Prepare a report and submit to your professor.

TEAM TIME

Forming a Successful Team

A shoe retailer's sales and earnings have a history of lagging during the spring and summer months. The company wants to reverse this trend by appealing to young people, a rapidly growing consumer base with increasing amounts of disposable income. The company has decided to give one team almost unlimited resources and freedom to develop a flip-flop sandal for modern youth. You need to apply the principles of best practices in team formation to determine the personalities and strengths of each member and assign roles in which the members will be motivated and contribute.

PROCESS

Step 1. Break up into teams of three or four individuals.
Step 2. Begin by deciding what tool you will use to evaluate each member for personality traits, strengths, and weaknesses.

Step 3. Develop a strategy for assessing what work needs to be done and then how your team will assign appropriate responsibilities to each member.
Step 4. How will you evaluate the level of motivation and creativity for the team? What changes can be made if the team's performance is not adequate?
Step 5. Present your findings to the class for discussion.

CONCLUSION

Teamwork can lead to creative, exciting results, but only if the team is designed well and managed well. It takes a combination of technical skills, emotional intelligence, and leadership to create a team that motivates people to contribute and thrive.

ETHICS AND RESPONSIBILITY

Ethics in Teamwork

Being a member of a team means that you are accountable for your actions and the actions of your fellow teammates. Review the following scenario.

SCENARIO

Imagine you work at an advertising firm. You're on a team that is developing an ad campaign proposal for a chain of fitness centres. The firm has been struggling and needs your team to land this account. At a meeting, one of your teammates reveals that he has hacked into a competing firm's network and has a draft of its proposal for the same account. Your teammate wants to steal the idea and use it in your team's proposal. Most of your teammates agree with this idea, but you think it is unethical.

DISCUSSION QUESTIONS

1. How would you handle this situation? Would you voice your objection or go along with the team?
2. If you decide to voice your objection, do you address the entire team or speak to members individually? Why?
3. How would you reconcile your role as a loyal employee and team player with your need to uphold ethical standards?

CLOSING CASE

Toyota Teamwork and the Prius

If you watch a movie set in the future, you may see cars that are fuelled by the sun, water, or even garbage. Those scenarios seemed improbable, and even laughable, ten years ago, but the birth of the Toyota Prius has changed the way we think about alternative power for vehicles. When the Prius hit the market in 2000, it became the car of the future: a gasoline-electric hybrid that could be purchased at the consumer level. Creating this futuristic car was no easy feat. The Toyota Prius design team realized early on that it was on its own. "We had to invent something completely original," states Satoshi Ogiso, the team's chief power train engineer. "We'd have to build it from scratch, blueprint and all."[62] The team knew it would take countless hours and strong teamwork to create this innovative piece of machinery.

The Prius might not have existed if it were not for the tenacity of its engineering team. For years, Toyota had toyed with idea of creating a car with a gasoline-electric motor. However, the idea was a continuous source of conflict. Engineers believed that this type of car would be the solution to the world's problem with carbon emissions. The executives saw other issues. They believed that the premium price, about US$25 000, would not be worth it to their average consumer. Akihiro Wada, Toyota's executive vice-president, sided with the engineers. He asked the team to develop a concept model of the Prius for the 1995 Toyota Motor Show. It was a lofty goal to achieve, especially in only twelve months.

Wada's decision to listen to the engineers, instead of the executives, may be unusual in most corporate settings, but it is a common practice at Toyota. In fact, in Toyota's list of guiding principles, "foster a corporate culture that enhances individual creativity and teamwork value, while honouring mutual trust and respect between labour and management" is listed as number five.[63] The confidence Wada showed in his design team provided the motivation the team needed to have the concept model ready on time. Impressed with the results, Toyota president Hiroshi Okuda put the Prius into production.

The original ten-person Prius design team quickly grew to thousands. The team encountered many problems while trying to turn a concept into a fully functional product. The battery was the main issue. The team had to come up with a way to make a battery that was big enough to power a car engine but not so big that it would overheat. The production of the engine became an ongoing process of trial and error. The first prototype wouldn't even start. The second only went 330 feet (100 metres) before puttering to a stop. The constant stream of failures and setbacks did not thwart the design team's mission. After gathering vital input from all engineers involved and testing meticulously for months, all the design kinks were worked out. In October 1997, Toyota revealed the Prius: a five-passenger car that could get 66 miles per gallon (almost 4 litres per 100 kilometres).

The car was not an immediate success during its first few years on the market. However, after celebrities such as Leonardo DiCaprio and Cameron Diaz purchased the Prius, sales gained tremendous momentum. "It's the hottest car we've ever had," stated Jim Press, president of Toyota Motor North America.[64] The Prius design team proved it could lower carbon emissions while raising Toyota's sales. The team's hard work and innovation even prompted *Time* magazine to name it "Heroes of the Environment."

DISCUSSION QUESTIONS

1. Why do you think the Toyota Prius design team was so motivated to create the car? What needs were being fulfilled in the development and production process? Where do you think it would fall in Herzberg's two-factor model of the workplace?
2. Review Toyota's guiding principle above, what style of leadership does this principle encourage?
3. Since the design of the Toyota Prius was completely new to all members of the design team, how do you think the phenomenon of groupthink affected the process? Why do you think the Toyota Prius design team was ultimately successful?

MyBusinessLab CHAPTER RESOURCES

MyBusinessLab in an online learning and testing environment that features the perfect study tools to help you master the concepts covered in this chapter. Log in to MyBusinessLab at www.pearsoned.ca/mybusinesslab to test your knowledge of key chapter concepts, participate in simulations modelled on real-world business situations, and explore the following additional practice tools:

- Study Plan
- Audio Chapter Summaries
- Glossary Flashcards
- eText
- BizChat Discussion Boards
- BizSkills Simulation: Team Management
- Decision-Making Mini-Simulations: Motivation; Leadership
- Document Makeovers: Team Meeting Email; Team Performance Memo
- Video Activity: Leading

Video Case:

To access the Chapter 7 Video Case: Joie de Vivre Hospitality: Employee Motivation, see the Activities folder in the Assessment section of MyBusinessLab.

Web Case:

To access the Chapter 7 Web Case, see the Activities folder in the Assessment section of MyBusinessLab

Human Resource Management

LEARNING OBJECTIVES

After studying this chapter, you should be able to:

1 Define human resource management and discuss its importance to an organization. (pp. 208–210)

2 Explain how organizations determine and plan for human resource needs. (pp. 210–211)

3 Describe some of the methods used and issues faced by companies when recruiting, selecting, and hiring employees. (pp. 211–215)

4 Discuss some of the types of training and development programs organizations offer employees. (pp. 215–217)

5 Explain why performance management processes are more effective than performance appraisals at evaluating employee performance. (pp. 217–219)

6 Describe how compensation is determined and the various ways employees are compensated. (pp. 219–221)

7 Describe the different types of workweek schedules and how these meet the needs of both the company and its employees. (pp. 221–224)

8 Explain how employees transition through a company over time by way of promotions, transfers, retirement, and termination. (pp. 224–227)

9 Identify the ways in which Canada's demographics are changing and how this affects the workforce. (pp. 227–230)

10 Outline the objectives of unions and the process of collective bargaining. (pp. 230–233)

11 Describe some of the key legislation regulating the hiring, compensating, and managing of employees in today's workplace. (pp. 233–235)

OPENING DISCUSSION: EMPLOYEE RETENTION

How Can Employers Keep Their Top Performers?

Employees who produce quality work and enhance a company's image are prized assets to any organization. Employers want to keep their top performers because the costs of replacing them are high. When experienced employees leave a company, they take valuable skills and knowledge with them, possibly to a competing company, and are usually replaced with new employees who require significant training and time before they become productive. Training and time cost the company money, and if the new employee is not successful in the job role, the costs incurred by the company are even greater. Due to Canada's shrinking available workforce (because of an aging population) and talent mismatch (job seekers skilled in areas where jobs are not available), companies may not only have difficulty finding right-fit employees but are also in continuous competition to hire these employees before their competitors do. Employers may have a difficult time retaining top-performing employees if they don't understand what employees want. Managers do not always motivate employees in a fashion that aids retention. Studies repeatedly show that the number one reason why employees choose to stay at or leave their current employment is their relationship with their supervisor or manager.[1] Employers need to offer incentives that motivate and encourage employees to stay with the company.

One company that has successfully created a working environment that engages employees and supports the creative experience is SAS, the world's largest privately held software company, with more than 12 000 employees in 400 offices worldwide.[2] By providing employees amenities such as health care, subsidized child care, a recreation and fitness centre, numerous wellness programs, flexible work hours, free car parking, religious observance room, profit-sharing, tuition subsidies, and a number of other wonderful benefits, the company boasts one of the lowest employee

(continued)

turnover rates in the industry: 2.6 percent, while the info-tech industry average is 22 percent.[3] The company welcomes employees to provide confidential feedback on their manger's performance and each year contracts independent consultants to conduct confidential employee satisfaction and engagement surveys.

Selected multiple times over the past few years as one of Fortune's 100 Best Companies to Work For,[4] SAS believes that happy, healthy employees drive the innovation that keeps SAS in a leadership position among

business analytics vendors; such an atmosphere is in part thanks to the policies of SAS CEO Jim Goodnight. According to Goodnight, SAS fosters a creative environment by:[5]

- Keeping employees intellectually engaged.
- Removing distractions so employees can do their best work.
- Making managers responsible for sparking creativity.
- Eliminating the arbitrary distinctions between administrative "suits" and more abstract "creatives."
- Engaging customers as creative partners.

In addition to encouraging strong professional lives, SAS supports its employees in their private lives. "The corporate philosophy is, if your fifth grader is in his first school play, you should be there to see it," says Goodnight.[6] Such a philosophy has placed SAS on Working Mother magazine's list of best companies multiple times.

DISCUSSION QUESTIONS

1. What would make you want to quit your job?
2. Besides the costs involved in hiring and training a new employee, what other losses might a company incur when a new employee does not work out and is asked to leave?
3. What do you think is the biggest motivator for most employees—money, interesting work, recognition on the job (employee of the month), or something else? Which incentives most appeal to you?

Define human resource management and discuss its importance to an organization.

HIRING FOR OPTIMUM ORGANIZATIONAL PERFORMANCE

The Importance of Managing Human Resources

Why are people considered valuable company resources?
When you think about the resources required to run a business, you probably think about money, space, equipment, supplies, and so on. Although financial and material resources are key aspects of a business, the resource often taken for granted but that is arguably the most important is the "human" resource—or people. People are valuable company assets because they provide the ideas, creativity, knowledge, and ingenuity that make a business run. An organization can have all the money and materials in the world, but without the right people doing the right things, it will not be successful.

Human resources (HR) are the people in an organization and need to be managed just as carefully as the material and financial resources of a business.

Human resource management (HRM) is the organizational function that deals with the people in the business, from the executives and the managers to the front-line production, sales, and administrative staff.

What is human resource management?
Human resources (HR)—the people in an organization—need to be managed just as carefully as the material and financial resources of a business. **Human resource management (HRM)** is the organizational function that deals with the people in the business, from the executives and the managers to the front-line production, sales, and administrative staff. HRM aims to ensure that

the organization is correctly staffed at all times by the right number of employees with the right skills required to meet company goals. Proper management of human assets builds value in the company and ensures time and money is not wasted.

What are the functions of HRM?

HRM functions encompass every aspect of the "human" in a business, including planning, recruiting, selecting and hiring, training, evaluating, compensating, scheduling, motivating, and transitioning employees. HRM also oversees employee–management relations and must always work within the limits of the law (see **Figure 8.1**). HRM works through the many challenges in today's society, such as diversity issues, work/lifestyle preferences, and global business considerations. Human resource

Management

HRM

Planning
Recruiting
Hiring
Training
Scheduling
Evaluating
Motivating
Compensating
Transitioning
Labour Relations

Employees

Legal

Job Seekers

Figure 8.1 The Functions of Human Resource Management

managers work with people, but they are also deeply involved in planning, record keeping, and other administrative duties. In recent years, HRM has become more focused on aligning its core responsibilities with the organization's vision, goals, and strategies for success. This alignment will allow HRM to take advantage of applicants' unique qualifications, which will enable it to provide strategic value to the company and the company's customers. Most HRM functions are shared between the professional human resource manager and the other managers.

What is the purpose of an HR department?

The human resources department, working with other department managers, is responsible for the people in an organization and helps to maximize organizational productivity by optimizing the effectiveness of employees. A company may create an HR department to establish, develop, maintain, and communicate company policies throughout the organization or to facilitate communication between management and employees. This is fairly easy to do in small companies and may not require a dedicated department. For large companies and multinational companies with many employees, however, a department specializing in human resource functions and solutions is required.

The HR department represents employees and offers them advice while keeping the overall best interests of the company in mind. A human resources department:

- develops hiring plans and recruiting policies
- handles compensation and salary administration
- handles employee relations, transitions, contracts, performance reviews, benefits, and pension plans
- develops official documentation, workplace ethics/codes of conduct, employee handbooks, employee training programs, award/reward programs, and community connections[7]

Determining and Planning Human Resource Needs

Why is it important for a company to plan for its human resource needs?

When an entrepreneur starts up a business, he or she may initially serve as the company's chief executive officer and financial manager, as well as the sales executive and

HRM functions encompass every aspect of the "human" in a business, including planning, recruiting, selecting and hiring, training, evaluating, compensating, scheduling, motivating, and transitioning employees. HRM also oversees employee–management relations and must always work within the limits of the law.

The **human resources department,** working with other department managers, is responsible for the people in the organization and helps to maximize organizational productivity by optimizing the effectiveness of employees.

marketing director. As a business expands, new people are brought into the organization. At that point, the owner may still serve as the HR director, hiring, firing, and realigning employees to fill the growing needs of the expanding business. Although keeping track of HR needs at small businesses can be fairly simple, companies that add employees and continue to grow require more specific HR planning. **Human resource planning** is creating a strategy for meeting future human resource needs within an organization. Poor staff planning can be costly. Being overstaffed burdens a company with the unnecessary expense of maintaining salaries, benefits, and training for surplus employees. An understaffed organization can lead to loss of sales and competitiveness if customer needs are not met. Planning staffing needs therefore involves 1) assessing the supply of and demand for current and future employee resources and 2) evaluating job requirements.

Human resource planning is the creation of a strategy for meeting future human resource needs within an organization.

Explain how organizations determine and plan for human resource needs.

How does a company determine how many employees it needs?

First, managers need to determine what jobs are required within the organization in order for the company to meet organizational goals. For instance, a company may be incurring growth and additional jobs need to be created in order for the company to maintain quality standards or increase production levels. Managers review trends in the company's human resource usage over time, economic trends that may affect the supply of available workers, economic trends that may increase or decrease possible future sales revenues, and future organizational goals before making any decisions about whether an increase or decrease in the number of employees is required. Planning human resource needs is done by assessing the jobs required within the organization, then assessing the current supply of, and demand for, employees. Many organizations use an **employee information system (EIS)** to create a **workforce profile**, in which a company can record and track their employees' skills and abilities, creating a "personnel inventory." Then when a promotion, special project, or transfer position is available, the EIS can be searched to find an internal candidate who possesses the skills required to do the job. The skills inventory may include the following types of information about each employee: education, training, experience, specialized skills, and current and previous positions held within the company.

An **employee information system (EIS)** creates a **workforce profile**, in which a company can record and track employee skills and abilities to generate a "personnel inventory."

Forecasting is the process of determining the future demand for employees as well as the future supply of employees.

Forecasting—an essential part of HR planning—is the process of determining the future demand for employees as well as the future supply of employees. Forecasting demand for employees is based on several factors, such as predicted sales of the company's goods or services, current workforce skill level, the effect of technology changes on staff needs, and changes in employment practices (such as using more or less temporary staff). In addition, staffing changes expected through normal turnover, retirement, and any planned reassignments are taken into consideration. Forecasting internal supply means tracking the number of current employees who will be available to fill various jobs at some future time. Forecasting external supply means examining labour market trends. If forecasting indicates an imbalance between the supply and demand for employees, further action must be taken. Such actions may include recruitment, training, retraining, labour reductions, or changes in workforce utilization.

A **job analysis** identifies and defines in detail the particular duties and requirements of the tasks and responsibilities an employee is required to perform.

A **job description** is a formal statement summarizing what the employee will do in that job role. It includes the job responsibilities, the conditions under which the job will be performed, and the job's relationship to other functions in the organization.

How do companies identify the skills needed to perform a particular job?

Human resource planners complete an analytical study of the tasks being performed in specific jobs throughout the organization. Information about a specific job is discovered through a job analysis. **A job analysis** identifies and defines in detail the particular duties and requirements of the tasks and responsibilities an employee is required to perform. In a job analysis, each task is defined by a **job description**, a formal statement summarizing what the employee will do in that job role. It includes the job responsibilities, the conditions under which the job will be performed, and the job's relationship to other functions in the organization. Job descriptions are important because they define job objectives used later in performance appraisals. They also can become a part of the legal contract between the employee and the employer. To assist in recruiting the right person to fulfill the job's requirements, job specifications are also defined during the job analysis. **Job specifications** are the skills, education, experience, and personal attributes that candidates need to possess to successfully fulfill the job role. **Figure 8.2** shows a sample job description and job specifications.

Job specifications are the skills, education, experience, and personal attributes that candidates need to possess to successfully fulfill the job role.

Company: Nelson Wireless	
Position title: Marketing manager	
(a) Job description	**(b) Job specifications**
Join a team of marketing professionals focused on mobile technologies in the consumer market segment. The marketing manager is responsible for coordinating and/or implementing marketing projects designed for the consumer market segment. Working in cooperation with the sales team, product offers, and other headquarters marketing teams, the marketing manager will coordinate public relations projects and other promotional activities to drive Nelson Wireless brand awareness and product demand and generate consumer purchases. The marketing manager will provide strategic oversight for regional-level industry events, and be responsible for planning and executing customer events. The marketing manager will be responsible for coordinating budgets and timelines, maintaining accurate records of expenditures, and compiling reports of activity results. Additionally, he/she will be responsible for managing a team of 8-10 marketing associates. The marketing manager role will also include administrative elements such as invoice processing, event scheduling, and maintenance of a promotional calendar.	• College degree required with emphasis in marketing, business administration, or communications preferred • 3+ years marketing/communications experience required • Excellent demonstrated verbal and written communication skills • Demonstrated experience in event execution • Demonstrated ability to coordinate cooperative working relationships across multiple parties • Ability to work well under pressure • Extremely well organized, strong project management and time management skills, and strong ability to multitask • Proven ability to operate in a fast-paced, high-growth professional environment

Figure 8.2   Sample (a) Job Description and (b) Job Specifications

Recruiting

What is the recruitment process?   Finding and attracting capable applicants for employment depends on a well-devised recruiting plan. The **recruitment process** provides the organization with a pool of potentially qualified job candidates from which judicious selection can be made to fill vacancies. The recruitment process begins when new recruits are sought and ends when their applications are submitted. Usually, the process starts when a manger initiates an employee requisition for a specific vacancy or an anticipated vacancy. **Internal recruiting**—filling job vacancies with existing employees from within the business—is the first choice of many companies. Often, companies post job openings on the company intranet, staff notice boards, in-house newsletters, and in staff meetings. Internal recruitment has several advantages. It tends to be a morale booster for employees because they know that the company has an interest in promoting their own. And because employer and employee have established a working relationship, there is a reduced risk of selecting an inappropriate candidate for the desired position. Finally, choosing from within is potentially quicker and less costly as it reduces costs associated with outside recruiting and shortens the length of training time.

However, there are disadvantages to not considering outside sources. This includes the possibility of not getting the best candidate due to a limited search process. In addition, another internal vacancy is created that must be subsequently filled. Moreover,

Describe some of the methods used and issues faced by companies when recruiting, selecting, and hiring employees.

The **recruitment process** provides the organization with a pool of potentially qualified job candidates from which judicious selection can be made to fill vacancies.

Internal recruiting is the process of filling job vacancies with existing employees from within the business.

8

Figure 8.3   External Recruitment Resources

External recruiting looks outside the business to fill vacancies using various resources and methods.

Employment agencies—which often specialize in accounting, sales, or clerical services—provide a screened pool of candidates, which reduces the hiring company's administrative burden of recruitment.

relying on internal employees may discourage new perspectives and ideas and eventually make the business resistant to change. As a result, businesses also rely on external recruiting to meet staffing needs. **External recruiting** looks outside the business to fill vacancies using various resources and methods (see **Figure 8.3**).

Depending on the type of position, companies often use employment agencies or consulting firms. **Employment agencies**—which often specialize in accounting, sales, or clerical services—provide a screened pool of candidates, which reduces the hiring company's administrative burden of recruitment. However, these agencies can be costly. Recruitment consultants, often referred to as "headhunters," conduct specialized searches, usually for senior management or key employees. Recruitment consultants are often expensive, but the costs of finding the wrong candidate can be even higher. Posting ads in local newspapers, on Internet job sites, or in specialized trade magazines can be advantageous methods because they are not expensive and reach a wide audience.

What are the challenges in recruiting?   One of the newer challenges facing recruiting specialists is the use of technology. Online job and resumé posting sites, Web and video blogs, virtual job fairs, podcasts, and other online media are all being used by both those looking to find a job and those looking to fill a position. While online job postings yield many responses and thus a large pool of candidates, sifting through these responses to find the right person for the job can be time-consuming for HR professionals. Therefore, HR managers must know how to use technology skilfully. At a basic recruiting level, this means learning how to make a posted job description appeal to the most qualified candidates as well as stand out from competitors in the online environment so the right person can find the open position more readily. It also means becoming familiar with the new social networking technologies and Web 2.0 techniques to post jobs and to find recruits.

BizChat

Explore on MyBusinessLab

What Is Recruiting 2.0?

You're probably familiar with social networking sites such as Myspace and Facebook. The same concept is applied to the professional community through sites such as LinkedIn (www.linkedin.com), ZoomInfo (www.zoominfo.com), and Spoke (www.spoke.com). LinkedIn is an online network of more than 135 million experienced professionals worldwide whose connections are made through college and university, graduate school, or professional affiliations.[8] Most people would like to hire or work with someone they know, and LinkedIn can provide helpful colleague and customer recommendations. Additionally, LinkedIn may assist job seekers by providing insiders' information on companies and employees. If you've scheduled an interview, you might find a LinkedIn page for the person with whom you are meeting. This can give you some information on that person's professional background, including where he or she went to school, as well as information on hobbies. Knowing these details may provide for good conversation starters during the interview.

Discussion Questions

1. Do you think it is appropriate for an employer to view your Facebook page before an interview or before they hire you? Why or why not? If an employer viewed your Facebook page, do you think it would affect their decision to hire you? Why or why not?
2. Have you established an online "professional" image using a professional networking tool such as LinkedIn? If you don't have an online image now, do you think you should create one? What will it say about you? What can you do to ensure your online image is portraying you in a positive way to potential employers?
3. Some people say they don't care what others think of them. Should you care about what others think of your online image? Why or why not?

One of the greatest recruiting challenges cited is the difficulty finding qualified candidates for critical positions.[9] At the 2010 World Economic Forum, Manpower Inc. identified several top concerns for business leaders, including that many aging employees will be retiring soon, taking with them much talent, and new employees with similar skills and abilities will be difficult to find. Another concern was that job seekers who do have sought-after skills will have the power to choose which company they will work for, and, as a result, companies will have to define jobs differently and adapt how they recruit and retain scarce talent.[10]

Selecting and Hiring

BizSkills Simulation: Hiring a New Employee. Located in MyBusinessLab.

How do employers select potential job candidates from many job applicants?

The large group of applicants that has been identified at the beginning of the recruitment process needs to be narrowed down into a select pool of candidates. **Selection** entails gathering information about candidates, evaluating their qualifications, and choosing the ones that best fit the job specifications. Many companies use special applicant-tracking system software to sort through resumés and job applications quickly. HR managers also use systems that build assessments into the application process to help pre-screen for certain personality traits. Through the selection process, HR personnel, in collaboration with department managers, compare the candidates' qualifications to the job specifications. Every employer is looking for a specific set of skills from job seekers that match the skills necessary to perform the particular job. Beyond the job-specific technical skills, employers demand certain critical employability skills. The Conference Board of Canada developed an Employability Skills profile, based on input from employers and validated by a wide range of stakeholders. The profile has quickly become the benchmark used by businesses to identify skills that potential employees require to enter, stay in, and progress in the world of work. These skills are grouped into three main areas: fundamental skills (communication, problem-solving, mathematics, and technology), personal management skills (positive attitudes and behaviours), and teamwork skills (working with others).[11]

Selection entails gathering information about candidates, evaluating their qualifications, and choosing the ones that best fit the job specifications.

What happens when an appropriate candidate is found?

After identifying a small pool of appropriate candidates, department and HR managers meet with each

A **job interview** is a one-on-one meeting of the company and the job candidate, through which the company is able to gauge the candidate's personality, clarify information in the candidate's resumé, and determine whether the candidate is the best match for the position.

Behavioural interviews are conducted to evaluate a candidate's experience and behaviours so the employer can determine the applicant's potential for success in the job.

candidate to conduct a **job interview**, a one-on-one meeting between the company and the job candidate, in which the company is able to gauge the candidate's personality, clarify information in the candidate's resumé, and determine whether the candidate is the best match for the position. At the same time, the interview is an opportunity for the candidate to evaluate whether the company is a desirable place of employment. The candidate may also need to complete one or more skills-related or behavioural tests. More and more organizations are hiring candidates who show they have the most "trainable fit." Employers look for and test candidates for the ability to fit in with the organization's culture and values, as well as the ability to learn quickly and adapt to new challenges. **Behavioural interviews** are conducted to evaluate a candidate's experience and behaviours so the employer can determine the applicant's potential for success in the job. In certain types of jobs, such as those in which a candidate may be handling money, working in safety-sensitive positions, or giving care to others, a candidate may be asked to undergo drug testing, get bonded, or obtain a police record check. Interviews may be conducted by one interviewer or a panel of interviewers, and the candidate may be asked to attend a single interview or several interviews before a hiring decision is reached.

During this process, the employer and the interviewee will discuss what they each bring to the prospective relationship. If agreement is reached, most employers will impose a standard form contract, leaving details to be clarified "on the job." Well-organized employers are careful to document all offers made to candidates to reduce the risk of statements later being remembered as promises that might give rise to expectations. Employers want to reduce the risk of raising false expectations followed by disappointment. When someone is hired into a company, both the employer and employee form a psychological contract (unwritten expectations). A **psychological contract** represents the mutual beliefs, perceptions, and informal obligations held between an employer and an employee. Employers expect employees to provide a fair day's work, to accept the authority within the organization, and to report to work regularly. A psychological contract breach may occur if employees perceive that the company has failed to deliver on what was perceived as promises. Negative responses may occur in the form of reduced loyalty and commitment to the company. Do you think a psychological contract means that employees have an obligation to work for an organization for their entire career? Does it mean that a company has an obligation to employ an employee until they retire? Why or why not? How might answers to these questions vary based on a person's age or the country in which one works?

Before offering a candidate a position, it is important that the company complete thorough background and reference checks. It is not uncommon to hear stories about companies that failed to conduct background checks and hired someone who falsified his

A **psychological contract** represents the mutual beliefs, perceptions, and informal obligations held between an employer and an employee.

Decision-Making Mini-Simulation: Human Resources. Located in MyBusinessLab.

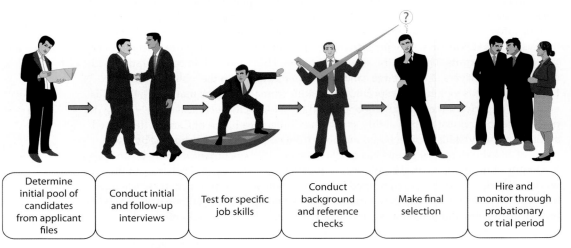

| Determine initial pool of candidates from applicant files | Conduct initial and follow-up interviews | Test for specific job skills | Conduct background and reference checks | Make final selection | Hire and monitor through probationary or trial period |

Figure 8.4 Hiring Process

or her educational or professional experiences or who had been in trouble with the law. For example, the Treaty Group Inc. relied on a global personnel and training firm to help with its hiring needs. Unfortunately, the person whom Treaty hired to assist with bookkeeping functions defrauded the company of more than $250 000. It was discovered later that the hired bookkeeper had been convicted of defrauding a former employer prior to joining Treaty.[12]

What happens after an applicant has progressed satisfactorily through all the selection steps?   If an applicant progresses satisfactorily through all the selection steps, a decision to hire the individual is made. The manager of the new employee is nearly always involved in the decision to hire. As shown in **Figure 8.4**, hiring is a multistep process. The **hiring process** begins with developing the job requirements and ends when a job offer is made. Where a company has a collective labour agreement (a union contract with its employees), the selection process must also follow the provisions of that agreement. When hiring for full-time, permanent employees, companies often hire on a probational condition. **Probation** is a specific timeframe (typically three to six months) during which the new hire proves their skills and worth on the job. If the employee proves himself or herself on the job, they move from probational employee status to permanent employee status.

DEVELOPING EMPLOYEES FOR OPTIMUM PERFORMANCE

Training

Why is it important to train employees?   Training employees can enhance the success of a business and ensure that employees stay in top form. Companies that emphasize training and development experience greater productivity, loyalty, and retention. Employee training is important for many reasons, as it often contributes to:[13]

- increased job satisfaction, motivation, and morale among employees
- greater efficiency in work, resulting in financial gain
- more effective use of new technologies and methods
- development of new strategies and products
- lower employee turnover
- fewer interpersonal conflicts and better communication

What kind of training do new employees receive?   Initially, when an employee is hired, the organization uses an **orientation program** to introduce the employee to the company's people, policies, and procedures. Orientation can be as simple as an overview of the organization and the distribution of basic information, such as company procedures and expectations. Employees should be introduced to associates in their department as well as the associates in other departments with whom the employee will be interacting; this will help them feel at ease so they can quickly become as productive as possible. The employee should be shown their workspace; given IDs and passwords necessary to log in to computers, printers, phones, and faxes; and provided information about company policies and procedures and employee benefits. Orientation is more effective if it becomes a means of familiarizing the employee with the company's mission and discussing how the new employee's contribution can add to the company's success. Over the first few weeks, the manager should schedule brief daily meetings with the new employee to review expectations and responsibilities and answer any questions the new employee may have. Failure to integrate new hires into a company adequately leads to low retention rates.

What other training is required of new and present employees?   Training begins where orientation ends. Training should teach employees skills or ways to

top 10

Ten of Canada's Top 100 Employers

(Canada's Top 100 Employers project is a national competition to determine which employers lead their industries in offering exceptional workplaces for their employees. The list below is shown in alphabetical order and includes multiple-year winners.)

Company	Industry
1. AMEC Americas Limited	Professional Services and Communications
2. Cameco Corporation	Industrial and Resources
3. Enbridge Inc.	Industrial and Resources
4. Goldcorp Inc.	Industrial and Resources
5. Loblaw Companies Limited	Consumer Services
6. Procter & Gamble Inc.	Consumer Services
7. Research In Motion Limited	Technology
8. SAS Institute Canada Inc.	Technology
9. Statistics Canada	Public Sector and Non-Profit
10. Toyota Motor Manufacturing Canada Inc.	Industrial and Resources

Source: Canada's Top 100 Employers, "Canada's Top 100 Employers," http://www.canadastop100.com/index.html, Accessed January 16, 2011, and Richard Yerema, "Canada's Top 100 Employers," www.macleans.ca, October 14, 2009, http://www2.macleans.ca/2009/10/14/the-top-100-2009/, Accessed January 16, 2011.

8

The **hiring process** begins with developing the job requirements and ends when a job offer is made.

Discuss some of the types of training and development programs organizations offer their employees.

Probation is a specific timeframe (typically three to six months) during which the new hire proves their skills and worth on the job.

An **orientation program** is used to introduce the employee to the company's people, policies, and procedures.

On-the-job training is when employees learn skills by performing them.

Mentoring is a form of on-the-job training whereby an experienced employee provides direction and information to the new employee as they learn the job.

Mentors are experienced individual employees who help a less-experienced person by explaining how to perform specific tasks, creating opportunities to learn new skills, and counselling about the consequences of particular actions and decisions.

Apprentice training program trains individuals through classroom or formal instruction and on-the-job training.

Programmed learning is an approach in which the employee is asked to perform step-by-step instructions or to respond to questions.

Off-the-job training and development techniques require employees to participate in outside seminars, university-conducted programs, and corporate universities.

Simulation training provides realistic job-task training in a manner that is challenging but does not create the threat of failure.

improve on existing skills. For example, a salesperson may know how to sell a product but may not know all the intricacies of selling a new product. Often, other employees in the department or the recent hire's mentor can conduct on-the-job training. In **on-the-job training**, employees learn skills by performing them. **Mentoring** is a form of on-the-job training whereby an experienced employee provides direction and information to the new employee as they learn the job. **Mentors** are experienced individual employees who help a less-experienced person by explaining how to perform specific tasks, creating opportunities to learn new skills, and counselling about the consequences of particular actions and decisions. Like other forms of training, mentoring increases employee performance, satisfaction, and loyalty. Sometimes, however, an apprentice training program is required. An **apprentice training** program trains individuals through classroom or formal instruction and on-the-job training.

Some jobs are more readily learned through a **programmed learning** approach, in which the employee is asked to perform step-by-step instructions or to respond to questions. These often come in the form of computerized multiple-choice tests, which provide immediate feedback. The benefit of programmed learning is that the employee can progress at his or her own pace, picking up information piece by piece, and the employer can track the employee's progress.

Some companies use **off-the-job training and development** techniques that require employees to participate in outside seminars, university-conducted programs, and corporate universities. Hamburger University, McDonald's corporate training facility, aligns training with employees' specific career paths, including development paths for crew, restaurant managers, mid-managers, and executives. Their curriculum is delivered using a combination of classroom instruction, hands-on lab activities, goal-based scenarios, and computer e-learning modules. Management hopefuls enroll in extensive classroom and field instruction and can earn credit that can even be applied toward a two-year or four-year degree.[14]

What kind of impact has technology had on training?
Improvements in technology provide companies with other training options such as simulated training and interactive multimedia training. **Simulation training** provides realistic job-task training in a manner that is challenging but does not create the threat of failure. **Vestibule training** is a type of simulation most suitable to airline pilots, astronauts, and surgeons, for whom making mistakes during training is not an option or is too costly.

Online training, or **distance learning**, allows employees to take college or university classes on the Internet at their convenience, enabling them to obtain specific job-related education or to pursue a degree. Other forms of Internet-based distance training have instructors in a centralized location teach groups of employees at remote locations

via television hook-ups (teletraining) or a combination of audio/video equipment (videoconferencing). **Games-based learning (serious games)** is a training method whereby employees play virtual reality games that simulate real-life events. SubSafe is a recent example of a games-based training system for submarine safety and spatial awareness, providing end users with a real-time, interactive, three-dimensional model of part of a Trafalgar class submarine.[15] Canadian Forces is using games-based training for air traffic control to increase the speed with which trainees gain experience.[16] SAP, which creates enterprise resource planning (ERP) software, introduced games-based training in France and in several African countries "to drive adoption of business strategies and increase employees' business skills."[17] Colleagues split into teams to compete on a live SAP ERP system to manage a mock company. According to SAP's South Africa education director, Johan Pretorius, "The simulation game won wide acclaim for achieving these goals through a fun, interactive, and informative process."[18]

Electronic performance support systems (EPSSs) automatically provide employees with information, advice, and training when they need it so they can accomplish specific tasks quickly. EPSSs are especially useful to train and support help-desk and on-call operators as well as to act as an in-house help-desk alternative. When Pitney Bowes, a provider of mail and messaging management equipment, previously upgraded its information management system, few employees took advantage of the half-day instructor-led training programs the company offered. Instead, employees inundated the company's help desk with their questions, which turned out to be a very inefficient and costly result. With their next software upgrade, Pitney Bowes implemented an

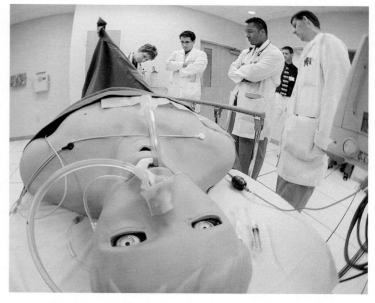

Robots are used in simulation training for medical students.

EPSS mentor program and found that the volume of help-desk call requests declined by more than 2000 calls per week, saving the company an estimated US$50 000 per week.[19]

How are managers trained?   Because of their roles in the organization, managers require different training than their front-line co-workers. **Management development training** focuses on leadership, communication, teamwork, and relationship-building skills. In addition, managers need to keep abreast of the changes in employment laws such as discrimination and harassment, as well as updates in the use of electronic communication resources. In addition to training for current managers, many companies offer management development programs that prepare management-trainees to become managers within the organization. These programs may have the trainees participate in an on-the-job training program, which may include **job rotation**, in which the employee rotates through different departments to learn first-hand the various aspects of the business, or a **coaching/understudy program**, in which the employee works directly with senior management in planning and other managerial functions. **Action learning**, another management development training approach, focuses on solving real problems on actual work projects. Action learning allows trainees to work together in teams to analyze real-time corporate problems that extend beyond their areas of expertise. Companies such as General Electric and Johnson & Johnson have successfully implemented action-learning teams as part of their management development programs.[20]

Senior managers often use executive coaches to further develop their effectiveness. Executive coaches identify the manager's strengths and weaknesses by interviewing those who work closely with the manager. They then meet with the manager to work on eliminating weaknesses and further developing strengths. Mentoring is another option that companies use to enable their experienced managers to work closely with inexperienced managers.

Evaluating

How is employee performance evaluated?   **A performance appraisal** is an evaluation of an employee's performance that gives feedback about how well the employee is doing, as well as where changes and improvements are needed (see **Figure 8.5**). Managers use the results of performance appraisals in decisions about promotion, raises,

Vestibule training is a type of simulation most suitable to airline pilots, astronauts, and surgeons, for whom making mistakes during training is not an option or is too costly.

Online training, or distance learning, allows employees to take college or university classes on the Internet at their convenience, enabling them to obtain specific job-related education or to pursue a degree.

Games-based learning (serious games) is a training method whereby employees play virtual reality games that simulate real-life events.

Electronic performance support systems (EPSSs) automatically provide employees with information, advice, and training when they need it so they can accomplish specific tasks quickly.

Management development training focuses on leadership, communication, teamwork, and relationship-building skills.

Explain why performance management processes are more effective than performance appraisals at evaluating employee performance.

Annual Employee Performance Evaluation

Employee's Name:		Supervisor:	
Job Title:		Date Hired:	
Department:		Date of Review:	

Evaluation

This form is design to assess your current performance and to help in setting goals for the future. This form is considered confidential and will only be reviewed by you and your supervisor(s).

Overall Job Knowledge/Experience Level

	Consistently meets requirements
	Generally meets requirements
	Does not meet requirements
Comments:	

Quality of Work

	Exceeds expectations
	Meets expectations
	Does not meet expectations
Comments:	

Attendance

	Rarely tardy or absent
	Sometimes tardy or absent
	Frequently tardy or absent
Comments:	

Cooperation

	Consistently participates and contributes to the team
	Generally participates and contributes to the team
	Does not participate or contribute to the team
Comments:	

Future Goals:

Figure 8.5 A Sample Performance Appraisal

Job rotation is when the employee rotates through different departments to learn firsthand the various aspects of the business.

Coaching/understudy program is when the employee works directly with senior management in planning and other managerial functions.

Action learning, another management development training approach, focuses on solving real problems on actual work projects.

A **performance appraisal** is an evaluation of an employee's performance that gives feedback about how well the employee is doing, as well as where changes and improvements are needed.

Performance management is an approach that combines goal setting, performance appraisal, and training and development into a unified and ongoing process.

additional training, or reassignments. The performance appraisal process is important for both employees and the organization as a whole. The process includes:

1. Determining standards that employees should aim for in their work.
2. Evaluating the employee's performance in comparison with these standards.
3. Providing feedback to reduce and eliminate poor performance and improve or enhance positive performance.

When employees are hired, they should have a good understanding of what is expected of them. These expectations become the performance standards upon which they'll be measured. Appraisals act as a confirmation of these standards and help employees establish quantifiable and measurable goals for improvement in the upcoming year.

Are performance appraisals effective?

Although performance appraisals, when conducted properly, are very helpful to the employee and ultimately the organization, they are often not effective. Since appraisals often lead to criticism, many managers shy away from them because they are uncomfortable handing out bad or harsh comments. Despite the fact that annual raises are often tied to the performance evaluation, manages avoid doing them as long as possible. This results in unmotivated employees who feel that the manager does not care about them enough to facilitate their annual raise. Additionally, some managers have a difficult time quantifying performance, and fear not being able to defend their ratings if questioned. Although performance appraisals often suggest means to improve weak performance or to enhance solid performance, the process does not always offer the opportunity to follow up and ensure that such means have been acted on. Often, it's not until the next performance appraisal that it is recognized that such training and development have not happened. And when the next appraisal can be a year away, the benefits of appraisals become diluted.

Is there an alternative to performance appraisals?
An alternative to a performance appraisal is performance management. **Performance management** is an approach that combines goal setting, performance appraisal, and training and development into a unified and ongoing process. As such, it is more of a cyclical and fluid process than the single occurrence of a performance appraisal. Employees are constantly receiving feedback and given opportunities for training and development to ensure that they have the right tools with which to perform their job. The vibrancy and performance of the organization is ensured because managers put focus on developmental plans and opportunities for each staff member. Thus, it is much more effective than the traditional method of using performance appraisals. **Table 8.1** summarizes several aspects of the performance management process. The concept, while often applied to employees, is also applicable to other components of the organization, including an entire department, a product or service, or the organization as a whole. Performance management, appraisals, and training can play a significant role in keeping a business productive and efficient. Although they often require an investment of time and money, the investment often pays off.

Table 8.1 Aspects of Performance Management

Direction sharing	Communicating organization's higher-level goals such as vision, mission, values, and strategy
Role clarifying	Defining roles in terms of daily work tasks
Goal setting and planning	Redefining organizational or departmental goals into specific employee goals, which includes the employee's development of the steps necessary to achieve goals
Ongoing performance monitoring and feedback	Periodic performance reports regarding progress on meeting goals as well as feedback regarding progress toward goals
Coaching and support	Ongoing as a part of the feedback process
Performance assessment (appraisal)	An element in performance management process that offers specific defined knowledge on how employee's performance is improving company results
Rewards, recognition, and compensation	Given as appropriate to motivate employee toward achieving current and future goals
Workflow, process control, and return on investment management	Making sure employee's measurable performance is linked to measurable goals of company

Source: Gary Dessler, Human Resource Management, 11th edition. Upper Saddle River, NJ: Prentice Hall, p. 338.

COMPENSATING, SCHEDULING, AND TRANSITIONING EMPLOYEES

Compensating

What is compensation?   In today's workplace, **compensation**, payment for work performed, comes in a variety of forms, including money, bonuses, work/life benefits, health insurance, and retirement plans. Having the right pay system in place is very important for a company to become and remain competitive. A fair and comparable compensation package attracts high-quality employees and keeps them from leaving. Moreover, employees have a greater incentive to work harder and more efficiently if they know their compensation is tied to their efforts and to the overall success of the company. A low turnover rate and a productive workforce help to keep costs low, which has a positive impact on the company's profits. Because there are many ways to structure compensation, the decision is not an easy one. It is often a delicate balance between paying to attract and keep the best and not jeopardizing the financial security of the company.

Are all employees compensated in the same way?   Employers have to consider many factors when determining an employee's pay rate. Employees are evaluated on prior work experience and education as well as contribution to the company. The employer considers how competing companies are compensating their employees and in so doing may find the company needs to offer more wages or benefits in order to attract top talent. Legislation and the cost of living play a role in determining compensation and the amount of pay increases. Laws prescribe minimum wage amounts as well as equal pay for equal work. As well, the employer needs to consider the company's ability to pay wages (i.e., having enough revenue to permit adding employees to the workforce or raising current wages). Not all company employees receive the same amount of pay, nor are they paid by the same methods. Pay varies depending on the type of job role and the industry an employee is working in. Regarding specific individuals and positions, companies typically determine the type and amount of compensation on a balance of the following: federal and provincial legislation (the law), what the company can afford, what competitors are paying, and what skills and talents each employee brings to the company.

There are many ways to pay workers for their time and effort. The most common types of compensation in Canada today are wages and salary. In addition to wages and salary, many companies compensate employees based on performance. Refer to **Table 8.2** for descriptions of various types of compensation.

⑥
Describe how compensation is determined and the various ways employees are compensated.

Compensation, payment for work performed, comes in a variety of forms, including money, bonuses, work/life benefits, health insurance, and retirement plans.

8

Table 8.2 Various Types of Compensation

Wages	Compensation based on the number of hours or days worked. Each province has a minimum hourly wage that varies depending on the positions and job market.
Salary	Fixed annual compensation usually paid on a weekly, bi-weekly, or monthly basis. The employee's compensation level has the potential to increase based on the results of employee evaluations, which usually occur on an annual basis. Many companies pay employees a base salary plus some sort of incentive-based payment.
Piecework	Compensation based on the number of items produced or sold. For instance, employees may receive $1 for every pie they make, so the more pies they make, the more money they make. Many assembly line workers are paid by the number of pieces they produce. Although this method may motivate workers to work faster, quality of work may suffer.
Commissions	Some salespeople are paid a percentage of the amount they sell. This is called a commission on sales (compensation based directly on employee performance).
Accelerated commissions	Increased commission based on levels. For instance, a salesperson may receive 2 percent commission on the first $75 000 they sell, plus 4 percent commission on the next $75 000 they sell, and so on.
Bonuses	Extra pay for reaching certain goals in work performance, lifelong learning, or other predetermined targets. Bonus may be money or gifts, trips, time off, and so on.
Profit sharing	Bonuses based on total corporate profits, which help tie employees' efforts to the company's bottom line. Higher corporate profits mean higher bonuses.
Gain sharing	Bonuses paid to employees when company costs are reduced through greater work efficiency, such as improving quality measures or production targets.
Stock options	Stock option plans offer shares of company stock to employees for purchase on a set date. The shares can be purchased at the value of the stock when it was originally offered or at an agreed-upon price. Employee stock purchase plans allow employees to buy company stock at a discount (usually 85 percent of market value). Companies typically provide payroll deductions for these purchases and limit amounts to 10 percent of total pay. An advantage of providing employees with ownership in the company via stock transactions is that employees feel more connected to the business and are motivated to ensure that the business succeeds. Starbucks uses stock options to give its employees a sense of ownership in the business.[21]

In what other ways are employees compensated? An important part of the business planning and management process is determining the type and amount of employee benefits, or indirect financial and nonfinancial payments, an employer offers that supplement cash compensation. Benefit compensation often enables a company to attract, motivate, and retain the best employees. **Benefits** come in many forms and provide additional compensation to employees beyond base wages. Some benefits are required by law, such as employment insurance (EI) and the Canada and Quebec Pension Plans (CPP/QPP)—each paid partially by the employer—paid vacations, statutory holiday pay, and maternity leave. Other benefits come voluntarily from the employer or as a result of employer–union agreements, and may include: health and disability insurance plans (dental, eyewear, massage, etc.); company pension plans (retirement plans); sick leave; bonuses; maternity leave top-up pay; termination pay; retirement packages; paid professional development (training); and paid time off.

Some companies offer **flexible benefits plans** (or cafeteria plans) that permit the employee to pick from a "menu" of several choices of taxable and non-taxable forms of compensation. Flexible benefit plans allow employees to choose the benefits most important to them while reducing the cost of offering all benefits to all employees. Vacation, holidays, and pensions constitute a significant percentage of total compensation. Other non-cash benefits help employees balance the demands of their professional and personal lives, also known as work/life benefits.

Work/life benefits help an employee achieve a balance between the demands of life both inside and outside the workplace. Work/life benefits include flexible schedules, relaxed atmospheres, free meals, child care, fitness/gym programs, and much more.

Benefits come in many forms and provide additional compensation to employees beyond base wages.

Flexible benefits plans (or cafeteria plans) permit the employee to pick from a "menu" of several choices of taxable and non-taxable forms of compensation.

Work/life benefits help an employee achieve a balance between the demands of life both inside and outside the workplace.

For example, you'll recall from the chapter opening discussion that SAS offers employees a range of amenities, including an on-site fitness club with indoor pool, on-site car detailing, massages, and a hair salon. Although seemingly expensive, this strategy of keeping its employees happy saves the company approximately $70 million per year because it experiences low turnover. Offering an employee discounted prices, free merchandise, or a sabbatical (leave from work with or without pay) are other types of work benefits (also known as job perks). Procter & Gamble offers up to twelve weeks unpaid leave, while McDonald's offers eight weeks paid leave, and Nike offers five weeks paid leave.[22] The sabbatical is thought to rejuvenate employees and increase their passion for their jobs.

Compensating, motivating, scheduling, and promoting employees comprise an important part of HR management. Companies identified as "The Best Companies to Work For" have revolutionized the way that businesses approach these issues with their implementation of innovative work/life benefits and a dynamic, employee-friendly work environment. Indeed, many of the highest-quality applicants nowadays expect companies to offer these perks. Such is the nature of the modern workplace.

Do most employers offer medical, pension, and wellness benefits? Employers are becoming more concerned with employee wellness, both physical and mental. They are recognizing that happy, healthy employees are more productive and more likely to stay with the company. Low productivity, absenteeism, and high employee turnover rates cost companies money. **Employee assistance programs (EAPs)** are employee benefit programs offered by many employers, typically in conjunction with a health insurance plan. EAPs are intended to help employees deal with personal and workplace problems that may adversely affect their work performance. According to the Sun Life Canadian Health Index, "employers with highly effective workplace wellness programs have performed more than 55% better than their industry peers, achieved higher average revenue per employee and seen less absence, disability, total turnover and lower annual medical costs."[23]

A competitive group benefits plan allows employers to help attract and retain employees by satisfying their needs and demands. But employers need affordable benefits plans. As the population ages, they spend more on health care. The government already spends a substantial portion of its revenue on health care and is likely to continue to limit and eliminate health services in order to shift costs to private plans.[24] Statistics Canada projects that by about 2031, seniors will comprise between 23 percent and 25 percent of the total population. Bell Canada, Nortel, and Sears Canada, among others, are taking steps toward the growing concern over retiree health benefits. For example, Bell plans to phase out all post-retirement benefits for retirees over the age of fifty-five and eliminate all post-retirement benefits for those retiring after 2017.[25]

Multinational corporations need to understand the cultural and legal standards in the countries in which they operate. The variances between each country's human resource practices and laws make managing employees and their benefits especially complicated. As the world continues to engage in global business, Canadian human resource practices will be influenced by conditions in other countries and cultures.

Employee assistance programs (EAPs) are employee benefit programs offered by many employers, typically in conjunction with a health insurance plan. EAPs are intended to help employees deal with personal and workplace problems that may adversely affect their work performance.

8

Scheduling

What is the traditional workweek schedule? An increasing number of employees are finding that managing the demands of work and personal life results in doing neither well. The added stresses that face employees today from child care, elder care, commuting, and other work/life conflicts have led to a decrease in productivity and an increase in employee absenteeism and tardiness. As a result, more and more employers are offering alternatives to the traditional 9:00 a.m. to 5:00 p.m., Monday to Friday workweek.

7

Describe the different types of workweek schedules and how these may meet the needs of both the company and its employees.

Creating work schedules requires meeting the needs of the company while satisfying the needs of the employees.

Some companies have flexible scheduling policies in place and others approach scheduling issues on an individual basis. Flexible schedules provide employees with many benefits, such as:

- reduced child care costs (e.g., when parents are home, child care is not needed)
- additional personal time (e.g., to attend appointments, work out at the gym, or get the shopping done)
- additional savings (e.g., money saved by a decreased frequency in dry cleaning or purchasing business attire)
- opportunity to pursue other interests (e.g., community involvement, volunteerism, or academic goals)

A **flexible work schedule** can take many different forms, yet not every job is well suited for an alternative structure. Flexible work schedules help people juggle work and family responsibilities, making them happier and more satisfied with their jobs, which can be measured in increases in productivity and morale and decreases in stress, absenteeism, and burnout. The employee that values this arrangement is motivated to keep it in place. Despite the costs associated with designing and implementing flexible working arrangements, employers can expect positive bottom-line results. Similarly, reductions in employee turnover lead to a decrease in time and costs associated with employee recruiting and replacement training. It is an excellent way to retain top talent.

State Farm believes employees are more engaged and productive when they work a schedule best suited for their individual work style and personal circumstances. State Farm offers several flexible scheduling options (compressed workweek, flextime, telecommuting, and job sharing) to help employees balance their personal and professional responsibilities.[26] IBM, Sun Microsystems, and Best Buy, among others, have successfully fostered ROWE (Results Only Work Environment), which debunks the old theory that the longer employees stay at the office, the higher their productivity. Instead, ROWE suggests that employees be paid for the work they accomplish, regardless of the hours it took or the work location. Best Buy's chief executive, Brad Anderson, states, "Orders processed by people who are not working in the office are up 13% to 18% over those who are."[27]

What alternate work arrangements are there?

The most popular flexible work arrangements include the following:

1. *Flextime.* In flextime scheduling, management defines a total number of required hours as a core workday and is flexible with starting and ending times. Managers must rise to the challenge of ensuring that required hours are met and monitoring employee performance. However, overall, flexible arrangements allow for increased productivity due to reductions in absenteeism and tardiness. For example, some employees may work 8:00 a.m. to 4:30 p.m., others 9:00 a.m. to 5:30 p.m., and so on. Of course, flextime may not be feasible in some types of jobs where everyone must work at the same time or when there are shift-work schedules in place.
2. *Permanent Part-Time.* Permanent part-time employees are hired on a permanent basis to work a part-time week. Unlike temporary part-time workers who are employed to fill short-term needs, permanent part-time employees enjoy the same benefits that full-time employees receive.
3. *Job Sharing.* Job sharing is an arrangement in which two employees work part-time sharing one full-time job. Those who share a job have been found to be very motivated to make this flexible situation work, so productivity and employee satisfaction increase. On the other hand, conflicts may arise if the job sharers don't have a clear understanding of who is in charge of what or if there is confusion from other employees about whom to contact and when. Therefore, job sharers must carefully coordinate and communicate both with one another and with their employer to ensure that all responsibilities are met.
4. *Compressed Workweek.* A compressed workweek allows employees to work fewer but longer days: four 10-hour days per week or 9-hour days with one day off every two weeks. Such arrangements can reduce worker overtime, make more efficient use of facilities, and provide employees with longer blocks of personal time and less

*A **flexible work schedule** can take many different forms, yet not every job is well suited for an alternative structure. Flexible work schedules help people juggle work and family responsibilities, making them happier with their jobs, which can be measured in increases in productivity and morale and decreases in stress, absenteeism, and burnout.*

commuting time. The disadvantages are a potential increase in employee fatigue and possible conflicts with labour laws that cite overtime requirements for hours worked in excess of eight a day.

5. *Telecommuting*. Telecommuting allows employees to work in the office part-time and work from home part-time, or to work completely from home, making only occasional visits to the office. Telecommuting reduces commuting costs and allows employees to take care of home needs while also fulfilling work responsibilities. Telecommuting arrangements are also necessary for those employees dealing with clients, colleagues, or suppliers who are on the other side of the globe. Taking calls at 2:00 a.m. is much easier at home than at the office. The disadvantages of telecommuting include monitoring employees' performance at a distance, servicing equipment for off-site employees, and communication issues. Additionally, employees who telecommute may become isolated from other employees.

Flexible Scheduling

- **Flextime**
- **Part-time**
- **Job Sharing**
- **Compressed Workweek**
- **Telecommuting**

Shift work is not considered as flexible as some of the flexible scheduling options discussed above because it doesn't give employees much say over their schedules. There are advantages, however. One advantage may be that employees don't waste time and fuel sitting in traffic as they may if all employees poured out of work at the same time. It also means that employees are not working 9:00 a.m. to 5:00 p.m. each day of the week, thus giving some flexibility in personal time to schedule medical or other personal appointments. Employees may work the 8:00 a.m. to 4:00 p.m. shift, the 4:00 p.m. to 12:00 a.m. shift, or 12:00 a.m. to 8:00 a.m. shift (or some variation of this pattern). Often employees will cycle through the shifts, working an entire week on each.

Why does a company hire contingent workers?

Contingent workers (temporary employees) are hired on an as-needed basis; therefore, they lack the status that comes from being a regular, full-time employee. These workers often fulfill important and specific functions. Contingent workers are most likely to be hired by companies in business and professional services, education and health care services, and construction industries. Companies hire temporary workers to fill in for absent employees (e.g., maternity leave) or to augment the staff during busy periods (e.g., holidays, promotions, events). Long-term temporary staff is often hired for indefinite periods to work on specific projects. In many cases, temporary staffing is part of a company's human resource "temp to perm" strategy.

Independent contractors and consultants are contingent workers who are generally self-employed and are hired on a temporary basis to perform specific tasks. Often contractors are hired for those jobs that are commonly hard to fill that involve state-of-the-art skills in construction, financial activities, and professional and business services. For example, it may be most cost efficient to hire a webpage developer as an independent contractor rather than keeping one on staff permanently. Consultants are hired to assist with long-term projects, often at a strategic level, but also with a specific end in sight. For example, a company that is reviewing its executive management compensation arrangements may hire a compensation consultant.

What are the advantages of temporary work?

Many people cite flexibility and variety as a benefit of working for a temporary agency. Many staffing agencies offer job seekers (applicants) free training, no-charge registration, some health benefits, choice of company location, and a variety of short- to longer-term assignments. The world's largest staffing companies have Canadian presences, including Kelly Services Inc., Manpower Inc., Adecco SA, and Spherion Corp. Because many of their assignments are short-term, temporary workers are able to experience working in many different companies, doing different jobs, and meeting numerous people. In many instances, temporary workers are hired permanently. Recent college and university graduates and students find temporary

Contingent workers (temporary employees) are individuals who are hired on an as-needed basis; therefore, they lack the status that comes from being a regular, full-time employee.

Independent contractors and consultants are contingent workers who are generally self-employed and are hired on a temporary basis to perform specific tasks.

Better Business **Better World**

The Home Depot Canada Foundation[28]

Established in 2008, The Home Depot Canada Foundation expands "The Home Depot Canada's commitment to giving back to the communities it serves." As a private, Canadian charitable organization, the foundation brings together volunteerism, do-it-yourself expertise, product donation, and monetary grants to meet community needs. It supports the development of affordable housing built responsibly and builds healthy neighbourhoods by supporting local initiatives such as restoring and creating much-needed community green spaces and other outdoor beautification projects. The foundation now works with a number of national community partners, including Habitat for Humanity Canada, Evergreen, Volunteer Canada, Boys & Girls Clubs of Canada, and Great Canadian Shoreline Cleanup.

The foundation's associate volunteer program—Team Depot—encourages and empowers associates (employees)

to take a leadership role in their community by organizing and volunteering on projects with local and national partners. Annually, The Home Depot associates contribute more than 60 000 volunteer hours to community projects across Canada.

Discussion Questions

1. **What advantages might The Home Depot or any other organization gain by engaging in philanthropy (goodwill, charity)? Are there any disadvantages to doing so?**
2. **With Team Depot, employees volunteer their time and talents to work on community projects. How might this lead to improved employee motivation and job satisfaction?**
3. **How do philanthropic initiatives influence the employee-employer relationship? Do you think employees would view such a volunteer program as a positive or negative workplace initiative? Why?**

work as a means to gain real-world experience in an industry they are interested in pursuing on a full-time basis. Other temporary workers are retired professionals who want to do something productive in their free time but still maintain some flexibility. Also, parents who need to earn income but also require a flexible schedule find that temporary work enables them to accomplish both. Companies need temporary employees with diverse skills, educational backgrounds, and work experiences. In-demand Manpower positions include call centre agents, customer service representatives, assemblers, business analysts, sales managers, and electrical engineers, with 40 percent of Manpower's temporary assignments leading to permanent job opportunities.[29]

Explain how employees transition through a company over time by way of promotions, transfers, retirement, and termination.

Transitioning: Promoting, Transferring, Retiring, and Terminating

What is meant by transitioning employees? Employees don't always stay in the same position for which they were hired. Sometimes they transition into different positions within the company or sometimes they leave the company (by their own choice or by the employer's choice). HRM performs various functions to help transition employees through changing job roles.

How can employees increase their level of responsibility in the firm?   After performing successfully in a position, many employees look to increase their level of responsibility and stature in the firm or department through a promotion. **A promotion** may be an upward or lateral move into a new position that allows employees to develop and display new skills and to learn more about the company overall. Promotions from within the company to well-qualified, deserving candidates improve employee morale because when employees know that management is going to promote based on merit, they are more likely to work hard and feel satisfied with the fair method of promotions, which creates a positive work environment and boosts morale. Promotions from within are also cost-effective in that the promoted employees are already familiar with corporate culture and business procedures, do not need to spend valuable time on basic orientation, and are already registered in the HR system as an employee. Employers like to promote from within because they can reward exceptional behaviour and fill positions with tested employees. However, promotion may not always result in a positive situation if it is seen as being draped in secrecy, unfairness, or arbitrariness. Therefore, management must ensure that promotions are based on a distinct set of criteria such as seniority or competency.

> A **promotion** may be an upward or lateral move into a new position that allows employees to develop and display new skills and to learn more about the company overall.

What kinds of promotion paths are available?   Consider an engineer who succeeds on the job but has no desire to manage. Some companies provide two career paths: one toward management and the other for "individual contributors" with no management aspirations. Therefore, engineers, for example, with a desire to manage can pursue one track, and other engineers without managerial aspirations or capabilities can be promoted to a position such as "senior engineer." Alternatively, it's always possible to keep employees in their same job but give them more responsibility, thus enriching their experience while continuing to prepare them for further advancement.

Why would a company transfer an employee?   **A transfer** occurs when an employee is appointed to the same or a similar position elsewhere within the organization. Transfers usually refer to a lateral move (a horizontal job assignment). Organizations transfer employees either to satisfy organizational requirements or to meet employee requests. Employees may request a transfer to a different department or a different position because they are not satisfied with their current work or manager. When vertical advancements are not available or possible, employees can transfer laterally to another department to develop new skills and learn more about the company. Employers may transfer employees due to a need for an employee's specific talent elsewhere in the organization. Also, a transfer may occur when the employee's current position is eliminated due to restructuring or reclassification. Multinational corporations sometimes transfer specific managers to new sites in foreign countries to help get the new location up and running.

> A **transfer** occurs when an employee is appointed to the same or a similar position elsewhere within the organization. Transfers usually refer to a lateral move (a horizontal job assignment).

When do employees retire?   It used to be that employees retired when they reached the age of sixty-five, but the current Canadian labour laws do not specify a retirement age.[30] **Retirement** is the point in a person's life when he or she stops participating full-time in his or her career. The average retirement age in Canada is sixty-two. About 6 percent of workers continue to work full-time after the age of sixty-five.[31] Reasons for staying on the job after age sixty-five include financial need as well as a desire to remain active and enjoy office camaraderie. For employers, an aging workforce may present other challenges, such as decreasing morale among workers or age-discrimination lawsuits if they aggressively lay off older workers. Therefore, to encourage older (and more expensive) workers to retire, companies have offered financial incentives, known as worker buyouts, early retirement plans, or severance pay. Retiring senior workers increase promotion opportunities for younger employees. For instance, in 2010, General Motors offered US$60 000 buyouts (with full benefits) to several thousand skilled trades workers when

> **Retirement** is the point in a person's life when he or she stops participating full-time in his or her career.

the company estimated that it had 2000 more skilled trades workers than it needed.[32] Ford also reduced its workforce with buyouts and early retirement offers as part of a massive restructuring plan in 2009.[33] The term *golden parachute* or golden handshake is sometimes used to refer to the package bestowed upon top-level managers who retire or otherwise leave the company. For example, when Citigroup CEO Charles Prince retired after four years and a poor third-quarter performance, he took nearly US$100 million with him.[34]

Why do employees leave their jobs? Even the most attractive benefits package and high wage incentives don't always retain valuable employees. Some employees leave their jobs to work for another company and some leave for personal reasons (possibly to raise a family). Others may quit their jobs because they do not feel motivated by or satisfied with their work tasks, co-workers, or manager. Employees are free to resign voluntarily from work at any time. Employees resigning on good terms would choose to give their employer notice of leave, mainly because they wish to keep a good working relationship with the employer, to obtain a positive reference, and to keep future opportunities open. Employers may accept an employee's notice or may ask the employee to leave immediately. Note that if an employee quits without just cause, he or she may not be eligible to collect employment insurance.

Companies are always looking for experienced, talented employees, and they will offer higher wages and more incentives in an effort to find them. Sometimes that may even mean luring talented employees away from their competitors. Learning about the reasons employees leave can give valuable insight to an employer and may help prevent the loss of additional employees in the future. **Exit interviews** are often conducted (in person, online, or on the telephone) by an outside contractor or by HR department personnel to gather feedback before employees leave the company. The **turnover rate** tracks the number of employees that leave the company each year. Companies monitor the turnover rate to compare it to previous years as an aid in analyzing and determining staffing needs and trends.

Why do companies terminate employment? At times it is necessary to re-evaluate an employee's contribution or tenure at the company, or to re-evaluate the composition and size of the workforce altogether. Companies that find themselves struggling to survive in the business world may be forced to reduce the size of their workforce (downsize). Downsizing and restructuring, the growth of outsourcing and offshoring, the pressures of global competition, and the increased uses of technology are all reasons companies look to reduce the number of employees. **Termination** of employment reduces the number of employees by permanently laying off workers due to poor performance or a discontinued need for their services. Companies may offer outplacement services such as resumé writing and career counselling to help employees transition out of the company. When large numbers of employees have been laid off (either permanently or temporarily), the employees that remain often feel insecure and uncertain about the future of their own jobs with the company. Insecurity undermines motivation, so HRM must deal with the issue.

Terminating employment due to an employee's poor performance or illegal activities can be a rather complex process. It is imperative for employers to have a good record-keeping system in place regarding poorly performing employees. In general, employment standards legislation requires that notice of termination be given to workers who have been employed for three consecutive months or more unless the employee is dismissed for just cause.[35] In some cases, employers may give pay in lieu of notice of termination.

Before firing an employee for wrongful doings or incompetence, managers must take steps to avoid a wrongful dismissal lawsuit. These steps include maintaining solid records so that they can build a case for dismissal with sufficient documentation and evidence. Courts have sided with the terminated employee, especially when not enough evidence of poor behaviour is brought forth. Written evidence is the only material evidence accepted, which makes building an employee's personnel file with documented

Exit interviews are often conducted to gather feedback before employees leave the company.

The turnover rate tracks the number of employees that leave the company each year.

Termination of employment reduces the number of employees by permanently laying off workers due to poor performance or a discontinued need for their services.

proof of poor performance critical. Hearsay and rumours do not stand up in legal proceedings. It is always up to the employer to prove to the judge that the dismissal was for just cause.

Some reasons considered just cause include dishonesty, absenteeism or lateness, wilful disobedience, alcoholism, sexual harassment, insolence, and conflict of interest.[36] In addition, companies cannot terminate employees because of whistleblowing, filing a worker's compensation claim, jury duty, or testifying against the company in a legal proceeding. Traditionally, U.S. employers have possessed the right to discharge their employees at will for any reason. The United States is the only major industrial power that maintains a general employment-at-will rule. Canada, France, Germany, Great Britain, Italy, Japan, and Sweden all have statutory provisions that require employers to show cause before discharging employees.[37]

MANAGING WORKPLACE DIVERSITY

Demographic Projections

What are the demographic changes occurring in the Canadian workforce?

Look around you. Most likely you work, study, and socialize with people of different genders, ages, religions, races, sexual orientations, mental and physical abilities, and educational backgrounds. Several demographic changes have brought forth HR challenges—some new and some that have existed for many years—and Canada will continue to grow in human diversity (see **Table 8.3** for Statistics Canada's diversity projections).

Workplace diversity encompasses all the ways in which people differ (keep in mind that people are often more similar than they are different). **Diversity-friendly organizations** are very inclusive. They don't just tolerate those who are different but instead celebrate their members' differences. These companies realize that by fostering an environment of involvement, respect, and inclusion, they create business value. Their diverse workforce equips them to understand evolving markets, connect with their global customer base, develop innovative solutions, and attract and retain the best talent.

Technological advancements have made it possible for businesses to operate with relative ease on a global basis. It is not unusual to read about companies offshoring work to other countries to lessen labour costs or establishing operations in other countries to broaden their market reach. Moreover, companies are hiring workers who have emigrated from other countries to Canada, where greater opportunities exist. European and Middle Eastern companies are experiencing similar increases in immigration. Many companies are seeking to increase the cultural diversity of their workforce because it has been proven to have positive results on the bottom line.

What challenges come from hiring a culturally diverse workforce?

The workforce today comprises employees from many different cultures and religions, which can lead to challenges in helping employees understand one another. Companies need to address diversity with training and other initiatives in order to be successful. Failure to do this can lead to lawsuits and embarrassment.

A more culturally diverse population naturally brings about a wider variety of religious beliefs and practices, with more employees trying to integrate their religious practices into their workday. As employers struggle to accommodate workers' religious needs, they must also try to avoid the potential friction that open demonstrations of religious practices may provoke. Many employers strike a balance by allowing employees to take prayer breaks, enabling employees to take time off to observe religious holidays, catering to dietary requirements, and permitting differences in dress. Some companies have set up quiet prayer rooms for their employees, and some employers encourage workers to form religious-based support groups.

What challenges come from hiring a gender-diverse workforce?

More women are entering the workforce than ever before. However, statistically, relatively few females hold top executive positions. High-performing women don't have the sponsorship they

Reasons Employees Get Fired

1. Dishonesty, evasion, or lack of integrity on the job.
2. Lying on a resumé.
3. Refusing to follow directions and orders.
4. Talking too much and conducting personal business at work.
5. Inconsistency—unreliable work and behaviours.
6. Inability to get along with other people.
7. Inability to actually do assigned job tasks.
8. Performing tasks slowly, with numerous errors.
9. High absenteeism rate.
10. Drug and/or alcohol abuse.

Source: Patty Inglish, "Top 10 Reasons Employees Get Fired, Among Surveyed Companies 2008–2012," *HubPages.com*, http://hubpages.com/hub/Fired, Accessed January 12, 2011.

Identify the ways in which Canada's demographics are changing and how this affects the workforce.

Workplace diversity encompasses all the ways in which employees differ.

Diversity-friendly organizations are very inclusive. They don't just tolerate those who are different but instead celebrate their members' differences.

Table 8.3 Statistics Canada: Diversity Projections

For year 2017*	For year 2031†
• Between 19% and 23% of Canadians would be a visible minority person. • The number of people whose mother tongue is neither English nor French will be between 21% and 25% of the total population in Canada. • For every 100 visible minority persons at the age to exit the labour force, there would be 142 at the age of entry. In the rest of the population there would be only 75 potential entries for every 100 potential exits. • Alberta's Aboriginal population is expected to grow by 39%.** • 75% of visible minority persons will be living in one of Canada's three largest metropolitan areas—Toronto, Vancouver, and Montreal.	• Between 25% and 28% of the population could be foreign-born. About 55% of this population would be born in Asia. • Visible minority groups will comprise 63% of the population of Toronto, 59% in Vancouver, and 31% in Montreal. • In Toronto, 24% of the population will be South Asian, which would continue to be its largest visible minority group. • Chinese residents will be the largest visible minority group in Vancouver, at 23% of the population. • 14% of people in Canada would have non-Christian religion. • 71% of visible minority persons will be living in one of Canada's three largest metropolitan areas—Toronto, Vancouver, and Montreal.

*Statistics Canada, "Study: Canada's Visible Minority Population in 2017," The Daily, March 22, 2005, http://www.statcan.gc.ca/daily-quotidien/050322/dq050322b-eng.htm, Accessed November 12, 2011.

†Statistics Canada, "Study: Projections of the Diversity of the Canadian Population," The Daily, http://www.statcan.gc.ca/daily-quotidien/100309/dq100309a-eng.htm, Accessed January 24, 2011.

**Human Rights, Citizenship and Multiculturalism, Education Fund, "A Snapshot of Demographic Trends in Alberta," http://justice.alberta.ca/programs_services/humanrights/hremf/Documents/Trends.pdf, Accessed November 12, 2011

need to reach the top—there is an absence of male advocacy. Many women underestimate the impact sponsorship may play in their advancement and fail to cultivate it. Others feel that hard work alone should be the basis of advancement and not the "connections" they make. Sponsorship can be misconstrued as sexual interest, so ambitious women and top executive men avoid it. The Financial Post 500 Catalyst Census states that "from 2005 to 2009, the number of female seats on corporate boards in the top 500 Canadian companies increased by half a percentage point per year, from 12% to 14%."[38] At that rate, Canadian women won't hold half the board seats in these companies until 2082. Unfortunately, this snail's pace does not reflect women's educational qualifications; for example, in 2010, 71 percent of women aged twenty-five to forty-four years had completed post-secondary education as compared to 65 percent of men of the same age.[39] Companies that foster sponsorships of their standout women will gain a competitive advantage in talent markets around the world.

What challenges come from hiring an age-diverse workforce?
Baby boomers (those born between 1943 and 1960) represent about one-third of the Canadian workforce. Many baby boomers indicate that they would like to, and need to, work beyond the traditional retirement age. This aging demographic group creates several workforce challenges. Compared with younger workers in the same position, older workers often expect higher salaries and better benefits. Health care costs, for example, are higher with an older workforce. However, many employers find that hiring and retaining older employees has several benefits, including less turnover and absenteeism, lower training costs, and a willingness to learn new skills and to help and train younger co-workers. These benefits offset the higher costs of retaining senior workers. Companies that hire an age-diverse workforce have a unique opportunity to utilize the insight of different generations and capitalize on the unique attributes each age group brings to the workplace.

Diversity-Friendly Organizations

How is a diverse workforce beneficial?
As discussed earlier, diversity is an important component of the modern workplace. For many companies, hiring to diversify the workforce initially meant complying with a government requirement by filling positions with a certain number of Aboriginal peoples, women, visible minorities, or persons with disabilities. Some criticized this strategy as unfair and bad for the company if the best candidate was not hired in favour of meeting such a requirement. Over time, however, many companies have come to embrace the idea of diversity beyond just satisfying a requirement. It is now becoming clear that companies should embrace diversity as a strategy and a resource to become more competitive in the global market. Promoting diversity in the workplace is more than abiding by the law; diversity should be aggressively pursued as a means to improve a company's competitiveness and its bottom line.

Canada's Top 100 Employers' annual competition aims to identify the best diversity employers.[40] A range of diversity initiatives is examined in five major employee groups: 1) women, 2) visible minorities, 3) persons with disabilities, 4) Aboriginal peoples, and 5) lesbian, gay, bisexual, and transgendered/transsexual (LGBT) peoples.

Procter & Gamble (P&G) Inc. was selected as one of Canada's best diversity employers in 2011 for some of the following initiatives:

- P&G's Women's Leadership Council provides mentorship to women employees and hosts events and seminars on inclusion, gender issues, and related topics.
- P&G established representation goals for visible minority, women, and LGBT employees and hosts annual recruitment events in Toronto for LGBT post-secondary students.
- P&G requires all employees to complete a diversity training workshop and holds a special diversity workshop for leaders and managers.
- P&G's diversity leadership assessment tool allows employees to evaluate how well their managers create inclusive, diverse work environments.

Boeing Canada Operations Limited was also selected as one of Canada's best diversity employers in 2011 for some of the following actions:

- Boeing provides BlackBerries to staff who are deaf to help in their communications with co-workers.
- Boeing has an employment equity and diversity team.
- Boeing recruits Aboriginal employees through partnership with the Centre for Aboriginal Human Resource Development's aerospace training program.
- Boeing hosts an onsite, one-year management development program for women employees in conjunction with the University of Manitoba.

A diverse workforce benefits organizations by supplying a broad range of viewpoints necessary to compete in a globalized marketplace. Such variety promotes creativity in problem solving with improved results. Products and services need to cater to customers and clients with diverse backgrounds, and if a company's workforce does not understand the nuances of different cultural needs, it may be missing some opportunities.

PepsiCo's Frito Lay launched a Doritos Guacamole Flavoured Tortilla chip to appeal especially to Latino consumers. The Latino Employee Network at PepsiCo's Frito Lay division provided valuable feedback on taste and packaging to ensure that these chips would be regarded as authentic in the Latino community. The product generated more than US$100 million in sales in its first year, making it the most successful product launch in the company's history. Additionally, a diverse staff helps strategize ways to handle markets that have become segmented, both culturally and demographically.[42]

top10

Canada's Best Diversity Employers

(The partial list of employers below, from the annual Canada's Best Diversity Employers competition, is shown in alphabetical order rather than rank.)

1. BC Hydro
2. Boeing Canada
3. HSBC Bank Canada
4. L'Oréal Canada Inc.
5. Manitoba Lotteries Corp.
6. McGill University
7. Mount Sinai Hospital
8. Procter & Gamble Inc.
9. Shell Canada Limited
10. The Home Depot Canada

Source: Canada's Top 100 Employers 2010, "Canada's Top 100 Employers," http://www.canadastop100.com/index.html, Accessed January 16, 2011, and Richard Yerema, "Canada's Top Employers," *Macleans*.ca, October 14, 2009, http://www2.macleans.ca/2009/10/14/the-top-100-2009/.

Harley-Davidson realized that in order to remain competitive, it needed to understand the needs and wants of customers beyond the traditional stereotype of the white male. Since then, the motorcycle manufacturer has made a significant effort to hire and retain women and minority managers.[41]

On Target

One Diversity Training Does Not Fit All

Because promoting diversity is a priority for most companies in today's global marketplace, so, too, is the implementation of diversity training programs. These often-costly programs typically involve workshops and seminars that teach managers about the benefits of a diverse workforce. Yet researchers found that most of them simply don't work.[43] While training was by far the most popular approach, it was also the least effective at getting companies to hire and promote women and minorities. Why? Some theorize that mandatory training inevitably leads to backlash; others say altering people's inner biases is a nearly impossible task. Hope for promoting diversity in the workplace is not lost, however; researchers also found that two techniques had significant, beneficial effects on workplace diversity. The first,

the appointment of a specific person or committee specifically accountable for addressing diversity issues within the company, led to 10-percent increases in the number of women and minorities in management positions. The second, creating minority mentoring programs in which executives are designated a protégé to mentor, increased the number of women of visible minorities in leadership positions by 23.5 percent. A combination of several approaches leads to the best results.

Discussion Questions

1. What might happen to companies that don't diversify their workforce?
2. Are most people unbiased and unprejudiced by nature or is this something they have to work at?
3. Why do you think a combination of approaches to diversity training seems to work best?

10
Outline the objectives of unions and the process of collective bargaining.

Employer–employee relations is the communication that takes place between employers and employees

What does it mean to "manage" diversity?   Unfortunately, a diverse workforce can have its obstacles. Differences in culture, age, religion, and sexual orientation can create misunderstandings and conflict, even over the most well-intentioned behaviours. Therefore, it is important that employers provide effective diversity training for their employees. It is also important for co-workers to learn to look at situations from a perspective different from their own. While implementing a diversity and equity plan, it is important to ensure that non-targeted groups do not feel undervalued if they are passed up for promotion in lieu of someone from a more diverse background. Ultimately, managing diversity is developing a workforce that has a capacity to accept, incorporate, and empower the diversity of human talents and perspectives.

EMPLOYER-EMPLOYEE RELATIONS

Labour Unions

What is meant by employer–employee relations?   **Employer–employee relations** refer to the communication that takes place between employers and employees. Much of employee relations involve employers and employees working together. Discussions between employers and employees typically cover the following areas: work schedules, bonuses, compensation, the work environment, hours of work, safety, production targets, and disputes. Employer–employee relations are affected by a number of factors, including labour organizations, labour market, government policy, the structure of the economy, labour law, technical change, and the collective bargaining power of the union (explained below).

Employers and employees seem to approach employment from vastly different perspectives. So how can the two sides reach any sort of agreement? One answer lies in labour unions. **A labour union** is a legally recognized group dedicated to protecting the interests of workers. They negotiate employment issues such as salary, benefits, and working hours with corporations, businesses, and other organizations on behalf of union members (workers).

A labour union is a legally recognized group dedicated to protecting the interests of workers.

What are the objectives of labour unions?   Labour unions began as a means to protect workers from the terrible injustices employers inflicted upon their workers in the nineteenth century during the Industrial Revolution. During that time, employers took advantage of workers, subjecting them to long hours, low pay, and health risks. Women and children were often treated worse and were paid less than men. Labour unions formed to fight for better working conditions and employee rights. These individual labour unions, by joining, proved to be more effective in bettering working conditions.

Unions have played a role in the employer–employee dialogue for centuries. Historically, unions were formed in manufacturing and resource companies, companies operating in steel mills, textile factories, and mines. Over time, unions have grown into other industries. Today, large memberships can be found in transportation, construction (e.g., roofers, plumbers, engineers), government (e.g., teachers, hospitals, firefighters), and utilities. Entertainers and supporting industries, such as actors and writers, also have unions. Nearly 30 percent of Canadian workers belong to unions.[44]

Unions in Canada are regulated by federal and provincial legislation, and most are affiliated with larger central labour bodies. These include:

■ *The Canadian Labour Congress (CLC).* Headquartered in Ottawa with regional offices across Canada, the CLC represents Canadian union members on national issues, such as unemployment, child care, human rights, immigration, the environment, and many other subjects. It is the main administrative body for numerous affiliated Canadian and international unions and provincial federations of labour and regional labour councils.

■ The *Provincial Federations of Labour*. Most workers are covered by provincial labour laws, and every province has a federation that lobbies for better laws for workers.

■ *Labour Councils:* Labour councils are made up of unions in a city and its surrounding area and represent workers on local issues, such as fair wage policies and other issues that affect the community.

Canada's largest labour unions include:

■ The *Canadian Union of Public Employees (CUPE)*, Canada's largest national union, has around 600 000 members. CUPE represents workers in health care, education, libraries, social services, public utilities, universities, transportation, municipalities, emergency services, and airlines. More than half of CUPE members are women and about one-third are part-time workers.[45]

■ The *United Food and Commercial Workers Canada (UFCW Canada)*, Canada's largest private sector union (especially in the retail and services industries), comprises forty-seven UFCW Canada local unions and has more than 250 000 members. Some of the sectors it represents include agriculture, breweries, distillers and soft drinks, call centres, cereal and flour mills, clothing manufacturing, credit unions and financial services, department stores, drug stores, food processing, health care services, restaurants, nursing, pharmaceutical, and warehouse and distribution. Nearly half of all UFCW Canada members are younger than thirty, and membership is made up equally of men and women, both full-time and part-time.[46]

■ The *Canadian Auto Workers (CAW)* union began as the Canadian region of the American United Auto Workers (UAW) union. Eventually the CAW split from the UAW and developed a distinct set of collective bargaining objectives. It has 200 000 national members from every sector of the Canadian economy, including aerospace, mining, fishing, auto and specialty vehicle assembly, auto parts, hotels, airlines, rail, education, hospitality, retail, road transportation, health care, manufacturing, and shipbuilding.[47]

How are labour unions structured?   To form a union, a group of workers must either have their employer voluntarily recognize them as a group or have a majority of workers form a bargaining unit for union representation. **A bargaining unit** is a group of employees who negotiate with the employer for better working conditions or pay. When a union forms, workers join and pay membership dues. Most unions have paid full-time staff as well as a substantial number of volunteer workers. In addition to dues, some unions create strike funds that help support workers in the event of a strike. Union members elect **officers and shop stewards**, who make decisions for the entire body and represent the members in dealings with management. So that unions can better represent specific interests, union locals are created by workers of the same industry, company, region, or business sector. There are three main functions of the local union: collective bargaining, member services and worker relations, and community and political activities.

Collective Bargaining

What is the collective bargaining process?   One of the main tasks performed by a union is **collective bargaining**, a process in which workers (through a union) negotiate with the employers for better work conditions and terms of employment. Negotiation is between union representatives and employers usually over concerns including wages, benefits, working hours, and grievance procedures. In recent decades, unions have experienced limited growth due to a shift from manufacturing and large companies to small and medium-sized companies outside of manufacturing. Potential union members have spread into a larger set of companies, making collective bargaining a more complicated task as union leaders must work with a larger set of managers and often have a harder time organizing employees. **A collective bargaining agreement** is the result of union–employer negotiations and forces the employer to abide by the conditions specified in the agreement. Change can only be made through subsequent negotiations.

If management violates some part of the collective bargaining agreement, employees or the union may file a **grievance**, which is a formal complaint by an employee, employees, or the union usually brought to the supervisor's attention either in person or in writing. If the problem is not resolved, the grievance is put in writing, and perhaps a union official, the employee, and one or more managers discuss the grievance. If top management and the local union cannot resolve the grievance, it goes to arbitration.

What happens if an agreement cannot be reached through collective bargaining?   If negotiating does not produce a collective bargaining agreement, and both parties seem to be at an impasse, then other means to settle the dispute are used before workers go on strike. **Mediation** is a process that involves a neutral third party that assists the two parties both privately and collectively to identify issues and to develop proposals for resolution.[48] The mediator works with both sides to understand their genuine interests and helps each side generate proposals that address those interests. **Arbitration** is a process in which the disputing parties present their case to a third-party intermediary (or a panel of arbitrators) who examine all the evidence and then make a decision (usually binding) for the parties. Sometimes, arbitration is nonbinding, meaning that neither party is required to accept the arbitrator's decision.

What happens when negotiations break down?   When negotiation reaches an impasse, union workers can take several actions to prompt management to accept union demands. Union members and those sympathetic to their cause can stage a **boycott**, in which supporters refuse to buy or handle the company's products or services. On the other hand, companies can use a **lockout** in which management refuses to allow union

---

A bargaining unit is a group of employees who negotiate with the employer for better working conditions or pay.

Officers and shop stewards are elected by union members to make decisions for the entire body and represent the members in dealings with management.

Collective bargaining is a process in which workers (through a union) negotiate with the employers for better work conditions and terms of employment.

A collective bargaining agreement is the result of union-employer negotiations and forces the employer to abide by the conditions specified in the agreement. Change can only be made through subsequent negotiations.

A **grievance** is a formal complaint by an employee, employees, or the union usually brought to the supervisor's attention either in person or in writing.

Mediation is a process that involves a neutral third party that assists the two parties both privately and collectively to identify issues and to develop proposals for resolution.

Arbitration is a process in which the disputing parties present their case to a third-party intermediary who examines all the evidence and then makes a decision (usually binding) for the parties.

A boycott occurs when union members and their supporters refuse to buy or handle the company's products or services.

A lockout occurs when management refuses to allow union members to enter the work premises.

members to enter the work premises. Lockouts are legal only if negotiations have come to an impasse and the company is defending a legitimate position.

A **strike** occurs when union workers agree to stop work until certain demands are met. As a last resort, union workers may vote to go on strike and agree to stop working. Strikes jeopardize the productivity of the organization, so they are used to force management into making concessions that they may not have made otherwise. Strikes also gain considerable media publicity, especially when the workers picket the workplace by walking outside the company's entrances with signs that reflect the employees' grievances. Workers do not easily make the decision to strike, as they risk losing income throughout the strike period. For example, a six-week strike would cost a worker earning $700 a week a total of $4200 in lost wages. Assuming the new contract negotiated an hourly wage increase of $1, it would take about two years to recover the lost wages. Additionally, strikers may be fired or replaced, as management has the authority to hire replacement personnel, known as **strikebreakers (or scabs)**. Some public service workers such as police officers, firefighters, and hospital workers are prohibited from going on strike because these services are deemed essential to society. In these cases, workers often have "sick-outs," during which union members are not officially on strike but instead call in sick, refusing to come to work.

A strike occurs when union workers agree to stop work until certain demands are met.

Strikebreakers (or scabs) are replacement personnel hired by management during a strike.

The summer of 2009 saw the longest strike in Toronto's history, as 24 000 city workers walked off the job after six months of unsuccessful contract bargaining, bringing a halt to garbage collection, fifty-seven city-run day cares, public swimming pools, ferries, and a host of other public services. One of the main reasons for the contract dispute was an existing perk allowing workers to bank unused sick days and cash them in when they retired, which the city of Toronto wanted to abolish because it would cost hundreds of millions in payouts. Job security was another major issue.[49] After thirty-nine days on strike, the two sides reached an agreement. The deal phased out banked sick days by ending the practice for new hires and giving the 18 000 current workers a choice to sell out their sick days or hold on to them. In the end, this deal will save the city well over $100 million. An agreement over wage increases was also made.[50]

What is the future of unions and employer–labour relations?   In response to a more globalized working community, unions have begun to build alliances worldwide. They recognize that when multinational corporations make decisions to move production abroad, for example, there may be a negative impact on local and international workers. Consequently, in an effort to protect their interests, they must broaden their reach and make a commitment to international labour solidarity. Unions will need to transform themselves to survive the effects of globalization.

Human Rights and Labour Laws

How do laws and regulations affect human resource management?   Several federal, provincial, and territorial labour laws—aimed at safeguarding employee rights and mediating many aspects of the relationship between employers, unions, and employees—must be observed in HRM. In Canada, laws related to unionized workplaces (collective labour law) differ from those relating to non-unionized workplaces. (In most countries, however, no such distinction is made.[51]) There is a constitutional division between the federal government and the governments of Canada's ten provinces and three territories. Only 10 percent of all Canadian employees are working in jobs covered by the federal labour law. The remaining 90 percent of Canada's employees are covered by provincial or territorial statutes.[52] Industries such as banks, broadcasting and

11

Describe some of the key legislation around hiring, compensating, and managing workers in today's workplace.

8

telecommunications, airlines, railways, pipelines, uranium mines, and marine transport and related services are regulated by the federal government. Most other industries fall under provincial or territorial jurisdiction.

Legislation affects all areas of HRM, from hiring and training to compensating and transitioning employees. There have been many court cases where employees have accused employers of wrongful dismissal, and most often the courts decided in favour of the employee. Terminating an employee's employment because the employee is a certain race, nationality, religion, sex, or age may constitute wrongful dismissal. A court-proven wrongful dismissal tends to result in either a reinstatement of the dismissed employee and/or financial compensation for the wrongfully dismissed.[53] Similarly, employers must use equitable practices and offer equal opportunities to all when hiring for a position in order to avoid discrimination. To ensure a company is in compliance with the laws governing HRM, managers need to know the regulations pertaining to human rights, employment standards, occupational health and safety, labour, privacy, and workers' compensation. A few essential topics include: wrongful termination, discrimination or harassment, rules on drug testing, rules on accommodating employees with disabilities, personal liability, and various provincial laws within the provinces the company operates.[54] Such standards protect the rights of workers, foster a positive workplace environment, enhance relationships between managers and employees, and, ultimately, benefit the bottom line of any business.

The **Canada Labour Code** (at the federal level) *and the* **provincial Employment Standards Acts and Labour Codes** (at the provincial level) define the rights and obligations of individuals as workers, union members, and employers in the workplace.[55]

The *Canada Labour Code* applies to federally regulated employers with 100 or more employees and contains three parts:

> The **Canada Labour Code** (at the federal level) and the **provincial Employment Standards Acts and Labour Codes** (at the provincial level) define the rights and obligations of individuals as workers, union members, and employers in the workplace.

1. *Industrial relations:* certification of unions, labour-management relations, collective bargaining, and unfair labour practices.
2. *Workplace health and safety:* ensures health and safety of employees by preventing accidents and injury to health arising out of, linked with, or occurring in the course of employment. All workers in Canada have the right to work in a safe and healthy environment. WHMIS (Workplace Hazardous Materials Information System) is an amendment to the *Occupational Health and Safety Act* and dictates that information must be shared with employees on hazardous materials in the workplace.
3. *Employment standards:* deals with the terms and conditions of employment such as general holidays, annual vacations, leaves, working hours, unjust dismissals, minimum wage, layoff procedures, and severance pay. Labour law prohibits companies from terminating employment because of whistleblowing, filing of a worker's compensation claim, jury duty, or testifying against the company in a legal proceeding.

How does the Canadian Human Rights Act affect recruiting practices?　The *Canadian Human Rights Act* promotes equal opportunity and prohibits discrimination and a wide variety of practices in recruiting, selecting, promoting, and dismissing employees or prospective employees (discussed in Chapter 3). An ability genuinely needed to perform a job is called a **bona fide job requirement**. A person who lacks such a necessary ability can be legitimately denied employment (e.g., a person with a visual impairment will be denied employment as a bus driver).

A **bona fide job requirement** is an ability genuinely needed to perform a job. A person who lacks such a necessary ability can be legitimately denied employment (e.g., a person with a visual impairment will be denied employment as a bus driver).

Does employment equity mean that every employee receives the same pay?
While employers must ensure they compensate employees equally for equal work and equal qualifications, the act pertaining to employment equity is about correcting an imbalance in the workforce that has occurred over time. The Employment Equity Act (discussed in Chapter 3), applies to federally regulated industries. The act states that no person shall be denied employment opportunities or benefits for reasons unrelated to ability. It seeks to improve the employment conditions experienced by women, Aboriginal peoples, persons with disabilities, and members of visible minorities.[56] Equitable treatment does not mean preferential treatment, nor does it mean treating everyone the

same. It means treating people as equals through the reasonable accommodation of their differences or using special measures designed to remedy past discrimination.

Are employers expected to provide employees with a safe work environment?

The **Occupational Health and Safety (OHS) Acts and Regulations** are enabled at the federal, provincial, and territorial levels and are designed to secure workers and self-employed persons from risks to their safety, health, and physical well-being arising out of, or in connection with, activities in their workplaces. OHS legislation outlines the general rights and responsibilities of the employer, the supervisor, and the worker. Employers are required to provide a safe environment for workers as well as provide safety equipment and training where necessary. For example, **WHMIS (Workplace Hazardous Materials Information System)** is a comprehensive plan for providing information on hazardous materials to employees. Employees are required to conduct themselves in accordance with safety procedures and regulations and have the right to refuse work on a job if they believe it is unsafe; a legal procedure exists for resolving any disputes in this area. In most provinces, the Ministry of Labour appoints inspectors to enforce health and safety regulations. For instance, working at heights without proper fall protection is a primary safety issue in the commercial construction sector, and if OHS officers find a violation of this during an inspection, they will issue a "stop work" order.[57]

HR managers are responsible for knowing the legislation in detail and for ensuring that management throughout the organization implements the legislation effectively. In addition, managers must be sensitive to union contracts as well as social standards and expectations. HR managers can stay abreast of what is happening in the HR world by networking, joining relevant associations, subscribing to HR publications, and reviewing labour and employment laws.

Occupational Health and Safety (OHS) Acts and Regulations are enabled at the federal, provincial, and territorial levels and are designed to secure workers and self-employed persons from risks to their safety, health, and physical well-being arising out of, or in connection with, activities in their workplaces.

WHMIS (Workplace Hazardous Materials Information System) is a comprehensive plan for providing information on hazardous materials to employees.

CHAPTER SYNOPSIS

① Define human resource management and discuss its importance to an organization. *(pp. 208–210)*

Human resources (HR)—the people in an organization—need to be managed just as carefully as the material and financial resources of a business.

Human resource management (HRM) is the organizational function that deals with the people in the business, from the executives and the managers to the front-line production, sales, and administrative staff. HRM aims to ensure that the organization is correctly staffed at all times by the right number of employees with the right skills required to meet company goals. Proper management of human assets builds value in the company and ensures time and money is not wasted.

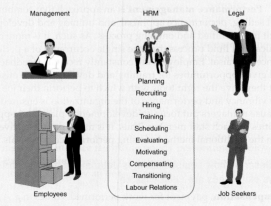

Functions of Human Resource Management

HRM functions encompass every aspect of the "human" in a business, including planning, recruiting, selecting and hiring,

training, evaluating, compensating, scheduling, motivating, and transitioning employees. HRM also oversees employee–management relations and must always work within the limits of the law (see Figure 8.1). HRM works through the many challenges in today's society, such as diversity issues, work/lifestyle preferences, and global business considerations. Most HRM functions are shared between the professional human resource manager and the other managers.

The **human resources department**, working with other department managers, is responsible for the people in the organization and helps to maximize organizational productivity by optimizing the effectiveness of employees.

② Explain how organizations determine and plan for human resource needs. *(pp. 210–211)*

Human resource planning is creating a strategy for meeting future human resource needs within an organization. Poor staff planning can be costly. Being overstaffed burdens a company with unnecessary expenses for salaries, benefits, and training for surplus employees. An understaffed organization can lead to loss of sales and competitiveness if customer needs are not met. Planning staffing needs therefore involves 1) assessing the supply of and demand for current and future employee resources and 2) evaluating job requirements.

Forecasting is the process of determining the future demand for employees as well as the future supply of employees.

A **job analysis** identifies and defines in detail the particular duties and requirements of the tasks and responsibilities an employee is required to perform.

A **job description** is a formal statement summarizing what the employee will do in that job role. It includes the job responsibilities, the conditions under which the job will be performed, and the job's relationship to other functions in the organization.

9

Business Technology

1. Describe the functions of a company's chief information officer (CIO) and information technology (IT) department. (pp. 244–246)

2. Explain how information technology, information systems, information, and data are interrelated within a business. (pp. 246–248)

3. Summarize how major types of hardware, software, and networks are used in business. (pp. 248–251)

4. Outline the benefits and risks of technology in the workplace, taking into account safety, creativity, communication, productivity, privacy, and ethics. (pp. 251–258)

5. With regard to e-business, explain what is meant by viral marketing, secure Internet connection, and phishing. (p. 258)

6. Describe two e-business challenges. (pp. 258–264)

OPENING DISCUSSION: RESPONSIBLE BUSINESS

The Tablet Race: Apple Wins, for Now!

A few years ago, most consumers had never heard of a tablet, let alone knew the difference between tablets and computers. Then Apple unleashed the iPad on an unsuspecting world, and computer manufacturers joined the race to catch up. Apple is far ahead, of course, but a couple contenders—Research In Motion's BlackBerry PlayBook and Samsung's Galaxy Tab—are coming on strong.

Generally, tablets are not full-fledged computers supporting a PC-style operating system. Instead, they use a simplified operating system such as Apple's iOS, Google's Android, or Palm's webOS. Most consumers use their tablets for listening to music, watching videos, updating social media, reading e-books, and playing games. Rarely are iPad-style consumer tablets being purchased as business tools, but business-use tablets are beginning to emerge. As soon as apps are ready, there will be many opportunities for iPad-like tablets to enter the health care, education, food services, law enforcement, transportation, and utilities industries. For instance, wait staff might use a tablet to record food orders that are sent electronically to the kitchen staff, or doctors might use one to record notes from a patient's appointment for uploading directly to the patient database.

Tablets have become one of the hottest consumer electronic gadgets around, and just about every hardware manufacturer is making one. RBC Capital Markets expects that by 2014, 185 million tablets will have been sold (generating US$70 billion), which is an 83 percent increase from 17 million tablets sold (US$11 billion) in 2010[1] (of which Apple alone sold 14.8 million iPads).[2] By 2014, RBC expects shipments of tablets and smartphones to comprise 64 percent of total computing shipments around the world.[3] Can you imagine 400 million tablet users worldwide?

As additional companies enter the tablet market, prices will be driven down, which in turn will increase demand. "So far, Apple is leading the tablet market in

(continued)

both quality and price, which is unusual for a company whose products are usually premium priced," said Consumer Reports electronics editor Paul Reynolds in April 2011. "However, it's likely we'll see more competitive pricing in tablets as other models begin to hit the market."[4] Clearly, iPads won't be the right solution for everything and everyone. There will still be lots of room for other players—Research In Motion, Samsung, Microsoft, and Motorola, to name a few.

In April 2011, "Consumer Reports tested tablets from Archos, Dell, Motorola, Samsung, and ViewSonic, as well as several models from Apple. Each tablet was evaluated on 17 criteria, including touch-screen responsiveness, versatility, portability, screen glare, and ease of use, and testers found several models that outperformed the rest. The Apple iPad 2 with Wi-Fi plus 3G (32G), $730, topped the ratings, scoring Excellent in nearly every category. The first-generation iPad, $580, also outscored many of the other models tested but tied with the Motorola Xoom, $800."[5] With each new generation of iPad, the tablet gains new features and uses. I can't wait for the next-generation iPad, can you?

DISCUSSION QUESTIONS

1. How might sales not reach the predicted US$70 billion in 2014? What might cause sales to slow?
2. Why will it be difficult for Apple's competitors to get market share? How will they steal Apple's consumers away?
3. Apple does not have channels in place to sell directly to organizations, so how do you think they will get their tablets into enterprises?

INFORMATION TECHNOLOGY (IT) BASICS

IT Professionals and the IT Organization

1 Describe the functions of a company's chief information officer (CIO) and information technology (IT) department.

Information technology (IT) is the design and implementation of computer-based information systems.

The **chief information officer (CIO)** is responsible for the information technology of an organization, including systems design and development, data centre operations, creating policies regarding security and intellectual property, and updating or replacing computer systems and software.

What role does information technology play in business?   Try to imagine a type of business that doesn't use computer systems for some primary functions—it's hard to do! Any modern business must be able to reach consumers via electronic communications media such as e-mail and websites. Accounting information can be managed electronically so that taxes are filed easily, and word processors and databases are vital to any business. In retail, point-of-sale terminals collect information that is fed into inventory and sales computer systems so that stock can be reordered, fast-moving products can be identified, and accounting information can be kept current and accurate. At Apple's retail stores, employees roam the store with mobile "cash registers" in hand. They complete credit card transactions, e-mail sales receipts, and have customers in and out of the store in no time. Many grocery stores—as well as The Home Depot, Zellers, and Canadian Tire—provide self-service automated checkout systems, reducing the need for cashiers. It's clear that technology is changing fundamental aspects of how business is conducted. Whether it's a small, family-owned business getting its first electronic accounting system or a huge corporate conglomerate launching a new interactive website, the business world is getting more technologically advanced every day.

The IT department is responsible for everything from hardware to software to networking.

Who is in charge of business technology?   **Information technology (IT)** is the design and implementation of computer-based information systems. In many organizational structures, the person responsible for such technology is the **chief information officer (CIO)**. This is typically a position at the same level as the chief financial officer (CFO) of the firm. As **Figure 9.1** shows, the CIO is in charge of information processing, including systems design and development, data centre operations, and creating policies regarding security and intellectual property. He or she is responsible for updating or replacing the computer systems and the software the company uses. Because technology is spread across all divisions and major functions of a modern business, a CIO requires excellent leadership and organizational skills. The CIO must also manage a budget that balances the benefits of technology against the ever-rising costs of

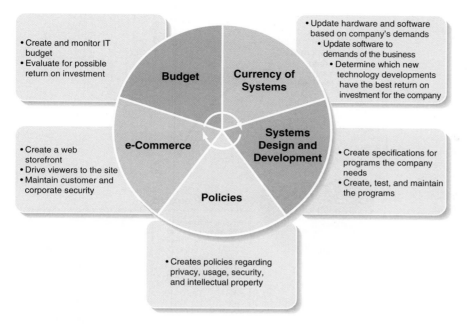

Figure 9.1 Functions of a CIO

upgrading to the latest systems. In addition, CIOs are involved in creating business and e-business opportunities.

What happens in an IT department? The **IT department** comprises a number of professionals responsible for everything from hardware components and software programs to networking and database strategies. This department is also responsible for security both in response to computer virus attacks and emergency recovery from power outages and system failures. In addition, the department keeps all the computers, printers, and other equipment operational and current. The IT department manages the design of the company's networks and databases where information is stored. The department is also responsible for selecting the appropriate software programs as well as often providing training to employees. Sometimes, IT professionals must also create custom software to bridge the gaps between the products available and the needs of the firm. The IT department also maintains and manages the use of mobile computing throughout the company. Equipment includes notebook computers, tablet PCs, smartphones, and other devices. Finally, the IT department is responsible for implementing remote access to computing resources, such as employees' access to work files or e-mail when they are working outside the office.

Information Systems

What is an information system? As mentioned above, information technology (IT) is the design and implementation of computer-based information systems. The main difference between information technology (IT) and **information systems (IS)**, or **management information systems (MIS)**, is that MIS is focused on applying IT to solve business and economic problems. For example, the payroll department may come to MIS asking for an upgrade to a new accounting system or software package. It is MIS's role to investigate the impact of that change on the other technology systems in the company and to rate the amount of gain against the cost required for the new software. So, MIS professionals bridge the gap between purely technical knowledge and how it will affect a business.

The **IT department** comprises a number of professionals responsible for everything from hardware components and software programs to networking and database strategies.

Information systems (IS), or **management information systems (MIS)**, focus on applying information technology (IT) to solve business and economic problems.

top 10

Questions to Ask Before Adopting a New Piece of Technology

Question	Reason for Asking
1. Who makes it?	Adopting new technology is like adopting a new partner, so you want to make sure that the partner is strong and reliable.
2. Who supports it?	If something goes wrong, you want to know who will fix it.
3. What are *all* the costs?	The initial cost of new technology can double once installation, training, and customization are calculated.
4. What other technology is required to make it work?	Some software might require certain hardware, and vice versa.
5. What services are required to make it work?	Additional communication partners, such as telephone, cable, or Internet providers, might be needed to connect new technology to outside systems.
6. How long has it been around?	A new system might still have some glitches, and an old system might be out of date.
7. Who else is using it?	It is valuable to know if your competitors are using the same product.
8. How will it generate profits for my company?	You must know if the cost of the system will be recouped by increased profits.
9. Can I take a test-drive?	It is important to know and see how the technology works.
10. Will it speak to my other systems?	An incompatible system can hinder, rather than help, operations.

9

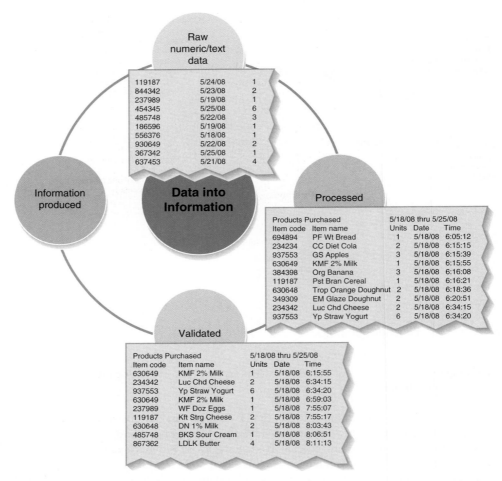

Figure 9.2   Processing Data into Useful Information

The raw data from a grocery store's sales log can be processed into information that will help the storeowner know when to schedule the store's milk shipments.

Data are the representations of a fact or idea. They may be a number, a word, an image, or a sound.

Information is data that have been organized or arranged in a way that make them useful.

The ***Personal Information Protection and Electronic Documents Act (PIPEDA)*** distinguishes proper use of personal information from improper use and disclosure.

Explain how information technology, information systems, information, and data are interrelated within a business.

Decision support systems (DSSs) are software systems that enable companies to analyze collected data so they can predict the impact of business decisions.

Executive information systems (EISs) are software systems that are specially designed for the needs of management.

What is the difference between data and information?   The terms *data* and *information* are often used interchangeably, but they have different meanings. **Data** are the representations of a fact or idea, which may be a number, a word, an image, or a sound. **Information**, however, is data that have been organized or arranged in a way that makes them useful (see **Figure 9.2**). The extraction of information from raw data is critical to the success of many business enterprises. Businesses try to use all the resources at their disposal to gather raw data. For example, media, credit bureaus, and information brokers often purchase data made public in court proceedings. These data are processed into useful information for that business. Businesses in Canada are subject to the ***Personal Information Protection and Electronic Documents Act (PIPEDA)***, which distinguishes proper use of personal information from improper use and disclosure. For example: If you own a pizzeria, you most likely collect personal information from clients, including the person's name, telephone number, and address, for the purpose of confirming a food order and providing home delivery. You would need that customer's consent to use the information for a different purpose, such as sending out promotional information.

How can collecting data help an organization?   Businesses can easily collect and store large amounts of data, but turning it into useful information is a challenging task. **Decision support systems (DSSs)** are software systems that enable companies to analyze collected data so they can predict the impact of business decisions. A DSS can also retrieve data from external sources and display results tied to the decision making of the business. **Executive information systems (EISs)** are software systems specially designed for the needs of management. These systems can consolidate and summarize the transactions within an organization by using both internal and external sources. The terms *DSS* and *EIS* are sometimes used interchangeably, but usually an EIS has a more graphical interface compared to a DSS, which often uses spreadsheets and can only show one department or product at a time.

Enterprise resource planning (ERP) is a way to integrate the data and processes of an organization into one single information system. It stores data from various functions found throughout the organization using sub-systems that include hardware, software, and databases in order to achieve integration. The SAP NetWeaver **business intelligence (BI) software** can assist managers in reporting, planning, and forecasting workforce performance. Business intelligence packages allow managers to analyze financial states, customer satisfaction, sales analysis, and supply chain status. Managers can quickly display the answers to several questions:[6]

- Who are my top ten revenue-generating customers?
- What factors (e.g., regions, products, or customers) are the greatest contributors to bad debt?
- Which vendors have unpaid invoices, and how much money do these vendors owe?
- How many days' worth of inventory is in each warehouse?
- Which plants have completed the highest number of work orders on time

How can companies make sense of all their data?

Data are stored in **database management systems (DBMSs)**, which are collections of tables of data that organize the data and allow simple analysis and reporting. As companies begin to store vast amounts of data in database systems separate from their production databases, **data warehouses** are created. Data warehouses can hold terabytes (thousands of gigabytes) of transaction data. Sometimes, subsets are created to isolate one product or one department. These smaller data sets are called **data marts**. The process of exploring and analyzing the data mart to uncover the relationships and patterns that will help a business is referred to as **data mining**. Data mining can be used in many ways. For example, suppose a supermarket uses data mining to help decide whether to restock a product that isn't selling well. If data mining reveals that the few people who typically buy the product are among the supermarket's most profitable customers, it will most likely be worth keeping the product on the shelves to retain their business. Although data mining has not yet lived up to its full potential, new advances in hardware and software are making it a larger part of business decision making.

Walmart seems to use data mining to its advantage: it stores huge amounts of customer data, and then uses it to predict future sales trends. For example, when the news struck that yet another hurricane would hit Florida, Walmart CIO Linda M. Dillman asked the experts to mine the data warehouse to determine whether, in the past, there had been certain trends in sales prior to major storms. Sure enough, they discovered that in the days before a major storm, consumers purchased more of specific, sometimes surprising items: flashlights but also Pop-Tarts (seven times normal sales) and beer (which is available for sale in U.S. Walmarts).[7] Thanks to these insights, Walmart increased its supply of these items and was able to make additional sales that might have been lost without data mining. Such knowledge, Walmart has learned, is not only power, it is profit too.

Enterprise resource planning (ERP) is a way to integrate the data and processes of an organization into one single information system. It stores data from various functions found throughout the organization using subsystems that include hardware, software, and databases in order to achieve integration.

Database management systems (DBMSs) are collections of tables of data that organize the data and allow simple analysis and reporting.

Data warehouses are created to store vast amounts of data in database systems separate from a company's production databases.

Data marts are subsets created to isolate one product or one department.

Data mining is the process of exploring and analyzing data marts to uncover the relationships and patterns that will help a business.

Many businesses use software programs to organize and analyze the data they collect.

COMPUTER SYSTEMS

③ Hardware

Is business computing the same as personal computing?   You're probably familiar with the hardware basics of a home computing system. A well-designed personal computer has a balance between the amount of (slow) hard disk storage, the amount of (faster) volatile memory called random access memory (RAM), and the speed of the central processing unit (CPU). In a business computing setting, these measurements are still critical to the design of a system, but there is a different emphasis. Entertainment features, such as powerful video graphics processing for video games or 7.1 channel sound cards, are typically not part of a business system. Hard disk storage, however, becomes incredibly important. If a hard drive with critical information fails, it can affect an entire organization. For this reason, business systems often use a hard disk backup design called **RAID (redundant array of independent drives)**. RAID 1

RAID (redundant array of independent drives) is a hard disk backup design.

systems use two disk drives instead of one and copy each piece of information stored onto both drives at the same time, making a perfect backup on a completely separate drive. Other types of RAID are more efficient, but the idea of using multiple drives to increase data security is the same.

Depending on the type of analysis being done at a particular business workstation, the processing power and speed of the CPU may need to be more advanced than that of the typical home computer. Because the amount of RAM is also related to the overall processing speed of the system, business workstations often have more memory. The exact speed of the processor and the amount and speed of memory vary dramatically each year as new systems are introduced. To be able to understand and compare specifications, it is useful to be familiar with the common units used in computing, shown in **Table 9.1**.

What role do mobile devices play in a modern business strategy?   Although the availability of Internet access enables workers to make decisions and conduct meetings virtually, business travel is still in huge demand. Business travellers, whether salespeople or field engineers, no longer need to be out of touch with their workplace or their customers when spending time in cars, airports, and hotels. Cellphones and more fully featured smartphones such as the BlackBerry 9900/9930 (with touchscreen) or the iPhone allow employees to access their e-mail and the Internet from virtually anywhere. Furthermore, smartphones running the Windows Mobile operating system enable users to read Microsoft Word, Excel, and Access files. Devices such as the Garmin Nüvi use a GPS to provide turn-by-turn directions to travellers and can locate the nearest restaurant, hospital, or gas station. Projectors and printers are available in mobile sizes as well. Projectors as light as 450 grams (1 pound) make it easy to bring your own complete presentation ready to play at any location. Mobile printers are small enough to tuck into a carry-on bag, and they allow users on the go to print documents.

Table 9.1   Common Units Used in Computing

Unit	Number of bytes	Equivalent to	Common measures
Kilobyte (KB)	1000	1 k	Small files
Megabyte (MB)	1 000 000	1000 KB	Video card memory
Gigabyte (GB)	1 000 000 000	1000 MB	Hard drive storage
Terabyte (TB)	1 000 000 000 000	1000 GB	Large server farms of stored data, data warehouse

As more and more devices appear on the market and as prices continue to drop, CIOs find they need to have a consistent policy to manage mobile devices. The requests for IT support can quickly cause a heap of technical support demands. One approach some companies are using is to restrict mobile devices to only those issued by the company itself. At Tastykake, a snack food company, CIO Brendan O'Malley makes it a point to provide the leading-edge, connected handheld devices so employees aren't tempted to get their own devices. "We figure out what people need and give it to them," he says.[8]

Mobile devices, such as smartphones, GPS devices, and portable printers and projectors, enable business travellers to stay in touch when they're out of the office.

Software

What analytical software is common in business?

Managers need to make decisions driven by data. Many different software products are available to analyze the large amounts of data needed to make business decisions. In addition, a variety of analytical software packages is used to support numerical analysis, such as the following:

1. *Spreadsheet Programs.* Microsoft Excel and similar spreadsheet programs can run hundreds of different statistical and financial functions with no programming required. They support "what if?" calculations, allowing managers to change one or two variables and easily interpret the results.
2. *Database Programs.* Database programs allow businesses to quickly enter data, filter and sort information, and generate reports. Forms can be easily designed so that data can be entered and validated for accuracy. These forms—such as weekly timecards or customer surveys—can be delivered through e-mail, and the responses automatically added into the database. The collected data can be queried to create lists of data that meet specific conditions, such as the addresses of all employees who worked overtime in the past week.
3. *Online Analysis Packages.* Online analysis packages (OLAPs) are software applications that enable very quick analysis of combinations of different business factors. OLAP systems are designed to help analysts combine multiple pieces of information into a clear picture of the state of the business. These software applications are used for tasks such as reporting sales figures and budgeting and forecasting. OLAP products in the marketplace include MS Analysis Studio, the open-source product Openi (pronounced "open eye"), and Jedox Palo software.

What software applications help manage the details of a business effectively?

Software packages can help businesses make strategic decisions about the use of resources, the direction of new marketing campaigns, or daily operations. Software can also help with the mechanics of the business world—such as payroll, accounting, and tracking benefits for individual employees. For example, many companies use software that allows employees to check the number of remaining personal leave days they have available, the insurance options they have selected, the amount of money they have placed into retirement, and other aspects of their benefits package. QuickBooks is a very popular accounting package used by small businesses worldwide to handle accounting and budgeting needs. It can also handle many other common business tasks, such as processing UPS and FedEx shipments or paying income taxes from payroll. In addition, QuickBooks can help a business become more tech-savvy with the package's full-service Web storefront program that allows businesses to set up an online store, take credit card payments, and automatically record all transactions into the accounting system.

Human resource management systems are software tools that organize people-related management tasks such as employee reviews, compensation calculations, and applicant management. Packages such as PeopleTrak and eAppraisal make it easier to execute and document the management of employees from the hiring process through performance evaluations. These tools help employers know when to offer additional training and how to assist employees in achieving their future career goals.

9

What communications technology is commonly used in businesses? E-mail and instant messaging aren't the only forms of business communication using modern technology. Other communications technologies frequently used by businesses today include:

1. *VoIP.* Standard telephone communications have evolved using the *voice over internet protocol (VoIP)*. VoIP technology lets users check their voicemail messages from any Internet browser. Products such as Skype use VoIP allow national and international calls to be made free over the Internet instead of over traditional phone networks.

2. *Remote Conferencing.* Remote conferencing allows many people to join a common discussion regardless of their physical location. Conferences can be conducted with or without video cameras at each workstation, and participants can each work collaboratively on a single document using a common virtual whiteboard. Some products even allow a participant to take control of another's desktop to demonstrate software to the group or to make a presentation. With more attendees participating in virtual meetings, the environmental impact of such a shift in business practices is significant. For example, one businessperson moving her sales presentation online instead of flying from Ottawa to Calgary saves 441 kilograms (972 pounds) of carbon dioxide emissions; if the plane does not make the trip at all, multiply the individual savings by the number of persons that would have filled the plane to get a total CO_2 emissions savings.[9] The shift to online conferencing across large sections of the business world could have a powerful, positive impact on the environment.

3. *Marketing Technologies and Services.* Marketing is an aspect of business that has responded to changes in business technology by redefining itself. In today's world, a marketing department must consider the Internet as a tool for both collecting information on its customers and distributing information about its products and services. Companies such as Lyris, Topica, and Constant Contact can organize and control mass e-mail campaigns by providing templates for e-mail newsletters or advice on how to create e-mail surveys. They also provide services that generate reports to track the number of people who read the e-mail message, how many followed the links inside, and how many forwarded the e-mail to another contact.

Networks

Why are business networks created? In many homes, a family may have more than one computer but only one printer or Internet connection. Each computer user in the household can share accessories or connections by implementing a home network— a set of communication links between computer systems that allow an exchange of information. This means a printer can receive printing jobs from multiple computers, and scanners can send files to multiple computers. This sharing capability helps households save on expensive resources only needed for brief periods. In business, companies want to utilize resources efficiently as well. Expensive devices such as colour laser printers or important collections of secure, protected data may need to be accessed by numerous employees in the organization. The most efficient way to provide needed resources to everyone is to create a network. In business, a **network** is a system of computers and other devices joined using cables, fibre optic links, or wireless connections.

But only techies need to know about networks, right? Some employees may be interested enough in networking to follow that as a career path, but even those who do not work in the IT department need to have a basic understanding of networks. In most workplaces, employees use networks to access shared files and documents, to access their private personnel data, and to communicate with others in the firm. Understanding the basic structure and operation of networks helps employees do their jobs more efficiently. Managers need to know about networking because the use and maintenance of networks as a company resource are important in their decision making.

What types of networks are in the workplace? There are two types of networks, other than the public Internet, commonly used in the workplace: an intranet and an extranet. An **intranet** is a network accessible only to employees or others with authorization. An intranet's website looks just like any other website. However, specialized

In business, a **network** is a system of computers and other devices joined using cables, fibre optic links, or wireless connections.

An **intranet** is a network accessible only to employees or others with authorization.

An **extranet** is an intranet partially accessible to authorized outsiders. Customers or vendors with a valid username and password are able to see certain parts of the network.

Local area networks (LANs) include only machines in close physical proximity to one another, such as the computers in one office building.

A **wireless LAN (WLAN)** is a network connected wirelessly by a Wi-Fi (wireless fidelity) signal instead of by cables.

A **wide-area network (WAN)** is a network of LANs.

firewall software surrounding an intranet keeps unauthorized users from gaining access to the site. An **extranet** is an intranet partially accessible to authorized outsiders. Customers or vendors with a valid username and password are able to see certain parts of the network. Extranets are becoming a very popular means for business partners to exchange information.

Do networks come in different sizes?   Some networks include only machines in close physical proximity to one another, such as the computers in one office building. These are known as **local area networks (LANs)**. The different computers on the network may be joined by physical cables, run through the walls and floors of a building, or by using a Wi-Fi (wireless fidelity) signal. If the LAN is connected wirelessly instead of with cables, it is referred to as a **wireless LAN (WLAN)**. Often, Wi-Fi hotspots, places where access to a wireless LAN is available, are advertised in airport terminals, coffee houses, and hotels trying to appeal to business travellers who need to reach server files or e-mail using the Internet. A collection of LANs can be joined into one network, forming a **wide-area network (WAN)**.

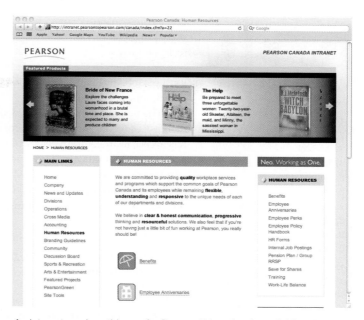

An intranet, such as this one for Pearson Education, is available only to employees and others with authorization.

As networks begin to link sites very far apart geographically, **virtual private networks (VPNs)** are often used. A VPN may connect some of its systems by cables that the company owns, but other sections of the network will be joined using the public Internet. This requires the encryption of information so that the company's private information is kept secure as it travels across public sections of the network. For example, if a company merged offices in two different cities into one network, a VPN would ensure secure flow of information.

Is the Internet just a network?   The **Internet** is a global system of interconnected computer networks that use the standard Internet Protocol Suite (TCP/IP) to send communications to billions of users worldwide. Put simply, the Internet is a large network that connects millions of computers internationally. The **Internet2**, a network of networks that can communicate at speeds a hundred to a thousand times faster than Internet1, is a collaboration of more than 200 universities and 120 companies and has been running since 1996. Businesses and individuals use the Internet for many reasons, such as to collaborate and communicate with others, to connect to remote devices, to buy and sell products or services, and to gather research.

As you may know, the Internet and the World Wide Web are not the same thing. The **World Wide Web (WWW)** is a way of accessing information available on the Internet. The Web uses a specific protocol, named hypertext transfer protocol (HTTP), to send data between systems. **Protocols** are the different "languages" used to transfer information across the Internet. Some examples of other protocols include FTP, a file transfer protocol to move files, and SMTP, simple mail transfer protocol, which handles outgoing e-mail.

BENEFITS AND CHALLENGES OF TECHNOLOGY

IT Benefits and Challenges for Employees

How does technology benefit employees?   Consider this example. Mark Dagostino has been a successful IT specialist at an insurance firm for fifteen years. He was excited by the prospect of being able to access his work files from home because he figured it would allow him to spend more time with his family. However, Mark now finds that the

Virtual private networks (VPNs), often used when networks begin to link sites very far apart geographically, may connect some of its systems by cables that the company owns, but other sections of the network will be joined using the public Internet.

The **Internet** is a global system of interconnected computer networks that use the standard Internet Protocol Suite (TCP/IP) to send communications to billions of users worldwide.

The **Internet2**, a network of networks that can communicate at speeds a hundred to a thousand times faster than Internet1, is a collaboration of more than 200 universities and 120 companies.

The **World Wide Web (WWW)** is a way of accessing information available on the Internet.

Protocols are the different "languages" used to transfer information across the Internet.

Outline the benefits and risks of technology in the workplace, taking into account safety, creativity, communication, productivity, privacy, and ethics.

World's Most Innovative Companies (2011)

1. Apple
2. Twitter
3. Facebook
4. Nissan
5. Groupon
6. Google
7. Dawning Information Industry
8. Netflix
9. Zynga
10. Epocrates

Source: "The World's Most Innovative Companies 2011," *FastCompany. com*, http://www.fastcompany.com/most-innovative-companies/2011/, Accessed April 9, 2011.

office is in constant contact with him. The insurance agents work shifts around the clock, processing claims from clients, and Mark is frequently asked to work at all hours to solve technological problems. He even had to work on a computer crisis on Christmas morning one year, much to the chagrin of his family. Mark has reached a new level of frustration with his job, and he is strongly considering taking a pay cut at a new job in exchange for a less chaotic schedule.

The boundary between work and home has blurred dramatically because of the increase of technology. Once a worker has access from home to office files, and the office has access to the employees through smartphones or live videoconferencing, the workday can extend dramatically. However, there are aspects of technology that clearly benefit employees. In rescue operations, robots and robotic assistance have relieved human rescue personnel of dangerous tasks. In automotive plants, robots have taken over most of the very monotonous, unfulfilling work, freeing humans for more creative positions.

What challenges does technology create for employees?

Some uses of technology in the workplace have brought about difficult changes. The increasing volume of e-mail can contribute to a breakdown in communication as fewer personal exchanges take place. Communication experts agree that in face-to-face discussions, up to 93 percent of the meaning of the messages exchanged is communicated in nonverbal ways—through gestures, glances, body position, and facial expression.[10] As more office discussions take place in e-mails, the chance of misunderstandings and errors starts to rise.

Has technology increased productivity?

What is the business value of IT? Many studies have been conducted to answer this question, and their findings differ widely. Some conclude that corporate investment in IT has led to increased output from employees, whereas others find that the investment has actually led to a drop in productivity. It's a complex question, and some of the discrepancies depend on the actual definition of productivity. Are they looking at knowledge workers only or blue-collar workers as well? How was the impact of the overall strength of the economy factored into the measurement of productivity? Other researchers question whether profitability, consumer benefit, and productivity are actually related. Although employees certainly have more access to information through technology, it is up to the individual to use that information appropriately. If you cannot guarantee that new technology is going to make a workforce more productive, then the task of selecting the IT solutions and tools that will yield enough benefit to outweigh the investment of purchase, training, and maintenance becomes all the more difficult.

How do intellectual property laws affect knowledge workers?

With more technology in place at businesses, more employees are becoming "knowledge-based" workers. Their contribution to the company is measured by their creativity and originality. But who owns the idea that an employee has while at work? In most businesses, the idea is the property of the company, even the brainstorm occurred during lunch instead of during an afternoon meeting. For example, a software engineer working at a health information management centre is struggling to come up with a way to store large files of hospital records on one drive. Suddenly, an idea for the design of a microchip comes to her while she is driving to work. Even though the idea was formed outside the work environment, the idea belongs to the company because it was based on previous work. Intellectual property and copyright law are constantly evolving. As technology creates a higher percentage of knowledge workers, the issue of ownership of ideas will affect more and more employees.

How does technology affect employee privacy?

At home, Canadian citizens are guaranteed specific levels of privacy and freedoms. In the workplace, however, the expectation of privacy is quite different. Electronic monitoring is commonly used to track employees' keystrokes and e-mails, examine their Internet browsing histories, and even monitor their cellphone and instant messaging usage.[11] Camera surveillance can be conducted with recording devices so small that employees do not realize they are being recorded. Used appropriately, these technical tools can help a company eliminate a drain of business resources for personal use. But to some employees, the work environment then begins to feel so monitored that they no longer produce their best work. In a study conducted at Bell Canada, researchers found that 50 percent of employees in the customer service department reported an increase in stress and anxiety when their calls were being monitored. Employee stress can lead to job dissatisfaction and prompt health problems.[12] Finding the balance between an appropriate level of monitoring and an optimal work environment is a continuous challenge.

Can technology support ethical conduct?

Charitable organizations use the Internet for fundraising, and intranets and e-mail are used every day to inform employees of ethical policies (e.g., a code of conduct). Law enforcement uses technology to track criminal activity occurring over the Internet. Several corporations now use their intranet to allow whistleblowers (those reporting wrongdoings) to submit reports (some anonymous, some not). Canada Post asks employees to report any improper activities to their immediate supervisor without fear of reprisal, but should the employee not feel comfortable doing so, he or she may submit a report by telephone, Internet, or mail.[13] Social networking sites—such as Facebook, Twitter, Flickr, and Myspace—have become very popular, and many of us use these sites to keep in touch with loved ones and friends. Business-focused social sites—such as LinkedIn—help us build a network of business contacts. Social networking sites can also be used to make the world a better place. Care2 (www.care2.com) is devoted to making a difference and all things green. Avaaz (www.avaaz.org) has over ten million members worldwide working on democracy and social justice initiatives through the Internet. International human rights organization Breakthrough (www.breakthrough.tv) uses social media to reshape public attitudes and advance equality, justice, and dignity. The Best Friends Animal Society (www.bestfriends. org) is devoted to educating people on proper pet care. Turn Your World Around (www. turnyourworldaround.org) empowers youth all over the world to take action in matters such as climate change, health care, peace, and civil liberties. With so many people joining these "good global citizenship" projects, these websites really can become powerful forces for shaping the world we live in.

Off the **Mark**

Hewlett-Packard Spying Scandal

Hewlett-Packard (HP) crossed the ethical lines of employee privacy in 2006 in an attempt to discover the source of an anonymous article that leaked private company information. Chairman Patricia Dunn hired private investigators and allegedly authorized them to use illegal tactics to uncover the source of this leak. The private investigators used pretexting, or lying about one's identity, to gain access to phone records, tracer e-mails containing spyware, and the surveillance of journalists. Placing physical spies in a newsroom was even discussed. Dunn resigned from HP in 2006, as well as board member George Keyworth, who was discovered to be behind the information leak. The scandal ended up costing the company several board members, millions of dollars, and bad press.

Employee privacy concerns are a big issue today, as technology makes it easier to spy on employees. Although HP engaged in illegal methods of observation, companies can legally screen the e-mail and Internet histories of employees, raising ethical concerns about the right of companies to do so.

Discussion Questions

1. Does it bother you to know your employer can read any e-mails you send or receive from your company e-mail account? Why or why not?
2. Do you think business and government should be permitted to place video cameras within the halls of their buildings or meeting rooms? Why or why not?
3. Do you think most people who post information on the Internet (e.g., Facebook, Flickr, YouTube, or LinkedIn) worry about privacy? What's the worst that can happen by having your pictures and information out there for anyone to see? Should you be concerned?

IT Benefits and Challenges for Management

What risks does technology pose for management?

Although the increase in IT has allowed many advances for businesses, it also has added risks. The stability of the business can be jeopardized if technology is not implemented reliably. Even a short black-out of vital services, such as internal e-mail or customer access to the corporate Internet presence, can damage a company's reputation and value. In June 2007, the Hawaiian airline Go! attempted to sell 1000 tickets for $1. The promotion caused so many people to access the company's website that it crashed, and customers could not get tickets. The company was forced to double the number of $1 tickets it was offering to placate upset customers.[14] One survey of managers in the United Kingdom found that 70 percent said IT failure was the top threat to their organization, whereas only 2 percent cited a concern over terrorism disrupting their business.[15]

Another challenge IT brings to management is security. With so much of the value of a modern business stored in electronic material—whether as documents, software pro-grams, or e-mail files—a company can be vulnerable to hackers. **Hackers** are individuals who gain unauthorized entry into a computer system either to disrupt the operation of the system or to gain access to protected data. According to the Canadian Anti-Fraud Centre (CAFC), 11 095 Canadian victims reported identity fraud in 2009, totalling a loss of more than $10 million. The most commonly reported incident was payment card fraud.[16] Hackers illegally gain access to credit and debit cards through technology. Criminals use your information to access your bank accounts, apply for loans, make purchases, obtain

Hackers are individuals who gain unauthorized entry into a computer system either to disrupt the operation of the system or to gain access to protected data.

BizChat

Explore on MyBusinessLab

Customers Exposed[17]

Epsilon, an online marketer for Alliance Data Systems Corp., controls e-mail databases for more than 2500 clients and sends out more than 40 billion e-mails a year. When Epsilon was hacked on April 1, 2011, customer names and e-mails of Citigroup Inc. and other large North American companies, and student data from the U.S. College Board, were exposed in a massive data breach.

Epsilon said that someone from outside the company accessed their customer database but obtained only names and e-mail addresses, not any financial or other sensitive information.

Some of the companies involved include:

1. Hilton Hotels
2. AbeBooks
3. Marriott
4. Citigroup
5. Air Miles
6. Best Buy
7. Kraft Foods
8. Target

"While we are cooperating with authorities and doing a thorough investigation, we cannot say anything else," said Epsilon spokesperson Jessica Simon.[18] Best Buy notified its Canadian and American customers that their information had been accessed by an "unauthorized party"[19] and advised them to delete any e-mails asking for personal information. Air Miles reminded its customers that it does not ask for personal information or login credentials via e-mail and cautioned them about opening e-mail links or attachments from unknown third parties.

The biggest risk in this type of data breach is that criminals could use the e-mail addresses to trick customers into providing more personal information by posing as one of companies affected—a technique known as phishing (see page 263). About three years before this attack, hacker Albert Gonzalez led a team who stole more than 40 million payment card numbers from Heartland Payment Systems, a credit and debit card processor. For his role in one of the biggest identity-theft cases in history, Gonzalez was sentenced to twenty years in prison.

Discussion Questions

1. Do you think companies have an obligation to alert customers when their personal information has been accessed without approval?
2. Do you think these hackers will be able to use the information they obtained to their advantage?
3. You can see from the case of Albert Gonzalez that stealing credit and debit card numbers is certainly a punishable crime. Yet criminals try this all the time. Research the Internet to find another example where someone was attempting to steal debit or credit information. What were their methods? Did they go to jail or receive a fine? How did they get caught?

passports, or receive government benefits. Using identity theft to facilitate organized criminal and terrorist activities seems to be a growing trend. Risk of a security breach becomes even greater if unprotected wireless networks are in use. If no encryption scheme is used, then the data travelling through a wireless network are available to anyone in range.

Does keeping pace with technology put a financial burden on businesses?

Another challenge IT poses for business is the financial burden placed on companies trying to stay up to date. The full cost of any new piece of technology includes not only the purchase of the software and hardware itself, but also potential hardware upgrades required to make the new product useful. For example, say management decides it wants to upgrade the operating system that runs on the company's computers. This requires that the firm buy not just licences for the operating system software but also memory upgrades for computer systems. In addition, the IT department will need to take time to test the software prior to deployment, establish a support staff, install the software, and train users on how to interact with the programs. Before adopting new technology, business managers must evaluate whether the benefits of new technology will exceed the costs.

Sometimes, management may feel pressure to upgrade software or hardware because the entire market has switched to a new product or because customers or vendors have already moved to a new version of a program or device. In such circumstances, the CIO must evaluate the available workforce and determine whether there are sufficient people trained with the new software or hardware to make the return on investment significant and worthwhile. Occasionally, software products are released and working, but not yet supported by other companies' software products. For example, when Microsoft released the Windows Vista operating system, many midsized companies found they would be required to upgrade their hardware, adding hard disk drives, more memory, or possibly even buying completely new computers because their existing processors were too slow for Vista.[20] However, Microsoft predicted a savings of US$340 a year per machine in IT labour and support costs. In these cases, the CIO must evaluate whether adopting a new piece of technology is in the best interest of the company.

What are the pros and cons of conducting business online?

Taking advantage of cyberspace storefronts is a major benefit of increased technology in business. But it does bring with it a set of concerns that managers must be prepared to face. Because customers are justifiably worried about possible online threats to their privacy, every aspect of an online store must be secure and inspire consumer trust. This can create some complicated decisions for management. For example, some companies use cookies, small text files written to a user's hard disk that track customer preferences and Web clicks, or they store previous responses to online forms. This allows a company to customize its Web storefront for each customer. Sophisticated analysis programs try to predict consumer behaviour when processing those data. This valuable information can then be sold to marketing firms or used to justify high prices for ad space. Some people feel this practice compromises their security so they change browser settings not to accept cookies, but when they do this, the sites may not function. That perception alone, whether accurate or not, can cost a company business. So, should a company use cookies or not? Some companies say yes, while others refuse to collect such information about their users.

Technology Creates a Global Village

BizSkills Simulation: Technology Direction. Located in MyBusinessLab.

Where will the next generation of workers live?

On one hand, employees with skills that stand out in the global talent pool will be able to live anywhere. With employees relocating often and internationally, the demand for workers with language and communication skills will increase. On the other hand, the introduction of millions of talented knowledge workers worldwide may cause workers who have only average or marginal skills to be displaced.

What skills will be expected in the global workplace?   Flexibility on the part of employees will be expected in the global workplace. Communication skills and social understanding of a range of cultures will be invaluable, as will mathematical skills, which transcend language boundaries. Demonstrated fluency in learning new technologies will let employers know a prospective employee can handle a multitude of projects. Knowledge of other languages in addition to English will be a key asset to business technology employees. Considering the fact that the population of China is 1.3 billion and growing, the demand for Chinese-language speakers is increasing. Other developing countries also continue to grow, thus, so will the demand for foreign language skills.

How does an understanding of digital culture help in business?   Those raised with Internet access, digital media, and easily available computer-processing power have developed a different set of skills, strengths, and demands than the generations before them. In today's workplace, three different generations are often working on the same project; being able to understand and adapt between the different styles of each generation is key to a successful team. It is also critical to understanding the marketplace, which is also composed of both "digital natives" and "digital immigrants." Improvements in business technology have allowed for greater coordination between countries in business.

 Better Business **Better World**

Electronics Recycling

As global environmental problems become more urgent, and as resources deplete and populations climb, the shift to a sustainable society has become a significant issue worldwide. One group doing good for the world is the Electronic Recycling Association (ERA), which is a non-profit organization helping companies and the public across Canada deal with unwanted electronic items. Not only does ERA donate computers to local schools, libraries, charities and non-profit groups, elderly homes, and other community-based organizations at no charge, but it also runs a reuse and recycle program. And its asset maximization program collects, refurbishes, and sells old equipment from companies, ensuring that all data is removed according to RCMP and U.S. Department of Defence standards. ERA states, "Initial trials found that a typical organization can recover 5 percent of the initial cost of redundant IT equipment."[21]

Another organization committed to environmental sustainability is Panasonic, which is a for-profit business whose "eco ideas" declaration states: "The Panasonic Group strives to be a Green Innovation Company with a global perspective."[22] By 2018, when Panasonic marks its one hundredth anniversary, it aims to become the number-one Green Innovation Company in the electronics industry. Among other green endeavours outlined on its website, Panasonic will strive to:

- develop innovative energy-saving products
- reduce total CO_2 emissions from production activities
- minimize the amount of total resources used
- minimize the environmental impact caused by chemicals used in manufacturing
- recycle water within its factories and reduce its use
- maximize the use of recycled materials

"We will make the 'environment' central to all our business activities and spur innovation."[23]

Discussion Questions

1. Why is it important for companies with initiatives such as these to set targets, write policies, and publicly display their intentions?
2. Do you think if more companies took these steps, it would slow global warming? Why or why not?
3. Knowing the initiatives Panasonic is taking toward environmental sustainability, does it make you want to pledge your patronage to Panasonic products? Research on the Internet to discover what other electronic companies are doing in the area of environmental sustainability.

Companies commonly use practices such as offshoring and outsourcing to lower costs. These practices allow companies to pay lower wages for work and choose from a greater pool of skilled employees. Workers are challenged to compete in an international skills market. Advances in business computing allow for global marketing campaigns, and consumers expect interactive Web media. Telecommuting to work has become increasingly popular, as employees can complete tasks from home while being able to care for their children or parents. The spread of work to foreign countries will force employees to develop greater communication skills and cultural awareness.

International Business Environment

How does technology change marketing in a global marketplace?
Internet technology allows every company with a website to advertise to the entire world. The site must support multiple languages, but more importantly, it must also make sure the content for different countries is culturally customized. Every marketing campaign is now global. In 2007, when Hewlett Packard launched its new Print 2.0 Web printing service, it began with a US$300 million global marketing campaign.[24] The campaign used interactive Web technologies to create "achiever experiences" designed to give customers printable content they could customize with their own images and text. HP also established two print communities for consumers and small businesses and wikis to allow customers to collaborate on print projects, marketing, and branding. HP found it needed to use Internet technologies joined with excellent content to deliver its worldwide marketing message.

How can technology redefine boundaries of business cooperation?
Business technology has helped fuel the collapse of fixed boundaries between international divisions of a business. Time and distance are no longer barriers between the collaboration of two parts of a business. Instead, different countries can bring the energy needed to foster breakthrough, high-impact innovation.[25] It can be challenging to take the necessary risk to create new ideas, especially once executives and business units have a record of proven success. The use of international, high-stakes competitions within a firm can ignite new designs. Mazda used this approach when it designed the Miata sports coupe in the 1990s. Two teams, one from the United States and one from Japan, were tasked with the job of designing an affordable sports car reminiscent of the classic British roadsters of the past. Technology allowed them to communicate easily and keep an eye on what the other team was doing, leading to a healthy competitive environment that resulted in one of the most successful sports car designs in the industry.

How is technology affecting the world's production and design centres?
For several decades, China has grown as a production centre for the world. "Made in China" is stamped on products from clothing to machinery. But the design centres drafting the products have been traditionally located in the United States and Western Europe. As business technology and education continue to blossom in China, design is shifting there as well. General Motors owns a plant in a suburb of Shanghai. The design of the latest model Buick LaCrosse was left to an open internal competition between American and Chinese designers in design studios 9600 kilometres (6000 miles) apart. Both teams excelled in the competitive environment. Ultimately, the Chinese GM design team was given the redesign for the LaCrosse interior and overall flow, and

Thanks to Internet technology, every company with a website is now capable of advertising globally. This page, for the company Charles Schwab, is designed for Chinese-speaking investors.

online distribution, advertising, networking, and accessing customers. Many B2C sites have call centres or request forms so customers can ask questions or submit comments to improve the site. Most advertise online at social networking sites that consumers frequent.

Consumer-to-consumer (C2C) transactions take place between consumers. In this e-business model, consumers sell goods and services to other consumers, sometimes with the involvement of a third party. A popular C2C marketplace with an intermediary is eBay. File and music sharing are types of C2C exchanges, sometimes referred to as *P2P*, or peer-to-peer. Social networking sites, including Facebook and Myspace, can fill this role as well.

What are some of the challenges in e-business?   E-business is all about convenience, but it can become complicated when *tax* and *jurisdiction* issues are taken into consideration.

Businesses pay taxes, but there are many questions around taxation when it comes to e-business. For instance, who's taxing who and for how much? How is sales tax handled when something is sold online? Do you charge the customer taxes according to where they live or where the product is being shipped, or do you charge taxes in accordance with company location? What if you don't have a specific brick-and-mortar location, but instead you have several computer server sites in various locations around the world? What about when the e-tailer (online retailer) is in one country and the consumer is in another? Complicated? Yes. But complicated or not, most merchants doing business online collect sales taxes on just about all transactions. It is bound to happen. E-business taxation is a very complex and technical area. For example, you may have legal obligations to collect or withhold taxes, such as GST/HST, or you may be subject to an exemption. Your customer may also have to withhold taxes on your bill. You should be sure to obtain good accounting, tax, and legal advice, particularly if you are selling across provincial or international borders.

Jurisdiction is the authority of a government to legislate and enforce its many laws. It is usually territorial, but since the Internet has a geographic territory too broad to define, it is difficult to address legal jurisdiction issues for online-only businesses.[28] With business-to-consumer e-business, goods could be sold anywhere in the world, making it very difficult or even impossible to comply with the laws of every potential relevant jurisdiction. Once a website is posted, it is instantly available worldwide through the Internet. Disputes over legal jurisdiction of e-business have been occurring since the introduction of the Internet. A large corporation might have offices or stores in several different countries, and it becomes very difficult to comply with the laws of all those countries. The *Canadian Code of Practice for Consumer Protection in Electronic Commerce* outlines good business practice standards for merchants conducting business with customers online.[29] The *Competition Act* prohibits false or misleading advertising in all media, including websites.[30] The World Intellectual Property Organization (WIPO) provides international coordination and agreement with legal matters pertaining to copyrights, trademarks, and patents.[31]

Has the Internet become the preferred way to advertise?   The rise of e-business has revolutionized the way goods and services are advertised. While the Internet hasn't completely replaced traditional advertising, online marketing has boosted sales in two significant ways. For a company trying to get its message out to young, web-savvy consumers, the Internet appears to be the best option. Moreover, for businesses that have historically relied on traditional forms of advertising, such as television and newspapers, the Internet has become a new source for revenue. For marketing experts, taking advantage of new advertising outlets offers many opportunities.

Online advertising is any form of advertising that uses the Internet to market its message to customers. This includes everything from banner ads to pop-up ads and spam. More often than not, the online ad is hyperlinked to another website and tracks how many "clicks" are registered. The ability to track how many eyes have viewed an ad is, in fact, one of the great allures of Internet advertising.

Consumer-to-consumer (C2C) transactions take place between consumers.

Online advertising is any form of advertising that uses the Internet to market its message to customers.

As the number of households with high-speed broadband Internet access has increased, online advertising has become much more sophisticated. Flash and Java technology allow advertisers to embed animated ads and full-motion video. In addition to the abundance of such rich media advertisements, programs such as Google's AdWords service and AdSense network utilize the process of pay-per-click (PPC) advertising. With **pay-per-click (PPC)** advertising, advertisers only have to pay for the number of times a Web surfer clicks on their ad. Google's AdWords and AdSense have been able to translate this simple technique into a successful source of revenue for the company.

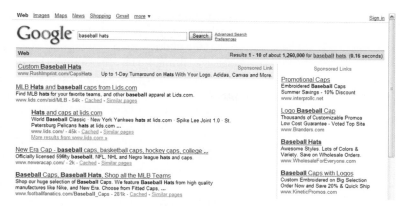

Google utilizes pay-per-click ads, like the sponsored links shown here, as an example of online advertising.

PPC ads are effective because they are associated with keywords and are highly relevant to what potential consumers are searching for. The idea was initially conceived by the GoTo.com search engine before Google began to develop its own AdSense network. Google's popular AdSense network takes PPC ads to the next level. By placing PPC ads on third-party sites, such as blogs and Web forums, they reach readers depending on the content of the particular page instead of search results. Also known as **contextual advertising**, these ads are automatically generated by the content on a specific site. This way, readers of a popular golf blog might see simple text ads promoting the latest Tiger Woods–endorsed golfing equipment. Moreover, the AdSense network also allows individual bloggers to generate revenue by hosting these ads on their site. Blogs with a significant readership can earn a great deal of money by giving such ads visibility.

There are drawbacks to online advertising. "Click fraud" can occur, in which a competing company clicks on ads in order to run up the cost of its competitor's advertising.[32] Spam annoys people by filling up their in-boxes. Web surfers also complain about pop-up ads, which open their advertisements in new browser windows, and interstitials, which are displayed before a viewer can get to the desired content. Also, because the integration of ads on the Internet is so prevalent, many people have grown so used to seeing Web ads that they may not even notice them. **Table 9.2** summarizes the pros and cons of online advertising.

How do companies get their advertisements noticed online?
To get people to notice their advertisements, many marketers are turning to a technique known as **viral marketing**, which involves using social networks, e-mail, and websites to spread the awareness of a particular brand. Rather than being an overt advertising campaign that relies on airwaves with commercials, a viral campaign is more subtle and dependent on the user to be an active participant in the spreading of the message. It is designed to appeal to consumers who may be resistant to traditional advertising. Essentially, viral

Pay-per-click (PPC) advertising involves advertisers only having to pay for the number of times a Web surfer clicks on their ad.

Contextual advertising are ads automatically generated by the content on a specific site. By placing PPC ads on third-party sites, such as blogs and Web forums, they reach readers depending on the content of the particular page instead of search results.

Viral marketing uses social networks, e-mail, and websites to spread the awareness of a particular brand.

Table 9.2   Pros and Cons of Online Advertising

Pros	Cons
Reasonable cost: With pay-per-click, the cost of advertising depends on frequency of use.	**Fear of spam:** Web users may avoid clicking ads to avoid receiving spam.
Hitting target markets: Contextual advertising allows for high probability of reaching intended viewers.	**Annoyance factor:** Rather than be drawn in, Web users may become annoyed with flashing ads or pop-ups.
Tracking: Companies are able to keep records of who is clicking ads and where they are located—essential information in designing future campaigns.	**Click fraud:** Companies who invest in pay-per-click advertising may receive unexpectedly large invoices if a competitor purposefully clicks ads in excess.

marketing is a Web 2.0 version—that is, a more consumer-friendly, interactive, and collaborative type—of old-fashioned word of mouth.

One of the earliest examples of a business promoting itself virally is the Webmail service Hotmail. The programmers behind Hotmail integrated an advertisement for the service into every piece of e-mail that was sent. Therefore, simply by sending an e-mail to your best friend, you were unwittingly promoting the service. This practice proved so successful that, in 1996, Hotmail grew to 12 million accounts by the end of its first year.[33] Another example of marketing-gone-viral is Burger King's "Subservient Chicken," which promoted a new type of sandwich and gained notoriety in 2004. Television commercials featured an actor in a chicken costume with the tagline "Chicken the way you like it." In an interesting twist, the advertisements did not feature the Burger King logo. Instead, these commercials pointed viewers to a website that allowed visitors to manipulate the chicken character in various ways. Interested participants eventually spread links to the website, helping it gain tens of millions of hits and spreading Burger King's message "virally" to millions of potential customers.[34] This kind of interactivity between product, message, and consumer sets viral marketing apart from other advertising media.

Viral marketing gives a company more than the opportunity to promote a product or brand; it allows potential consumers to feel a personal connection to the brand by becoming a part of a communal experience. Hollywood movie studios have been on the forefront of this kind of viral advertising. In 1999, Artisan Entertainment was one of the first studios to embrace the practice when promoting the horror film *The Blair Witch Project*. Warner Bros.' 2008 *Batman* sequel, *The Dark Knight*, took the interactivity of viral marketing to another level by incorporating the concept of alternate reality gaming—a completely immersive "narrative" experience that requires participants to engage through multiple platforms, both online and in the real world.[35] Through the alternate reality gaming firm 42 Entertainment, promotion for the summer blockbuster debuted online more than a year before the film's opening. Rather than using traditional movie marketing practices, like hosting the film's trailer on a website, the marketing team launched a series of seemingly unrelated URLs and cryptic clues on billboards and in comic book shops across the country. These clues then led fans to even more elaborate sites online. Along the way, active participants who successfully pieced together every hint and puzzle were treated to exclusive stills, theatrical posters, and actual footage from the movie.[36] The campaign's ultimate goal was to generate buzz for the film's release by giving consumers an environment in which to completely immerse themselves.[37] This dedication to using advertising as a means to develop content and create an entertainment experience is one way the Internet and viral marketing is changing the capabilities of advertising.

How do banks use the Internet to do business with customers?   The Internet

has also transformed the way people interact with their financial institutions. The rise of **online banking**—using the Internet rather than visiting a bricks-and-mortar bank to manage finances—has allowed people to do everything from shopping for interest rates to paying bills without ever leaving their houses or buying a postage stamp. That convenience is the biggest advantage of online banking.

Online banking involves using the Internet rather than visiting a bricks-and-mortar bank to manage finances.

Most traditional banks and credit unions have some sort of presence online. Most large national banks, such as TD CanadaTrust, offer their customers services online. Customers may transfer money between accounts, pay bills, download account balances, or make mortgage payments online. Online banking may prove challenging when it comes to making cash deposits. Unless you have direct deposit set up, making cash deposits involves travelling to your local branch or, in the case of Internet-only virtual banks, sending the money through the mail. In addition, most banks charge a fee for online services.

How do banks and businesses protect your personal online information?

Online security is an issue for businesses. The widespread access to information that the Internet affords affects business in a variety of ways. Personal information such as Social Insurance Numbers, credit card numbers, addresses, and passwords are all accessible online. This sensitive information, even when it is secured, can be vulnerable to hackers. Since businesses are the ones who often store this and other types of personal information, the responsibility is on them to take measures to protect consumers' online privacy. It is no coincidence that as the number of people and businesses who trade and store personal information online rises, so does the number of people who are victims of identity theft—the illegal gain and use of personal information. According to statistics from Internet security companies Akamai and Symantec, malicious computer programs originate from more than 190 countries.[38] Its no wonder, then, that Public Safety Canada reports that 77 percent of Canadians are worried about the security of personal information—even though 63 percent still conduct sensitive transactions online and 57 percent store sensitive information on their computers.[39]

The security of online financial transactions presents another challenge. Businesses that receive payments online and banks that provide online banking to customers require **secure Internet connections**, which are Internet protocols (such as Secure Socket Layer) whereby data can be transmitted over the World Wide Web securely—unauthorized persons cannot access the data. With online sites such as eBay and Amazon.com, using the Internet to shop is easier than ever. However, in order to purchase goods and services, many consumers must share credit card information with these retailers over what they hope are secure connections. Some sites, such as PayPal, which is owned by eBay, allow consumers to make payments without sharing their personal information.[40] But this is the exception, not the rule.

While most banks' websites have secure connections for doing online banking, you might still be uncomfortable sending such sensitive information via the Internet. Moreover, while the connection to your bank may be secure, it is still wise to handle any online transactions from a home computer. Accessing your financial records on a public computer—at a library or in an airport lobby—has the potential to leave your personal information accessible to the next person who uses that particular computer, and if it's an unsecured wireless connection, it can be vulnerable to hackers. Banks such as TD CanadaTrust ensure that your transactions are secure and your records are safe by using firewalls, monitoring, and encryption. The bank even has an "online security guarantee."[41]

Although online businesses or businesses with an online component have the most potential for growth and expansion, they are also the most vulnerable to threats such as security breaches and viruses. If you've ever clicked on a banner ad or downloaded a program, you've run the risk of allowing adware or spyware onto your computer. **Adware** is any software application that displays banner ads or pop-up ads while the program is running. At best, this is annoying. At worst, it installs spyware that tracks your personal information and passes it on to a third party without your knowledge. **Spyware** collects data and relays it back to interested persons who wish to commit fraud or identity theft.[42] This can cripple businesses, as hackers can use spyware to steal money, erase valuable information, or even crash an entire company's system. The most insidious spyware can capture keystrokes, thereby stealing passwords and other confidential information, which can grant hackers unlimited access to company networks.[43]

Any business that processes transactions online is at risk of having their customers' credit card information stolen by hackers. Spyware is not the only method that hackers use to obtain private information. **Phishing** is a common way to trick online users into sending their credit card numbers straight to hackers.[44] Suppose you have a chequing account with TD CanadaTrust and you receive an e-mail from them informing you that your online banking account is about to expire. This e-mail requests that you fill out a secure form with your personal information so TD CanadaTrust can reactivate your account. The e-mail has the bank's logo and background, and it includes a link to the secure form to be filled out. You click on the link, which takes you to an online

Secure Internet connections are Internet protocols whereby data can be transmitted over the World Wide Web securely—unauthorized persons cannot access the data.

Adware is any software application that displays banner ads or pop-up ads while the program is running.

Spyware collects data and relays it back to interested persons who wish to commit fraud or identity theft.

Phishing is a common way to trick online users into sending their credit card numbers straight to hackers.

To maintain the security of your online financial records, avoid accessing them from public computers.

Hackers "phish" for private banking information, which they can use to make fraudulent purchases.

form on the bank's website. After completing the form, which asks for your name, address, password, credit card number, and credit card expiration date, you click the Submit button and send all that information to TD CanadaTrust.

Surprise! You've just been phished. That e-mail was not from your bank but from hackers who had broken into the bank's network and copied its logo and e-mail design. The link you clicked took you to a fake website designed to look like an authentic registration form. You just sent your banking information to phishers, who can now use your credit card to make fraudulent purchases in your name. Such identity theft can destroy your credit rating. It also hurts TD CanadaTrust because the bank will have to track and cancel any illegal transactions and issue you a new credit card account.

Banks are not the only businesses that suffer from phishing. Online retailers such as eBay or payment services such as PayPal have been victims of spyware and phishers. This can cost them dearly because many customers no longer trust these websites after being scammed. Businesses that have been hacked often spend thousands of dollars on reclaiming lost information and updating their antivirus programs and security systems to prevent future break-ins. Although these security breaches seem to foretell an unstable future for e-business, they also force online businesses to remain current in their network protection and to take extra precautions to protect consumers. As businesses become more sophisticated and secure, consumers will become more confident and interested in e-business.

The rise of the Internet and, in turn, e-business has brought about revolutionary changes in the business world. E-business has played a key role in the advancement of globalization and has opened up a vast array of opportunities and possibilities in the B2B, B2C, and C2C facets. Although online security and privacy remain challenging issues within the realm of e-business, they are unlikely to hamper this burgeoning area's continued growth in the future.

CHAPTER SYNOPSIS

❶ Describe the functions of a company's chief information officer (CIO) and information technology (IT) department. *(pp. 244–246)*

Information technology (IT) is the design and implementation of computer-based information systems. In many organizational structures, the person responsible for such technology is the **chief information officer (CIO)**. This is typically a position at the same level as the chief financial officer (CFO) of the firm. As **Figure 9.1** shows, the CIO is in charge of information processing,

including systems design and development, data centre operations, and creating policies regarding security and intellectual property. He or she is responsible for updating or replacing the computer systems and the software the company uses. Because technology is spread across all divisions and major functions of a modern business, a CIO requires excellent leadership and organizational skills. The CIO must also manage a budget that balances the benefits of technology against the ever-rising costs of upgrading to the latest systems. In addition, CIOs are involved in creating business and e-business opportunities.

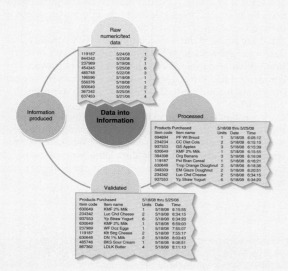

Functions of a CIO

The **IT department** comprises a number of professionals responsible for everything from hardware components and software programs to networking and database strategies. This department is also responsible for security both in response to computer virus attacks and emergency recovery from power outages and system failures. In addition, the department keeps all the computers, printers, and other equipment operational and current. The IT department manages the design of the company's networks and databases where information is stored. The department is also responsible for selecting the appropriate software programs as well as often providing training to employees. Sometimes, IT professionals must also create custom software to bridge the gaps between the products available and the needs of the firm. The IT department also maintains and manages the use of mobile computing throughout the company.

❷ Explain how information technology, information systems, information, and data are interrelated within a business. *(pp. 246–248)*

The terms *data* and *information* are often used interchangeably, but they have different meanings. **Data** are the representations of a fact or idea, which may be a number, a word, an image, or a sound. **Information**, however, is data that have been organized or arranged in a way that makes them useful (see **Figure 9.2**). The extraction of information from raw data is critical to the success of many business enterprises.

Processing Data into Useful Information

Information technology (IT) is the design and implementation of computer-based information systems. The main difference between information technology (IT) and

information systems (IS), or **management information systems (MIS)**, is that MIS is focused on applying IT to solve business and economic problems.

❸ Summarize how major types of hardware, software, and networks are used in business. *(pp. 248–251)*

Although the availability of Internet access enables workers to make decisions and conduct meetings virtually, business travel is still in huge demand. Business travellers, whether they are salespeople or field engineers, no longer need to be out of touch with their workplace or their customers when spending time in cars, airports, and hotels. Cellphones and more fully featured smartphones allow employees to access their e-mail and the Internet from virtually anywhere. Furthermore, smartphones running the Windows Mobile operating system enable users to read Microsoft Word, Excel, and Access files. Projectors and printers are available in mobile sizes as well. Projectors as light as 450 grams (1 pound) make it easy to bring your own complete presentation that is ready to play at any location. Mobile printers are small enough to tuck into a carry-on bag, and they allow users on the go to print documents.

Software packages can help businesses make strategic decisions about the use of resources, the direction of new marketing campaigns, or daily operations. Software can also help with the mechanics of the business world—such as payroll, accounting, and tracking benefits for individual employees.

E-mail and instant messaging aren't the only forms of business communication using modern technology. Other communications technologies frequently used by businesses today include voice over internet protocol (VoIP), remote conferencing, and market technologies and services.

As networks grow and begin to link sites very far apart geographically, **virtual private networks (VPNs)** are often used. A VPN may connect some of its systems by cables that the company owns, but other sections of the network will be joined using the public Internet.

❹ Outline the benefits and risks of technology in the workplace, taking into account safety, creativity, communication, productivity, privacy, and ethics. *(pp. 251–258)*

There are aspects of technology that clearly benefit employees. In rescue operations, robots and robotic assistance have relieved human rescue personnel of dangerous tasks. In automotive plants, robots have taken over most of the very monotonous, unfulfilling work, freeing humans for more creative positions. But some uses of technology in the workplace have brought about difficult changes. As more office discussions take place in e-mails, the chance of misunderstandings and errors starts to rise. Once a worker has access from home to office files, and the office has access to the employees through smartphones or live video conferencing, the workday can extend dramatically.

Electronic monitoring is commonly used to track employees' keystrokes and e-mails, examine their Internet browsing histories, and even monitor their cellphone and instant messaging usage. Camera surveillance can be conducted with recording devices so small that employees do not realize they are being recorded. Used appropriately, these technical tools can help a company eliminate a drain of business resources for personal use. But to some employees, the work environment then begins to feel so monitored that they no longer produce their best work.

Another challenge IT brings to management is security. With so much of the value of a modern business stored in electronic material—whether as documents, software programs, or e-mail files—a company can be vulnerable to hackers. **Hackers** are individuals who gain unauthorized entry into a computer system either to disrupt the operation of the system or to gain access to protected data.

9

⑤ **With regard to e-business, explain what is meant by viral marketing, secure Internet connection, and phishing.**
(p. 258–264)

To get people to notice their advertisements, many marketers are turning to a technique known as **viral marketing**, which involves using social networks, e-mail, and websites to spread the awareness of a particular brand. Essentially, viral marketing is a Web 2.0 version—that is, a more consumer-friendly, interactive, and collaborative type—of old-fashioned word of mouth.

Businesses that receive payments online and banks that provide online banking to customers require **secure Internet connections**, which are Internet protocols (such as Secure Socket Layer) whereby data can be transmitted over the World Wide Web securely—unauthorized persons cannot access the data.

Phishing is a common way to trick online users into sending their credit card numbers straight to hackers.

E-business is all about convenience, but it can become complicated when *tax* and *jurisdiction* issues are taken into consideration. With business-to-consumer e-business, goods could be sold anywhere in the world, making it very difficult or even impossible to comply with the laws of every potential relevant jurisdiction. E-business taxation is a very complex and technical area.

KEY TERMS

adware   *(p. 263)*
business-to-business (B2B)
    transactions   *(p. 258)*
business-to-consumer (B2C)
    transactions   *(p. 259)*
chief information officer
    (CIO)   *(p. 244)*
consumer-to-consumer (C2C)
    transactions   *(p. 260)*
contextual advertising   *(p. 261)*
data   *(p. 246)*
data marts   *(p. 247)*
data mining   *(p. 247)*
data warehouses   *(p. 247)*
database management
    systems (DBMSs)   *(p. 247)*

decision support systems
    (DSSs)   *(p. 246)*
electronic commerce
    (e-commerce)   *(p. 258)*
enterprise resource planning
    (ERP)   *(p. 247)*
executive information systems
    (EISs)   *(p. 246)*
extranet   *(p. 251)*
hackers   *(p. 254)*
information   *(p. 246)*
information systems (IS), or
    management information
    systems (MIS)   *(p. 245)*
information technology (IT)
    (p. 244)

Internet   *(p. 251)*
Internet2   *(p. 251)*
Intranet   *(p. 250)*
IT department   *(p. 245)*
local area networks (LANs)
    (p. 251)
network   *(p. 250)*
online advertising   *(p. 260)*
online banking   *(p. 262)*
pay-per-click (PPC)   *(p. 261)*
*Personal Information
    Protection and Electronic
    Documents Act (PIPEDA)*
    (p. 246)
phishing   *(p. 263)*
protocols   *(p. 251)*

RAID (redundant array of
    independent drives)
    (p. 248)
secure Internet connections
    (p. 263)
spyware   *(p. 263)*
viral marketing   *(p. 261)*
virtual private networks
    (VPNs)   *(p. 251)*
wide-area network (WAN)
    (p. 251)
World Wide Web (WWW)
    (p. 251)
wireless LAN (WLAN)
    (p. 251)

CRITICAL THINKING QUESTIONS

1. How does electronic monitoring impact your life as a student? Should the IT resources of the university or college be monitored? How might the goals of the institution come into conflict with the needs of the students on this issue? What if a student sends a threatening e-mail, should IT notify authorities? Who should judge what is deemed threatening?

2. Think about the difference between data and information. Using the credit card application process as an example, identify and discuss what type of data is supplied to the credit card company and what type of information is generated by the credit card company.

3. Reitmans Company, a fashion retail store, operates more than 950 stores throughout Canada. Consider these three Reitmans management positions: store manager (in charge of day-to-day operations), district manager (in charge of several stores),

and CEO of Reitmans (Canada) Limited (in charge of operations throughout Canada). Identify the information needs of managers at each of these levels.

4. What are some of the ways companies try to protect their data against hackers? What is a firewall? What is encryption? What other things can companies do to protect company data? What does your school do to keep student information confidential? What can you do to protect yourself?

5. Does constant connection to the workplace increase employee productivity or employee frustration? Is having employees work from home beneficial to employers? What are the pros and cons for each? Would you like a job where you work from home? What types of people do you think might prefer to work from home?

APPLICATION EXERCISES

1. **Data Breach!** Visit http://breachalerts.trustedid.com/ and review the recent data breach reports posted on the homepage. Select one of these reports and note relevant information about the breaches, such as the source(s) of data loss, the date(s) of the occurrence, the sizes of loss, and the individuals

or geographic area(s) affected. How did the loss occur? How might it have been prevented?

2. **Meeting Online.** Visit three or four remote conferencing sites such as www.webex.com, www1.gotomeeting.com, www. dimdim.com, or www.webhuddle.com. Do all sites offer

cross-platform meetings (Windows, Mac, etc.)? Which sites offer free meetings? How many participants may be included in each meeting?

3. **Website Comparison.** Review and compare two of the following three company websites: www.walmart.com, www.hp.com, and www.nike.com. Answer these questions:
   a. How easy is it to order merchandise from the website?
   b. How easy is it to change the language from English to French or Chinese?
   c. Can you notice differences in design or approach when you switch languages or go to other country sites?
   d. Do these companies offer links to a company blog, Twitter, Facebook, or other such social media?
   e. As a potential customer, are you satisfied with these sites? Do you think their websites meet the needs of their customers? Why or why not?
   f. Which one did you like using the most? Why?
   g. How might the company website help or hurt business opportunities?

4. **Did the Internet Kill Print?** How has the Internet, with its availability of immediate online news and information, affected the demand for newspapers and other printed materials (such as magazines and textbooks)? Complete a PEST analysis (see Chapter 1) on *Canadian BusinessMagazine*, and then complete a SWOT analysis (see Chapter 6). Discuss the impact of technology on the printing industry—newspapers, magazines, and books.

5. **Identity Theft.** Imagine owning a business and learning that the personal information of your customers has been stolen. What legal trouble would you be in? What could you have done to prevent it? Use the Internet to research the answers to these questions. Several good websites to help get you started include:
   - Royal Canadian Mounted Police at http://www.rcmp-grc.gc.ca/index-eng.htm
   - Department of Public Safety and Emergency Preparedness at http://www.publicsafety.gc.ca/index-eng.aspx
   - Department of Justice at http://www.justice.gc.ca/eng/news-nouv/nr-cp/2007/doc_32178.html
   - Consumers Measures Committee at http://cmcweb.ic.gc.ca/eic/site/cmc-cmc.nsf/eng/fe00091.html.

GLOBAL 500 RESEARCH PROJECT

INSTRUCTIONS

1. Choose a Global 500 company from the *Fortune* magazine's annual rankings at http://money.cnn.com/magazines/fortune/global500/.
2. Research:
   a. Do they have a website? What other social media or sites do they have?
   b. Do they market through these sites? Which ones?
   c. What information do they share on their sites?
   d. Can you shop through their site (e-commerce)? Can you communicate with the company through their site? If so, do you feel comfortable giving your information to the company in this way?
   e. What type of public image are they creating through the technology of the Internet?
   f. Have people posted anything negative about this company on the Internet? If so, what was it? If not, can you locate a positive story or a news article? What does it say? Are these comments consistent with the image the company is trying to make for itself in the digital world?
   g. Locate one piece of information that tells you something about the computer systems this company uses. Do they have global locations that are networked? Are they using an enterprise resource planning (ERP) software? What can you discover about the technology this company uses? Validate your findings by listing the sources you used to gather this information.
3. Prepare a report and submit to your professor.

TEAM TIME

The Winds of Change

Assemble into groups of three. Each member of the group should select one of the following areas:
   a. Business hardware/software/networking
   b. Ethical impact of business technology
   c. Global impact of business technology

PROCESS

Step 1. As a group, determine what innovation in business technology will have the most impact over the next year, five years, and ten years. Once the group has selected a specific innovation, each member will create a short presentation on why that particular technology change will be significant in his or her area.

Step 2. Evaluate the innovation by asking the following:
   - How many businesses will be impacted?
   - How many aspects of business activity will be impacted?
   - How many consumers and/or vendors will be impacted?
   - Will the innovation lead to additional changes in the business in the future?

Step 3. Optional: As a class, compare the group results. Decide which innovation has the most likelihood of coming to fruition. How will it change your career and the world you will be part of in the future?

ETHICS AND RESPONSIBILITY

Computer Hacking: A High Price to Pay

Read the following case study. Then, as a class, discuss the questions that follow.

In 2004, twenty-one-year-old Adam Botbyl and his roommate were driving around in Adam's car with a couple of antennas hanging out the window and a laptop powered up looking for open wireless networks they could access. As they drove past the Lowe's home improvement store, they found one. Lowe's had set it up so that scanners and other devices could connect to its network without cabling. Six months later, Adam Botbyl and his friend Brian Salcedo decided to place a modified program onto Lowe's computer system. When credit card transactions were processed, a copy of the number would be sent to a special file they could use later. The FBI investigated and arrested them before they ever saw a single credit card number. They pleaded guilty and worked with Lowe's to boost its security. Even so, Brian Salcedo was sentenced to nine years in prison, and Adam Botbyl was sentenced to twenty-six months.

Discussion Questions

1. Who holds responsibility for Lowe's customers?
2. How can consumers know their purchases are safe?
3. Were the sentences given to the pair appropriate? Why or why not?

CLOSING CASE

Business Intelligence (BI) Systems at Mark's Work Wearhouse[45]

As a leading Canadian retailer of high-quality casual, business, and work apparel and footwear, Mark's Work Wearhouse has used business intelligence (BI) tools to organize its products and price them more strategically. Generally, BI tools are a type of application software designed to retrieve data from a data warehouse or data mart, analyze the data, and report results. BI software allows management to understand an organization's strengths and weaknesses better and to see the relationship between different data for better decision making and optimal deployment of resources. It plays a key role in an organization's strategic planning.

"We had been using the best planning system known to man, which is Excel," said Dale Trybuck, general manager of merchandise planning at Mark's Calgary headquarters. Mark's found it very difficult to quantify the benefits of proper planning in isolation (separate systems at individual locations). The company was growing at a quick pace, which made tracking and reporting results much more complicated; they needed a corporate-wide approach to merchandise management.

Mark's chose SAS—a leader in business analytics software for retail—to help restructure its merchandising systems and to help sustain the continued expansion of its product line. Mark's had worked with business intelligence tools before, including the implementation of a Web-based reporting tool, but it adopted components of SAS's Merchandise Intelligence suite of products because they would provide Mark's with the capabilities the company's growth was demanding. The new BI system would permit Mark's to get the right products into the right stores at the right times. Mark's would know if there was enough to sell in each store, what was on the shelves in each store, which days had the highest sales volumes in each store, and which items were being sold most frequently and least frequently in each store. It would give Mark's the type of connectivity needed to get very granular details about what items needed to go into each store, based on sales and inventory levels, thereby increasing inventory turnover.

There are large savings because of optimizing inventory, improving inventory practices, and increasing inventory turnover rates. By not having inventory sitting on store shelves for long periods, not being sold, the company saves money. When a company can optimize inventory levels by shipping supplies that are selling (in demand) to the stores that need them (running low on inventory) at the times they are needed (when customers want them), it can increase revenues and decrease expenses and losses.

Companies that effectively transform and optimize their merchandise planning process and focus on customer demand and preferences will be the ones to lead the retail market space. As Mark's Dale Trybuck comments, "With SAS, we'll be able to maximize profitability while continuing our tradition of giving customers a reason to come back to Mark's again and again."

DISCUSSION QUESTIONS

1. How do you think the purchase of such a BI system would benefit a company like Mark's? How do you think the company might save money by implementing such a system? Do you think customer service would improve? Do you think sales might increase due to this improved system? Why or why not?
2. What other companies have used SAS solutions? Visit the SAS website to find out. Choose one other customer, besides Mark's, that SAS has served and summarize what was done and how it helped the company.
3. Who are SAS's major competitors? Using Porter's Five Forces Model (see Chapter 2), analyze the competitive environment for SAS (in Canada as well as globally).

MyBusinessLab **CHAPTER RESOURCES**

MyBusinessLab in an online learning and testing environment that features the perfect study tools to help you master the concepts covered in this chapter. Log in to MyBusinessLab at www.pearsoned.ca/mybusinesslab to test your knowledge of key chapter concepts, participate in simulations modelled on real-world business situations, and explore the following additional practice tools:

- Study Plan
- Audio Chapter Summaries
- Glossary Flashcards
- eText
- BizChat Discussion Boards
- BizSkills Simulations: Technology Direction; E-commerce
- Document Makeover: Order Confirmation Email

Video Case:

To access the Chapter 9 Video Case: ZipCar: IBusiness Technology, see the Activities folder in the Assessment section of MyBusinessLab.

Web Case:

To access the Chapter 9 Web Case, see the Activities folder in the Assessment section of MyBusinessLab

10

Operations Management: Goods and Services

LEARNING OBJECTIVES

After studying this chapter, you should be able to:

1. Explain how operations management produces finished goods that provide utility to consumers. (pp. 272–274)

2. Explain the differences between goods and service operations. (pp. 274–275)

3. Describe mass production, mass customization, flexible manufacturing, and lean production, and the benefits and challenges of each. (pp. 275–276)

4. Explain how technology influences the production process. (pp. 277–279)

5. Summarize the transportation, human, and physical factors involved in choosing a manufacturing location. (pp. 279–282)

6. Explain how facility layout affects efficiency. (pp. 282–283)

7. Explain how a company determines that it requires a supplier, selects a supplier, and strives to manage its supply chain. (pp. 283–285)

8. Describe what value-stream mapping is, and what its benefits are. (pp. 285–287)

9. Explain the benefits of just-in-time (JIT) production and enterprise resource planning (ERP). (pp. 287–289)

10. Describe quality control and how ISO standards help companies produce high-quality goods and services. (pp. 289–292)

OPENING DISCUSSION: SUPPLY CHAIN

McDonald's . . . From Farm to Front Counter

Every item on a McDonald's menu starts with its ingredients; where they come from, how they are processed, and how they are prepared in each restaurant determine the taste and quality of the finished product. According to its 2010 Corporate Responsibility Report, McDonald's focuses on "on every aspect of this journey in order to ensure quality and safety, work toward greater sustainability and continuously create opportunities for people and communities—all while delivering a great value to our customers."[1] Let's examine how it's all done.

Potato Suppliers and Social Responsibility

Farms around the world abide by a set of good agricultural practices (GAP) developed by McDonald's employees, suppliers, and outside consultants to plant, grow, and harvest potatoes. Out of the hundreds of potato varieties that exist, only four types (following strict requirements for size, shape, and consistency) are used

to achieve the perfect appearance and texture of McDonald's fries. Working with the National Potato Council, the Integrated Pest Management Institute, and growers in the United States and Canada, McDonald's developed a comprehensive process to analyze the use of pesticides, fertilizer, and water on potato crops. McDonald's U.S.A. has initiated a plan to reduce pesticide use among potato growers in its supply chain. According to John Keeling of the National Potato Council, "Growers now have a state-of-the-art tool to benchmark their performance and learn from the efficient production of high quality potatoes. McDonald's has been a real leader in identifying a path forward that is truly a win/win for all involved."[2]

The Production Process and Quality Control[3]

Potatoes are brought into the processing plant by conveyor belts, shakers, slides, or flumes (small stainless steel canals that use water to move the potatoes along).

(continued)

A combination of steaming and tumbling peels the potatoes, followed by a rinsing to remove any particles. The potatoes are separated by size, conforming to McDonald's strict length specifications, and inspected for blemishes, which are trimmed away. After being pre-cooked in boiling water for three minutes to soften them, they are then pushed along by water pressure into a series of blades that cuts them into shoestring-style strips. These strips are inspected, blanched in hot water, dried, and inspected again before being partially fried in pure vegetable oil for fifty seconds (at 360°F). They continue along the conveyor to the de-oiler shaker, which does exactly what it sounds like it does. After the fries cool for six minutes, they are transferred to the blast freezer for six chilly minutes (at 14°F). The frozen fries move down the conveyor for another quality inspection and length check before being packaged in bags (3 kg/6 lb. each). The bags are packed six to a carton (case), sealed by a glue press, and then placed on pallets (thirty-six cases to a pallet), dated, shrinkwrapped, and moved on rollers to the freezers. Refrigerated trucks deliver the fries to McDonald's restaurants by truck and are stored in walk-in freezers until use. Fries are then cooked in pure vegetable oil at 360°F temperature for three and a half minutes,

salted, and served crisp, hot, and fresh to customers. Each restaurant could quite possibly use 120 cases of fries every four days. McDonald's developed a next-generation "low oil volume" (LOV) fryer that uses about 40 percent less cooking oil and 4 percent less energy than regular fryers. Electric and gas fryers are available in McDonald's around the world.

Environmental Sustainability[4]

In partnership with Conservation International, McDonald's developed an Environmental Scorecard—measuring energy, water, air, and waste impacts—for potato suppliers to complete each year. For example, one of the restaurant chain's largest suppliers, McCain Foods, began using the scorecard in 2005 to track the use of "biogas" (a wastewater treatment by-product that replaces fossil fuels in plant boilers or to generate "green" electricity). McCain was able to identify opportunities that increased biogas usage from about 65 percent to more than 86 percent (a good thing). As a result, this increase generated enough clean, renewable energy to power a city of about 20 000 people for one year. Using fewer natural resources makes McDonald's supply chain more efficient and cost effective.

DISCUSSION QUESTIONS

1. Do you think McDonald's has the power to prompt changes in standards used around the world (technology, environmental, employment, agricultural)? Why or why not?

2. How do McDonald's operational methods show evidence of quality control? Is it necessary to have so many steps in the production of fries? Why or why not?

3. How do you think McDonald's attempts to keep input costs low while continuing to supply consumers with quality products and services?

OPERATIONS OVERVIEW

Producing Goods and Services

Explain how operations management produces finished goods that provide utility to consumers.

Production is the process of getting a good or service to the customer; it is a series of related activities, with value being added at each stage.

Why is the production of goods and services a critical component of any business?   Every business that produces goods or provides services has a specific production process. **Production** is the process of getting a good or service to the customer; it is a series of related activities, with value being added at each stage. Both businesses that produce manufactured goods ("things")—such as bicycles, automobiles, and computers—and businesses that offer services—such as restaurants, repair shops, and retail stores—require an efficient production process. GE and IBM, for example, are considered manufacturing companies, and both are considered two of the largest, most competitive service operations in the world. All businesses are service operations to some extent.

Companies strive to make a profit by providing goods and services to consumers. To increase their profits and decrease production costs, businesses must find the most efficient production process possible. Increasing global competition, increasing costs of resources such as labour, and changing customer needs are just a few of the issues that require companies to scrutinize the efficiencies of their production process. If a business utilizes a production process that's inefficient or costly, the company might go bankrupt, even if there is demand for its product. Companies that spend too much on production have to raise prices to break even, which can drive consumers away. A cost-effective, efficient, innovative, and flexible production process is crucial to the success of a business. For example, in 1908, the Model T Ford was less expensive than most other cars on the market. However, it still wasn't affordable "for the great multitude,"[5] which was Henry Ford's ultimate goal. The changes that Ford introduced during the production process—division of labour, interchangeable parts, precise speed and motions, and, most famously, the use of an assembly line—allowed the Ford Motor Company to produce an automobile that truly was affordable for a great number of people.

How a company handles the production processes can either help or hurt their chances for success. Swedish furniture manufacturer IKEA is a great example of a company using intelligent production management to enhance its business. What sets IKEA apart from other furniture companies is that it purchases mass quantities of production resources worldwide and most of its products are shipped in flat packs for assembly at the consumer's home, which minimizes storage and transportation costs. Ultimately, these processes result in high-quality products at a low cost.[6]

Is there a difference between production and operations?

Operations management (or **production management**) refers to the organized direction and control of the processes that transform resources (inputs) into finished goods and services (outputs). As shown in **Figure 10.1**, the act of production gives these finished products and services *value*. Whenever a business satisfies a need or want, it creates *value* for the customer. The **value** of a product equals the ratio of the product's benefits to its costs (value = benefits/costs). With

Operations management (or **production management**) refers to the organized direction and control of the processes that transform resources (inputs) into finished goods and services (outputs).

The **value** of a product equals the ratio of the product's benefits to its costs (value = benefits/costs).

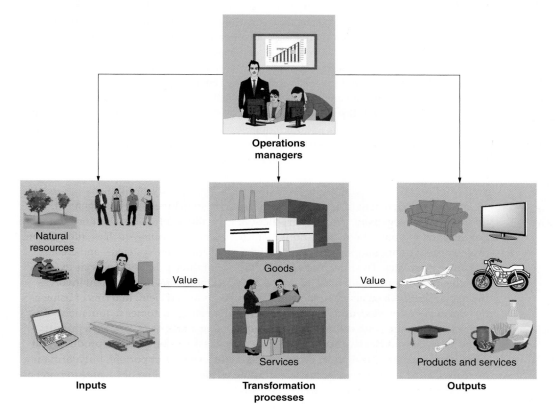

Figure 10.1 The Transformation Process

a high-value product, its benefits far exceed its costs. Businesses that offer the highest-value products gain the most customers and thrive.

Products and services provide businesses with economic results (profits, wages, suppliers) and provide customers with **utility**, which is the power of a product or service to satisfy a human want or need, something of value to the person. There are four types of utility:

1. *Time utility.* The ability of the product or service to satisfy a human want because of the time at which it is made available (e.g., holiday decorations, summer garden supplies).
2. *Place utility.* The ability of the product or service to satisfy a human want because of where it is made available (e.g., a grocery store right down the street).
3. *Form utility.* The ability of the product or service to satisfy a human want because of its form; this requires raw materials to be transformed into a finished product (e.g., it would be difficult for you to form rubber into tires for your car).
4. *Ownership utility.* The ability of the product or service to satisfy a human want during its consumption or use (e.g., a lawn mower that is yours, so you don't have to borrow or rent one each time the lawn needs to be cut).

To buy groceries, for example, most of us go to the grocery store. As a customer, you expect the store to be open at convenient times (time utility), be conveniently located (place utility), offer quality food products (form utility) that you can take home to eat (ownership utility), all at reasonable prices (value). As a consumer, you affect the operations process because the manager sets the store hours to meet customer requirements, orders food supplies to meet customer demand, and so on.

> **Utility** is the power of a product to satisfy a human want or need, something of value to the person.

Operations Management

> Explain the differences between goods and service operations.

How do firms manage and control the creation of products and services?
The business plans and forecasts developed by top managers guide operations planning. Planning and controlling operation processes are critical to business success. There are four decisions that must be made in **operations planning**: 1) the type of production process, 2) the facility location, 3) the facility layout, and 4) resource planning. To ensure that a product provides utility, production managers must successfully develop and carry out a **production plan**, which helps ensure a smoothly run operations process. **Operations managers** are responsible for managing and supervising all the activities that occur when transforming resources into goods or services, such as setting schedules, making buying decisions, and overseeing quality control. Managers who plan effectively are able to increase productivity, reduce costs, and improve customer satisfaction.

Operations control means that managers check to ensure that production decisions are being implemented. If schedules or quality standards are not being met, managers need to take corrective action. Through operations management—controlling production processes—managers can ensure schedules are met and production goals are fulfilled, in both quality and quantity. We'll examine these concepts later in this chapter.

> **Operations planning** includes four steps: 1) the type of production process, 2) the facility location, 3) the facility layout, and 4) resource planning.

> A **production plan** that is well developed and efficiently executed ensures a smoothly run operations process and a product that provides utility.

> **Operations managers** are responsible for managing and supervising all the activities that occur when transforming resources into goods or services, such as setting schedules, making buying decisions, and overseeing quality control.

What is meant by "a company must be effective" to stay in business?
Operations management includes forecasting, purchasing, inventory management, information management, production scheduling, quality control, distribution, and more. For instance, in your school, operations management takes inputs—such as information, professors, students, supplies, buildings, offices, and computer systems—and creates outputs—graduates. The operations function is one of three primary functions of organizations; the other two are marketing and finance. Operations management involves the responsibility of ensuring that business operations are efficient, in terms of using as few resources as needed, and effective, in terms of meeting customer requirements. In operations management, **efficiency** means completing a task or producing a product at the lowest cost. **Effectiveness** means completing tasks and producing products that create the greatest value. Both effectiveness and efficiency are important, but a firm may produce a good at the lowest cost, thereby being efficient, but if no one wants to purchase that good, the firm will not be effective and won't be in business.

> **Efficiency** means completing a task or producing a product at the lowest cost.

> **Effectiveness** means completing tasks and producing products that create the greatest value.

What are the differences between service and manufacturing operations?
Both service and manufacturing operations transform raw materials (inputs) into finished

products (outputs), but in service operations the outputs are people with their needs met and possessions serviced. Goods are produced; services are performed. There are three areas where services differ from goods:

1. *Services are intangible.* Goods are tangible—they have a physical form and can be seen, touched, and handled—while services can only be experienced because they do not have a physical form.
2. *Services are unstorable.* Goods can be stored in inventory, but services are consumed when they are produced. Trash collection, child care, or mail services cannot be produced ahead of time and then stored for high-demand periods.
3. *Services are more customizable than goods.* Each person receives service customized for his or her specific needs.

A useful way of classifying services is to determine the degree to which the customer is involved in the production system. **High-contact service processes** require the customer to be present, such as a public transit system, a hair salon, or an accountant. Companies offering high-contact services, where the customer is present, must ensure their locations are clean and inviting. **Low-contact service processes** do not require the customer to be present, such as a utility company, the chequing processes at a bank, or an auto-repair shop. Since customers are not present while the service is occurring, the attractiveness and atmosphere of the location are not of much concern.

There are some inherent differences between the industrial sector and the service sector. Service providers have more contact with their customers than manufacturers do. In addition, services are usually customized to satisfy the specific needs of a customer. For example, a house painter applies the colours chosen by the customer, and a doctor treats each patient's specific symptoms. However, despite these differences, the ultimate goal of providing a quality product in a cost-efficient manner is similar to manufacturers and service providers.

OPERATIONS PLANNING
The Production Process

What types of production processes are usually used by businesses?   Businesses can use several types of production processes. The type chosen depends on the business and what types of goods or services it produces. The most common types of production processes and techniques include the following:

- mass production
- mass customization
- flexible manufacturing
- lean production

The production process plays a major role in determining the profitability of a business. Efficiency and low production costs are essential in successfully producing any product. Let's examine each type of production process in detail.

How are large quantities of goods produced?   The method of producing large quantities of goods at a low cost is called **mass production**. This method relies on machines and automated assembly lines to mass-produce goods that are identical and adhere to certain standards of quality. Mass-produced goods are usually manufactured along an **assembly line** (or **production line**), in which partially complete products are moved from one worker to the next on a conveyor belt.

The cost to run an assembly line is kept low because machines do the majority of the work and the labourers don't need to be especially skilled to perform their repetitive tasks. This method also cuts down on production time, allowing a large quantity of goods to be produced very quickly. Because machinery is the main component, risk of human error is virtually eliminated. A major disadvantage, however, is that mass production is inflexible. After a production line is established, it's very difficult to change or alter the process if an unexpected problem occurs.

High-contact service processes require the customer to be present, such as a public transit system, a hair salon, or an accountant.

Low-contact service processes do not require the customer to be present, such as a utility company, the chequing processes at a bank, or an auto-repair shop.

3
Describe mass production, mass customization, flexible manufacturing, and lean production, and the benefits of each.

10

Mass production is a method of producing large quantities of goods at a low cost and relies on machines and automated assembly lines to mass-produce goods that are identical and adhere to certain standards of quality.

An **assembly line** (or **production line**) is used to move partially complete products from one worker to the next on a conveyor belt.

Mass customization combines the low unit cost of mass production processes with the flexibility of producing goods or services tailored to meet individual customer's needs.

A **flexible manufacturing system (FMS)** uses one central computer to link together several machines that can process different part types simultaneously.

Can product customization be done with mass production?
When mass production was first implemented, if any customization of product design was desired, the process had to be stopped or slowed down to do so in small batches. With advances in technology, customization is now accessible and affordable to a wide variety of markets. **Mass customization** combines the low unit cost of mass production processes with the flexibility of producing goods or services tailored to meet individual customer's needs. More and more manufacturers are learning to customize their products. For example, Dell permits customers to customize their computer design (i.e., laptop colour) and specifications (i.e., hard drive space) online when ordering new computer systems.[7] At Walmart Photo Centres, you can not only customize your photo prints with borders and text but also purchase calendars, mugs, or photo albums that feature your photos in the style and layout of your choice.[8] You can even order personalized M&Ms.[9]

How is mass customization achieved?
A solution to the rigid system of mass production is *flexible* production, also known as a **flexible manufacturing system (FMS)**. An FMS uses one central computer to link together several machines that can process different part types simultaneously. Unlike a mass production system, an FMS can adapt to changes in schedules and product specifications. There are four components to a flexible manufacturing system: processing machines, a material-handling system, a central computer, and human labour.[10]

A flexible manufacturing system includes four components: processing machines, a material-handling system, a central computer, and human labour.

Can mass customization be used in service industries?
The technologies of mass customization have also enabled many service-based organizations—such as the fast-food industry—to meet the individual needs of their customers. When you think about Burger King, McDonald's, and Wendy's, for example, realize that they are using a mass customization process every time you choose a specific drink or side dish with your order or even a certain salad dressing. The hospitality industry is also enhancing customer service through mass customization. Hotel chains note unique habits, likes, and dislikes of each guest in their database, so that the next time the same guest visits one of the hotel chain's locations, staff retrieves these preferences to provide a more individualized, customized service. For example, a guest may have his or her favourite newspaper waiting for them in the room or have non-allergenic pillows on the bed. Hotel staff seems to anticipate a customer's every need. The result of this type of customized program at the Ritz Carlton Hotel, for instance, has shown a 23 percent increase in guest retention.[11]

What type of production focuses on efficiency?
Although efficiency has always been a concern, the success of lean production has made efficiency a primary focus for many companies. **Lean production** is a set of principles concerned with reducing waste and improving flow that evolved from the original Toyota Production System (TPS) first used in Japan in the 1980s. Its objective is to focus all resources and energies into producing products and services with value-added characteristics (utility to the consumer) while eliminating activities that are of no value.[12] Lean production can be used in goods- or service-producing companies to eliminate wasteful overproduction, unnecessary wait time, needless transportation, excess inventory, superfluous motion, redundant overprocessing, and careless defective units.

Lean production is a set of principles concerned with reducing waste and improving flow that evolved from the original Toyota Production System (TPS) first used in Japan in the 1980s.

Technology in the Production Process

What is the role of technology in the production process?   With thousands of goods to produce at a given time, you might guess that technology plays an inte-

④
Explain how technology influences the production process.

gral role in facilitating the flow of any production process. When managed efficiently, the technological aspect of a production process should lead to increases in production and reductions in costs. Technology may also improve the quality and increase the variety of products, which influences the customer's buying decisions. Customers are more likely to buy a product that is not only low-priced compared to other similar products, but also of high quality and readily available in many varieties. It is essential for businesses in today's globally competitive environment to be up-to-date on new technologies that can improve any or all aspects of the production process.

Robots play a big part in automobile manufacturing, but they are also used to weld, paint, assemble, package, inspect, and test many other types of products.

What has helped automate the production process?   Humans are sometimes at a disadvantage when it comes to performing a task repetitively for many hours and with great precision and accuracy. This is where robots come in; an industrial robot is any device that performs automatically, typically completing repetitive tasks.[13] Not only can robots work around the clock tirelessly, and with accuracy, but they can also work in potentially hazardous conditions, thereby protecting human workers from dangerous environments.

Robots offer consistency in reducing production costs, raising productivity, and producing high-quality products. Industrial robots may take away some jobs, but they also create many new jobs for technicians and engineers. Companies that can effectively apply robotic technology in their production process are more likely to gain an economic advantage in the global marketplace.

How has technology improved the design process?   **Computer-aided design (CAD)** refers to the use of a computer to create two-dimensional or three-dimensional models of physical parts. With CAD systems, the models displayed onscreen can be modified in size or shape, viewed internally, and rotated on any axis. CAD also enables testing of a part by simulating real-world environments. CAD, however, cannot design a model of a product on its own. A designer must first translate the design into a geometri-

Computer-aided design (CAD) refers to the use of a computer to create two-dimensional or three-dimensional models of physical parts.

10

cal model for the CAD system to display. Once the model data are received, the CAD system provides the designer with tools and a flexible environment. By programming a simple design change into the CAD system, a manufacturer can produce custom-designed products such as clothing and cars without incurring higher costs. CAD is not only used to design smaller products; it can also be used to design houses, machinery, tools, and commercial structures.

Some manufacturing processes that are more complicated, such as those for motor vehicles, airplanes, and ships, need more than one CAD program to design and incorporate all the different model parts. For instance, the design of a ship may require one CAD application for the steel structure and another CAD program for the propeller. A disadvantage to this method is that it requires knowledge of all the different software applications

CAD uses computer technology for the design of objects in two or three dimensions.

used as well as knowledge of how to integrate them in the end. On the other hand, the Boeing Company's 757 model is a good example of how integration can be achieved. Because the 757 model is composed of parts from fifty different firms, Boeing's CAD system effectively integrates all the parts, ensuring a precise fit. This system then effectively reduces the number of prototypes needed and the working hours for assembly.[14]

Computer-aided manufacturing (CAM) uses the design data to control the machinery used in the manufacturing process.

How is CAD information incorporated into the manufacturing process?   Once a design is approved, **computer-aided manufacturing (CAM)** uses the design data to control the machinery used in the manufacturing process. The integration of the CAD and CAM systems with the various aspects of a firm's production process is referred to as *simultaneous engineering*. Ford Motor Company's engine division, for example, successfully integrated all its production and design systems into one database that could be accessed by PCs and workstations of employees and suppliers involved with design and production.[15] This type of facilitated communication is a huge benefit for firms with complex systems. One of the main disadvantages of using CAD/CAM systems is that they require considerable time and investment to set up and to learn the necessary software, hardware, communications, and integration.

Computer-integrated manufacturing (CIM) combines design and manufacturing functions with other functions such as order taking, shipment, and billing.

Can an entire facility be automated?   Yes, and **computer-integrated manufacturing (CIM)** takes it even further by combining design and manufacturing functions with other functions such as order taking, shipment, and billing. For example, printing company VistaPrint uses CIM not only to manufacture its products but also to help customers create and place orders for custom-designed business cards, brochures, and T-shirts. Using CIM, the company has expanded its business and is able to serve more customers while continuing to offer affordable prices.[16]

What effect has automation had on the production process?   CAD, CAM, and CIM have dramatically improved the process of producing goods by reducing the time between design and manufacturing, thus making a sizable impact on productivity. These systems have also increased the scope of automated machinery usage in the production process. Through the rapid pace of technological advancement, the use of CAD, CAM, and CIM is not limited to large mass-production facilities; they are entering smaller companies as well.

BizChat

Explore on MyBusinessLab

Technology: Too Much of a Good Thing?

In 1995, the new Denver International Airport boasted a fully automated baggage-handling system. The technology, however, turned out to be too much of a good thing. The system was designed to move luggage along an automated track between airport terminals and baggage-claim areas, some of which were as far as 1 mile (1.6 kilometres) apart in the large airport. A centralized computer system would control the entire operation, eliminating the need for human baggage handlers to move the baggage physically from one point to another. But after ten years of misplaced luggage, glitches in the system, and soaring maintenance costs, the error-prone system was finally shut down. In 2005, the only airline ever to use the system, United Airlines, went back to using baggage handlers to complete the tasks previously handled by the automated system. In a test run before the switch was made, human baggage handlers beat the automated system's error rate handily. With the help of mobile devices, such as handheld scanners, United Airlines is now able to track luggage better than the automated system ever could. In some cases, a little technology goes a long way.

Discussion Questions

1. As a whole, do you think technology plays a positive or negative role in our society? Why?
2. In what ways can technology make you more productive? Less productive?
3. How long do you think you could live comfortably without a cellphone? An MP3 player? A laptop/PC? Access to the Internet?

How has social networking affected production?   Social media capabilities enable consumers to influence directly what products and services companies bring to market. They also permit customers and potential customers to give companies instant feedback, which enables companies to gather market statistics and utilize consumer feedback to enhance processes in the hopes of obtaining greater profits. For example, Adidas created Mi Adidas, which is a custom design extension of its product line. It has a company Twitter account (Miadidas) and blog (Adidas Group), as well as an interactive website that helps announce and discuss new styles.[17] Social media helps Adidas to better understand which product features are most attractive to customers and to collect information that will help it make future product decisions.

Best Buy Canada's Community page on its website invites customers and potential customers to join in blog discussions and forums about brands and products. It also provides online support from its Geek Squad, and includes some common troubleshooting Q&As. Twelpforce Best Buy (Twitter) is a collective force of Best Buy technology pros offering technical advice in Tweet form.[18] Starbucks has a MyStarbucks-Ideas site and Dell has an IdeaStorm site, where they invite customers to share product development ideas.[19] Third-party sites, such as Engadget web magazine, have been running "How Would You Change or Improve" topics that give users a place to voice their insights and suggestions about products.[20] The Internet and social media have created a virtually new world of opportunities.

Facility Location Planning

What factors must be considered when determining the location of facilities?   The location of a factory, office, or retail business affects its production costs and flexibility, sound location planning is crucial. In goods-producing operations, facility location decisions are influenced by the availability and proximity of raw materials, transportation costs, labour availability, physical factors such as electrical power, water, and communication capabilities, local regulations and taxes, and community living conditions. In low-contact service-producing operations, facilities can be located near resource supplies, labour, or transportation outlets. In high-contact service-producing operations, facilities must be located near customers. For example, businesses such as restaurants, supermarkets, and hair salons choose their locations based on their *proximity to market;* they need to be close to their potential customer base. A restaurant easily visible to passing motorists and pedestrians has more of an advantage in attracting business than a restaurant tucked away in a remote part of town where few people visit.

What are the transportation factors a company must consider?   Transportation costs are one of the major expenses that many manufacturing companies must consider. In fact, transportation costs for supplies coming in and goods going out can

⑤
Summarize the transportation, human, and physical factors involved in choosing a manufacturing location.

top10

Critical Decisions for Operations Management

1. Product and service design
2. Location selection
3. Process and layout design
4. Capacity decisions
5. Aggregate planning (forecast demand, production, and capacity strategies)
6. Scheduling decisions
7. Human resources
8. Quality strategy
9. Inventory decisions
10. Preventative maintenance

Source: Reva Wibowo, "10 Strategic Operations Management Critical Decisions," *associatedcontent .com*, November 7, 2008, http:// www.associatedcontent.com/article/ 1144036/10_strategic_operations_ management.html?cat=3, Accessed May 17, 2011.

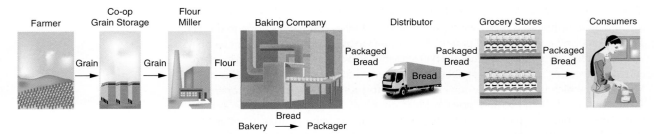

Figure 10.2 Supply Chain for Bread

be as much as five times the costs of operating a production facility.[21] Therefore, locating a facility with easy access to natural resources or suppliers helps a business keep transportation costs low. Many automotive companies outsource their transportation systems to logistics companies that plan and execute this complex operation through logistics networks.

Transportation systems become more complex and costly when a company's supply chain is global. A **supply chain** is the sequence of organizations—their facilities and activities—that are involved in producing (right from the raw materials) and delivering (all the way to the consumer) a good or service. Supply chain facilities include warehouses, factories, processing centres, office, distribution centres, and retail outlets (see **Figure 10.2**). For example, in October 2006, CNH (Case New Holland) Global N.V., a top manufacturer of agricultural and construction equipment, hired the software company Oracle as part of its plan to help the company gain control of spiralling transportation costs.[22] Previously, CNH had outsourced its transportation operations, but then the company realized it could significantly lower costs if the transportation system was operated in-house. With the help of the software application Oracle Transportation Management, CNH was able to efficiently plan and control its manufacturing cycles, manage and adjust for unexpected supply chain events, and help customers know when a product left the factory and when it would reach the end user. Global companies such as CNH that learn how to reduce transportation costs, manage transportation processes more efficiently, and improve customer service are more likely to have a competitive edge over other large-scale companies that have less efficient and more costly transportation operations.

Just as with technology, labour, and material expenses, transportation costs can only be limited to a certain point before they start to affect a business negatively. Businesses look to different transportation methods when receiving materials from suppliers and delivering orders to customers. A business might rely on one method of transportation or a combination of methods. Each type of transportation comes with its advantages and disadvantages.

- The most common transportation mode used by suppliers and businesses is *road transport.* Not only is this method cheaper than other transportation modes, the delivery time is relatively quick, and the goods can be tracked easily by communicating with the driver. This method is especially ideal for delivering perishable goods such as fresh fruit and vegetables. The disadvantages of transporting by road include possible damage to goods from rough driving, delays due to heavy traffic or bad weather, the effects of high gas prices, and vehicle breakdowns or accidents.
- Another cost-effective transportation mode is *rail transport*, which may be the choice mode for delivering heavy goods such as coal or steel. Railroads provide a quick and safe mode of transportation. However, rail schedules may be inflexible and wrought with unexpected delays. Some areas may not be close to a rail station either, meaning longer delivery times and higher costs due to additional forms of transportation to and from the rail station.

A **supply chain** is the sequence of organizations—their facilities and activities—that are involved in producing (right from the raw materials) and delivering (all the way to the consumer) a good or service.

Decision-Making Mini-Simulation: Supply Chain. Located in MyBusinessLab.

- When businesses receive supplies from abroad or when they export goods to foreign markets, *sea transportation* is usually the preferred mode for heavy, bulky goods such as stone slabs. Sea tankers are also used to carry goods such as oil and coal. Transportation by water naturally takes more time, entails higher costs, and is subject to delays from bad weather.

- Another transportation option for companies with distant suppliers and customers is *air transport*. Although this option may not be ideal for huge or bulky goods, businesses that want to transport fragile goods are likely to use transportation by air as opposed to land. The rapid delivery time also improves service, satisfying customers who are in a rush. This method is usually the most costly. Like other transportation modes, it can be affected by bad weather, which can cause flights to be cancelled or delayed.

- Advantages of using *pipeline* as a transportation mode include its low cost, but disadvantages include slow speed and the fact that not many products can travel by pipeline.

What else affects location selection?

The second consideration when deciding on a location for production is the **human factor**, which refers to how the location decision affects the people in a surrounding community and vice versa. Companies need to hire employees to maintain their operations, but they also need to be aware of how their presence affects the community overall. The human factor has three separate, though interrelated, components:

- *Labour availability.* Seeking skilled workers is only part of the decision-making process. Many businesses need to find a workforce that they can afford financially as well. One of the reasons some corporations send their manufacturing operations outside Canada is because those countries contain highly skilled workers who require lower wages than their Canadian counterparts. India is the number-one destination for outsourced high-tech labour because it offers an experienced, skilled, and affordable labour pool.[23]

- *Living conditions.* On the one hand, a business brings opportunities to citizens of a community by creating jobs and a higher standard of living. Similarly, many businesses seek out areas where the quality of life is already high (good schools, pleasant weather, low crime rates, etc.) before settling on a location. Some social entrepreneurs might take it upon themselves to locate their businesses in an impoverished area to revitalize the local economy. Environmentally aware politicians advocate "green collar" jobs precisely for their ability to rejuvenate economically depressed communities. Conversely, a business could also have negative effects on the surrounding area. Some corporations have been accused of worsening a community's living conditions by exploiting workers or polluting the environment.

- *Laws and regulations.* To try to maintain a balance between business and community interests, governments have created many laws and regulations to protect individuals and the environment. These may vary from province to province, and from one country to another; companies need to understand which business practice laws affect their business operations, and then determine whether the location is right for the company.

What are the physical factors a company must consider?

When selecting a location for production, a company must also consider physical factors such as hazardous-waste disposal and supply of utilities. These factors are often determined by local ordinances that may vary from province to province—and even from city to city. The **utility supply** refers to the availability of public infrastructure services such as power, water, and communications. For example, a company establishing a large facility—like a bottling plant or a warehouse—wouldn't want to situate it in a remote location with little public infrastructure, even if the land is cheap. Because such a large facility requires ample amounts of electricity or running water to operate properly, the cost to establish this infrastructure could be enormous. Moreover, locating manufacturing operations in an area where easy access to these utilities and resources is inexpensive greatly reduces costs. Another common

---

The **human factor** refers to how the location decision affects the people in a surrounding community and vice versa.

top10

Supply Chain Innovations of All-Time

1. The Toyota Production System
2. P & G's Continuous Replenishment
3. The Ocean Shipping Container
4. Economic Order Quantity (EOQ)
5. The Ford Assembly Line
6. The Universal Product Code
7. The FedEx Tracking System
8. Distribution Requirements Planning (DRP)
9. 3M's Transportation Load Control Center
10. Taylorism (Frederick Taylor)

Source: Dan Gilmore, "The Top 10 Supply Chain Innovations of All-Time," *SupplyChainDigest.com*, December 3 2010, http://www.scdigest.com/ASSETS/FIRSTTHOUGHTS/10-12-03.php?cid=3973, Accessed May 17, 2011.

The **utility supply** refers to the availability of public infrastructure services such as power, water, and communications.

public utility—waste management—is also essential for business operations. Just as being "off the grid" wouldn't make much sense in terms of selecting a business location, a remote location would also render waste disposal and treatment difficult.

Knowing how to handle hazardous waste is essential. Regardless of the type of business, understanding how to dispose of unwanted material—and the regulations involved—is an important factor to consider when selecting a location. Even everyday materials such as paint and cleaning fluids are considered hazardous waste and must be disposed of properly.[24] Many businesses, as part of their day-to-day operations, create large amounts of hazardous waste. The proper disposal of this waste has ramifications on a business's immediate vicinity. Each municipality, province, and other local government will have its own guidelines and procedures for dealing with hazardous waste. Responsible organizations must be aware of the disposal options available in their areas.

Taking transportation, human, and physical factors into consideration, businesses ultimately choose a manufacturing location in order to remain competitive. These decisions are influenced and measured by their efficiency and practicality.

Facility Layout and Capacity Planning

 Explain how facility layout affects efficiency.

Facility layout is the physical arrangement of resources, the people in the production process, and how they interact.

Why is facility layout important? A production manager must be responsible for determining the layout of a facility. **Facility layout** is the physical arrangement of resources, the people in the production process, and how they interact. The design of a facility's layout is important to maximize efficiency and satisfy employees' needs. It involves everything from the arrangement of cubicles in an office space to the position of robotic arms in an automobile-manufacturing plant. When determining or renovating a facility layout for maximum effectiveness and efficiency, business owners must also consider many operational factors. For example, facilities should be designed so that they can be easily adjusted to meet changing production needs. Having to undergo extensive renovations or completely relocate as a company's operations change or expand can be a costly endeavour; therefore, managers need to be prepared to factor possible growth at the planning stage. Additionally, the facility layout should be in accordance with Canada's *Occupational Health and Safety Act* and *Regulations* to ensure worker safety. Service organizations are concerned with how the layout affects customers' behaviour, while manufacturers are concerned with efficient processes that will reduce costs.

Capacity is the amount of a product or service that a company can produce under normal working conditions in a given time period.

How big should the facility be? **Capacity** is the amount of a product or service that a company can produce under normal working conditions in a given time period. Capacity is dependent upon the size of the facility, the number of workers employed, and the technology and processes used. When managers plan for capacity, they must consider that if capacity is too small to meet demand, the company will have to turn customers away and forgo profits; yet if capacity is too large, the firm wastes money by having

employees, space, and equipment underutilized. For manufacturing facilities, capacity is determined by the extent of the production processes, whereas for service facilities, capacity is determined by peak demand and fluctuations in demand.

How does facility layout affect production?   A facility layout should be able to handle materials orderly and efficiently to ensure a smooth flow of production. To do so, designers need to utilize available space effectively. Warehouses, for instance, need to have enough space to stack goods, and products need to be easily accessible for workers using equipment such as forklifts and conveyor belts.

The distance that a work-in-progress must travel within a facility must also be taken into account. This is not only true for the production of goods, but in service industries as well. For example, the layout of a fast-food restaurant can help the employees involved in the different parts of the process—preparing food and serving customers—to work in a more integrated fashion.

What are the most common types of facility layouts?   Different manufacturing processes require different types of facility layouts based on the following four common types:

- **Process layout** (or **job-shop** or **functional layout**) is a format in which workers who perform similar tasks on similar equipment are grouped together. The partially assembled product travels from one work area to the next, but not necessarily to all work areas, for workers to perform a particular process on the product. Each work area is one step in the production process. For example, all painting of parts would be done in one work area, all welding of parts in another, and all assembling in yet another, but not all products require welding so they would skip over that functional area.
- **Product layout** (or **flow-shop layout**) arranges equipment or work processes according to the progressive steps by which the product is made. It is used mostly when large quantities of a product must be produced. Products move along a straight line (assembly line), with the workstations arranged along the line. Production of toilet paper, shoes, chemicals, and candy, as well as services such as car washes, all use product layout. With **fixed-position layout**, the product stays in one place (fixed position) while workers and machinery move to the product to complete tasks rather than vice versa. Fixed-position layouts are ideal for manufacturing large items, such as ships, airplanes, and modular homes. Examples of fixed-position layouts in the services might include house cleaning, landscaping, and interior painting.
- **Cellular layout** (or **group technology layout**) combines aspects from both product and fixed-position layout: workers are arranged into self-contained, stand-alone production units (or *cells* of small work teams). Each cell completes all tasks necessary to complete a manufacturing order. Each team is equipped with the machinery, parts, and tools necessary to produce a product from start to finish. Clothing manufacturing often use cellular layout.

Resource Planning

How are materials acquired?   One of the challenges in production planning is to ensure that the resources needed, such as raw materials, parts, and equipment, will be available at strategic moments in the production process. Resource planners create a **bill of material** for each product in the production process that lists the items and the number of each required to make that specific product. **Purchasing** (or **procurement**) is the task of buying the materials and services needed in the production process. Production managers need to find reliable suppliers who can provide high-quality resources at the best price.

What is a make-or-buy decision?   When starting the production process, one of the first decisions that must be made is a **make-or-buy decision**: deciding what needs to be manufactured and what needs to be purchased from outside suppliers. If a company plans to manufacture a product that will carry both the company's name and reputation, it has to decide if it will make the entire product in-house or if the product will be assembled from

Process layout (or **job-shop** or **functional layout**) is a format in which workers who perform similar tasks on similar equipment are grouped together.

Product layout (or **flow-shop layout**) is one in which equipment or work processes are arranged according to the progressive steps by which the product is made. It is used mostly when large quantities of a product must be produced.

Fixed-position layout is a format in which the product stays in one place (fixed position) while workers and machinery move to the product to complete tasks rather than vice versa.

Cellular layout (or **group technology layout**) combines aspects from both product and fixed-position layout: workers are arranged into self-contained, stand-alone production units (or *cells* of small work teams).

Explain how a company determines that it requires a supplier, selects a supplier, and strives to manage its supply chain.

A **bill of material** lists the items and the number of each required to make that specific product.

Purchasing (or **procurement**) is the task of buying the materials and services needed in the production process.

A **make-or-buy decision** decides what needs to be manufactured and what needs to be purchased from outside suppliers.

a combination of parts manufactured in-house and other parts purchased from suppliers. It is not always necessary for a company to make everything in-house, so how does a company decide what to make and what to buy? A company needs to consider factors such as cost and quality. If it is less expensive to outsource the production of certain parts elsewhere, that may be the best decision. However, it is important that a manager can trust the quality of any parts produced elsewhere and that appropriate quantities are delivered in a timely manner.

How does a company decide which suppliers to use?

Selecting suppliers is a significantly less complicated task than making a make-or-buy decision, but that doesn't mean that deciding which suppliers to use should be made with any less consideration. After all, establishing a business relationship with a supplier is like entering into a partnership. Customers don't see a product that is supplied by one company with parts provided by different suppliers; they see a total product. Customers will hold the company responsible even if an individual supplier is to blame for making a faulty part or missing a deadline and causing a delay. For example, Mattel had to recall close to one million toys because its supplier in China had coated the toys in lead paint. Mattel was later fined $US2.3 million by the Consumer Product Safety Commission.[25] Such recalls can be costly and damaging to a company's reputation. So having a good supplier that meets the company's needs and cares about the company's customers as if they were its own is an invaluable asset.

A company's first step in finding suppliers involves clearly defining and understanding its needs so that it can find suppliers that truly fit its requirements. Cost is always a factor, but it should never be the sole factor. For example, if several potential suppliers offer similar products with similar prices, other factors will come into play: the company may need a supplier that is reliable or one that is fast. Likewise, one supplier may offer a part for significantly less, but of such poor quality that later repairs or recalls would end up costing the company more than the cost of quality parts; its reputation would also be affected. Understanding these needs before choosing a supplier will make the process easier and more beneficial in the end.

There's a vast collection of resources designed to help businesses connect with suppliers. These resources include the Better Business Bureau, the local chamber of commerce, exhibitions, trade magazines, the Internet, and old-fashioned recommendations from friends and business acquaintances. The challenge is in finding the best people for the job and determining which of those suppliers offer optimal solutions for production needs.

Supply chain management involves the logistics of obtaining all the necessary inputs that go into a production process (*inbound logistics*), managing the actual production process (*materials handling* and *operations control*), and managing the physical distribution (or *outbound logistics*) of getting the proper quantities of produced products to customers when and where they want them. When applying supply chain management, companies are trying to reduce costs, increase flexibility and speed, and improve quality and customer service. It is crucial that companies develop tighter bonds with suppliers, as many suppliers play an important role in supporting the operations of their business customers, offering suggestions for reducing costs, and even contributing to new product design.

E-procurement is an online purchasing system connecting companies and their business processes directly with suppliers while managing all interactions between them. For example, authorized Canada Post employees have access to an e-procurement system, which gives them a single portal for the acquisition of goods and services from suppliers.[26]

Supply chain management involves the logistics of obtaining all the necessary inputs that go into a production process (*inbound logistics*), managing the actual production process (*materials handling* and *operations control*), and managing the physical distribution (or *outbound logistics*) of getting the proper quantities of produced products to customers when and where they want them.

E-procurement is an online purchasing system connecting companies and their business processes directly with suppliers while managing all interactions between them.

Better Business **Better World**

Ethical Standards for Suppliers

Many multinational companies now demand that their suppliers enforce legal and ethical business practices before they will order from them. While the notion of what is ethical varies around the globe, as do the laws, multinational companies in North America and other developed nations are putting pressure on global suppliers to do business legally and ethically or forgo the business relationship.

According to Walmart's "Standards for Suppliers," the chain has "fundamental expectations from its suppliers regarding their activities in relation to the workers producing merchandise for sale by Walmart and the impact of their manufacturing practices on the environment."[27] Standards include, but are not limited to:

- abiding by the law
- not employing workers through forced or involuntary labour practices
- hiring and compensating employees in accordance with labour laws
- not giving gifts or entertainment to Walmart associates
- not using bribery or corruption in dealings with public officials or individuals in the private sector
- adhering to local environmental laws for air emissions, water discharges, toxic substances and hazardous waste disposal

In the "Ethical Standards" section of The Home Depot's *Supplier Reference Manual*, it states that the company "expects that all suppliers will abide by all applicable local laws, rules and regulations,"[28] as well as adhere to company's ethical standards. The *Supplier Reference Guide* outlines key contractual obligations suppliers need to follow to conduct business with The Home Depot. The obligations include, but are not limited to:

- providing transparent operations, policies, processes, and relevant records
- not employing any persons under the age of sixteen
- not employing workers through forced or involuntary labour practices
- abiding by the law
- compensating employees in accordance with labour laws
- not discriminating against employees
- providing safe workplaces
- providing workplaces free from corruption and fraud

Discussion Questions

1. **When multinational companies put pressure on developing countries' governments and businesses to improve workplace conditions and ethical practices are they making a difference? Why or why not?**
2. **By creating rules that suppliers must follow are companies possibly chasing away potential low-cost suppliers?**
3. **What problems might you foresee with this type of ethical procurement? How can companies ensure their suppliers are ethical?**

OPERATIONS CONTROL

Operations Scheduling

How does routing shape the production process?   **Routing** is the way in which goods are transported, via water, rail, truck, or air. It includes transporting goods to a client, transporting materials from suppliers, or any of the other many combinations. Routing is actually the first step in production control. It sets out workflow, the sequence of machines and operations through which a product or service progresses from start to finish. The management of routing ensures that any transportation of goods, from the supplier, through the facility, and to the customer, is done at a minimum of cost, time, and distance without sacrificing quality. One useful tool for routing is **value-stream mapping**, which identifies all the flows and resources required to deliver a product: people, technologies, physical facilities, communication and transportation channels, policies, and procedures. It enables a company to identify and eliminate waste, thereby streamlining work processes, cutting lead times, reducing costs, and increasing quality. Anything that does not add value to the end-customer is waste.

 Describe what value-stream mapping is, and what its benefits are.

Routing is the way in which goods are transported (to a client, from a supplier, or any other combination), via water, rail, truck, or air.

Value-stream mapping identifies all the flows and resources required to deliver a product: people, technologies, physical facilities, communication and transportation channels, policies, and procedures.

Scheduling involves specifying and controlling the time required for each step in the production process as well as making the most efficient use of equipment, facilities, labour, and materials.

A master production schedule shows which products will be produced, when production will occur, and what resources will be used during the scheduled time.

A **Gantt chart**, formatted similarly to a horizontal bar graph, is used to lay out each task in a project, the order in which these tasks must be completed, and how long each task should take.

How does scheduling shape the production process? Related to routing is scheduling. **Scheduling** involves specifying and controlling the time required for each step in the production process as well as making the most efficient use of equipment, facilities, labour, and materials. There are two different types of scheduling: *forward* and *backward*. With *forward scheduling,* you start with the date that materials are available, create the most efficient schedule, and then determine a shipping date based on that schedule. *Backward scheduling* is the exact opposite, where you are given a shipping or due date and you have to determine the start date and the most efficient schedule based on when everything has to be finished.

Two major components go into making an effective schedule: loading and sequencing. *Loading* is assigning a job to a specific machine or work centre. *Sequencing* is assigning the order in which jobs are processed. A **master production schedule** shows the resources that will be used to produce specific products during the scheduled time. There are numerous tools designed to help managers ensure that all the right resources are working on the right jobs at the right times. Two of the most commonly used tools are *Gantt charts* and *PERT charts*.

What is a Gantt chart? One method for monitoring the progress of a given project is a Gantt chart, a tool developed by Henry Gantt in the 1920s. A **Gantt chart**, formatted similarly to a horizontal bar graph, is used to lay out each task in a project, the order in which these tasks must be completed, and how long each task should take. **Figure 10.3** shows an example of a Gantt chart for a remodelling project. Originally used for large-scale construction projects, such as building the Hoover Dam between Nevada and Arizona in the 1930s, Gantt charts are still used today to manage a variety of both large-scale and small-scale projects. At any point in the process, project managers and manufacturers can see at a glance which tasks have been completed and whether these tasks were completed on schedule.

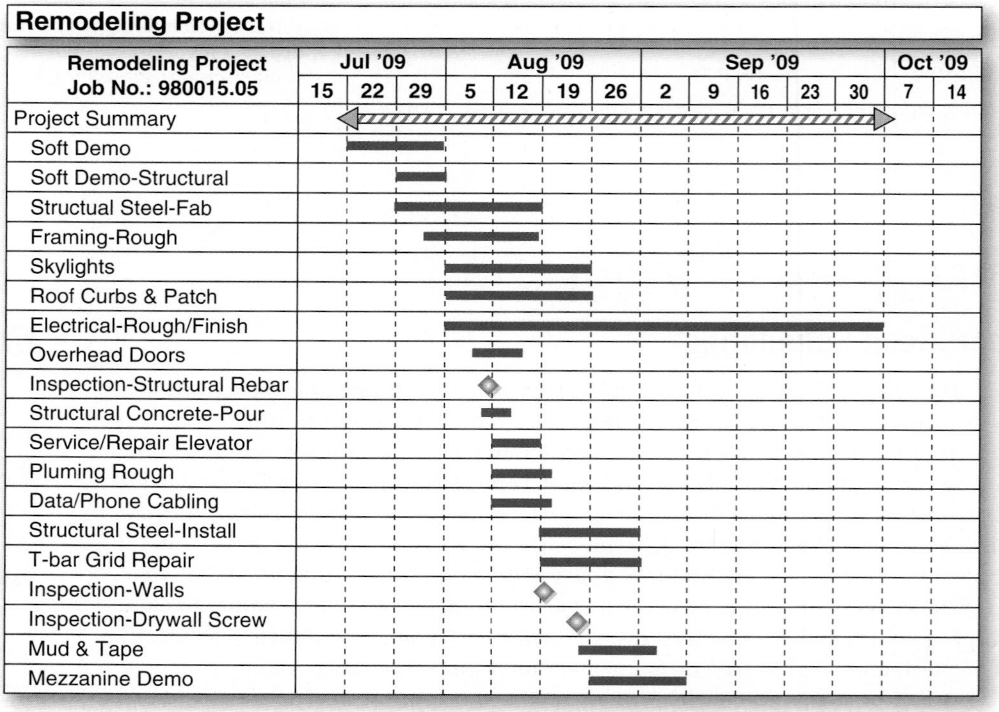

Figure 10.3 Sample Gantt Chart

What is a PERT chart?

The **program evaluation and review technique (PERT)** was first used in the development of submarines in the 1950s. This method maps out the various steps involved in a project, differentiating tasks that must be completed in a certain order from tasks that may be completed simultaneously. The result is a web-like diagram similar to the example shown in **Figure 10.4**.

In creating a PERT chart, time estimates are assigned to each task. Creating the chart helps identify the *critical path*, or the path of sequential tasks that will take the longest amount of time to complete. This helps managers determine an overall timeline for completing a project or, from a manufacturing standpoint, producing a particular good or service. However, because delays can cause the critical path in a project to change, PERT charts are limited in their ability to predict project completion times.

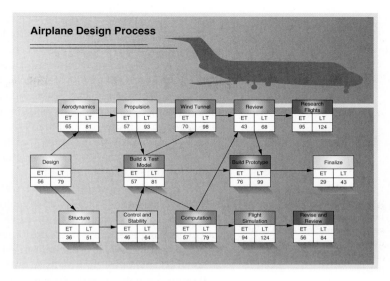

Figure 10.4 Sample PERT Chart

The **program evaluation and review technique (PERT)** maps out the various steps involved in a project, differentiating tasks that must be completed in a certain order from tasks that may be completed simultaneously.

Is scheduling for service operations the same as scheduling for production operations?

In low-contact service operations, schedules may be based either on the desired completion date or on the time of order arrival. For example, an auto-shop may schedule various customer jobs on different days of the week and at different times; although you'd like your car serviced today, you may be on the schedule for tomorrow. In such businesses, appointment systems help to balance demand. In high-contact service operations, precise scheduling of service may not be possible because it is difficult to balance. For example, some health clinics take appointments as well as accommodate walk-in patients. If a patient with an appointment cancels at the last minute or does not show up, then the appointment time is wasted unless there is a walk-in patient to take that time slot. Walk-in patients don't want to have long wait times, nor do schedule patients, but if the doctor sees too many walk-in patients throughout the day then scheduled patients will have longer wait times and may begin to look for another clinic to use in the future. If the doctor does not see enough walk-in patients throughout the day, then this group will have longer wait times or may not be seen at all, and they will begin to look for another clinic to use in the future. Due to the difficulty of balancing the schedule, some clinics do not accept walk-in patients.

Inventory Control

What's the best way to manage inventory?

Inventory control includes the receiving, storing, handling, and tracking of everything in a company's stock, from raw materials to finished products. Inventory often makes up a large portion of a business's expenses. Therefore, proper management is not only just a way to stay informed, it's necessary to keep costs low while ensuring that all necessary materials are in stock and stored in the proper place. There are four main types of stock: raw materials, unfinished products, finished products, and consumables (such as pens and paper). Maintaining each of these kinds of stock helps determine where money should and shouldn't be spent. Proper maintenance keeps track of things such as products that have shelf lives that could deteriorate or products that have become obsolete, or where more stock than necessary is being purchased. Ensuring an adequate supply of finished products or other types of stock is further complicated when customer demand is variable.

Managing stock can be achieved in a number of different ways, and no single method works best for every business. Factors such as the size of the business, the amount of inventory necessary, the amount of inventory storage space, and the proximity to

9

Explain the benefits of just-in-time (JIT) production and enterprise resource planning (ERP).

Inventory control includes the receiving, storing, handling, and tracking of everything in a company's stock, from raw materials to finished products. Inventory often makes up a large portion of a business's expenses.

10

suppliers all contribute to which inventory control method will work best for an individual company. The least involved way to manage inventory is simply to estimate it. This method works really well for smaller companies or companies that don't maintain large amounts of stock. When accuracy is a necessity, a *stock book solution*, where stock on hand is tallied in a book along with stock on order and stock that has been sold, would probably work best. Another less complicated management system is called the *reserve stock system*. This is where stock is set aside in reserve so that it cannot be used. The company goes through its inventory as it regularly would, and when it has to dip into the reserve stock, it knows it is time to reorder that item. It is important for managers to keep in mind when using this system that however much stock is in reserve should be enough to last the amount of time it takes to resupply.[29]

> A **just-in-time (JIT) inventory control** system keeps the smallest amount of inventory on hand as possible, and everything else that is needed is ordered so that it arrives just in time to be used.

Whereas these systems can work well with smaller businesses, larger businesses generally require a more complicated inventory-management system. A **just-in-time (JIT) inventory control** system keeps the smallest amount of inventory on hand as possible, and everything else that is needed is ordered so that it arrives just in time to be used. Storing fewer items and using items right away can reduce storage costs. Dell Computers adopted JIT inventory control. By manufacturing computers to customer specifications, Dell orders only the specific parts needed to complete those orders, thereby reducing expenses (less storage, fewer damaged parts, fewer obsolete parts).[30]

This system, however, is not without its drawbacks. To work properly, a company must have a very good relationship with its suppliers to ensure that appropriate quantities arrive on time and arrive where they are needed. Even then, if a supplier is far away, there may be shipping delays due to weather. The shipping costs, too, may become quite high.

> A **radio frequency identification (RFID)** tag allows a computer to keep track of the status and quantity of each item.

How is technology used to streamline inventory control?   Many

organizations rely on a computerized inventory system that uses a barcode or **radio frequency identification (RFID)** tag on each item, allowing a computer to keep track of the status and quantity of each item. Each item is logged and classified when it is stocked and an identifying barcode or RFID is attached to the item. Both barcodes and RFIDs store all the specific information for each item, such as cost, stock number, and storage location. Using these systems, items in inventory can be scanned when they are used or sold, and the computer can continuously update the information for each item. Depending on the system used, computerized inventory makes it easier to analyze the quantitative factors of managing stock, such as how quickly each item is sold, how much really needs to be held in inventory at once, and when it's time to restock items.

With the use of barcodes and RFIDs, items can be scanned and inventory can be monitored electronically.

> **Materials requirement planning (MRP)** is a type of software system used to schedule and monitor the use of components and other materials in a manufacturing operation.

What is materials requirement planning (MRP)?   **Materials requirement planning (MRP)** is a type of software system used to schedule and monitor the use of components and other materials in a manufacturing operation. When an order is made, the specifics of that order are put into the MRP. The MRP then determines which parts will be needed to finish the job and compares these findings to the current inventory. Based on this information, it highlights what needs to be obtained, either through production or a supplier, as well as when the parts will be needed. It uses previous manufacturing data to break the job into parts. A process is input into the system, and the MRP portion of the system determines which components are needed when to meet customers' order quantities and due dates. The result should be the best estimate based on previous data. Knowing these estimates helps determine both part and labour

shortages before a project even starts. There are many limitations to MRP, the biggest being that it is only as effective as its data. So if its data are not well maintained, the estimates that it provides will only become increasingly useless. Another limitation to MRP is its scope: it only focuses on the management of needed component parts in the *manufacturing* processes of a company.

While MRP is concerned primarily with manufacturing materials, **manufacturing resource planning (MRPII)** is concerned with integrating and coordinating data from many departments, including manufacturing, finance, marketing, and human resources. MRPII can not only generate a production plan but also various management reports, forecasts, and financial statements.

Enterprise resource planning (ERP) systems (also discussed in Chapter 9) allow companies the ability to streamline the various workflows and share information across departments by consolidating information into a central database accessible to various system modules (company departments). This allows for improved productivity from all employees. With an ERP system in place, the various aspects of an organization can work together without worrying about compatible software. Unfortunately, there are disadvantages for a business that fails to invest fully in an ERP system. These problems can range from inadequate tech support to limited customization of the system. Companies that specialize in ERP systems include Oracle, SAP, and Microsoft.

Quality Control

Has quality control always been part of the production process? The use of techniques, activities, and processes to guarantee that a certain good or service meets a specified level of quality is referred to as **quality control**. Quality control is essential in maintaining both the reputation of a business and consumer safety. Customers demand quality and expect products they purchase to be reliable, safe, and provide utility (value). They also expect quality service from the company employees they interact with. If customers do not perceive that they have received a quality product or service, they will not make a repeat purchase. Customer loyalty is an important element to company success, and to create a satisfied customer a company must deliver a high-quality product or service as well as excellent customer service.

The old method of quality assurance was to delegate quality control to a separate department that would inspect and test products for flaws after the product had been manufactured. This inspection method of quality control involves checking work at the *end* of the process before products are delivered. Unfortunately, several problems arise using this method, including the expense in terms of time, labour, and employee confidence. Because inspection is performed by outside people instead of by the workers, each inspector can pass or fail a product using his or her own standards and procedures. Moreover, inspecting finished products and discovering defects means some of these defects have to be scrapped or reworked. This can be costly.

What methods are used to improve quality? Merely controlling for quality through inspection and monitoring employees is like visiting the doctor for treating symptoms as opposed to the source of an illness. Since the 1980s, firms have been focusing on building quality into every step of the production process instead of merely taking action to scrap or fix defects. This concept of "total quality" at every stage of a production process was only embraced in North America after Japanese manufacturers implemented company-wide quality-improvement methods and strengthened their presence in the global market.[31] Unlike the old inspection method of quality control, in which products are reviewed at certain points of the process (usually the end), total quality management involves every factor in producing high-quality goods—management, customers, employees, and suppliers. At any point, employees and leaders are aiming to produce high quality.

Total quality management (TQM) involves ongoing improvement of products, services, and processes. This can be accomplished by undertaking a Plan, Do, Check, Act (PDCA) cycle, created by American statistician W. Edwards Deming.[32] Using the PDCA, organizations first formulate a plan to reduce potential errors, carry out the plan on a

Manufacturing resource planning (MRPII) uses software to integrate data from many departments, including manufacturing, finance, marketing, and human resources.

Quality control is the use of techniques, activities, and processes to guarantee that a certain good or service meets a specified level of quality.

Deming's concept of **total quality management (TQM)** emphasizes the use of quality principles in all aspects of a company's production and operations.

Describe quality control and how ISO standards help companies produce high-quality goods and services.

BizSkills Case Simulation: Improving Business Operations and Quality. Located in MyBusinessLab.

Companies for Quality Products and Services (2010)

1. Walt Disney
2. Intel
3. UPS
4. Apple
5. Singapore Airlines
6. Nordstrom
7. Altria Group
8. Adobe Systems
9. Procter & Gamble (P&G)
10. Phillip Morris International

Source: "World's Most Admired Companies (2010)," *Fortune* (online), March 22, 2011, http://money.cnn.com/magazines/fortune/mostadmired/2010/best_worst/best8.html, Accessed May 17, 2011.

Off the **Mark**

Quality Catastrophes

There was a time when people would buy Toyota vehicles solely based on the automaker's reputation for excellent quality and durability, but its longstanding reputation has been heavily questioned in the last few years. While trying to recover from a painful PR blow over the "sticky" accelerator pedal recall, among sixteen others in 2010 (involving more than 700 000 vehicles), Toyota Canada took yet another hit in 2011 when it had to notify 11 700 Lexus owners about the possibility of improperly installed fuel pressure sensors that could eventually leak. The Lexus recall in Canada was part of a larger Lexus recall in Japan (affecting 1.3 million models), a sedan and station wagon recall in Europe and New Zealand, and a Daihatsu Motors truck recall. Toyota Canada officials said the recalls have hurt sales, but the company has put teams in place around the world to address customer concerns and resolve problems quickly.[33]

In 2007, Mattel Toys' long history of producing safe, high-quality toys also came into question. Two weeks after the toymaker recalled more than 1 million Chinese-made toys in the United States because of excessive lead in the paint (lead is toxic if ingested), it had to recall another 18 million toys worldwide because of small magnets that posed a swallowing hazard *and* excessive lead in the paint. Mattel stated that it did not know whether the contracted Chinese manufacturer substituted paint from a non-certified supplier or if a certified paint supplier caused the problem, but it would ensure that Chinese-made toys are safe for U.S. consumers. Mattel offered replacement products to all consumers who had purchased the recalled products, and estimated that the first recall alone would cost US$30 million in profits. This was Mattel's seventeenth recall in ten years.[34]

The Bridgestone/Firestone tire company had to endure a major crisis because of poor quality assurance.

In 2000, millions of its ATX, ATX II, and Firestone Wilderness radial tires had to be recalled due to tire tread separation, which caused SUV rollovers. These tires had not been adequately tested for quality and safety, and they caused numerous accidents due to their defects. Many people were injured and some were killed because of this lack of quality management, and Bridgestone/Firestone had to pay the Ford Motor Company US$240 million to settle claims from injured motorists.[35] This crisis could have been prevented had the company taken greater quality-control measures in the production of these tires.

Discussion Questions

1. **How do companies recover their good reputation after such a blunder? How does it make you feel with regard to purchasing from these companies?**
2. **How much time and money do you estimate companies spend recovering from these types of situations? How do companies stay in business after these types of mistakes?**
3. **How could such mistakes be avoided?**

Statistical process control (SPC) uses statistical sampling of products at every phase of production and displays the results on a graph to show potential variations that need to be corrected.

Six Sigma is a method that seeks to eliminate defects by removing variation in outcomes and measuring and analyzing manufacturing processes to see if standards are being met.

small scale, check the outcome and effectiveness of the change, and then implement the plan on a larger scale while monitoring results continually. One popular tool used to check or measure if quality goals are being met is **statistical quality control (SQC)**, or the continual monitoring of each stage of the entire production process to ensure that quality standards are being met at every stage. **Statistical process control (SPC)** uses statistical sampling of products at every phase of production and displays the results on a graph to show potential variations that need to be corrected. A common SPC tool is **Six Sigma**, a method that seeks to eliminate defects by removing variation in outcomes and measuring and analyzing manufacturing processes to see if standards are being met. A company with Six Sigma quality produces at a low defect rate of just 3.4 defects per million opportunities.

How does TQM cater to the customer?   It is not enough simply to implement quality-management tools. A significant aspect of TQM is catering to the customer's

needs and desires. SGL Carbon, a manufacturer of graphite specialties, emphasizes adherence to a TQM approach by giving its customers the final say in determining whether a product meets the requirements of high-quality standards. Although firms may define in the beginning what makes their products high quality or low quality, those companies that learn how to simultaneously emphasize quality throughout the production process and incorporate the desires of customers will make a greater presence in the global marketplace.

What is the ISO?

The **International Organization for Standardization (ISO)** is an organization dedicated to creating worldwide standards of quality for goods and services. ISO was established in 1947 and is headquartered in Geneva, Switzerland. The organization has published more than 18 500 International Standards, and more than 1000 new ISO standards are published every year.[36] ISO standards facilitate trade, spread knowledge, share technological advances, and share good management and leadership practices. The ISO standards apply not to the products themselves, but to the production methods and systems used to manufacture them, as well as other areas, such as communication within the company and leadership. Such a standardized system is necessary to avoid trying to comply with various conflicting systems.

The **International Organization for Standardization (ISO)** is an organization dedicated to creating worldwide standards of quality for goods and services.

What is the ISO certification process?

The **ISO 9000** is a set of five technical standards of quality management created by the International Organizations for Standardization to provide a uniform way of determining whether organizations conform to sound quality procedures. Since then, more than ninety countries have adopted these standards, and thousands of companies require their products to be ISO 9000 certified. Some industries have even developed their own industry-specific set of ISO standards. Certification is usually done by a third-party registrar who assesses the company's quality-assurance manuals and practices. First, a pre-assessment must be conducted, during which the registrar reviews the documents that outline the company's standards and processes. If the manual and other printed documents pass the review, the company can proceed with the rest of the assessment. If the registrar finds errors in these documents, further review will have to be delayed until the mistakes are corrected.

The **ISO 9000** is a set of five technical standards of quality management created by the International Organizations for Standardization to provide a uniform way of determining whether organizations conform to sound quality procedures.

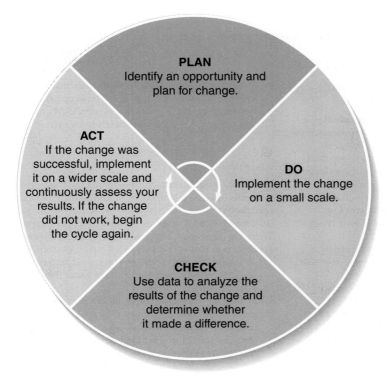

PLAN
Identify an opportunity and plan for change.

ACT
If the change was successful, implement it on a wider scale and continuously assess your results. If the change did not work, begin the cycle again.

DO
Implement the change on a small scale.

CHECK
Use data to analyze the results of the change and determine whether it made a difference.

Figure 10.5 Quality – PDCA

During the formal assessment, the registrar reviews the corrected documents and interviews the employees and administrators of the company. The goal of this part of the assessment is to ensure that written policies and procedures are being implemented in the company's production methods. Finally, the registrar issues an audit report summarizing the results of the assessment and listing any areas that need improvement. If corrections are required at this stage, the company can make them and document them in a report to the registrar. After satisfactory corrections have been made, the registrar can then award certification tothe company. Once it has earned certification, the company can put the ISO 9000 seal in advertising and on letterhead.

After certification, the registrar returns to the company twice a year to make sure the company complies with the ISO standards. These spot checks are conducted without advance warning, and the registrar focuses on areas that were notably weak during the initial assessment. Every three years, the registrar will complete another assessment and issue a new audit report. The company must also establish an internal auditing program that is responsible for keeping the ISO standards in practice.

The **ISO 14000**, launched after ISO 9000, is designed to promote clean production processes in response to environmental issues such as global warming and water pollution. Requirements for certification include documenting an environmental policy, invoking an environmental management system, and keeping control records pertaining to both. ISO 14000 ensures that "environmental management" is a continuously improving process to minimize harmful environment affects.[37]

The **ISO 14000**, launched after ISO 9000, is designed to promote clean production processes in response to environmental issues such as global warming and water pollution.

CHAPTER SYNOPSIS

❶ **Explain how operations management produces finished goods that provide utility to consumers.** *(pp. 272–274)*

Operations management (or **production management**) refers to the organized direction and control of the processes that transform resources (inputs) into finished goods and services (outputs). The act of production gives these finished products and services *value*, or *utility*. Products and services provide businesses with economic results (profits, wages, suppliers) and provide customers with **utility**, which is the power of a product or service to satisfy a human want or need, something of value to the person. There are four types of utility:

1. *Time utility*. The ability of the product or service to satisfy a human want because of the time at which it is made available (e.g., holiday decorations, summer garden supplies).
2. *Place utility*. The ability of the product or service to satisfy a human want because of where it is made available (e.g., a grocery store right down the street).
3. *Form utility*. The ability of the product or service to satisfy a human want because of its form; this requires raw materials to be transformed into a finished product (e.g., it would be difficult for you to form rubber into tires for your car).

4. *Ownership utility*. The ability of the product or service to satisfy a human want during its consumption or use (e.g., a lawn mower that is yours, so you don't have to borrow or rent one each time the lawn needs to be cut).

❷ **Explain the differences between goods and service operations.** *(pp. 274–275)*

Both service and manufacturing operations transform raw materials (inputs) into finished products (outputs), but in service operations the outputs are people with their needs met and possessions serviced. Goods are produced; services are performed. There are three areas where services differ from goods:

1. *Services are intangible.* Goods are tangible—they have a physical form and can be seen, touched, and handled—while services can only be experienced because they do not have a physical form.
2. *Services are unstorable.* Goods can be stored in inventory, but services are consumed when they are produced. Trash collection, child care, or mail services cannot be produced ahead of time and then stored for high-demand periods.
3. *Services are more customizable than goods.* Each person receives service customized for his or her s pecific needs.

❸ **Describe mass production, mass customization, flexible manufacturing, and lean production, and the benefits of each.**   *(pp. 275–276)*

The method of producing large quantities of goods at a low cost is called **mass production**. This method relies on machines and automated assembly lines to mass-produce goods that are identical and adhere to certain standards of quality. The cost to run an assembly line is kept low because machines do the majority of the work and the labourers don't need to be especially skilled to perform their repetitive tasks. This method also cuts down on production time, allowing a large quantity of goods to be produced very quickly. Because machinery is the main component, risk of human error is virtually eliminated. A major disadvantage, however, is that mass production is inflexible. After a production line is established, it is very difficult to change or alter the process if an unexpected problem occurs. **Mass customization** combines the low unit cost of mass production processes with the flexibility of producing goods or services tailored to meet individual customer's needs.

A solution to the rigid system of mass production is *flexible* production, also known as a **flexible manufacturing system (FMS)**. An FMS uses one central computer to link together several machines that can process different part types simultaneously. Unlike a mass production system, an FMS can adapt to changes in schedules and product specifications.

Lean production is a set of principles concerned with reducing waste and improving flow that evolved from the original Toyota Production System (TPS) first used in Japan in the 1980s. Its objective is to focus all resources and energies into producing products and services with value-added characteristics (utility to the consumer) while eliminating activities that are of no value.

❹ **Explain how technology influences the production process.** *(pp. 277–279)*

With thousands of goods to produce at a given time, you might guess that technology plays an integral role in facilitating the flow of any production process. When managed efficiently, the technological aspect of a production process should lead to increases in production and reductions in costs. Technology may also improve the quality and increase the variety of products, which influences the customer's buying decisions. Customers are more likely to buy a product that is not only low-priced compared to other similar products, but also of high quality and readily available in many varieties. It is essential for businesses in today's globally competitive environment to be up-to-date on new technologies that can improve any or all aspects of the production process.

Computer-aided design (CAD) refers to the use of a computer to create two-dimensional or three-dimensional models of physical parts.

Once a design is approved, **computer-aided manufacturing (CAM)** uses the design data to control the machinery used in the manufacturing process.

Computer-integrated manufacturing (CIM) takes it even further by combining design and manufacturing functions with other functions such as order taking, shipment, and billing.

❺ **Summarize the transportation, human, and physical factors involved in choosing a manufacturing location.** *(pp. 279–282)*

In goods-producing operations, facility location decisions are influenced by the availability and proximity of raw materials, transportation costs, labour availability, physical factors such as electrical power, water, and communication capabilities, local regulations and taxes, and community living conditions.

In low-contact service-producing operations, facilities can be located near resource supplies, labour, or transportation outlets. In high-contact service-producing operations, facilities must be located near customers.

❻ **Explain how facility layout affects efficiency.**   *(pp. 282–283)*

Facility layout is the physical arrangement of resources, the people in the production process, and how they interact. When determining or renovating a facility layout for maximum effectiveness and efficiency, business owners must also consider many operational factors. For example, facilities should be designed so that they can be easily adjusted to meet changing production needs. Having to undergo extensive renovations or completely relocate as a company's operations change or expand can be a costly endeavour; therefore, managers need to be prepared to factor possible growth at the planning stage. Additionally, the facility layout should be in accordance with *Occupational Health and Safety Act* and *Regulations* to ensure worker safety. Service organizations are concerned with how the layout affects customers' behaviour, while manufacturers are concerned with efficient processes that will reduce costs. Four common types of layouts are process, product, cellular, and fixed-position.

Capacity is the amount of a product or service that a company can produce under normal working conditions in a given time period. Capacity is dependent upon the size of the facility, the number of workers employed, and the technology and processes used. When managers plan for capacity, they must consider that if capacity is too small to meet demand, the company will have to turn customers away and forgo profits; yet if capacity is too large, the firm wastes money by having employees, space, and equipment underutilized. For manufacturing facilities, capacity is determined by the extent of the production processes, whereas for service facilities, capacity is determined by peak demand and fluctuations in demand.

❼ **Explain how a company determines that it requires a supplier, selects a supplier, and strives to manage its supply chain.**   *(pp. 283–285)*

If a company plans to manufacture a product that will carry both the company's name and reputation, it has to decide if it will make the entire product in-house or if the product will be assembled from a combination of parts manufactured in-house and other parts purchased from suppliers. A company needs to consider factors such as cost and quality. If it is less expensive to outsource the production of certain parts elsewhere, that may be the best decision. However, it is important that a manager can trust the quality of any parts that are produced elsewhere and that appropriate quantities are delivered in a timely manner.

A company's first step in finding suppliers involves clearly defining and understanding its needs so that it can find suppliers that truly fit its requirements. Cost is always a factor, but it should never be the sole factor.

Supply chain management involves the logistics of obtaining all the necessary inputs that go into a production process (*inbound logistics*), managing the actual production process (*materials handling* and *operations control*), and managing the physical distribution (or *outbound logistics*) of getting the proper quantities of produced products to customers when and where they want them. When applying supply chain management, companies are trying to reduce costs, increase flexibility and speed, and improve quality and customer service. It is crucial that companies develop tighter bonds with suppliers, as many suppliers play an important role in supporting the operations of their business customers, offering suggestions for reducing costs, and even contributing to new product design.

10

❽ Describe what value-stream mapping is, and what its benefits are.   *(pp. 285–287)*

One useful tool for routing is **value-stream mapping**, which identifies all the flows and resources required to deliver a product: people, technologies, physical facilities, communication and transportation channels, policies, and procedures. It enables a company to identify and eliminate waste, thereby streamlining work processes, cutting lead times, reducing costs, and increasing quality. Anything that does not add value to the end-customer is waste.

❾ Explain the benefits of just-in-time (JIT) production and enterprise resource planning (ERP).   *(pp. 287–289)*

A **just-in-time (JIT) inventory control** system keeps the smallest amount of inventory on hand as possible, and everything else needed is ordered so that it arrives just in time to be used. Storing fewer items and using items right away can reduce storage costs.

   Enterprise resource planning (ERP) systems (also discussed in Chapter 9) allow companies the ability to streamline the various workflows and share information across departments by consolidating information into a central database accessible to various system modules (company departments). This allows for improved productivity from all employees. With an ERP system in place, the various aspects of an organization can

work together without worrying about compatible software. Unfortunately, there are disadvantages for a business that fails to invest fully in an ERP system. These problems can range from inadequate tech support to limited customization of the system. Companies that specialize in ERP systems include Oracle, SAP, and Microsoft.

❿ Describe quality control and how ISO standards help companies produce high-quality goods and services. *(pp. 289–292)*

The use of techniques, activities, and processes to guarantee that a certain good or service meets a specified level of quality is referred to as **quality control**. **The International Organization for Standardization (ISO)** is an organization dedicated to creating worldwide standards of quality for goods and services. ISO standards facilitate trade, spread knowledge, share technological advances, and share good management and leadership practices. ISO standards facilitate trade, spread knowledge, share technological advances, and share good management and leadership practices. The ISO standards apply not to the products themselves, but to the production methods and systems used to manufacture them, as well as other areas, such as communication within the company and leadership. Such a standardized system is necessary to avoid trying to comply with various conflicting systems.

KEY TERMS

assembly line (or production line)   *(p. 275)*
bill of material   *(p. 283)*
capacity   *(p. 282)*
cellular layout (or group technology layout)   *(p. 283)*
computer-aided design (CAD)   *(p. 277)*
computer-aided manufacturing (CAM)   *(p. 278)*
computer-integrated manufacturing (CIM)   *(p. 278)*
e-procurement   *(p. 284)*
effectiveness   *(p. 274)*
efficiency   *(p. 274)*
facility layout   *(p. 282)*
fixed-position layout   *(p. 283)*
flexible manufacturing system (FMS)   *(p. 276)*

Gantt chart   *(p. 286)*
high-contact service processes   *(p. 275)*
human factor   *(p. 281)*
International Organization for Standardization (ISO)   *(p. 291)*
inventory control   *(p. 287)*
ISO 9000   *(p. 291)*
ISO 14000   *(p. 292)*
just-in-time (JIT) inventory control   *(p. 288)*
lean production   *(p. 276)*
low-contact service processes   *(p. 275)*
make-or-buy decision   *(p. 283)*
manufacturing resource planning (MRPII)   *(p. 289)*
mass customization   *(p. 276)*
mass production   *(p. 275)*

master production schedule   *(p. 286)*
materials requirement planning (MRP)   *(p. 288)*
operations management (or production management)   *(p. 273)*
operations managers   *(p. 274)*
operations planning   *(p. 274)*
process layout (or job-shop or functional layout)   *(p. 283)*
production   *(p. 272)*
production plan   *(p. 274)*
Product layout (or flow-shop layout)   *(p. 283)*
program evaluation and review technique (PERT)   *(p. 287)*
purchasing (or procurement)   *(p. 283)*
quality control   *(p. 289)*

radio frequency identification (RFID)   *(p. 288)*
routing   *(p. 285)*
scheduling   *(p. 286)*
Six Sigma   *(p. 290)*
statistical process control (SPC)   *(p. 290)*
supply chain   *(p. 280)*
supply chain management   *(p. 284)*
total quality management (TQM)   *(p. 289)*
utility   *(p. 274)*
utility supply   *(p. 281)*
value   *(p. 273)*
value-stream mapping   *(p. 285)*

CRITICAL THINKING QUESTIONS

1. What are the advantages and disadvantages of mass production and the mechanized assembly line? Did this shift to machines and robots eliminate jobs, or did it create new ones?
2. What are the resources (inputs) needed and the finished products (outputs) for each of the following service companies: a child care, a bank, an auto-repair shop?
3. A sports equipment company is known for a special grip on its tennis rackets that is imported from South America. The cost of shipping these grips has grown steadily more expensive, and the business would like to produce the

   grips in-house. What factors does the business need to consider before adding another step to the production process?
4. How does a business decide what the best method of shipment is for its products? What factors, other than cost, are important in this decision?
5. Give an example of what the process of total quality management (TQM) would involve in the production of automobiles. What steps can manufacturers take to ensure that a high level of quality is maintained consistently in their production processes?

APPLICATION EXERCISES

1. **Leaders in the Industrial Robot Industry.** Search the Internet for several industrial robot production companies. What kinds of functions are robots being used to perform? In what kinds of industries are these robots best suited to perform?

2. **Facility Layout.** Think of the cafeteria at your college or university and redesign the layout (make a pencil drawing placing people and materials) so that the facility (employees included) could serve its customers more effectively and efficiently.

3. **Radio Frequency Identification.** The use of chips to track goods during the shipping process is becoming more widespread. Use the Internet to research options for radio frequency identification. What are some of the options for tracking goods? What kind of range can these products cover?

4. **Quality Control.** Use the Internet to research one company that has had recent recalls. What went wrong? Does the company not have quality checks/systems in place? How did the company correct the problems? Were there lawsuits? Write a short paragraph considering the situation and discuss how the company might have avoided this mistake and how they might have better handled the corrective measures.

5. **Bill of Material (BOM).** Create a manufacturing bill of materials for each of the following products: a baby carriage, chocolate chip cookies, and a pair of leather sneakers. You may research the Internet to learn more about BOM and gather your information. What software might be used to record a BOM and how could this information be used in an ERP system? Report your findings.

GLOBAL 500 RESEARCH PROJECT

INSTRUCTIONS

1. Choose a Global 500 company from *Fortune* magazine's annual rankings at http://money.cnn.com/magazines/fortune/global500/.

2. Research:
   a. What are the resources (inputs) for this company and the outputs for this company?
   b. What is the supply chain for this company? Which businesses supply products, services, or raw materials for this company?
   c. What type of quality control systems are in place? Is this company certified by ISO or some other quality standard?
   d. What type of transportation methods does this company use? What are the costs?
   e. Does this company use an ERP system? Which one?
   f. Does this company have an EDI setup with one of their suppliers for e-procurement?
   g. What types of technology does this company use to manage operations?

3. Prepare a report and submit to your professor.

TEAM TIME

To Outsource or Not to Outsource . . . That Is the Question

DIVIDE INTO TWO TEAMS TO REPRESENT BOTH SIDES OF THE ISSUE.

   a. group that thinks the company should make the component
   b. group that thinks the company should outsource the component

SCENARIO

The Grindstone Supply Company of New Jersey is attempting to expand its manufacturing of large wall clocks. In years past, the company has outsourced the manufacturing of clock springs to a company in Nebraska. This has been cost-effective in the past, but now that demand for the springs has increased, Grindstone is considering manufacturing the springs in-house. Although the cost of producing the springs in-house is lower, it is unclear whether it will be profitable in the end, as the manufacturing process will change greatly. New machines for the production of springs will be needed, as the factory works exclusively in wood and plastic. With the new machines comes the need for new technicians to monitor and service them. Should the Grindstone Supply Company alter its manufacturing process to include the production of clock springs, or should it continue outsourcing to Nebraska as it has in the past? What factors contribute to this decision? Will this be more profitable in the end? How will it affect employee morale and relations?

PROCESS

Step 1. Record your ideas and opinions about the issue presented in the scenario above. Be sure to consider the issue from your assigned perspective.

Step 2. Meet as a team and review the issue from both perspectives. Discuss together why the position of your group is the best decision.

ETHICS AND RESPONSIBILITY

Environmental Shipping Concerns

You have just been promoted to head of the shipping department for your office supply company, and it is now your responsibility to determine routing. The company is located on the eastern seaboard, near major highways as well as the ocean. In the past, trucking has been the preferred method of shipping, as it was deemed the most cost-effective. Shipping the freight by boat, however, would greatly reduce the negative effects on the environment caused by truck emissions. After calculating the cost on paper, you realize that shipping by sea would have a negative effect on the overall profit margin, but the company would still generate solid profits.

DISCUSSION QUESTIONS

1. What decision would you make in this situation, land or sea?
2. If you were told that you would take a personal pay cut from switching to the more environmentally friendly route, how would that affect your decision?
3. What kind of impact do you think one company switching to less environmentally damaging practices could have on the general atmosphere of the shipping world?

CLOSING CASE

Just in Time for Toyota

Since Toyota Motor Corporation's inception, it has prided itself on having a lean production system that manages equipment, people, and materials in the most effective manner. Toyota builds this system from two main principles: *jidoka* and just-in-time production. *Jidoka* is a Japanese term that refers to the power given to an employee to stop a production line if he or she detects a problem. Just-in-time production refers to the manufacturing of only "what is needed, when it's needed."[38] Toyota feels that these principles emphasize the company's philosophy that "good thinking means good production."

Toyota's desire for lean production can date back to the early 1900s with Sakichi Toyoda, the founder of the Toyota Group. When it came to producing goods, whether by hand or by machine, Toyoda knew that there was a difference between being quick and being efficient. He came to this conclusion after observing the automatic looms being used in Japanese textile mills. The looms formed fabrics quickly; however, threads would snap in the process, and the defective fabric would continue in the production line. Toyoda invented an automatic loom that would stop whenever a thread snapped so the problem could be fixed before the product moved on.[39] Toyoda used the word *jidoka* to describe this process, and his son, Kiichiro Toyoda, applied it to the company's automobile-manufacturing operations when they began in the 1930s.

The *jidoka* philosophy focuses on quality. It means a machine will safely stop if it encounters a quality or equipment problem. A production-line operator can fix the problem before any materials are passed down the production line. Operators are notified of any problems through the *andon*, or problem display board, which gives details about where and when the problems occurred. By stopping any potentially defective materials from continuing on in the production process, Toyota can guarantee that all products are made to the highest standards of quality.

Producing quality parts through *jidoka* allows the just-in-time system to function. This system strives to produce quality products efficiently through the complete elimination of waste, inconsistencies, and unreasonable requirements on the production line.[40] To achieve this, Toyota stocks its assembly line with only a small number of the parts needed to make different types of cars. For example, Toyota may have four different types of rear-view mirrors and only stock three of each type on the assembly line. When one type of rear-view mirror is used, a message is sent to the parts production department to construct a new rear-view mirror of that particular type. Then that mirror is sent back up to the assembly line to replenish the stock. By not mass-producing parts, Toyota minimizes the chance of having a large inventory of unneeded materials. Toyota also uses this process with parts it orders from outside suppliers. The company only orders parts on an as-needed basis and receives them "just in time" for the parts to be configured. Therefore, Toyota avoids being bogged down by excess inventory and can run its assembly line more efficiently.

The intricate methods of Toyota's production system may seem cumbersome and possibly overwhelming to employees, but the results state otherwise. Toyota Motor Manufacturing Kentucky, Inc., Toyota's largest production facility outside of Japan, produces about 2000 vehicles a day. "An environment where people have to think brings with it wisdom, and this wisdom brings with it *kaizen* (continuous improvement)," states Teruyuki Minoura, Toyota's chief officer of Business Development & Purchasing Group.[41] Toyota always looks to improve its *jidoka* and just-in-time production in order to make its production system as lean as possible, believing that wasted resources lead to wasted revenue.

DISCUSSION QUESTIONS

1. What lesson did Sakichi Toyoda learn from observing the Japanese looms? Why is it so important for a problem to be fixed when it happens instead of once it reaches the end of the assembly line?
2. What are the benefits of just-in-time production?
3. What problems might operators encounter with just-in-time production systems?

MyBusinessLab CHAPTER RESOURCES

MyBusinessLab in an online learning and testing environment that features the perfect study tools to help you master the concepts covered in this chapter. Log in to MyBusinessLab at www .pearsoned.ca/mybusinesslab to test your knowledge of key chapter concepts, participate in simulations modelled on real-world business situations, and explore the following additional practice tools:

- Study Plan
- Audio Chapter Summaries
- Glossary Flashcards
- eText
- BizChat Discussion Boards
- BizSkills Simulation: Improving Business Operations and Quality
- Decision-Making Mini-Simulation: Supply Chain
- Video Activities: Triple Rock Brewing; Zifty.com; Platinum Autobody

Video Cases:

To access the Chapter 10 Video Cases: Liquid Squids and Body Glove: Surfing the Production Tidal Wave, see the Activities folder in the Assessment section of MyBusinessLab.

Web Case:

To access the Chapter 10 Web Case, see the Activities folder in the Assessment section of MyBusinessLab

10

11

Marketing and Consumer Behaviour

How Sponsored Stories Work

 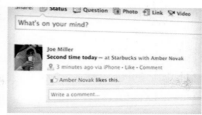 

Joe Miller, or any other Facebook user, likes a Facebook Page, for example, Starbucks.

This generates a News Feed story that his friends might see.

Sponsored Stories increase visibility of this story by highlighting it in the right column of his friends Facebook pages.

Source: Facebook at http://www.facebook.com/ads/stories/ retrieved July 2, 2011

OPENING DISCUSSION: MARKETING BUZZ

Facebook Turns the "Like" into Its Newest Ad

"People are naturally interested in things their friends care about," says Facebook, which is why its News Feed is a key feature of the social networking site.[1] Clicking Facebook's ubiquitous "Like" button allows you to share online what you like with your friends as your "likes" appear in their News Feed, updating them on what you're saying and doing. Essentially, Facebook is an electronic version of the in-person, word-of-mouth model we might use to tell friends where we like to shop, what products we like to buy, or how good the service is at our favourite restaurant. Marketers refer to this word-of-mouth advertising as guerrilla marketing, which is typically unexpected, unconventional, and potentially interactive. Its goal is to generate buzz (getting people to talk about a company's product or service) and sales: minimal resources achieving maximum results. Companies hope that by generating

buzz, their guerrilla marketing campaigns will turn viral. Viral marketing uses pre-existing social networks (i.e., you tell two friends, and they tell two friends, and so on) to increase brand awareness and generate more sales. The term *viral* describes how the ad reaches the masses. Companies want interest in their products and services to spread like a virus: one person reads an ad and likes it (is infected), then that person shares the ad with one or more other people and they like it (are infected), and so on exponentially. These types of marketing techniques have been further enhanced by the Internet's networking strength. Getting someone to "like" your company or product in Facebook is an endorsement and may generate additional business for a company.[2]

More and more companies are using social media and mobile devices to engage consumers and create a memorable brand experience. In 2011, Facebook launched a new ad format called "Sponsored Stories," which presents a friend's actions in the News Feed (likes, check-ins, etc.) as promoted content (ads) in

(continued)

the right-hand column of Facebook. Because, says Facebook, "a lot of impressions do get lost because there's so much content coming through," Sponsored Stories will give brand-related user action much more visibility. Users will be more likely to learn about places to go, apps to use, games to play, and organizations their friends like.[3] Launch partners included Starbucks, Coca-Cola, Levi's, Anheuser-Busch, Amnesty International, RED, and UNICEF.[4]

Jim Squires, Facebook product marketing lead, says, "The advertiser is not controlling the message; it's about actions."[5] For example, if Starbucks buys a Sponsored Story and one of your friends "liked" Starbucks, the ad would run twice: once in your friend's News Feed and again as a paid ad clearly titled Sponsored Story.[6] These relatively inexpensive ads yield a generally higher engagement rate because they target people who are already engaged. A potential area for concern exists should users become dissatisfied with the fact that they cannot stop their Facebook actions from becoming sponsored ads broadcast to all their connections. Friends may gain some control over the viewing of Sponsored Stories by setting their privacy options to hide their activities from each other, but doesn't that defeat the purpose of being a Facebook user?

A check-in post will show up in the Sponsored Story exactly as the user wrote it, which means that a dissatisfied customer could post a negative comment about a company or product. Facebook has obviously anticipated this possibility, providing a "flag" button for "inappropriate content" and giving advertisers the option to avoid any negative postings by limiting their ad purchases to "likes" only.

TBG Digital conducted a test of about two billion ad impressions (whenever an ad is displayed on a website), which showed that Sponsored Stories performed better in click-through rate and cost-per-click (measurement of cost on a per-click basis) than standard Facebook ads—in fact, there was a 46 percent higher click-through rate.[7] Click-through rate measures the success of an online advertising campaign and is calculated by dividing the number of mouse clicks the ad received by the number of times the ad was shown (impressions). Historically, it has been very difficult for companies to buy word-of-mouth advertising, but Sponsored Stories allow companies to leverage their investment in Facebook further by amplifying their brands so they are noticed—which, ultimately, is what companies want.

DISCUSSION QUESTIONS

1. Would you like your posts to be used as ads? Do you think Facebook users will decrease the amount of "likes" they do knowing that their "likes" and other activities may become a Sponsored Story? Why or why not?

2. Do you think that Facebook users who do post a Sponsored Story should be paid for it? Why or why not? Do you think Facebook users may turn away from Facebook because they feel "spammed" on? Why or why not? Do you think businesses will consider that their Sponsored Stories may be viewed by Facebook users as "spam," which might in turn create a negative image of the company instead of the intended positive one? Why or why not?

3. Use the Internet to locate information on why some businesses have failed when trying to implement a social media campaign. Why did they fail? Are these factors present in the Facebook Sponsored Stories strategy?

MARKETING FUNDAMENTALS

Evolution of Marketing

Summarize how marketing has evolved over the production concept era, sales concept era, marketing concept era, and customer relationship era.

How does the Canadian Marketing Association (CMA) define marketing?

CMA members follow a code of ethics to ensure that their marketing practices are fair to consumers. But how responsible are marketers who work with products that may do a disservice to society? For example, what is the moral responsibility for a caffeinated energy drink called "Cocaine"? Does this glamorize drug use or is it just a cheeky, attention-grabbing name created by marketers to generate buzz?

The CMA defines **marketing** as "a set of business practices designed to plan for and present an organization's products or services in ways that build effective customer relationships."[8] Marketing departments serve a variety of functions. First, marketers are responsible for keeping an eye on what people need and want, then communicating these desires to the rest of the organization. Marketing departments help establish desirable pricing strategies and promote the organization by persuading customers that their products are the best. A **product** is any good, service, or idea available for purchase in a market, as well as any intangible benefits derived from its consumption. Marketing departments are also responsible for distributing products to customers at a place and time most suitable to the customer. But perhaps the most important aspect of marketing is to establish meaningful relationships with customers to instill loyalty and ensure repeat business. Marketing is one of the most visible functions of any organization; however, the public only sees the tip of the iceberg.

Marketing is "a set of business practices designed to plan for and present an organization's products or services in ways that build effective customer relationships."

A **product** is any good, service, or idea available for purchase in a market, as well as any intangible benefits derived from its consumption.

How has marketing evolved over time?

The nature of marketing has evolved over four general eras:

The Production Concept Era   From the Industrial Revolution until the 1920s, most companies focused solely on production. The prevailing mindset was that a good-quality product would simply sell itself. This approach worked for many organizations during this era because of a strong demand and a limited supply of products. Whenever demand outstrips supply, it creates a "seller's market."

The Sales Concept Era   From the mid-1920s through the early 1950s, technological advances meant that production increased more sharply than demand for goods and services. The competition for customers became more intense, and businesses began to undertake aggressive sales tactics to sell or "push" their products. The use of heavy public advertising in all available forms of media became prevalent. During this era, marketing generally took place after the product was developed and produced. Heavy emphasis was placed on selling existing products. Even today, many people associate marketing with selling or advertising; however, it has become much more than that.

The Marketing Concept Era   By the 1950s, production continued to expand more quickly than the growth in demand for goods and services, creating a "buyer's market." Soldiers returning from the Second World War were getting married, starting families, and were willing to spend their money on goods and services. Businesses began to realize that simply producing quality products and pushing them onto customers through clever advertising and promotional campaigns didn't guarantee sales. Companies needed to determine what customers wanted and then produce products, as opposed to produce products and then try to convince customers to buy them.

The **marketing concept** changed the focus from finding the right customer for a product to producing the right product for a customer and doing it better than the competition (see **Figure 11.1**). More specifically, the marketing concept focuses on:

1. identifying customer needs before the product is designed and produced
2. aligning all functions of the entire organization to meet or exceed these customer needs through superior products and customer service
3. realizing a profit (not just sales) by satisfying customers over the long term

This requires constantly taking the pulse of changing customer needs and wants and then quickly adapting to meet them. Moreover, it may mean anticipating customers' changing preferences—before they are expressed or even known by consumers—and satisfying these preferences before competitors. For example, Apple has become a master of anticipating customers' desires and fulfilling them with its range of iPods, iPhone, iPads, and all the accessories that go with each.

The **marketing concept** changed the focus from finding the right customer for a product to producing the right product for a customer and doing it better than the competition.

11

Figure 11.1 The Marketing Concept

 Decision-Making Mini-Simulation: What Is Marketing? Located in MyBusinessLab.

Customer relationship management (CRM) is the process of establishing long-term relationships with individual customers to foster loyalty and repeat business.

The Customer Relationship Era Since the late 1990s, organizations have tried to build on their marketing concept successes by intensifying the entire organization's focus on customer satisfaction over time. The result has been the creation of **customer relationship management (CRM)**, the process of establishing long-term relationships with individual customers to foster loyalty and repeat business. The marketing concept is good for *acquiring* customers by offering customized products, among other things, but customer relationship management goes one step further by trying to please customers *after the sale*. It combines computer information technology with customer service and marketing communications to *retain* customers in order to stimulate future sales of similar or supplementary products. Several popular clothing stores, including Gap, Banana Republic, and Old Navy, offer coupons to customers who join their mailing lists. Customers on the list also receive information about sales and promotions to keep them up-to-date on the latest deals at the store.

The idea is to learn as much as possible about customers and create a meaningful one-on-one interaction with each of them. In practice, CRM often involves the sales force gathering information about specific customers to create a customer database. CRM software allows e-mail or other communications to be personalized. It enables the company to offer products tailored to these specific customers' needs and desires. CRM databases also mean that customers visiting the organization's website or customer service call centre can be recognized quickly and easily, and offerings can be adapted to their preferences. Customer relationship management is part of why airlines offer frequent flyer programs to selected customers and why credit card companies offer customized services and low-interest balance transfer to certain targeted customers.

Although each concept experienced a peak in popularity during a specific period, some companies still use marketing concepts from an earlier era. Today's most successful marketing campaigns are a sophisticated combination of the best of each of these times.

Benefits and Criticisms of Marketing

How does marketing benefit stakeholders? *Stakeholders*, or interested parties, include customers, sellers, investors, employees, and society. Each group of stakeholders has a different set of motives for their interest in the success of the business. Through marketing, companies sell products and services that satisfy human needs and wants (the product or service has value and offers utility). Businesses that are most successful in satisfying customers generate higher profits, and investors benefit from the profits earned.

- *Customer and Seller Benefits.* As consumers, we have many needs—food, clothing, housing, medical care, and transportation, among others. Marketers don't really *create* needs. Instead, they *respond* to them. Indeed, many businesses have become extremely profitable by finding a need and satisfying it. Although marketers do not

Outline the benefits of marketing to customers, sellers, investors, employees, and society, and summarize the criticisms of marketing.

create needs, they do work very hard to convince you to choose their specific product over competing products. Hence, sellers, as stakeholders, benefit from successful marketing because their profits enable the organization not only to sustain itself but also to prosper and continue to provide value to customers.

- *Investor and Employee Benefits.* Investors, as stakeholders, receive profits to reward them for devoting their financial resources to organizations that are successful. Employees benefit from successful marketing as well because their jobs and livelihoods are more secure. In addition, new job opportunities are created as production expands to satisfy the growing demand for high-value products.
- *Societal Benefits.* Society benefits from successful marketing because scarce resources are more efficiently allocated or channelled into the production of those goods and services most desired by society. When resources are utilized more efficiently, society is able to consume more products, increasing the average standard of living.

What is non-traditional marketing?   To understand non-traditional marketing, let's first be clear about the definition of traditional marketing. The objective of traditional marketing is to generate a profit. However, many non-profit organizations also have an interest in marketing. Rather than looking to market a product or service, these organizations market an event, cause, place, or person. This is non-traditional marketing. For example, environmental organizations such as the Sierra Club, the National Wildlife Federation, and the Nature Conservancy and other non-profits such as the Red Cross and the Cancer Society rely on marketing to raise awareness of and increase donations to their causes. Likewise, churches and other civic organizations market their missions to attract new membership. Countries, provinces, and cities also run marketing campaigns to attract tourists and businesses to their locations. Museums and zoos also undertake "place marketing" by emphasizing the value of visiting their locations.

Politicians and political parties market candidates for elected office. Agents for athletes, movie stars, television personalities, and musicians market their clients. We market ourselves when we interview for a job. You may have marketed yourself for acceptance to your college or university. To a certain extent, we're all marketing ourselves every day at work and play. Regardless of what is being marketed—an event, a cause, a place, a person, a good, or a service—the essence of marketing remains the same. The only difference between non-traditional and traditional marketing practices is the stakeholders involved and their objectives.

What are the criticisms of marketing?   Over time, certain social shortcomings have emerged from marketing techniques. Some of the questionable tactics criticized include price gouging (asking for a price that is widely considered unfair), high-pressure selling, the production of shoddy or unsafe products, planned obsolescence (the product becomes obsolete after a period of time planned by the manufacturer), poor customer service, misuse of customer information, confusing and deceptive labelling, and other deceptive practices such as hidden fees and charges.

Let's consider a few examples of the costs to society of questionable marketing:

- *Misuse of personal information.* Marketing often involves the collection of personal information about customers. Companies conduct marketing surveys to find out the marital status, annual income, age, sex, race, and other characteristics of their primary customers. Many of us feel violated when this personal information is not adequately protected or is resold without our permission, especially in the age of identity theft.
- *Hidden fees.* Many of us feel taken advantage of when we must pay "hidden" fees and charges not included in the advertised price. Products that require additional parts or shipping and service fees often make customers upset.
- *Consequences of purchase.* Unscrupulous marketing may take advantage of less sophisticated members of society. To what extent is it reasonable to hold buyers responsible for being aware of the consequences of their purchases? This is especially important when purchasing expensive or sophisticated goods and services, such as a car or a mortgage on a home. Similar concerns emerge when marketing is directed at children.

Canadian Marketing Association's (CMA) Code of Ethics and Standards of Practice[9]

Marketers need to inform themselves about the relevant laws in their jurisdiction, including but not limited to the federal *Competition Act* and federal, provincial, and territorial consumer, privacy, and language laws. Marketing activities in Canada are governed by the federal Competition Bureau and Office of Consumer Affairs while consumer protection is regulated by the provincial and territorial governments.

CMA's Code of Ethics and Standards of Practice is the marketing community's cornerstone of self-regulation but does not replace legal advice or provide legal guidance. It establishes and maintains standards for the conduct of marketing in Canada. Unlike many other codes that serve only as guidelines, CMA's code is compulsory for members and as such is a comprehensive regulatory framework governing members' conduct. A series of guidelines assist members to understand their obligations under the code, providing practical information relevant to today's marketing practices, technologies, and channels.

Some of the code's guidelines include:

- Marketing communications must be clear and truthful. Marketers must not knowingly make a representation to a consumer or business that is false or misleading.
- Organizations selling abroad are governed by this Code unless doing so contravenes the laws of foreign jurisdictions.
- Marketers must not knowingly exploit the credulity, lack of knowledge or inexperience of any consumer, taking particular care when dealing with vulnerable consumers. The term "vulnerable consumer" includes, but is not limited to children, teenagers, people with disabilities, the elderly and those for whom English or French is not their first language.

- All consumer marketers must abide by the *Personal Information Protection and Electronics Documents Act* (PIPEDA), and/or applicable provincial privacy laws and the following ten Privacy Principles from the National Standard of Canada and five additional CMA requirements.
- Marketers recognize and acknowledge a continuing responsibility to manage their businesses to minimize environmental impact.

Marketers know they have a core responsibility to the public to establish and maintain high standards of practice, which are also essential to winning and holding consumer confidence. CMA members are obligated to conduct themselves according to the highest standards of honesty, accuracy, fairness, and professionalism not only to serve consumers and businesses but also to preserve the integrity of the discipline in which they operate and to each other.

Discussion Questions

1. Visit the CMA website and review the Code of Ethics and Standards of Practice documentation. Who does the code apply to? How are "must" and "should" used in the code? What do you think of the areas covered in the code? Is this a legal requirement? Will companies abide by the terms? Why or why not?
2. How will a CMA member company ensure that their employees follow the membership guidelines? Would a company lose membership if an employee were in non-compliance with the Code of Ethics and Standards of Practice? Can you find a case of a company having been in a situation of non-compliance? If so, summarize the situation and outcome.
3. Compare the CMA's Code and Standards to those in other countries. Did you find a country that does not seem to have a marketing association? If so, does this country have laws pertaining to marketing strategy and tactics? Do you think other countries should have a similar association? Why or why not?

The many criticisms of marketing should not be taken lightly. These concerns may help explain the strong support for consumer protection laws and other regulations governing business behaviour. Too often, the social costs of marketing stem from unethical business behaviour.

The Marketing Mix (4 Ps of Marketing)

What is a marketing strategy?   A marketing strategy consists of two major elements: the organization must determine its *target market* and then develop a *marketing mix* to meet the needs of that market. The **target market** is the specific group of consumers, with similar needs and wants, toward which a firm directs its marketing efforts. The **marketing mix** is the combination of four factors, called the "4 Ps" of marketing, designed to serve the target market: product, price, promotion, and place (the marketing mix will be discussed in detail in Chapter 12). A marketing strategy must not only define the target market, it must define goals and outcomes, timeline, resources, and opportunities as well.

Does effective marketing require a blend of the 4 Ps?
The idea is to provide the *product* that customers need and want at an appropriate *price* and to *promote* its sale and *place* or distribute the good or service in a convenient location for the customer to purchase (see **Figure 11.2**). Effective marketing requires the appropriate blend of the 4 Ps directed at targeted customers. This blend is constrained by forces outside the firm's control that are found within the broader market environment.

Product   Distinguishing your product from that of your competitors is critical. If you don't do something that's different from and superior to the competition, why should customers buy from you? Product differentiation is the creation of a real or perceived difference in a product designed to attract customers. Product differentiation is one of

③ Describe the two major elements of a marketing strategy and the 4 Ps of the marketing mix.

④ Explain how firms implement a marketing strategy by applying the five steps of the marketing process.

🔲 **Decision-Making Mini-Simulation:** Strategic Marketing. Located in MyBusinessLab.

A **target market** is the specific group of consumers, with similar needs and wants, toward which a firm directs its marketing efforts.

The **marketing mix** is the combination of four factors, called the "4 Ps" of marketing, designed to serve the target market: product, price, promotion, and place.

11

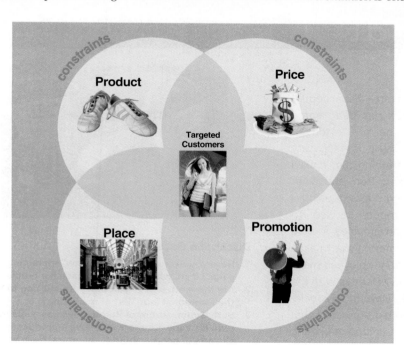

Figure 11.2   The Marketing Mix

the most critical ingredients to success for most businesses. Product differentiation can take the form of functionality, styling, quality, safety, packaging, warranty, accessories, or brand name image. A brand is a name, term, symbol, or design that distinguishes a company and its products from all others.

Price There is a lot to consider when deciding on the price for a product. Of course, the price will have to be sufficient to cover costs if you wish to make a profit. However, the product must be competitively priced to appeal to customers.

Promotion The promotion part of the marketing mix consists of all the methods to inform and persuade targeted customers to buy a product and to build positive customer relationships. Communicating the benefits of your good or service to customers includes advertising, sales promotions, personal selling, public relations, direct marketing, and publicity.

Place The place (or distribution) component of the marketing mix refers to all the methods involved in getting the product into the hands of customers. A product isn't beneficial to a customer if it can't be purchased when and where it is needed. When a business is providing a good instead of a service, the delivery component is often more complicated. Many goods, such as grocery store items, go through a distribution channel, which is a series of firms or individuals that participate in the flow of a product from manufacturer to consumer. The intermediaries in a distribution channel are sometimes called distributors or wholesalers. Some goods, such as food products, go through many wholesalers before reaching a retail outlet (such as a grocery store) and, finally, the consumer. Other goods, such

Costco offers its warehouse members a more direct distribution channel and therefore saves them money.

BizChat

❖ Explore on MyBusinessLab

Is There a Fifth P?

Although the "4 Ps" of marketing are the accepted criteria for the marketing mix, there has been some discussion of adding a fifth "P" to the mix. In today's competitive business world, some say it is necessary to have a "purple cow" factor—something that makes your business or product stand apart from the competition. A company that has attained success using a "purple cow" is the Geek Squad computer service. An affiliate of Best Buy, the Geek Squad provides a wide range of technical services to customers. What makes it stand apart is its image. Geek Squad employees make house calls, driving black-and-white VW Beetles with the Geek Squad logo on the door. The IT world is considered a nerdy field, and the Geek Squad embraces that image and runs with it. Because of its unique marketing approach, Geek Squad is one of the most recognizable technical service businesses.

Discussion Questions

1. Have you ever seen a "purple cow" marketing campaign? If so, what was it that made it a purple cow?
2. Are there other "Ps" you thing are missing from the traditional four "Ps" of marketing?
3. Seth Godin, author of *Purple Cow*, has a special term for early adopters who love a product and tell all sorts of people about it: sneezers. Have you ever been a sneezer for a particular product or service?

as automobiles, typically move from the manufacturer to just one wholesaler, the car dealership, and then on to the consumer. Still other goods bypass wholesalers altogether and move from the manufacturer directly to the consumer. Today, many of these "direct to consumer" manufacturers have convenient websites whereby consumers can make purchases online and have the products delivered directly to them.

What are the steps in the marketing process?   There are five steps in the marketing process, as outlined in **Figure 11.3**.

1. *Identify a Market Need.* Is there a need for pool cleaning services in your area? To identify a new business, new product, or new service need, you must observe your potential customer base. For example, if there are many pools in the area in which you wish to run your pool cleaning business and there are not too many other businesses already servicing those pools, then, yes, there is probably a need.

2. *Conduct Market Research and Develop a Marketing Plan.* The next step is to conduct research on the profitability of a potential business, product, or service. (How to conduct market research and develop a marketing plan are discussed later in this chapter.)

3. *Identify Target Customers.* The third step is to select a target market. Without this focus, you will waste effort and money promoting a product or service to individuals not interested in your product or service. When selecting a target market, visualize your ideal customer. What does your ideal customer need or want, and how will you provide this? Are your targeting customers who are individual/household consumers or other businesses for which you will be a supplier?

4. *Implement the 4 Ps.* Once you have selected a target market, the fourth step is to implement the marketing mix, or the 4 Ps of marketing—product, price, promotion, and place.

   Once an unfilled customer need has been identified, it is important to develop a product that not only meets that need but also fulfills it better than the competition. Start by coming up with a memorable brand to distinguish your business and services from all others. Having a memorable brand name will make it easier to find investors and to attract customers.

   Having developed a set of goods and services and a brand that distinguishes your business from all others, you will now want to contemplate a pricing strategy. What price are people willing to pay, and how sensitive are customers to price changes? Will different hourly rates be charged on weekends as compared to weekdays? Will seasonal differences influence prices?

   Promotion is the most visible part of the marketing mix. It can be very expensive, yet very fruitful. How should your business be promoted?

   The place component of the marketing mix often involves finding the best location for the business. You will want to be within a reasonable distance of your customers. Whether providing products or services the "place" (or delivery) component of the marketing mix is equally important.

5. *Nurture Customer Relationships.* The final step in the marketing process is to manage customer relationships. As we noted earlier, the goal of customer relationship management (CRM) is to establish long-term trusting relationships with individual customers to foster loyalty and repeat business. You must develop a rapport with customers by learning which customers are returning customers and note any particular preferences they may have. You might even offer discounts for repeat customers. You should not only solicit but also respond to suggestions by customers on how to improve products or services. To build customer trust, you should also offer customers their money back if they are unsatisfied. To maintain and foster interest in your products or services, you may want to create a mailing list for select customers. You will want to establish relationships with suppliers. Above all, it is critical to personalize and maintain good customer relationships. Marketing is an ongoing process of tweaking a business to satisfy customers in order to ensure quality, value, and repeat business.

Is the marketing process easy to implement?   The marketing process may seem simple when it's written on the page, but it's as much art as it is science. For instance, a mobile pool cleaning service would have a completely different marketing strategy

Figure 11.3   The Five Steps in the Marketing Process

The **marketing environment** includes environmental influences outside the firm's control that constrain the organization's ability to manipulate its marketing mix.

than a non-mobile standalone pool business selling goods and offering cleaning services. Each product needs to be looked at individually in order to tailor an appropriate marketing plan.

Common ingredients for marketing success include producing a high-quality product (with a unique brand that is properly promoted) that consistently delivers value to customers at a "fair" price, where they want it, and when they want it.

THE MARKETING ENVIRONMENT

The Competitive Environment

5 Describe how the various factors in the marketing environment influence a firm's ability to manipulate its marketing mix.

Decision-Making Mini-Simulation: Marketing Environment. Located in MyBusinessLab.

Why is analyzing the competitive environment important? Assessing the competitive environment, or the degree of competition facing a firm, is critical to creating an effective marketing mix. You may recall from Chapter 2 the four basic market environments with respect to the varying degrees of competition facing firms: perfect competition, monopolistic competition, oligopoly, and monopoly. The degree of competition affects the firm's production, pricing, promotion, and place (distribution) strategies in many ways. A successful business must be aware of competition and always try to stay one step ahead.

How do marketing managers control the competitive environment? Generally, the marketing mix (the blend of the 4 Ps) can be controlled by marketing managers; however, the **marketing environment** includes environmental influences outside the firm's control that constrain the organization's ability to manipulate its marketing mix. These external environmental influences (see **Figure 11.4**) include the competitive environment (discussed in Chapter 2) as well as the political, economic, socio-cultural, and technological (PEST) environment (discussed in Chapter 1).

Scanning the Environment

How do companies stay informed about changes in the external marketing environment? Marketers must be keenly aware of the marketing environment when selecting their marketing mix. In fact, one of the key responsibilities of managers in any organization is to undertake **environmental scanning**, the process of surveying the market environment to assess external threats and opportunities. A successful business detects changes in the market environment and adjusts its marketing mix (product, price, promotion, and distribution) quickly and appropriately, inasmuch as the overall market environment will allow it to do so. Let's look at each of the elements of the marketing environment in a bit more detail.

How does the competitive environment affect marketing? Assessing the competitive environment, or the degree of competition facing the firm, is critical to creating an effective marketing mix. You may recall from Chapter 2 the four basic market environments with respect to the varying degrees of competition facing

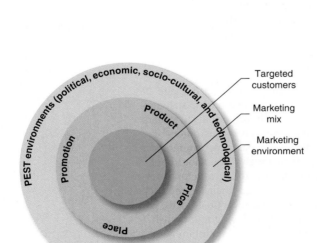

Figure 11.4 The Marketing Mix and the Marketing Environment

firms: perfect competition, monopolistic competition, oligopoly, and monopoly. The degree of competition affects the firm's production, pricing, promotion, and place (distribution) strategies in many ways. A successful business must be aware of competition and always try to stay one step ahead.

Environmental scanning is the process of surveying the market environment to assess external threats and opportunities.

How does the political environment affect marketing?
It has been said that in a democracy, the squeaky wheel gets the grease. Special-interest groups try to influence the political process in various ways. Businesses are no exception. They try to wield political influence through contributions to political parties, individual candidates, and political action committees (PACs) because government laws and regulations significantly influence business interests. In addition, several agencies enforce laws and regulations constraining marketing efforts, such as Environment Canada and Health Canada, and the Federal Trade Commission (FTC). Businesses are forced to consider the political (and legal) environment in making marketing decisions, as these factors can play a major role in overall success.

How does the economic environment affect marketing?
The economic environment can affect customers' willingness and ability to spend their money on a firm's product. Therefore, marketers must keep abreast of changes in inflation, interest rates, unemployment, and economic growth rates over the course of the business cycle. Part of this is keeping up with changes in consumer confidence levels and government fiscal and monetary policies. Moreover, because of globalization, prudent firms follow global economic trends as well. This is especially important if the firm is involved in international business.

The economic environment affects the firm's marketing strategy in many ways. For example, a rising inflation rate reduces the purchasing power of money, and sales may fall. A recession will reduce the demand for most products. Even the best-laid marketing plans will fail when customers can no longer afford to buy your product. If interest rates are high, then the cost of borrowing is up, and consumers who buy on credit will purchase less and your sales may fall. As a final example, suppose the value of the dollar falls (gets weaker) in foreign exchange markets. This will cause imported goods to become more expensive. Importing firms may need to raise their prices, which could significantly reduce sales. Savvy marketers try to keep their fingers on the changing pulse of the economy to forecast looming problems or potential opportunities and make the necessary adjustments.

How does the socio-cultural environment affect marketing?
Domestic, and to a stronger extent multinational, businesses must realize that culture is dynamic, and effective marketers must be able to adapt to different attitudes and keep up with changing social trends. Demographic shifts—such as age, gender, ethnicity, and marital status—and changing values can signal opportunities for businesses. For example, we can expect the demand for medical care, pharmaceuticals, and nursing homes to increase as the average age of the population increases. We've also observed greater demand for convenience foods, restaurant services, and cellphones over the years as lifestyles have changed. Products such as Wii Fit attempt to deal with society's concern about children's lack of exercise.

How does the technological environment affect marketing?
The technological environment can also influence the marketing mix. Indeed, advances in communications and transportation technologies may be one of the most influential factors affecting modern business. The Internet alone has enabled many small businesses to compete with large corporations around the world by marketing and selling their products online. Moreover, modern, sophisticated manufacturing innovations have enabled many firms to customize their products more easily and to offer them at dramatically reduced prices to satisfy the varying tastes of targeted customers. Successful marketing requires use of the latest technologies to reach and satisfy target customers wherever they may be. This also includes the use of computer databases to enhance customer relationship management (CRM). Technological advances over the past decade have changed the way we work, live, and do business.

Technological Advances of the Decade That Changed Our Lives

1. Pocket-sized networked computers (e.g., iPhone)
2. Social networks (e.g., Facebook)
3. Online video streaming (e.g., YouTube)
4. Internet purchasing (e.g., Amazon)
5. Digital still and video cameras
6. Mass acceptance of cellphones
7. Networked gaming (e.g., Xbox Live)
8. Global outsourcing
9. Democratization of information (e.g., Wikipedia)
10. GPS in our pockets

Source: Peter Brauer, "Top Ten Technological Advances of the Decade that Changed My Life," *Popten.net*, December 14, 2009, http://www.popten.net/2009/12/top-ten-technological-advances-of-the-decade-that-changed-my-life/, Accessed May 28, 2011.

11

MARKETING RESEARCH AND PLANNING

The Marketing Research Process

Identify the five steps of the marketing research process and the four elements of a good marketing plan.

Decision-Making Mini-Simulation:
Marketing Research.
Located in MyBusinessLab.

Market research is the process of gathering and analyzing market information for making marketing decisions.

Primary data are raw data collected by the researcher. The data are frequently collected through observation, questionnaires, surveys (via mail, e-mail, or telephone), focus groups, interviews, customer feedback, samples, and controlled experiments.

A **focus group** is typically a group of eight to ten potential customers who are asked for feedback on a good or service, advertisement, idea, or packaging.

Secondary data are data that have already been collected and processed. An example of secondary data is census data.

What is involved in researching the market?   For a business example, let's look at Tiara Watson's salon supply business. Tiara thinks the business will be a great investment because the next closest supplier is more than 100 kilometres (70 miles) away, so salons have to pay unnecessarily high shipping costs. Tiara started researching and found more than thirty salons around the city, so she has a strong target market. She's already met with a few of the owners to see whether they'd be willing to switch suppliers, and they seem interested. She knows she can't start out selling supplies to every salon in the city, but she isn't sure where to start. How can she figure out which salons to target for her start-up?

Look back at the five-step marketing process shown in Figure 11.3. You'll notice that after a market need is identified, a firm needs to conduct *market research* to determine the profitability of a venture, develop a marketing plan, and determine its target market. In this section, we'll explore each of these processes in more detail.

Market research is the process of gathering and analyzing market information for making marketing decisions. The marketing research process consists of five steps:

1. *Define the Need, Problem, or Objective.* Marketing managers and researchers need to work together to clearly define the objective of the research. They should determine the exact nature of the business need, problem, or opportunity, and the information desired. They should also determine why that information would be helpful to the manager. This step will help the researcher collect relevant and appropriate data for analysis. Tiara has defined the need for a salon supply company that is in close proximity to city salons.
2. *Collect Relevant Data.* Determining which types of data will be collected and how the information will be collected is the next step. Two general types of data exist: primary and secondary. **Primary data** are raw data collected by the researcher. The data are frequently collected through observation, questionnaires, surveys (via mail, e-mail, or telephone), focus groups, interviews, customer feedback, samples, and controlled experiments. A **focus group** is typically a group of eight to ten potential customers who are asked for feedback on a good or service, advertisement, idea, or packaging.

   Secondary data have already been collected and processed. An example of secondary data is census data. This information is usually much cheaper to obtain. Tiara Watson has collected secondary data about the location of the closest salon supply companies and primary data about the interest of the salon owners in changing to a closer, cheaper supplier. Examples of primary and secondary data sources are summarized in **Table 11.1**.
3. *Analyze Data.* Analysis of data requires knowledge of appropriate statistical techniques beyond the scope of this textbook. Nevertheless, honest analysis is necessary. You should never adjust your data to get the results you want. For example, Apple's honest assessment of marketing data led the company not to introduce the iPod wristwatch.
4. *Interpret Results.* Statistics never speak for themselves. Careful analysis will lead to conclusions about marketing strategies that have more favourable benefits in relation to their costs. For example, a company's profit numbers for the previous year might appear to indicate a lack of growth, but when inflation and the falling value of the dollar are taken into account, the statistics may actually show that the company expanded its business.
5. *Act on Conclusions.* The whole purpose of marketing research is to point managers toward better marketing decisions. Marketing research should therefore be ongoing. Changing market conditions require businesses to continually adapt and constantly search for better ways to provide value to customers. Part of acting on the conclusions of marketing research is creating a marketing plan (discussed in the next section).

Table 11.1 Examples of Sources of Primary and Secondary Data

Primary Sources of Data	Secondary Sources of Data
• Observation • Questionnaires • Surveys • Focus groups • Interviews • Customer feedback • Sampling • Controlled experiments	**Government Resources** • Industry Canada—Economic research and analysis; company directories; trade and investment • Statistics Canada—census; labour statistics; demographics • *CIA World Fact Book* (U.S.) • Human Resources and Skills Development Canada (HRSDC) • Foreign Affairs and International Trade Canada • Bank of Canada **Company, Industry, and Product Resources** • Ipsos Canada—marketing research • Euromonitor International—marketing research • Marketing Resources Links—by Decision Analyst, Inc. at SecondaryData.com • Canadian Business Resource—www.cbr.ca • Hoover's Online—Listings include 12 million companies worldwide • *Fraser's Canadian Trade Directory* • *Moody's Industry Review* • Standard & Poor's Industry Surveys **Trade Publications** Chamber of Commerce, Board of Trade, Canadian Marketing Association, Retail Council of Canada, Conference Board of Canada, Dun & Bradstreet Canada **Magazines** *BusinessWeek, Canadian Business, Fortune, Fast Company, Entrepreneur, Forbes, Marketing Magazine* **Newspapers** *The Globe and Mail, National Post, Wall Street Journal* **Internal sources** Accounting records; annual reports; prior research reports; company records

top10

Statistics Every Marketer Should Know (2011)

1. 91% of Canadian Internet users go online to research product information.
2. 78% of businesspeople use their mobile devices to check e-mail.
3. 20% of Canadian shoppers use their smartphones to search product recommendations while shopping in-store.
4. More than 9 million Canadians have registered on the "National Do Not Call List."
5. 84% of twenty-five- to thirty-four-year-olds have left a favourite website because of intrusive or irrelevant advertising.
6. 57% of businesses have acquired a customer through their company blogs.
7. 64% of Facebook users have become "fans" of at least one company.
8. Inbound marketing costs 62% less per lead than traditional outbound marketing.
9. 41% of B2B companies and 67% of B2C companies have acquired a customer through Facebook.
10. More than 100 million active users currently access Facebook through mobile devices.

Sources: **1.** "Quality Healthcare Publications," *PatientDirectory.ca*, from http://www.patientdirectory.ca/online.htm, Accessed May 28, 2011. **2.** Marta Kagan, "12 Mind-Blowing Statistics Every Marketer Should Know," *HubSpot Blog*, April 1, 2011, http://blog.hubspot.com/blog/tabid/6307/bid/11414/12-Mind-Blowing-Statistics-Every-Marketer-Should-Know.aspx, Accessed May 28, 2011. **3.** Canadian Marketing Association, "Weekly Watching Brief," *the-cma.org*, February 25, 2011, http://www.the-cma.org/public/?WCE=C=47IK=230095, Accessed May 28, 2011. **4.** Canadian Radio-television and Telecommunications Commission, "National Do Not Call List (DNCL) Status Report," *CRTC.gc.ca*, http://www.crtc.gc.ca/eng/dncl/status-etape.htm, Accessed May 28, 2011. **5.–9.** Kagan, "12 Mind-Blowing Statistics Every Marketer Should Know." **10.** Erick Schonfeld, "Facebook Drives 44% of Social Sharing on the Web," *TechCrunch.com*, February 16, 2011, http://techcrunch.com/2010/02/16/facebook-44-percent-social-sharing/, Accessed May 28, 2011.

How is social media used in market research? For brands, reputation is a key foundation to building a successful fan-driven online community. Social media sites such as Facebook, Twitter, and YouTube are becoming invaluable sources of information for company research. Companies can follow discussions in Twitter to find out what people are saying about their company, brand, products, and services. The value social media has over focus groups is in breadth, the great number of people that can be surveyed, and in the speed at which people can be surveyed. Not every company or marketing research project will lend itself to social media tools, but if a fit is there, then social media gives marketers valuable, inexpensive, broad-ranging, and speedy tools for obtaining consumer insight. Of all people identified as marketers in Twitter, 15 percent follow more than 2000 people, compared with 0.29 percent of all Twitter users who follow more than 2000 people.[10]

The Marketing Plan

A **marketing plan** is a written document that specifies marketing activities designed to reach organizational objectives.

What is a marketing plan?
A **marketing plan** is a written document that specifies marketing activities designed to reach organizational objectives. It is a critical component of a business plan. A marketing plan is typically a *written* document because details about tasks to be performed by employees can be lost easily if communicated orally. Moreover, written objectives can be compared with actual measurements to see whether objectives are being met.

What are the elements of a good marketing plan?
Four elements emerge from all good marketing plans:

- a clearly written marketing objective
- performance of situational analysis
- selection of a target market
- implementation, evaluation, and control of the marketing mix (4 Ps)

A **marketing objective** is a clearly stated goal to be achieved through marketing activities. It should be realistic, quantifiable, and time specific.

Why is a marketing objective necessary?
A **marketing objective** is a clearly stated goal to be achieved through marketing activities. It should be realistic, quantifiable, and time specific.[11] The objective is the starting point for the marketing plan. A marketing objective of having every home in Canada purchase a specific product is unrealistic. Selling 100 000 units in a year is a more realistic, quantifiable, and time-specific marketing objective. When objectives are realistic, they are attainable and can motivate employees toward their goal. When they are measurable, the firm can determine whether they are being achieved. If deadlines are also imposed, then firms know whether they are reaching their goals in a timely manner.

What is a situational analysis?
Creating clearly stated objectives is the first step in any good marketing plan. The next step is conducting a *situational (or SWOT) analysis*. As you learned in Chapter 6, this is an evaluation of the organization's internal *strengths* and *weaknesses*, as well as the *opportunities* and *threats* found in the external environment.

The **5 Cs of marketing** include company, collaborators, customers, competitors, and climate (see Figure 11. 5).

Scanning the environment by analyzing the **5 Cs of marketing** (company, collaborators, customers, competitors, and climate) is another useful situational analysis framework that can be used alone or in conjunction with a SWOT (see **Figure 11.5**). It covers the internal, the micro-environment, and the macro-environment situation (these environments were discussed in Chapter 1). By combining regional and market analysis with knowledge of the firm's own capabilities and partnerships, the firm can select more favourable opportunities to provide value to the customer. The 5 C analysis is an extension of the 3 C analysis (company, customers, and competitors), with the addition of collaborators and climate (which is a macro-environmental analysis, or PEST analysis).[12]

What do we mean by internal strengths?
In terms of marketing, a company's internal strengths refer to the competitive advantages or core competencies that the

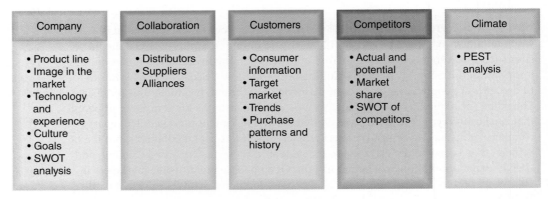

Figure 11.5 Situational Analysis: 5 Cs of Marketing

company has at its disposal to meet a specified marketing objective. Core competencies provide customer benefits and are not easily imitated by other companies, setting the company apart from the competition.

How does a company assess its weaknesses? Assessing internal weaknesses means that a company must perform an audit of current managerial expertise, manufacturing and financing capabilities, and the organization's execution of the 4 Ps in the marketing mix. By honestly assessing its weaknesses, a company can determine a realistic marketing objective. For example, a company that makes handmade watches and has only three employees cannot expect to produce 75 000 watches a week.

Why look to the external environment? The dynamic and ever-changing external environment offers many opportunities and creates many threats. Changes in the degree of competition facing firms, the economic, technological, and socio-cultural forces, as well as changes in the political, legal, and regulatory environments, have caused some firms to thrive while damaging others. This is especially true for international businesses because the number of market environments compounds the analysis. Rapid changes in technology create new opportunities, such as expanding sales over the Internet, but pose new threats, such as requiring additional technological expertise to protect against hackers. Successful companies continually evaluate environmental factors as part of their SWOT analysis to match their strengths with opportunities and to address their weaknesses to avoid threats.

Target Markets

How are target markets determined? Once an organization has evaluated its internal strengths and weaknesses, as well as the external opportunities and threats of the market environment, then it is ready to select its target market. If a business doesn't focus its marketing efforts, it will likely waste time and money promoting its product to individuals who are not interested.

 Describe how target markets are determined and how a firm positions itself to satisfy a target market.

 BizSkills Simulation: Market Research Matters. Located in MyBusinessLab.

Off the **Mark**

The Tale of Pets.com

The Pets.com sock puppet signalled an advertising frenzy for a brief period in the late 1990s. These ads were so popular that the company's spokesperson, a sock puppet dog, ended up being the company's best-selling product.

Unfortunately, sock puppet sales alone were not enough to sustain the business. Selling dog food and other pet products online did not pan out the way that the young Pets.com entrepreneurs had hoped or the way that the venture capitalists who supplied them with US$110 million had counted on. Pets.com made the crucial error of buying expensive advertising slots and going public before the company had generated significant revenue. In 2000, Pets.com announced that it was selling all its assets, including the rights to the sock puppet. Perhaps running a successful business takes more than producing catchy sock puppet commercials. Had the company given more thought to its target market, maybe this company wouldn't have ended up in the doghouse.[13]

Discussion Questions

1. Who was the target market for this company's products?
2. What are some of the real and imagined errors this company's management made?
3. Before they started the business, how could these entrepreneurs have determined whether pet owners would buy pet food online?

Market segmentation is the process of separating the broader market into smaller markets (or market segments) that consist of similar groups of customers.

Niche marketing occurs when a product is marketed to a very narrowly defined set of potential customers.

Positioning is the process of developing a unique marketing mix that best satisfies a target market.

 Decision-Making Mini-Simulation: Segmentation, Targeting, and Positioning. Located in MyBusinessLab.

Geographic segmentation is market segmentation according to geographic characteristics.

Demographic segmentation is market segmentation according to age, race, religion, gender, ethnic background, and other demographic variables.

Psychographic segmentation is market segmentation based on lifestyles, personality traits, motives, and values.

How do you find a target market?　The marketing concept's recognition of consumers' various needs and wants leads marketing managers to think in terms of target markets. As mentioned earlier, a target market is the specific group of consumers, with similar needs and wants, toward which a firm directs its marketing efforts. Finding a target market begins with **market segmentation**, the process of separating the broader market into smaller markets (or market segments) that consist of similar groups of customers. A **market segment** is a subgroup of potential customers who share similar characteristics and therefore have similar product needs and preferences. Some firms focus so much on one specific market that they undertake **niche marketing**, or marketing a product to a very narrowly defined set of potential customers. A company that sells specialized gear shifters for racing bicycles is operating in a niche market.

Marketers choose those market segments that offer the greatest profit potential, and these become the target markets. For each target market, the company tries to blend the 4 Ps of the marketing mix to best satisfy the targeted customers. The process of developing a unique marketing mix that best satisfies a target market is known as **positioning**.

How are consumer markets segmented?　Consumer markets can be segmented based on many variables or characteristics of consumers. Four of the most common consumer market segmentation classifications are geographic, demographic, psychographic, and behavioural (summarized in **Table 11.2**).

Geographic segmentation is market segmentation according to geographic characteristics. For example, clothing apparel, skis, snow blowers, four-wheel-drive vehicles, air conditioning, and heating needs differ by regional climate differences. Taste in food products also varies by region.

Demographic segmentation is market segmentation according to age, race, religion, gender, ethnic background, and other demographic variables. Few businesses want to miss a growing market segment. It is now common to find product labels, television stations, and newspapers published in languages other than English. The number of people whose mother tongue is neither English nor French will be between 21 percent and 25 percent of the total population in Canada by 2017[14] (Canadian demographics was discussed in Chapter 8).

Automobile companies also use demographic segmentation. They are keenly aware of how important it is to position their models to appeal to different age groups, income levels, and differences in gender.

Psychographic segmentation is market segmentation based on lifestyles, personality traits, motives, and values. Cat food advertisements are cleverly focusing on "cat lover" personalities, whereas many beer commercials target specific personality types. When motives are used to determine the appropriate market, marketers focus on why consumers make a purchase. For example, Volvo has been very successful in selling cars to consumers motivated by safety concerns, and Gold's Gym sells memberships to customers concerned with their health. Sophisticated marketers closely

Table 11.2　Consumer Market Segmentation

Geographic	Demographic	Psychographic	Behavioural
• Region	• Age	• Lifestyle	• Benefit sought
• Suburban	• Race	• Personality traits	• Volume usage
• Rural	• Religion	• Motives	• Brand loyalty
• City	• Family size	• Values	• Price sensitivity
• County	• Ethnicity		• Product end use
• Population density	• Gender		
• Climate	• Income		
• Terrain	• Education		

examine their customers' lifestyles, personality traits, motives, and values because, unlike geographic and demographic variables, these psychographic variables can be manipulated by marketing efforts. Whatever consumers may value, whether it be quality, social status or affiliation, safety, health, privacy, technology, or appearance, you can bet that businesses will offer a good or service to satisfy that real or perceived need. They will be rewarded with profits for doing so.

Behavioural segmentation is market segmentation based on certain consumer behaviour characteristics, such as the benefits sought by the consumer, the extent to which the product is consumed, brand loyalty, price sensitivity, and the ways in which the product is used. For example, a company that produces herbal supplements is appealing to the specific benefits sought by its consumers.

Brand loyalty is another kind of behavioural segmentation. It can influence price sensitivity—the more loyal the customer, the less sensitive he or she is to a price increase. If a customer has been using the same brand of toothpaste for twelve years and has had no cavities in that time, a small price increase will most likely not be an issue. Finally, knowing how the product is actually used can help companies develop packages that appeal to customers. For example, when pills are taken daily, having pills placed in a package where the day of the week is written below each pill can be useful for consumers.

What personality traits and motives would marketers target when marketing a gym membership?

Behavioural segmentation is market segmentation based on certain consumer behaviour characteristics, such as the benefits sought by the consumer, the extent to which the product is consumed, brand loyalty, price sensitivity, and the ways in which the product is used.

CONSUMER BEHAVIOUR

Consumer Markets

8
Describe the purchase decision process and the major influences affecting a consumer's buying decision.

Why study consumer behaviour?   Knowledge of consumer behaviour helps marketers select the most profitable target markets and guides the implementation, evaluation, and control of the marketing mix (4 Ps) for selected targeted markets. For example, consumers are becoming increasingly concerned about gas mileage. Automobile companies that realize this can create more gas-efficient cars or drop the prices on less-efficient models to compensate for poor gas mileage.

Consumer behaviour refers to the ways individuals or organizations search for, evaluate, purchase, use, and dispose of goods and services. Notice that consumer behaviour involves the study of individual consumers or business organizations as buyers in the market. Most of us intuitively think of a market as being a consumer market. Consumer markets are the markets we, as consumers, are most familiar with. In a **consumer market**, individuals purchase goods and services for personal consumption. But there are also business-to-business markets. In **business-to-business (B2B) markets**, businesses purchase goods and services from other businesses. In this section, we'll explore both markets and examine the buying behaviour differences between consumer markets and business-to-business markets.

Consumer behaviour refers to the ways individuals or organizations search for, evaluate, purchase, use, and dispose of goods and services.

In a **consumer market**, individuals purchase goods and services for personal consumption.

In **business-to-business (B2B) markets**, businesses purchase goods and services from other businesses.

11

How does a consumer make a buying decision?   The consumer buying process involves five steps:

1. need recognition
2. information search
3. evaluation of alternatives
4. purchase or no purchase decision
5. post-purchase evaluation

- -

Consumer Behaviour **quiz**

Answer the following questions to test your consumer behaviour IQ.

1. In a consumer market, who is the primary buyer of goods?

    a. Businesses

    b. Households

2. Which of the following is a major influence on what people buy?

    a. Education

    b. Income

3. Which step comes first in the buying decision process?

    a. Information search

    b. Evaluation of alternatives

4. Which product is a result of psychological influences on society?

    a. Hybrid cars

    b. Bottled water

5. Which of the following statements is true?

    a. Consumer behaviour doesn't help marketers identify target markets.

    b. The marketing process is the same for all markets.

Answers: 1. B; 2. B; 3. A; 4. A; 5. B

Not all consumers go through each step in the process, and the steps do not need to be completed in the same order. As well, the process can be interrupted at any time with a "no purchase" decision.

Consider your decision to purchase the educational services of your college or university. You first recognized the need for higher education. You likely obtained information about schools from many sources, including your friends, family, counsellors, and the Internet. You may have also visited a few campuses to gather first-hand information. You then evaluated your choices based on a number of factors, including the tuition (price), geographic location, or maybe where your friends were going to school. Your final choice may have been based on "rational analysis" or the result of an emotional decision (based on some "gut feelings"). After making a purchase, we also evaluate our decision in terms of how well our expectations are being met. You'll likely continue to evaluate your college or university choice long after you graduate.

What influences consumer decision making?   The five-step consumer decision-making process is part of a broader environmental context that influences each step. Effective marketing attempts to help consumers with their information search and the evaluation of alternatives. These environmental influences are shown in **Figure 11.6**.[15]

1. *Socio-cultural Influences.* Socio-cultural influences on buying decisions include the buyer's culture, subculture, social class, family, and peers. Culture is the set of learned attitudes, beliefs, and ways of life that are unique to a society and are handed down through generations. Subcultures are specific groups within a culture that

Most Popular Searches for Brands (2010)

1. Nokia
2. Samsung
3. Airtel
4. Micromax
5. Dell
6. Maruti
7. Vodafone
8. Apple
9. Sony Ericsson
10. HP

Source: Arun Prabhudesai, "Top Most Popular Searches of 2010," *Trak.in*, December 10, 2010, http://trak.in/tags/business/2010/12/10/top-search-terms-of-year-2010/, Accessed May 25, 2011.

Figure 11.6   Major Influences Affecting a Consumer's Buying Decision

share attitudes and life experiences. Some examples of subcultures include churches, community organizations, and online communities such as Facebook and Myspace. Cultural values change over time. For example, many people today value healthier lifestyles. Social class refers to a combination of factors such as education, income, wealth, and occupation common to a group of people. Social class can have an impact on purchasing decisions, as some possessions are considered status symbols.

2. *Personal Influences.* Personal influences on a buyer's consumption choice are often shaped by his or her age, economic situation, lifestyle, and personality. A person who enjoys spending time outdoors hiking is more likely to purchase a tent than a person who spends time playing video games.

3. *Psychological Influences.* Psychological influences include differences in the buyer's motivation, perception, attitudes, and learning. One goal of marketing is to shape the perception of a product in the minds of consumers. Attitudes toward a product put customers in a frame of mind that either predisposes them to view the product favourably or not. For example, changing attitudes toward the environment have increased the demand for hybrid cars. Learning refers to changes in buying behaviour based on experience. Good experiences with brands result in repeat business. Bad experiences stunt future sales.

4. *Situational Influences.* Situational influences include the physical surroundings, social surroundings, and the type of product purchased. Complex, expensive, and infrequently purchased products, such as a new home, will elicit a greater degree of information searching and evaluation of alternatives than a frequently purchased product that has few substitutes, such as table salt.

5. *Marketing Mix Influences.* Marketing mix (4 Ps) influences include the product, price, promotion, and place (distribution) aspects of purchases. As stressed throughout this chapter, marketing is interested in producing a product that buyers want at an affordable price, promoting awareness of the attributes of the product, and placing the good or service in a timely and convenient location for consumers to buy.

Knowledge of consumer buying behaviour and the influences on the buying decision is critical to effective marketing. Some of these influences, such as personal influences, are outside the control of marketers, while other influences, such as psychological influences, can be affected by businesses. All these influences should be kept in mind when selecting a target market, implementing, evaluating, controlling the marketing mix, and building customer relationships.

Business-to-Business (B2B) Markets

What is the difference between consumer markets and business-to-business markets? The difference between consumer and B2B markets hinges on who's doing the buying. If a good or service is purchased in a B2B market, it is purchased by a business for further processing or for resale or to facilitate general business activity. The B2B market is significantly larger compared to consumer markets because virtually all consumer products go through a number of distributors or wholesalers before reaching the final consumer at a retail outlet. In fact, each time an unfinished product is bought and sold through the many stages of a product's development, a separate B2B market exists. Think of all the transactions involved in producing a car. Most of the components are produced by separate firms. Moreover, each of these firms derives its inputs from different businesses.

There are several key differences between consumer and B2B markets.[16] The more important characteristics of B2B markets include the following:

1. *A few buyers that purchase in large quantities.* Business-to-business markets typically involve a few buyers that purchase very large quantities. For example, only a few airline companies buy most of Boeing's jets.

2. *Highly trained buyers.* Most business purchasing agents are highly skilled at their jobs. They often weigh the benefits and the costs in a more systematic fashion and are less influenced by emotional factors than buyers in consumer markets. This requires sellers to pitch their products at a much more sophisticated level.

9

Compare the buying decisions and marketing processes in business-to-business markets to those in the consumer market.

11

3. *Group purchasing decision.* A team of individuals within purchasing departments usually collaborate in making a purchasing decision in B2B markets. This means marketers must be prepared to be patient and mindful of all decision-makers' concerns to seal a deal.

4. *Close customer relationship.* Because there are only a few sophisticated buyers that purchase large quantities, marketers find it necessary to establish a much closer relationship with customers compared to the relationship with buyers in consumer markets. As a result, B2B marketing is more focused on personal selling compared to the mass advertising campaigns that typify consumer markets.

5. *Geographically concentrated buyers.* Most buyers in B2B markets are concentrated in a few of the most industrialized areas where most large businesses are located. This reduces the costs of reaching buyers.

6. *Direct purchasing.* Often buyers in B2B markets purchase directly from sellers, as opposed to consumer markets, where products typically go through many wholesalers before the product arrives to the end user.

These key differences between consumer and B2B markets are summarized in **Table 11.3**. These differences can be organized by differences in market structure, the nature of the buying unit, and the purchasing process.

How does a business make a buying decision, and what influences that decision?

The five-step consumer decision-making process is equally applicable to business purchasing decisions. Businesses begin by recognizing a need; they seek out information to aid them in the purchase decision; evaluate alternatives; decide to either purchase or not to purchase; and undertake a post-purchase evaluation. However, business purchases are generally more rational, reasoned, objective decisions based on influences such as the state of the economy, technological factors, the degree of competition, political and regulatory concerns, and organizational objectives, policies, and procedures.

Is the marketing process different for B2B markets?

The marketing process remains the same for all markets: identify a need, undertake research to come up with a marketing plan, select a target market, implement and control the marketing mix, and nurture customer relationships.

Think back to the quiz you took at the beginning of this section. Would you ace the quiz now based on what you've learned? Understanding consumer behaviour and the buying and marketing process are essential for marketers when selecting a target market and managing the marketing mix.

Table 11.3   Differences between Business-to-Business and Consumer Markets

	Business-to-Business Market	Consumer Market
Market Structure	• Few customers • Large-volume purchases • Geographically concentrated	• Many customers • Small-volume purchases • Geographically dispersed
Nature of the Buying Unit	• More professional and rational purchase decision	• Less sophisticated and more emotional purchase decision
Purchasing Process	• Highly trained buyers • Group purchasing decision • Complex buying decisions • Formalized buying procedures • Close and personal selling relationship between marketer and buyer • Personal selling • Geographically concentrated	• Untrained buyers • Individual purchasing decision • Relatively simple buying decisions • Informal buying decision • Impersonal relationship between marketer and buyer • Mass advertising • Geographically dispersed

CHAPTER SYNOPSIS

❶ **Summarize how marketing has evolved over the production concept era, sales concept era, marketing concept era, and customer relationship era.** *(pp. 300–302)*

During the production concept era (from the Industrial Revolution until the 1920s), most companies focused solely on production. Demand was often greater than supply, and the prevailing mindset was that a good-quality product would simply sell itself.

During the sales concept era (from the mid-1920s through the early 1950s), technological advances meant that production increased more sharply than demand for goods and services. The use of heavy public advertising in all available forms of media became prevalent.

During the marketing concept era (from the 1950s through the 1990s), production continued to expand more quickly than the growth in demand for goods and services. The **marketing concept** changed the focus from finding the right customer for a product to producing the right product for a customer and doing it better than the competition.

During the customer relationship era (from the late 1990s to the present), organizations have worked to establish long-term relationships with individual customers to foster loyalty and repeat business (referred to as **customer relationship management (CRM)**.

❷ **Outline the benefits of marketing to customers, sellers, investors, employees, and society, and summarize the criticisms of marketing.** *(pp. 302–305)*

Stakeholders, or interested parties, include customers, sellers, investors, employees, and society. Each group of stakeholders has a different set of motives for their interest in the success of the business. Through marketing, companies sell products and services that satisfy human needs and wants (the product or service has value and offers utility). Businesses that are most successful in satisfying customers generate higher profits, and investors benefit from the profits earned. Employees benefit from successful marketing as well because their jobs and livelihoods are more secure. Society benefits from successful marketing because scarce resources are more efficiently allocated or channelled into the production of those goods and services most desired by society.

Criticisms of marketing include price gouging, the production of shoddy or unsafe products, and confusing and deceptive practices. The criticisms of marketing should not be taken lightly. All companies should have a code of ethics and policies in place to curb unethical behaviour within their organizations.

❸ **Describe the two major elements of a marketing strategy and the 4 Ps of the marketing mix.** *(p. 305)*

A marketing strategy consists of two major elements: the organization must determine its *target market* and then develop a *marketing mix* to meet the needs of that market. The **target market** is the specific group of consumers, with similar needs and wants, toward which a firm directs its marketing efforts. The **marketing mix** is the combination of four factors, called the "4 Ps" of marketing, designed to serve the target market: product, price, promotion, and place.

The idea is to provide the *product* that customers need and want at an appropriate *price* and to *promote* its sale and *place* or distribute the good or service in a convenient location for the customer to purchase (see Figure 11.2). Effective marketing requires the appropriate blend of the 4 Ps directed at

targeted customers. This blend is constrained by forces outside the firm's control that are found within the broader market environment.

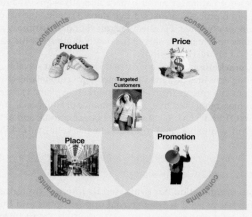

The Marketing Mix

❹ **Explain how firms implement a marketing strategy by applying the five steps of the marketing process.** *(pp. 305–308)*

The Five Steps in the Marketing Process

The marketing process may seem simple when it's written on the page, but it's as much art as it is science. Common ingredients for marketing success include producing a high-quality product (with a unique brand that is properly promoted) that consistently delivers value to customers at a "fair" price, where they want it, and when they want it.

❺ **Describe how the various factors in the marketing environment influence a firm's ability to manipulate its marketing mix.** *(pp. 308–310)*

The **marketing environment** includes environmental influences such as the competitive environment (discussed in Chapter 2) and the political, economic, socio-cultural, and technological (PEST) environment (discussed in Chapter 1). Because these

11

factors are outside the firm's control, they constrain the organization's ability to manipulate its marketing mix.

❻ Identify the five steps of the marketing research process and the four elements of a good marketing plan. *(pp. 310–313)*

Market research is the process of gathering and analyzing market information for making marketing decisions. The marketing research process consists of five steps: 1) define the need, problem, or objective; 2) collect the relevant data (primary and secondary sources); (3) analyze the data; (4) interpret the results; and (5) act on the conclusions.

A **marketing plan** is a written document that specifies marketing activities designed to reach organizational objectives. Four elements emerge from all good marketing plans: 1) a clearly written marketing objective, 2) performance of situational analysis (e.g., SWOT and 5 Cs), 3) selection of a target market; and 4) implementation, evaluation, and control of the marketing mix (4 Ps).

❼ Describe how target markets are determined and how a firm positions itself to satisfy a target market. *(pp. 313–315)*

Once an organization has evaluated its internal strengths and weaknesses, as well as the external opportunities and threats of the market environment, then it is ready to select its target market. A **target market** is the specific group of consumers, with similar needs and wants, toward which a firm directs its marketing efforts. Finding a target market begins with **market segmentation**, the process of separating the broader market into smaller markets (or market segments) that consist of similar groups of customers. A **market segment** is a subgroup of potential customers who share similar characteristics and therefore have similar product needs and preferences. Four of the most common consumer market segmentation classifications are geographic, demographic, psychographic, and behavioural. For each target market, the company tries to blend the 4 Ps of the marketing mix to best satisfy the targeted customers. The process of developing a unique marketing mix that best satisfies a target market is known as **positioning**.

❽ Describe the purchase decision process and the major influences affecting a consumer's buying decision. *(pp. 315–317)*

The consumer buying process involves five steps:
1. need recognition
2. information search
3. evaluation of alternatives

4. purchase or no purchase decision
5. post-purchase evaluation

Not all consumers go through each step in the process, and the steps do not need to be completed in the same order. As well, the process can be interrupted at any time with a "no purchase" decision.

The five-step consumer decision-making process is part of a broader environmental context that influences each step. Effective marketing attempts to help consumers with their information search and the evaluation of alternatives. These environmental influences are shown in **Figure 11.6**.

Major Influences Affecting a Consumer's Buying Decision

❾ Compare the buying decisions and marketing processes in business-to-business markets to those in the consumer market. *(pp. 317–318)*

In a **consumer market**, buyers are households that purchase final consumer goods. In a **business-to-business (B2B) market**, businesses buy from other businesses. There are many more B2B markets compared to consumer markets. In B2B markets, purchases are often undertaken by a small group of highly trained individuals who buy in large volumes and have a much closer relationship with marketers. B2B buyers are also more geographically concentrated and often avoid distributors.

KEY TERMS

5 Cs of marketing *(p. 312)*
behavioural segmentation *(p. 315)*
business-to-business (B2B) markets *(p. 315)*
consumer behaviour *(p. 315)*
consumer market *(p. 315)*
customer relationship management (CRM) *(p. 302)*

demographic segmentation *(p. 314)*
environmental scanning *(p. 308)*
focus group *(p. 310)*
geographic segmentation *(p. 314)*
market research *(p. 310)*
market segmentation *(p. 314)*

marketing *(p. 300)*
marketing concept *(p. 301)*
marketing environment *(p. 308)*
marketing mix *(p. 305)*
marketing objective *(p. 312)*
marketing plan *(p. 312)*
niche marketing *(p. 314)*
positioning *(p. 314)*

primary data *(p. 310)*
product *(p. 301)*
psychographic segmentation *(p. 314)*
secondary data *(p. 310)*
target market *(p. 305)*

CRITICAL THINKING QUESTIONS

1. Can you think of an example of how a specific organization (for-profit or non-profit) tried to establish a better customer relationship with you? What did the organization do? Was it effective? Why or why not? What recommendations would you make to these organizations?

2. Select a product or service you use regularly, such as a cosmetic or toiletry item, a snack food, article of clothing, cellphone, laptop, and so on. Explain how the 4 Ps of the marketing mix (product, price, promotion, and place) relate to this product. Who is the target market for this product? How can this product be changed or the marketing strategy be adjusted to appeal to other market segments?

3. You're interested in starting a limousine service in your community. How might you best segment the market for your services? What is your target market and why? What marketing mix strategies would you employ? How would you nurture customer relationships?

4. Retailers such as Hudson's Bay Company (HBC) and Canadian Tire Corporation offer loyalty programs. Walmart has a loyalty program now with its own credit card that offers consumers Walmart bucks that can be used toward future purchases. What other such programs can you think of? What are companies trying to do by offering such programs?

5. Think of the last major purchase you made. Discuss how the socio-cultural, personal, psychological, situational, and marketing mix influences influenced this purchase.

APPLICATION EXERCISES

1. **Apple's Marketing Mix.** Go to Apple's website that focuses on the iPhone: www.apple.com/iphone. Describe Apple's marketing mix strategy: product, price, promotion, and place. How does Apple attempt to foster good customer relations? What marketing recommendations would you make to Apple?

2. **SWOT Analysis.** Go to www.marketingteacher.com/SWOT/walmart_swot.htm to see a SWOT analysis for Walmart. What strengths, weaknesses, opportunities, and threats would you add or delete? Why? How could Walmart take advantage of its strengths in terms of its marketing mix? How do Walmart's weaknesses affect its marketing mix? What market environmental forces do you think gave rise to its opportunities and its threats? How much control does Walmart have over its market environment? What recommendations would you make for Walmart? Why?

3. **Mission and Values as Marketing Tools.** Go to the Phillip Morris website at www.philipmorrisusa. com/en/cms/Company/Mission_Values/default.aspx?src=top_nav. What kind of advertising techniques does this site use? Do you feel that this company is genuine in its concerns about public health?

4. **Freebies: Long-Term Gain or Loss?** Go to www.sephora.com. This company gives three free samples with every purchase from its website. Do you think that this strategy will be profitable for the company in the end, or will it cause it to lose money?

5. **The Jeep Experience.** The Jeep brand uses a non-traditional marketing approach by offering Jeep owners invitations to special events. Go to www.jeep.com/en and research the events that this company offers to its customers. How effective do you think engaging customers in ongoing events is in getting them to be repeat buyers?

GLOBAL 500 RESEARCH PROJECT

INSTRUCTIONS

1. Choose a Global 500 company from *Fortune* magazine's annual rankings at http://money.cnn.com/magazines/fortune/global500/.

2. Research:
   a. Does this company have a "purple cow"? What is it?
   b. What strategies does this company use to market its products or services? Does the company use different strategies for different areas of the world? What is the marketing mix—the 4 Ps?
   c. What are the company's flagship products or services (the most popular)? Does this vary in different countries?
   d. How does the company differentiate its products or services from competitors' products or services?
   e. Has this company made a marketing blunder in the past (have they attempted to market some product or service and failed miserably)? Summarize the situation.
   f. Does this company engage in social media as a marketing tool and/or a consumer research, or image-building tool? How?
   g. How much money did the company spend on marketing strategies last year (or the year before if you cannot find last year's information)? You might find this information in the company's annual report, in a business index, or on the Internet at several popular business sites (*Forbes, BusinessWeek*, etc.). How much revenue did the company make last year? What percentage was spent on marketing?
   h. Over the past three to five years, how has the external marketing environment (competitive and PEST) affected this company?
   i. Choose one product or service this company sells and discuss how you, as a potential customer, would work through the purchase decision process. Be specific about what features you require, who the competition is, what comparisons you would make, and how you would evaluate whether or not it was a good decision to buy or not to buy this company's product or service.

3. Prepare a report and submit to your professor.

TEAM TIME

Tobacco Wars

Divide into two even teams, one to represent each of the following:

a. tobacco company employees; pro-cigarette advertising in magazines
b. anti-tobacco advertising activists

SCENARIO

Does a company have a fundamental right to market its products wherever it wishes? Cigarette advertising in magazines has been a topic of great controversy. The large tobacco companies provide publications with a great deal of revenue by purchasing expensive advertising space, but many anti-smoking groups and some magazine publishers are questioning the ethical nature of this. Anti-smoking groups argue that these advertisements appeal to children and glamorize smoking. Tobacco companies claim that they are merely making attractive advertisements with no intention of encouraging children to use their products. The European Union has banned tobacco advertisements from magazines entirely, and many U.S. publications have stopped selling ad space to tobacco companies. The Canadian government has taken bold steps to control tobacco marketing. Do tobacco companies have the right to advertise their products as they see fit? Is it morally wrong to advertise a product that is known to cause health problems?

PROCESS

Step 1. Collaborate with team members to discuss both sides of the issue, analyzing the arguments from each perspective.
Step 2. Prepare the most effective argument for your team's perspective, and think about counterpoints to arguments that the other team may raise.

ETHICS AND RESPONSIBILITY

Subprime Mortgage Crisis

In the United States, subprime loans are home loans made available at temporarily reduced or zero interest rates that adjust or increase to much higher interest rates over time. These allowed many people to qualify for loans to buy expensive homes that they otherwise would not have been qualified to buy. Because of the long-standing expectation that home prices would continue to rise over time, as they have historically, and that recipients of subprime loans would be able to refinance their loans into traditional fixed-interest loans, many people thought these subprime loans were going to turn out to be great deals. However, when the price of homes began to fall in 2006 and 2007, it became difficult to refinance these subprime loans. At the same time, the temporary low interest rates on subprime loans were rapidly adjusting upward as specified in the loan contracts. Some people found themselves unable to make their monthly house payments, and they couldn't sell their homes because they owed more than the homes were worth. Many people were forced into foreclosure and lost their homes. Foreclosures also hurt many banks, and this downturn has negatively affected the U.S. economy as a whole.

DISCUSSION QUESTIONS

1. Do you feel that it is unethical to offer loans at "teaser" low rates that adjust upward rapidly over time to people who may not fully understand the consequences of increased house payments, or to allow people to purchase homes that they otherwise would not be able to afford?
2. As a bank owner, would you feel that the benefits of giving subprime loans outweigh their potential risks?
3. Do you think the banks that gave the loans should take responsibility for their payment?
4. Should the government provide assistance at taxpayers' expense to those people who received these subprime loans and now have trouble keeping their homes?

CLOSING CASE

The iPod Started a Love Affair[17]

Today, the original Mac 128k computer is likely viewed more as a technological dinosaur than as an innovative machine. However, when Apple introduced it in 1984, the Mac 128k began a revolutionary way of developing and marketing new technology. Its simple design, easy-to-use operating system, and accessible cost made it the first personal computer created with the consumer in mind. Apple continued to produce successful products in its first decade but fell into a bit of a slump starting in the late 1980s, losing its grip on its target market and having difficulty competing with companies such as IBM and Hewlett-Packard. It took the dawning of a new millennium and the return of a founding member to turn Apple around.

In 1997, Steve Jobs's return to Apple Computer Inc. as interim chief executive officer sparked a sort of renaissance for the company. Jobs wanted to revive what had made Apple a flourishing company in the first place: making products based on the customer's needs. The key to Apple's success was marketing to a very specific target audience: a young, creative demographic who valued advanced technology and sleek design. The true brilliance of this marketing strategy was that Apple didn't just identify its target audience; it actually predicted what the target audience wanted. "A lot of times, people don't know what they want until you show it to them," Jobs told *BusinessWeek* in 1998. And what Jobs showed the world three years later was exactly what his target audience wanted.

Generation Y (those born between 1982 and 2000) was already accustomed to getting its music digitally through websites such as Napster and Lycos, but it needed a way to take music from the computer to the streets. In 2001, Apple introduced the iPod, a portable digital music player that fulfilled such a need. The iPod's sleek geometric design and durability made it easy to slide in a pocket or toss in a backpack. The iPod also met customer need to have creative control over the media outlet. The iPod allowed music files to be organized in a variety of ways, and customers could make playlists of their favourite songs.

When the iPod was introduced, it was not an immediate worldwide success, but that was to be expected. Jobs knew he could not market to everyone. He was willing to alienate some consumers in order to appeal to the core group of people for which the product was designed. He knew it would take time to turn some skeptics into customers. In 2003, Apple announced the second-generation iPod and iTunes, a digital music store that allowed customers to buy song files. It was then that the iPod/iTunes juggernaut emerged. The iPod was no longer just a product. Part status symbol, part entertainment, the iPod created a love affair between young adults and all things Apple. "Apple's products often elicit an emotional response and connection with customers that is extremely unique and very rewarding,"[18] states Apple's Marketing Department.

That emotional connection translates into big numbers for Apple. Currently, the iPod holds a majority market share for digital music players.[19] Its presence in the market is so dominant that, like Kleenex, Xerox, and Post-it, the brand name has become synonymous with the product, which makes all competing brands look generic. Jobs's decision to streamline its customer base proved that a focused marketing strategy could dominate a target market, whereas an expansive strategy must submit to the many needs of a broad market. With his keen ability to anticipate future trends, Jobs (who passed away October 5, 2011) helped Apple become a giant in the digital markets. As Apple continues to improve upon the iPod with new editions such as the iPod shuffle, iPod nano, and iPod touch, it's inevitable that the original iPod will join the ranks of the Mac 128k as a technological fossil, but Apple's marketing methods behind these and other products, including the iPhone and the iPad, will likely influence Apple's success for decades to come.

DISCUSSION QUESTIONS

1. What was Apple's target demographic for the iPod? Why do you think that Apple chose to market specifically to this audience? How would Apple have to change its product if it wanted to appeal to a broader market?
2. How did Apple meet the socio-cultural, personal, psychological, and behavioural needs of its target audience?
3. Consider what you've learned about marketing to audiences in this chapter. What methods do you think companies should use to help them establish a target market?

MyBusinessLab CHAPTER RESOURCES

MyBusinessLab in an online learning and testing environment that features the perfect study tools to help you master the concepts covered in this chapter. Log in to MyBusinessLab at www.pearsoned.ca/mybusinesslab to test your knowledge of key chapter concepts, participate in simulations modelled on real-world business situations, and explore the following additional practice tools:

- Study Plan
- Audio Chapter Summaries
- Glossary Flashcards
- eText
- BizChat Discussion Boards
- BizSkills Simulation: Market Research Matters
- Decision-Making Mini-Simulations: What is Marketing?; Segmentation, Targeting, and Positioning; Marketing Environment; Marketing Research; Strategic Marketing
- Document Makeovers: Competitive Analysis; Dusty Strings Letter; Lektonik Presentation

Video Cases:
To access the Chapter 11 Video Cases: Live Nation; Jones Soda: Marketing and Consumer Behaviour, see the Activities folder in the Assessment section of MyBusinessLab.

Web Case:
To access the Chapter 11 Web Case, see the Activities folder in the Assessment section of MyBusinessLab

Marketing Mix: Product, Price, Promotion, and Place

OPENING DISCUSSION: PRODUCT PROMOTION

Kraft Is a Champion Marketer

Kraft Foods Inc. is a food, beverage, and confectionery company ranked number one in North America and number two (after Nestlé) in the world. According to its 2010 annual report, Kraft sells products in approximately 170 countries, and eleven of its seventy brands earn more than US$1 billion annually worldwide: Oreo, Nabisco, and LU biscuits; Milka and Cadbury chocolates; Trident gum; Jacobs and Maxwell House coffees; Philadelphia cream cheeses; Kraft cheeses, dinners, and dressings; and Oscar Mayer meats.[1] Kraft Canada brands include Kraft cheeses, dinners, and dressings; Caramilk chocolate; Christie cookies and crackers; Kool-Aid and Del Monte beverages; Maynards candy; and Stride and Dentyne gum.[2] People around the world consume about 900 million servings of Kraft products daily, which resulted in Kraft earning net revenues of US$49.2 billion in 2010.[3]

Kraft's marketing efforts include consumer marketing in print, on-air, outdoor, and digital media;

consumer incentives such as contests and coupons; and trade promotions (e.g., gifts, demonstrations, special pricing, and display).[4] It is essential to Kraft's business success to continue to extend its brands into new markets, expand its brand image by developing new products, and maintain its brand image for existing products. This is done through product innovation and marketing investments in advertising and consumer promotions. *Advertising Age* estimated that Kraft's global measured advertising expenditure of US$2.12 billion in 2009 placed Kraft in tenth place as a world advertiser.[5]

Kraft's marketing services division is a collection of teams that supply marketing strategies to Kraft's business divisions. Positions include market research analysts, consumer promotion coordinators, and Kraft Kitchens members. The market research team helps transform consumer data and demographic information into business-building initiatives. The consumer promotions team develops and executes consumer awareness programs such as in-store promotions, couponing, contests, and

(continued)

loyalty programs. The Kraft Kitchens team develops recipes and provides ideas about entertaining, healthy eating, and other cuisine tips.[6]

A few of Kraft's recent marketing strategies include:

- *Mobile Marketing.* "Big Fork Little Fork" is an iPad app that helps parents teach kids smart eating habits and an appreciation for food. It offers recipes, how-to videos, and educational games to encourage the whole family to cook together, eat together, and live well together. It targets parents in their twenties and thirties, and aims to teach users healthy eating while promoting love and loyalty for the Kraft's brands such as Kraft Singles, Ritz Crackers, Jell-O, and Mac & Cheese.[7]
- *Epic Campaign.* "The Real Women of Philadelphia" cream cheese contest asked women to invent their own dishes and shoot and upload instructional videos to the contest's website. Aligning itself with a popular television personality who was already using Philadelphia cream cheese on her cooking show, Paula Deen, the campaign tapped into an existing network rather than having to start from scratch. Intended to run for only one year with an estimated 400 responses, "The Real Women of Philadelphia" received about 6000 entries and blossomed into a thriving social network of more than 30 000 women. And it sold 5 percent more cream cheese.[8]
- *Product Innovation.* When Post, a division of Kraft, launched the "Diamond Shreddies" campaign, it positioned an historic product prominently in people's minds without changing the product. The campaign compared how the old square Shreddies were "boring" and the new Diamond Shreddies were "exciting." Customers laughed along with the light-hearted notion that by turning old Shreddies 45 degrees, new Diamond Shreddies can be made exciting![9] The advertising industry seemed to appreciate Post's "innovation" too, as the campaign won several awards, including a Grand Clio, a Bronze Pencil at the One Show, and a finalist spot in Cannes in the Integrated category.[10]

- *Power Brand.* Increased marketing and new packaging in regions including Latin American and Asia Pacific have seen Kraft's Tang's sales grow 30 percent in 2009, to more than US$750 million. Tang's resurgence is part of Kraft's strategy to grow ten of its key brands overseas. In China, market research showed that children thought water was boring and bland, while mothers believed their children needed about six glasses of water per day; this lead to the campaign and slogan: "Tang makes water more exciting." Kraft's market research also showed that Chinese consumers preferred drinks by the glass, rather than by the pitcher, so single-serve powder sticks were created for sale in China instead of pitcher packs.[11]
- *Positive Image and Social Media.* Since 2006, Kraft Canada has sponsored an annual Kraft Hockeyville program along with the Canadian Broadcasting Corporation (CBC), the National Hockey League (NHL), and the National Hockey League Players Association (NHLPA) to find Canada's "most passionate" hockey community. Each year the winner receives $100 000 for arena upgrades and earns a spot as guest-host for a pre-season NHL game. The marketing program has become one of Kraft's most successful, with sales of products featured in the program—such as Kraft Dinner, Maxwell House, Ritz, Oreo, and Cracker Barrel cheese—increasing between 4 percent and 6 percent. Kraft Hockeyville is supported by TV, in-store materials, Facebook, Twitter, and YouTube.[12]

Over the years, Kraft has launched numerous successful marketing campaigns. Kraft joins mainstay marketers such as Campbell, General Mills, Heinz, and Kellogg in boosting ad spending, launching new products, and restaging old favourites.[13]

DISCUSSION QUESTIONS

1. You may recall the TV commercial about college students cooking Kraft Dinner on a hot water radiator in their dorm room. Choose a different Kraft advertisement or commercial you can recall and research the specific gains or losses incurred by the company due to this marketing effort. What were they?

2. Review Kraft's online annual and sustainability reports. What types of projects, practices, initiatives, or endeavours is Kraft working on that will help build its good reputation and at the same time market its company and brands to potential consumers?

3. Which Kraft products do you use? Why do you choose Kraft? Are Kraft products more expensive than generic products? Do you prefer the Kraft brand over other brands? Why or why not?

THE MARKETING MIX (4 Ps): PRODUCT
The Total Product Offer

Which do you prefer: Diet Coke or Coke Zero?   You may think they're the same, but they're not. They have different flavours, marketing strategies, and targeted demographics. After having moderate success with flavoured versions of Coke products, the company came up with an idea to differentiate Diet Coke to appeal more to men.[14] Coke Zero's marketing strategy reflects this new target market. The can is darker to convey a bigger flavour, and advertisements for the beverage are male dominated, with plots built around sports such as auto racing. The website for Coke Zero also includes pages with information about NCAA and NFL football. Coke Zero shows it is not only important to differentiate products from their competitors, but also to differentiate current products to meet the needs of a broader market.

The application of the marketing process is as much an art as a science. Making a high-quality product with a unique, properly promoted brand that consistently delivers value to customers at a "fair" price, when and where they want it, presents significant challenges to marketers all over the world.

What is the total product offer?   As you'll recall from Chapter 11, a product is any good, service, or idea available for purchase in a market, as well as any intangible benefits derived from its consumption. An Apple iPad, a Toyota Sienna, a college education, E*Trade financial services, a doctor's advice, and even a Caribbean vacation package are all products. Consumers buy products for a number of tangible and intangible benefits. The **total product offer** (or **value package**) consists of all the benefits associated with a good, service, or idea that affect a consumer's purchasing decision. When you buy a car, you're not just buying a mode of transportation; you're also buying some intangible benefits, such as style or an image. Marketers know this, and when planning a total product offering, they think about products on three levels: the *core product*, the *actual product*, and the *augmented product*. Each level adds more value to a product.

- The *core product* provides the core benefit or service that satisfies the basic need or want that motivates the consumer's purchase. For a car, that core benefit is the convenient transportation it provides. For a soft drink, it is the product's thirst-quenching capability. For a camera, it is the ability to capture and share memories. Notice that the core product is intangible. You can't touch it. This is because the core product is the basic *benefit* the product provides. Companies use the benefits of their products to lure customers. That is why car companies such as Toyota use "Moving Forward" as an advertising slogan. Similarly, the soft drink Sprite uses "Obey Your Thirst," and camera conglomerate Kodak once used "Share a Moment, Share a Life" to draw in customers.
- Of course, an *actual product* must be developed in order to provide the core benefit or service desired. The actual product is the tangible aspect of the purchase that you can touch, see, hear, smell, or taste. It provides core benefits when it is used. Consumers often assess the tangible benefits of actual products by comparing brands, quality (often associated with a brand's reputation), features, styling, or packaging. For a car, the actual product is the automobile itself. Benefits of an actual product such as a Volvo station wagon could be a high-quality brand, numerous safety features, seating for seven passengers, or leather seats. For a soft drink, the actual product might provide a refreshing taste, desirable colour, or pleasant aroma. The product could even provide the "pick-me-up" caffeine buzz that consumers are looking for when they purchase some sodas. For a camera, the actual product may provide features such as an LCD screen or a lightweight design.
- The *augmented product* consists of the core product and the actual product *plus* other real or perceived benefits that provide additional value to the customer's purchase.

1 Define "product" and "total product offer" as they pertain to marketing.

The **total product offer** (or **value package**) consists of all the benefits associated with a good, service, or idea that affect a consumer's purchasing decision.

12

Ben & Jerry's Homemade Ice Cream differentiated itself from other ice cream makers by offering original and unique flavours and product names such as Goodbye Yellow Brickle Road, Cherry Garcia, and Phish Food.

For a Caribbean vacation package, the core product is an opportunity to take a break from your everyday life. The actual product includes airplane tickets and accommodations at a resort. Together, these products aim to produce an augmented product that includes benefits such as having fun, resting, and relaxing.

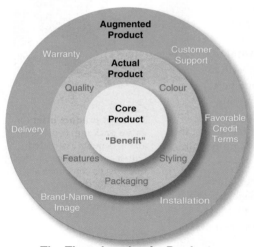

The Three Levels of a Product

Figure 12.1   Three Ring Model

The three levels of a product define the benefits to be derived from a total product offering.

②

Describe product differentiation, and explain its role in product development.

Product differentiation
is the creation of a real or perceived difference in a product designed to attract customers.

These benefits might include customer service and support, delivery, installation, a warranty, or favourable credit terms. The value-enhancing elements of an actual product are an important part of the total product offering because they help provide a more satisfying customer experience. For a product such as a car, augmented benefits might include a reasonable price, an easy payment plan, a ten-year warranty, or just the security of owning a brand-new car.

Figure 12.1 summarizes the three levels of a product. Remember that when developing products, marketers must begin with a basic customer need or want to be satisfied by a product. Then marketers develop an actual product to satisfy that need for targeted customers. Successful product developers then augment the product to create a total product offering that provides a benefit package superior to that of the competition. This is the essence of successful *product differentiation*, which we'll discuss next.

Product Differentiation

How important is product differentiation?   **Product differentiation** is the creation of a real or perceived difference in a product designed to attract customers. A company can distinguish a product from its competitors by establishing concrete or intangible differences between similar products. For example, a luggage company might offer suitcases in unique colours or shapes. It might also offer a lifetime guarantee on certain models. Product differentiation is critical for a product's success. If a product doesn't possess qualities that make it stand out, then customers will not be motivated to buy that product instead of a competitor's product.

How does consumer input affect product development?   Companies rely on customer input and feedback to help shape their products. Listening to customers and incorporating their suggestions are effective ways to foster good customer relationships, which is a critical component in establishing repeat business and long-term success. In fact, listening to customers is one of the most important elements of sound customer relationship management. You have to know what your customers want to tailor a product offering that best satisfies their needs.

Consumer input often provides information that prompts companies to segment a large market and focus on narrowly defined targeted customers. For example, a breakfast cereal company might find that most consumers buy its cereal because it is high in fibre. That company can differentiate its product from competing products by labelling the cereal "a good source of fibre" and target the product to health-conscious adults. Companies might also use consumer input to differentiate their products by improving an existing product or creating an entirely new product. Product differentiation is the result of carefully segmenting markets into clearly defined targeted customers and developing a variety of total product offerings that best meet these varying customer needs—and doing it better than the competition.

New Product Development

What are the steps in developing a new product? As outlined in **Figure 12.2**, **new product development** involves five steps:

1. *Idea Generation*. Ideas for entirely new products or improved versions of existing products are often obtained by listening closely to customers or focus groups. In fact, customer complaints may signal a need for a new product. Suppliers, employees, and salespeople also generate ideas by assessing the competition and through trade shows.
2. *Idea Screening*. The objective of idea screening is to eliminate unsound concepts before devoting costly resources to their development. Screening involves estimating

3 Outline the five steps in new product development, and describe the product life cycle.

Decision-Making Mini-Simulation: New Product Development. Located in MyBusinessLab.

New product development involves five steps: idea generation; idea screening; product analysis; product development and concept testing; and commercialization.

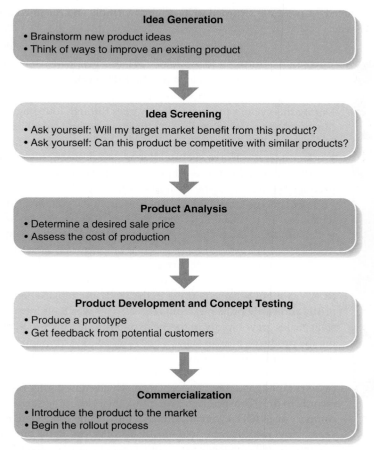

Figure 12.2 The Five Steps in the New Product Development Process

12

the level of consumer demand for the product, its profitability, and its production feasibility given the company's current technical capabilities.

3. *Product Analysis.* Product analysis estimates costs of production, selling price, sales volume, and profitability. Costs of production depend on the features of the product deemed necessary to meet the targeted customers' needs. The selling price, sales volume, and profitability may depend on the degree of competition in the market.

4. *Product Development and Concept Testing.* At this stage, product ideas that survive the screening and analysis steps are analyzed further. This often begins with a physical prototype of the good. Computer-aided design systems are helpful in quickly making design changes even before a physical prototype is manufactured. In the testing phase of a new service offering, management determines the details concerning staffing needs and equipment requirements to ensure the service is delivered properly. Concept testing involves soliciting customer responses to a new product idea. Potential targeted customers are asked to evaluate different features, prices, packages, and a host of other factors surrounding the product. The idea is to come up with the best, most profitable total product offering.

5. *Commercialization.* If a product makes it this far in the process, it is ready to be launched. Commercialization is the decision to market a product. Introducing a new product can be costly due to manufacturing investments, advertising, personal selling, and other promotional activities. The returns from such investments can take time. This may explain why many companies introduce their new products in one region at a time—sometimes called *rolling out the product.*

BizSkills Simulation: Product Development. Located in MyBusinessLab.

A **product life cycle** is a theoretical model describing a product's sales and profits over the course of its lifetime.

Despite the scientific nature of new product development, a large proportion of new products still fail. In contrast to the success of Coke Zero discussed earlier, one of the most interesting cases of a new product failure was Coca Cola's "New Coke," launched in 1985. In an attempt to revitalize its brand, the company toyed with the formula of its popular soda and almost destroyed it. People didn't want their favourite soft drink to be modified, and New Coke was pulled from the shelves only three months after the product was introduced.[15] Coca-Cola returned to its original formula and renamed the cola Coca-Cola Classic.

Crocs footwear was originally marketed as an outdoor shoe useful for boating, but in 2007, it gained popularity as an everyday casual shoe. Crocs have been considered a fad, but only time will tell if this product will continue to grow or hit a declining stage.

What is a product's life cycle?   Once a product is developed, it begins the product life cycle. A **product life cycle** is a theoretical model describing a product's sales and profits over the course of its lifetime. During this cycle, a product typically goes through four stages: an introductory stage, a growth stage, a maturity stage, and a declining stage. The product life cycle can be applied to a specific product or to an entire product category. However, like all models, it is a simplified version of reality and should not be used prescriptively because the duration of a product's entire life can be as short as a few months, as is often the case for fad items such as Beanie Babies. The product's life can also be as long as a century or more for such products as baking soda. In addition, not all products strictly follow these stages. Some products are introduced but never grow in sales, whereas others never seem to decline.

You can see how the theory works if you consider the life cycle of vinyl musical recordings. Vinyl records were first introduced in 1930 by RCA Victor but became popular in the 1950s as a replacement for the brittle and easily broken 78-rpm records. This was their introductory stage. Sales grew rapidly in the 1950s and through the 1960s, representing the product's growth stage. They came in 33 1/3-rpm long-playing records, or LPs, and 45-rpm single records. In the early 1970s, vinyl records hit their maturity stage. By the late 1970s and early 1980s, cassette tapes gained wide acceptance, which caused sales of vinyl records to drop drastically, representing their declining stage. After compact discs (CDs) were introduced, the decline continued. For many years, vinyl records were sold mostly as collectors' items but have been making a small comeback in recent years among avid music fans who believe the sound quality is better than digital formats.

How do marketing decisions affect the product's life cycle? The product life cycle model may be useful as a general description of a product's sales and profits over time, but it should be used with caution when forecasting or predicting future sales and profits. Not all products strictly follow these stages, and the period involved with each stage can vary dramatically. In fact, marketing decisions can affect each of the phases of a product's life cycle, while knowledge of a product's life cycle stage also helps determine the appropriate marketing mix strategy for that stage. **Figure 12.3** summarizes the characteristics, marketing objectives, and strategies for each of the four stages of a product's life cycle.

Characteristics	Introduction	Growth	Maturity	Decline
Sales	Low sales	Radically rising sales	Peak sales	Declining sales
Costs	High cost per customer	High cost per customer	Low cost per customer	Low cost per customer
Profits	Negative	Rising	High	Declining
Customers	Innovators	Innovators	Middle majority	Laggards
Competitors	Few	Growing number	Stable number beginning to decline	Declining number

Marketing Objectives

	Introduction	Growth	Maturity	Decline
	Create product awareness and trial	Maximize market share	Maximize profit while defending market share	Reduce expenditure and milk the brand

Strategies

	Introduction	Growth	Maturity	Decline
Product	Offer a basic product	Offer product extensions, services, warranty	Diversify brands and models	Phase out weak items
Price	Charge cost-plus	Price to penetrate market	Price to match or beat competitors	Cut prices
Distribution	Build selective distribution	Build intensive distribution	Build more intensive distribution	Go selective; phase out unprofitable outlets
Advertising	Build product awareness among early adopters and dealers	Build awareness and interest in the mass market	Stress brand differences and benefits	Reduce to level needed to retain hard-core loyals
Sales Promotion	Use heavy sales promotion to entice trial	Reduce to take advantage of heavy customer demand	Increase to encourage brand switching	Reduce to minimal level

Figure 12.3 The Product Life Cycle Model

12

Because most products eventually decline and may have to be withdrawn from the market, companies must continuously seek to develop new products to replace older ones. At the same time, marketers work hard to extend the life of existing products to milk as much profit from them as possible. Some auto companies have used discounted prices, rebates, and low-interest loans to extend the life of their models. Arm & Hammer, a company that produces baking soda, extended its product's life by advertising and *creating a new use* for its product as a refrigerator deodorizer. The Home Depot and Lowe's tried to *create new markets* for their businesses by expanding into do-it-yourself training on home projects within their stores. Jell-O extended its knowledge (*extended technology*) of raw gelatin to create puddings and other snacks. *Repackaging*, or using new labels or different container types, is another popular method to extend a product's life. For example, Coca-Cola switched from six-ounce glass bottles to eight-ounce cans. A company can also *reposition* its product as Oldsmobile attempted with its "This isn't your father's Oldsmobile" campaign. These strategies are not always effective—the Oldsmobile, for example, has been discontinued.[16]

As you've just learned, developing a high-quality product is not so much an end in itself as it is a beginning. After a product is developed, the product life cycle begins, and appropriate marketing strategies must be conceived and implemented accordingly.

Product Lines and the Product Mix

What do we call a group of similar products?

Customer feedback guides product development and product differentiation. It also gives rise to the creation of a **product line**, a group of similar products intended for a similar market. A **product mix** is the combination of all product lines offered for sale by a company. For example, Coca-Cola has many product lines, including its soft drinks, energy drinks, and sports drinks, which collectively make up its product mix. Toyota offers a full line of automotive products, which can be broken down into various product lines, including its cars, minivans, trucks, SUVs, motorcycles, ATVs, and vehicle-related parts and accessories. Toyota also offers a financial-services product line to dealers and their customers for the purchase or lease of Toyota vehicles. Toyota is involved in a number of other non-automotive business activities as well. One of these product lines is the manufacture and sale of prefabricated housing.[17] All Toyota's combined activities constitute its product mix.

How long can a product line be?

An important marketing decision involves product line length. **Product line length** is the number of items in any given product line. Product line length is determined by how the addition or removal of items from a product line affects profits. Coca-Cola has found it very profitable to pursue a long product line length given the huge variety of drinks it offers for sale. Although Coca-Cola is the biggest-selling soft drink in history, the company still offers more than 500 brands and 3500 beverage products in order to satisfy the specific tastes of the customers in more than 200 countries who purchase 1.7 billion servings per day.[18] Consumers who like Coca-Cola but desire a low-calorie alternative can purchase Diet Coke or Coke Zero. Consumers who want a low-calorie soda without caffeine can purchase Caffeine-Free Diet Coke. Those who do not want a soft drink can choose from one of Coca-Cola's many beverage offerings that appeal to the various wants and needs of the company's wide consumer base.[19]

How do companies decide how many product lines to offer?

Product mix width refers to the number of different product lines a company offers. This, too, is determined by profitability. General Electric (GE) has hundreds of product lines, ranging from light bulbs and home appliances to jet engines and medical machinery.[20] GE aims to achieve maximum profitability by stretching the company's capabilities across multiple markets. Product line length and product mix width are the result of companies striving to offer differentiated products to satisfy targeted customers.

Decision-Making Mini-Simulation: Product Life Cycle. Located in MyBusinessLab.

A **product line** is a group of similar products intended for a similar market.

A **product mix** is the combination of all product lines offered for sale by a company.

Product line length is the number of items in any given product line. Product line length is determined by how the addition or removal of items from a product line affects profits.

Product mix width refers to the number of different product lines a company offers.

Consumer and Business-to-Business Products

What is the difference between consumer products and business-to-business products?
In Chapter 11, we explored the differences between consumer markets and business-to-business (B2B) markets; now we'll explore the differences between consumer products and B2B products. **Consumer products** are goods and services purchased by households for personal consumption. They are traded in consumer markets. **Business-to-business (B2B) products** (sometimes called *industrial products*) are goods and services purchased by businesses for further processing or resale or are used in facilitating business operations. They are traded in B2B markets.

Most products can be classified as either consumer or B2B products. The distinction depends on their use. For example, if a homeowner purchases a lawn mower for personal use, then it would be a consumer product. If a landscaper purchases the same lawn mower but uses it to run his business, then it would be a B2B product. It is convenient for marketers to classify various consumer and B2B products because the buying behaviour is different between these two categories. This behaviour affects how the marketer prices, promotes, and distributes the product.

How are consumer products classified?
Four **consumer product classifications** emerge from strategic marketing mix plans for consumer products: convenience, shopping, specialty, and unsought goods and services. Let's look at each in more detail.

- *Convenience goods and services* are those that the customer purchases frequently, immediately, and effortlessly. Convenience goods are typically *nondurable goods*—goods normally used or consumed quickly. Gum, soap, tobacco, and newspapers are all considered convenience goods, as are common grocery items such as ketchup and milk. A car wash is an example of a convenience service. These purchases are usually based on habitual behaviour, meaning consumers routinely purchase a particular brand with which they're familiar and comfortable. Convenience goods and services are relatively low-priced items. They're usually promoted through brand awareness and image (which we'll discuss shortly) and are widely distributed through convenience stores or local grocery stores. Consumers make purchasing decisions for these goods based on the convenience of location and brand-name image.

- *Shopping goods and services* are products purchased less frequently than convenience goods and services and typically require more effort and time for comparison. Consumers usually base their comparison on attributes such as suitability, quality, price, and style. Shopping goods are typically *durable goods*—goods that can be used repeatedly over a long period. Examples of shopping goods include clothes, shoes, televisions, cameras, stereos, bicycles, lawn mowers, furniture, and major appliances. These products are often sold at shopping centres that allow for easy comparison between stores, such as Best Buy, Sears, and The Home Depot. Examples of shopping services include hotels and airline services. Since consumers carefully compare brands, companies that sell shopping services compete based on price, quality, and brand-name image.

- *Specialty goods and services* are unique to the point that buyers are willing to spend a considerable amount of time and effort searching for particular brands or styles. Customers know exactly what they want and they will not accept substitutes. Examples of specialty goods and services include Ferrari sports cars, Rolex watches, high-fashion designer clothing, and the services of prestigious legal experts. Because there are no suitable substitutes, buyers of specialty products do not comparison shop. They already know the specific good or service they want, and they are willing to seek it out regardless of its price and location. Businesses that successfully differentiate their product to the point that it is considered a specialty good or service can set a much higher price than similar products considered shopping goods or services.

- *Unsought goods and services* are products buyers don't usually think about buying, don't know exist, or buy only when a specific problem arises. We don't usually think about or want to think about buying some products such as life insurance or cemetery plots. These goods and services require a lot of persuasive advertising and

4

Summarize the different classifications of consumer products and business-to-business products.

Consumer products are goods and services purchased by households for personal consumption.

Business-to-business (B2B) products (sometimes called *industrial products*) are goods and services purchased by businesses for further processing or resale or are used in facilitating business operations.

Consumer product classifications include convenience, shopping, specialty, and unsought goods and services.

12

Pharmaceutical companies have stepped up their direct-to-consumer advertising efforts because they realize their products are unsought until consumers become aware of them and their benefits.

Five **B2B product (or industrial product) classifications** emerge from strategic marketing mix plans for B2B products: equipment; maintenance, repair, and operating (MRO) products; raw and processed materials; component parts; and specialized professional services.

Logos are representations of brands that help build an image for a company.

A **brand** is a name, term, symbol, or design that distinguishes a company and its products from all others.

personal selling to encourage consumers to buy products that will help them prepare for life's uncertainties. Other unsought goods and services are products that are completely new to consumers. New and innovative products, such as pharmaceutical drugs, must be introduced to consumers through promotional advertising before consumers can actively seek out these products. Automobile repairs are also unsought purchases where pre-purchase planning is rarely considered. In these cases, resolving the immediate problem is more important than comparison-shopping based on price or other features. Notice that sales of unsought products require personal selling or promotional advertising, and price may not be an important consideration if the good or service is urgently needed.

How are business-to-business products classified?

Five **B2B product (or industrial product) classifications** emerge from strategic marketing mix plans for B2B products: equipment; maintenance, repair, and operating (MRO) products; raw and processed materials; component parts; and specialized professional services. Each of these types of products has unique pricing, promotion, and distribution strategies. Let's look at each in more detail.

- *Equipment,* also known as *installations* or *capital items,* includes all the physical facilities of a business, such as factories, warehouses, office buildings, heavy equipment, and other less costly equipment, such as computers, printers, and copiers. Many of these capital items are expensive, unique, and intended to last for a long time; therefore, they may require special negotiations involving top management that can stretch over many months or even years. Marketers frequently offer a variety of services to help sell this type of equipment, including financial assistance with the purchase, maintenance, and repairs after the sale.
- *Maintenance, repair, and operating (MRO) products* facilitate production and operations but do not become a part of the finished product. They include printer paper, pens, cleaning materials, tools, and lubricants for machines. They are often marketed based on convenience, just like consumer convenience goods and services.
- *Raw and processed materials* are the basic inputs that become part of a finished good. Many raw products and some processed farm products, such as eggs or butter, go into the production of our grocery items. Raw materials such as wood and processed materials such as steel are used to make a variety of products, such as buildings or bridges. Raw and processed materials are usually purchased in large quantities at prices based on the quality of the materials.
- *Component parts* are assembled portions of the finished product. Examples include brakes, engines, transmissions, and steering columns for a car, or lumber, cement, drywall, and electrical wire for a house. Businesses purchasing component parts make their decisions based on quality and brand-name recognition because, ultimately, the quality of a business's product will be based on the quality of its component parts.
- *Specialized professional services* help support a firm's operations. They include advertising, management consulting, legal, accounting, and information technology services. Managers compare the costs and the quality of these specialized services with their in-house operations before deciding whether to *outsource* these activities. For example, a local grocery store owner might assess his or her ability to handle the business's financial records before hiring an outside accounting firm.

Considering the variety of types and classifications of products, it is clear that product development is an exciting yet challenging area of business. As Coca-Cola showed with the development of Coke Zero, new product development can lead to great success. The key is considering and understanding the many complex factors involved in creating a differentiated product.

Branding

Why do companies use logos?   **Logos** are representations of brands that help build an image for a company. Many logos are trademarked so the company alone has rights to the symbol. Which logos do you remember best? What does the logo say about the brand? What are the benefits of a brand? These questions are important components of another complex aspect of product development: branding.

What are the benefits of branding?   A **brand** is a name, term, symbol, or design that distinguishes a company and its products from all others. Branding is one of the most important tools of product differentiation, and it benefits both buyers and sellers. For buyers, well-recognized brands reduce the shopping time necessary to find the quality and consistency they desire in a product. Branding also reduces the risks involved in some purchases for which buyers are unable to determine quality objectively. We rely on established brand names to deliver an expected level of quality consistently. Imagine the frustration you'd feel if all the products in your grocery store were packaged with generic labels. How would you decide what type of peanut butter or frozen pizza to buy? Comparing product descriptions and ingredients takes a lot longer than simply picking up your favourite brand. Consumers are also able to express themselves by buying brand names with which they wish to be identified. For example, some buyers seek prestige by buying exclusive brands such as Mercedes-Benz, Rolex, or Dom Pérignon.

Branding also helps sellers define their products' special qualities, thus promoting repeat purchases as well as new sales at higher prices. Because certain brands, such as Coca-Cola, are associated with quality and value, these companies are able to introduce new products quickly and at a relatively low cost. In doing so, they add length to their product lines, widen their product mix (also known as *brand extension*), and enhance their profitability. Because Coca-Cola has a large amount of diversity in its product mix, the company can market its brand to just about any person in the world. To those who don't enjoy cola, Cola-Cola claims it is "so much more than soft drinks. Our brands also include milk products, soup, and more so you can choose a Coca-Cola Company product anytime, anywhere for nutrition, refreshment or other needs."[21] Well-branded companies usually establish a trademark so their products are easily identifiable. A trademark, a legally protected brand, can also benefit sellers by distinguishing them from competitors' *knockoff brands*, or illegal copies or cheap imitations of a product.

Brand Loyalty and Brand Equity

Does customer satisfaction create loyalty to a brand?   Another major benefit of branding for sellers is the creation of **brand loyalty**, the degree to which customers consistently prefer one brand over all others. In fact, companies hope their brands are not just recognized (*brand recognition*) and then preferred (*brand preference*), but that customers will eventually insist on their brand name (*brand insistence*). **Brand insistence** is the highest degree of brand loyalty. It can turn a product into a specialty good or service that can command a much higher price. Ultimately, the degree of brand loyalty depends on satisfied customers. Perhaps the most significant contemporary example of brand loyalty is the passionate devotion of many Mac users to Apple and its products.

Brand loyalty is the degree to which customers consistently prefer one brand over all others.

 5
Explain why branding is beneficial to both buyers and sellers, and describe some different types of brands.

Brand insistence is the highest degree of brand loyalty. It can turn a product into a specialty good or service that can command a much higher price.

One benefit of branding for sellers is brand loyalty, such as that displayed by many Mac users for Apple products.

12

World's Most Valuable Brands (2011)

Rank	Brand	Brand Value (US$mil)
1.	Apple	153 285
2.	Google	111 498
3.	IBM	100 849
4.	McDonald's	81 016
5.	Microsoft	78 243
6.	Coca-Cola	73 752
7.	AT&T	69 916
8.	Marlboro	67 522
9.	China Mobile	57 326
10.	GE (General Electric)	50 318

Source: MaryLou Costa, "The Most Valuable Brands in the World," *MarketingWeek* (online), May 12, 2011, http://www.marketingweek.co.uk/the-most-valuable-brands-in-the-world/3026256.article, Accessed June 25, 2011.

Brand equity is the overall value of a brand's strength in the market.

Brand awareness refers to the extent to which a particular brand name is familiar within a particular product category.

Brand association involves connecting a brand with other positive attributes, including image, product features, usage situations, organizational associations, brand personality, and symbols.

A **brand manager** (or **product manager**) is responsible for the 4 Ps of marketing a specific product or product line. Brand managers attempt to increase the product's perceived value to customers in order to increase brand equity.

How do companies build equity in their brands?   Strong brand loyalty contributes to **brand equity**, the overall value of a brand's strength in the market. Perceptions of quality contribute significantly to brand equity. Quality products are not just free from defects; they consistently perform at high levels. For example, many of Apple's customers will purchase another Apple product because of the brand's high quality. This adds significantly to Apple's brand equity. *Interbrand* annually ranks the top 100 brands in the world based on their brand equity (see the Top 10 World's Most Valuable Brands).

Perceptions of *brand awareness* and *brand association* also contribute to brand equity. **Brand awareness** refers to the extent to which a particular brand name is familiar within a particular product category. Companies participate in mass advertising as a way to help their product's brand name become synonymous with the actual name of the product. For example, what brand first comes to mind when you think of diapers? If it's Pampers, then Procter & Gamble has succeeded in its brand awareness campaigns for its disposable diapers.

Brand association involves connecting a brand with other positive attributes, including image, product features, usage situations, organizational associations, brand personality, and symbols. Hiring celebrities to endorse a product can be an effective tool for nurturing brand associations. Nike was so successful with Michael Jordan's endorsement that it launched its Air Jordan line of sport shoes. Disney has been successful in associating its brand with wholesome family values. The images invoked by symbols and slogans can be very powerful brand association techniques.

What does a brand manager do?   Branding has become such an important part of marketing that businesses have created brand manager positions within their organizations. A **brand manager** (or **product manager**) is responsible for the 4 Ps of marketing a specific product or product line. Brand managers attempt to increase the product's perceived value to customers in order to increase brand equity. Brand managers are also responsible for new product development.

Since 1934, the breakfast cereal Wheaties has featured professional and Olympic athletes on the cover of its box. These images allow the Wheaties brand to associate itself with desired values such as athleticism and success.

BizChat

Explore on MyBusinessLab

Who's Behind Those Catchy Slogans?

The American Advertising Council is a non-profit public service advertising organization that markets many causes. Funding is received strictly through donations. A main goal of this volunteer organization is to address important social issues with public service campaigns. Much of its work is probably familiar to you. It is behind the "Friends don't let friends drive drunk" and "Buzzed driving is drunk driving" campaigns for the prevention of drunk driving. It created the Crash Test Dummies: "You could learn a lot from a dummy," and Smokey the Bear: "Only you can prevent forest fires." The Ad Council also helps to further high school dropout prevention with "A mind is a terrible thing to waste," and crime prevention for the National Crime Prevention Council with "Take a bite out of crime"—just to name a few.[22]

Canada has similar bodies that help to guide advertising in an ethical direction. Advertising Standards Canada is a non-profit, self-regulatory organization committed to encouraging community confidence in advertising and administers the *Canadian Code of Advertising Standards*.[23] The Consumers Council of Canada helps business and government manage today's consumer issues and aims to create a safe, equitable, efficient, and effective marketplace.[24]

Discussion Questions

1. **Are you familiar with any of these Ad Council's campaigns? Which one do you think has been most effective? Why?**
2. **If you could choose an issue to be covered by an Ad Council campaign, what would it be? Why?**
3. **Currently, the Ad Council is funded through public donations. Do you think all taxpayers should help pay for Ad Council ads? Why or why not?**

The slogan "Got Milk?" released in 1993 became so popular it spawned endless parodies, such as "Got Faith?" and "Got Soy?"

top10

Characteristics of a Good Brand Name

1. Evokes positive associations
2. Easy to remember
3. Suggests product benefits
4. Easy to pronounce
5. Unique within its industry
6. Copyright protected
7. Promotes company image
8. Timeless
9. Transferable to other products
10. Recognizable and meaningful

Source: "Top 10 Characteristics of a Good Name," *Brighter Naming*, http://www.brighternaming.com/ Top_10_Naming_Factors.html, Accessed January 22, 2012, and "Brands - Brand names," Tutor2u.net, http://tutor2u.net/business/market-ing/brands_names.asp on January 22, Accessed January 22, 2102.

Packaging and Labelling

How does packaging affect a product and the brand?   How a product is packaged sends a message about the product and the brand. Packaging serves four functions:

1. to contain and protect the product
2. to facilitate use and convenience
3. to promote the product
4. to be environmentally friendly

Effective packaging is crucial to the success of a product, because the customers typically see the packaging before they see the product.

The Association for Dressings & Sauces named Hellman's Easy Out! mayonnaise squeezable bottle the 2007 package of the year.[25]

Why is convenient packaging so important?   Packaging

should facilitate use and convenience. Sellers want packages that are easy to ship, store, and stock on shelves. More importantly, consumers want products that handle easily, open and reseal, store conveniently, and have a long shelf life. We dislike bulky, heavy packages that are difficult to handle and open. Packages that don't reseal or result in easy spoilage are also unpopular.

Packages that are convenient to use and physically attractive sell better. Heinz ketchup experienced a significant increase in sales when it began offering ketchup in a squeezable bottle. Hellman's mayonnaise now offers a similar squeezable bottle for its product. Campbell's soup is responding to changing consumer tastes and preferences for greater convenience and healthier foods by offering sippable soups, microwave soup lines, and ready-to-serve soups. For example, Campbell's Soup Healthy Request microwavable bowls come in six varieties, and Soup At Hand sippable soups are low in calories, saturated fat, and cholesterol.[26] This shift toward healthy eating has helped the company gain 70 percent market share of the microwavable, ready-to-go soup category.[27] Many sellers also offer different sized packages dependent on frequency of use. For example, salt, sugar, and breakfast cereal packages come in many different sizes for added convenience.

How does packaging help promote the product?   Getting

the consumer to notice a product and pick it up from crowded

 ## Off the Mark

Q-tips Brand Cotton Swabs

Branding acts as a tool to help differentiate a product from other similar products. However, what happens when the brand itself becomes the category? When was the last time you purchased a box of cotton swabs? How about Q-tips? Well if you bought cotton swabs that didn't display the brand name Q-tips, then you didn't buy Q-tips. The Q-tips brand has been so effective in establishing itself that the brand name has become synonymous with its product category. Someone shopping for Q-tips may actually buy another brand of cotton swabs. The competitor's price and/or packaging could convince a consumer to choose that particular brand over the Q-tips brand. Perhaps the issue Q-tips hasn't made clear is explaining why a box of Q-tips cotton swabs is better than a competitor's brand. Nevertheless, all companies want to guard against their brand name becoming a generic description for a product category because then their brand name becomes public property, which means the owner loses all rights to it!

Companies hope that consumers will think of their brand name before all others, and they spend billions to turn their products into "household names." With that said, they also spend millions trying to prevent these household names from being applied to products other than their own. Coca-Cola and Xerox are probably the best-known examples of companies fighting to ensure their brand name is not used generically. Although Coke has lost the proprietary right to the name *cola* because it is considered descriptive of the product, it has won lawsuits against restaurants who serve another brand of cola when their customers ask for a Coke.[28]

Some products that have retained their registered trademarks despite the generic use of their names include Q-tip, Band-Aid, Jell-O, Frisbee, Kleenex, Play-Doh, and Scotch Tape. Former trademarks that have been legally declared as descriptive words and are therefore no longer owned by the companies or individuals who invented them include aspirin, cellophane, raisin bran, thermos, yo-yo, and zipper.[29]

Through obtaining trademarks for their brands, companies can help prevent their brand names from becoming public property and preserve their product differentiation.

Discussion Questions
1. Can you think of any other brand names now used as generic descriptors? If so, which ones?
2. How can having your brand name used as a generic descriptor be a good thing for your company?
3. How can a company get their brand known, but not have it become a generic description?

shelves is extremely important. The package design, shape, colour, and texture all influence buyers' perceptions and buying behaviour. Luxury items such as jewellery or high-end cosmetics typically package their products to create an impression of extravagance, sophistication, and exclusiveness.

What does the government have to say about product labels?   Labelling serves two functions: to inform and to persuade. The *Consumer Packaging and Labelling Act* and *Regulations* requires companies to identify:[30]

- the product name or function
- the name and place of business of the manufacturer, packer, or distributor
- the size, age, material content, or such information about the nature of the contents

Administration and enforcement of the act and regulations, as they relate to non-food products, is the responsibility of the Competition Bureau, Industry Canada. Labelling of food products enforcement is the responsibility of the Canadian Food Inspection Agency (CFIA). Clearly, labels should inform consumers about the product, its uses, and any safety concerns. However, labels can be confusing and misleading. For example, what does the label "organic product" really mean? Are all ingredients in that product organic, or just one ingredient? Businesses that wish to foster good customer relationships must be careful to label their products ethically.

Why is labelling important to establishing a brand image?   Labels are also used to promote and to persuade customers to buy the product. Labels can educate consumers of the features and other benefits of the product. Many companies label their products with their brand logo to distinguish their product from that of their competitors. If the label comes to represent consistent quality and dependability, then the label can perpetuate a positive brand-name image.

Decision-Making Mini-Simulation: Pricing. Located in MyBusinessLab.

The Marketing Mix (4 Ps): Price
Revenue Generating Component

Why is price an important component in the marketing mix?   Pricing is so important to consumers and producers alike that it ranks as one of the 4 Ps in the marketing mix. Prices are sometimes called *fees*, *fares*, *tolls*, *rates*, *charges*, or *subscriptions*. **Price** is the only revenue-generating component of the marketing mix—product, promotion, and place (distribution) strategies are all cost components. In fact, *revenue* to a business equals the price multiplied by the number of units sold or services performed. *Profit* equals total revenue minus total costs. So, you can see that the pricing decision has a huge impact on profitability.

Trying to set the right price can be a real challenge for marketers. The price of a product has to be low enough to generate enough value to customers to motivate sales, yet high enough to enable the company to cover costs and earn a profit. Setting the right price is challenging because market conditions are always changing. As a result, companies must constantly tweak prices to remain competitive. Moreover, some companies operating in very competitive markets may have little to no control over their price. Instead, price is determined in the market through the interaction of demand and supply. These companies may therefore be *price-takers* (not *price-setters*). For example, farmers have virtually no control over the prices of their agricultural commodities. However, most companies have at least some control over the price they charge.

What are some pricing objectives?   Some of the most common pricing objectives include the following:

- *Maximizing profits.* This occurs when price is set so that total revenue exceeds total cost by the greatest amount.
- *Achieving greater market share.* A company's market share is the percentage of total industry sales or revenues it is able to capture. Unfortunately, achieving greater market share does not always translate into higher profits.
- *Maximizing sales.* Maximizing sales often means charging low prices that can result in losses. Firms cannot survive for long with losses. However, maximizing sales may

6

Describe three major approaches to pricing strategy, and outline some pricing tactics used to launch a new product, to adjust prices, and to affect price perceptions.

Price is the only revenue-generating component of the marketing mix—product, promotion, and place (distribution) strategies are all cost components.

12

be an appropriate short-run objective to rid the company of excess inventory, such as last year's models.

- *Building traffic.* Many retail stores, such as grocery stores, pharmacies, hardware stores, and department stores, may advertise a sale price on a few goods to increase traffic in their stores and build a stronger customer base. They also hope customers will purchase other, more profitable items while they are shopping for the bargains.
- *Status quo pricing.* The objective of status quo pricing is simply to match competitors' prices, possibly to avoid a price war that could be damaging to everyone. The airfare wars of the past hurt all the airline carriers, so they have chosen to compete on non-price factors instead.
- *Survival.* If a company is struggling to build a customer base, it may choose to set prices to generate just enough revenues to cover costs. However, this is not a suitable long-term objective. Survival prices might generate sales, but they will not generate profits.
- *Creating an image.* Some products are priced high because firms hope that consumers will associate high prices with high quality. This is the case for many specialty goods such as luxury cars, perfume, and designer jewellery.
- *Achieving social objectives.* Some companies may charge low prices to enable the poor to afford their products. For example, many governments have been involved in ensuring that staple food products such as grains are affordable to all.

Marketers must develop their pricing strategies in coordination with their product branding, packaging, promotion, and distribution strategies as well. Indeed, price is only one element in the marketing mix.

Pricing Strategies

BizSkills Simulation: Pricing Strategies. Located in MyBusinessLab.

The most common **pricing strategies** include *cost-based pricing*, *demand-based pricing*, and *competition-based pricing*.

Cost-based pricing (or **cost-plus pricing**) is charging a price in relation to the costs of providing the good or service.

Break-even analysis determines the production level for which total revenue is just enough to cover total costs.

Fixed costs (or **overhead costs**) are any costs that do not vary with the production level. Total fixed costs typically include salaries, rent, insurance expenses, and loan repayments.

Variable costs are costs that vary with the production level. Examples include wages, raw materials, and energy costs. *Average variable costs* (or *per unit variable costs*) equal total variable costs divided by the production level.

What are the major pricing strategies? Although there is no one right way to determine the price of a good or service, there are a number of strategies a seller can use. The most common **pricing strategies** include *cost-based pricing*, *demand-based pricing*, and *competition-based pricing*.

What is cost-based pricing? **Cost-based pricing** (or **cost-plus pricing**) is charging a price in relation to the costs of providing the good or service. It is the simplest and one of the more popular pricing strategies. Suppose you manufacture 100 units of a product at a total cost of $2000. The per unit cost would be $20. If you want to make a unit profit margin, or *markup*, of 20 percent, which is $4 (0.20 x $20), you would price the product at $24. Total revenue would equal $2400 and profit would equal $400, or 20 percent above costs.

There are many advantages of cost-plus pricing. Besides being easy to calculate and easy to administer, it requires a minimum amount of information. However, it has several disadvantages as well. It ignores whether the price is compatible with consumer demand or expectations and the prices charged by competitors. It also provides little incentive to be efficient and to hold costs down. Many pharmaceutical companies undertake cost-plus pricing to recoup their expensive research and development costs associated with a new drug and to earn a targeted profit level. The monopoly power granted by patents on new drugs means there is no competition, and pharmaceutical companies find little need to consider consumer demand when setting prices on drugs.

Cost-based pricing can be facilitated by **break-even analysis**, which determines the production level for which total revenue is just enough to cover total costs. Total costs equal total fixed costs plus total variable costs. **Fixed costs** (or **overhead costs**) are any costs that do not vary with the production level. Total fixed costs typically include salaries, rent, insurance expenses, and loan repayments. **Variable costs** are costs that vary with the production level. Examples include wages, raw materials, and energy costs. *Average variable costs* (or *per unit variable costs*) equal total variable costs divided by the production level. A convenient formula for calculating the break-even production level is

$$\text{Break-even volume of production} = \frac{\text{Total Fixed Costs}}{\text{Price} - \text{Average Variable Costs}}$$

For example, suppose that the total fixed costs equal $600, the selling price is $24, and average variable costs are $14. The break-even volume of production is therefore $600/($24 – $14), or 60 units. Any production level below the break-even volume will result in losses, and any production level above the break-even level will result in profits. Any changes in fixed or variable costs, as well as changes in the price, will affect the break-even volume of production. Many book publishers use this strategy.

What is demand-based pricing?   **Demand-based pricing** (or **value-based pricing**) is pricing a good or service based on the demand for the product or its perceived value. A high price will be charged when demand or the perceived value of the product is high, and a lower price will be charged when demand or perceived value is low. This pricing strategy assumes firms can accurately estimate perceived value or the demand for their goods or services. Sometimes this is the case, but it is usually very difficult to do in practice. Nevertheless, many firms try.

One of the specific demand-based pricing strategies that firms employ is target costing. **Target costing** estimates the value customers receive from a product and therefore the price they are willing to pay, and then subtracts an acceptable profit margin to obtain a desired cost. Firms then work to get costs down to this targeted level. The Boeing Company, Caterpillar, DaimlerChrysler, and Continental Teves (a supplier of automotive brake systems) have successfully used target costing as a pricing strategy.[31]

Another demand-based pricing technique is **price discrimination**, charging different prices to different customers when these price differences are not a reflection of cost differences. Successful price discrimination charges higher prices to targeted customers who are price insensitive and lower prices to other targeted customers who are more price sensitive. Price discrimination requires firms to be able to segment customers successfully based on their differences in demand and price sensitivity, and it requires that the product cannot be easily resold among customers. One example of price discrimination includes hotels and resorts charging different rates based on different days of the week or seasonal variations. Movie theatres may also charge higher prices to view a movie during the evening showing as opposed to the matinee viewing time. Airline companies also price discriminate on the airfares they charge. Those who place their reservations well in advance pay less than those who book a flight on short notice. Restaurants price discriminate with early bird specials and discounted happy hour rates. Grocery stores price discriminate by offering clip-out coupons that price-sensitive customers may use to buy grocery items at lower prices. In some cases, even salespeople charge different prices to customers based on their perceived demand for big-ticket items such as cars and furniture, so don't tell them how much you value or love their good or service! Many organizations price discriminate because it is profitable to do so.

What is competition-based pricing?   **Competition-based pricing** is a pricing strategy based on what the competition is charging. Revenues and costs are secondary. The degree of competition in markets affects a company's price-setting ability. *Monopolistically competitive markets*, markets in which many firms compete based on doing something unique, have some firms that charge higher prices if they are successful in their product differentiation strategies. Other companies may charge lower prices to get an edge on the competition. *Oligopolies*, a market with a few dominant sellers such as those in the airlines and oil industries, often avoid competing based on price to avoid price wars. Instead, they compete aggressively on product differentiation and charge higher prices if their total product offerings are unique. However, periodically, a *price leader* may charge a different price and all other firms follow with similar price changes. Finally, a *monopoly*, a market that is controlled by one dominating firm, possesses the greatest price-setting ability because there is no competition. In some extreme cases, monopolies may have captured their markets through *predatory pricing*, the practice of charging very low prices with the intent to destroy the competition. Predatory pricing is illegal, but that hasn't prevented it from occurring. Most real-world competition rests on product differentiation and customer's perception of value. Companies such as

Demand-based pricing (or **value-based pricing**) is pricing a good or service based on the demand for the product or its perceived value.

Target costing estimates the value customers receive from a product and therefore the price they are willing to pay, and then subtracts an acceptable profit margin to obtain a desired cost.

Price discrimination involves charging different prices to different customers when these price differences are not a reflection of cost differences.

Competition-based pricing is a pricing strategy based on what the competition is charging. Revenues and costs are secondary.

12

Harley-Davidson have successfully differentiated their products and can charge higher prices than for comparable models produced by Honda, Yamaha, and Kawasaki.

Are there alternate pricing strategies?
When launching a new product, companies may need to use a different type of pricing strategy than they would on an existing product. One pricing strategy for introducing a new product is **price skimming**. It involves charging a high price for a product initially, then lowering the price over time. Price skimming coincides with the introductory stage of a product's life cycle during which there are few, if any, competitors. The idea is to skim off as high a price as possible to recoup the expensive new product development costs. However, the high price may encourage competitors to enter the market at a lower price.

At the other end of the spectrum is **penetration pricing**, a strategy of charging the lowest possible price for a new product. This pricing strategy is designed to build market share for the product quickly. If the increased production to satisfy growing sales results in lower per unit costs, then profits can actually rise even though the price is lower. Penetration pricing is appropriate during the growth stage of a product's life cycle and when customers are price sensitive. It may also create goodwill among consumers and inhibit competitors from entering the market. Its drawbacks include the establishment of low price expectations or a poor-quality image for the brand and the company. This may make it difficult to raise prices later.

What are the common types of price adjustments?
Most businesses adjust their prices to promote their products. Several tactics are used. One way to adjust prices is to use **discounts**, a deduction from the regular price charged. Discounts come in many forms:

- quantity discounts (a lower price for buying in large quantities)
- cash discounts (a reduced price for paying with a method that does not require processing)
- seasonal discounts (a price reduction if you buy out of season)
- forms of allowance, such as a trade-in allowance (a reduced price if you trade your old good for a new good)

Another way to adjust prices is to use rebates. **Rebates** are partial refunds on what a customer has already paid for a product. An example is mail-in rebates, where the manufacturer writes a cheque to the customer after the customer provides proof of purchase.

Bundling is another type of price adjustment. In **bundling**, two or more products that usually complement one another are combined and sold at a single price. To be attractive, the single price is usually lower than the sum of the individual products' prices. Bundling is quite common in the fast-food industry where products are bundled to make a complete meal. Bundling also occurs with cable or satellite TV sales, when a package of channels is sold at a single price. Many vacation packages are also bundled products consisting of airfare, car rental, hotel accommodations, and other amenities bundled together.

Dynamic pricing is another price-adjustment technique. In **dynamic pricing**, prices are determined directly between the buyer and seller, unlike the more traditional fixed pricing in which prices are set by the seller. Auctions are a traditional form of dynamic pricing. More recent examples exist in e-commerce, such as eBay and Priceline.com. Dynamic pricing often results in quick price adjustments.

Price skimming involves charging a high price for a product initially, then lowering the price over time.

Penetration pricing is a strategy of charging the lowest possible price for a new product.

Discounts are deductions from the regular price charged.

Rebates are partial refunds on what a customer has already paid for a product.

Bundling occurs when two or more products that usually complement one another are combined and sold at a single price.

Dynamic pricing determines prices directly between the buyer and seller, unlike the more traditional fixed pricing in which prices are set by the seller.

Everyday low pricing (EDLP) is a strategy of charging low prices with few, if any, special promotional sales.

In dynamic pricing, prices are determined directly between the buyer and the seller, a practice seen in traditional auctions such as the one shown here.

Finally, some retail stores choose not to adjust their prices at all, but instead offer **everyday low pricing (EDLP)**, a strategy of charging low prices with few, if any, special promotional sales. Walmart has successfully used this strategy because it has been able to give the impression that its brand means everyday low cost. However, it risks taking the excitement out of shopping for bargain hunters.

What are some strategies used to affect price perceptions?
For many consumers, a high price indicates good quality. Although this is not always the case, many consumers make this association when products are complex, do not have a strong brand identity, or are services with which they are unfamiliar. **Prestige pricing** (or **premium pricing**) is the practice of charging a high price to invoke perceptions of high quality and privilege. For those brands for which prestige pricing may apply, the high price itself is a motivator for consumers. The higher perceived value because of the higher price actually increases demand and creates a higher price that becomes self-sustaining. Some people have called this the *snob effect*. Examples of this strategy include the pricing of cars made by Mercedes-Benz, Lexus, and Rolls-Royce.

Another pricing strategy that affects price perceptions is **psychological pricing** (or **odd** or **fractional pricing**), the practice of charging a price just below a whole number to give the appearance of a significantly lower price. For example, charging $9.99 as opposed to $10.00 is an example of psychological pricing. Gas stations often use psychological pricing.

A **loss leader** is a product priced below its cost. Stores use loss leaders to attract customers and motivate them to buy items that are more expensive as well. Reference pricing is another strategy used to attract customers. **Reference pricing** refers to listing an inflated price (the "regular retail price" or "manufacturer's suggested retail price") that is then discounted to appear as if it is a good value. A variation of this strategy occurs when stores provide both a more expensive "gold-plated" version of a product and a lower-priced alternative. This makes the alternative appear to be a bargain.

These are just a few pricing strategies—many others exist. Indeed, the pricing component of the marketing mix is one of the most difficult for marketers to grapple with.

Mercedes-Benz uses the pricing strategy known as prestige pricing to invoke perceptions of high quality and privilege.

Prestige pricing (or **premium pricing**) is the practice of charging a high price to invoke perceptions of high quality and privilege.

Psychological pricing (or **odd** or **fractional pricing**) is the practice of charging a price just below a whole number to give the appearance of a significantly lower price.

A **loss leader** is a product priced below its cost. Stores use loss leaders to attract customers and motivate them to buy items that are more expensive as well.

Reference pricing refers to listing an inflated price (the "regular retail price" or "manufacturer's suggested retail price") that is then discounted to appear as if it is a good value.

The **promotion** part of the marketing mix consists of all the methods to inform and persuade targeted customers to buy a product and to build positive customer relationships.

THE MARKETING MIX (4 Ps): PROMOTION AND THE PROMOTIONAL MIX

Promotion

What does it mean to "promote" a product?
Few products—no matter how well developed, priced, and distributed—will sell well if they are not properly promoted. The **promotion** part of the marketing mix consists of all the methods to inform and persuade targeted customers to buy a product and to build positive customer relationships. Promotion involves all the techniques marketers use to inform targeted customers of the benefits of a product and to persuade them to purchase the good, service, or idea. Promotion is designed to increase brand awareness, brand loyalty, and sales, and is therefore one of the most visible components of the marketing mix. Finding the best way to communicate the benefits of a product and to persuade consumers to buy it is a critical job of marketers. Should the product be advertised, or is personal selling more appropriate? If advertising is used, is it best to advertise through newspapers, magazines, radio, television, or

7
Define a promotional mix, and explain its function in a promotional campaign.

 BizSkills Simulation: Promoting a Product. Located in MyBusinessLab.

12

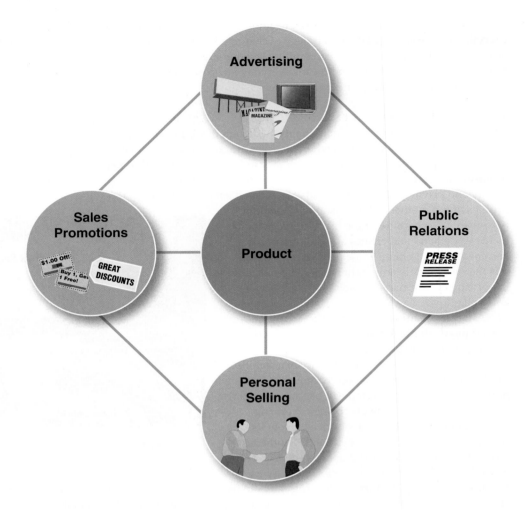

Figure 12.4 The Promotional Mix

another source? Beyond advertising and personal selling, what types of public relations activities might be most appropriate? These are just a few of the questions that marketers must ask themselves when promoting a product.

What are the most popular tools marketers use to promote a product? Four basic **promotional tools** are used to promote a good or service: advertising, public relations, personal selling, and sales promotions. The **promotional mix** is the strategic combination of promotional tools used to reach targeted customers to achieve marketing objectives. These elements of the promotional mix are illustrated in **Figure 12.4**. Notice that the product itself can be a promotional tool because its features may be promoted by giving away free samples of the good or service.

Efficient organizations search for the optimal or most cost-effective promotional mix, given their marketing objectives and their budgetary constraints. If a firm's major objective is to maximize profits, then it will juggle the amounts of advertising, public relations, personal selling, and sales promotion until a mix is found that maximizes profits, given the company's limited promotional budget. The optimal, or best, promotional mix for a given product will vary depending on the goals of the business.

What are the steps involved in a promotional campaign? Six steps emerge from all **effective promotional campaigns**:

1. *Identify target market.* The first step in any promotional campaign is to identify the specific group of potential customers on which to focus marketing efforts.

Promotional tools, used to promote a good or service, include advertising, public relations, personal selling, and sales promotions.

The **promotional mix** is the strategic combination of promotional tools used to reach targeted customers to achieve marketing objectives.

Effective promotional campaigns include six steps: identify target market; determine marketing objectives; design the message; determine the budget; implement the promotional mix; and evaluate and adjust as needed.

2. *Determine marketing objectives.* Is the business trying to maximize profits, sales, or market share? Is the goal to build traffic, brand awareness, or brand image? Is the business trying to introduce a new product or respond to an attack by a competitor? Whatever the marketing objective is, the goal should be clearly understood and measurable.

3. *Design the message.* The message should inform customers of the benefits of the business's product and be echoed by all elements of the promotional mix to give a unified message.

4. *Determine the budget.* The best combination of promotional activities can be determined by finding that mix with the biggest bang for the buck.

5. *Implement the promotional mix.* Businesses must always integrate and coordinate all promotional efforts. For example, public relations, sales promotions, and direct marketing efforts should try to produce results at the same time advertisements are scheduled to appear.

6. *Evaluate and adjust as needed.* The effectiveness of any promotional mix depends on clearly understood and measurable objectives. Each element of the mix, as well as the entire combination of the mix, will need to be adjusted as necessary for growth, for changing marketing objectives, or to correct ineffective promotional techniques.

How do companies create consistency across an entire promotional campaign?
An **integrated marketing communication (IMC)** is a strategy to deliver a clear, consistent, and unified message about the company and its products to customers at all contact points. Consistency nurtures good customer relations and repeat business. It is essential that all members of the marketing team—whether they are involved with advertising, public relations, personal selling, or sales promotions—work together to foster and sustain a consistent and compelling message to create a positive brand image. In short, everyone in the organization needs to be on the same page and communicate with one voice.

Promotional Mix: Advertising

How do companies persuade consumers to buy their products?   **Advertising** is paid, impersonal mass communication from an identified sponsor to persuade or influence a targeted audience. When we think of advertising, many of us first think of television commercials, such as those during the Super Bowl. But as we shall see, advertising is much more than this.

Advertising plays a huge role in business as one of the promotional tools designed to communicate with targeted customers. It is especially important in the introduction and growth stages of a product's life cycle, as it helps build mass brand awareness and brand association. In the maturity stage, advertising is often used to stress product differentiation. Effective advertising also builds brand loyalty and brand equity. Although it is costly, advertising also often leads to lower prices for consumers because advertising is a mass-marketing tool. The more people know about a product and like it, the higher its sales and the greater its production level. Given the frequent economies of scale associated with increased volumes of production, we, as consumers, get lower per-unit costs and lower priced products. Advertising can also inform consumers of the value inherent in products and educate the public in their uses. However, critics argue that advertisers are less concerned about informing or educating consumers and are instead more interested in misleading the public into perceptions of value that may not really exist. This debate continues. It echoes the need for ethical business behaviour and can explain the existence of government laws and regulations that constrain advertising and other marketing practices.

Advertising also affects the economy because of the huge sums of money spent on it. This creates many jobs in advertising agencies as well as related and supporting industries. Companies spend so much on advertising because it is economically in their best self-interest to do so. It doesn't just cost, it pays! For example, a business that advertises online with Google can exponentially increase traffic to its company website, leading to more sales.

Decision-Making Mini-Simulation: Advertising. Located in MyBusinessLab.

An **integrated marketing communication (IMC)** is a strategy to deliver a clear, consistent, and unified message about the company and its products to customers at all contact points.

Explain the advantages and disadvantages of the various types of media used for advertising.

Advertising is paid, impersonal mass communication from an identified sponsor to persuade or influence a targeted audience.

Below are some of the most successful advertising campaigns of all time. Can you connect each advertising campaign to its product? **quiz**

1. "Have it your way" 1973   **A.** Maxwell House coffee
2. "When it rains it pours" 1912   **B.** AT&T
3. "Takes a licking and keeps on ticking" 1950s   **C.** Morton's Salt
4. "Good to the last drop" 1959   **D.** Campbell's Soup
5. "Ring around the collar" 1968   **E.** Burger King
6. "Reach out and touch someone" 1979   **F.** Hallmark
7. "Breakfast of champions" 1930s   **G.** Wisk Detergent
8. "Mmm mm good" 1930s   **H.** Timex
9. "When you care enough to send the very best" 1930s   **I.** Kellogg's Rice Krispies
10. "Snap! Crackle! Pop!" 1940s   **J.** Wheaties

Answers: 1. E; 2. C; 3. H; 4. A; 5. G; 6. B; 7. J; 8. D; 9. F; 10. I

Source: Bob Garfield, "The Top 100 Advertising Campaigns of the Century," *AdAge.com*, http://adage.com/century/campaigns.html, Accessed May 29, 2011.

How did you do? Did these campaigns succeed in making a lasting impression on you? Some of these campaigns date back more than fifty years and are still used today. Can you think of others?

What are the different types of advertising?

Advertising is undertaken by virtually all organizations in one form or another. Different organizations use different types of advertising. The following are some of the more common types of advertising:

- *Product advertising*—advertising that promotes a specific product's uses, features, and benefits. This is the type of advertising we most often think of.
- *Corporate (or institutional) advertising*—advertising that focuses on creating a positive image toward an organization or an entire industry as opposed to a specific product (i.e. "Got Milk?"). Government entities can also undertake institutional advertising. For example, provincial governments do it when they run advertisements that promote tourism in their provinces.
- *Comparative advertising*—advertising that compares a brand's characteristics with those of other established brands. Examples include television commercials comparing toothpaste, pain relievers, and detergents.
- *Retail (or local) advertising*—advertising that focuses on attracting customers to a fixed location such as a department store or a grocery store.
- *Business-to-business advertising*—advertising directed to other businesses rather than to consumers. For example, Caterpillar, the earth-moving equipment company, advertises to construction companies.
- *Non-profit advertising*—advertising that focuses on promoting not-for-profit organizations such as the Red Cross and the Nature Conservancy.
- *Public service advertising*—advertising that communicates a message on behalf of a good cause, such as the prevention of wildfires.
- *Advocacy advertising*—advertising that promotes an organization's position on a public issue, such as global warming or immigration. We are familiar with advocacy advertising undertaken during political campaigns by organizations independent of a political party or candidate.
- *Interactive advertising*—advertising that uses interactive media, such as interactive video catalogues on the Internet or at kiosks at shopping malls, to connect directly with consumers in a personal and engaging way.
- *Internet advertising*—advertising that uses pop-up and banner ads and other techniques to direct people to an organization's website. Internet advertising is growing rapidly. Revenues to businesses from this type of advertising are expected to continue to grow.[32]

What are the different types of advertising media?

Advertising media are the means of conveying a message about a product. Media conveying informative and persuasive messages exist all around us, including on seats of grocery carts, on sides of buses and trucks, on billboards, in magazines, in newspapers, and in brochures. Advertisements are also heard on telemarketing and telephone hold messages, on in-store public address systems, and on the radio. And of course we see ads on television, on the Internet, in movies, in video games, and in our mailboxes every day. Advertising is pervasive and has been around for many years. Some of the more modern, traditional media for advertising include television, newspapers, magazines, radio, the Internet, and outdoor media. Outdoor media include billboards; signs in sports arenas; ads painted on the sides of cars, trucks, and buses; and even skywriting.

Beyond these advertising media, *direct mail advertising* remains one of the largest forms of advertising. You're probably familiar with direct mail advertising; you just have a different name for it—junk mail. Direct mail advertising comes in many forms, ranging from coupon offers to brochures and catalogues. However, it continues and may even grow because it's generally a very effective advertising tool.[33] Direct mail advertising allows companies to target their advertising dollars to the customers most likely to buy their products and to offer customized product offerings to these customers. Besides direct mail, the *Yellow Pages* are also frequently used to advertise. This medium is particularly important for small businesses.

What are the advantages and disadvantages of the different types of advertising media?

Many advantages and disadvantages accompany each of these advertising media. For example, television advertising reaches a huge audience, but is very expensive. In fact, TV commercials are so effective that networks can command huge sums of money for commercial airtime during popular or prime-time TV events. For example, as of 2011, a thirty-second spot during the Super Bowl would cost around US$3 million.[34] But remember, the marketer's task is to find the most effective and efficient medium for transmitting his or her message to targeted customers—given marketing objectives and budget constraints. **Table 12.1** lists some of the advantages and disadvantages of each major medium.

What are some important recent trends in advertising?

One of the most important trends to emerge from modern advertising has been the development of Internet advertising. In fact, it is one of the fastest-growing media in part because it allows firms to focus their advertising dollars on targeted customers. Other trends include product placement, infomercials, and global advertising.

Internet Advertising   Internet advertising includes spam ("junk" e-mail), pop-ups, banner ads, and other links found at websites to attract potential customers to a company's Web page. Google, Yahoo!, and other search engine sites can determine customers' perceived needs and wants based on their searches. If you search for a vacation package, for example, then Disney or Norwegian Cruise Lines may pay Google or Yahoo! to have its banner ad appear on your search. Once customers have been persuaded to visit

Table 12.1   Advantages and Disadvantages of Advertising Media

Media	Advantages	Disadvantages
Television	Good mass-market coverage; low cost per contact; combines sight, sound, and motion; good attention span	High cost; low recall; channel surfing or digital video recorders skip over ads; short exposure
Newspaper	Timing and geographic flexibility; good local market coverage; high credibility and acceptability	Short life span; lots of competition for attention; poor-quality reproductions
Magazine	High market segmentation; high-quality colour; long life; longer attention span; high credibility	Declining readership; lots of competition for attention; high cost; long ad-purchase lead time
Radio	High geographic and demographic selectivity; low cost; creative opportunities with sound	Low attention span; short exposure time; information overload; limited coverage
Internet	Global and interactive possibilities; ease of segmentation; high audience interest; easy to measure responses	Audience controls exposure; clutter on each site; skewed demographically to surfers
Outdoor	Able to select key geographic areas; low cost per impression; high frequency on major commuter routes	Short exposure time; brief messages; creative limitations; little segmentation possible
Direct Mail	High levels of segmentation; allows personalization; high flexibility; ad can be saved; measurable impact	High cost; can be rejected as "junk mail" and viewed as a nuisance
Yellow Pages	Inexpensive; commonly used and accessible; good local coverage and segmentation possible; long life	Costly for very small businesses; lists the competition as well

Leading Global Advertisers by Expenditures (2009, US$billion)

1. Procter & Gamble	8.68
2. Unilever	6.03
3. L'Oreal	4.56
4. General Motors Co.	3.27
5. Nestlé	2.62
6. Coca-Cola Co.	2.44
7. Toyota	2.31
8. Johnson & Johnson	2.25
9. Reckitt Benckiser	2.24
10. Kraft Foods	2.12

Source: "Leading Global Advertisers," *Adbrands.net*, http://www.adbrands .net/top_global_advertisers.htm, Accessed June 3, 2011.

Product placement is the placement of products in TV shows, movies, and video games where they will be seen by potential customers.

Infomercials are television commercials that run as long as regular TV programs.

a firm's website, the company can learn a lot about potential customers depending on where and how many times they click within the company's website. Businesses then attempt to interact with their customers through videos or even through starting a chat based on their perceived needs and wants. The idea is to work with customers to create a customized product offering that best meets the customers' unique tastes and preferences. If the business is able to deliver consistently high-quality value using these modern techniques, then Internet advertising can help businesses maintain positive customer relations.

Product Placement and Infomercials   The placement of products in TV shows, movies, and video games where they will be seen by potential customers has increased vastly in recent years. This is known as **product placement**. For example, the superhero in the movie *Iron Man* drives an Audi R8, while his leading lady cruises around in an Audi S5.[35] The advent of digital video recorders (DVRs), which allow viewers to record shows and then fast-forward through advertisements, has driven product placement on TV. Another variant of strategic placement is the banners of brand names, symbols, and slogans found on the walls of professional sports stadiums so that camera shots of the televised games will frequently display the banners' messages.

Another significant trend on TV is the use of **infomercials**, television commercials that run as long as regular TV programs. Infomercials typically appear as actual television programs, often in the form of a talk show, with little direct reference to the fact that they are actually advertisements. Unlike normal commercials, infomercials are designed to elicit a specific, direct, and quantifiable response from viewers. The pitches are similar to "call this toll-free number and order yours today" or "if you call within the next few minutes we will also . . ." Infomercials often use "experts" or celebrities as guests or hosts to endorse and push their products. Infomercials have the advantage of showing the features of the products in detail. Some of the most successful infomercials include Bowflex Home Gym, Proactiv Solution Acne Treatment, Ronco Showtime Rotisserie Oven, and Ionic Breeze Air Purifier.[36]

Global Advertising   The globalization of advertising is another important trend. Most products have to be customized to satisfy foreign customers. This means that products are tailored to meet the unique local tastes, preferences, and cultural sensitivities of foreign customers or to satisfy the regulatory standards of different governments around the globe. Likewise, some advertising campaigns can be exported intact, while others have to be changed. Advertisers prefer to use the same message because it is cheaper, it allows for a more globally integrated communication message, and it allows for the pooling of talent to design the most compelling advertising message. But transferring domestically successful advertising messages abroad can be tricky. As we discussed in Chapter 4, marketers have to consider the interpretations of their messages carefully in the underlying cultural context of the foreign market. Increasingly, marketers are realizing that customized advertising campaigns to globally segmented markets work much better, just as domestic market segmentation is more effective.

 Promotional Mix: Public Relations

Define *publicity* and describe how a company might generate positive publicity as well as manage negative publicity.

Public relations is the management function that establishes and maintains mutually beneficial relationships between an organization and its stakeholders.

How much control do businesses have over their public image?   Another important part of the promotional mix is public relations. **Public relations** is the management function that establishes and maintains mutually beneficial relationships between an organization and its stakeholders.[37] Stakeholders for businesses include all interested parties, including consumers, stockholders, employees, suppliers, the government, and the public in general. All organizations—for-profits, non-profits, and even governments—are interested in public relations.

The idea behind public relations is to create and maintain a positive image of the organization in the minds of stakeholders. This begins with assessing public attitudes and perceptions of the organization. Sometimes, public opinion may be based on perceptions that have little to do with facts. Nevertheless, an honest audit of public opinion is necessary before specific public relations programs can be implemented to shape the image and reputation of the organization. Once an organization has listened carefully to public concerns and interests, it needs to respond by changing its behaviour or by correcting misperceptions. Finally, the organization needs to inform the public of any changes it has made or educate the public about the facts associated with the organization.

Several specific types of public relations tools exist to build a positive business image. They can be classified by whether the news transmitted is controlled, semi-controlled, or uncontrolled by the organization.[38] The degree of control hinges on how and when the message is delivered. **Controlled messages** include corporate (or institutional) advertising, advocacy advertising, and public service advertising. An organization may also disseminate annual reports, brochures, flyers, and newsletters, or provide films or speakers to send a controlled message to targeted audiences. **Semi-controlled messages** are placed on websites, in chat rooms, and on blogs. In these forums, what people say about the company is not strictly regulated. Other forms include sporting or special events sponsorships because participation by the press and stakeholders is not under the control of the sponsoring company. A company also may use **uncontrolled messages**, which generally take the form of publicity.

Publicity is information about an individual, organization, or product transmitted through mass media at no charge. Publicity has two advantages over advertising. First, it is free. Second, it is more believable because it is often presented as a news story. However, publicity is *not* controlled by the seller—it is controlled by the media, and this is its disadvantage. If, when, and how a news release, a press conference, a captioned photograph, an appearance on a talk show, or a staged event will be covered by the media is outside the control of public relations managers.

How does a company generate positive publicity?

Naturally, keeping friendly relations with the press increases the probability that a "newsworthy" story will be covered and treated with a favourable spin. Nevertheless, public relations managers need to ensure that publicity releases are timely, interesting, accurate, and in the public interest. For example, in May 2005, GE launched its "ecomagination" campaign to portray itself as an environmental leader. Was General Electric sincere about the environment, or was it just jockeying for a favourable marketing impression? The consensus was that GE was sincere. This may explain why the campaign won the prestigious 2006 Silver Effie Award in the category of Corporate Reputation, Image & Identity.[39] GE's publicity releases were timely, interesting, accurate, and in the public interest.

It appears green business is good business, and not just for GE. For example, The Home Depot, the world's largest seller of lumber, now gives preference to vendors that offer FSC-certified wood. The FSC (Forest Stewardship Council) determines whether lumber is grown and harvested responsibly to preserve environmental integrity. Shoppers can identify FSC-certified lumber by its greentree logo. IKEA, based in Sweden, where nearly half the forests are certified, produces as much furniture as possible from FSC-certified wood. These companies received a lot of publicity when the documentary *Buyer Be Fair* first aired on Public Television in March 2006. You can bet these companies appreciate the publicity for their efforts.

Another example of positive publicity is the favourable press that McDonald's Ronald McDonald House Charities receive for providing families with temporary living quarters while their children are in the hospital. Corporate philanthropy is generally good publicity, especially if it results in getting your name on a building, an annual event, a scholarship, or volunteer programs visible to the community. Many smaller companies give to local schools, hospitals, and arts programs. Some of the larger corporations renowned for their philanthropic and charitable efforts include Microsoft, Target, Avon, Hewlett-Packard, AOL, and Timberland.[40]

Controlled messages include corporate (or institutional) advertising, advocacy advertising, and public service advertising.

Semi-controlled messages are placed on websites, in chat rooms, and on blogs, and are not strictly regulated. Other forms include sporting or special events sponsorships because participation by the press and stakeholders is not under the control of the sponsoring company.

Uncontrolled messages generally take the form of publicity.

Publicity is information about an individual, organization, or product transmitted through mass media at no charge.

The names of companies and brands on NASCAR drivers' clothes and cars demonstrate companies undertaking event sponsorship.

12

Companies such as Avon generate positive publicity through philanthropic efforts, such as hosting a Walk for Breast Cancer.

Whether motivated by publicity needs or a sense of social responsibility, giving back to the community doesn't just *cost* companies, it *pays* them. Most of us like buying products from companies if we believe that some of our money will be used to give back to the community or to reward companies for doing the right thing.

How does a company respond to negative publicity?
A final role of public relations personnel is managing a crisis. **Damage control** is a company's effort to minimize the harmful effects of a negative event. Negative publicity, in a matter of days, can tear down a firm's image that took decades to build up. For example, Exxon-Mobil still suffers from the *Exxon Valdez* oil spill accident that occurred more than two decades ago. Sometimes, bad news doesn't come from the media but from word of mouth. In the event of bad news, a company must stand ready to react, and react quickly. No easy remedies exist for crises, but being honest, accepting responsibility and making other ethical responses are the first steps toward regaining credibility and re-establishing a positive image.

Damage control is a company's effort to minimize the harmful effects of a negative event.

Advertising, public relations, and publicity are important elements in the promotional mix. Review the ad campaign quiz at the beginning of the chapter. You're probably familiar with many of the ads, which means that they were highly successful, well-crafted campaigns. These campaigns were effective because they resonated with customers, created memorable brand awareness, and made people want to buy the products. In doing so, they demonstrated the power of promotion.

 Promotional Mix: Personal Selling

List the six steps in the personal selling process.

What is "personal" selling and why is it an important promotional technique?
Personal selling is direct communication between a firm's sales force and potential buyers to make a sale and to build good customer relationships. For example, a laboratory supplies company may deploy a representative to a research facility to demonstrate new products. Good salespeople don't just want to sell their products; they want to serve customers. A salesperson should help customers with their buying decisions by understanding their needs and presenting the advantages and disadvantages of a product. Salespeople most effectively represent their companies by establishing good customer relationships that foster repeat business and long-term company success.

 Decision-Making Mini-Simulation: Personal Selling. Located in MyBusinessLab.

Personal selling is direct communication between a firm's sales force and potential buyers to make a sale and to build good customer relationships.

The sales staff is often the first contact point for many customers. To build good customer relationships, a salesperson should be customer oriented, competent, dependable, honest, and likeable. Good salespeople are also able to listen carefully to customer needs. They possess knowledge of the company's total product offerings and make the buying process as easy as possible for the customer. In many business-to-business or industrial sales, millions of dollars may be involved in a single purchase, such as buying an airplane or building an office building.

Obtaining and keeping good salespeople is expensive. This helps explain why personal selling is the most expensive part of the promotional mix for most companies, along with the fact that sales, unlike advertising, is labour-intensive and deals with only one buyer at a time. Generally, personal selling is preferred over advertising when selling a high-value, custom-made, or technically complex product. Advertising is more cost-effective when selling a low-value, easily understood, standardized product.

What are the steps in the selling process?
The best way to understand the personal selling process is to look at an example. Suppose your company sells a sophisticated global positioning system (GPS) for use in the trucking industry. Your latest model

allows trucking firms to keep track of their tractor-trailer rigs via a password-protected website that features a digital map display of vehicle location and speed, engine use, refrigerated load temperature, door alarms or other motion-sensing devices that have been activated, cargo weight, and odometer reports. You can imagine the benefits of such a system for trucking companies. Although this is a business-to-business (B2B) example, the steps involved in the selling process are essentially the same for selling a consumer product, even though selling a B2B product is usually more complex. In all cases, the salesperson has to be knowledgeable about his or her product and competitors' products.

No two salespeople are alike, and no two selling situations are the same. However, six steps emerge from all personal selling: prospecting, approaching the prospect, presenting, overcoming objections, closing the sale, and following up. This six-step personal selling procedure is outlined in **Figure 12.5**.

STEP 1: Prospecting. The first step in the personal selling process is to identify qualified potential customers. This is known as prospecting. Notice that businesses need not only to find potential customers, they need to identify those who are qualified to buy. To be qualified to buy means that the potential customer has the ability and the authority to purchase, plus the willingness to listen to the sales message. Prospecting can be a daunting task. Good salespeople find leads at trade shows from those who have scouted the company's website or, better yet, from currently satisfied customers willing to recommend the salespeople to others for their superior product and service.

STEP 2: Approaching the Prospect. This step divides into two parts: the pre-approach and the actual approach. The pre-approach involves salespeople doing their homework. This is especially critical if they are trying to sell a B2B product such as a GPS device. Salespeople must learn as much as possible about their potential customers to determine their likely needs and think about how they might be able to satisfy those needs. In our trucking example, you would need to determine the people in the trucking firm who would be most interested in buying your GPS product and learn as much about them as you can. Are they currently using a GPS system? If so, what brand is it? How is your product better? You should also decide on the best approach. Should you phone them, send a letter, or make a personal visit? The timing decision of the actual approach should also be carefully planned not to catch the prospect at a busy time.

In the actual approach, the idea is to meet, greet, and put the prospect at ease. First impressions are lasting impressions! This is the salesperson's first chance at building a long-lasting relationship. Good salespeople present themselves as knowledgeable and friendly professionals who are genuinely interested in serving customers. The first impression is followed by asking some questions to learn about the potential customers' needs. Then, the salesperson must listen carefully to those responses. In our example, because GPS hardware and software is often complicated, you may want to remind them that your product is not only superior, but your service is better than that of the competition as well. You can offer to help install the system, train employees in its use, and offer free twenty-four-hour service and upgrades when necessary.

STEP 3: Presenting. In the actual presentation of the GPS technology, you'll need to tell your product's "story" and detail how your product can help the trucking firm. You should demonstrate the product and let the prospect use it as well. Your presentation should be carefully planned using the most advanced presentation technologies that allow for the full use of multimedia effects. Most importantly, you should ask probing questions during your presentation and listen carefully to answers. Listening is more important than talking. You can't serve the customer until you fully understand his or her needs or problems.

STEP 4: Overcoming Objections. Objections to buying are common. Good salespeople anticipate them and are prepared to counter them. Once objections surface, you should

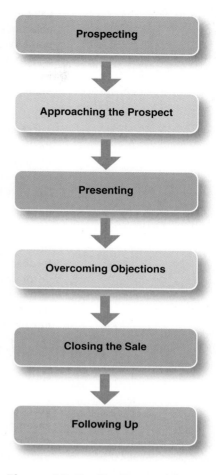

Figure 12.5 The Personal Selling Process

use this opportunity to provide more information on your GPS product and turn these objections into reasons to buy. You may invite others from your company to join in at this point to address any objections via a teleconference or a virtual meeting. This provides an opportunity to establish a rapport based on trust between you, your company, and the prospect. Overcoming objections can be the beginning of a mutually beneficial and lasting relationship.

STEP 5: Closing the Sale. After overcoming objections, the next step is to close the sale and ask for a purchase. You should look for physical cues, comments, or questions that signal the time to ask the buyer for an order. You may want to review points of agreement, ask the buyer which model he or she prefers, ask how many units are needed, or sweeten the deal by offering more favourable credit terms or by throwing in an extra quantity free of charge. Closing the sale is an art that is learned with practice.

STEP 6: Following Up. To ensure a long-term relationship and repeat business, be sure to follow up with the customer to ensure he or she is happy with his or her new GPS product. Stand ready to help him or her with any problems promptly after the sale. Ask for feedback. Relay that feedback to your company as input for improving existing products or for designing new ones. Periodically check up on customers by phone or by sending birthday cards. Good follow-up service and rapport can give rise to referrals or testimonials that can be used to enhance future sales. Following up is all about building and nurturing relationships.

Promotional Mix: Sales Promotion

Describe the two main types of sales promotions and the types of tools commonly used as incentives.

Sales promotions are short-term activities that target consumers and other businesses for generating interest in a product.

How can a company generate interest in a product?   The final element of the promotional mix is sales promotion. **Sales promotions** are short-term activities that target consumers and other businesses for generating interest in a product. Sales promotions encompass all those activities designed to inform, to persuade, and to remind targeted customers about the product—and that have not already been undertaken by advertising, public relations, or personal selling. As consumers, we see sales promotions almost everywhere: from clip-out coupons in our newspaper, to rebate offers on a new car purchase, to e-mail announcements offering discounted prices on airline tickets, to end-of-aisle displays of potato chips at our local grocery store tempting impulse purchases.

Trade (or business-to-business) sales promotions are incentives to push a product through the distribution system to final consumers.

Consumer sales promotions are incentives designed to increase final consumer demand for a product.

What are two general types of sales promotions?   Most companies' products go through a distribution system before they ever reach the final consumer. These companies encourage the intermediaries (such as wholesalers) to push their products on through the distribution channel to end users. Any incentives to push a product through the distribution system to final consumers are called **trade (or business-to-business) sales promotions**. In addition, **consumer sales promotions** are incentives designed to increase final consumer demand for a product. The whole idea behind all sales promotions is to generate interest and excitement around a product. Businesses need to create a reason why stores should not only carry their product, but also encourage its purchase by consumers. Companies want consumers to be so excited about their products that they seek the products out and ask for them by name. In short, companies want to create a tipping point so that all involved will opt for their products instead of the competitors' alternatives.

Trade Sales Promotional Tools   If you want other businesses to become interested and excited about carrying your product, then you must first generate in-house enthusiasm. You will need to educate your entire staff, especially your sales staff, about your product and its many uses, features, and benefits. This may require some formal training of your sales staff on how to best present your product. In order to generate leads, you may need to send your sales staff to trade shows equipped with sophisticated multimedia presentations, full-colour brochures, shirts, hats, coffee mugs with your product logo, and a lot of excitement. You have to create some internal buzz and excitement for your product before you can ever expect other businesses to be interested in carrying and promoting your product. Once your staff is energized, then you can work on creating the same

level of energy and excitement for distributors. Some of the specific trade sales promotion tools include:

- trade shows and conventions
- trade allowances (deals and price reductions to wholesalers, dealers, and retailers)
- co-operative advertising (a manufacturer agrees to pay for some of the advertising costs of the retailer)
- free merchandise
- sales contests (e.g., a free trip to Hawaii for those who sell the most)
- dealer listings (advertisements of your product that mention retail outlets where it can be found)
- catalogues and store demonstrations
- in-store displays
- quantity discounts
- training and support programs

When it comes to trade sales promotional techniques, firms have many options from which to choose. If one doesn't work, they can easily adopt new strategies until they find the best combination.

Consumer Sales Promotion Tools

Consumer sales promotions are aimed at the end users, or final consumers. Consumer sales promotions are intended to increase demand for a good or service, or at least provide that extra incentive to tip consumers in favour of a specific brand. Sales promotions are also aimed at providing customers with another reason to feel good about their purchases. Timing of consumer sales promotions is important to get maximum impact. They need to be strategically coordinated with the other elements in the promotional mix. Some of the most common consumer promotional tools include:

- *Coupons.* Coupons are discount certificates that reduce the price of a product and are redeemable at the time of purchase. Coupons are found in print ads, on packages, in direct mail, at checkout counters, and on the Internet. They are used to encourage the purchase of a new product or to generate repeat sales. Coupons are the most common consumer promotional tool. They are popular because consumers like the sense of getting a bargain.
- *Rebates.* Rebates provide for a reduced price if the rebate form is mailed in along with a proof of purchase. Unlike coupons, the discounted price is not realized at the point of purchase. Because most people do not redeem the rebates, they are an inexpensive way for businesses to promote sales.
- *Frequent-user incentives.* Some credit card companies encourage customers to use their credit cards for purchases that accumulate points redeemable for merchandise. Airlines sometimes offer frequent-flyer miles redeemable for free tickets for additional travel. Hudson's Bay Company (HBC) has a points program whereby customers accumulate points for the purchases they make which are redeemable for merchandise or store credit. These incentives encourage customer loyalty and repeat business.
- *Point-of-purchase (POP) displays.* These are displays strategically located to draw attention and encourage impulse purchases. Examples are items placed in racks close to checkout counters at grocery stores and end-of-aisle stacks of soft drink bottles. Studies indicate that POP displays really work.[41]
- *Free samples.* Free samples are an effective way to introduce a new product, to get non-users to try it, or to get current users to use it in a new way—especially if the samples are made available where the product is sold. Most of us have sampled small portions of foods at our local grocery stores. Some companies also mail samples of products such as cereal and shampoo directly to consumers.
- *Contests and sweepstakes.* Many companies use contests and sweepstakes to increase the sales of their products. As a reward for participating, consumers might win cash, free products, or vacations.
- *Advertising specialties.* Companies frequently create and give away everyday items such as bottle or can openers, caps, and key rings with their names and logos printed on them. Companies prefer to use inexpensive handouts that will yield constant free advertising when used by the recipient.

12

Table 12.2 The Advantages and Disadvantages of Promotional Tools

Promotional Tool	Advantages	Disadvantages
Advertising	• Builds brand awareness and brand loyalty • Reaches a mass audience	• Expensive • Impersonal • Not good at closing a sale
Public Relations	• Often seen as more credible than advertising • Inexpensive way of reaching many customers	• Risk of losing control • Cannot always control what other people write or say about your product
Personal Selling	• Highly interactive communication between the buyer and seller • Excellent for communicating a complex product, information, and features • Good for building customer relationships and closing a sale	• Expensive • Not suitable if there are thousands of buyers
Sales Promotions	• Can stimulate quick increases in sales by targeting promotional incentives on particular products • Good short-term tactical tool	• If used over the long term, customers may get used to the effect • Too much promotion may damage the brand image

Other consumer sales promotion tools include bonuses (buy one, get one free), catalogues, demonstrations, special events, lotteries, premiums, and cents-off deals. Consumer sales promotions are becoming more common because they help segment markets and they are cost-effective.

What are the advantages and disadvantages of the promotional mix? When developing the best promotional mix for a product, companies must weigh the advantages and disadvantages of each of the four main options—advertising, public relations, personal selling, and sales promotions. **Table 12.2** summarizes some of these key advantages and disadvantages.

THE MARKETING MIX (4 Ps): PLACE (DISTRIBUTION)

Marketing Intermediaries and Distribution Channels

How do companies get their products into the hands of customers? Imagine walking through a drugstore, looking for cough syrup. Did you ever wonder how far the products on the shelves have travelled? Consider that cough syrup you're looking for. After it was bottled, it had to travel to a wholesaler and then to the retailer. If you cut out all the travelling and intermediaries, how much would the cough syrup actually cost? What are wholesalers and intermediaries? Why are they needed? And how do they affect the price of a product?

The **place** (or **distribution**) component of the marketing mix refers to all the methods involved in getting the product into the hands of customers. Distribution is the process that makes products available to consumers when and where the consumers want them. Managing the entire process of getting products out the door and eventually into the hands of final consumers is known as *supply chain management* (discussed in Chapter 10). Although somewhat limited in scope, this is still a very complicated process in the real world of business today. Most of us don't think about the transfer and storage of the products we buy—unless something goes wrong and we are unable to get the products we want, when and where we want them. You can imagine the challenges companies face trying to guarantee that customers have access to the products at the right time and in the

Define marketing intermediaries and distribution channels, and explain why these are important elements in marketing.

Decision-Making Mini-Simulation: Marketing Mix. Located in MyBusinessLab.

The **place** (or **distribution**) component of the marketing mix refers to all the methods involved in getting the product into the hands of customers.

right quantity and place. Despite proper distribution being critical and extremely complicated in practice, the distribution function of the 4 Ps of marketing is often overshadowed by the more visible product, pricing, and sales promotional strategies.

A **marketing intermediary** is a business firm that operates between producers and consumers or business users. Intermediaries are sometimes referred to as *middlemen* or *resellers* because they pass along products from manufacturers to end users.

Many goods, such as grocery store items, go through a **distribution channel**, which is a series of firms or individuals that participate in the flow of a product from manufacturer to consumer. The intermediaries in a distribution channel are sometimes called **distributors** (or **wholesalers**).

What are the different types of intermediaries?
There are three types of intermediaries:

- **Wholesalers** are intermediaries that buy and resell products to other wholesalers, to retailers, and to industrial users. For example, your local grocery store probably purchased the Tide laundry detergent on its shelves from a wholesaler who bought it from Procter & Gamble, the manufacturer.
- **Agents/brokers** are intermediaries that facilitate negotiations between buyers and sellers of goods and services but never take title (ownership) of the products traded. Examples include real estate agents and brokers, stockbrokers, and agricultural brokers. Even eBay, which never owns the various items it sells, can be considered an agent/broker because the company facilitates the transfer of ownership from sellers to buyers.
- **Retailers** are intermediaries that buy products for resale to ultimate consumers. As consumers, we buy most of our products from retail outlets, such as the Tide laundry detergent from our local supermarket.

Why are intermediaries needed?
You might wonder why we need all these intermediaries and whether they serve only to drive up prices. It is certainly true that each link in the distribution channel incurs costs, and intermediaries must cover these costs and earn a profit to remain in business. However, these costs and the higher prices we must pay are usually less than the time and money we would otherwise spend to obtain the products directly from the manufacturer. In short, intermediaries add costs, but these costs are offset by the value added.

To examine the efficiencies provided by intermediaries, review **Figure 12.6**, which shows five manufacturers and five retail outlets. Without an intermediary, each retailer would have to contact each manufacturer to order desired goods. That would entail five times five, or twenty-five, exchange relationships. Now suppose a wholesaler is established to stock and resell each of the five manufacturers' products to each of the five retailers. Now the five manufacturers and five retailers have only one intermediary to deal with. This reduces the number of exchange relationships from twenty-five to ten. Intermediaries reduce

A **marketing intermediary**, or middleman, is a business firm that operates between producers and consumers or business users.

A **distribution channel** is a series of firms or individuals that participate in the flow of a product from manufacturer to consumer.

Distributors (or **wholesalers**) are often the intermediaries in a distribution channel.

Decision-Making Mini-Simulations: Retailing/Wholesaling. Located in MyBusinessLab.

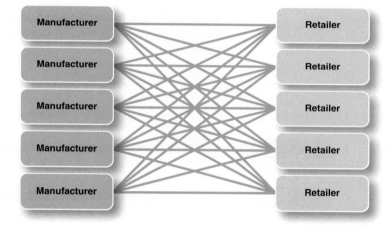

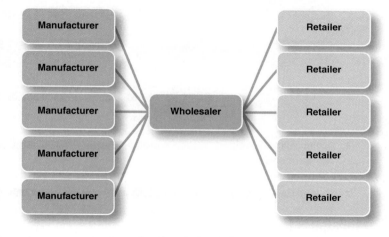

Figure 12.6   The Efficiencies of Intermediaries

The introduction of an intermediary reduces the number of exchange relationships between manufacturers and retailers.

Wholesalers are intermediaries that buy and resell products to other wholesalers, to retailers, and to industrial users.

Agents/brokers are intermediaries that facilitate negotiations between buyers and sellers of goods and services but never take title (ownership) of the products traded.

Retailers are intermediaries that buy products for resale to ultimate consumers.

the time and costs of providing products to customers. Of course, the wholesaler will incur some costs that will be pushed onto the consumer. But these costs are less than the costs without the involvement of the intermediary. The most efficient intermediaries get most of the business and survive in a competitive environment. This is why intermediaries are always looking for more advanced technologies to facilitate their operations. The modern distribution system is high-tech business.

What are the different types of distribution channels?

Many distribution channels exist, as illustrated in **Figure 12.7**. As you can see, the type of distribution channel used varies depending on the type of product being brought to the consumer. The number of intermediaries depends on whether greater efficiency or adding value is possible by adding another link to the chain in the distribution system. If greater efficiency is possible, then another link will be added in order to increase profits. Competitive markets determine what number of intermediaries will be most efficient.

An important recent development in the distribution of products has been the increased use of ecommerce, buying and selling on the Internet. It is now possible for consumers to buy thousands of products online. Businesses are also using the Internet to buy and sell to other businesses. For example, customer relationship software can be purchased and downloaded online for sales to other businesses. These direct channels (channels 1 and 6 in Figure 12.7) bypass all intermediaries.

E-commerce is prevalent in all distribution channels, not just the direct channel. Almost all firms—manufacturers, agents, brokers, wholesalers, or retailers—have websites that allow customers to shop, place an order, and pay. Many sites also use interactive videos to enable customers to explore the features of products from their homes or offices. E-commerce is expected to continue to grow because of the convenience it provides.

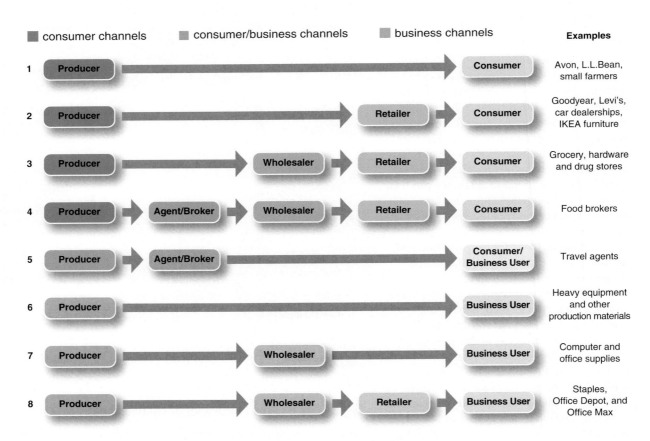

Figure 12.7 Different Channels of Distribution

Remember the questions you had about the cough syrup in the drugstore? You now know that the cough syrup likely travelled from the manufacturer to a wholesaler and then to a retailer before landing in your hands. You also know that although intermediaries do add costs to products, these costs are offset by the value they add. As you purchase your cough syrup, consider that while it may seem at first cheaper to buy products directly from the producer, the time and money it would take to do so would ultimately make it more expensive.

Wholesalers, Agents, and Brokers

What services do wholesalers provide?

As we've already discussed, wholesalers are intermediaries that buy and resell products to other wholesalers, to retailers, and to industrial users. They are different from retailers because retailers only sell products to final consumers. It can be confusing because some of us, as households, purchase products at wholesale distributors, such as Costco or Office Depot, which also sell to other businesses. One of the most effective ways to distinguish wholesalers from retailers is to remember that wholesalers *primarily* sell business-to-business products, while retailers sell *only* consumer products. Nevertheless, wholesalers provide a host of services to their customers. Some of these are listed in **Table 12.3**.[42]

What are the different types of wholesalers?

Wholesalers are technically known as merchant wholesalers, independently owned businesses that take ownership (title) of the products they handle. They are sometimes called *jobbers, mill supply firms,* or *distributors.* Merchant wholesalers include *full-service wholesalers* and *limited-service wholesalers.* **Full-service wholesalers** provide a full line of services: carrying stock, maintaining a sales force, offering credit, making deliveries, and providing management assistance. There are two types: *Wholesale merchants* who sell primarily to retailers, and *industrial distributors* who sell to manufacturers and institutions such as hospitals and the government. As intermediaries, **limited-service wholesalers** offer fewer services than full-service wholesalers. There are four major types:

- *Cash-and-carry wholesalers* carry a limited line of fast-moving goods and sell to small retailers for cash. They normally do not deliver. For example, a small fish store may drive to a cash-and-carry fish wholesaler, buy fish for cash, and bring the merchandise back to the store.
- *Truck wholesalers* (or *truck jobbers*) perform primarily a selling-and-delivery function. For example, soft-drink trucks that deliver to supermarkets and restaurants are truck wholesalers.

Full-service wholesalers provide a full line of services: carrying stock, maintaining a sales force, offering credit, making deliveries, and providing management assistance.

Limited-service wholesalers offer fewer services than full-service wholesalers. There are four major types: Cash-and-carry wholesalers, truck wholesalers, drop shippers, and rack jobbers.

Table 12.3 Services Provided by Wholesalers

Service	Description
Bulk Breaking	Wholesalers save retailers money by buying in bulk and breaking bulk packages down into smaller quantities.
Financing	Wholesalers finance retailers by giving credit, and they finance manufacturers by ordering early and paying bills on time.
Management Service and Advice	Wholesalers often help retailers train their sales clerks, improve store layouts and displays, and set up accounting and inventory control systems.
Market Information	Wholesalers give information to manufacturers and retailers about competitors, new products, and price developments.
Risk Bearing	Wholesalers absorb risk by taking title to merchandise and bearing the costs of theft, damage, spoilage, and obsolescence.
Selling and Promoting	Wholesalers' sales forces help manufacturers reach many smaller retailers at a low cost. The wholesaler has more contacts and is often more trusted by the retailer than the distant manufacturer.
Transportation	Wholesalers can provide quicker delivery to buyers because they are closer than the producers.
Warehousing	Wholesalers hold inventories, thereby reducing the inventory costs and risks of suppliers and retailers.

■ *Drop shippers* don't carry inventory or handle the product. On receiving an order, they select the manufacturer, who ships the merchandise directly to the customer. Drop shippers assume title and risk from the time of the order to delivery. They operate in bulk industries such as lumber, coal, and heavy equipment.

■ *Rack jobbers* serve grocery stores and drug retailers, mostly in non-food items. They send delivery trucks to stores, where the delivery people set up racks or displays within the stores. Rack jobbers retain title to the goods and bill the retailer only for the goods sold to consumers.

Because of their limited functions, these limited-service wholesalers usually operate at a lower cost than wholesale merchants and industrial distributors.

What are some common types of agents?

Agents and brokers are unique among intermediaries because they do not take title to the products traded. They merely facilitate the buying and selling of products and earn a commission on the selling price. What distinguishes agents from brokers is that agents represent the buyers or sellers who hired them on a more permanent basis than brokers do. Three common types of agents are manufacturers' agents, selling agents, and purchasing agents.[43]

■ *Manufacturers' agents* represent two or more manufacturers of complementary lines. A formal written agreement with each manufacturer covers pricing, territories, order handling, delivery service and warranties, and commission rates. Manufacturers' agents are often used in such lines as apparel, furniture, and electrical goods. Most manufacturers' agents are small businesses with only a few skilled salespeople. Small manufacturers may hire an agent if they cannot afford their own field sales force, while larger manufacturers rely on agents to open new territories or to cover territories that cannot support full-time salespeople.

■ *Selling agents* have contractual authority to sell a manufacturer's entire product line. The manufacturer is either not interested in the selling function or feels unqualified. The selling agent serves as the sales department for the manufacturer. Selling agents are common in the industrial machinery and equipment businesses as well as for coal, chemicals, and metals.

■ *Purchasing agents* generally have long-term relationships with buyers and make purchases for them, often receiving, inspecting, warehousing, and shipping the merchandise to the buyers. They provide helpful market information to clients and help them obtain the best goods and prices available.

Retailers

What are three important retail strategies?

Retailers primarily sell their products to final consumers. All companies need to decide how intensively they wish to cover any geographic market. Undertaking an **intensive distribution** entails selling the product through all available retail outlets. This seems most appropriate when selling convenience goods such as tobacco, newspapers, soft drinks, chewing gum, potato chips, bread, and milk. Companies want these products to obtain the widest possible exposure in the market. As a result, they try to make these products convenient for purchase at as many convenience stores and supermarkets as possible.

Selective distribution uses only a portion of the many possible retail outlets for sale of a product. This approach is appropriate for the sale of shopping products and durable goods such as stereos, TVs, and furniture. Buyers spend more time comparing competitors' prices and features when buying shopping products. A sale often depends on providing buyers with information on these features to differentiate one brand's product from another successfully. Naturally, producers want to determine selectively where their products will be sold to ensure successful differentiation. Moreover, customers often want other services such as installation to be properly distributed. Again, producers are selective in determining outlets and may provide training to outlets to ensure the best service.

At other times, sellers want to undertake **exclusive distribution**, the use of only one outlet in a geographic area. This is most appropriate when selling specialty products

Intensive distribution entails selling the product through all available retail outlets.

Selective distribution uses only a portion of the many possible retail outlets for sale of a product.

Exclusive distribution is the use of only one outlet in a geographic area.

Table 12.4   Types of Retail Stores

Type of Store	Description	Examples
Specialty Store	A retail store that carries a wide selection of products in one category	Pay Less Shoes, Foot Locker, EB Games
Department Store	A retail store that carries a wide variety of products organized by departments	Sears, The Bay, Zellers
Supermarket	Large, low-cost, high-volume grocery stores that also sell household products	Loblaw's Super Store
Convenience Store	Small stores located near residents that are open long hours seven days a week and carry the most frequently purchased convenience goods	Mac's Milk, 7-Eleven
Discount Store	Stores that offer lower prices by accepting lower profit margins and sell at a higher volume than department stores	Giant Tiger, Walmart
Category Killer	Large specialty stores that specialize in selling a particular product line and are staffed by knowledgeable sales staff	Toys "R" Us, Best Buy, Chapters, Bass Pro Shops
Factory Outlet	Stores owned and operated by a manufacturer that normally carries surplus, discontinued, or irregular goods	Nike Factory Outlet, Nordstrom Rack
Warehouse Club	Stores that sell a limited selection of brand-name food and non-food items at deep discounts that usually require an annual membership fee	Costco

such as expensive, high-quality sports cars, jewellery, or high-fashion clothing. Because these products carry a certain degree of prestige, sellers often require distributors to carry a full line of inventory, offer distinguished high-quality service, and meet other exclusive requirements. Another common form of exclusive distribution exists with franchises such as McDonald's and Subway. Only one outlet is chosen in a given geographic area, and the retail distributors are required to meet strict quality and service standards to protect brand-name integrity.

What are the different types of retailers?

Retailing constitutes a major sector of our economy. You're likely familiar with retail distributors because most of your personal shopping experiences have occurred at retail stores. **Table 12.4** describes the major types of retail stores and lists some examples of each.

Little has drawn as much attention in modern retailing than the growth of non-store retailing. Non-store retailing is a form of retailing in which consumer contact occurs outside the confines of a traditional brick-and-mortar retail store. Examples include the use of electronic shopping, vending machines, at-home personal selling, and catalogue buying.

The rapid growth of technology and especially the Internet has made it possible for consumers to shop online—comparing prices, ordering, and paying for a product from the convenience of their homes. Electronic retailing, or the selling of consumer goods and services over the Internet, is a fast-growing trend. This poses many risks for some businesses that don't adapt to this trend. Online shopping offers many benefits as well. In fact, many small businesses have found the Internet to be the great equalizer. They can establish websites offering an interactive environment that allows for the full use of state-of-the-art multimedia to attract sales.

Many other forms of non-store retailing exist beyond electronic retailing. You have seen vending machines, kiosks, and carts before. Vending machines provide many convenience goods, such as soft drinks, at locations where they are most often desired, such as airports, swimming pools, and college dorms. Kiosks are familiar in shopping malls. They are an inexpensive way to sell many goods, as are carts that often sell food on the street. Here are some other important non-store retailers:

- *Telemarketing* is selling products over the phone. Sometimes the sales pitches are recorded messages. Many people, annoyed by telemarketers, sign up for the National Do Not Call List. However, many consumers do use the telephone to place orders, even though these sales may not have been solicited by phone.

12

Mall kiosks are a relatively inexpensive way to sell goods and services in a non-store retail environment.

Warehousing is the storing of products at convenient locations ready for customers when they are needed.

■ *Direct selling* is selling goods and services door-to-door at people's homes and offices, or at temporary or mobile locations. Avon and Mary Kay cosmetics, Pampered Chef kitchen products, and Herbalife health products are sold through direct selling.

■ *Direct marketing* refers to any aspect of retailing a good or service that attempts to bypass intermediaries. It includes catalogue sales, direct mail, and telemarketing.

Physical Distribution

How important are warehousing and inventory control?   **Warehousing**, or storing products at convenient locations ready for customers when they are needed, is critical for customer service. It is often much easier to sell products than to get them to their destinations. This is especially true when selling products globally. There are tradeoffs between maximizing customer service and minimizing physical distribution costs. Increasing customer service requires rapid delivery and large inventories to reduce the probability of being under stocked. But this is expensive. On the other hand, lowering distribution costs can cause slower deliveries and lower inventory levels that increase the risk of being out of stock of a desired product. Given these tradeoffs, the goal of any physical distribution system should be to first determine the desired level of customer service and then work toward achieving that level of customer service at the lowest cost. Those companies that are most efficient at this survive and prosper. Inefficient businesses lose market share and risk failure.

Two types of warehouses emerge from marketing products. *Storage warehouses* store goods from moderate-to-long periods. *Distribution warehouses* (or distribution centres) are designed to gather and move goods quickly to consumers. Warehousing today uses sophisticated technologies to effectively store and distribute products. A host of technologies allows companies to manage their entire supply chain systems more effectively. As you learned in Chapter 10, one of the challenges in managing a supply chain is managing inventory levels to ensure there is neither too much nor too little inventory on hand.

What are the benefits and costs of various transportation methods?   Transportation is the most expensive distribution cost. If a company wants one of its products to remain price competitive, then the selection of the most effective transportation mode is obvious. When deciding on transportation modes, companies also have to consider other factors beyond cost—such as speed, dependability, flexibility in handling products, frequency of shipments, and accessibility to markets. As you learned in Chapter 10, there are benefits and costs associated with each of the five major types of transportation—railroads, trucks, waterways, airways, and pipelines. Businesses have to weigh these benefits and costs carefully in making a mode-of-transportation decision. It is often the job of the supply-chain manager is to find the most efficient combination of these forms of transportation.

CHAPTER SYNOPSIS

❶ Define "product" and "total product offer" as they pertain to marketing. *(pp. 327–328)*

A **product** is any good or service, along with its perceived attributes and benefits, that creates value for the customer. Consumers buy products for a number of tangible and intangible benefits. The **total product offer** (or **value package**) consists of all the benefits associated with a good, service, or idea that affects a consumer's purchasing decision. When you buy a car, you're not just buying a mode of transportation; you're also buying some intangible benefits, such as style or an image.

❷ Describe product differentiation, and explain its role in product development. *(pp. 328–329)*

Product differentiation is the creation of a real or perceived difference in a product designed to attract customers. A company can distinguish a product from its competitors by establishing concrete or intangible differences between similar products. For example, a luggage company might offer suitcases in unique colours or shapes. It might also offer a lifetime guarantee on certain models. Product differentiation is critical for a product's success. If a product doesn't possess qualities that make it stand out, then customers will not be motivated to buy that product instead of a competitor's product.

❸ Outline the five steps in new product development, and describe the product life cycle. *(pp. 329–332)*

As outlined in **Figure 12.2**, **new product development** involves five steps: idea generation; idea screening; product analysis; product development and concept testing; and commercialization.

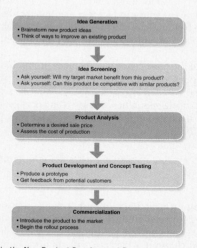

The Five Steps in the New Product Development Process

A **product life cycle** is a theoretical model describing a product's sales and profits over the course of its lifetime. During this cycle, a product typically goes through four stages: an introductory stage, a growth stage, a maturity stage, and a declining stage.

❹ Summarize the different classifications of consumer products and business-to-business products. *(pp. 333–334)*

Four **consumer product classifications** emerge from strategic marketing mix plans for consumer products: convenience, shopping, specialty, and unsought goods and services.

Five **B2B product** (or **industrial product**) **classifications** emerge from strategic marketing mix plans for B2B products: equipment; maintenance, repair, and operating (MRO) products; raw and processed materials; component parts; and specialized professional services. Each of these types of products has unique pricing, promotion, and distribution strategies.

❺ Explain why branding is beneficial to both buyers and sellers, and describe some different types of brands. *(pp. 335–339)*

A **brand** is a name, term, symbol, or design that distinguishes a company and its products from all others. Branding is one of the most important tools of product differentiation, and it benefits both buyers and sellers. For buyers, well-recognized brands reduce the shopping time necessary to find the quality and consistency they desire in a product. Branding also reduces the risks involved in some purchases for which buyers are unable to determine quality objectively.

Branding also helps sellers define their products' special qualities, thus promoting repeat purchases as well as new sales at higher prices. Because certain brands, such as Coca-Cola, are associated with quality and value, these companies are able to introduce new products quickly and at a relatively low cost. In doing so, they add length to their product lines, widen their product mix (also known as *brand extension*), and enhance their profitability.

❻ Describe three major approaches to pricing strategy, and outline some pricing tactics used to launch a new product, to adjust prices, and to affect price perceptions. *(pp. 339–343)*

Cost-based pricing (or **cost-plus pricing**) is charging a price in relation to the costs of providing the good or service.

Demand-based pricing (or **value-based pricing**) is pricing a good or service based on the demand for the product or its perceived value.

Competition-based pricing is a pricing strategy based on what the competition is charging. Revenues and costs are secondary.

One pricing strategy for introducing a new product is **price skimming**. It involves charging a high price for a product initially, then lowering the price over time. Price adjustments may consist of **discounts**, a deduction from the regular price charged; **rebates**, which are partial refunds on what a customer has already paid for a product; and **bundling**, when two or more products that usually complement one another are combined and sold at a single price.

Prestige pricing (or **premium pricing**) is the practice of charging a high price to invoke perceptions of high quality and privilege. Another pricing strategy that affects price perceptions is **psychological pricing** (or **odd** or **fractional pricing**), the practice of charging a price just below a whole number to give the appearance of a significantly lower price. A **loss leader** is a product priced below its cost. Stores use loss leaders to attract customers and motivate them to buy items that are more expensive as well. **Reference pricing** refers to listing an inflated price (the "regular retail price" or "manufacturer's suggested retail price") that is then discounted to appear as if it is a good value.

❼ Define a promotional mix, and explain its function in a promotional campaign. *(pp. 343–345)*

Four basic **promotional tools** are used to promote a good or service: advertising, public relations, personal selling, and sales

12

promotions. The **promotional mix** is the strategic combination of promotional tools used to reach targeted customers to achieve marketing objectives. Six steps emerge from all **effective promotional campaigns**: identify target market; determine marketing objectives; design the message; determine the budget; implement the promotional mix; and evaluate and adjust as needed.

⑧ Explain the advantages and disadvantages of the various types of media used for advertising. *(pp. 345–348)*

Table 12.1   Advantages and Disadvantages of Advertising Media

Media	Advantages	Disadvantages
Television	Good mass-market coverage; low cost per contact; combines sight, sound, and motion; good attention span	High cost; low recall; channel surfing or digital video recorders skip over ads; short exposure
Newspaper	Timing and geographic flexibility; good local market coverage; high credibility and acceptability	Short life span; lots of competition for attention; poor-quality reproductions
Magazine	High market segmentation; high-quality colour; long life; longer attention span; high credibility	Declining readership; lots of competition for attention; high cost; long ad-purchase lead time
Radio	High geographic and demographic selectivity; low cost; creative opportunities with sound	Low attention span; short exposure time; information overload; limited coverage
Internet	Global and interactive possibilities; ease of segmentation; high audience interest; easy to measure responses	Audience controls exposure; clutter on each site; skewed demographically to surfers
Outdoor	Able to select key geographic areas; low cost per impression; high frequency on major commuter routes	Short exposure time; brief messages; creative limitations; little segmentation possible
Direct Mail	High levels of segmentation; allows personalization; high flexibility; ad can be saved; measurable impact	High cost; can be rejected as "junk mail" and viewed as a nuisance
Yellow Pages	Inexpensive; commonly used and accessible; good local coverage and segmentation possible; long life	Costly for very small businesses; lists the competition as well

⑨ Define *publicity* and describe how a company might generate positive publicity as well as manage negative publicity. *(pp. 348–350)*

Publicity is information about an individual, organization, or product transmitted through mass media at no charge. Naturally, keeping friendly relations with the press increases the probability that a "newsworthy" story will be covered and treated with a favourable spin. Nevertheless, public relations managers need to ensure that publicity releases are timely, interesting, accurate, and in the public interest. Corporate philanthropy is generally good publicity, especially if it results in getting your name on a building, an annual event, a scholarship, or volunteer programs that are visible to the community.

Damage control is a company's effort to minimize the harmful effects of a negative event. Negative publicity, in a matter of days, can tear down a firm's image that took decades to build up. In the event of bad news, a company must stand ready to react, and react quickly. No easy remedies exist for crises, but being honest, accepting responsibility and making other ethical responses are the first steps toward regaining credibility and re-establishing a positive image.

⑩ List the six steps in the personal selling process. *(pp. 350–352)*

No two salespeople are alike, and no two selling situations are the same. However, six steps emerge from all personal selling: prospecting, approaching the prospect, presenting, overcoming objections, closing the sale, and following up.

⑪ Describe the two main types of sales promotions and the types of tools commonly used as incentives. *(pp. 352–354)*

Any incentives to push a product through the distribution system to final consumers are called **trade** (or **business-to-business) sales promotions**. In addition, **consumer sales promotions** are incentives designed to increase final consumer demand for a product.

Some of the specific trade sales promotions tools include: trade shows and conventions, trade allowances (deals and price reductions to wholesalers, dealers, and retailers), cooperative advertising (a manufacturer agrees to pay for some of the advertising costs of the retailer), free merchandise, sales contests (e.g., a free trip to Hawaii for those who sell the most), dealer listings (advertisements of your product that mention retail outlets where it can be found), catalogues and store demonstrations, in-store displays, quantity discounts, and training and support programs.

Some of the most common consumer promotional tools include coupons, rebates, frequent-user incentives, point-of-purchase (POP) displays, free samples, contests and sweepstakes, advertising specialties, bonuses (buy one, get one free), catalogues, demonstrations, special events, lotteries, premiums, and cents-off deals.

⑫ Define marketing intermediaries and distribution channels, and explain why these are important elements in marketing. *(pp. 354–360)*

A **marketing intermediary**, or middleman, is a business firm that operates between producers and consumers or business users. Many goods, such as grocery store items, go through a **distribution channel**, which is a series of firms or individuals that participate in the flow of a product from manufacturer to consumer. Intermediaries reduce the time and costs of providing products to customers. Of course, the wholesaler will incur some costs that will be pushed onto the consumer. But these costs are less than the costs of sourcing the product without the involvement of the intermediary.

KEY TERMS

advertising   (p. 345)
agents/brokers   (p. 355)
B2B product (or industrial product) classifications   (p. 334)
brand   (p. 335)
brand association   (p. 336)
brand awareness   (p. 336)
brand equity   (p. 336)
brand insistence   (p. 335)
brand loyalty   (p. 335)
brand manager (or product manager)   (p. 336)
break-even analysis   (p. 340)
bundling   (p. 342)
business-to-business (B2B) products   (p. 333)
competition-based pricing   (p. 341)
consumer product classifications   (p. 333)
consumer products   (p. 333)
consumer sales promotions   (p. 352)
controlled messages   (p. 349)

cost-based pricing (or cost-plus pricing)   (p. 340)
damage control   (p. 350)
demand-based pricing (or value-based pricing)   (p. 341)
discounts   (p. 342)
distribution channel   (p. 355)
distributors (or wholesalers)   (p. 355)
dynamic pricing   (p. 342)
effective promotional campaigns   (p. 344)
everyday low pricing (EDLP)   (p. 343)
exclusive distribution   (p. 358)
fixed costs (or overhead costs)   (p. 340)
full-service wholesalers   (p. 357)
infomercials   (p. 348)
integrated marketing communication (IMC)   (p. 345)
intensive distribution   (p. 358)

limited-service wholesalers   (p. 357)
logos   (p. 335)
loss leader   (p. 343)
marketing intermediary   (p. 355)
new product development   (p. 329)
penetration pricing   (p. 342)
personal selling   (p. 350)
place (or distribution)   (p. 354)
prestige pricing (or premium pricing)   (p. 343)
price   (p. 339)
price discrimination   (p. 341)
price skimming   (p. 342)
pricing strategies   (p. 340)
product differentiation   (p. 328)
product life cycle   (p. 330)
product line   (p. 332)
product line length   (p. 332)
product mix   (p. 332)
product mix width   (p. 332)
product placement   (p. 348)

promotion   (p. 343)
promotional mix   (p. 344)
promotional tools   (p. 344)
psychological pricing (or odd or fractional pricing)   (p. 343)
public relations   (p. 348)
publicity   (p. 349)
rebates   (p. 342)
reference pricing   (p. 343)
retailers   (p. 355)
sales promotions   (p. 352)
selective distribution   (p. 358)
semi-controlled messages   (p. 349)
target costing   (p. 341)
total product offer (or value package)   (p. 327)
trade (or business-to-business) sales promotions   (p. 352)
uncontrolled messages   (p. 349)
variable costs   (p. 340)
warehousing   (p. 360)
wholesalers   (p. 355)

CRITICAL THINKING QUESTIONS

1. What types of consumer products are sold by a gas station? By an automotive repair shop? By a shoe store? By an orthodontic dentist? How might these goods and services be best differentiated in terms of the "product" and "price" components of the marketing mix?

2. What are the differences between cost-based pricing, demand-based pricing, and competition-based pricing?

3. Describe the conditions when it might be appropriate to use each of the following pricing strategies: discounting, rebates, bundling, dynamic pricing, prestige pricing, psychological pricing, loss leader pricing, and reference pricing.

4. Describe which distribution strategy—intensive, selective, or exclusive—would be most appropriate for each of the following products, and explain why: laundry detergent, cigarettes, Mercedes sports cars, and Snickers candy bars.

5. Suppose you are the distribution manager for a high-tech producer of big-screen televisions. Which mode of transportation would you select in distributing your products to customers and why?

APPLICATION EXERCISES

1. **The iPhone as a Product.** Go to Apple's iPhone website: www.apple.com/iphone. Describe Apple's marketing mix strategy for its product and its price. When would an iPhone be a consumer product, and when would it be a B2B product? What does Apple do to augment its product? What type of branding strategy is Apple pursuing? What stage of the product life cycle is the iPhone experiencing? Is Apple undertaking the appropriate strategies, given this stage of the product's life cycle?

2. **Research a Brand.** Choose a favourite brand of clothing or food and use the Internet to gather information about it. What type of brand is it—a manufacturer's, private, individual, or other? Is it part of a brand extension? Is it associated with a co-brand or a licensing arrangement? How do packaging and labelling affect the image the brand projects? Summarize your findings in a brief report.

3. **The Dynamics of Dynamic Pricing.** Visit an online auction website such as www.ebay.com. Choose a few products and compare their prices on the website with their prices at a retail store.

   What do the higher or lower prices on eBay indicate about supply and demand? How does dynamic pricing differ from fixed pricing? What other factors must buyers take into account when purchasing products from eBay?

4. **Read All About It.** Search the websites of a variety of large companies for recent press releases. For example, visit Apple's press release library (www.apple.com/pr/library) or GE's updates about ecomagination (www.ge.ecomagination.com/site/index.html#press). What type of language is used in these press releases? How does this publicity advance promotional goals? Do you think it is effective? Why or why not?

5. **Tracking a Product.** Use the Internet to research the likely distribution path of a product of your choice. Where was it produced? Through which countries and/or states did it travel? Which intermediaries were involved in its distribution? Make a chart or diagram tracing its channel of distribution.

12

GLOBAL 500 RESEARCH PROJECT

INSTRUCTIONS

1. Choose a Global 500 company from *Fortune* magazine's annual rankings at http://money.cnn.com/magazines/fortune/global500/.
2. Research:
   a. What are the company's main product lines?
   b. Who is the target market for these product lines?
   c. What products or services are the biggest sellers for this company?
   d. How does the company differentiate its products or services?
   e. What type of marketing strategy changes would this company need to do in order to sell its products or services in another country—for instance, in China, Germany, or India?
   f. Choose one popular product or service this company sells and describe how the 4 Ps apply?
   g. What is the promotional mix used by this company?
   h. What do you think is this company's most memorable advertisement? Why?
   i. How much money did this company spend on advertising last year (or the year before)? *Hint:* Check the company annual report.
   j. Complete a Porter's Five Forces analysis for this company on any of its products or services.
3. Prepare a report and submit to your professor.

TEAM TIME

Developing a Promotional Mix

The company you work for, FitFoods, is launching a new product: Shine Breakfast Bars, all-natural, vitamin-fortified granola bars. The company has enlisted you and your teammates to design an optimal promotional mix for this product.

PROCESS

1. Assemble into teams of four. Each team member should be assigned as the "lead" for one of the four components of the promotional mix—advertising, public relations, personal selling, and sales promotions.
2. Use the knowledge gained from this chapter to develop a promotional mix for Shine Breakfast Bars that integrates each of the four components. What will be the key aspects of the advertising campaign? What media will be used? What public relations tools will be used? What will a sales pitch for this product consist of? How will sales promotions be implemented?
3. Summarize the key points of the promotional mix plan in a poster or PowerPoint presentation.
4. Present your findings to the class for discussion.

ETHICS AND RESPONSIBILITY

The Ethics of Rx

The pharmaceutical drug industry is an ethical minefield. The development of prescription medications is one topic among many that can present significant ethical challenges. Consider the questions raised by the following scenario. If possible, discuss your thoughts with a classmate or participate in a group debate on the topic.

You are an executive at one of the top drug companies in the United States. At the most recent product development meeting, two teams of scientists reported that each is within one year of having a new drug ready for clinical trials. Team A is developing a drug to cure a rare but fatal bone disease. Team B is developing a drug to treat a common, non-life-threatening skin condition. In order to make the deadline, however, both teams need an additional 10 million dollars in funding. You know that the company can only afford to fund one team. According to the product analysis, Team A's drug will be expensive to produce, difficult to market, and will yield only modest profits. Team B's drug has the potential to yield massive profits.

1. Which team would you recommend the company fund? Why?
2. How do the potential profits of Team B's drug affect your stance, from both financial/business and medical/ethical perspectives?
3. What about pricing? How might you reconcile the need to keep the drug company profitable with the ethical responsibility to make medications affordable for those in need?

CLOSING CASE

The iPhone: Revolutionary Product or Rip-off?

Then entire auditorium was buzzing with excitement as the crowd waited for Steve Jobs, CEO of Apple, Inc. and keynote speaker, to take the stage at the 2007 Macworld Conference and Expo.[44] Executives, reporters, and Apple enthusiasts alike were anxiously anticipating the introduction of Apple's latest advancement in portable technology: the iPhone. Rumours about the iPhone's capabilities floated around for months, but few people had actually seen the product. Jobs's presentation of the iPhone wowed the audience. Its touch screen design and Web browsing capabilities were nothing short of revolutionary.[45]

On June 29, 2007, thousands of people stood in line for hours at the retail stores of AT&T, the iPhone's exclusive wireless carrier, to get their hands on the first iPhone.[46] The hefty price of US$599 for the 8-gigabyte device did not deter customers. The premium cost seemed a small price to pay for some tech junkies, many of who were eager to be the first person in their school or office to have the cutting-edge piece of technology. Apple sold an impressive 270 000 iPhones within the first thirty hours it was available for purchase.[47] Just seventy-four days after its initial release, on September 10, Apple sold its one millionth iPhone.[48]

Although Apple's millionth iPhone sale should have been a celebrated milestone, Apple, Inc. and Jobs were busy dealing with a much bigger issue involving iPhone sales. On September 5, less than ten weeks after the product hit the market, Apple announced that it would drop the price of the popular 8-GB iPhone from US$599 to US$399. The US$200 reduction was intended to boost iPhone sales during the 2007 holiday season. "We've clearly got a breakthrough product, and we want to make it affordable for even more customers as we enter this holiday season," said Jobs. The price cut made the iPhone accessible to a larger market, but it enraged many of Apple's loyal customers. Many felt betrayed by the reduced price, believing that Apple had ripped off its most devoted supporters. Early iPhone owners let Jobs know how they felt about his sales decision by flooding his inbox with heated e-mails.

Jobs did not shy away from the price-drop backlash. After reading hundreds of e-mails from iPhone customers,[49] Jobs decided to offer anyone who purchased an iPhone within fourteen days of the price drop a US$100 credit toward other Apple products. Jobs defended his initial decision to cut the iPhone price, stating, "It benefits both Apple and every iPhone user to get as many new customers as possible under the iPhone 'tent.'" Jobs explained that the purpose of this credit was to mend ties with loyal customers. "Our early customers trust us, and we must

live up to that trust with our actions in moments like these," he continued. The US$100 credit not only helped repair the image of the iPhone, but of Apple in general.

Although the original price of the iPhone may have ruffled feathers among Apple aficionados, it is a customary practice in the specialty goods market. The latest video game, luxury car, and designer handbag often have inflated prices when they are first released. The snob appeal alone can be most alluring for customers who want something that only a select few can afford. What is different for Apple is that their products are tailored so tightly to their customers' needs, that customers feel personally connected to products. If that personal connection is broken, Apple can lose its greatest asset, brand loyalty.

DISCUSSION QUESTIONS

1. What do you think might have happened if Apple originally set its price at US$399? Would this have increased or decreased sales of the iPhone in the end? What do you think might have happened if Steve Jobs had not issued the US$100 credit?
2. Why is brand loyalty so important to a company such as Apple? How does regaining the trust of iPhone customers affect all Apple brands?
3. Consider what you've learned about the different types of product pricing. Do you think it was ethical for Apple to practise price skimming with the iPhone? Do you think price skimming is always unfair to the customer, or is it a legitimate way of doing business?

MyBusinessLab CHAPTER RESOURCES

MyBusinessLab is an online learning and testing environment that features the perfect study tools to help you master the concepts covered in this chapter. Log in to MyBusinessLab at www.pearsoned.ca/mybusinesslab to test your knowledge of key chapter concepts, participate in simulations modelled on real-world business situations, and explore the following additional practice tools:

- Study Plan
- Audio Chapter Summaries
- Glossary Flashcards
- eText
- BizChat Discussion Boards
- BizSkills Simulations: Product Development; Pricing Strategies; Promoting a Product
- Decision-Making Mini-Simulations: Pricing; Personal Selling; Retailing/Wholesaling; Product Life Cycle; Advertising; New Product Development; Marketing Mix
- Document Makeover: Laptops 4U Letter

Video Cases:

To access the Chapter 12 Video Cases: MCCI: Developing and Pricing Space-Age Products; Joby: Product Distribution, see the Activities folder in the Assessment section of MyBusinessLab.

Web Case:

To access the Chapter 12 Web Case, see the Activities folder in the Assessment section of MyBusinessLab

13

Financial Management and Accounting

OPENING DISCUSSION: ACCOUNTING STANDARDS

2011 Was a Pivotal Year in Accounting History

For years, Canadian businesses used the Generally Accepted Accounting Principles (GAAP)—a common set of accounting principles, standards, and procedures—to compile their financial statements. GAAP gives investors a minimum level of consistency in the financial statements they use to analyze companies for investment purposes. While companies were expected to follow GAAP when reporting financial data, there was still room within GAAP for unscrupulous accountants to distort figures, so even when companies followed GAAP, investors still needed to scrutinize their financial statements.[1]

For fiscal years commencing in 2011 and thereafter, Canadian GAAP for most public companies transitioned to the International Financial Reporting Standards (IFRS)—a set of accounting standards developed by the International Accounting Standards Board (IASB) that is becoming a global standard for the preparation of financial statements of publicly accountable enterprises (PAEs). In general, PAEs are enterprises other than government, public sector, or non-profit organizations that trade their debt or equity in a public market or that hold assets in a fiduciary capacity for a broad group of outsiders.[2] Approximately 120 nations (many in Europe) and reporting jurisdictions have for several years now required or permitted IFRS.[3] Using IFRS, a business's financial statements are presented on the same basis as its foreign competitors, which makes comparisons easier. Companies with subsidiaries in foreign countries that use IFRS may need only one accounting language company-wide. Adopting IFRS does not only affect how items are accounted for but also calls for more extensive disclosures. The Canadian Accounting Standards Board (AcSB), the Canadian Institute of Chartered Accountants (CICA), and the Certified General Accountants Association of Canada (CGA-Canada), along with numerous accounting firms and other associations,

(continued)

offer businesses an abundance of literature, guides, advice, training, and services to help them accomplish this conversion and understand how implementing IFRS affects their financial reporting methods.

Since private companies are reporting to a much smaller user group than publicly traded companies, and investors may request additional information from the company if not satisfied with the annual financial statements, there is no need for private corporations to issue "general purpose" financial statements.[4] The Canadian Accounting Standards Board and the Public Sector Accounting Board will continue to issue and maintain separate accounting standards for private enterprises (not publicly traded), non-profit organizations, and public sector (government) organizations. Canada has developed its own standards for private enterprises called the Accounting Standards for Private Enterprises (ASPE), which are similar to IFRS but are usually simpler and may provide additional information for special industries (e.g., mining) that the IFRS doesn't examine in detail. Canadian private companies may choose to use either the full IFRS, just like a public company, or ASPE for non-publicly accountable enterprises. By not using the full IFRS, a private company takes a chance that potential capital providers (sources of money) may assess the company at a higher risk level because the company is not using IFRS, which may hinder the company's chances of obtaining capital. In Canada, non-profit organizations (including government organizations) are not publicly traded so the typical primary user of the businesses financial statements is non-existent. These organizations generally are required to follow ASPE standards, although larger non-profits (such as hospitals, universities, and colleges) are usually required to get an audit and are often required to provide special-purpose financial statements for specific users (such as government ministries).

As of 2011, Canada had a four-pronged approach to accounting standards:[5]

1. Public (publicly traded enterprises) and publicly accountable enterprises (such as banks) will follow IFRS;
2. Private enterprises (not publicly traded) have an option to follow full IFRS or a less complex IFRS created specifically for small and medium enterprises (ASPE);
3. Non-profit organizations have an option to follow IFRS or accounting standards for non-profit organizations;[6]
4. The Public Sector Accounting Board (PSAB) will continue to make recommendations to all levels of government organizations (national, provincial, territorial, and municipal).

When countries each used their own accounting standards, users were forewarned that financial statements were not comparable, but with IFRS a new concern is growing . . . that users will be misled into thinking that international comparison is simple. This is indeed not the case; there are three factors that limit comparability:[7]

1. IFRS standards are not accepted to the same extent in each country.
2. The quality of reporting under IFRS depends on the quality of the accounting profession within each country and the effectiveness of each country's financial reporting enforcement mechanism.
3. Even when IFRS standards are fully accepted, some standards will be applied differently in different nations because of local conditions (e.g., taxes, interest, ways of doing business, and economic and political factors).

DISCUSSION QUESTIONS

1. Do you think this move to IFRS is needed? Why or why not? Whom does it benefit?
2. Do you think IFRS should apply to all business, not only those publicly traded? Why or why not?
3. Do you think foreign countries will follow the IFRS? Why or why not?

FINANCIAL MANAGEMENT

The Financial Manager

What is financial management? Producing, marketing, and distributing a product are important aspects of generating a profit. Even more important, however, is the company's ability to *pay* for the resources required to accomplish these tasks. Without management of finances, there is no business! Without good financial controls and planning, a company will not be able to respond to unexpected challenges or planned expansion. **Financial management** involves the strategic planning and budgeting of short- and long-term funds for current and future needs. Tracking past financial transactions, controlling current revenues and expenses, and planning for future financial needs of the company are the foundation of financial management.

In most companies, the finance department comprises two divisions: accounting (which will be discussed later in the chapter) and financial management. Just as you might save money to ensure that you can pay next month's rent, or make plans for a big purchase such as a car or home, businesses must also plan and save. To remain competitive, businesses must make large strategic investments such as buying or building a new factory or investing in more advanced machinery or technology. At the same time, they also must ensure that they can pay their monthly bills. Financial management involves setting up and monitoring controls to make certain the plans and budgets are monitored sufficiently so that the business can reach its financial goals.

What is the role of a financial manager? A **financial manager** or **chief financial officer (CFO)** oversees the financial operations of a company. Generally, a financial manager assumes accounting responsibilities for the company. A financial manager is responsible for planning and managing the company's financial resources, including the following:

- developing plans that outline the company's financial short-term and long-term needs
- defining the sources and uses of funds that are needed to reach goals
- monitoring the cash flow of a company to ensure that obligations are paid in a timely and efficient manner and that funds owed to the company are collected efficiently
- investing any excess funds so that those funds can grow and be used for future development
- raising capital for future growth and expansion

Although not all companies have a CFO, all successfully run businesses have some person or persons designated to manage the financial needs of a company. In smaller companies, the financial manager may have other business-related responsibilities as well. Some entrepreneurs might serve as both owner and financial manager of a company.

Planning for Financial Needs

How does the financial manager plan for financial needs? A company's financial needs are both short-term and long-term in nature, and a financial manager must plan for both. In addition, he or she must ensure that funds are used optimally and that the firm is ultimately profitable. In order to meet these objectives, a financial manager oversees three important processes: forecasting financial needs, developing budgets and plans to meet financial needs, and establishing controls to ensure that the budgets and plans are being followed.

What is involved in forecasting financial needs? In most large companies, the executive management team and the board of directors formulate a strategic plan that sets out corporate goals and objectives. For example, if one of a company's goals and objectives were to produce a new device to compete directly with a competitor's product,

---

① Summarize the implications of financial management and how financial managers fulfill their responsibilities.

Financial management involves the strategic planning and budgeting of short- and long-term funds for current and future needs.

A **financial manager** or **chief financial officer (CFO)** oversees the financial operations of a company.

② Describe how financial managers plan for financial needs.

13

it would be the CFO's responsibility to manage revenues and expenses for this plan. In addition, the CFO would need to develop short- and long-term financial forecasts to ensure that the strategic goals and objectives were financially feasible. Financial managers coordinate with other areas of the company to formulate answers to certain questions: How much product do we need to sell? Do we need to expand to meet demand? Do we have the resources to expand our product line? Financial forecasts are especially important when strategic goals include large capital projects, such as acquiring new facilities, replacing outdated technology, or expanding into a new product line. It is critical that such forecasts are relatively accurate, as erroneous forecasts can have serious consequences.

Forecasts predict revenue, costs, and expenses for a specific future period.

Forecasts predict revenue, costs, and expenses for a specific future period. Short-term forecasts would include predictions within the upcoming year, while long-term forecasts would include predictions for a period longer than one year into the future. In developing forecasts, the financial manager considers many factors, including the current and future plans of the company, the current and future state of the economy, and the current and anticipated actions of the competition. In addition, the financial manager must anticipate the impact such factors will have on the company's financial situation. If, for example, national economic forecasts predict a recession in six months, a financial manager knows such a forecast will affect the company in many ways. Therefore, additional planning is required during general economic downturns to handle the possibility that payments might be harder to collect or that sales could be lower. Because of the result from either or both of these possibilities, plans for expansion of buildings or equipment might need to be postponed.

A **budget** is a financial plan that outlines the company's planned cash flows, expected operating expenses, and anticipated revenues.

An **operating (master) budget** includes all the operating costs for the entire organization, including inventory, sales, purchases, manufacturing, marketing, and operating expenses.

How does a company know it has enough resources to meet forecasted needs?

The accounting area of the finance department generates financial statements, such as the income statement, balance sheet, and statement of cash flows. Financial statements will be discussed in more detail later in the chapter, but generally they create a financial landscape that explains where the company has been over the current and past years. Moreover, they serve as a basis for management to develop expectations of where the company will be in future periods. Using these expectations, a financial manager puts together a **budget**, a financial plan that outlines the company's planned cash flows, expected operating expenses, and anticipated revenues. An **operating (master) budget** includes all the operating costs for the entire organization, including inventory, sales, purchases, manufacturing, marketing, and operating expenses. The operating budget maps out the projected number of units to be sold and estimated income for the coming year, in addition to all anticipated costs of operating the business to manufacture and sell the estimated level of business.

The **capital budget** considers the company's long-range plans and outlines the expected financial needs for significant capital purchases such as real estate, manufacturing equipment, plant expansions, or technology.

For financial managers, ensuring that the business stays within the budget is a priority.

How are funds made available for large projects?

Another component of the budgeting process is the **capital budget**, which considers the company's long-range plans and outlines the expected financial needs for significant capital purchases such as real estate, manufacturing equipment, plant expansions, or technology. Since capital projects are often financed with borrowed money or money raised through the sale of stocks or bonds, it is important to plan ahead to ensure that necessary funds are available when needed. During the capital budget process, each department in the organization puts together a list of its anticipated capital needs. Then senior management and the board evaluate these needs to determine which will best maximize the company's overall growth and profitability. Some requests are routine replacement of equipment or technology and may not need much evaluation. Other requests might be necessary in order to move the company in a new direction and should be evaluated closely.

Addressing the Budget

What helps plan for short-term needs?   **Cash flow** is the movement of money in and out of a business over a defined period (weekly, monthly, or quarterly). If cash going out of the business exceeds the cash coming into the business, then the business has a negative cash flow (a gap). To create a positive cash flow, a company would need to generate more cash and collect the cash in a more timely fashion, and at the same time maintain or reduce expenses. The cash flow budget is a short-term budget that estimates cash inflows and outflows and can predict a business's cash flow situation (see **Figure 13.1**). Cash flow budgets help financial managers determine whether the business needs to seek outside sources of funds beyond sales to manage anticipated cash shortages. Cash flow budgets also indicate future investment opportunities due to surges in cash inflow, as well as show whether a business will have enough cash to grow. Moreover, the financial manager uses the cash flow budget to help plan for debt repayment or to cover unusual operating expenses.

Cash flow is the movement of money in and out of a business over a defined period (weekly, monthly, or quarterly).

Why is monitoring cash flow important?   A company can have the bestselling product on the market, but if the flow of funds coming in and going out of the company is not managed properly, the company can easily fail. Monitoring cash flow is important because it measures a company's short-term financial health and financial efficiency. Cash flow specifically measures whether there are sufficient funds to pay outstanding bills. For seasonal businesses such as ski shops and pool installation companies, cash management is critical to carry a business through the slow months. Although many investors focus on a company's profitability as an indicator of strength, a company's **liquidity**—how quickly assets can be turned into cash—is often a better indicator.

Liquidity is how quickly assets can be turned into cash.

How does a company know if it is staying on budget?   A budget allocates the use of specific resources throughout the firm in accordance with management's expectations. After the budget is developed, it must be compared periodically to the actual performance of the company. It is very important that management compare actual performance regularly to the budget. This generally occurs every month. Without such a comparison, it is hard to determine whether the company is actually performing as expected. For example, let's say you decide to save some money, and at the end of the month, you have $50 in your savings account. Is that good or bad? It all depends on what you originally planned on saving. If you intended on saving only $35, then ended up with $50, that's great. If you intended on saving $75, then the outcome is not as good.

The same is true with the financial performance of a company. If the actual numbers generated by the company closely match the budget, this shows the company is fulfilling

Figure 13.1   Business Cash Flow

13

Table 13.1   Sources of Short-Term and Long-Term Financing

Short-Term Financing	Long-Term Financing
Friends and family	**Debt Financing**
Credit cards	• Commercial banks (e.g., line of credit, loans)
Commercial banks (e.g., line of credit, loans)	• Commercial finance companies (e.g., loans)
Commercial finance companies (e.g., loans)	• Selling bonds
Trade credit	**Equity Financing**
Promissory note	• Selling stock
Factoring	• Venture capital
Commercial paper	• Retained earnings

its plans. On the other hand, if the actual numbers differ greatly from those projected by the budget, this indicates that corrective actions must be taken. Businesses strive to stay on budget and fund needs through monies generated by business operations. However, there are many situations, even with the best planning, when a financial manager needs to consider funding operations by using internal cash sources or by finding outside sources (e.g., donations or grants to help fund large projects).

What must a financial manager consider when seeking outside funds?   In your personal life, you most likely have different types of financing to help you manage your financial needs. For example, you may have a credit card to pay for expenses. In addition, you might also have loans to pay for bigger, long-term expenses such as school, a car, or your home. Like you, a company may have several different types of borrowing needs to finance small operating costs as well as large projects. There are many sources of outside funds available to a company. How does a financial manager evaluate the best financing option? The financial manager must first match the length of the financing to the length of the need. Then, the financial manager must evaluate the cost of obtaining the funds and determine whether it is best to finance by raising *equity*—ownership interest in the form of stocks—or issuing *debt*—funds borrowed that must be repaid.

Financial managers or CFOs have myriad responsibilities, some of which include controlling and collecting funds, managing taxes, auditing, and *budgeting*. In order to determine the feasibility of a company's project, CFOs develop short- and long-term financial *forecasts*. They take into account the state of the economy and the plans of the company. They also need to take a close look at the capital budget and evaluate funding options. The next two sections of this chapter discuss short-term and long-term funding options. **Table 13.1** lists the sources from which financial managers must choose when making decisions about financing both short-term and long-term business needs.

FINANCIAL NEEDS

Financing Short-Term Business Needs

Describe the different options available for companies to finance their short-term business needs, including friends and family, credit cards, commercial banks and finance companies, trade credit, promissory note, factoring, and commercial paper.

How are the operations of a company financed?   When businesses, both large and small, find it necessary to expand, they must make some important decisions regarding financing. You may recall from Chapter 5 that different forms of business ownership have varying short-term needs. It is important that all companies have a plan to finance those needs. As was mentioned above, cash flow budgets are prepared to predict a company's cash flow gaps—periods when cash outflows are greater than cash inflows. When these gaps are expected, depending on the size of the business and the cash flow gap, there are several short-term sources available to help fill the temporary gap.

Short-term financing is any type of financing repaid within a year or less. It is used to finance day-to-day operations such as payroll, inventory purchases, and overhead (utilities, rent, leases). As discussed in Chapter 5, smaller start-up businesses often fund cash flow gaps first by appealing to friends and family. This is not a recommended strategy as it can lead to severed relationships if loans are not paid back promptly. However, when it is used, it is important that both parties understand and agree to formal payment arrangements. Another approach that many smaller businesses take to fund cash flow gaps is the use of credit cards. Credit cards are a good way to defer payments, but they can become very expensive if credit balances are not paid off completely every month.

Larger businesses with good credit and an established relationship with their suppliers take advantage of another credit relationship to help bridge the temporary gap. Companies will often purchase inventory and supplies on trade credit. **Trade credit** is the ability to purchase inventory and supplies on credit without interest. Suppliers will typically request payment within thirty, sixty, or ninety days. Deferring payment with trade credit is a good strategy to bridge a temporary cash flow gap because it does not tie up cash unnecessarily. Moreover, using trade credit keeps debt levels down, which is always attractive to outside investors and lenders. However, there are disadvantages associated with using trade credit. Sometimes, buyers are offered a discounted rate if they pay their creditor early. Trade credit will negate this early payment discount. Additionally, if payments extend beyond the trade credit period, delinquency penalties are charged, and, if allowed to accrue, can be very costly.[8] Financial managers must weigh the costs and benefits of paying early for a discount or paying on time without a discount so that their cash is available longer. **Figure 13.2** illustrates this decision. Some suppliers hesitate to give trade credit to organizations with a poor credit history. In such cases, the supplier may insist that the customer sign a promissory note as a condition of obtaining credit. A **promissory note** is a written promise to pay a supplier a specific amount of money by an agreed-upon date. A supplier might decide to sell a promissory note to a bank at a discounted rate (the amount of the note less a fee for the bank's services in collecting the amount due).

> **Short-term financing** is any type of financing repaid within a year or less.

> **Trade credit** is the ability to purchase inventory and supplies on credit without interest.

> A **promissory note** is a written promise to pay a supplier a specific amount of money by an agreed upon date.

Figure 13.2 Trade Credit

Using trade credit can be advantageous, but always must be evaluated and monitored carefully.

In addition to trade credit, often companies will rely on commercial banks, savings and loans institutions, or other commercial lenders for interim credit arrangements and other banking services.

How do commercial banks help with financial management?   Commercial banks are financial institutions that raise funds from businesses and individuals in the form of chequing and savings accounts and use those funds to make loans to businesses and individuals. Small start-up businesses rely on commercial banks for savings and chequing services to pay bills and to store excess funds. Chequing and savings accounts are a form of demand deposit, funds that can be withdrawn (or demanded) at any time without prior notice.

As a business develops and establishes a good relationship with a bank, the business owners may seek to open a line of credit. You can think of a business **line of credit** as having available credit that a manager can access at any time up to an amount agreed upon between the bank and the company. The funds can be withdrawn all at once or in multiple withdrawals during the stated period. This is a common way of covering cash flow shortages, purchasing seasonal inventory, or financing unforeseen operating expenses.

Many commercial banks also offer loans for the purchase of equipment, property, or other capital assets. A **secured loan** requires collateral, which is generally the asset that the loan is financing, to guarantee the debt obligation. For example, if a bank were to give a loan to a company so it could purchase a building, the building would serve as the collateral. If the company were unable to pay down the loan, the bank would then take possession of the building as a substitute for the remaining loan payments. If the firm has an excellent credit history and solid relationship with the lending institution, it may get an **unsecured loan**, which does not require collateral.

Are there other short-term financing options?   Sometimes, a company is unable to secure a short-term loan from a commercial bank. In these cases, an alternative source of financing is a **commercial finance company**, a financial institution that makes short-term loans to borrowers who offer tangible assets as collateral. Commercial finance companies, such as General Electric Credit Corporation, provide businesses with loans but are not considered banks. Other non-bank or private lenders include credit unions, factors, and credit card companies. Non-bank lenders are becoming increasingly popular among entrepreneurs, particularly owners of start-up businesses.

Soon after starting his own clothing manufacturing business, Ken Seiff needed additional short-term financing. He was looking to expand his product line for the next season, but he had no cash—it was tied up in receivables (money he is owed by customers) and business expenses. Commercial banks were not interested in helping him because of his perceived risk as a recent start-up business. Being in the apparel industry added even more risk. On the advice of his accountant, Seiff turned to a commercial finance company, which ultimately helped him through his short-term cash crunch.[9]

One of the strategies that the commercial finance company used in Seiff's case was factoring. **Factoring** is the process of selling accounts receivable for cash. The finance company agreed to give Seiff money, and in exchange, it would collect the accounts receivable and keep the money that was owed Seiff's company. The money given to Seiff is equal to the amount his company would have received had he waited to collect the funds directly, minus a fee charged by the factoring agent. The fee applied is dependent on how long the receivable has been outstanding, the nature of the business, and the economy. While costly at times, factoring can be an important strategy for companies to bridge cash flow gaps.

Do larger corporations do anything differently for short-term financing?   Large corporations have the advantage over smaller start-up companies in that they have a greater ability to establish a credit or debt rating. Those companies who have a high-quality debt rating can issue commercial paper. When a company has a high-quality debt rating, it means it is looked upon favourably by lenders as being a company that has a good or excellent likelihood of paying off its debt. **Commercial paper** is an

---

Commercial banks are financial institutions that raise funds from businesses and individuals in the form of chequing and savings accounts and use those funds to make loans to businesses and individuals.

A **line of credit** is available credit that a manager can access at any time up to an amount agreed upon between the bank and the company.

A **secured loan** requires collateral, which is generally the asset that the loan is financing, to guarantee the debt obligation.

An **unsecured loan** does not require collateral.

A **commercial finance company** is not considered a bank, but rather a financial institution that makes short-term loans to borrowers who offer tangible assets as collateral.

Factoring is the process of selling accounts receivable for cash.

Commercial paper is an unsecured (that is, it does not need collateral) short-term debt instrument of $100 000 or more, typically issued by a corporation to bridge a cash flow gap created by large accounts receivable, inventory, or payroll.

unsecured (that is, it does not need collateral) short-term debt instrument of $100 000 or more, typically issued by a corporation to bridge a cash flow gap created by large accounts receivable, inventory, or payroll. Commercial paper is a type of promissory note (promise to pay back) which comes due (matures) in 270 days or less and is not required to go through the same registration process as other longer-term debt and equity instruments, which we'll discuss next. When companies have extra cash, they may choose to buy commercial paper from other companies that need cash. The company that purchases the commercial paper will make money from the interest earned (that is the interest paid on the promissory note by the debtor). Therefore, commercial paper can be a means of short-term financing for companies in need of cash, and for other companies, commercial paper can be a short-term investment.

Financing Long-Term Business Needs

BizSkills Simulation: Financial Management. Located in MyBusinessLab.

Why do companies need long-term financing solutions?
Remember that in order to grow, new or small companies need expansion projects such as establishing new offices or manufacturing facilities, developing a new product or service, or buying another company. These projects may cost millions of dollars and take several years to complete. Long-term financing is needed because it provides funds for a period longer than one year (often up to ten years). In most cases, a company will use several sources of long-term financing, even for one project.

What are the different types of long-term financing?
In general, a company can choose from two different types of long-term financing: debt financing and equity financing. **Debt financing** occurs when a company borrows money that it is legally obligated to repay, with interest, by a specified time. Contrary to debt financing, the funds for **equity financing** are generated by the owners of the company rather than an outside lender. These funds might come from the company's own savings or partial sale of ownership in the company in the form of stock. The choice depends on many factors, including the maturity and size of the company, the number of assets a company already owns, and the size and nature of the project being financed.

Construction of large capital projects often requires long-term financing.

4 Summarize the pros and cons of debt and equity financing.

5 Outline the differences between each of the following types of long-term financing options: selling bonds, selling stock, venture capital, and retained earnings.

Debt financing occurs when a company borrows money that it is legally obligated to repay, with interest, by a specified time.

Equity financing is the generation of funds by the owners of the company rather than an outside lender. These funds might come from the company's own savings or partial sale of ownership in the company in the form of stock.

What kinds of debt financing are available?
There are mainly two types of debt financing for companies to choose between to raise funds: loans and bonds.

Loans   In our personal lives, when we want to buy something such as a house or a car that costs more than what we have saved, our best option is to borrow money. We take out a loan specifically to pay for an item, and that item is used as collateral, which permits the lender to claim ownership of the item in the event the loan is not repaid. A **loan** is an arrangement in which a lender gives money to a borrower, under the agreement that the borrower repays the loan amount, usually with interest, at some future point in time. Similarly, when a company has a project or purchase that it cannot finance with existing company assets, it can take out a business loan. For larger projects that demand big loans with long payment terms, long-term financing is available from financial institutions such as insurance companies and pension funds, as well as large commercial banks and finance companies. Most long-term loans require some form of collateral, such as real estate, machinery, or stock. Often, as in a home mortgage, the asset being financed serves as the collateral. Large long-term loans usually have a higher interest rate (rate charged for borrowing the money) because of the added risk associated with a large project and the longer term of the loan. The rate of interest is also determined by the prevailing

13

A **loan** is an arrangement in which a lender gives money to a borrower, under the agreement that the borrower repays the loan amount, usually with interest, at some future point in time.

A **corporate bond** is a type of loan issued by a company, not a commercial bank or commercial finance company. It is a formal written agreement to reimburse a loan at a regular interest rate at a given date in time.

Interest is the payments the bond issuer makes to the bondholder for use of the borrowed money (most interest payments are semi-annual).

A **sinking fund** is a type of savings fund in which companies set aside money regularly to help repay a bond issue.

Secured bonds require some form of collateral pledged as security.

Unsecured bonds (or **debenture bonds**) are issued with no collateral.

A **convertible bond** gives the bondholder the right (but not the obligation) to convert the bond into a predetermined number of shares of the company's stock.

market interest rates and the general financial worthiness of the borrower. Loans are easiest to obtain, when a firm has established a relationship with a bank or other financial institution and has a good credit standing.

Bonds   Some companies issue bonds when loans aren't obtainable or are not the most economical option; perhaps the rates are too high or the project requires a greater amount of financing than loans can provide. A **corporate bond** is a type of loan issued by a company and not a commercial bank or commercial finance company. It is a formal written agreement to reimburse a loan at a regular interest rate at a given date in time. Bonds are issued by companies or governments with the purpose of raising capital to finance a large project. The company issuing the bond is the borrower, who owes money to the lender, who is the investor and holder of the bond. There are two types of payments made to bond investors: interest and principal. **Interest** is the payments the bond issuer makes to the bondholder for use of the borrowed money (most interest payments are semi-annual). At the end of the loan period, the company is responsible for paying back the entire initial amount of the bond (the principal). There is a legal contract between the company (borrower) and the investor (lender) that outlines the terms of the bond, the interest due, and the date when the principal amount of the loan must be paid back (the bond's maturity date). Corporate bonds are generally more risky to invest in than government bonds because companies can only stay in business as long as they remain profitable, while governments have a ready source of funds through taxes. Because they are riskier, corporate bonds often pay higher interest rates than government bonds in order to attract investors. To ensure there is enough money at the end of the loan period to pay off all the bondholders, companies use a **sinking fund**—a type of savings fund in which companies set aside money regularly to help repay a bond issue.

As attractive as bond financing sounds, financial managers must consider several factors before deciding to finance with bonds. First, the cost of the loan—the rate of interest the lender will demand—is an important consideration. If the interest rate is too high, it can force the cost of the project into something that is not affordable or that just doesn't make economic sense. The interest rate is determined by a combination of many factors, including *issuer risk*—whether the lender (bond purchaser) thinks the company can meet its obligations to pay back the loan. As the risk increases, so does the interest rate. Often bond issuers use *bond insurance* to help lower the risk. Although there is a cost to having such insurance, the amount of money saved by having a lower interest rate is greater than the cost of the bond insurance. In addition to issuer risk, the *length of the bond term* affects the rate. Bonds that have a longer length of term have a greater chance of default; therefore, they carry additional risk and a higher interest rate. Last, *the general state of the economy* affects the interest rate. Before making a final decision to issue bonds, a financial manager must also consider how this additional debt obligation affects the overall financial health of the company.

Secured bonds require some form of collateral pledged as security. The collateral is generally corporate-owned property that will pass to the bondholders (or be sold to reimburse bondholders) if the issuer does not repay the amount borrowed. **Unsecured bonds** (or **debenture bonds**) are issued with no collateral. They are only backed by the general creditworthiness and reputation of the issuer. A **convertible bond** gives the bondholder the right (but not the obligation) to convert the bond into a predetermined number of shares of the company's stock. Convertible bonds generally carry a lower interest rate since the investor will benefit from investing in the underlying stock.

What kinds of equity financing are available?

The most common forms of financing for small businesses are personal savings or contributions from family, friends, or business associates. As a business grows, venture capital or funds from angel investors are also possible sources of new capital, but eventually, those options are not sufficient to finance large capital needs. Without an established credit history, it is difficult to obtain a loan from a financial institution. Looking inside the company for long-term funding (equity financing) is an alternative to looking outside. Equity financing primarily takes three forms: 1) issuing common stock, 2) obtaining venture capital, or 3) retaining the company's earnings.

Why finance with stock (equity)?

Most companies issue stock (often referred to as equity) to finance long-term general funding and ongoing expansion rather than a specific project or need. **Equity** is money received in exchange for ownership in a business. There are two main types of stock that companies issue: *common* and *preferred*. **Stock** is a unit of ownership in a company sold with the intention of raising capital to finance ongoing or future projects and expansions. **Issuing common stock** by selling common shares of ownership in the company to the public—in other words, "going public"—can be a great option to generate funds through equity financing. A company can choose to go public when it feels it has enough public support to attract new shareholders. For instance, Google Inc. went public on the NASDAQ (National Association of Securities Dealers Automated Quotations) American stock exchange in 2004. The first time a company offers to sell new stock to the public is called an **initial public offering (IPO)**. Google's IPO was of 19 605 052 shares of common stock at an opening price of US$85 per share.[10] Imagine the funding the company generated from selling shares to the public. Going public provides companies with equity financing opportunities to grow their businesses, from expansion of operations to buying other companies (acquisitions).

What are the disadvantages of financing with stock?

Common shares are the most basic form of ownership and shareholders have the right to 1) to vote for the company board of directors and on important company issues, and 2) to share in the company profits through dividends. The biggest disadvantage of financing with stock is the dilution of ownership. Another disadvantage is the payment of dividends. **Dividends** are a portion of a company's profits distributed to shareholders as either cash payments or additional shares of stock. Legally common share dividends and preferred share dividends (discussed next) never have to be paid if the company makes no profit, nor do they ever have to be repurchased by the company. Of course, if a company does not pay dividends, it would become difficult to entice new investors to purchase shares in the company. Paying dividends to shareholders is more expensive for a company than paying interest to bondholders, which is tax deductible while paying dividends to shareholders is not (dividends are paid out of profit after taxes and are not an allowable income tax deduction). Shareholders do not have direct control over the day-to-day management of a company, but they do directly control who manages the company through voting rights. As a result, shareholders can have a strong influence on management's decisions.

What are preferred stocks?

Preferred stock is a hybrid investment because it has some of the features of common stock (i.e., it never matures) and some of the features of corporate bonds (i.e., payments on stock are for fixed amounts, such as $5 per share per year). Preferred stock is a class of ownership in which the preferred shareholders have a claim to assets before common shareholders if the firm goes out of business. In addition, preferred shareholders receive a fixed dividend that must be paid before the payment of any dividend to common shareholders. A major advantage of preferred stock for the issuing company is that funds can be obtained without giving up control of the company because preferred shareholders usually do not have voting rights.

Why finance with venture capital?

If a company does not feel it is ready to go public, it may look for long-term financing in the form of venture capital. Venture capital is an investment in the form of money that includes a substantial amount of risk for the investors. Because of the high level of risk, the group of outside investors, called venture capitalists (discussed in Chapter 5), command an active role in the management decisions of the company. Venture capitalists seek their return in the form of equity, or ownership, in the company. They anticipate a large return on their investment when the company is sold or goes public. Venture capitalists are willing to wait longer than other investors, lenders, or shareholders for returns on their investment, but they expect higher than normal results.

Why finance with retained earnings?

A successful company, making a profit, could find long-term funding by simply looking at its balance sheet for *retained earnings*, or *accumulated profits*. **Retained earnings** represent the profits (money remaining after taxes

---

Equity is money received in exchange for ownership in a business.

Stock is a unit of ownership in a company sold with the intention of raising capital to finance ongoing or future projects and expansions.

Issuing common stock by selling common shares of ownership in the company to the general public—in other words, "going public"—can be a great option to generate funds through equity financing.

An **initial public offering (IPO)** is the first time a company offers to sell new stock to the public.

Dividends are a portion of a company's profits distributed to shareholders as either cash payments or additional shares of stock.

Preferred stock is a hybrid investment because it has some of the features of common stock (i.e., it never matures) and some of the features of corporate bonds (i.e., payments on stock are for fixed amounts, such as $5 per share per year).

Retained earnings represent the profits (money remaining after taxes and other expenses are paid) not paid out in dividends.

13

and other expenses are paid) not paid out in dividends. Using retained earnings is an ideal way to fund long-term projects because it saves companies from paying interest on loans or underwriting fees on bonds. Unfortunately, not all companies produce enough retained earnings to fund large projects. In particular, start-up businesses find themselves with few options for long-term financing. Each business owner can contribute money to the company for expansion, purchases, operations, and so on. However, at some point the individual owners contribute as much as they can or are willing to and still need additional funds to keep their business growing.

How do companies decide between debt and equity financing?

For large capital-intensive projects or general expansion, business owners can use securities—**investment instruments** such as bonds (debt) or stock (equity). The choice between financing large projects with debt or equity is a decision managers reach by understanding the financing needs of the project itself and the impact the financing decision has on corporate earnings, cash flow, and taxes. In addition, a company must take into consideration how much debt it already has before issuing bonds or whether it wants to dilute ownership by issuing stock. Lastly, the company must also consider external factors at the time of financing, such as the state of the bond or stock market, the economy, and the anticipated interest of the investors.

> **Investment instruments** such as bonds (debt) or stock (equity) are used for large capital-intensive projects or general expansion.

Most companies use debt to finance operations, which increases the company's leverage. **Leverage** is the amount of debt used to finance a firm's assets with the intent that the rate of return on the assets is greater than the cost of the debt. One measure of a company's financial leverage is determined by its debt to equity ratio (or total liabilities divided by shareholders' equity—discussed in the next section). Using leverage wisely is beneficial because a company can invest in business operations without losing equity by increasing the number of owners in the company. For example, if a company formed with $3 million from five investors (who become the company's shareholders), the equity in the company is $3 million. If the company also uses debt financing to borrow $17 million, the company now has $17 million to invest in business operations without having to take on more shareholders. This creates additional opportunities for the original shareholders to make more money. Although there is a cost to borrowing, the intention is that the project or company expansion will ultimately have a positive rate of return after paying for the cost of the debt. However, it can be risky to take on too much debt, so lenders consider how much debt a company has relative to the amount of equity (or assets) a company owns before they issue a loan. A common leverage ratio is for a company to have at least twice the amount of equity (67 percent) as it has debt (33 percent).

> **Leverage** is the amount of debt used to finance a firm's assets with the intent that the rate of return on the assets is greater than the cost of the debt.

If a company is unwilling or cannot take on additional debt, it must consider equity financing to meet its long-term business needs. Unlike bonds and other forms of debt, equity financing does not need to be repaid, even if the company goes bankrupt, and no assets need to be pledged as collateral. In addition, financing with equity enables the company to retain cash and profits in the company rather than using the funds to make interest and principal payments. In many instances, financing with equity can make the company look stronger, as high levels of debt can be problematic to lenders and investors.

Financial planners try to find a mix between equity and debt financing that will maximize stockholders' wealth. The balance between debt and equity varies according to industry and size of the business. For example, capital-intensive manufacturing industries, such as car manufacturers, will have more debt than service industries, such as health care providers. Other industries that are expanding rapidly but have large capital reserves, such as computer hardware manufacturers, have a minimal need for debt or equity financing. Companies aim to achieve an **optimal capital structure**, which refers to the optimal balance between equity and debt financing. The most conservative strategy would be to use all equity financing and no debt because a company has no formal obligations for financial payouts. The riskiest strategy would be to use all debt financing because indebtedness increases the risk that the company will be unable to meet its obligations and will go bankrupt. See **Table 13.2** for a comparison of debt and equity financing.

> **Optimal capital structure** is the optimal balance between equity and debt financing.

Table 13.2   Comparison of Debt and Equity Financing

Debt Financing	Equity Financing
What are the repayment obligations?	
Interest must be paid.	Not obligated to pay dividends.
Principal must be repaid at maturity date.	Stock has no maturity date.
	Never required to repay equity.
What are the tax implications?	
Interest paid is tax deductible.	Dividends are not tax deductible.
What are the implications for management control?	
None, unless special conditions apply.	Common shareholders have voting rights.
	May cause challenge for corporate control.

Companies that need large amounts of money in addition to profits gained through regular business operations often acquire funding through various investments and financing (debt and equity) options. For a more in-depth discussion of stock, bonds, and the risks and rewards that come with various types of investments, refer to MyBusinessLab, Appendix 13A: "Securities and Investments."

ACCOUNTING FUNCTIONS
Accounting Fundamentals

What is accounting?   **Accounting** is the recording, classifying, summarizing, and interpreting of financial events in order to communicate useful financial information. It involves tracking a business's income and expenses through a process of recording financial transactions. The transactions are then summarized into key financial reports that are further used to evaluate the business's current and expected financial status. Accounting is not just for large organizations, it is quite important for businesses of all sizes. Accounting defines the heart and soul of even the smallest business as it helps to "account for" what the business has done, what it is currently doing, and what it has the potential to do. While accounting involves a great deal of precision, there are also some degrees of interpretation in the process of accounting. This makes accounting both an art and a science.

Arnold Sawyer was pretty good at handling figures. When his niece Josephine asked him to oversee finances for her vegan catering business, he figured he could handle it. Arnold's background was in sales, but he assumed he was smart enough to handle accounting. He used QuickBooks to create a basic bookkeeping system. Since the company only had a small but steady stream of clients, the accounting side didn't seem complicated. However, after Josephine appeared on a newscast to talk about the benefits of a vegan diet, sales skyrocketed. With the significant increase in catering contracts, the workload doubled. Josephine needed to increase her staff and supplies, but the company didn't have enough cash to cover the initial costs. Arnold must decide how his niece's catering business will acquire the extra funds it needs to keep the business moving. Arnold will need to review the company's financial information and possibly enlist outside consultants before making a decision.

Accounting is often called the language of business because it provides financial information used for decision making, planning, and reporting. When companies are small, it can seem relatively simple. However, as a company grows and diversifies, accounting becomes increasingly complex. In this section, the fundamentals of

Accounting is the recording, classifying, summarizing, and interpreting financial events in order to communicate useful financial information. It involves tracking a business's income and expenses through a process of recording financial transactions.

A **private accountant** is employed by an organization and may perform one or more different accounting functions.

A **public accountant** provides a broad range of accounting, auditing, tax, and consulting activities for various corporate clients.

A **certified general accountant (CGA)** provides the financial information for use by stockholders, government, creditors, and others "outside" an organization.

A **certified management accountant (CMA)** provides financial information to managers and other corporate decision makers "inside" the corporation and helps formulate policy and strategic plans.

A **chartered accountant (CA)** provides financial information for use by stockholders, government, creditors, and others "outside" an organization. The CA can work in both public and private sector fields of business and finance.

accounting, the types of accounting, and accounting standards and processes will be discussed.

Is there more than one type of accountant?   It is critical for firms to keep accurate financial information. A company may employ a *private* accountant or hire the services of a *public* accountant. A **private accountant** is employed by an organization and may perform one or more different accounting functions. A **public accountant** provides a broad range of accounting, auditing, tax, and consulting activities for various corporate clients.

Three professional accounting organizations have developed in Canada to certify accounting expertise:

1. *Certified General Accountants (CGA).* The Certified General Accountants Association of Canada grants the CGA designation. The duties of a CGA include accounting, auditing, taxation, and business consulting.[11] A **certified general accountant (CGA)** provides the financial information for use by stockholders, government, creditors, and others "outside" an organization.
2. *Certified Management Accountants (CMA).* The Society of Management Accountants of Canada grants the CMA certification. A **certified management accountant (CMA)** provides financial information to managers and other corporate decision makers "inside" the corporation and helps formulate policy and strategic plans.[12]
3. *Chartered Accountants (CA).* The Canadian Institute of Chartered Accountants (CICA) grants the CA designation. A **chartered accountant (CA)** provides the financial information for use by stockholders, government, creditors, and others "outside" an organization. A CA is widely recognized as the leading financial and accounting professional in Canada and has satisfied rigorous requirements; it is in no way less than the CGA or CMA. CA firms typically provide tax, audit, and management services.[13] The CA is a professional and can work in both public and private sector fields of business and finance.

Off the **Mark**

Accounting Error Reduces Share Value[14]

TUI Travel PLC is the world's leading leisure travel group, owning First Choice and Thomson travel companies and servicing more than 30 million customers. In 2009, auditors KPMG discovered an accounting error in TUI Travel's books that had compounded over four or five years to total £117 million (more than CDN$167 million). The audit revealed that reductions offered by Thomson travel agents, including waiving of booking charge fees and discounts for e-tickets, as well as some cancellations, were not recorded when UK cash sales data was transferred to TUI Travel's accounts department.

TUI was forced to issue a series of statements to investors detailing how £117 million, said to be owed to TUI Travel, was in fact an illusory figure in its accounts. The discovery led to the resignation of TUI's chief financial officer, Paul Bowtell, which forced a complete overhaul of its UK management team. Peter Long, TUI's chief executive,

said he was sorry about Bowtell's resignation and that the former CFO was not directly at fault.

The company had to reduce its reported earnings by £120 million for the past few years and restate its accounts. The adjustments erased much of the strong operating profit gains recorded by its UK and Ireland businesses during 2009. Share prices fell 11 percent soon after the accounting error was publicized. TUI said that the balance corrections would not harm its cash position or net debt, and that it expected to stay profitable.

Discussion Questions
1. How can such errors go on for years without being noticed? Is this any one person's fault?
2. How might a company prevent such errors from occurring? Is it important for the company to publicize and correct the errors? Why or why not?
3. Isn't this just a small oversight with nothing to be concerned about? Why do you think share prices fell? What happened to TUI's public image?

Types of Accounting

What are the types of corporate accounting? *Accounting* is a general term, to say the least. Since different forms of business have varying needs, there is a multitude of specialty areas under the accounting umbrella.

As stated in the beginning of this chapter, financial managers must make many important decisions. Some decisions may involve determining whether the company's financial assets are working most efficiently (that is, earning as much money as possible), evaluating what kind of financing strategy is best, or choosing a way to obtain needed funds. The answers to these decisions, and many more, are found in the reports and analysis done by corporate accountants. **Corporate accounting** is the part of an organization's finance department responsible for gathering and assembling data required for key financial statements. Corporate accounting has two separate functions: *managerial accounting* and *financial accounting*.

Managerial accounting is used to provide information and analyses to managers within the organization to assist them in making good business decisions. More specifically, managerial accounting is responsible for tracking sales and the costs of producing the sales (production, marketing, and distribution). By doing so, it helps determine how efficiently a company is run. Moreover, managerial accountants help determine which business activities are most and least profitable. Based on their analysis, management is better equipped to make decisions about whether to continue with, expand, or eliminate certain business activities. Managerial accounting produces budgets so senior management can make informed decisions. For example, a managerial accounting budget can help management decide whether it should increase staff or institute layoffs. In addition, by monitoring the activities involved in planned budgets, managerial accountants help determine and anticipate in what areas the company strays from its budgeted expectations.

While individuals inside a company use managerial accounting to make decisions, interested parties outside a company depend on financial accounting to make financial decisions. **Financial accounting** produces financial documents to aid decision makers outside an organization in making decisions regarding investments and credibility. Investors and shareholders rely on financial accounting to help them evaluate a company's performance and profitability. Such information is generally found in key documents such as quarterly statements or **annual reports**—documents produced once a year that present the current financial state of a company and future expectations. These documents help investors determine whether it is wise to put funds into the company. Banks and other creditors analyze financial accounting statements to determine the business's financial health and creditworthiness.

Is auditing considered an area of accounting? **Auditing** is responsible for reviewing and evaluating the accuracy of financial reports. Large corporations may have private accountants on staff who work in-house to determine whether the company's financial information is recorded correctly and by using proper procedures. Generally, companies hire independent auditors from outside the company to ensure their financial reports have been prepared accurately and are not biased or manipulated in any way. Companies can avoid devastating budget problems, such as the one experienced by TUI Travel (described in the Off the Mark box above), by performing audits.

Do businesses hire outside accounting firms to complete their income tax returns? Paying taxes is an important part of running a business. Government require individuals and organizations to file tax returns annually. **Tax accounting** involves preparing taxes and giving advice on tax strategies. The process for filing taxes can be complicated and is ever changing, so companies often have tax accountants on staff or hire an outside accounting firm such as H&R Block or BDO Canada to prepare their taxes.

6
Describe the functions of corporate accounting, managerial accounting, financial accounting, auditing, tax accounting, and government and non-profit accounting.

Corporate accounting is the part of an organization's finance department responsible for gathering and assembling data required for key financial statements.

Accounting Scandals of All Time (US$)

1. Enron: Shareholders Lose $74 Billion
2. Lehman Brothers: $50 Billion in Disguised Loans
3. Madoff Scandal: Cash Losses of $21.2 Billion for Investors
4. Worldcom: $11 Billion Accounting Fraud
5. Freddie Mac: $5 Billion in Misstated Earnings
6. HealthSouth: $2.7 Billion Accounting Fraud
7. Waste Management, Inc.: $1.9 Billion in Fake Earnings
8. AIG: $1.7 Billion Improper Accounting
9. Satyam: $1 Billion Fraud
10. Tyco: Execs Steal $120 Million and Inflate Income by more than $500 Million

Source: "The Biggest Accounting Scandals of All Time," *Huffingtonpost.com*, March 28, 2010, http://www.huffingtonpost.com/2010/03/17/biggest-accounting-scanda_n_502181.html#s74418&title=Madoff_Scandal_, Accessed June 30, 2011.

Managerial accounting is used to provide information and analyses to managers within the organization to assist them in making good business decisions.

Financial accounting produces financial documents to aid decision makers outside an organization in making decisions regarding investments and credibility.

Annual reports are documents produced once a year to present the current financial state of a company and future expectations.

Auditing is responsible for reviewing and evaluating the accuracy of financial reports.

Tax accounting involves preparing taxes and giving advice on tax strategies.

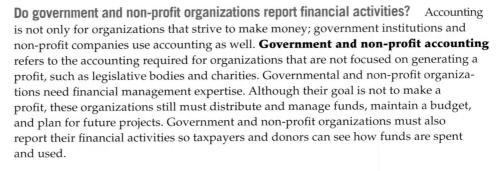

Government and non-profit accounting refers to the accounting required for organizations that are not focused on generating a profit, such as legislative bodies and charities.

Do government and non-profit organizations report financial activities? Accounting is not only for organizations that strive to make money; government institutions and non-profit companies use accounting as well. **Government and non-profit accounting** refers to the accounting required for organizations that are not focused on generating a profit, such as legislative bodies and charities. Governmental and non-profit organizations need financial management expertise. Although their goal is not to make a profit, these organizations still must distribute and manage funds, maintain a budget, and plan for future projects. Government and non-profit organizations must also report their financial activities so taxpayers and donors can see how funds are spent and used.

Explain how double entry bookkeeping is used to maintain the balance of the fundamental accounting equation.

Accounting Standards and Processes

Are there specific standards accountants must adhere to? For any financial information to be useful, it is critical that the information is accurate, fair and objective, and consistent over time. Therefore, accountants in Canada follow the Generally Accepted Accounting Principles (GAAP) defined by the Canadian Accounting Standard Board (see this chapter's opening discussion). Although GAAP provides accountants with general rules, they are often subject to different interpretations, which can lead to problems. Companies such as WorldCom, Enron, and Tyco made headlines and fell into financial ruin in the early 2000s due to very aggressive and fraudulent accounting practices. Hundreds of thousands of investors also lost millions of dollars due to the accounting fraud that occurred in corporate financial disclosures, and one of the five big accounting firms, Arthur Andersen, was found guilty of criminal charges related to the firm's handling of auditing of Enron. The conviction was later reversed, but the damage to Arthur Andersen's image has subsequently made it difficult for the firm to return as a viable business. Due to a series of major corporate scandals, the U.S. introduced the *Sarbanes-Oxley Act (SOX)* in 2002 to restore investor confidence in the markets and prevent occurrences of corporate fraud. Given that 15 percent of Canadian firms listed on the Toronto Stock Exchange (TXE) were also listed on a U.S. stock exchange, Canadian regulators adopted similar reforms.[15] The regulatory reforms are an ongoing process, and in Canada, the Canadian Securities Administrators (CSA) has introduced a series of national instruments and policies to cover major *SOX* provisions.

With the growing number of business-related investigations and the growing complexity of the business environment, the use of forensic accountants has increased.

A **forensic accountant** provides investigative accounting services and litigation support.

A **forensic accountant** provides investigative accounting services and litigation support. *Forensic* means "pertaining to or used in a court of law," and forensic accountants are often involved in investigating and analyzing financial evidence and assisting in legal proceedings by providing reports, advice, and evidence to clients, lawyers, and courts. This may include testifying in court as an expert witness and preparing visual aids to support trial evidence.[16]

In an attempt to make accounting practices country-neutral and financial information comparable between countries, the International Accounting Standards Board (IASB) developed International Financial Reporting Standards (IFRS) (see this chapter's opening discussion). By doing so, multinational companies that have operations in Canada and other countries, such as Toyota, Walmart, and Research In Motion (RIM), may avoid the need to convert regional financial reports into foreign accounting specifications.

Bookkeeping is the systematic recording of a company's every financial transaction.

Assets are what the company owns.

Liabilities are what the company owes to its creditors.

Owners' equity is what the company owes to its owners.

The **fundamental accounting equation** is assets = liabilities + owners' equity.

What is the accounting process? When people think of accounting, most think of the systematic recording of a company's every financial transaction, which is a small but important part of accounting called **bookkeeping**. The process of bookkeeping centres on the fundamental concept that what a company owns (**assets**) must equal what it owes to its creditors (**liabilities**) plus what it owes to its owners (**owners' equity**). This balance is illustrated in **Figure 13.3** and is better described as the **fundamental accounting equation:** assets = liabilities + owners' equity.

Assets = Liabilities + Owners' Equity

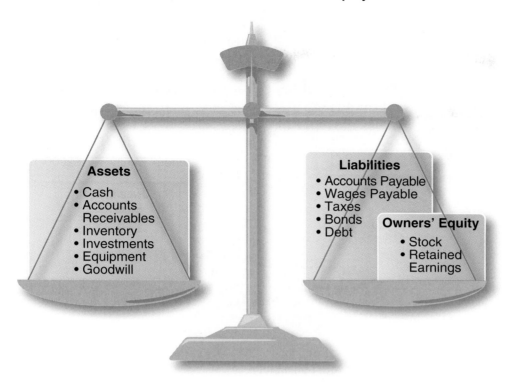

Assets
- Cash
- Accounts Receivables
- Inventory
- Investments
- Equipment
- Goodwill

Liabilities
- Accounts Payable
- Wages Payable
- Taxes
- Bonds
- Debt

Owners' Equity
- Stock
- Retained Earnings

Figure 13.3 The Fundamental Accounting Equation

Explore on MyBusinessLab

Fraudulent Bigwigs Face Hard Time

Since the implementation of the *Sarbanes-Oxley Act* of 2002, fraud cases being handled by the FBI have risen 70 percent. Oscar Wyatt Jr. was eighty-three years old when he was sentenced to eighteen to twenty-four months in jail for consenting to bribes that lead to the build-up of the Iraqi military.[17]

In 1996, the United Nations set up a program, Oil-for-Food, that allowed Iraq to trade oil for food, medicine, and other needs. This would allow Iraqi people to have basic necessities while preventing the Iraqi government from getting money to aid the military. Iraqi officials began manipulating the system by demanding monetary bribes in order for companies to gain oil contracts. It is estimated that the Iraqi government collected US$10 billion to US$11 billion in illegal bribes.

Before the Oil-for-Food program even started, Oscar Wyatt, Jr., was so close to Iraqi officials that he personally met with Saddam Hussein to discuss the release of American prisoners in Iraq. Wyatt even worked with the Iraqi government after the U.S. invasion of Iraq in 2003. In October 2007 Wyatt plead guilty to conspiring, under the Oil for Food program, to make illegal payments to Saddam Hussein's Iraq. Wyatt was only one of the many American oilmen who consented to bribes that led to the build-up of the Iraqi military.

Discussion Questions
1. Do you think Oscar Wyatt Jr.'s punishment fit his crime? Why or why not?
2. The FBI considers insider trading an example of corporate fraud. If you got word through an in-the-know friend that a stock you owned would plummet in price tomorrow, would you sell your stock today? Do you think you would be guilty of insider trading? Why or why not?
3. Visit the FBI White Collar Crime page and click on Corporate Fraud. What are some of the recent cases of corporate fraud being investigated? Are you surprised at these findings?

13

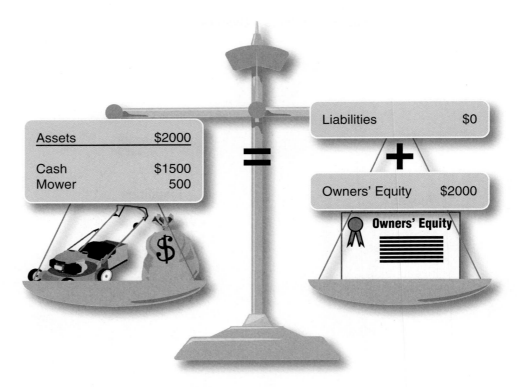

Figure 13.4 Business with No Liability

Without any liabilities, assets equal owners' equity.

Does the accounting equation always stay in balance? To maintain the balance of assets and liabilities plus owner's equity, accountants use a recording system called double entry bookkeeping. **Double entry bookkeeping** recognizes that for every transaction that affects an asset an equal transaction must also affect either a liability or owners' equity. For example, say you were to start a business mowing lawns. Your initial assets are a lawn mower worth $500 and $1500 in cash that you have saved and are willing to use to start the business. Your assets total $2000. Because the cash and lawn mower were yours to begin with, you do not owe anyone any money, so you have zero liabilities. If you we re to close the business tomorrow, the cash and the lawn mower would belong to you; therefore, they are considered owners' equity. The accounting statement for your lawn mowing business would look like the one in **Figure 13.4**.

Now imagine that the business is growing rapidly. You realize you need to buy another lawn mower and you also want to buy a snow blower so you can expand your business to include snow removal. Together these items cost $2500. You don't have enough cash to buy either outright, so you have to borrow the money. Although you are increasing your assets with a new lawn mower and a new snow blower, you are also adding a liability—the debt you have incurred to buy the new equipment. If the business closed tomorrow, your owners' equity would not change because you could sell the lawn mower and the snow blower to pay off the debt. The accounting statement for your lawn mower business would look like the one in **Figure 13.5**.

Accounting is necessary for businesses of all sizes to help figure out what they have the potential to do. Arnold Sawyer was able to handle finances for his niece's catering business for a while, but when business boomed he didn't know what to do. He realized he was in over his head and convinced his niece that she needed to hire an accountant to handle these important matters. Having someone on staff who is knowledgeable about accounting is vital to a company's success.

Double entry bookkeeping recognizes that for every transaction that affects an asset an equal transaction must also affect either a liability or owners' equity.

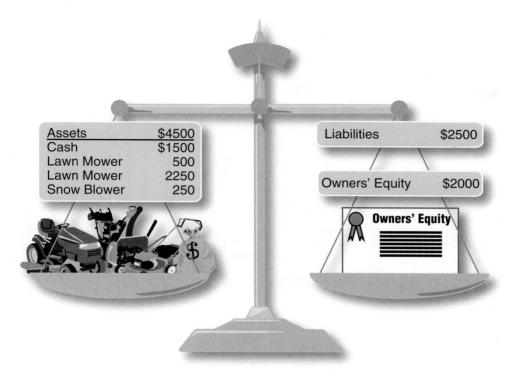

Assets	$4500
Cash	$1500
Lawn Mower	500
Lawn Mower	2250
Snow Blower	250

Liabilities	$2500

Owners' Equity	$2000

 Owners' Equity

Figure 13.5 Business with Liability

Borrowing to buy assets increases assets and liabilities.

FINANCIAL STATEMENTS

The Balance Sheet

Are companies required to publish financial information? **Financial statements** are the formal reports of a business's financial transactions that accountants prepare periodically. They represent what has happened in the past and provide management, as well as various outsiders such as creditors and investors, with a perspective of what is going to happen in the future. Publicly owned companies are required to publish three financial statements:

- A **balance sheet** shows what the company owns and what it has borrowed (owes) at a fixed point in time and shows the net worth of the business.
- An **income statement** shows how much money is coming into a company and how much money a company is spending over a period. It shows how well a company has done in terms of profit and loss.
- A **statement of cash** flows shows the exchange of money between a company and everyone else it deals with over a period. It shows where cash was used.

    Let's look more closely at each of these financial statements.

What is the balance sheet used for? A balance sheet is a snapshot of a business's financial condition at a specific point in time. It reflects what the company owns (assets), what it owes to its creditors (liabilities), and what it owes to the owners (owners' equity). At any point in time, the information in the balance sheet is used to answer questions such as "Is the business in a good position to expand?" and "Does the business have enough cash to ride out an anticipated slow-down in sales?" In addition, by analyzing how a balance sheet changes over time, financial managers can identify trends and then suggest strategies to manage accounts receivable and payable in a way that is most beneficial to the company's bottom line. **Figure 13.6** is a condensed balance sheet for Google.

8
Describe the function of balance sheets, income statements, and statements of cash flow.

Financial statements are the formal reports of a business's financial transactions that accountants prepare periodically.

A **balance sheet** shows what the company owns and what it has borrowed (owes) at a fixed point in time and shows the net worth of the business.

An **income statement** shows how much money is coming into a company and how much money a company is spending over a period. It shows how well a company has done in terms of profit and loss.

A **statement of cash** flows shows the exchange of money between a company and everyone else it deals with over a period. It shows where cash was used.

13

Google Inc.
Summary of Balance Sheet
as of December 31 2010
(in millions of U.S. Dollars)

Assets		**Liabilities**	
Current Assets		Current Liabilities	
Cash and Cash Equivalents	13 630	Accounts Payable	6137
Short-Term Investments	21 345	Short/Current Long Term Debt	3465
Net Receivables	5261	Other Current Liabilities	394
Inventory	0	**Total Current Liabilities**	**9996**
Other Current Assets	1326		
Total Current Assets	**41 562**	Long-Term Liabilities	
		Long-Term Debt	0
Fixed Assets		Other Liabilities	1579
Property, Plant, and Equipment	7759	Deferred Long-Term Liability Charges	35
Other Assets	1230	**Total Long-Term Liabilities**	**1614**
Total Fixed Assets	**8989**		
		Total Liabilities	**11 610**
Intangible Assets			
Goodwill	6256	**Owners' Equity**	
Other Assets	1044	Common Stock	18 235
Total Intangible Assets	**7300**	Retained Earnings	27 868
		Other Owners' Equity	138
		Total Owners' Equity	**46 241**
Total Assets	**57 851**	**Total Liabilities and Owners' Equity**	**57 851**

Figure 13.6 Condensed Balance Sheet for Google Inc.

Source: Based on Yahoo! Finance, Google Inc. (GOOG) Balance Sheet, Retrieved on June 25, 2011 from http://ca.finance.yahoo.com/q/bs?s=GOOG&annual

What does the balance sheet track? Balance sheets are based on the most fundamental equation in business accounting:

$$\text{assets} = \overbrace{\text{liabilities} + \text{owners' equity}}^{\text{claims on assets}}$$

It is important to remember that assets (the items on the left side of the balance sheet) must always equal claims on assets, which are liabilities plus owners' equity (the items on the right side of the balance sheet). Let's look at each of these components in a bit more detail, and then see how they all fit together on a balance sheet.

Assets Assets are the things a company owns, which include cash, investments, buildings, furniture, and equipment. On a balance sheet, assets are organized into three categories: current, fixed, and intangible. These categories are listed on the balance sheet in order of liquidity—the speed at which assets can be turned into cash.

Current assets are those assets that can be turned into cash within a year.

Accounts receivable are amounts due to the company from customers who have purchased goods or services on credit.

Fixed assets are assets with long-term use, such as real estate, buildings, machinery, and equipment.

Depreciation spreads out the cost of the equipment over its useful life.

■ **Current assets** are those assets that can be turned into cash within a year. Examples of current assets include cash, accounts receivable, inventory, and short-term investments such as money market accounts. **Accounts receivable** are amounts due to the company from customers who have purchased goods or services on credit. As you can see in Figure 13.6, as of December 31, 2010, Google had more than US$41.5 billion in current assets.

■ **Fixed assets** are assets with long-term use, such as real estate, buildings, machinery, and equipment. Often, the value of a fixed asset, such as machinery or equipment, decreases over time due to usage or obsolescence. To compensate for such reduction in value over time, accountants use **depreciation** to spread out the cost of the equipment over its useful life. Depreciation helps keep the accounting equation in balance by matching the expense of the asset with the revenue that asset is expected to generate. As you can see in Figure 13.6, as of December 31, 2010, Google had approximately US$8.9 billion in fixed assets.

- **Intangible assets** do not have physical characteristics (you can't touch or see them), but they have value nonetheless. Trademarks, patents, and copyrights are examples of intangible assets, in addition to strong brand recognition and excellent customer or employee morale. Intangible assets are often reflected on financial statements and reports as *goodwill*. **Goodwill** is an accounting concept meaning the value of an entity over and above the value of its assets. **Amortization** is the process of applying those long-term expenses to intangible assets such as goodwill or patents. Sometimes the term "amortization" is used to indicate the length of time given to pay off the principal and interest of a debt, as with a mortgage or other loan. However, for accounting purposes, only the narrower definition applies. As you can see in Figure 13.6, Google's goodwill and intangible assets amounted to approximately US$7.3 billion.

Liabilities   Liabilities are all debts and obligations owed by the business to outside creditors, suppliers, or other vendors. Liabilities are listed on the balance sheet in the order in which they will come due.

- **Current liabilities** (or **short-term liabilities**) are obligations a company is responsible for paying within a year or less and are listed first on the balance sheet. They consist of accounts payable, accrued expenses, and short-term financing. **Accounts payable** are obligations a company owes to vendors and creditors. They are similar to those bills you need to pay every month, such as cable fees, credit card payments, cell phone charges, and other obligations paid less frequently such as taxes and insurance. **Accrued expenses** include payroll, commissions, and benefits earned but not paid to employees. Trade credit and commercial paper make up short-term financing. As you can see in Figure 13.6, Google had approximately US$9.9 billion in current liabilities.
- **Long-term liabilities** include debts and obligations owed by the company and due more than one year from the current date, such as mortgage loans for the purchase of land or buildings, long-term leases on equipment or buildings, and bonds issued for large projects. As you can see in Figure 13.6, Google's long-term liabilities are approximately US$11.6 billion.

Owners' Equity   The easiest way to think of owners' equity is what is left over after you have accounted for all your assets and taken away all that you owe. For small businesses, owners' equity is literally the amount the owners in the business can call their own. Owners' equity increases as the business grows, assuming debt has not increased. It is often referred to as the owners' capital account. For larger publicly owned companies, owners' equity becomes a bit more complicated. Shareholders are the owners of publicly owned companies. Owners' equity, in this case, is the value of the stock issued as part of the owners' (shareholders') investment in the business and retained earnings, which are the accumulated profits a business has held onto for reinvestment into the company. As you can see in Figure 13.6, the owners' equity (or stockholders' equity because it is a public company) for Google is approximately US$46.2 billion.

Analyzing a Balance Sheet

How do you analyze a balance sheet?
A lot of information about a company can be determined by the balance sheet. For example, just looking at the amount of inventory a company keeps on hand can be an indicator of a company's efficiency. **Inventory** is the merchandise a business owns but has not sold. Inventory on hand is necessary to satisfy customers' needs quickly, which makes for good business. However, there are costs associated with keeping inventory, the most obvious being the money spent to purchase the merchandise. In addition to the initial cost, storing unused inventory incurs warehousing costs and ties up money that could be used elsewhere. An even worse situation can arise

Intangible assets do not have physical characteristics (you can't touch or see them), but they have value nonetheless. Trademarks, patents, and copyrights are examples of intangible assets, in addition to strong brand recognition and excellent customer or employee relations.

Goodwill is an accounting concept meaning the value of an entity over and above the value of its assets.

Amortization is the process of applying those long-term expenses to intangible assets such as goodwill or patents.

Current liabilities (or **short-term liabilities**) are obligations a company is responsible for paying within a year or less and are listed first on the balance sheet.

Accounts payable are obligations a company owes to vendors and creditors.

Accrued expenses include payroll, commissions, and benefits that have been earned but not paid to employees.

Long-term liabilities include debts and obligations owed by the company and due more than one year from the current date such as mortgage loans for the purchase of land or buildings, long-term leases on equipment or buildings, and bonds issued for large projects.

Inventory is the merchandise a business owns but has not sold.

if the value of unused inventory decreases over time, causing the company to lose money. This is a big concern for computer companies such as Apple, whose inventory consists of computer parts and other technology-related components that can become obsolete very quickly. Generally, it is okay to have a lot of inventory on hand if it is being sold quickly enough to avoid becoming outdated or spoiled. Inventory turnover varies greatly by industry, and companies must always have enough inventory to keep business moving and keep up with competitors.

Ratio Analysis   Although looking at a balance sheet is a good way to determine the overall financial health of a company, the data presented on the sheet can be overwhelming and useless to investors if they are not organized. This is why ratio analysis is crucial when analyzing financial statements. **Ratio analysis** is a comparison of numbers and therefore is used to compare current data to data from previous years, competitors' data, or industry averages. Ratios eliminate the effect of size, so you can reasonably compare a large company's performance to a smaller company's performance. There are three main calculations one can do using information from a balance sheet to determine a company's financial health and liquidity:

> **Ratio analysis** is a comparison of numbers and therefore is used to compare current data to data from previous years, competitors' data, or industry averages.

1. *Working capital:* current assets − current liabilities
2. *Current ratio:* current assets ÷ current liabilities
3. *Debt to equity ratio:* total liabilities ÷ owners' equity

Let's examine these measurements in more detail.

Working Capital   One of the most important reasons one looks at a company's balance sheet is to determine the company's working capital. **Working capital** tells you what is left over if the company pays off its short-term liabilities with its short-term assets. Working capital is a measure of a company's short-term financial fitness, as well as its efficiency. Working capital is calculated as:

> **Working capital** is the amount left over if the company pays off its short-term liabilities with its short-term assets. It is a measure of a company's short-term financial fitness, as well as its efficiency.

$$\text{current assets} - \text{current liabilities} = \text{working capital}$$

If a company has positive working capital (its current assets are greater than its current liabilities), that means it is able to pay off its short-term liabilities. If a company has negative working capital (its current assets are less than its current liabilities), that means it is currently unable to offset its short-term liabilities with its current assets. In this case, even after adding up all of a company's cash, collecting all funds from accounts receivable, and selling all inventory, the company would still be unable to pay back creditors in the short term. When a company's current liabilities surpass its current assets, many financial difficulties develop, bankruptcy being the most severe. It is important to watch for changes in working capital, as a decline in positive working capital over time can be an indication that a company's finances are in trouble. For example, a company experiencing a decrease in sales will have a decrease in accounts receivable (current assets).

On the other hand, situations such as the one faced by Arnold Sawyer and the catering company can arise when a company experiences a sudden spike in sales. It is possible to have positive working capital, but not have enough immediately available to handle a large, unexpected cash need. A good financial manager and accountant must maintain a balance between having enough cash on hand and keeping the available short-term assets from being idle. Because of this, working capital can also be an indicator of a company's underlying operational efficiency.

Current Ratio (Liquidity Ratio)   Although working capital is an important measurement, it is hard to compare how efficient a company is to the rest of the industry or to its competitors, especially if companies vary significantly in size. The **current ratio** (or **liquidity ratio**) is a measurement used to determine the extent to which a company can meet its current financial obligations. Current ratio is calculated

> The **current ratio** (or **liquidity ratio**) is a measurement used to determine the extent to which a company can meet its current financial obligations.

$$\text{current ratio} = \frac{\text{current assets}}{\text{current liabilities}}$$

As you can see in Figure 13.6, Google's current ratio (41 562/9996) equals 4.15, which means Google has US$4.15 of current assets for every US$1 of current liabilities. Usually a company with a current ratio of 2 or better is considered a safe risk for granting short-term credit because it has two or more times current assets than current liabilities, so if need be, the current assets could be converted to cash to pay off the current liabilities. It is important that for a company to compare its current ratio to that of the industry average as well. For example, if during 2010 the current ratio for automotive manufacturers was 1.42, and during the same year Toyota Motor Corp. had a current ratio of 1.2,[18] then Toyota would rank slightly below the industry average. Having a current ratio that is too high indicates the company may not be very efficient with its cash, but having a current ratio that is too low may indicate the company will face potential problems paying back its creditors.

Debt to Equity Ratio (Leverage Ratio)   Another way to analyze the activities of a company is to use the debt to equity ratio. Although leverage can be beneficial by freeing up cash for other investments, too much debt can become a problem. Companies with too much long-term debt may end up financially overburdened with interest payments. The **debt to equity ratio** (**leverage ratio**) measures how much debt a company has relative to its assets by comparing a company's total liabilities to its total owners' (or shareholders') equity. Debt to equity ratio is calculated as

The **debt to equity ratio (leverage ratio)** measures how much debt a company has relative to its assets by comparing a company's total liabilities to its total owners' (or shareholders') equity.

$$\text{debt to equity ratio} = \frac{\text{total equity}}{\text{owners' equity}}$$

The debt to equity ratio can give a general idea of a company's financial leverage. As you may remember from the beginning of this chapter, *leverage* is the amount of debt used to finance a firm's assets. The debt to equity ratio will tell potential investors how much a company is willing to go into debt with creditors, lenders, and suppliers over debt with shareholders. As you can see in Figure 13.6, Google's debt to equity ratio is .25, which means Google has 25 percent debt and 75 percent equity. A ratio above 1 (above 100 percent) shows that a firm has more debt than equity. Creditors and investors may perceive a company as quite risky if it has a very high debt to equity ratio. A lower debt to equity ratio number means that a company is using less leverage and has more equity. It is a good idea for a company to compare its debt to equity ratio with that of the industry standard because having a high debt to equity ratio in some industries is quite acceptable.

To get a better idea of how ratio analysis is used as a comparison tool, see the information displayed in **Table 13.3**. In this case, both companies are in the same industry but Google is much bigger than Yahoo! so comparing absolute numbers is not effective. It appears that Google has a better current ratio than Yahoo!, but the debt to equity ratios are about the same.

Table 13.3   Industry Comparison of Balance Sheet Data for Fiscal Year 2010*

Company	Working Capital Current Assets − Current Liabilities	Current Ratio Current Assets/Current Liabilities	Debt to Equity Ratio Total Liabilities/Owners' Equity
Google	$31 566	4.15	0.25
	($41 562 − 9996)	($41 562/9996)	($11 610/46 241)
Yahoo!	$2720	2.7	0.19
	($4345 − 1625)	($4345/1625)	($2369/12 558)

*Numbers in US$mil.

Sources: Based on Google Inc., Google 2010 Annual Report, *http://investor.google.com/pdf/2010_google_annual_report.pdf, and Yahoo! Inc., "Balance Sheet,"* Finance.Yahoo.com, *December 31, 2010, http://finance.yahoo.com/q/bs?s=YHOO&annual, Accessed June 25, 2011.*

Income Statements

Revenue is any monies received by a company from sales of goods or services or from other sources such as licensing fees, rental fees, or interest earned.

Expenses are the costs incurred (an outflow of money) while operating a business.

The **bottom line** refers to the difference of money in and money out, the profit or loss.

What does an income statement show?   An income statement reflects the profitability of a company by showing how much money the company takes in (*revenue*) and how much money it spends (*expenses*). **Revenue** is any monies received by a company from sales of goods or services or from other sources such as licensing fees, rental fees, or interest earned. **Expenses** are the costs incurred (an outflow of money) while operating a business. The difference of money in and money out is the profit or loss, sometimes referred to as the **bottom line**. Besides showing overall profitability, income statements also indicate how effectively management is controlling expenses by pinpointing abnormal or excessive expenditures, highlighting unexpected increases in costs of goods sold, or showing a change in returns.

What are the components of an income statement?   Recall that the balance sheet relates directly to the fundamental accounting equation: assets = liabilities + owners' equity. Similarly, income statements also work around an equation:

$$\text{revenues} - \text{expenses} = \text{profit (or loss)}$$

The income statement is grouped into four main categories: revenues, costs of goods sold, operating expenses, and net income, which are arranged in the following formula:

$$((\text{revenue} - \text{cost of goods}) - \text{operating expenses}) - \text{taxes} = \text{net income or (loss)}$$

Figure 13.7 shows an income statement for Google Inc. Let's look at each of these components in more detail, and then see how they all fit together on an income statement.

Revenue   If a company has several different product lines or businesses, the income statement shows each product or division in categories to distinguish how much each generated in revenue. For example, Starbucks breaks down its revenue into

Google Inc.
Summary Income Statement
as of December 31, 2010
(in millions of U.S. Dollars)

Total Revenue	**$29 321**
Cost of Goods Sold	(10 417)
Gross Profit	**$18 904**
Operating Expenses	
Research Development	$3762
Selling General and Administrative	4761
Total Operating Expenses	**(8523)**
Net Income Before Interest and Taxes	**$10 381**
Interest Income	579
Realized Gains on Marketable Securities, Net	185
Foreign Currency Exchange Losses, Net	(355)
Other	6
Less: Income Tax Expense	(2291)
Net Income	**$8505**

Figure 13.7   Summary Income Statement for Google Inc.

Source: Based on Google Investor Relations, Google Inc. (GOOG) 2010 Annual Report, Retrieved on June 25, 2011 from http://investor.google.com/pdf/2010_google_annual_report.pdf

two sources: retail and specialty. Revenue generated from retail sources is from sales made at all Starbucks stores. Specialty sales include revenue generated from licensing arrangements, food service accounts, and other initiatives related to core businesses.[19]

Cost of Goods Sold   An income statement delineates several categories of expenses. The first category of expenses, cost of goods sold (COGS), is a separate item on an income statement. **Cost of goods sold (COGS)** are the variable expenses a company incurs to manufacture and sell a product, including the price of raw materials used in creating the good along with the labour costs used to produce and sell the items. For Starbucks, obviously, the costs of coffee beans, cups, milk, and sugar are included in COGS. When you subtract cost of goods sold (or cost of sales) from revenue (total sales), the result is **gross profit**. Gross profit tells you how much money a company makes just from its products and how efficiently management controls costs in the production process. In addition, analysts use gross profit to calculate one of the most fundamental performance ratios used to compare the profitability of companies: *gross profit margin* (which will be discussed later in this chapter).

Operating Expenses   Although it is certainly important to identify the costs associated with producing the product or service, it is also important to identify **operating expenses**, the overhead costs incurred with running the business. Operating expenses include sales, general, and administrative expenses. These costs may consist of items such as rent, salaries, wages, utilities, depreciation, and insurance. Expenses associated with research and development of new products also are included in operating expenses. Unlike costs of goods sold, operating expenses usually do not vary with the level of sales or production and are constant or "fixed." Outside interested parties (lenders and investors) watch operating expenses closely as an indication of managerial efficiency. Management's goal is to keep operating expenses as low as possible without negatively affecting the underlying business. The amount of profit realized from the business's operations (**operating income**) is determined when operating expenses are subtracted from gross profit.

Management focuses on operating income as they prepare and monitor budgets. Some feel that operating income is a more reliable and meaningful indicator of profitability than gross profit since it reflects management's ability to control operating expenses. But, it is still not the "bottom line." Adding or subtracting any other income or expense, such as interest payments on outstanding debt obligations or earnings from investments, adjusts operating income further. Lastly, taxes paid to the local and federal governments are subtracted to determine net income (or net income after taxes). **Net income** (or **loss**) is the revenue remaining after all costs and expenses, including taxes, have been paid. It is the "bottom line" and is usually stated on the very last line of an income statement. For publicly owned companies, however, net income is further adjusted by dividend payments to stockholders, resulting in *adjusted net income*.

Analyzing Income Statements

How do I analyze an income statement?
One of the main purposes of the income statement is to report a company's earnings to its shareholders. However, an income statement reveals much more about a company, such as how effectively management controls expenses or how the company's profits compare to others in its industry. Specifically, the measurements that reveal this information are:

- gross profit margin
- operating profit margin
- earnings per share (EPS)

Let's look at each measurement in detail to understand the differences between them and learn how they are used to analyze a company's financial health.

How can I determine a company's overall profitability?
A company's profitability and efficiency can be determined at two levels: profitability of production, and profitability of operations. The **gross profit margin** determines a company's profitability of

Cost of goods sold (COGS) are the variable expenses a company incurs to manufacture and sell a product, including the price of raw materials used in creating the good along with the labour costs used to produce and sell the items.

Gross profit is calculated by subtracting cost of goods sold (or cost of sales) from revenue (total sales).

Operating expenses are the overhead costs incurred with running the business. They include sales, general, and administrative expenses. These costs may consist of items such as rent, salaries, wages, utilities, depreciation, and insurance.

Operating income is determined when operating expenses are subtracted from gross profit.

Net income (or **loss**) is the revenue remaining after all costs and expenses, including taxes, have been paid. It is the "bottom line" and is usually stated on the very last line of an income statement.

The **gross profit margin** determines a company's profitability of production. It indicates how efficient management is in using its labour and raw materials to produce goods.

13

Table 13.4   Benefit of Ratio Analysis

	Based on Annual Income Statement Data for Fiscal Year 2010	
Company	Gross Profit*	Gross Profit Margin
	Revenue − Cost of Goods Sold	Gross Profit/Revenue × 100
Google	$18 904	64.5
	($29 321 − 10 417)	($18 904/29 321 × 100)
Yahoo!	$3697	58.5
	($6324 − 2627)	($3697/6324 × 100)

* Numbers in US$mil.

Sources: Based on Google Inc., Google 2010 Annual Report, *http://investor.google.com/pdf/2010_google_annual_report.pdf, and Yahoo! Inc., "Balance Sheet," Finance.Yahoo.com, December 31, 2010, http://finance.yahoo.com/q/bs?s=YHOO&annual, Accessed June 25, 2011.*

production. It indicates how efficient management is in using its labour and raw materials to produce goods. A gross profit margin is calculated as

$$\text{gross profit margin} = \frac{(\text{total revenue} - \text{COGS})}{\text{total revenue}}$$

The **operating profit margin** determines a company's profitability of operations. It indicates how efficiently management is in using business operations to generate a profit.

The **operating profit margin** determines a company's profitability of operations. It indicates how efficiently management is in using business operations to generate a profit. An operating profit margin is calculated as

$$\text{operating profit margin} = \frac{(\text{total revenue} - \text{COGS}) - \text{operating expenses}}{\text{total revenue}}$$

Gross profit margin and operating profit margin are equally important to management as well as investors. You may notice they are both ratios, and, as you have learned in this chapter, ratios are best used when comparing two or more companies. Look at **Table 13.4**. Google's gross profit (revenue less cost of goods sold) for 2010 is more than US$18 billion. Yahoo!'s gross profit of US$3 billion seems to pale in comparison. However, you'll notice that while the two companies' gross profits are quite different, their gross profit margins are very close.

How much of the company's profit belongs to the shareholders?
The portion of a company's profit allocated to the stockholders on a per-share basis is determined by calculating **earnings per share**. The general formula for earnings per share is calculated as

Earnings per share determines the portion of a company's profit allocated to the stockholders on a per-share basis.

$$\text{earnings per share} = \frac{\text{net income}}{\text{outstanding shares}}$$

Again, looking at the earning per share number in isolation is not completely meaningful. For example, it might seem reasonable to assume that a company with higher earnings per share will be the better company to invest in than one with lower earnings per share. However, a highly efficient company—and potential good investment—can have low earnings per share ratio simply because it has a large number of outstanding shares. **Shares outstanding** are common shares authorized, issued, and purchased by investors. Still, shareholders and prospective investors monitor earnings per share closely. In some instances, the pressure of maintaining a continued growth record in net income or earnings per share has led management to "cook the books" or misrepresent financial information so that the business's bottom line appears better than it actually is. Such fraudulent behaviour was the notable downfall of companies such as Enron, World-Com, and Tyco, and is the reason why the *Sarbanes-Oxley Act* of 2002 was passed into law. Therefore, it is best not to rely on any one financial measure and to look at the financial statements and other information as a whole.

Shares outstanding are common *shares* authorized, issued, and purchased by investors.

Statement of Cash Flows

What is the statement of cash flows?
You have just looked at two important financial statements, the balance sheet and the income statement. The cash flow statement

Google Inc.
Summary Cash Flow Statement
as of December 31 2010
(in millions of U.S. Dollars)

Net Income	**$8505**
Operating Activities, Cash Flows Provided by or Used in	
Depreciation and Amortization of Property and Equipment	1067
Amortization of Intangible and Other Assets	329
Adjustments to Net Income	1279
Changes in Accounts Receivables	(1129)
Changes in Liabilities	1342
Changes in Inventories	0
Changes in Other Operating Activities	(312)
Total Cash Flow from Operating Activities	**$11 081**
Investing Activities, Cash Flows Provided by or Used in	
Capital Expenditures	($4018)
Investments	(7956)
Other Cash Flows from Investing Activities	1294
Total Cash Flows from Investing Activities	**($10 680)**
Financing Activities, Cash Flows Provided by or Used in	
Dividends Paid	$0
Net Proceeds (Payments) from Stock-Based Award Activities	294
Excess Tax Benefits from Stock-Based Award Activities	94
Sale Purchase of Stock	(801)
Net Borrowings	3463
Total Cash Flows from Financing Activities	**($3050)**
Effect of Exchange Rate Changes	(19)
Change in Cash and Cash Equivalents	**$3432**

Figure 13.8 Summary Cash Flow Statement for Google Inc.

Source: Based on Google Investor Relations, Google Inc. (GOOG) 2010 Annual Report, Retrieved on June 25, 2011 from http://investor.google.com/pdf/2010_google_annual_report.pdf

(or statement of cash flows) is the third important financial statement and gives some information that the other two financial statements do not show. The balance sheet is a snapshot of a company's financial position, and the income statement reflects a company's profitability over a specific period. A statement of cash flows is different because it does not reflect the amount of incoming and outgoing transactions that have been recorded on credit. Instead, it only displays cash transactions, similar to a chequebook register. As shown in **Figure 13.8**, the cash flow statement organizes and reports cash generated in three business components:

1. *Operating activities* measures cash used or provided by the core business of the company.
2. *Investing activities* represents the cash involved in the purchase or sale of investments or income-producing assets such as buildings and equipment.
3. *Financing activities* shows the cash exchanged between the firm and its owners (or shareholders) and creditors, including dividend payments and debt service.

Why is the statement of cash flows important? The statement of cash flows tells a story that the income statement does not. The income statement reports revenue receipts and expense payments. Because revenue and expenses often are accrued (earned but not paid), the income statement does not tell how efficiently management generates and uses cash. The statement of cash flows, because it focuses specifically on cash, provides this important information. It shows whether all the revenues booked on the income

worth of the business. At any point in time, the information in the balance sheet is used to answer questions such as "Is the business in a good position to expand?" and "Does the business have enough cash to ride out an anticipated slow-down in sales?" In addition, by analyzing how a balance sheet changes over time, financial managers can identify trends and then suggest strategies to manage accounts receivable and payable in a way that is most beneficial to the company's bottom line.

Balance sheets are based on the most fundamental equation in business accounting:

$$\overbrace{\text{assets} = \text{liabilities} + \text{owners' equity}}^{\text{claims on assets}}$$

There are three main calculations one can do using information from a balance sheet to determine a company's financial health and liquidity:

1. *Working capital:* current assets – current liabilities
2. *Current ratio:* current assets ÷ current liabilities
3. *Debt to equity ratio:* total liabilities ÷ owners' equity

An **income statement** shows how much money is coming into a company (**revenue**) and how much money a company is spending (**expenses**) over a period. It shows how well a company has done in terms of profit and loss.

$$\text{revenues} - \text{expenses} = \text{profit (or loss)}$$

The income statement is grouped into four main categories: revenues, costs of goods sold, operating expenses, and net income, which are arranged in the following formula:

$$((\text{revenue} - \text{cost of goods}) - \text{operating expenses})$$
$$- \text{taxes} = \text{net income or (loss)}$$

A company's profitability and efficiency can be determined at two levels: profitability of production, and profitability of operations, which have their own equations based on income statement information.

A **statement of cash** flows shows the exchange of money between a company and everyone else it deals with over a period. It shows where cash was used.

The statement of cash flows tells a story that the income statement does not. The income statement reports revenue receipts and expense payments. Because revenue and expenses often are accrued (earned but not paid), the income statement does not tell how efficiently management generates and uses cash. The statement of cash flows, because it focuses specifically on cash, provides this important information. It shows whether all the revenues booked on the income statement have actually been collected.

KEY TERMS

accounting   (p. 379)
accounts payable   (p. 387)
accounts receivable
   (p. 386)
accrued expenses   (p. 387)
amortization   (p. 387)
annual reports   (p. 382)
assets   (p. 382)
auditing   (p. 382)
balance sheet   (p. 385)
bookkeeping   (p. 382)
bottom line   (p. 390)
budget   (p. 370)
capital budget   (p. 370)
cash flow   (p. 371)
certified general accountant
   (CGA)   (p. 380)
certified management
   accountant (CMA)   (p. 380)
chartered accountant (CA)
   (p. 380)
commercial bank   (p. 374)
commercial finance company
   (p. 374)
commercial paper   (p. 374)
convertible bond   (p. 376)
corporate accounting
   (p. 381)
corporate bond   (p. 376)
cost of goods sold (COGS)
   (p. 391)

current assets   (p. 386)
current liabilities (or short-
   term liabilities)   (p. 387)
current ratio (or liquidity
   ratio)   (p. 388)
debt financing   (p. 375)
debt to equity ratio (leverage
   ratio)   (p. 389)
depreciation   (p. 386)
dividends   (p. 377)
double entry bookkeeping
   (p. 384)
earnings per share
   (p. 392)
equity   (p. 377)
equity financing   (p. 375)
expenses   (p. 390)
factoring   (p. 374)
financial accounting
   (p. 381)
financial management
   (p. 369)
financial manager or chief
   financial officer (CFO)
   (p. 369)
financial statements
   (p. 385)
fixed assets   (p. 386)
forecasts   (p. 370)
forensic accountant
   (p. 382)

fundamental accounting
   equation   (p. 382)
goodwill   (p. 387)
government and non-profit
   accounting   (p. 382)
gross profit   (p. 391)
gross profit margin   (p. 391)
income statement
   (p. 385)
initial public offering (IPO)
   (p. 377)
intangible assets   (p. 387)
interest   (p. 376)
inventory   (p. 387)
investment instruments
   (p. 378)
issuing common stock
   (p. 377)
leverage   (p. 378)
liabilities   (p. 382)
line of credit   (p. 374)
liquidity   (p. 371)
loan   (p. 376)
long-term liabilities
   (p. 387)
managerial accounting
   (p. 381)
net income (or loss)
   (p. 391)
operating (master) budget
   (p. 370)

operating expenses   (p. 391)
operating income   (p. 391)
operating profit margin
   (p. 392)
optimal capital structure
   (p. 378)
owners' equity   (p. 382)
preferred stock   (p. 377)
private accountant   (p. 380)
promissory note   (p. 373)
public accountant   (p. 380)
ratio analysis   (p. 388)
retained earnings   (p. 377)
revenue   (p. 390)
secured bonds   (p. 376)
secured loan   (p. 374)
shares outstanding
   (p. 392)
short-term financing
   (p. 373)
sinking fund   (p. 376)
statement of cash
   (p. 385)
stock   (p. 377)
tax accounting   (p. 382)
trade credit   (p. 373)
unsecured bonds (or
   debenture bonds)
   (p. 376)
unsecured loan   (p. 374)
working capital   (p. 388)

CRITICAL THINKING QUESTIONS

1. Jason worked in a deli for five years before starting his own sandwich delivery store. The business has been quite successful for two years. The quality of the service and the sandwiches has caused an increased demand for his products. Jason now thinks he needs to buy more cars to deliver the sandwiches. He is trying to decide on the most appropriate way of financing the acquisition of two cars.
   a. What methods of financing should Jason consider?
   b. What information will Jason need to have to help make his decision?
   c. How would the financing decisions change if Jason also decided to open another store at a new location?
2. What are the key financial statements, and what is the importance of financial statements? What information do they contain? Which statement do shareholders typically find most useful? Why? What about independent contractors considering working with a firm, which statements would be most useful for them?
3. Discuss the role of independent auditors for a company. Over the past decade, why have independent auditors been under scrutiny by the government?
4. Recall Arnold Sawyer from the third section. What advice would you give to him? Why was recording the transactions in QuickBooks not enough?
5. What is the relationship between the balance sheet and the income statement?

APPLICATION EXERCISES

1. **Cash Flow Simulation.** How well would you be able to manage the cash flow of a company? To find out, go to www.bized.co.uk/learn/business/accounting/cashflow/simulation/index.htm and play the Cash Flow simulation game. Go through the tutorial and then play the simulation. Even though this is based on a company in the United Kingdom, the principle of cash flow is universal. How did you do?
2. **Balancing a Budget.** Companies are not the only entities that must create budgets. Cities, provinces, and other governmental agencies must also prepare budgets, but unlike corporations, they can raise or lower taxes to help balance the budget. However, raising taxes is not always politically favourable, and while lowering taxes helps get the votes, it is not always fiscally prudent. How would you do if you were just hired to close the US$3.8 billion budget deficit for New York City? Find out by playing the Budget Game: http://www.gothamgazette.com/budgetgame.
3. **Exploring Career Possibilities.** Visit job search sites such as www.monster.ca and find postings for financial managers and accountants. What are the job specifications and requirements? What companies are advertising the openings? Are these careers you are interested in pursuing? Why or why not?
4. **Securing Financing.** Go to the website of a local bank and research its options for short-term business financing. What are the terms of its small business loans and lines of credit? Does it offer other commercial financing options, such as factoring? If you were going to open a small business, how would you go about financing it, based on what you learned?
5. **Analyzing Current Ratios.** Many trade associations and other specialized organizations publish financial ratios. Industry averages of various types of businesses can be obtained for a fee from organizations such as Statistics Canada, Dun & Bradstreet Canada, RMA Annual Statement Studies, Standard and Poor's Corporation, etc. You can also find this information online free of charge, visit http://www.bizminer.com/products/analysis/industry/financial-ratios-profiles.php (free sample reports), or http://www.reuters.com/finance/industries/allIndustries, or http://www.creditguru.com/ratios/inr.htm to get started in your search to locate the current ratios for several industries of your choice. How do the ratios compare? What does this number tell you about the industry? What conclusions can you draw based on your findings?

GLOBAL 500 RESEARCH PROJECT

INSTRUCTIONS

1. Choose a Global 500 company from *Fortune* magazine's annual rankings at http://money.cnn.com/magazines/fortune/global500/.
2. Research:
   a. Locate last year's annual report for the company. Calculate its current ratio. What did you discover? How does this ratio compare to the industry average?
   b. How much revenue did the company generate last year? How much of that was net profit or loss?
   c. Has the company been growing based on revenue? Locate these figures for the past five years and calculate the percentage of increase (or decrease) for each year.
   d. Calculate the company's debt to equity ratio. How much debt does this company have? How might this debt ratio be viewed by investors and creditors?
   e. Review the company's financial statements for last year and calculate the company's gross profit margin, operating profit margin, and earnings per share. How profitable is this company? Would you want to invest?
3. Prepare a report and submit to your professor.

13

TEAM TIME

Industry Analysis
Assemble into groups of four or five.

PROCESS

Step 1. As a group, decide on an industry. Alone or with a partner, pick a company in that industry. The company should be publicly traded so that financial records are easily available.

Step 2. Alone or with a partner, review the annual report and the three key financial statements for the company you chose and prepare a brief analysis of the company's financial situation.

Then, calculate the ratios covered in this chapter, and find three other ratios that are meaningful to your analysis.

Step 3. When your report is completed, combine your information with the information from others members of your group into an industry analysis, and determine how each company fits into the industry. Would the conclusions from your independent analysis change once you see the analyses of other companies in the industry?

Step 4. As a group, prepare a presentation summarizing your findings for the industry and each company in the industry and present it to the class.

ETHICS AND RESPONSIBILITY

Getting to the Bottom of the *Sarbanes-Oxley Act*
In 2002, U.S. president George W. Bush signed the *Sarbanes-Oxley Act* into law in the aftermath of some of the largest financial and accounting scandals in recent U.S. history. The intent of the law is to protect investors from accounting fraud.

Reports indicate that complying with the law's requirements has cost U.S. businesses tens of millions of dollars. In addition, critics state that complying with *Sarbanes-Oxley* has stripped CEOs of their creativity and is making U.S. companies less competitive internationally,[20] although support for the act's provisions is slowly gaining.

Exercise
Research the history behind the *Sarbanes-Oxley Act* as well as current compliance with the act's provisions. Then, prepare a brief report summarizing your answers to the following questions:

1. What specifically are companies asked to do?
2. How might these requirements affect "CEO creativity" and international competitiveness?
3. What are your thoughts as to the need for and effectiveness of this act? Is it effective, or is it causing more harm than good? Why, and what other measures, if any, do you think should be taken to address these issues?

CLOSING CASE

A Googol of Dollars for Google

Like many Silicon Valley success stories, Internet search engine Google arose from humble beginnings. The company started as a thesis project developed and refined by two students in their Stanford University dorm room. Larry Page and Sergey Brin wanted to organize the chaotic data on the Internet by developing a new way to search and retrieve information from the Web. Other Internet search engines already existed at the time, but Page and Brin wanted a system that was easy to use and could generate results in a split second. After leaving their Ph.D. studies behind, the two students formed Google Inc. The seemingly senseless company name was formed from the word *googol*, which is a mathematical term for a 1 followed by 100 zeros. A googol, or Google, represented the vast amount of information on the Web and the company's mission to organize it. What Page and Brin did not know was that those zeroes also represented the amount of money their search engine would eventually generate.[21]

Originally, Page and Brin had no interest in starting their own company. They simply wanted to sell their technology to a second party. It was actually David Filo, friend and founder of Yahoo!, who convinced the two young men to start a search engine company of their own. By the beginning of 1998, Page and Brin were ready to move forward, but they needed some long-term financing to get the company on its feet. The two students approached university faculty member Andy Bechtolsheim to be their first investor. Bechtolsheim provided Google with

US$100 000. The initial investment was an encouraging start. By the end of 1998, Brin was able to acquire nearly US$1 million in funding for their company. Soon, a staff of eight was running a system that answered more than 500 000 queries a day. Google was proving to be a very wise investment. Later that year, Google announced that it had secured US$25 million in funding from two venture capital firms in Silicon Valley.

Now that Google had the funds to set up an office, they needed to start turning a profit. Selling search services to Internet giants such as AOL/Netscape and Virgin Net generated Google's initial revenue. However, it was advertising programs that catapulted Google's balance sheet into the black. By the end of 2000, Google was receiving 100 million hits a day, giving the company a larger audience than the Super Bowl. It was clear to Google's financial management team that an advertising program would be a lucrative venture. Google developed a keyword-target advertising program that allowed website owners to purchase keywords or phrases that potential customers might use in a search. If one of those keywords is typed into the Google search engine, the company is placed at the top of the search results page as a sponsored link.

In order to tailor to the needs of smaller businesses, Google established AdWord. The program allowed businesses to place a small advertisement along the edge of a search results page for certain keywords. Google advertising programs were so successful that by 2001, only three years after its incorporation,

Google was a profitable company. The following year, Google looked to expand its advertising program to include AdSense. The program served as a way for advertisers to buy ad space on keyword-targeted sites outside Google and those site owners to profit from the sale of the space.

Over the last six years, Google has continued to make the majority of its revenue from advertising. In fact, in 2010 Google's advertising revenues totalled about US$28.2 billion, which accounts for 96 percent of the company's total revenue.[22] While Google continues to consider providing users with the ultimate search engine to be its primary goal, it still strives to be a profitable business. Google uses the statement "You can make money without doing evil" (or simply put "Don't do evil") as one of its business philosophies.[23] In following this philosophy, it does not use flashy or obtrusive advertisements and only provides users with advertisements that are relevant to their search. This

sharp form of managerial accounting has allowed Google to stay true to Page and Brin's original mission, as well as achieve a net income of more than US$8.5 billion in 2010.[24]

DISCUSSION QUESTIONS

1. Since Google is an Internet service company and does not have to worry about the cost of goods sold, why would Page and Brin need to get long-term financial support to start their business? What operating expenses might they encounter during their first year?
2. Why did Google choose to incorporate advertising into its business plan? What do you think Google's bottom line would look like if it only sold search services?
3. How much of Google's success can be attributed to strong managerial accounting? Explain.

MyBusinessLab CHAPTER RESOURCES

MyBusinessLab in an online learning and testing environment that features the perfect study tools to help you master the concepts covered in this chapter. Log in to MyBusinessLab at www.pearsoned.ca/mybusinesslab to test your knowledge of key chapter concepts, participate in simulations modelled on real-world business situations, and explore the following additional practice tools:

- Study Plan
- Audio Chapter Summaries
- Glossary Flashcards
- eText
- BizChat Discussion Boards
- BizSkills Simulation: Financial Management

Video Cases:
To access the Chapter 13 Video Cases: The Capital Structure Choice: Cisco; McDonald's: Accounting for Billions of Hamburgers, see the Activities folder in the Assessment section of MyBusinessLab.

Web Case:
To access the Chapter 13 Web Case, see the Activities folder in the Assessment section of MyBusinessLab

Appendix 13A:
"Securities and Investments": Visit MyBusinessLab, where the financing lesson from Chapter 13 is taken to a deeper level. You

will learn about investing in stocks and bonds, the differences among bond mutual funds, money market funds, and equity funds, and the factors that lead to changes in stock price.

Career Skills:
Visit the Career Skills module "Personal Finance" on MyBusinessLab, where you'll learn how to apply the principles of finance to managing the ways in which your personal monies are budgeted, saved, invested, preserved for future life events, and protected against risks. A plan for reducing expenses and increasing assets helps ensure that your money lasts throughout your lifetime.

Glossary

absolute advantage a country's ability to produce more of a good or service than any other country. (97)

accounting the recording, classifying, summarizing, and interpreting financial events in order to communicate useful financial information. It involves tracking a business's income and expenses through a process of recording financial transactions. (379)

accounts payable obligations a company owes to vendors and creditors. (387)

accounts receivable amounts due to the company from customers who have purchased goods or services on credit. (386)

accrued expenses include payroll, commissions, and benefits that have been earned but not paid to employees. (387)

acquisition occurs when one company or investor group buys a corporation and the identity of the acquired company might be lost. (145)

action learning another management development training approach that focuses on solving real problems on actual work projects. (217)

administrative trade barriers government rules designed to limit imports. (100)

advertising paid, impersonal mass communication from an identified sponsor to persuade or influence a targeted audience. (345)

advisory board a group of individuals who offer guidance to the new business owner . (132)

adware any software application that displays banner ads or pop-up ads while the program is running. (263)

agents/brokers intermediaries that facilitate negotiations between buyers and sellers of goods and services but never take title (ownership) of the products traded. (355)

amoral behaviour occurs when a person has no sense of right and wrong and no interest in the moral consequences of his or her actions. (61)

amortization the process of applying those long-term expenses to intangible assets such as goodwill or patents. (387)

Angel Investors wealthy individuals who are willing to put up their own money in hopes of a profit return later on. (134)

annual reports documents produced once a year to present the current financial state of a company and future expectations. (381)

apprentice training program trains individuals through classroom or formal instruction and on-the-job training. (216)

arbitration a process in which the disputing parties present their case to a thirdparty intermediary who examines all the evidence and then makes a decision (usually binding) for the parties. (232)

articles of incorporation lay out the general nature of the corporation, the name of the corporation and its directors, the type and number of shares to be issued, and location of the company's operations. (142)

assembly line (or production line) is used to move partially complete products from one worker to the next on a conveyor belt. (275)

assets what the company owns. (382)

auditing responsible for reviewing and evaluating the accuracy of financial reports. (381)

autocratic leader makes decisions without consulting others. (169)

B2B product classifications (or industrial product classifications) emerge from strategic marketing mix plans for B2B products: equipment; maintenance, repair, and operating (MRO) products; raw and processed materials; component parts; and specialized professional services. (334)

balance of payments a summary of a country's international financial transactions. (111)

balance of trade the difference between the value of a country's exports and the value of its imports during a specific time. (110)

balance sheet shows what the company owns and what it has borrowed (owes) at a fixed point in time and shows the net worth of the business. (385)

Bank of Canada acts as the federal government's financial advisor and is responsible for promoting the economic and financial well-being of Canada. It manages the country's money supply through its monetary policy to control inflation. (49)

bargaining unit a group of employees who negotiate with the employer for better working conditions or pay. (232)

bartering involves people trading goods or services without an exchange of money. The "price" of something is determined by the needs of each person in the bartering exchange and what they are willing to trade. (32)

behavioural interviews conducted to evaluate a candidate's experience and behaviours so the employer can determine the applicant's potential for success in the job. (214)

behavioural segmentation market segmentation based on certain consumer behaviour characteristics, such as the benefits sought by the consumer, the extent to which the product is consumed, brand loyalty, price sensitivity, and the ways in which the product is used. (315)

benefits come in many forms and provide additional compensation to employees beyond base wages. (220)

Big Five also referred to as the Five Factor Model, is one of the most widely accepted models of personality. The model categorizes most human personality traits into five broad dimensions and then assigns people a score for each dimension: openness, conscientiousness, extraversion, agreeableness, and neuroticism (emotional stability). (191)

bill of material lists the items and the number of each required to make that specific product. (283)

board of directors elected by shareholders to govern and handle the overall management of the corporation. (143)

bona fide job requirement an ability genuinely needed to perform a job. A person who lacks such a necessary ability can be legitimately denied employment (e.g., a person with a visual impairment will be denied employment as a bus driver). (234)

bookkeeping the systematic recording of a company's every financial transaction. (382)

bottom line refers to the difference of money in and money out, the profit or loss. (390)

boycott occurs when union members and their supporters refuse to buy or handle the company's products or services. (232)

brand a name, term, symbol, or design that distinguishes a company and its products from all others. (335)

brand association involves connecting a brand with other positive attributes, including image, product features, usage situations, organizational associations, brand personality, and symbols. (336)

brand awareness refers to the extent to which a particular brand name is familiar within a particular product category. (336)

brand equity the overall value of a brand's strength in the market. (336)

brand insistence the highest degree of brand loyalty. It can turn a product into a specialty good or service that can command a much higher price. (335)

brand loyalty the degree to which customers consistently prefer one brand over all others. (335)

brand manager (or product manager) is responsible for the 4 Ps of marketing a specific product or product line. Brand managers attempt to increase the product's perceived value to customers in order to increase brand equity. (336)

break-even analysis determines the production level for which total revenue is just enough to cover total costs. (340)

budget a financial plan that outlines the company's planned cash flows, expected operating expenses, and anticipated revenues. (370)

budget deficit occurs when the money being spent by government exceeds the money coming into government. (50)

budget surplus occurs when the money coming into the government exceeds the money being spent by government. (50)

bundling occurs when two or more products that usually complement one another are combined and sold at a single price. (342)

business any activity that provides goods or services in exchange for other goods and services or money, based on their perceived worth. (6)

business cycle describes how the economy fluctuates over time, going through periods of increased growth (expansion) and decreased growth (contraction). (48)

business ethics the application of ethical behaviour in a business context. It deals with internal values that are part of corporate culture and shapes decisions and actions concerning social responsibility. (66)

business incubators organizations that support start-up businesses by offering resources such as administrative services, technical support, business networking, and sources of financing that a group of startup companies share. (132)

business law refers to rules, statutes, codes, and regulations established to provide a legal framework within which business may be conducted. (75)

business plan a formal document that states the goals of the business as well as the plan for reaching those goals. (131)

business-to-business (B2B) market a market in which businesses purchase goods and services from other businesses. (315)

business-to-business (B2B) products (or industrial products) are goods and services purchased by businesses for further processing or resale or are used in facilitating business operations. (333)

business-to-business (B2B) sales promotions (or trade sales promotions) incentives to push a product through the distribution system to final consumers. (352)

business-to-business (B2B) transactions involve the exchange of products, services, and information between businesses on the Internet. (258)

business-to-consumer (B2C) transactions refer to e-business that takes place between businesses and consumers. (259)

bylaws the rules of a corporation, established by the board of directors during the process of starting a corporation. (143)

Canada Labour Code (federal level) together with the provincial Employment Standards Acts and Labour Codes (at the provincial level), defines the rights and obligations of individuals as workers, union members, and employers in the workplace. (234)

Canadian Charter of Rights and Freedoms a binding legal document that protects the basic human rights of all Canadians, such as fundamental freedoms, democratic rights, mobility rights, legal rights, equality rights, and language rights. (75)

Canadian Federation of Independent Business (CFIB) an advocacy organization representing more than 108 000 small and medium-sized enterprises. (127)

Canadian Human Rights Act extends the law to ensure equal opportunity to individuals who may be victims of discriminatory practices based on a set of prohibited grounds (e.g., gender, disability, or religion). (76)

capacity the amount of a product or service that a company can produce under normal working conditions in a given time period. (282)

capital investments in the form of money, equipment, supplies, computers, and any other tangible thing of value. (141)

capital budget considers the company's long-range plans and outlines the expected financial needs for significant capital purchases such as real estate, manufacturing equipment, plant expansions, or technology. (370)

capital flight the transfer of domestic funds into foreign currency held outside the country. (112)

capitalism also called a market economy, free market, or free enterprise, allows freedom of choice and encourages private ownership of the resources required to make and provide goods and services consumers enjoy. (31)

cash flow the movement of money in and out of a business over a defined period (weekly, monthly, or quarterly). (371)

Cattell 16 personality factors (16 PF) suggest that each of us has a consistent and constant underlying personality. (193)

cellular layout (or group technology layout) combines aspects from both product and fixed-position layout: workers are arranged into self-contained, stand-alone production units (or cells of small work teams) (283)

certified general accountant (CGA) provides the financial information for use by stockholders, government, creditors, and others "outside" an organization. (380)

certified management accountant (CMA) provides financial information to managers and other corporate decision makers "inside" the corporation and helps formulate policy and strategic plans. (380)

Charities Directorate of the Canada Revenue Agency (CRA) registers qualifying organizations as charities, provides information to donors, and handles audit and compliance activities. (78)

chartered accountant (CA) provides financial information for use by stockholders, government, creditors, and others "outside" an organization. The CA can work in both public and private sector fields of business and finance. (380)

chief financial officer (CFO) (or financial manager) oversees the financial operations of a company. (369)

chief information officer (CIO) responsible for the information technology of an organization, including systems design and development, data centre operations, creating policies regarding security and intellectual property, and updating or replacing computer systems and software. (244)

circular flow of Canada's economy an economic cycle in which businesses and households provide government with tax payments generated from revenue and wages, and government uses the tax money to provide businesses and households with incentives, programs, and services. (29)

coaching/understudy program when the employee works directly with senior management in planning and other managerial functions. (217)

collective bargaining a process in which workers (through a union) negotiate with the employers for better work conditions and terms of employment. (232)

collective bargaining agreement the result of union-employer negotiations and forces the employer to abide by the conditions specified in the agreement. Change can only be made through subsequent negotiations. (232)

commercial banks financial institutions that raise funds from businesses and individuals in the form of chequing and savings accounts and use those funds to make loans to businesses and individuals. (374)

commercial finance company not considered a bank, but rather a financial institution that makes short-term loans to borrowers who offer tangible assets as collateral. (374)

commercial paper an unsecured (that is, it does not need collateral) short-term debt instrument of $100 000 or more, typically issued by a corporation to bridge a cash flow gap created by large accounts receivable, inventory, or payroll. (374)

communism an economic system in which government makes all economic decisions and controls all the social services and many of the major resources required for production of goods and services. (30)

comparative advantage a country's ability to produce a good or service relatively more efficiently than any other country. (97)

compensation payment for work performed, comes in a variety of forms, including money, bonuses, work/life benefits, health insurance, and retirement plans. (219)

competition arises when two or more businesses contend with one another to attract customers and gain an advantage. (38)

Competition Act a federal law regulating most business conduct in Canada. Its criminal and civil provisions are aimed at preventing anti-competitive practices in the marketplace. (77)

competition-based pricing a pricing strategy based on what the competition is charging. Revenues and costs are secondary. (341)

computer-aided design (CAD) refers to the use of a computer to create two-dimensional or threedimensional models of physical parts. (277)

computer-aided manufacturing (CAM) uses the design data to control the machinery used in the manufacturing process. (278)

computer-integrated manufacturing (CIM) combines design and manufacturing functions with other functions such as order taking, shipment, and billing. (278)

conceptual skills involve the ability to think abstractly in order to picture the organization as a whole and to understand its relationship to the rest of the business community. (156)

consumer behaviour refers to the ways individuals or organizations search for, evaluate, purchase, use, and dispose of goods and services. (315)

consumer market a market in which individuals purchase goods and services for personal consumption. (315)

consumer price index (CPI) a benchmark used to track changes in prices over time. The CPI measures price changes by creating a "market basket" of a specified set of goods and services (including taxes) that represent the average buying pattern of urban households. (46)

consumer product classifications include convenience, shopping, specialty, and unsought goods and services. (333)

consumer products goods and services purchased by households for personal consumption. (333)

consumer sales promotions incentives designed to increase final consumer demand for a product. (352)

consumerism a social movement that seeks to increase and strengthen the rights and powers of buyers in relation to sellers. (77)

consumer-to-consumer (C2C) transactions take place between consumers. (260)

contextual advertising ads automatically generated by the content on a specific site. By placing PPC ads on third-party sites, such as blogs and Web forums, they reach readers depending on the content of the particular page instead of search results. (261)

contingency leadership is a more adaptive style of leadership in which managers recognize that they need to be flexible and use whatever style works best for the particular situation. (169)

contingency planning a set of plans that ensures that the organization will run as smoothly as possible during an unexpected disruption. (162)

contingent workers (temporary employees) are individuals who are hired on an as-needed basis; therefore, they lack the status that comes from being a regular, full-time employee. (223)

contract manufacturing occurs when a firm subcontracts part or all of its goods to an outside firm as an alternative to owning and operating its own production facility. (109)

contractionary measures include raising taxes and decreasing government spending in an attempt to slow the economy. (49)

controlled messages include corporate (or institutional) advertising, advocacy advertising, and public service advertising. (349)

controlling ensures that the plans and strategies set in place by management are properly carried out. (170)

convertible bond gives the bondholder the right (but not the obligation) to convert the bond into a predetermined number of shares of the company's stock. (376)

co-operative a business owned and governed by members who use its products or services, not by outside investors. (144)

core values the fundamental beliefs about what is important and appropriate when conducting company activities—affect a company's overall planning processes and operations. (159)

corporate accounting the part of an organization's finance department responsible for gathering and assembling data required for key financial statements. (381)

corporate bond a type of loan issued by a company, not a commercial bank or commercial finance company. It is a formal written agreement to reimburse a loan at a regular interest rate at a given date in time. (376)

corporate code of ethics a formal statement of the organization's commitment to certain values regarding ethics and social issues. (67)

corporate culture a collection of values, norms, and behaviour shared by management and workers that defines the character of the organization. (159)

corporate philanthropy occurs when companies donate some of their profits or resources to charitable organizations. (72)

corporate social responsibility (CSR) a company's obligation to conduct its activities with the aim of achieving social, environmental, and economic development. (68)

corporation a specific form of business organization that is a separate legal entity, that is liable for its own debts, and whose owners' liability is limited to their investment in the company. (142)

cost of goods sold (COGS) the variable expenses a company incurs to manufacture and sell a product, including the price of raw materials used in creating the good along with the labour costs used to produce and sell the items. (391)

cost of living the average monetary cost of the goods and services required to maintain a particular standard of living. It is closely related to the CPI. (46)

cost-based pricing (or cost-plus pricing) is charging a price in relation to the costs of providing the good or service. (340)

cost-plus pricing (or cost-based pricing) is charging a price in relation to the costs of providing the good or service. (340)

countertrade a form of international barter, the swapping of goods and services for other goods and services. (112)

cross-cultural awareness an understanding, appreciation, and sensitivity to foreign culture. (113)

crown corporations businesses owned by the federal government that provide important services to Canadians, including Canada Post, the Canadian Broadcasting Corporation (CBC), and the Royal Canadian Mint. (31)

culture the complex set of values, behaviours, lifestyles, arts, beliefs, and institutions of a population that are passed on from generation to generation. (113)

currency a unit of exchange for the transfer of goods and services, provides a consistent and equitable standard, the value of which is based on an underlying commodity, such as gold. (32)

currency appreciation an increase in the exchange rate value of a nation's currency, causes the relative price of imports to fall as the relative price of exports rises. (110)

currency depreciation a decrease in the exchange rate value of a nation's currency, has the opposite effect on the relative prices of exports and imports. A weak currency causes exports to become cheaper and imports to become more expensive. (110)

current assets those assets that can be turned into cash within a year. (386)

current liabilities (or short-term liabilities) are obligations a company is responsible for paying within a year or less and are listed first on the balance sheet. (387)

current ratio (or liquidity ratio) a measurement used to determine the extent to which a company can meet its current financial obligations. (388)

customer relationship management (CRM) the process of establishing long-term relationships with individual customers to foster loyalty and repeat business. (302)

damage control a company's effort to minimize the harmful effects of a negative event. (350)

data the representations of a fact or idea. They may be a number, a word, an image, or a sound. (246)

data marts subsets created to isolate one product or one department. (247)

data mining the process of exploring and analyzing data marts to uncover the relationships and patterns that will help a business. (247)

data warehouses created to store vast amounts of data in database systems separate from a company's production databases. (247)

database management systems (DBMSs) collections of tables of data that organize the data and allow simple analysis and reporting. (247)

debenture bonds (or unsecured bonds) are issued with no collateral. (376)

debt financing occurs when a company borrows money that it is legally obligated to repay, with interest, by a specified time. (375)

debt to equity ratio (or leverage ratio) measures how much debt a company has relative to its assets by comparing a company's total liabilities to its total owners' (or shareholders') equity. (389)

decision support systems (DSSs) software systems that enable companies to analyze collected data so they can predict the impact of business decisions. (246)

decision-making skills involve the ability to identify and analyze a problem, examine the alternatives, choose and implement the best plan of action, and evaluate the results. (155)

deflation a continuous decrease in prices over time. (45)

demand refers to how much of a product or a service people want to buy at any given time. (33)

demand-based pricing (or value-based pricing) is pricing a good or service based on the demand for the product or its perceived value. (341)

democratic leader delegates authority and involves employees in decision-making. (169)

demographic segmentation market segmentation according to age, race, religion, gender, ethnic background, and other demographic variables. (314)

depreciation spreads out the cost of the equipment over its useful life. (386)

depression a severe or long recession. (48)

discounts deductions from the regular price charged. (342)

disinflation a decrease in the rate of inflation. (45)

distance learning (or online training) allows employees to take college or university classes on the Internet at their convenience, enabling them to obtain specific job-related education or to pursue a degree. (216)

distribution (or place) a component of the marketing mix that refers to all the methods involved in getting the product into the hands of customers. (354)

distribution channel a series of firms or individuals that participate in the flow of a product from manufacturer to consumer. (355)

distributors (or wholesalers) often the intermediaries in a distribution channel. (355)

diversity initiative outlines a company's goals and objectives for managing, retaining, and promoting a diverse workforce. It might include a non-discrimination policy, minority network, or diversity education. (19)

diversity-friendly organizations are very inclusive. They don't just tolerate those who are different but instead celebrate their members' differences. (227)

dividends a portion of a company's profits distributed to shareholders as either cash payments or additional shares of stock. (377)

double entry bookkeeping recognizes that for every transaction that affects an asset an equal transaction must also affect either a liability or owners' equity. (384)

double taxation means that the corporation must pay income taxes on its profits and the shareholders must pay personal income taxes on the dividends they receive from the corporation. (143)

due diligence involves research and analysis of the business to uncover any hidden problems associated with it. (138)

dumping selling a product at a price below the price charged in the producing country; it is illegal but can be difficult to prove. (103)

dynamic pricing determines prices directly between the buyer and seller, unlike the more traditional fixed pricing in which prices are set by the seller. (342)

earnings per share determines the portion of a company's profit allocated to the stockholders on a pershare basis. (392)

ecological footprint a measure of human demand on Earth's ecosystems based on consumption and pollution. It compares the human demand with the planet's capacity to regenerate. (84)

economic environment consists of factors that affect consumer purchasing power and spending patterns. (16)

economic indicators such as gross domestic product (GDP), consumer and producer price indexes, and the unemployment rate are used by economists to determine how well businesses are performing overall. (44)

economics the study of how individuals, businesses, and government make decisions about how to allocate limited (scarce) resources to best satisfy people's wants, needs, and desires. (28)

effective promotional campaigns include six steps: identify target market; determine marketing objectives; design the message; determine the budget; implement the promotional mix; and evaluate and adjust as needed. (344)

effective teams made up of people with diverse skills, talents, and points of view. Team members' attributes should complement one another in order for the team to perform at the optimal level. (198)

effectiveness means completing tasks and producing products that create the greatest value. (274)

efficiency means completing a task or producing a product at the lowest cost. (274)

electronic commerce (e-commerce) a paperless exchange of business information and consists of the buying and selling of products or services over electronic systems such as the Internet and other computer networks. The term e-business was introduced to identify that the term e-commerce was too narrow to encompass everything required for successful online business. (258)

electronic performance support systems (EPSSs) automatically provide employees with information, advice, and training when they need it so they can accomplish specific tasks quickly. (217)

embargo a total restriction on an import (or an export). (100)

emotional intelligence involves a skills set (including self-awareness, self-management, social awareness, and relationship management) that enables one to understand both one's own and others' emotions. (189)

employee assistance programs (EAPs) employee benefit programs offered by many employers, typically in conjunction with a health insurance plan. EAPs are intended to help employees deal with personal and workplace problems that may adversely affect their work performance. (221)

employee information system (EIS) creates a workforce profile, in which a company can record and track employee skills and abilities to generate a "personnel inventory." (210)

employer–employee relations the communication that takes place between employers and employees. (230)

employment agencies often specializing in accounting, sales, or clerical services, provide a screened pool of candidates, which reduces the hiring company's administrative burden of recruitment. (212)

Employment Equity Act states that no person shall be denied employment opportunities or benefits for reasons unrelated to ability. It seeks to improve the employment conditions experienced by women, Aboriginal peoples, persons with disabilities, and members of visible minorities. (76)

Employment Standards Acts and Labour Codes (provincial level) together with the Canada Labour Code (at the federal level), defines the rights and obligations of individuals as workers, union members, and employers in the workplace. (234)

employment-related legislation covers the following subjects: employment standards legislation, human rights legislation, federal and provincial privacy legislation, occupational health and safety legislation, workers' compensation legislation, and labour relations legislation. (76)

engaged employee one who is fully involved in, and enthusiastic about, their work, and thus will act in a way that furthers their organization's interests. (179)

enterprise resource planning (ERP) a way to integrate the data and processes of an organization into one single information system. It stores data from various functions found throughout the organization using subsystems that include hardware, software, and databases in order to achieve integration. (247)

entrepreneur someone who assumes the risk of creating, organizing, and operating a business and who directs all the business resources. (10, 122)

entrepreneurial team a group of qualified individuals with varied experiences and skills that come together to form a new venture. (125)

environmental scanning the process of surveying the market environment to assess external threats and opportunities. (308)

e-procurement an online purchasing system connecting companies and their business processes directly with suppliers while managing all interactions between them. (284)

equity money received in exchange for ownership in a business. (377)

equity financing the generation of funds by the owners of the company rather than an outside lender. These funds might come from the company's own savings or partial sale of ownership in the company in the form of stock. (375)

equity theory focuses on social comparisons—people evaluating their treatment by the organization relative to the treatment of others. (186)

ethical behaviour (moral behaviour) behaviour that conforms to a set of approved standards of social or professional behaviour. (60)

ethical decision entails making a right-versus-wrong decision—one in which there is a right (ethical) choice and a wrong (unethical or possibly illegal) choice. (64)

ethical dilemma a morally problematic situation in which guiding moral principles cannot determine which course of action is right or wrong. (64)

ethical lapse an error in judgement that produces a harmful outcome but does not show a complete lack of integrity. (64)

ethical norms standards in moral behaviour and tend to be broader and more informal than laws. (75)

ethics moral principles and values that govern human conduct, with respect to the rightness and wrongness of the choices humans make. (60)

ethnocentrism a belief that one's own culture is superior to all other cultures (113)

European Union (EU) with 27 member nations, the oldest and largest free trade area. (104)

everyday low pricing (EDLP) a strategy of charging low prices with few, if any, special promotional sales. (343)

exchange rates the rates at which currencies are converted into another currency. (110)

exclusive distribution the use of only one outlet in a geographic area. (358)

executive information systems (EISs) software systems that are specially designed for the needs of management. (246)

exit interviews often conducted to gather feedback before employees leave the company. (226)

expansionary measures include decreasing taxes and increasing government spending to boost the market and put money back into the hands of businesses and consumers, encouraging businesses to expand and consumers to buy more goods and services. (49)

expenses the costs incurred (an outflow of money) while operating a business. (7, 390)

exporting the act of selling domestically produced products to other countries. (95)

external environment (what occurs outside the organization) consists of micro and macro factors, including the micro-environment and the macro-environment. (13)

external recruiting looks outside the business to fill vacancies using various resources and methods. (212)

extranet an intranet partially accessible to authorized outsiders. Customers or vendors with a valid username and password are able to see certain parts of the network. (251)

extrinsic motivators (within managers' control) include such things as pay, promotion, and verbal praise. (184)

facility layout the physical arrangement of resources, the people in the production process, and how they interact. (282)

factoring the process of selling accounts receivable for cash. (374)

factors of production the resources used to produce goods and services. (10)

Federal Accountability Act (Fed AA) helps strengthen accountability and increases transparency and oversight in government operations. (78)

financial accounting produces financial documents to aid decision makers outside an organization in making decisions regarding investments and credibility. (381)

financial capital money used to facilitate a business enterprise. (10)

financial management involves the strategic planning and budgeting of short- and long-term funds for current and future needs. (369)

financial manager (or chief financial officer) oversees the financial operations of a company. (369)

financial statements the formal reports of a business's financial transactions that accountants prepare periodically. (385)

first-line managers carry out operational planning. (164)

fiscal policy in which the government determines the appropriate level of taxes and spending. (48)

five Cs of marketing include company, collaborators, customers, competitors, and climate. (312)

fixed assets assets with long-term use, such as real estate, buildings, machinery, and equipment. (386)

fixed costs (or overhead costs) are any costs that do not vary with the production level. Total fixed costs typically include salaries, rent, insurance expenses, and loan repayments. (340)

fixed-position layout a format in which the product stays in one place (fixed position) while workers and machinery move to the product to complete tasks rather than vice versa. (283)

flexible benefits plans (or cafeteria plans) permit the employee to pick from a "menu" of several choices of taxable and non-taxable forms of compensation. (220)

flexible manufacturing system (FMS) uses one central computer to link together several machines that can process different part types simultaneously. (276)

flexible work schedule can take many different forms, yet not every job is well suited for an alternative structure. Flexible work schedules help people juggle work and family responsibilities, making them happier with their jobs, which can be measured in increases in productivity and morale and decreases in stress, absenteeism, and burnout. (222)

flow state happens when you are completely involved and focused on what you are doing. Often people produce their best work, make the best use of their skills, and feel the most pleasure when they are in such a flow state. (179)

flow-shop layout (or product layout) is one in which equipment or work processes are arranged according to the progressive steps by which the product is made. It is used mostly when large quantities of a product must be produced. (283)

focus group typically a group of eight to ten potential customers who are asked for feedback on a good or service, advertisement, idea, or packaging. (310)

forecasting the process of determining the future demand for employees as well as the future supply of employees. (210)

forecasts predict revenue, costs, and expenses for a specific future period. (370)

forensic accountant provides investigative accounting services and litigation support. (382)

four degrees of competition monopoly, oligopoly, monopolistic competition, and perfect competition. (40)

franchise a method of doing business whereby the business (the franchisor) grants the buyer (the franchisee) the right to use its brand name and to sell its goods and services for a specified time. (134)

franchising involves selling a well-known brand name or a proven method of doing business to an investor in exchange for a fee and a percentage of sales or profits. The seller is the franchisor, and the buyer is the franchisee. (108)

free trade he unencumbered flow of goods and services across national borders. (100)

free trade areas or agreements (FTA) abolish trade barriers among member countries. (104)

freely floating (or flexible) exchange rate system uses the global supply and demand for currencies to determine exchange rates. (112)

free-reign leaders (or laissez-faire leaders) encourage employees to contribute ideas rather than specifically directing their tasks. (169)

friendly takeover occurs when the target company's management and board of directors support the acquisition. (145)

Front-Page-of-the-Newspaper Test asks you to envision how a reporter would describe your decision on the front page of the newspaper the next day. (82)

full-service wholesalers provide a full line of services: carrying stock, maintaining a sales force, offering credit, making deliveries, and providing management assistance. (357)

functional areas often separate departments where business activities are grouped by similar tasks or skills. (12)

functional layout (or process or job-shop layout) a format in which workers who perform similar tasks on similar equipment are grouped together. (283)

fundamental accounting equation assets = liabilities + owners' equity. (382)

games-based learning (serious games) a training method whereby employees play virtual reality games that simulate real-life events. (216)

Gantt chart formatted similarly to a horizontal bar graph, is used to lay out each task in a project, the order in which these tasks must be completed, and how long each task should take. (286)

GDP per capita (per person) measures the country's total GDP divided by a country's population. (45)

General Agreement on Tariffs and Trade (GATT) created in 1948 with 23 member nations to provide rules for world trade; its membership grew to 123 countries by 1994. (103)

general partners full owners of the business, are responsible for all the day-to-day business decisions, and remain liable for all the debts and obligations of the business. (140)

general partnership similar to the sole proprietorship in that all the (general) partners are jointly liable for the obligations of the business. (140)

geographic segmentation market segmentation according to geographic characteristics. (314)

global strategy involves competing primarily based on price while selling a standardized (or homogenous) product. (107)

globalization the movement toward a more interconnected and interdependent world economy. (16, 95)

globalization of markets the movement away from thinking of the market as being only local or national to including the entire world. (96)

globalization of production the trend of individual firms moving production to different locations around the globe to take advantage of lower costs or to enhance quality. (96)

goals broad, long-term accomplishments an organization wants to achieve within a certain period. (157)

goods any physical products offered by a business. (10)

goodwill an accounting concept meaning the value of an entity over and above the value of its assets. (387)

government and nonprofit accounting refers to the accounting required for organizations that are not focused on generating a profit, such as legislative bodies and charities. (382)

grants financial awards usually offered by federal and provincial governments and some private organizations. (134)

great leaders characterized by the ability to be both managers and leaders: they define a vision, foster agreement across the company, and then implement the strategy. (188)

green economy factors ecological concerns into its business decisions. (19)

greenwashing occurs when a company makes claims about its environmental record that aren't supported by its actions. (84)

grievance a formal complaint by an employee, employees, or the union usually brought to the supervisor's attention either in person or in writing. (232)

gross domestic product (GDP) measures economic activity—the overall market value of final goods and services produced in a country in a year. (44)

gross national product (GNP) attributes earnings to the country where the firm was owned, not where the product was manufactured. (45)

gross profit calculated by subtracting cost of goods sold (or cost of sales) from revenue (total sales). (391)

gross profit margin determines a company's profitability of production. It indicates how efficient management is in using its labour and raw materials to produce goods. (391)

group flow occurs when a group knows how to work together so that each individual member can achieve flow. (197)

group technology layout (or cellular layout) combines aspects from both product and fixed-position layout: workers are arranged into self-contained, stand-alone production units (or cells of small work teams) (283)

groupthink a type of narrow-mindedness that can emerge in a group situation if team members have not been carefully selected for a range of skills and attributes. (196)

growth entrepreneurs strive to create fast-growing businesses and look forward to expansion. (125)

hackers individuals who gain unauthorized entry into a computer system either to disrupt the operation of the system or to gain access to protected data. (254)

Hawthorne effect describes the increase in productivity caused by workers being given special attention. (187)

Herzberg's motivator-hygiene (two-factor) theory suggests that two factors influence a person's motivation—hygiene factors (cause job dissatisfaction) and motivation factors (cause job satisfaction). (183)

Hidden Video Test allows you to measure how you would feel about what you are doing if you found a video of yourself on YouTube the next day. (82)

high-contact service processes require the customer to be present, such as a public transit system, a hair salon, or an accountant. (275)

hiring process begins with developing the job requirements and ends when a job offer is made. (215)

HMIS (Workplace Hazardous Materials Information System) a comprehensive plan for providing information on hazardous materials to employees. (235)

horizontal organization (or flat organization), the traditional managerial pyramid is flattened, and the management layers are collapsed. (165)

hostile takeover occurs when the takeover goes against the wishes of the target company's management and board of directors. (145)

HRM functions encompass every aspect of the "human" in a business, including planning, recruiting, selecting and hiring, training, evaluating, compensating, scheduling, motivating, and transitioning employees. HRM also oversees employee–management relations and must always work within the limits of the law. (209)

human factor refers to how the location decision affects the people in a surrounding community and vice versa. (281)

human resource management (HRM) the organizational function that deals with the people in the business, from the executives and the managers to the frontline production, sales, and administrative staff. (208)

human resource planning the creation of a strategy for meeting future human resource needs within an organization. (210)

human resources (HR) the people in an organization and need to be managed just as carefully as the material and financial resources of a business. (208)

human resources department working with other department managers, responsible for the people in the organization and helps to maximize organizational productivity by optimizing the effectiveness of employees. (209)

importing the act of buying products from other countries. (95)

income statement shows how much money is coming into a company and how much money a company is spending over a period. It shows how well a company has done in terms of profit and loss. (385)

independent contractors and consultants contingent workers who are generally self-employed and are hired on a temporary basis to perform specific tasks. (223)

industrial product classifications (or B2B product classifications) emerge from strategic marketing mix plans for B2B products: equipment; maintenance, repair, and operating (MRO) products; raw and processed materials; component parts; and specialized professional services. (334)

industrial products (or business-to-business (B2B) products) are goods and services purchased by businesses for further processing or resale or are used in facilitating business operations. (333)

industrial psychology studies scientifically how to manage employees and work optimally. (187)

inflation a rise in the general level of prices over time. (45)

infomercials television commercials that run as long as regular TV programs. (348)

information data that have been organized or arranged in a way that make them useful. (246)

information and knowledge quickly becoming the key factors of production as the new competitive business environment places a premium on these factors. (11)

information systems (IS) or management information systems (MIS), focus on applying information technology (IT) to solve business and economic problems. (245)

information technology (IT) the design and implementation of computerbased information systems. (244)

initial public offering (IPO) the first time a company offers to sell new stock to the public. (377)

intangible assets do not have physical characteristics (you can't touch or see them), but they have value nonetheless. Trademarks, patents, and copyrights are examples of intangible assets, in addition to strong brand recognition and excellent customer or employee relations. (387)

integrated marketing communication (IMC) a strategy to deliver a clear, consistent, and unified message about the company and its products to customers at all contact points. (345)

intensive distribution entails selling the product through all available retail outlets. (358)

interest the payments the bond issuer makes to the bondholder for use of the borrowed money (most interest payments are semi-annual). (376)

internal environment (what occurs within the organization) includes the five Ms: Management, Materials, Machinery (equipment), Money (wages, finance), and eMployees (internal customers). (13)

internal recruiting the process of filling job vacancies with existing employees from within the business. (211)

International Monetary Fund (IMF) promotes trade through financial cooperation. (103)

International Organization for Standardization (ISO) an organization dedicated to creating worldwide standards of quality for goods and services. (291)

Internet a global system of interconnected computer networks that use the standard Internet Protocol Suite (TCP/ IP) to send communications to billions of users worldwide. (251)

Internet2 a network of networks that can communicate at speeds a hundred to a thousand times faster than Internet1, is a collaboration of more than 200 universities and 120 companies. (251)

interpersonal skills enable a manager to interact with other people in order to motivate them. (155)

intranet a network accessible only to employees or others with authorization. (250)

intrapreneurs employees who work in an entrepreneurial way within the organizational environment. (125)

intrinsic motivators (outside managers' control) are internal to each individual employee, such as the sense of purpose or value a person derives from their work. (184)

inventory the merchandise a business owns but has not sold. (387)

inventory control includes the receiving, storing, handling, and tracking of everything in a company's stock, from raw materials to finished products. Inventory often makes up a large portion of a business's expenses. (287)

investment instruments such as bonds (debt) or stock (equity) are used for large capital-intensive projects or general expansion. (378)

ISO 14000 launched after ISO 9000, is designed to promote clean production processes in response to environmental issues such as global warming and water pollution. (292)

ISO 9000 a set of five technical standards of quality management created by the International Organizations for Standardization to provide a uniform way of determining whether organizations conform to sound quality procedures. (291)

issuing common stock the process of selling common shares of ownership in the company to the general public—in other words, "going public"—can be a great option to generate funds through equity financing. (377)

IT department comprises a number of professionals responsible for everything from hardware components and software programs to networking and database strategies. (245)

job analysis identifies and defines in detail the particular duties and requirements of the tasks and responsibilities an employee is required to perform. (210)

job description a formal statement summarizing what the employee will do in that job role. It includes the job responsibilities, the conditions under which the job will be performed, and the job's relationship to other functions in the organization. (210)

job interview a one-on-one meeting of the company and the job candidate, through which the company is able to gauge the candidate's personality, clarify information in the candidate's resumé, and determine whether the candidate is the best match for the position. (214)

job rotation when the employee rotates through different departments to learn first-hand the various aspects of the business. (217)

job specifications are the skills, education, experience, and personal attributes that candidates need to possess to successfully fulfill the job role. (210)

job-shop layout (or process or functional layout) a format in which workers who perform similar tasks on similar equipment are grouped together. (283)

joint ventures involve shared ownership in a subsidiary firm. International joint venture partners involve an international business teaming up with a local partner in order to enter a foreign market. (108)

just-in-time (JIT) inventory control system keeps the smallest amount of inventory on hand as possible, and everything else that is needed is ordered so that it arrives just in time to be used. (288)

labour the human resource that refers to any physical or intellectual work people contribute to business production. (10)

labour union a legally recognized group dedicated to protecting the interests of workers. (231)

laissez-faire leaders (or free-reign leaders) encourage employees to contribute ideas rather than specifically directing their tasks. (169)

law of demand states that people will buy more of an item at a lower price than at a higher price. (33)

law of supply states that the amount supplied will increase as the price increases; if the price is lower, less of the product is supplied. (33)

leadership the processes and behaviours used by managers to motivate, inspire, and influence subordinates to work toward certain goals. (188)

leading the process of influencing, motivating, and enabling others to contribute to the success and effectiveness of the organization by achieving its goals. (166)

lean production a set of principles concerned with reducing waste and improving flow that evolved from the original Toyota Production System (TPS) first used in Japan in the 1980s. (276)

legal compliance refers to conducting a business within the boundaries of all the legal regulations of that industry. (75)

legal monopolies occur when a company receives a patent giving it exclusive use of an invented product or process. (41)

leverage the amount of debt used to finance a firm's assets with the intent that the rate of return on the assets is greater than the cost of the debt. (378)

leverage ratio (or debt to equity ratio) measures how much debt a company has relative to its assets by comparing a company's total liabilities to its total owners' (or shareholders') equity. (389)

liabilities what the company owes to its creditors. (382)

liability the obligation to pay a debt such as an account payable or a loan. (139)

licensing an agreement in which the licensor's intangible property—patents, trademarks, service marks, copyrights, trade secrets, or other intellectual property—may be sold or made available to a licensee in exchange for a royalty fee. (108)

lifestyle entrepreneurs look for more than profit potential when they begin their business. (125)

limited liability safeguards personal assets from being seized as payment for debts or claims. (139)

limited partners don't participate actively in the business, and their liability is limited to the amount they invested in the partnership. (140)

limited partnerships consist of at least one general partner (who has unlimited liability) and one or more limited partners who cannot participate in the day-to-day activities of the business or they will risk the loss of their limited liability status. (140)

limited-service wholesalers offer fewer services than full-service wholesalers. There are four major types: Cash-and-carry wholesalers, truck wholesalers, drop shippers, and rack jobbers. (357)

line of credit available credit that a manager can access at any time up to an amount agreed upon between the bank and the company. (374)

liquidity how quickly assets can be turned into cash. (371)

liquidity ratio (or current ratio) a measurement used to determine the extent to which a company can meet its current financial obligations. (388)

loan an arrangement in which a lender gives money to a borrower, under the agreement that the borrower repays the loan amount, usually with interest, at some future point in time. (376)

local area networks (LANs) include only machines in close physical proximity to one another, such as the computers in one office building. (251)

local content requirement a requirement that some portion of a good be produced domestically. (100)

lockout occurs when management refuses to allow union members to enter the work premises. (232)

logos representations of brands that help build an image for a company. (335)

long-term liabilities include debts and obligations owed by the company and due more than one year from the current date such as mortgage loans for the purchase of land or buildings, long-term leases on equipment or buildings, and bonds issued for large projects. (387)

loss (or net income) the revenue remaining after all costs and expenses, including taxes, have been paid. It is the "bottom line" and is usually stated on the very last line of an income statement. (7, 391)

loss leader a product priced below its cost. Stores use loss leaders to attract customers and motivate them to buy items that are more expensive as well. (343)

low-contact service processes do not require the customer to be present, such as a utility company, the chequing processes at a bank, or an auto-repair shop. (275)

macroeconomics the study of the behaviour of the overall economy. Economy-wide occurrences, such as changes in unemployment, interest rates, inflation, and prices, are all part of the study of macroeconomics. (29)

macro-environment the external environment over which the organization can exert little influence. This environment is often referred to by the acronym PEST (politicallegal, economic, socio-cultural, and technological). (13)

make-or-buy decision decides what needs to be manufactured and what needs to be purchased from outside suppliers. (283)

management the process of working with people and resources to accomplish the goals of the organization. (154)

management by objectives (MBO) a performance goal–setting method in which anagement and employees work together to set goals and evaluate performance. (186)

management development training focuses on leadership, communication, teamwork, and relationship-building skills. (217)

management information systems (MIS) or information systems (IS), focus on applying information technology (IT) to solve business and economic problems. (245)

managerial accounting used to provide information and analyses to managers within the organization to assist them in making good business decisions. (381)

manufacturing resource planning (MRPII) uses software to integrate data from many departments, including manufacturing, finance, marketing, and human resources. (289)

market research the process of gathering and analyzing market information for making marketing decisions. (310)

market segmentation the process of separating the broader market into smaller markets (or market segments) that consist of similar groups of customers. (314)

marketing "a set of business practices designed to plan for and present an organization's products or services in ways that build effective customer relationships." (Canadian Marketing Association) (300)

marketing concept a philosophy that businesses should analyze the needs of their customers and then make decisions to satisfy those needs, better than the competition. (5, 301)

marketing environment includes environmental influences outside the firm's control that constrain the organization's ability to manipulate its marketing mix. (308)

marketing intermediary (or middleman) a business firm that operates between producers and consumers or business users. (355)

marketing mix the combination of four factors, called the "4 Ps" of marketing, designed to serve the target market: product, price, promotion, and place. (305)

marketing objective a clearly stated goal to be achieved through marketing activities. It should be realistic, quantifiable, and time specific. (312)

marketing plan a written document that specifies marketing activities designed to reach organizational objectives. (312)

Maslow's hierarchy of needs suggests that our primary needs are met first before our higher-level needs are addressed. (181)

mass customization combines the low unit cost of mass production processes with the flexibility of producing goods or services tailored to meet individual customer's needs. (276)

mass production a method of producing large quantities of goods at a low cost and relies on machines and automated assembly lines to mass-produce goods that are identical and adhere to certain standards of quality. (275)

master production schedule shows which products will be produced, when production will occur, and what resources will be used during the scheduled time. (286)

materials requirement planning (MRP) a type of software system used to schedule and monitor the use of components and other materials in a manufacturing operation. (288)

McClelland's "three needs" theory suggests there are three main motivators: 1) the need for achievement (to accomplish something difficult on your own); 2) the need for affiliation (to form close personal relationships); and 3) the need for power (to be able to control the behaviour of others). (182)

McGregor's Theory X suggests that people inherently dislike work and want to avoid it. (184)

McGregor's Theory Y suggests that people view work as being as natural as playing and resting. (185)

mediation a process that involves a neutral third party that assists the two parties both privately and collectively to identify issues and to develop proposals for resolution. (232)

mentoring a form of on-the-job training whereby an experienced employee provides direction and information to the new employee as they learn the job. (216)

mentors experienced individual employees who help a less-experienced person by explaining how to perform specific tasks, creating opportunities to learn new skills, and counselling about the consequences of particular actions and decisions. (216)

merger occurs when two or more firms combine to form one new company, which often takes on a new corporate identity. (145)

microeconomics the study of how individual businesses, households, and consumers make decisions to allocate their limited resources in the exchange of goods and services. (29)

micro-environment may be defined as including groups and organizations that have a direct relationship with the business and have a direct interest in the activities of the company because they are clearly affected by its actions. (13)

micropreneurs start their own business but are satisfied with keeping the business small in an effort to achieve a balanced lifestyle. (125)

middle-level managers top managers for only one division or a part of an organization. (164)

middleman (or marketing intermediary) a business firm that operates between producers and consumers or business users. (355)

mission statement a description of the organization's purpose, basic goals, and philosophies. (158)

mixed economies a blend of market and planned economies with a mixed economy of privately owned businesses and government control of selected social programs, such as health care. (31)

monetary policy in which the government manages the supply of money, are applied by governments to smooth out the fluctuations in the business cycle. (48)

monopolistic competition occurs when there are many buyers and sellers and little differentiation between the products, but there is a perceived difference among consumers, who therefore favour one product offering over another. (42)

monopoly occurs when there is only one provider of a service or product and no substitutes for the product exist. (41)

moral relativism maintains that there is no universal moral truth but instead only people's individual beliefs, perspectives, and values. (60)

multi-domestic strategy involves competing primarily by customizing or differentiating the product to meet unique local needs, tastes, or preferences. (107)

national debt the accumulated total yearly deficits. (50)

natural monopolies include public utilities, such as those that sell gas or water. These organizations require huge investments, and it would be inefficient to duplicate the products they provide. (41)

natural resources the raw materials provided by nature and used to produce goods and services. (10)

near-shoring a form of offshoring in which a company moves jobs to a foreign location geographically close or linguistically and culturally similar to its own country. (97)

net income (or loss) the revenue remaining after all costs and expenses, including taxes, have been paid. It is the "bottom line" and is usually stated on the very last line of an income statement. (391)

network a system of computers and other devices joined using cables, fibre optic links, or wireless connections. (250)

network organizations collections of independent, mostly single-function firms that collaborate on a product or service. (166)

new product development involves five steps: idea generation; idea screening; product analysis; product development and concept testing; and commercialization. (329)

niche marketing occurs when a product is marketed to a very narrowly defined set of potential customers. (314)

nominal GDP includes all of the changes that have occurred in market prices during the year due to inflation and deflation. (45)

nonconvertible currency a currency that can't be converted into another currency in the foreign exchange market. (112)

non-profit and voluntary sector includes non-governmental, non-profit organizations that receive support from individual Canadians, governments, and businesses. (8)

North American Free Trade Agreement (NAFTA) an ongoing agreement to move Canada, the United States, and Mexico closer to true free trade. (106)

objectives the short-term targets designed to help achieve these goals. (157)

Occupational Health and Safety (OHS) Acts and Regulations enabled at the federal, provincial, and territorial levels and are designed to secure workers and self-employed persons from risks to their safety, health, and physical wellbeing arising out of, or in connection with, activities in their workplaces. (235)

odd or fractional pricing (or psychological pricing) is the practice of charging a price just below a whole number to give the appearance of a significantly lower price. (343)

officers and shop stewards elected by union members to make decisions for the entire body and represent the members in dealings with management. (232)

offshoring a practice in which work is shifted from its original domestic location to other foreign locations. (97)

off-the-job training and development techniques require employees to participate in outside seminars, universityconducted programs, and corporate universities. (216)

oligopoly a form of competition in which only a few sellers exist. (41)

online advertising any form of advertising that uses the Internet to market its message to customers. (260)

online banking involves using the Internet rather than visiting a bricks-and-mortar bank to manage finances. (262)

online training (or distance learning) allows employees to take college or university classes on the Internet at their convenience, enabling them to obtain specific job-related education or to pursue a degree. (216)

on-the-job training when employees learn skills by performing them. (216)

operating (master) budget includes all the operating costs for the entire organization, including inventory, sales, purchases, manufacturing, marketing, and operating expenses. (370)

operating expenses the overhead costs incurred with running the business. They include sales, general, and administrative expenses. These costs may consist of items such as rent, salaries, wages, utilities, depreciation, and insurance. (391)

operating income determined when operating expenses are subtracted from gross profit. (391)

operating profit margin determines a company's profitability of operations. It indicates how efficiently management is in using business operations to generate a profit. (392)

operational plans determine the process by which tactical plans can be achieved. (161)

operations management (or production management) refers to the organized direction and control of the processes that transform resources (inputs) into finished goods and services (outputs). (273)

operations managers responsible for managing and supervising all the activities that occur when transforming resources into goods or services, such as setting schedules, making buying decisions, and overseeing quality control. (274)

operations planning includes four steps: 1) the type of production process, 2) the facility location, 3) the facility layout, and 4) resource planning. (274)

opportunity niche a need in the marketplace that is not being adequately fulfilled. (122)

optimal capital structure the optimal balance between equity and debt financing. (378)

organizational chart shows how groups of employees fit into the larger organizational structure. (164)

organizational psychology studies how to create a workplace that fosters motivation and productivity among employees. (179)

organizing the process of structuring the capital, personnel, raw materials, and other resources to carry out the plans in a way that best matches the nature of the work. (163)

orientation program used to introduce the employee to the company's people, policies, and procedures. (215)

outsourcing occurs when a company contracts with an outside firm to handle a specific part of its business activities. (97)

overhead costs (or fixed costs) are any costs that do not vary with the production level. Total fixed costs typically include salaries, rent, insurance expenses, and loan repayments. (340)

owners' equity what the company owes to its owners. (382)

participative management and empowerment involves encouraging employees to become engaged in their jobs and loyal to the company by inspiring them to be self-motivated and giving them responsibility with the power (empowerment) to make decisions. (186)

partnership a type of business entity in which two or more owners (or partners) share the ownership and the profits and losses of the business. (140)

pay-per-click (PPC) advertising involves advertisers only having to pay for the number of times a Web surfer clicks on their ad. (261)

penetration pricing a strategy of charging the lowest possible price for a new product. (342)

perfect competition occurs when many buyers and sellers of products are virtually identical, and any seller can easily enter and exit the market. (42)

performance appraisal an evaluation of an employee's performance that gives feedback about how well the employee is doing, as well as where changes and improvements are needed. (217)

performance management an approach that combines goal setting, performance appraisal, and training and development into a unified and ongoing process. (218)

personal code of ethics a set of principles that guide the decisions you make in your life with respect to what is right or wrong. (61)

Personal Information Protection and Electronic Documents Act (PIPEDA) distinguishes proper use of personal information from improper use and disclosure. (246)

personal motivation what drives us internally and externally to succeed in whatever we want to succeed in. (178)

personal selling direct communication between a firm's sales force and potential buyers to make a sale and to build good customer relationships. (350)

PEST model (Political-D97legal, Economic, Sociocultural, and Technological) used to measure changes in the external business environment that might affect the company's ability to prosper. (14)

phishing a common way to trick online users into sending their credit card numbers straight to hackers. (263)

place (or distribution) a component of the marketing mix that refers to all the methods involved in getting the product into the hands of customers. (354)

planned economic system a system in which the government plays a greater role in determining the goods and services provided and how they are produced and distributed. Both communism and socialism are planned economic systems. (30)

planning the process of establishing goals and objectives and determining the best ways to accomplish them. (157)

political-legal environment reflects the government's relationship with business. (15)

Porter's Five Forces analysis model depicts the five forces that affect industry competition: threat of new entrants, threat of substitutes, bargaining power of buyers, bargaining power of suppliers, and rivalry among existing competitors. The intensity of the competition within an industry has a big influence on how a company operates. (39)

positioning the process of developing a unique marketing mix that best satisfies a target market. (314)

preferred stock a hybrid investment because it has some of the features of common stock (i.e., it never matures) and some of the features of corporate bonds (i.e., payments on stock are for fixed amounts, such as $5 per share per year). (377)

price the only revenuegenerating component of the marketing mix—product, promotion, and place (distribution) strategies are all cost components. (339)

price discrimination involves charging different prices to different customers when these price differences are not a reflection of cost differences. (341)

price fixing occurs when a group of companies agree among themselves to set the products' prices, independent of market demand or supply. (66)

price skimming involves charging a high price for a product initially, then lowering the price over time. (342)

pricing strategies most commonly include cost-based pricing, demand-based pricing, and competition-based pricing. (339)

primary data raw data collected by the researcher. The data are frequently collected through observation, questionnaires, surveys (via mail, e-mail, or telephone), focus groups, interviews, customer feedback, samples, and controlled experiments. (310)

private accountant employed by an organization and may perform one or more different accounting functions. (380)

private business sector includes goods and services produced and delivered by private individuals or groups as a means of enterprise for profit. (8)

private corporations companies whose shares of stock are held by only a few people and not generally available for sale. (142)

privatization the conversion of government-owned production and services to privately owned, profitseeking enterprises. (31)

probation a specific timeframe (typically three to six months) during which the new hire proves their skills and worth on the job. (215)

process layout (or job-shop or functional layout) a format in which workers who perform similar tasks on similar equipment are grouped together. (283)

procurement (or purchasing) the task of buying the materials and services needed in the production process. (283)

producer price index (PPI) tracks the average change in prices at the wholesale level (from the seller's perspective). Therefore, it tracks prices of goods sellers use to create their products or services, such as raw materials, product components that require further processing, and finished goods sold to retailers. The PPI excludes energy prices and prices for services. (46)

product any good, service, or idea available for purchase in a market, as well as any intangible benefits derived from its consumption. (301)

product differentiation the creation of a real or perceived difference in a product designed to attract customers. (328)

product layout (or flow-shop layout) is one in which equipment or work processes are arranged according to the progressive steps by which the product is made. It is used mostly when large quantities of a product must be produced. (283)

product life cycle a theoretical model describing a product's sales and profits over the course of its lifetime. (330)

product line a group of similar products intended for a similar market. (332)

product line length the number of items in any given product line. Product line length is determined by how the addition or removal of items from a product line affects profits. (332)

product manager (or brand manager) is responsible for the 4 Ps of marketing a specific product or product line. Brand managers attempt to increase the product's perceived value to customers in order to increase brand equity. (336)

product mix the combination of all product lines offered for sale by a company. (332)

product mix width refers to the number of different product lines a company offers. (332)

product placement the placement of products in TV shows, movies, and video games where they will be seen by potential customers. (348)

production the process of getting a good or service to the customer; it is a series of related activities, with value being added at each stage. (272)

production concept emerged from the mid-1700s to the mid-1800s, in which mass production took hold and huge factories were built, creating goods that were inexpensive and widely available. (5)

production line (or assembly line) is used to move partially complete products from one worker to the next on a conveyor belt. (275)

production management (or operations management) refers to the organized direction and control of the processes that transform resources (inputs) into finished goods and services (outputs). (273)

production plan when well-developed and efficiently executed, ensures a smoothly run operations process and a product that provides utility. (274)

productivity measures the quantity of goods and services that human and physical resources can produce in a given time. (45)

profit a profit is earned when a company's revenue is greater than its expenses. (6)

program evaluation and review technique (PERT) maps out the various steps involved in a project, differentiating tasks that must be completed in a certain order from tasks that may be completed simultaneously. (287)

programmed learning an approach in which the employee is asked to perform step-by-step instructions or to respond to questions. (216)

promissory note a written promise to pay a supplier a specific amount of money by an agreed upon date. (373)

promotion (1) may be an upward or lateral move into a new position that allows employees to develop and display new skills and to learn more about the company overall. (225)

promotion (2) a part of the marketing mix that consists of all the methods to inform and persuade targeted customers to buy a product and to build positive customer relationships. (343)

promotional mix the strategic combination of promotional tools used to reach targeted customers to achieve marketing objectives. (344)

promotional tools used to promote a good or service, include advertising, public relations, personal selling, and sales promotions. (344)

protocols the different "languages" used to transfer information across the Internet. (251)

psychographic segmentation market segmentation based on lifestyles, personality traits, motives, and values. (314)

psychological contract represents the mutual beliefs, perceptions, and informal obligations held between an employer and an employee. (214)

psychological pricing (or odd or fractional pricing) is the practice of charging a price just below a whole number to give the appearance of a significantly lower price. (343)

public accountant provides a broad range of accounting, auditing, tax, and consulting activities for various corporate clients. (380)

public business sector includes goods and services produced, delivered, and allocated by the government and public sector organizations (publicly controlled government business enterprises). (8)

public corporations companies whose shares of stock are widely held and available for sale to the public. (142)

public relations the management function that establishes and maintains mutually beneficial relationships between an organization and its stakeholders. (348)

publicity information about an individual, organization, or product transmitted through mass media at no charge. (349)

purchasing (or procurement) the task of buying the materials and services needed in the production process. (283)

purchasing power parity (PPP) When comparing GDP between countries to determine living standards, calculations are based on PPP, which takes into account the relative cost of living and the inflation rates of the countries, rather than just exchange rates, which might distort the real differences in income. (45)

Put-Yourself-in-the-Other-Person's-Shoes by asking yourself how you would feel if the other person (or company) was doing this to you, you may discover that what you are doing does not feel right. (82)

quality control the use of techniques, activities, and processes to guarantee that a certain good or service meets a specified level of quality. (289)

quality of life is subjective and intangible. It takes into account not only the material standard of living, but also more intangible aspects that make up human life, such as freedom from slavery, torture, and discrimination; the right to rest and leisure, education, safety, choice of employment, and equal treatment; and freedom of religion and of thought. (7)

quota a limitation on the amount of an import allowed to enter a country. (100)

radio frequency identification (RFID) tag allows a computer to keep track of the status and quantity of each item. (288)

RAID (redundant array of independent drives) a hard disk backup design. (248)

ratio analysis a comparison of numbers and therefore is used to compare current data to data from previous years, competitors' data, or industry averages. (387)

real capital refers to the physical facilities used to produce goods and services. (10)

real GDP takes inflation into account, allowing for comparisons against other historical periods. (45)

rebates partial refunds on what a customer has already paid for a product. (342)

recession a decline in the GDP for two or more successive quarters of a year. (48)

recruitment process provides the organization with a pool of potentially qualified job candidates from which judicious selection can be made to fill vacancies. (211)

reference pricing refers to listing an inflated price (the "regular retail price" or "manufacturer's suggested retail price") that is then discounted to appear as if it is a good value. (343)

resonant leader highly aware of others' emotional states and skilled at inspiring people to feel more positive. (189)

retailers intermediaries that buy products for resale to ultimate consumers. (355)

retained earnings represent the profits (money remaining after taxes and other expenses are paid) not paid out in dividends. (377)

retirement the point in a person's life when he or she stops participating full-time in his or her career. (225)

revenue the total amount of money received for goods and services provided. (7)

revenue any monies received by a company from sales of goods or services or from other sources such as licensing fees, rental fees, or interest earned. (390)

routing the way in which goods are transported (to a client, from a supplier, or any other combination), via water, rail, truck, or air. (285)

sales concept emerged during the 1920s, and the emphasis turned to selling and advertising to persuade customers to buy the existing mass-produced goods. (5)

sales promotions short-term activities that target consumers and other businesses for generating interest in a product. (352)

scabs (or strikebreakers) replacement personnel hired by management during a strike. (233)

scheduling involves specifying and controlling the time required for each step in the production process as well as making the most efficient use of equipment, facilities, labour, and materials. (286)

scientific management comprises methods aimed at determining the one best way for a job to be done. (187)

secondary data data that have already been collected and processed. An example of secondary data is census data. (310)

secure Internet connections Internet protocols whereby data can be transmitted over the World Wide Web securely—
unauthorized persons cannot access the data. (263)

secured bonds require some form of collateral pledged as security. (376)

secured loan requires collateral, which is generally the asset that the loan is financing, to guarantee the debt obligation. (374)

selection entails gathering information about candidates, evaluating their qualifications, and choosing the ones that best fit the job specifications. (213)

selective distribution uses only a portion of the many possible retail outlets for sale of a product. (358)

semi-controlled messages placed on websites, in chat rooms, and on blogs, and are not strictly regulated. Other forms include sporting or special events sponsorships because participation by the press and stakeholders is not under the control of the sponsoring company. (349)

services refer to intangible products that are bought or sold. (10)

Seven Habits developed by Stephen Covey, a model which lists the seven habits that successful people exhibit. (199)

shareholders investors in a corporation who buy shares of ownership in the form of stock. (143)

shares outstanding common shares authorized, issued, and purchased by investors. (392)

shortage occurs when sellers do not produce enough of a product to satisfy demand. (35)

short-term financing any type of financing repaid within a year or less. (373)

short-term liabilities (or current liabilities) are obligations a company is responsible for paying within a year or less and are listed first on the balance sheet. (387)

simulation training provides realistic job-task training in a manner that is challenging but does not create the threat of failure. (216)

sinking fund a type of savings fund in which companies set aside money regularly to help repay a bond issue. (376)

situational ethics maintain that people make decisions based on a specific situation instead of universal laws. (61)

Six Sigma a statistically based, proactive, long-term process designed to look at the overall business process to prevent problems; it seeks to eliminate defects by removing variation in outcomes and measuring and analyzing manufacturing processes to see if standards are being met. (171, 290)

Small Business Investment Companies (SBIC) private venture capital firms that make equity capital or long-term loans available to small companies. (134)

small or medium-sized enterprise (SME) independently owned and operated and has fewer than 500 employees. (127)

social audit a study of how well a company is doing at meeting its social responsibilities. (71)

socialism provides that the government plans and controls the economy. Government owns or controls many basic businesses and services, while individuals own and operate less crucial industries. (30)

socially responsible investing (SRI) is investing only in companies that have met a certain standard of corporate social responsibility. (73)

sociocracy a system of organization and management in which the interests of everyone are served equally. (188)

socio-cultural environment an interconnected system of different demographic factors such as race, ethnicity, gender, age, income distribution, sexual orientation, and other characteristics. (16)

sole proprietorship a business owned by one person and not protected by limited liability. (138)

spyware collects data and relays it back to interested persons who wish to commit fraud or identity theft. (263)

stakeholders individuals or groups to whom a business has a responsibility: employees, customers, investors, suppliers, government, community, and society overall (which includes environmental responsibility). (69)

standard of living the level of wealth, comfort, material goods, and necessities available to its people. It is the ease by which people living in a time or place are able to satisfy their needs and wants. It is generally measured by standards such as income per person and poverty rate. (7)

statement of cash shows the exchange of money between a company and everyone else it deals with over a period. It shows where cash was used. (385)

statistical process control (SPC) uses statistical sampling of products at every phase of production and displays the results on a graph to show potential variations that need to be corrected. (290)

stock a unit of ownership in a company sold with the intention of raising capital to finance ongoing or future projects and expansions. (377)

strategic alliances cooperative arrangements between actual or potential competitors. Unlike a joint venture, each partner retains its business independence. (109)

strategic plan the main course of action created by top-level managers that sets the approach for achieving the long-term goals and objectives of the organization. (157)

strength-based management a system based on the belief that, rather than improve weak skills, the best way to help employees develop is to determine their strengths and build on them. (187)

strike occurs when union workers agree to stop work until certain demands are met. (233)

strikebreakers (or scabs) replacement personnel hired by management during a strike. (233)

subsidy a payment that governments make to domestic producers. (100)

supply refers to how much of a product or service is available for purchase at any given time. (33)

supply and demand a complicated process involving multiple factors, such as income levels, tastes, and the amount of competition in the market. The need for an item is demand, and the availability of that item is supply. (32)

supply chain the sequence of organizations—their facilities and activities—that are involved in producing (right from the raw materials) and delivering (all the way to the consumer) a good or service. (280)

supply chain management involves the logistics of obtaining all the necessary inputs that go into a production process (inbound logistics), managing the actual production process (materials handling and operations control), and managing the physical distribution (or outbound logistics) of getting the proper quantities of produced products to customers when and where they w ant them. (284)

surplus occurs when sellers supply more of a product than buyers are willing to purchase. (34)

SWOT (Strengths, Weaknesses, Opportunities, and Threats) analysis situational analysis of strengths, weaknesses, and anticipated changes that helps determine the strategic fit between an organization's internal, distinctive capabilities, and external possibilities relative to the business and economic environments. (159)

synergy the achieved effect when two companies combine and the result is better than each company could achieve individually. (145)

tactical plans specifically determine the resources and the actions required to implement particular aspects of the strategic plan. (161)

target costing estimates the value customers receive from a product and therefore the price they are willing to pay, and then subtracts an acceptable profit margin to obtain a desired cost. (341)

target market the specific group of consumers, with similar needs and wants, toward which a firm directs its marketing efforts. (305)

tariff a tax that governments impose on an imported good or service, such as French wine. Governments prefer to impose tariffs because they raise tax revenues. (100)

tax accounting involves preparing taxes and giving advice on tax strategies. (381)

tax law the system of laws that describe government levies on economic transactions. (78)

team comprises a group of people linked in a common purpose. (195)

technical skills include the abilities and knowledge that enable an employee to carry out the specific tasks required of a discipline or department. (155)

technological environment includes human knowledge, work methods, physical equipment, electronics and telecommunications, and various processing systems used to perform business activities. (20)

technology includes human knowledge, work methods, physical equipment, electronics and telecommunications, and various processing systems used to perform business activities. (10)

termination of employment reduces the number of employees by permanently laying off workers due to poor performance or a discontinued need for their services. (226)

Thematic Apperception Test (TAT) presents a person with a series of images and interprets his or her responses. (194)

Theory X (or McGregor's Theory X) suggests that people inherently dislike work and want to avoid it. (184)

Theory X management proposes that employees have to be coerced and controlled by management in order to be productive. This leads to an authoritarian, hard-line management style. (185)

Theory Y (or McGregor's Theory Y) suggests that people view work as being as natural as playing and resting. (185)

Theory Y management assumes that, on average, people will accept and seek out responsibility. Such managers have a softer style of management that involves the participation of many. (185)

Theory Z based on a Japanese management style that relied heavily on collaborative decision making. (185)

Theory Z management a combination of American and Japanese management philosophies characterized by long-term employment security, consensual decision making, and slow evaluation and promotion procedures, with an emphasis on individual responsibility within a group context. (185)

Three Questions Model states that people faced with ethical dilemmas should ask themselves three questions before making a decision: 1) Is it legal? 2) Is it balanced? 3) How does it make me feel? (82)

time management skills involve the ability to achieve the maximum amount of productivity in a set amount of time. (156)

top-level managers the corporate officers responsible for the organization as a whole. (163)

total product offer (or value package) consists of all the benefits associated with a good, service, or idea that affect a consumer's purchasing decision. (327)

total quality management (TQM) Deming's concept emphasizes the use of quality principles in all aspects of a company's production and operations; it is an integrated approach focusing on quality from the beginning of the production process up through managerial involvement to detect and correct problems. (171, 289)

trade and investment barriers government barriers that prevent the flow of goods, services, and financial capital across national boundaries. (97)

trade credit the ability to purchase inventory and supplies on credit without interest. (373)

trade deficit or unfavourable balance of trade, exists when the value of a country's imports exceeds the value of its exports. (110)

trade sales promotions (or business-to-business sales promotions) incentives to push a product through the distribution system to final consumers. (352)

trade surplus or favourable balance of trade, occurs when the value of a country's exports exceeds the value of its imports. (111)

transfer occurs when an employee is appointed to the same or a similar position elsewhere within the organization. Transfers usually refer to a lateral move (a horizontal job assignment). (225)

transnational strategy involves competing by offering a customized product while simultaneously selling at the lowest possible price. (107)

triple-bottom-line reporting (also referred to as TBL, 3BL, or "People, Planet, Profit") used as a framework for measuring and reporting corporate performance against economic, social, and environmental parameters. (72)

turnkey project implemented when firms export their technological expertise in exchange for a fee. (107)

turnover rate tracks the number of employees that leave the company each year. (226)

uncertainty management theory suggests that when people face increased uncertainty, fairness becomes more important to them. (188)

uncontrolled messages generally take the form of publicity. (349)

unemployment rate measures the number of people who are at least fifteen years old, are seeking work, and are currently unemployed. (47)

unethical behaviour (immoral behaviour) behaviour that does not conform to a set of approved standards of social or professional behaviour. (61)

unlimited liability means that if business assets aren't enough to pay business debts, then personal assets, such as the sole proprietor's house, personal investments, or retirement plans, can be used to pay the balance. (140)

unsecured bonds (or debenture bonds) are issued with no collateral. (376)

unsecured loan does not require collateral to guarantee the debt obligation. (374)

utility the power of a product to satisfy a human want or need, something of value to the person. (274)

utility supply refers to the availability of public infrastructure services such as power, water, and communications. (281)

value the value of a product equals the ratio of the product's benefits to its costs (value = benefits/costs). (273)

value package (or total product offer) consists of all the benefits associated with a good, service, or idea that affect a consumer's purchasing decision. (327)

value-based pricing (or demand-based pricing) is pricing a good or service based on the demand for the product or its perceived value. (341)

value-stream mapping identifies all the flows and resources required to deliver a product: people, technologies, physical facilities, communication and transportation channels, policies, and procedures. (285)

variable costs costs that vary with the production level. Examples include wages, raw materials, and energy costs. Average variable costs (or per unit variable costs) equal total variable costs divided by the production level. (340)

venture capitalists contribute money to your business in return for some form of equity—a piece of ownership. (134)

vertical organization (or tall organization) in which the company is organized by specific function, such as marketing, finance, purchasing, information technology, and human resources. (164)

vestibule training a type of simulation most suitable to airline pilots, astronauts, and surgeons, for whom making mistakes during training is not an option or is too costly. (216)

viral marketing uses social networks, e-mail, and websites to spread the awareness of a particular brand. (261)

virtual private networks (VPNs) often used when networks begin to link sites very far apart geographically, may connect some of its systems by cables that the company owns, but other sections of the network will be joined using the public Internet. (251)

virtual team comprises members located in different physical locations but working together to achieve a goal. (198)

vision identifies what the business wants to be in the future. (158)

Vroom's Expectancy theory suggests an individual's motivation in any given situation can be described by the relationship among three psychological forces, illustrated in the formula: Motivation = Expectancy * Instrumentality * Valence. (185)

warehousing the storing of products at convenient locations ready for customers when they are needed. (360)

whistleblower an employee who reports misconduct, most often to an authority outside the firm. (79)

wholesalers intermediaries that buy and resell products to other wholesalers, to retailers, and to industrial users. (355)

16. Community Sector Council Newfoundland and Labrador, "Voluntary Sector in Canada," *Envision.ca,* http://www.envision.ca/templates/profile. asp?ID=54, Accessed June 18, 2011.

17. Industry Canada, "Goods-Producing Industries," http://www.ic.gc.ca/eic/ site/cis-sic.nsf/eng/h_00007.html, Accessed February 6, 2011.

18. Industry Canada, "Services-Producing Industries," http://www.ic.gc.ca/ eic/site/cis-sic.nsf/eng/h_00008.html, Accessed February 6, 2011.

19. "Nantucket Nectars from the Beginning," Nantucket Allserve, Inc., 2006, www.nantucketnectars.com/fullstory.php?PHPSESSID= 996c6c936ce6351082022525b73e9fce, Accessed June 25, 2008.

20. Jim Hopkins, "Surprise! There's a Third YouTube Co-Founder," USA Today, October 11, 2006, www.usatoday.com/tech/news/2006-10-11-youtube-karim_x.htm.

21. John Could, "The Gurus of YouTube," *Time.com,* www.time.com/time/ magazine/article/0,9171,1570721,00.html, Accessed February 6, 2011.

22. Better Business Bureau, "BBB Structure," www.bbb.org/canada/ BBB-Structure/, Accessed February 10, 2011.

23. Better Business Bureau, "BBB Code of Business Practices (BBB Accreditation Standards)," www.bbb.org/canada/SitePage.aspx?id=e5c68728-5d54-4537-9e03-f33673a2e125, Accessed February 10, 2011.

24. David K. Foot, "Population Aging: Some Economic and Social Consequences of Population Aging," Canadian Priorities Agenda/*www.irpp.org/ cpa,* http://www.irpp.org/cpa/briefs/foot.pdf, Accessed February 10, 2011.

25. CNBC, "American Boomers Now a $2 Trillion Market," *msnbc.msn.com,* September 28, 2006, http://www.msnbc.msn.com/id/12288534, February 10, 2011.

26. Statistics Canada, "Demographic Change," http://www.statcan.gc.ca/pub/ 82-229-x/2009001/demo/intl-eng.htm, Accessed February 10, 2011.

27. Statistics Canada, "Study: Projections of the Diversity of the Canadian Population," http://www.statcan.gc.ca/daily-quotidien/100309/dq100309a-eng. htm, Accessed February 10, 2011.

28. Canada's Top 100 Employers, "Canada's Best Diversity Employers 2010," http://www.canadastop100.com/diversity/, Accessed February 10, 2011.

29. Ryan Z. Cortazar, "Diversity Training Fails to Boost Minorities into Management," *Harvard University Gazette* (online), September 14, 206, http://www. news.harvard.edu/gazette/2006/09.14/25-dobbin.html, Accessed February 10, 2011.

30. Andrea Cooper, "The Influencers: What Forces Will Affect Your Business in the Coming Year?" *Entrepreneur* (online), February 8, 2008, http://www. entrepreneur.com/magazine/entrepreneur/2008/march/190234.html, Accessed February 10, 2011.

31. Daniel Gross, "Hummer vs. Prius," *Slate.com,* February 26, 2004, http:// www.slate.com/id/2096191, Accessed February 10, 2011.

32. Mark Kyrnin, "Upgrade or Replace a Desktop PC?" *About.com,* http://com-previews.about.com/od/general/a/UpgradeReplace.htm, Accessed February 10, 2011.

33. Patty Azzarello, "How to Overcome IT's Credibility Challenges," *CIOUp-date.com,* September 25, 2007, http://www.cioupdate.com/article.php/ 3701571, Accessed February 10, 2011.

34. Allan Schweyer, "Managing the Virtual Global Workforce," *Human Capital* (online), October 17, 2006, http://www.hcamag.com/resources/ hr-strategy/managing-the-virtual-global-workforce/113172/, Accessed February 10, 2011.

35. Dave Roos, "The History of E-commerce," *howstuffworks.com,* http:// communication.howstuffworks.com/history-e-commerce.htm/printable, Accessed February 10, 2011.

36. General Electric, "Thomas Edison & GE," www.ge.com/company/history/ edison.html, Accessed June 25, 2008.

37. General Electric, "A Tradition of Innovation," www.ge.com/innovation/timeline/index.html, Accessed June 25, 2008.

38. General Electric, "We Are GE," www.gelighting.com/au/company/brochure/we_are_ge_brochure.pdf, Accessed February 4, 2012.

Chapter 2

1. European Commission, "G7/G8, G20," http://ec.europa.eu/economy_finance/international/forums/g7_g8_g20/index_en.htm, Accessed February 16, 2011.

2. World Countries News, "PwC: E7 to Overtake G7 by 2020," January 12, 2011, http://world-countries.net/archives/109481, Accessed February 16, 2011.

3. Tushar Dhara, "India to Top China as Fastest Growing Economy by 2015, Morgan Stanley Says," *Bloomberg.com*, http://www.bloomberg.com/news/2010-08-16/india-to-top-china-as-fastest-growing-economy-by-2015-morgan-stanley-says.html, Accessed February 16, 2011.

4. PricewaterhouseCoopers, "Global Financial Crisis Accelerates Shift in Economic Power to Emerging Economics," *pwc.com*, January 7, 2011, http://www.pwc.com/gx/en/press-room/2011/global-financial-crisis-accelerates-shift-eco-power.jhtml, Accessed February 16, 2011.

5. CreditLoan, "International Tax Rate Comparison," http://www.creditloan.com/infographics/international-tax-rate-comparison/, Accessed February 14, 2011.

6. Ibid.

7. Alfred Poor, "HDTV Almanac—NeTV Sales to Grow," *HDTV Magazine*, February 2, 2011, http://www.hdtvmagazine.com/columns/2011/02/hdtv-almanac-netv-sales-to-grow.php, Accessed February 7, 2011.

8. Guinness World Records 2011, "Kinect Confirmed As Fastest-Selling Consumer Electronics Device,"http://community.guinnessworldrecords.com/_Kinect-Confirmed-As-Fastest-Selling-Consumer-Electronics-Device/blog/3376939/7691.html, Accessed March 17, 2011.

9. Nancy Gohring (IDG News), "Mundie: Microsoft's Research Depth Enabled Kinect," PCWorld Business Center, July 2010, www.pcworld.com/businesscenter/article/202184/mundie_microsofts_research_depth_enabled_kinect.html, Accessed March 17, 2011.

10. Scot Meyer / SwitchYard Media, "Products Back by Popular Demand," *msn.com*, http://articles.moneycentral.msn.com/SmartSpending/ConsumerActionGuide/products-back-by-popular-demand.aspx?slide-number=6, Accessed September 6, 2011.

11. Alfred Poor, "HDTV Almanac—Internet TV Is the Competition," *HDTV Magazine*, October 18, 2010, http://www.hdtvmagazine.com/columns/2010/10/hdtv-almanac-internet-tv-is-the-competition.php, Accessed February 7, 2011.

12. Joe Wilcox, "Microsoft, Apple Alliance at Key Juncture," CNET News, February 2, 2002, http://news.cnet.com/2100-1040-843145.html, Accessed February 6, 2011.

13. "Competition Bureau Denies Interac's Corporate Bid," *MONEY*, February 12, 2010, http://money.canoe.ca/money/business/canada/archives/2010/02/20100212-160037.html, Accessed February 21, 2011.

14. Competition Bureau Canada, "Competition Bureau Reaches Agreement in Principle in Real Estate Case," http://www.competitionbureau.gc.ca/eic/site/cb-bc.nsf/eng/03293.html, Accessed February 21, 2011.

15. OECD, "Members and Partners," www.oecd.org/pages/0,3417,en_36734052_36761800_1_1_1_1_1,00.html, Accessed March 28, 2011.

16. Government of Canada, "Canada and the OECD," http://www.canadainternational.gc.ca/oecd-ocde/canada_oecd-ocde.aspx?lang=eng&view=d, Accessed March 28, 2011.

17. Muhammed Afruzur Rahman, "WestJet Airlines: Critical Success Factors—From Marketing Point of View," *seriousopinion.com,* March 4, 2009, http://www.seriousopinion.com/westjet-airlines-critical-success-factors/, Accessed February 7, 2011.

18. Central Intelligence Agency, "Canada," *The World Factbook* (online), https://www.cia.gov/library/publications/the-world-factbook/geos/ca.html, Accessed March 28, 2011.

19. Statistics Canada, "Consumer Price Index and Major Components, Canada," July 5, 2011, http://www.statcan.gc.ca/daily-quotidien/110629/t110629a1-eng.htm, Accessed August 17, 2011.

20. Statistics Canada, "Labour Force Survey (LFS)," November 4, 2011, http://www.statcan.gc.ca/cgi-bin/imdb/p2SV.pl?Function=getSurvey&SDDS=3701&lang=en&db=imdb&adm=8&dis=2, Accessed March 19, 2011.

21. Bank of Canada, "Inflation and Price Stability," http://www.bank-banque-canada.ca/en/backgrounders/bg-i1.html, Accessed March 19, 2011.

22. Statistics Canada, "Exchange Rates, Interest Rates, Money Supply and Stock Prices," November 4, 2010, http://www40.statcan.gc.ca/l01/cst01/econ07-eng.htm, Accessed March 20, 2011.

23. Bank of Canada, "The Bank Rate," http://www.bankofcanada.ca/wp-content/uploads/2010/11/bank_rate.pdf, Accessed March 28, 2011.

24. Gabriel Madway and Jennifer Robin Raj. "Apple iPad 2 Sales Seen Clearing 1 million units," Reuters, March 14, 2011, www.reuters.com/article/2011/03/14/us-apple-research-idUSTRE72D30020110314, Accessed March 27, 2011.

25. Brian X Chen, "Live Blog: Apple Unveils Thinner, Lighter iPad 2,, *"Wired.com* "Gadget Lab," March 2, 2011, www.wired.com/gadgetlab/2011/03/apple-ipad-liveblog/, Accessed March 28, 2011.

26. Ibid.

27. Jim Dalrymple, "Apple Says Demand for iPad 2 Is 'Amazing,'" *The Loop,* March 14, 2011, www.loopinsight.com/2011/03/14/apple-says-demand-for-ipad-2-is-amazing/, Accessed March 27, 2011.

Chapter 3

1. IKEA, "Responsibility Beyond Home Furnishing," http://www.ikea.com/ms/en_CA/the_ikea_story/people_and_the_environment/index.html, Accessed April 13, 2011.

2. Kristina Leung and Richard Yerema, "IKEA Canada Limited Partnership: Chosen as One of Canada's Greenest Employers for 2010," *eluta.ca,* http://www.eluta.ca/green-at-ikea-canada, Accessed April 13, 2011.

3. Ibid.

4. Ontario Consultants on Religious Tolerance, "Shared Belief in the 'Golden Rule,'" http://www.religioustolerance.org/reciproc.htm, Accessed April 21, 2011.

5. Dr. Martin Seligman/University of Pennsylvania, "Authentic Happiness," http://www.authentichappiness.sas.upenn.edu/Default.aspx, Accessed April 13, 2011..

6. The character's name in this story has been changed from the name used in the original article. Ann Pomeroy, "The Ethics Squeeze," *HR Magazine,* March 2006, 53.

7. Trevor S. Harding, Donald D. Carpenter, Cynthia J. Finelli, and Honor J. Passow. "The Influence of Academic Dishonesty on Ethical Decision-Making in the Workplace: A Study of Engineering Students," Proceedings of the 2004 ASEE Annual Conference & Exposition: Salt Lake City, UT, June 2004, http://digitalcommons.calpoly.edu/cgi/viewcontent.cgi?article=1060&context=mate_fac, Accessed April 13, 2011.

8. Renae Merle, "Boeing CEO Resigns Over Affair with Subordinate," *Washington Post* (online), March 8, 2005, http://www.washingtonpost.com/wp-dyn/articles/A13173-2005Mar7.html?nav=rss_topnews, Accessed April 13, 2011.

9. The character's name in this story has been changed from the name used in the original article. Pomeroy, "The Ethics Squeeze."

10. Ibid.

11. Kurt Eichenwald, *The Informant: A True Story* (New York: Broadway Books, 2001).

12. Miriam Schulman, "Winery with a Mission: Fetzer Vineyards Husbands the Earth's Resources," Markkula Center for Applied Ethics/Santa Clara University *(scu.edu)*, http://www.scu.edu/ethics/publications/iie/v7n2/fetzer.html, Accessed April 13, 2011.

13. Ibid.

14. Gap Inc., Press Release: "Gap Inc.'s P.A.C.E. Program Honored with the ICRW Innovation Award," March 9, 2011, http://www.gapinc.com/content/gapinc/html/media/pressrelease/2011/med_pr_PACEAward03082011.html, Accessed April 13, 2011.

15. Brooks Barnes, "Bowing to Pressure, Disney Bans Smoking in Its Branded Movies," *The New York Times* (online), July 26, 2007, http://www.nytimes.com/2007/07/26/business/media/26disney.html, Accessed April 13, 2011.

16. Shell, "Air Emissions," http://www.shell.com/home/content/environment_society/environment/air/, Accessed April 13, 2011.

17. Archie B. Carroll, "The Pyramid of Corporate Social Responsibility: Toward the Moral Management of Organizational Stakeholders," *Business Horizons*, July–August 1991, http://www.cbe.wwu.edu/dunn/rprnts.pyramidofcsr.pdf, Accessed April 23, 2011.

18. Mark Young, "HR as the Guardian of Corporate Values at Cadbury Schwepps," *Strategic HR Review*, January–February 2006, 10.

19. Amnesty International, "Indian Government Must Stop Refinery Expansion Until Human Rights Are Addressed," February 9, 2010, http://www.amnesty.org/en/news-and-updates/report/Vedanta, Accessed April 14, 2011.

20. Jennifer Alsever, "Chiquita Cleans Up Its Act," *Business 2.0 Magazine (money.cnn.com)*, October 2, 2006, http://money.cnn.com/magazines/business2/business2_archive/2006/08/01/8382241/index.htm, Accessed April 14, 2011.

21. Kate Connolly, " *Brigitte*, Germany's Most Popular Women's Mag, Bans Professional Models," *The Guardian* (online), October 5, 2009, http://www.guardian.co.uk/lifeandstyle/2009/oct/05/brigitte-german-magazine-bans-models, Accessed April 14, 2011.

22. CBC News Online, "Walkerton Report Highlights," January 2002, http://www.cbc.ca/news/background/walkerton/walkerton_report.html, Accessed April 14, 2011.

23. Nestlé Waters Canada, "Good Neighbour Policy," 2008, http://www.nestle-waters.ca/en/community/Good_Neighbour_Policy.htm, Accessed April 14, 2011.

24. European Business Forum, *Corporate Social Responsibility*, Summer 2004, http://www.johnelkington.com/ebf_CSR_report.pdf, Accessed April 14, 2011.

25. "The WorldBlu List of Most Democratic Workplaces 2011," http://www.worldblu.com/awardee-profiles/2011.php, Accessed October 5, 2011.

26. "I Love Rewards Employee-Centric Culture Gains a Spot on WorldBlu's Democratic Workplaces List for Third Consecutive Year," *PRWeb.com*, April 12, 2011, http://www.prweb.com/releases/2011/04/prweb5243754.htm, Accessed October 5, 2011.

27. TimeWarner, "Corporate Responsibility," 2011, http://www.timewarner.com/our-company/corporate-responsibility/, Accessed April 14, 2011.

28. NewsofAP, "USA: Bill Gates Is Once Again the Richest Man in US," http://www.newsofap.com/newsofap-25709-26-usa-bill-gates-is-once-again-the-richest-man-in-us.html, Accessed April 14, 2011.

29. "Who's Who," *The Corporation* (documentary)/Big Picture Media Corporation, http://www.thecorporation.com/index.cfm?page_id=3, Accessed April 14, 2011.

30. "Worldwide HIV & AIDS Estimates, End of 2009," *AVERT.org*, http://www.avert.org/worldstats.htm, Accessed April 15, 2011.

31. World Health Organization, "Tuberculosis," http://www.who.int/mediacentre/factsheets/who104/en/print.html, Accessed April 15, 2011.

32. "Malaria Kills," *NothingButNets.net*, http://www.nothingbutnets.net/malaria-kills/, Accessed April 15, 2011.

33. Nesara International, "Canada's Constitution," http://nesara.insights2.org/Constitution.html, Accessed January 30, 2011.

34. Department of Justice, *Canadian Charter of Rights and Freedoms,* http://laws-lois.justice.gc.ca/eng/charter/page-1.html#anchorbo-ga:l_I-gb:s_1, Accessed April 18, 2011.

35. Human Resources and Skills Development Canada, Ministry of Labour, *Canada Labour Code, Part II–Overview,* http://www.hrsdc.gc.ca/eng/labour/health_safety/overview.shtml, Accessed June 27, 2011.

36. Department of Justice, *Canadian Human Rights Act,* http://laws-lois.justice.gc.ca/eng/H-6/page-1.html#anchorbo-ga:s_2, Accessed January 26, 2011.

37. Department of Justice, *Employment Equity Act,* http://laws-lois.justice.gc.ca/eng/E-5.401/page-1. *html*#anchorbo-ga:s_2, Accessed January 26, 2011.

38. Consumers' Association of Canada, "Consumer Rights," http://www.consumer.ca/1625, Accessed April 18, 2011.

39. Competition Bureau, "Our Legislation," http://www.competitionbureau.gc.ca/eic/site/cb-bc.nsf/eng/h_00148.html, Accessed April 16, 2011.

40. Canada Revenue Agency, "Charities and Giving," http://www.cra-arc.gc.ca/chrts-gvng/menu-eng.html, Accessed April 16, 2011.

41. Con Artist Hall of Infamy, "The Inductees: Bernard L. Madoff,"http://www.thehallofinfamy.org/inductees.php?action=detail&artist=bernard_madoff, Accessed April 16, 2011.

42. Con Artist Hall of Infamy, The Inductees: Bernie Ebbers," http://www.thehallofinfamy.org/inductees.php?action=detail&artist=bernie_ebbers, Accessed April 16, 2011.

43. "Corporate Social Responsibility: Companies in the News, Enron," *mallenbaker.net*, October 2, 2007, http://www.mallenbaker.net/csr/CSRfiles/enron.html, Accessed April 19, 2011.

44. FAIR, "Some Canadian Whistleblowers," http://fairwhistleblower.ca/wbers/canadian_wbs.html, Accessed April 19, 2011.

45. Parliament of Canada, *Bill C-13: An Act to Amend the Criminal Code,* http://www2.parl.gc.ca/Sites/LOP/LegislativeSummaries/Bills_ls.asp?Parl=37&Ses=3&ls=c13, Accessed April 21, 2011.

46. http://transparency.org/about_us, Accessed April 18, 2011.

47. http://transparency.org/about_us, Accessed April 18, 2011.

48. Heather Burke, "Salvation Army Says Target Ban May Cost $9 Million," *Bloomberg.com,* November 9, 2004, http://www.bloomberg.com/apps/news?pid=newsarchive&sid=aq0Ci588n96c&refer=us, Accessed June 27, 2011.

49. International Association of Chiefs of Police, "Ethics Training in Law Enforcement," http://www.theiacp.org/PolicServices/ExecutiveServices/ProfessionalAssistance/Ethics/ReportsResources/EthicsTraininginLaw Enforcement/tabid/194/Default.aspx, Accessed April 21, 2011.

50. Benjamin Freedman, rev. Patricia Bailey, "Medical Ethics," *The Canadian Encyclopedia* (online) http://www.thecanadianencyclopedia.com/index.cfm?PgNm=TCE&Params=A1ARTA0005197, Accessed April 21, 2011.

51. "Coca-Cola 'Misleading' Investors over Water Use in India," *Ecologist* (online), April 23, 2010, http://www.theecologist.org/News/news_round_up/470622/cocacola_misleading_investors_over_water_use_in_india.html, Accessed April 21, 2011.

52. Steve Kovach, "AT&T Blocks PlayBook Tethering to BlackBerry Devices," *Financial Post* (online), April 19, 2011, http://business.financialpost.com/2011/04/19/att-blocks-playbook-tethering-to-blackberry-devices/, Accessed April 21, 2011.

53. Mark Young, "HR as the Guardian of Corporate Values at Cadbury Schweppes," *Strategic HR Review*, Vol. 5, No. 2 (2006), pp. 10–11, www.emeraldinsight.com/journals.htm?issn=1475-4398&volume=5&issue=2&articleid=1728817&show=abstract, Accessed June 30, 2011.

54. Topia GreenStop (website), http://www.topiagreenstop.com/, Accessed April 20, 2011.

55. *Monmouth University Magazine*, vol. Xxvi, no. 3, 2006, http://www.monmouth.edu/about_monmouth/monmouth_magazine/MUFall2006.pdf, Accessed April 20, 2011.

56. "Malaria Prevention," *news-medical.net*, http://www.news-medical.net/health/Malaria-Prevention.aspx, Accessed April 20, 2011.

57. Steven Musil, "Week in Review: Google Slams China Censorship," CNET News (online), http://news.cnet.com/8301-1001_3-10435702-92.html, Accessed April 20, 2011.

58. Ben Elgin and Bruce Einhorn, "Outrunning China's Web Cops," *Businessweek* (online), February 20, 2006, http://www.businessweek.com/magazine/content/06_08/b3972061.htm, Accessed April 20, 2011.

59. Jennifer Beck, "Business Hero: Ray Anderson," *myhero.com*, March 18, 2009, http://myhero.com/go/hero.asp?hero=r_anderson, Accessed April 20, 2011.

60. Interface, "What Is Sustainability?" http://www.interfaceglobal.com/Sustainability/What-is-Sustainability-.aspx, Accessed April 20, 2011.

61. Interface, "Our Progress," http://www.interfaceglobal.com/Sustainability/Our-Progress.aspx, Accessed April 20, 2011.

62. Global Footprint Network, "Footprint Basics—Overview," http://www.footprintnetwork.org/en/index.php/GFN/page/footprint_basics_overview/, Accessed April 20, 2011.

63. Starbucks, "Global Responsibility Report: Goals & Progress 2010," http://www.starbucks.com/responsibility/learn-more/goals-and-progress/recycling, Accessed April 20, 2011.

64. Starbucks, "Shared Planet: Global Responsibility Scorecard 2009," http://assets.starbucks.com/assets/ssp-g-p-scorecard.pdf, Accessed April 20, 2011.

65. Managing Values, "The Ethics of Oil Spills—BP's 'Defining Moment'?"May 14, 2010, www.values.com.au/2010/05/14/the-ethics-of-oil-spills-bps-defining-moment/, Accessed April 23, 2011.

66. Ibid.

67. BP Global, "Deepwater Horizon Accident,"www.bp.com/sectiongenericarticle800.do?categoryId=9036575&contentId=7067541, Accessed April 23, 2011.

68. Alyssa Newcomb and Matt Gutman, "Spillionaires—Profiting off the BP Oil Spill," abcNews.com, April 17, 2011, http://abcnews.go.com/Business/bp-oil-spill-spillionaires-profit-off-gulf-disaster/story?id=13396181, Accessed October 11, 2011.

69. AFP, "US Report Spreads Blame for BP Oil Spill," News24.com, September 14, 2011, http://www.news24.com/SciTech/News/US-report-spreads-blame-for-BP-oil-spill-20110914, Accessed October 3, 2011.

Chapter 4

1. U.S. Chamber of Commerce/Business Civic Leadership Centre, "Corporate Aid Tracker—Japanese Earthquake and Tsunami, March 2011," http://bclc.uschamber.com/site-page/corporate-aid-tracker-japanese-earthquake-and-tsunami-march-2011, Accessed October 25, 2011.

2. Foreign Affairs and International Trade, "Canada Provides Relief Supplies to Japan," March 15, 2011, http://www.international.gc.ca/media/aff/news-communiques/2011/106.aspx?view=d, Accessed October 25, 2011.

3. BBC News "China, Japan, South Korea Seek Trade Pact," http://www.bbc.co.uk/news/13184570, Accessed April 25, 2011.

4. Len Jelinek, "Japan Earthquake Suspends Supply of Raw Material Used in 25 Percent of Global Chip Production—Memory Segment Hit Hard," *iSuppli.com,* March 21, 2011, http://www.isuppli.com/Semiconductor-Value-Chain/News/Pages/Japan-Earthquake-Suspends-Supply-of-Raw-Material-Used-in-25-Percent-of-Global-Chip-Production-Memory-Segment-Hit-Hard.aspx, Accessed October 25, 2011.

5. Scott Malone, "Japan Disaster Called Temporary Hit for Rare Earth," *Reuters.com,* March 16, 2005, http://in.mobile.reuters.com/article/businessNews/idININdia-55608020110315, Accessed April 25, 2011.

6. Laura Myers, "Japan Crisis Spurs Iodide Demand in U.S. and Canada," *Reuters.com,* March 15, 2011, http://www.reuters.com/article/2011/03/15/us-japan-quake-iodide-demand-idUSTRE72E8Y920110315, Accessed October 25, 2011.

7. Ken Belson and Hiroko Tabuchi, "Japan Finds Contaminated Food Up to 90 Miles From Nuclear Sites," *The New York Times* (online), March 20, 2011, http://query.nytimes.com/gst/fullpage.html?res=9A0DE2D61631F933A15750C0A9679D8B63&pagewanted=2, Accessed April 25, 2011.

8. Rabobank Group, Press Release: "Japan Food Trade Deficit Set to Rise After Earthquake," April 7, 2011, https://www.perscentrumrabobank.com/publications/food__agri/rabobank_says_japan_food_trade_deficit_set_to_rise_after_earthquake_.html, Accessed April 25, 2011.

9. Harumi Ozawa, "Trade Will Help Japan Quake Recovery: Ministers," *The Citizen* (online), April 24, 2011, http://www.citizen.co.za/citizen/content/en/citizen/world-news?oid=189917&sn=Detail&pid=333&Trade-will-help-Japan-quake-recovery-ministers, Accessed April 25, 2011.

10. Vittorio Hernandez, "China, South Korea Keep Japanese Food Import Restrictions," All Headline News (online), April 25, 2011, http://www.allheadlinenews.com/articles/90046246?China%2C%20South%20Korea%20keep%20Japanese%20food%20import%20restrictions#ixzz1KXQGTJjq, Accessed April 25, 2011.

11. Kounteya Sinha, "Govt Bans Food Imports from Japan for 3 Months," *The Economic Times* (online), April 6, 2011, http://economictimes.indiatimes.com/news/economy/foreign-trade/govt-bans-food-imports-from-japan-for-3-months/articleshow/7881681.cms, Accessed April 25, 2011.

12. Bonnie Burgess, "Global Impact of Japan Earthquake Disaster," *About.com,* April 15, 2011, http://tourism.about.com/od/globaltourismissues/a/Global-Impact-Of-Japan-Earthquake-Disaster.htm, Accessed April 24, 2011.

13. Ibid.

14. Ibid.

15. Agence France-Presse, "IATA Sees Sharp Slowdown in Japan Air Traffic," *ABS-CBNnews.com,* March 19, 2011, http://www.abs-cbnnews.com/business/03/19/11/iata-sees-sharp-slowdown-japan-air-traffic, Accessed April 25, 2011.

16. Charles W. L. Hill, *International Business: Competing in the Global Marketplace,* 8th ed. (Burr Ridge, IL: Irwin/McGraw-Hill Publishing Co., 2010), pp. 6–8.

17. Ibid.

18. Govindkrishna Seshan, "Fruit Punch," *Business Standard,* February 26, 2008, http://www.business-standard.com/india/storypage.php?autono=314923, Accessed April 26, 2011.

19. Guy Stanley, "Wal-Mart in the NAFTA Market," *GlobalStart.biz*, http://globalstart.biz/teaching-resources/wal-mart-nafta-market, Accessed October 26, 2011.

20. Democratic Leadership Council, "The World's Top 50 Economies: 44 Countries, Six Firms," http://www.dlc.org/ndol_ci.cfm?contentid=255173&kaid=108&subid=900003, Accessed April 26, 2011.

21. Hill, *International Business: Competing in the Global Marketplace,* pp. 10–16.

22. Daniel Trefler, "Policy Responses to the New Offshoring: Think Globally, Invest Locally," A Paper Prepared for Industry Canada's March 30, 2005 Roundtable on Offshoring, April 29, 2005, http://homes.chass.utoronto.ca/~trefler/Outsourcing_Final_TeX.pdf, Accessed April 9, 2011.

23. Justin Fox, "Where Your Job Is Going," *Fortune* (online), November 24, 2003, http://money.cnn.com/magazines/fortune/fortune_archive/2003/11/24/353752/index.htm, Accessed April 9, 2011.

24. U.S. Department of State, "Background Note: Cuba," http://www.state.gov/r/pa/ei/bgn/2886.htm, Accessed April 28, 2011.

25. Harley Richards, "Canada Lands Share of EU Beef Import Quota," *Red Deer Advocate* (online), November 23, 2010, http://www.albertalocalnews.com/reddeeradvocate/business/local_biz/Canada_lands_share_of_EU_beef_import_quota_110287579.html, Accessed April 28, 2011.

26. Eric Eldon, "Facebook Hasn't Signed Any Deals to Enter China—At Least Not Yet," InsideFacebook.com, April 11, 2011, http://www.insidefacebook.com/2011/04/11/facebook-hasnt-signed-any-deals-to-enter-china-at-least-not-yet/, Accessed April 24, 2011.

27. AFP, "China Warns Google not to Stop Filtering Web Searches," Google News, March 12, 2010, http://www.google.com/hostednews/afp/article/ALeqM5hyxPaSAvdmIPwKHXROKfG_a19YjQ, Accessed April 24, 2011.

28. Brendan Greeley and Mark Drajem, "China's Facebook Syndrome," Bloomberg Businessweek.com, March 10, 2011, http://www.businessweek.com/magazine/content/11_12/b4220029428856.htm, Accessed April 24, 2011.

29. Ibid.

30. "Google Stops China Services," PoliticolNews.com, July 22, 2011, http://www.politicolnews.com/google-stops-china-services/?utm_source=INK&utm_medium=copy&utm_campaign=share, Accessed April 24, 2011.

31. World Trade Organization, "The GATT Years: From Havana to Marrakesh," http://www.wto.org/english/thewto_e/whatis_e/tif_e/fact4_e.htm, Accessed May 1, 2011.

32. World Trade Organization, "Understanding the WTO," http://www.wto.org/english/thewto_e/whatis_e/tif_e/tif_e.htm, Accessed May 1, 2011.

33. World Trade Organization, "The Doha Round," http://www.wto.org/english/tratop_e/dda_e/dda_e.htm, Accessed May 1, 2011.

34. Central Intelligence Agency, "Rank Order: Exports," *The World Factbook* (online), https://www.cia.gov/library/publications/the-world-factbook/rankorder/2078rank.html, Accessed May 1, 2011.

35. Matt Rosenberg, "Euro Countries," *About.com*, March 17, 2011, http://geography.about.com/od/lists/a/euro.htm, Accessed May 1, 2011.

36. BBC News, "Microsoft Loses Anti-Trust Appeal," September 17, 2007, http://news.bbc.co.uk/2/hi/business/6998272.stm, Accessed May 1, 2011.

37. Asia-Pacific Economic Cooperation, "What Is Asia-Pacific Economic Cooperation?" http://www.apec.org/About-Us/About-APEC.aspx, Accessed May 1, 2011.

38. Franchise International, "Disney Signs India Master," November 7, 2006, http://www.franchise-international.net/page/walt-disney-company/disney-signs-india-master.php, Accessed May 1, 2011.

39. Franchise International, "Domino's Pizza Gunning for 10,000th Store," August 16, 2006, http://www.franchise-international.net/page/domino-s-pizza-group-limited/dominos-pizza-gunning-for-10-000th-store.php, Accessed May 1, 2011.

40. SRI International, "Intellectual Property and Licensing," http://www.sri.com/rd/hot.html, Accessed May 1, 2011.

41. Janaki Krishnan and Rina Chandran, ed. Dhara Ranasinghe, "Factbox: Indian Retail Attracts More Foreign Players," *Reuters.com,* May 21, 2010, http://us.mobile.reuters.com/article/businessNews/idUSTRE64K1CC20100521, Accessed May 1, 2011.

42. Hyundai Motor Company, "Hyundai's Russia Plant On-Schedule," http://worldwide.hyundai.com/company-overview/news-view.aspx?idx=273&nCurPage=1&strSearchColunm=&strSearchWord=&ListNum=189, Accessed May 1, 2011.

43. Industry Canada, "International Trade Canadian Economy (NAICS 11-91)," http://www.ic.gc.ca/eic/site/cis-sic.nsf/eng/h_00029.html#it1, Accessed May 1, 2011.

44. C.G. Alex and Barbara Bowers, "The American Way to Countertrade," *Barter News* (online), no. 17, 1988, http://www.barternews.com/american_way.htm, Accessed May 1, 2011.

45. Kwintessential, "Results of Poor Cross Cultural Awareness," http://www.kwintessential.co.uk/cultural-services/articles/Results%20of%20Poor%20Cross%20Cultural%20Awareness.html, Accessed May 1, 2011.

46. Kwintessential, "Business Hours in Spain," http://www.kwintessential.co.uk/articles/article/Spain/Business-hours-in-Spain/9, Accessed May 2, 2011.

47. Kwintessential, "Doing Business in Germany," http://www.kwintessential.co.uk/etiquette/doing-business-germany.html, Accessed May 2, 2011.

48. Kwintessential, "Results of Poor Cross Cultural Awareness." http://www.kwintessential.co.uk/cultural-services/articles/Results%20of%20Poor%20Cross%20Cultural%20Awareness.html, accessed May1, 2011.

49. Ibid.

50. Department of Justice, *The Corruption of Foreign Public Officials Act,* http://www.justice.gc.ca/eng/dept-min/pub/cfpoa-lcape/index.html, Accessed May 2, 2011.

51. Jeffrey Immelt, "Winning in the Essential Themes,"GE 2007 Annual Report, http://www.ge.com/ar2007/ltr_winning.jsp, Accessed June 28, 2011.

52. General Electric Company, "GE and the Olympic Games: A Legacy for Beijing," www.ge.com,http://www.ge.com/innovation/china/index.html, Accessed June 28, 2011.

53. Immelt, "Winning in the Essential Themes."

54. General Electric Company, "Worldwide Activities," www.ge.com, http://www.ge.com/company/worldwide_activities/index.html, Accessed June 28, 2011.

Chapter 5

1. Careerbuilder.com, "Forty-five Percent of Employers Use Social Networking Sites to Research Job Candidates, CareerBuilder Survey Finds," http://www.careerbuilder.com/share/aboutus/pressreleasesdetail.

aspx?id=pr519&sd=8%2f19%2f2009&ed=12%2f31%2f2009&siteid=cbpr&sc_cmp1=cb_pr519_&cbRecursionCnt=1&cbsid=4bbce0cfa8bc46909f7b09573e776c23-304007915-wy-6, Accessed May 4, 2011.

2. Patti Church and Andy Church, *Whyhire.me Reveal Your Potential,* Winter 2010, http://beta.whyhire.me/images/media/RevealYourPotential_Winter2010.pdf, Accessed November 11, 2011.

3. Patti Church, Patti, "Whyhire.me Mission Statement," Interview Questionnaire, February 17, 2011.

4. Ibid.

5. Yahoo! Finance, McDonald's Corp., http://finance.yahoo.com/q/pr?s=MCD+Profile, Accessed May 3, 2011.

6. Steven Almond, "Citizen Wayne—The Unauthorized Biography," *Miami New Times,* December 1–7, 1994, vol. 9, no. 33, http://www.corporations.org/wmi/huizenga.html, Accessed May 3, 2011.

7. Scott Allen, "Quotations from Famous Entrepreneurs on Entrepreneurship: Inspiring Words from the Best of the Best," *About.com,* http://entrepreneurs.about.com/od/famousentrepreneurs/a/quotations.htm, Accessed May 3, 2011.

8. Mary Bellis, "Henry Ford (1863–1947)," *About.com,* http://inventors.about.com/od/fstartinventors/a/HenryFord.htm, Accessed May 3, 2011.

9. Ben & Jerry's Homemade, Inc., http://www.benjerry.com/company/, Accessed May 3, 2011.

10. Adapted from Jack Kaplan and Anthony Warren, *Patterns of Entrepreneurship,* 2nd ed., John Wiley & Sons, Inc., p. 27 from U.S. Small Business Administration Report, "The State of Small Business: A Report of the President"(Washington, D.C.: U.S. Government Printing Office, 1995), p. 114

11. "When Taking Business Risks Is Necessary," *San Francisco Business Times,* August 4, 1996, http://www.bizjournals.com/sanfrancisco/stories/1996/08/05/smallb2.html, Accessed May 3, 2011.

12. CEO Challenges, "Kennedy Featured in Daily Camera Business Plus Chat," http://www.ceochallenges.com/news/2008/02/29/kennedy-featured-daily-camera-business-plus-chat, Accessed May 3, 2011.

13. Pete's Wicked, http://www.petes.com, Accessed May 3, 2011.

14. John Case, "The Gazelle Theory," *Inc. Magazine* (online), May 15, 2011, http://www.inc.com/magazine/20010515/22613.html, Accessed May 3, 2011.

15. Facebook, "Statistics," http://www.facebook.com/press/info.php?statistics, Accessed May 3, 2011.

16. Michael Arndt, "Creativity Overflowing," *Businessweek* (online), May 8, 2006, http://www.businessweek.com/magazine/content/06_19/b3983061.htm?chan=searchand, Accessed May 3, 2011.

17. Michael Arndt, "How Whirlpool Defines Innovation," *Businessweek* (online), March6, 2006, http://www.businessweek.com/print/innovate/content/mar2006/id20060306_287425.htm, Accessed May 3, 2011.

18. Aneliese Debus, *Small Business, Big Value,* Canadian Federation of Independent Business, October 2007, http://www.cfib.ca/research/reports/rr3040.pdf, Accessed May 3, 2011.

19. Industry Canada, "Canadian Industry Statistics," http://www.ic.gc.ca/eic/site/cis-sic.nsf/eng/h_00005.html#employment_size_category, Accessed May 3, 2011.

20. Industry Canada: Small Business and Tourism Branch, *Key Small Business Statistics,* July 2010, http://www.ic.gc.ca/eic/site/sbrp-rppe.nsf/vwapj/KSBS-PSRPE_July-Juillet2010_eng.pdf/$FILE/KSBS-PSRPE_July-Juillet2010_eng.pdf, Accessed May 3, 2007.

21. ProQuest, "Discovery Guides," http://www.csa.com/discoveryguides/scholarship/gloss.php, Accessed May 3, 2011.

22. Keith Girard, "GM Bankruptcy Spells Disaster for Small Suppliers," *The Washington Post* (online), May 28, 2009, http://allbusiness.washingtonpost.

com/government/elections-politics-campaigns/12344120-1.html, Accessed May 3, 2011.

23. "Small Business Online," *Entrepreneur* (online), http://www.entrepreneur.com/sbe/online/index.html, Accessed May 3, 2011.

24. Debus, *Small Business, Big Value.*

25. "Bruce Freeman," PROLine Communications, Inc., http://www.prolinepr.com/bruce_freeman.html, Accessed May 3, 2011.

26. Industry Canada: Small Business and Tourism Branch, *Key Small Business Statistics.*

27. Wim Venter, "Your Own Business–Risks vs. Rewards," *Ezinearticles.com*, http://ezinearticles.com/?Your-Own-Business—-Risks-Vs-Rewards&id=1464351, Accessed May 4, 2011.

28. Stacy Perman, Jeffrey Gangemi, and Douglas MacMillan, "Entrepreneurs Favorite Mistakes: Nina Riley, Water Sensations," *Businessweek* (online), http://images.businessweek.com/ss/06/09/favorite_mistake/index_01.htm, Accessed May 4, 2011.

29. Small Business Financing Centre, "Canadian Small Business Grants and Loans Can Be the Key to Success," http://www.grants-loans.org/small-business-grants.php, Accessed May 4, 2011.

30. Canadian Franchise Association, "Fast Franchise Facts," http://www.cfa.ca/Publications_Research/FastFacts.aspx, Accessed November 4, 2011.

31. Scotiabank: Get Growing for Business Blog, "Franchising Opportunities in Canada," http://getgrowingforbusiness.scotiabank.com/blog/franchising-opportunities-canada, Accessed November 4, 2011.

32. Canadian Franchise Association, "Franchise System Members," http://www.cfa.ca/MemberListing.aspx#M, Accessed November 4, 2011.

33. Tim Hortons, "Frequently Asked Questions," http://www.timhortons.com/ca/en/join/franchise_ca_faq.html, Accessed November 4, 2011.

34. CBC News Online, "Suncor, Petro-Canada Announce Merger," March 23, 2009, http://www.cbc.ca/news/business/story/2009/03/23/suncor-petro-canada-merge.html, Accessed May 10, 2011.

Chapter 6

1. "World's Top 20 Food & Beverage Companies," *FoodBev.com*, October 14, 2010, http://www.foodbev.com/gallery/worlds-top-20-food-beverage-companies; PepsiCo, "Letter to Shareholders," *2010 Annual Report* (online), http://www.PepsiCo.com/annual10/letter/todays-business.html; and "The World's Most Powerful Women: Indra Nooyi," *Forbes* (online), August 2011, http://www.forbes.com/profile/indra-nooyi/, All accessed November 6, 2011.

2. PepsiCo, "The PepsiCo Family," http://www.PepsiCo.com/Company/The-PepsiCo-Family/PepsiCo-Americas-Beverages.html; and PepsiCo, *2010 Annual Report*, http://www.PepsiCo.com/Download/PepsiCo_Annual_Report_2010_Full_Annual_Report.pdf, both accessed November 6, 2011.

3. Yale School of Management, "Alumni Profiles: Indra Nooyi '80," http://mba.yale.edu/alumni/alumni_profiles/nooyii.shtml, Accessed November 11, 2011.

4. Betsy Morris, "The Pepsi Challenge," *Fortune* (online), February 19, 2008, http://money.cnn.com/2008/02/18/news/companies/morris_nooyi.fortune/index.htm?postversion=2008021904, Accessed March 30, 2011.

5. Yale School of Management, "Alumni Profiles: Indra Nooyi '80."

6. Morris, "The Pepsi Challenge."

7. Ibid.

8. Diane Brady, "Indra Nooyi: Keeping Cool in Hot Water," *Businessweek* (online), June 11, 2007, http://www.businessweek.com/magazine/content/07_24/b4038067.htm, Accessed March 30, 2011.

9. Meghan Casserly, "The World's Most Powerful Women: Indra Nooyi," *Forbes* (online), October 7, 2010, http://money.ca.msn.com/savings-debt/gallery/forbes/gallery.aspx?cp-documentid=25850149&page=5, Accessed November 6, 2011.

10. Brady, "Indra Nooyi: Keeping Cool in Hot Water."

11. "The World's Most Powerful Women: Indra Nooyi," *Forbes* (online), August 2011.

12. Ibid.

13. Andrea Kostelas (ed.), "CEO of the Year: PepsiCo's Indra K. Nooyi," *Global Supply Chain Review,* July 2009, http://www.gsclg.com/images/GSC_Review_July2009.pdf, Accessed November 6, 2011.

14. Carter McNamara, "Free Basic Guide to Leadership and Supervision," Free Management Library, http://www.managementhelp.org/mgmnt/prsnlmnt.htm#anchor1012225, Accessed March 30, 2011.

15. Domino's Pizza Canada Ltd., "Domino's Pizza Careers," http://www.dominos.ca/pages/legal-join-ca.jsp, Accessed March 30, 2011.

16. Nikebiz, "Frequently Asked Questions," http://swoosh.custhelp.com/, Accessed November 6, 2011.

17. Adidas Group, "Corporate Mission Statement," http://adidas-group.corporate-publications.com/2010/gb/en/group-management-report-our-group/corporate-mission-statement.html, Accessed November 6, 2011.

18. McDonald's: Student Zone/Company Information, "What Is McDonald's Mission Statement?, http://www.aboutmcdonalds.com/mcd/our_company/mcd_faq/student_research.html#7, Accessed November 6, 2011.

19. Canadian Cancer Society, "Our Mission, Vision and Values," http://www.cancer.ca/Ontario/About%20us/OD-Mission.aspx?sc_lang=en, Accessed March 30, 2011.

20. Google, "Our Philosophy," http://www.google.com/corporate/tenthings.html, Accessed March 31, 2011.

21. The Coca-Cola Company, "Workplace Culture," http://www.thecoca-colacompany.com/citizenship/workplace_culture.html, Accessed March 31, 2011.

22. Volvo Car Corporation, "About Volvo," http://www.volvocars.com/intl/top/about/corporate/career/Pages/default.aspx, Accessed March 31, 2011.

23. Cara Foods, "Values & Principles,"http://www.dgp.utoronto.ca/~trendall/sfp/boycott/Cara_Values_and_Principles.html, Accessed March 31, 2011.

24. Canadian Tire, "Business Conduct Compliance," http://corp.canadiantire.ca/EN/Investors/Governance/Pages/CodeofConduct.aspx, Accessed March 31, 2011.

25. Vanguard, "Business Contingency Planning and Disaster Recovery Programs at Vanguard," 2011, www.vanguard.com/pdf/s509.pdf?2210035511, Accessed November 28, 2011.

26. International Institute for Organization Research, "Horizontal Organization," http://www.anarchy.no/horizon1.html, Accessed March 30, 2011.

27. James M. Kouzes and Barry Z. Posner, *The Leadership Challenge,* 3rd ed. (San Francisco: Jossey-Bass, 2003).

28. Fred Luthans, "Successful vs. Effective Real Managers," *Academy of Management Executive,* 1988, 2(2):127–132.

29. William Ouchi, "Markets, Bureaucracies, and Clans," *Administrative Science Quarterly*, March 1980, vol. 25, no. 1, pp. 129–141.

30. Adapted from Carey Toane, "Overall Winner—Loblaw's Craig Hutchinson: Back to the Future," *Strategy* (online), December 1, 2009, http://strategyonline.ca/2009/12/01/moyhutchison-20091201/?page=2, Accessed March 31, 2001 .

31. Loblaw Companies Ltd., "Training Developer-Supply Chain: Company Description," Linkedin.com, October 28, 2011, http://ca.linkedin.com/jobs/jobs-Training-DeveloperSupply-Chain-2121279, Accessed November 5, 2011.

32. Dana Flavelle, Price Fight: Superstores take on Wal-Mart," *the star.com*, October 2, 2009, http://www.thestar.com/Business/article/704193, Accessed November 5, 2011.

33. Rick Wartzman, "Has Toyota Lost Its Way?" BusinessWeek.com, November 26, 2007, http://www.businessweek.com/managing/content/nov2007/ca20071125_337938.htm; Charles Fishman. "No Satisfaction at Toyota" fast-company.com, December 2006, http://www.fastcompany.com/magazine/111/open_no-satisfaction.html; Toyota Motor Sales U.S.A., Inc., "Our Company," http://www.toyota.com/about/our_values/index.html, Accessed May 15, 2008.

34. Toyota Motor Manufacturing Kentucky, Inc., "Toyota Production System Terms," http://www.toyotageorgetown.com/terms.asp, Accessed May 15, 2008.

35. Katsuhiro Nakagawa, "The Toyota Way: Japanese Management in the Global Economy—Up Close and Personal," University of California, San Diego School of International Relations and Pacific Studies, September 27, 2004, http://irps.ucsd.edu/news/speeches/the-toyota-way.htm, Accessed May 15, 2008.

36. Ibid.

Chapter 7

1. General Electric Company, "Leadership," http://www.ge.com/company/leadership/index.html, Accessed April 2, 2011.

2. General Electric Company, "Jeff Immelt, CEO," http://www.ge.com/company/leadership/ceo.html, Accessed April 2, 2011.

3. Diane Brady, "Can GE Still Manage?" *Businessweek* (online), April 15, 2010, http://www.businessweek.com/magazine/content/10_17/b4175026765571.htm, Accessed November 7, 2011.

4. General Electric Company, "Executive Leaders," http://www.ge.com/company/leadership/executives.html, Accessed November 7, 2011.

5. Brady, "Can GE Still Manage?"

6. Ibid.

7. Steve Lohr, "G.E. Goes With What It Knows: Making Stuff," *The New York Times*, December 4, 2010, http://www.nytimes.com/2010/12/05/business/05ge.html, Accessed April 2, 2011.

8. Brady, "Can GE Still Manage?"

9. Leslie Knudson, "Generating Leaders GE Style," *HR Management* (online), no. 4, http://www.hrmreport.com/article/Generating-leaders-GE-style/, Accessed November 7, 2011.

10. Lohr, "G.E. Goes With What It Knows: Making Stuff."

11. Ibid.

12. Mihaly Csikszentmihalyi, *Flow* (New York: HarperCollins, 1990).

13. Towers Perrin, *Closing the Engagement Gap*, Towers Perrin Global Workforce Study 2007–2008, http://www.towersperrin.com/tp/getwebcachedoc?webc=HRS\USA\2008\200803\GWS_Global_Report20072008_31208.pdf, Accessed April 2, 2011.

14. Towers Watson, *Turbocharging Employee Engagement: Part 1—The Engagement Engine*, Two-Part White Paper 2010, http://www.towerswatson.com/assets/pdf/629/Manager-Recognition_Part1_WP_12-24-09.pdf, Accessed November 7, 2011.

15. Towers Watson, "Key Findings: An Interview with July Gebauer on Towers Perrin's Just Released Global Workforce Study, Part 2," http://www.towersperrin.com/tp/showhtml.jsp?url=global/publications/gws/key-findings_2.htm&country=global, Accessed April 2, 2011.

16. Towers Perrin, *Closing the Engagement Gap*.

17. Towers Perrin, *2007–2008 Towers Perrin Global Work force Study,* http://www .towersperrin.com/tp/getwebcachedoc?webc=HRS/USA/2008/200802/ GWS_handout_web.pdf, Accessed April 2, 2011.

18. Towers Watson, "Key Findings: An Interview with July Gebauer on Towers Perrin's Just Released Global Workforce Study, Part 2."

19. Best Employers in Canada, "Best Employers in Canada 2010 List," http:// was2.hewitt.com/bestemployers/canada/pages/the_list_2010.htm, Accessed November 7, 2011.

20. Towers Perrin, *Closing the Engagement Gap.*

21. Carnegie Management Group, "The Executor Mentor: The High Cost of Disengagement," http://www.carnegiemg.com.au/blog/the-disengagement-crisis/, Accessed April 2, 2011.

22. Nash Popovic, "What Really Motivates Us?" BBC News in Video, http://news.bbc.co.uk/nolavconsole/ukfs_news/hi/newsid_4760000/ newsid_4764500/nb_rm_4764545.stm, Accessed April 2, 2011.

23. Victor Vroom, *Work and Motivation,* (New York: Wiley, 1964); and Craig Pinder, *Work Motivation* (Glenview, IL: Scott, Foresman, 1984).

24. "The WorldBlu List of Most Democratic Workplaces 2010," http://www .worldblu.com/awardee-profiles/2010.php, Accessed November 7, 2011.

25. Charlton Communications, "The WestJet Story," lin.ca/Files/10721/vm091. pdf, Accessed April 4, 2011.

26. Gallup, "Strengths-Based Development," http://www.gallup.com/ consulting/61/strengths-development.aspx, Accessed April 2, 2011.

27. Ibid.

28. Fraya Wagner-Marsh, rev. Patricia A. Lanier, "Pioneers of Management," *Encyclopedia of Business*, 2nd ed. (online), http://www.referenceforbusiness. com/management/Or-Pr/Pioneers-of-Management.html, Accessed April 4, 2011.

29. Frank J. Landy and Jeffrey M. Conte, *Work in the 21st Century: An Introduction to Industrial and Organizational Psychology,* 2nd ed., (Malden, MA: Blackwell Publishing, 2007).

30. Kristina A. Diekmann, Zoe I. Barsness, and Harris Sondak, "Uncertainty, Fairness Perceptions, and Job Satisfaction: A Field Study," *Social Justice Research*, September 2004, vol. 17, no. 3.

31. "What is Sociocracy?: A New Power Structure for Ethical Governance," http://www.sociocracyinaction.ca/whatis.htm, Accessed April 2, 2011.

32. The Quotations Page, "Quotations by Author Peter Drucker," http://quotationspage.com/quotes/Peter_Drucker/, Accessed April 3, 2011.

33. Daniel Goleman, Richard Boyatzis, and Annie McKee, *Primal Leadership: Realizing the Power of Emotional Intelligence* (Boston, MA: Harvard Business Press, 2002).

34. Brian Grow, "Out of Home Depot: Behind the Flameout of Controversial CEO Bob Nardelli," *Businessweek* (online), January 9, 2007, http://www .msnbc.msn.com/id/16469224/ns/business-bloomberg_businessweek/, Accessed April 3, 2011.

35. The Coca-Cola Company press release, "Coca-Cola Raises Total Pledge to 2.5 Billion Yen (US$31 Million) for Relief and Rebuilding Efforts in Japan," www.thecoca-colcompany.com, March 24, 2011, http:// www.thecoca-colacompany.com/dynamic/press_center/2011/03/ coca-cola-japan-reconstruction-fund.html, Accessed Retrieved April 3, 2011.

36. David Markiewicz, "Aflac Pledges Aid to Japan after Disaster," Atlanta Journal-Constitution (online), March 11, 2011, http://www.ajc.com/ business/aflac-pledges-aid-to-868637.html, Accessed April 3, 2011.

37. Molson Coors press release, "Molson Coors Donates $50,000 to Japan Relief," www.businesswire.com, March 16, 2011, http://

www.businesswire.com/news/home/20110316006760/en/
Molson-Coors-Donates-50000-Japan-Relief, Accessed April 3, 2011.

38. Kraft Foods press release, "Kraft Foods Gives $200,000 to Red Cross for Relief Efforts in Japan," www.kraftfoodscompany.com, http://phx. corporate-ir.net/phoenix.zhtml?c=129070&p=irol-newsArticle&ID=1539037, Accessed November 7, 2011.

39. Jon Huntsman, *Winners Never Cheat: Everyday Values We Learned as Children (But May Have Forgotten)*, (Philadelphia: Wharton School Publishing, 2005).

40. G. Scott Acton, "Great Ideas in Personality: Five-Factor Model," 1997, http://www.personalityresearch.org/bigfive/costa.html; and Oliver D. John, "The Big Five Personality Test," 2009, http://www.outofservice.com/bigfive/, Both accessed April 3, 2011.

41. Adapted from Talya Bauer and Berrin Erdogan, *Organizational Behavior, FlatWorldKnowledge.com*, http://www.flatworldknowledge.com/node/34687#web-34687, Accessed April 4, 2011.

42. Sean Neubert, "The Five-Factor Model of Personality in the Workplace," Rochester Institute of Technology, http://www.personalityresearch.org/papers/neubert.html, Accessed April 4, 2011.

43. *Professional's Feedback: Couple's Counseling Report*, 16PF Fifth Edition, http://www.pearsonassessments.com/NR/rdonlyres/66658BFC-36EE-4D9F-9636-1B3DE8252644/0/16pf5couples.pdf, Accessed April 3, 2011.

44. Del Jones, "Does Height Equal Power? Some CEOs Say Yes," *USA Today*, July 18, 2007 http://www.usatoday.com/money/companies/management/2007-07-17-ceo-dominant-behavior_N.htm, Accessed April 3, 2011.

45. Ibid.

46. Adam Lashinsky, "RAZR's Edge: How a Team of Engineers and Designers Defied Motorola's Own Rules to Create the Cellphone that Revived Their Company," *Fortune* (online), June 1, 2006, http://money.cnn.com/2006/05/31/magazines/fortune/razr_greatteams_fortune/index.htm, Accessed November 7, 2011.

47. John R. Katzenbach and Douglas K. Smith, *The Wisdom of Teams* (Cambridge, MA: Harvard University Press, 1993).

48. Jerry Useem, Stuart R. Brown, Cait Murphy, Ellen McGirt, and Eugenia Levenson, "Six Teams that Changed the World," *Fortune* (online), http://money.cnn.com/2006/05/31/magazines/fortune/sixteams_greatteams_fortune_061206/index.htm, Accessed April 3, 2011.

49. Geoffrey Colvin, "Why Dream Teams Fail," Fortune (online), http://money.cnn.com/magazines/fortune/fortune_archive/2006/06/12/8379219/index.htm, Accessed April 3, 2011.

50. Yahoo Canada, "Michael Ovitz Biography," http://movies.yahoo.com/movie/contributor/1808503949/bio, Accessed April 3, 2011.

51. David Teather, "Investors Lose Battle with Disney over Ovitz's $140m," The Guardian (online), August 10, 2005, http://www.guardian.co.uk/media/2005/aug/10/citynews.filmnews, Accessed April 3, 2011.

52. Colvin, "Why Dream Teams Fail."

53. Jack A. Goncalo and Barry M. Staw, "Individualism-Collectivism and Group Creativity," *Organizational Behavior and Human Decision Processes*, November 2005, vol. 100, pp. 96-109, http://digitalcommons.ilr.cornell.edu/obpubs/1/, Accessed April 3, 2011.

54. Neil Howe and William Strauss, *Millennials Rising: The Next Great Generation* (New York: Vintage Books, 2000).

55. Stephanie Armour, "Generation Y: They've Arrived at Work with a New Attitude," *USA Today* (online), November 6, 2005, http://www.usatoday.com/money/workplace/2005-11-06-gen-y_x.htm, Accessed April 3, 2011.

56. LifeCourse Associates, "What's Ahead for Generation Y?" *The News & Observer* (Raleigh, N.C.) (online), February 5, 2006, http://www.lifecourse.com/media/articles/lib/2006/020506-ral.html, Accessed April 4, 2011.

57. Useem et al., "Six Teams that Changed the World."

58. Queen's School of Business, "Queen's Executive MBA Program: Now Available on Your Desktop," January 24, 2011, http://business.queensu.ca/news/2011/jan_24_queens_executive_MBA_program_now_available_on_your_desktop.php; and"Virtual Teams a First in Canada," *Financial Post* (online), January 19, 2011, http://business.financialpost.com/2011/01/19/mba-virtual-teams-a-first-in-canada/, Both accessed April 3, 2011.

59. Kerith Nicholl, "Second Life Recreates Border Patrol at Loyalist," *Online Pioneer Plus,* http://www.thepioneer.com/?q=node/3112, Accessed April 4, 2011.

60. J.S. Lurey and M.S. Raisinghani, "An Empirical Study of Best Practices in Virtual Teams," *Information & Management,* October 2001, vol. 38, no. 8, pp. 523–544.

61. Stephen R. Covey, *The 7 Habits of Highly Effective People* (New York: Free Press, 1989).

62. Bryan Walsh and Toko Sekiguchi, "Heroes of the Environment: Toyota Prius Design Team," Time (online), October 17, 2007, http://www.time.com/time/specials/2007/article/0,28804,1663317_1663323_1669899,00.html, Accessed May 5, 2008.

63. Toyota, "Contribution towards Sustainable Development," http://www.toyota.com/about/our_values/index.html, Accessed May 5, 2008.

64. Alex Taylor III, "Toyota: The Birth of the Prius," Fortune (online), February 21, 2006, http://money.cnn.com/2006/02/17/news/companies/mostadmired_fortune_toyota/index.htm, Accessed May 5, 2008.

Chapter 8

1. Nancy Germond, "Employee Retention Strategy Can Save Companies Millions," *all Business.com*, http://www.allbusiness.com/labor-employment/human-resources-personnel-management/14352477-1.html, Accessed January 14, 2011.

2. SAS, "About SAS," http://www.sas.com/company/about/index.html, Accessed June 29, 2011.

3. "A Culture That Values Employees," *Baldrige.com*, February 22, 2011, http://www.baldrige.com/criteria_workforce/a-culture-that-values-employees/, Accessed November 12, 2011.

4. Canada's Top 100 Employers 2012, "Canada's Top 100 Employers," http://www.canadastop100.com/national/; and "100 Best Companies to Work For 2011, 2010, 2009," CNNMoney, http://money.cnn.com/magazines/fortune/bestcompanies/2011/index.html, http://money.cnn.com/magazines/fortune/bestcompanies/2010/index.html, and http://money.cnn.com/magazines/fortune/bestcompanies/2009/full_list/, All accessed November 12, 2011.

5. Richard Florida and Jim Goodnight, "Managing for Creativity," *Harvard Business Review*, July–August 2005, http://www.zuhl.com/~mikez/Info/Software/SoftwareEng/ManagingCreativity.html, Accessed July 2, 2011.

6. Ibid.

7. "Purpose of Having a Human Resource Department," *Small Business Bible* (online), http://www.smallbusinessbible.org/purpose_having_humanr_department.html, Accessed January 19, 2011.

8. "About Us," www.LinkedIn.com, http://press.linkedin.com/about, Accessed November 3, 2011.

9. JCSI, *The New Age of Recruiting: 2010 Recruiting Survey Results,* http://www.jcsi.net/pdf/2010_recruitment_survey.pdf, Accessed January 15, 2011.

10. "Talent Mismatch Tops Manpower's Mega Trends," *Recruiter* (online), November 29, 2011, http://www.recruiter.co.uk/talent-mismatch-tops-manpower%E2%80%99s-mega-trends/1004089.article, Accessed January 27, 2011.

11. Conference Board of Canada, "Employability Skills 2000+," http://www
     .conferenceboard.ca/topics/education/learning-tools/employability-skills.
     aspx, Accessed January 30, 2011.

12. Stephanie Thiffeault, "Poor Reference Check Results in Damages," Mcmillian
     Binch Mendelsohn, February 2006, http://mcmillan.ca/Files/Poor Refer-
     ence Check_0106.pdf, Accessed January 15, 2010.

13. Carter McNamara, "Employee Training and Development: Reasons and Bene-
     fits," Free Management Library, http://www.managementhelp.org/trng_dev/
     basics/reasons.htm, Accessed January 1, 2011.

14. McDonald's, "Training & Education," http://www.mcdonalds.com/us/
     en/careers/training_education.html, Accessed January 22, 2011.

15. Robert Stone, Antoinette Caird-Daley, and Kevin Bessell, "SubSafe: A
     Games-Based Training System for Submarine Safety and Spatial Awareness
     (Part 1)," *Virtual Reality*, November 28, 2008, vol. 13, no. 1, http://www
     .springerlink.com/content/1p57h1h547734420/, Accessed January 26, 2011.

16. "Next-Generation Training," *Military Simulation & Training News*,
     Spring–Summer 2010, no. 22, http://www.cae.com/en/military/_pdf/
     Newsletter22.pdf, Accessed November 9, 2011.

17. Tintswalo Baloyi, "SAP Introduces Games-Based Training in South Africa,"
     ITnewsafrica.com, http://www.itnewsafrica.com/?p=8902, Accessed January
     25, 2011.

18. Ibid.

19. Karen O'Leonard, *Performance Support Systems*, Bersin & Associates, Febru-
     ary 2005, www.bersinassociates.com/free_research/epss_paper_2.9.pdf,
     Accessed January 22, 2011.

20. Human Resource Development Council, "Organizational Learning Strate-
     gies: Action Learning," http://www.humtech.com/opm/grtl/ols/ols2.cfm,
     Accessed January 22, 2011.

21. Matt Andrejczak, "Starbucks Completes Employees Stock-Option Swap,"
     MarketWatch.com, June 3, 2009, http://www.marketwatch.com/story/
     starbucks-completes-employee-stock-option-swap-200963143100, Accessed
     January 22, 2011.

22. "Workplaces for Sabbaticals 2011," *yourSABBATICAL.com*, http://yoursabbati-
     cal.com/learn/workplaces-for-sabbaticals/2011/, Accessed January 23, 2011.

23. "Canadians Don't Make Health a Priority," *BenefitsCanada.com*, January 18, 2011,
     http://www.benefitscanada.com/benefits/health-benefits/canadians-don%
     E2%80%99t-make-health-a-priority-13854, Accessed January 23, 2011.

24. Jim Pearse, "Premium Value," *BenefitsCanada.com*, May 1, 2008, http://
     www.benefitscanada.com/benefits/health-benefits/premium-value-8348,
     Accessed January 23, 2011.

25. Brooke Smith, "Out of Reach," *BenefitsCanada.com*, May 1, 2007, http://
     www.benefitscanada.com/benefits/health-benefits/out-of-reach-8361,
     Accessed January 23, 2011.

26. State Farm Insurance, "Worklife & Wellness," http://www.statefarm.com/
     careers/emp_worklife.asp, Accessed March 10, 2011.

27. Goldbeck Recruiting Inc., "Striving for the 'Clockless' Work Schedule," *HR
     Blog for Canadian Employers and Job Seekers*, October 26, 2010, http://hrblog.
     goldbeck.com/?tag=flexible-work-schedule, Accessed January 23, 2011.

28. The Home Depot Canada Foundation, http://www.homedepot.ca/
     foundation/html/en/index.html, Accessed November 12, 2011.

29. Manpower, "Temporary Work Life: Does It Fit Your Style?" http://man-
     power.ca/ca/en/multimedia/temporary-work-life-does-it-fit-your-style_
     tcm269-39676.pdf, Accessed January 23, 2011.

30. Labour Canada, "Legislative Framework: Mandatory Retirement," http://
     www.hrsdc.gc.ca/eng/lp/spila/wlb/aw/27retirement_legislative02.shtml,
     Accessed November 12, 2011.

31. CBC News Online, "Mandatory Retirement Fades in Canada," October 18, 2010, http://www.cbc.ca/news/canada/story/2009/08/20/mandatory-retirement-explainer523.html, Accessed March 10, 2011.

32. "GM Offers Buyouts to Skilled Trades Workers," *GazetteXtra.com*, December 15, 2010, http://gazettextra.com/news/2010/dec/15/gm-offers-buyouts-skilled-trades-workers/, Accessed January 23, 2011.

33. Associated Press, "Ford Offers Retirement, Buyout Packages to All 41,000 Factory Workers to Thin Ranks," *The News* (online), December 22, 2009, http://www.ngnews.ca/Business/Employment/2009-12-22/article-801621/Ford-offers-retirement,-buyout-packages-to-all-41,000-factory-workers-to-thin-ranks/1, Accessed January 23, 2011.

34. Wallstats.com, "Golden Parachutes: How the Bankers Went Down," *mint.com*, February 24, 2009, http://www.mint.com/blog/finance-core/golden-parachutes-how-the-bankers-went-down/, Accessed January 23, 2011.

35. Government of Canada Labour Program, *Information on Labour Standards:10 Terminations,* http://www.hrsdc.gc.ca/eng/labour/publications/employment_standards/pdf/terminations.pdf, Accessed November 12, 2011.

36. Lloyd Duhaime, "Wrongful Dismissal Law in Canada," *Duhaime.org,* http://www.duhaime.org/LegalResources/EmploymentLabourLaw/LawArticle-104/Wrongful-Dismissal-Law-in-Canada.aspx, Accessed January 23, 2011.

37. "Employment at Will," *TheFreeDictionary.com*, http://legal-dictionary.thefreedictionary.com/Employment+at+Will, Accessed January 23, 2011.

38. Scotiabank, *Investors & Shareholders: Investor Relations,* http://www.scotiabank.com/ca/en/0,,915,00.html, Accessed January 24, 2011.

39. Human Resources and Skills Development Canada, "Learning – Educational Attainment," http://www4.hrsdc.gc.ca/.3ndic.1t.4r@-eng.jsp?iid=29, Accessed November 13, 2011.

40. Canada's Top 100 Employers 2012, "Canada's Best Diversity Employers 2011," http://www.canadastop100.com/diversity/; Kristina Leung and Richard Yerema, "Boeing Canada Operations Limited," February 21, 2011, http://www.eluta.ca/diversity-at-boeing-canada; Kristina Leung and Richard Yerema, "Procter & Gamble Inc.," February 21, 2011, http://www.eluta.ca/diversity-at-procter-%26-gamble; Canada's Best Diversity Employers 2008, "Procter & Gamble Inc.," www.canadastop100.com/diversity/chapters/Procter.pdf, All accessed January 24, 2011.

41. Carol Hymowitz, "The New Diversity," *The Wall Street Journal* (online), November 14, 2005, http://www.tedchilds.com/files/TheNewDiversityWSJ.pdf, Accessed January 23, 2011.

42. Robert Rodriguez, "Diversity Finds Its Place," *HR Magazine,* August 1, 2006, vol. 51, no. 8, http://www.shrm.org/Publications/hrmagazine/EditorialContent/Pages/0806rodriguez.aspx, Accessed January 24, 2011.

43. Lisa Takeuchi Cullen, "Employee Diversity Training Doesn't Work," *Time.com,* http://www.time.com/time/magazine/article/0,9171,1615183,00.html, Accessed January 24, 2011.

44. United Food and Commercial Workers Canada, "Facts About Unions," http://www.ufcw.ca/index.php?option=com_content&view=article&id=29&Itemid=49&lang=en, Accessed November 13, 2011.

45. Canadian Union of Public Employees, "About CUPE," http://cupe.ca/about, Accessed November 13, 2011.

46. United Food and Commercial Workers Canada, "About UFCW Canada," http://www.ufcw.ca/index.php?option=com_content&view=article&id=59&Itemid=2&lang=en, Accessed November 13, 2011.

47. Canadian Auto Workers Union, "About the CAW," http://www.caw.ca/en/about-the-caw.htm, Accessed November 13, 2011.

48. The Social Studies Help Center, "Collective Bargaining," http://www.socialstudieshelp.com/Eco_collective_bargaining.htm, Accessed November 13, 2011.

49. CBC News Online, "Striking Toronto Workers Reach Tentative Deals," July 27, 2009, http://www.cbc.ca/canada/toronto/story/2009/07/27/toronto-strike.html; and Nina Lex and Frank Pingue, "Toronto Hopes for Quick End to City Workers' Strike," *Reuters.com*, June 22, 2009, http://ca.reuters.com/article/domesticNews/idCATRE55L2HN20090622?pageNumber=1&virtualBrandChannel=0, Both accessed January 24, 2011.

50. Alison Hanes, " Toronto on Strike: Council Approves Deal with Both Unions to End Strike," *National Post* (online), July 31, 2009, http://network.nationalpost.com/np/blogs/toronto/archive/2009/07/31/toronto-on-strike-workers-return-to-jobs-as-city-council-votes.aspx, Accessed January 24, 2011.

51. The Lawyers & Jurists, "Labour Law," http://www.lawyersnjurists.com/our-services/practice-areas-3/labour-law, Accessed November 13, 2011.

52. Human Resources and Skills Development Canada, Ministry of Labour, *Canada Labour Code, Part II–Overview,* http://www.hrsdc.gc.ca/eng/labour/health_safety/overview.shtml, Accessed June 27, 2011.

53. World Law Direct, "Wrongful Termination," http://www.worldlawdirect.com/forum/law-wiki/5940-wrongful-termination.html, Accessed November 13, 2011.

54. Bongarde, "HR Compliance," http://www.bongarde.com/bongarde-products/compliance/hr-compliance/, Accessed November 13, 2011.

55. Department of Justice, *Canada Labour Code,* http://laws.justice.gc.ca/eng/L-2/index.html, Accessed January 26, 2011.

56. Department of Justice, *Employment Equity Act,* http://laws.justice.gc.ca/eng/E-5.401/page-1.*html*#anchorbo-ga:s_2, Accessed January 26, 2011.

57. Government of Alberta, *Occupational Health and Safety Focused Inspection Project: Commercial Construction,* December 13, 2010, http://employment.alberta.ca/documents/WHS/WHS-PUB-Commercial-Construction-Focused-Inspection-Report-2010.pdf, Accessed November 13, 2011.

58. HR World Editors, "30 Interview Questions You Can't Ask and 30 Sneaky, Legal Alternatives to Get the Same Info," November 15, 2007, http://www.hrworld.com/features/30-interview-questions-111507/, Accessed May 5, 2008.

59. Toyota Motor Sales, "About T-Ten," *Toyota.com*, http://www.toyota.com/about/tten/whytten.html, Accessed June 28, 2011.

60. Toyota Motor Sales, "Certification You Will Receive," *Toyota.com*, http://www.toyota.com/about/tten/certification.html, Accessed June 28, 2011.

Chapter 9

1. Tommy Toy, "RBC: 185 Million Tablets Worth $70 Billion Will Be Sold in 2014, and a List of All iPad and Tablet Forecasts," PBT Consulting (website), March 9, 2011, http://tommytoy.typepad.com/tommy-toy-pbt-consultin/2011/03/rbc-capital-markets-expects-tablet-market-to-reach-185-million-units-in-calendar-2014-up-83-percent-compound-annual-growth-r.html, Accessed April 6, 2011.

2. Eric Zeman, "Apple Sells 15M iPads in 2010, Dismisses Competition," *InformationWeek.com*, January 19, 2011, http://www.informationweek.com/news/smb/mobile/showArticle.jhtml?articleID=229000915, Accessed April 6, 2011.

3. Toy, "RBC: 185 Million Tablets Worth $70 Billion Will Be Sold in 2014, and a List of All iPad and Tablet Forecasts."

4. ConsumerReports.org, "Apple's iPad 2 Tops Consumer Reports' Tablet Ratings," *PRNewswire.com*, http://www.prnewswire.com/news-releases/apples-ipad-2-tops-consumer-reports-tablet-ratings-119237109.html, Accessed April 6, 2011.

5. Ibid.

6. IBM, "Cognos Analytical Applications," http://www-01.ibm.com/software/analytics/cognos/analytic-applications/, Accessed June 30, 2011.

7. Constance L. Hays, "What Wal-Mart Knows About Customers' Habits," *The New York Times* (online), November 14, 2004, http://www.nytimes.com/2004/11/14/business/yourmoney/14wal.html?pagewanted=1&_r=1, Accessed April 4, 2011.

8. Galen Gruman, "Managing Mobile Devices," *CIO.com*, January 15, 2007, http://www.cio.com/article/28177/Managing_Mobile_Devices?page=1, Accessed April 7, 2011.

9. Google Maps, "Flight Carbon Dioxide (CO2) Emissions," http://www.cheap-parking.net/flight-carbon-emissions.php, Accessed April 7, 2011.

10. Susan M. Heathfield, "Listen with Your Eyes: Tips for Understanding Non-verbal Communication," *About.com*, http://humanresources.about.com/od/interpersonalcommunicatio1/a/nonverbal_com.htm, Accessed April 7, 2011.

11. "Electronic Eavesdropping," *Encyclopaedia Britannica* (online), http://www.britannica.com/EBchecked/topic/183788/electronic-eavesdropping, Accessed April 7, 2011.

12. D. DiTecco, G. Cwitco, A. Arsenault, and M. Andre, "Operator Stress and Monitoring Practices," *Applied Ergonomics*, February 1992, vol. 23, no. 1, pp. 29–34.

13. Canada Post, "Whistleblowing," http://www.canadapost.ca/cpo/mc/aboutus/corporate/whistleblowing.jsf, Accessed April 7, 2011.

14. Dan Nakaso, "$1 Tickets Crash Airline's Website," *USAToday.com*, June 12, 2007, http://www.usatoday.com/travel/flights/2007-06-12-one-dollar-tickets-crash-web_N.htm, Accessed April 4, 2011.

15. Andy McCue, "IT Failure Remains Top Cause of Business Disaster," *silicon.com*, March 11, 2005, http://hardware.silicon.com/storage/0,39024649,39128617,00.htm, Accessed April 7, 2011.

16. Royal Canadian Mounted Police, "Identity Theft and Identity Fraud," http://www.rcmp-grc.gc.ca/scams-fraudes/id-theft-vol-eng.htm, Accessed April 7, 2011.

17. Jonathan Spicer and Maria Aspan, "More Customers Exposed as Big U.S. Data Breach Grows," *Reuters.com*, April 4, 2011, http://www.reuters.com/article/2011/04/04/us-citi-capitalone-data-idUSTRE7321PI20110404, Accessed April 9, 2011, and "Air Miles Among Firms Hit by Huge Data Breach," *CBC.ca*, http://www.cbc.ca/news/canada/story/2011/04/05/business-data-breach.html, Accessed April 9, 2011.

18. Spicer and Aspan, "More Customers Exposed as Big U.S. Data Breach Grows."

19. "Air Miles Among Firms Hit by Huge Data Breach."

20. Ben Worthen, "Mid-Market: The Big Upgrade to Microsoft Vista," *CIO.com*, November 15, 2006, http://www.cio.com/article/26664/Mid_Market_The_Big_Upgrade_to_Microsoft_Vista, Accessed April 9, 2011.

21. Electronic Recycling Association, "Services," *Era.ca*, http://www.era.ca/donations/recycling/services.html, Accessed April 7, 2011.

22. Panasonic Group, "Eco Ideas," Panasonic.net, http://panasonic.net/eco/ecoideas/en/html/declaration/, Accessed April 7, 2011.

23. Panasonic Group, "Vision and Strategy," *Panasonic.net*, http://panasonic.net/eco/vision/ecoideas/, Accessed April 7, 2011.

24. Hewlett-Packard (HP) Development Company, Press Release: "HP Fuels Growth with Print 2.0, Launches $300 Million Global Marketing Campaign," August 28, 2007, http://www.hp.com/hpinfo/newsroom/press/2007/070828xc.html, Accessed April 9, 2011.

25. Jeneanne Rae, "The Keys to High-Impact Innovation," *Businessweek* (online), September 27, 2005, http://www.businessweek.com/innovate/content/sep2005/id20050927_002673.htm?chan=search, Accessed April 9, 2011.

26. Fara Warner, "Made in China," *Fast Company* (online), April 1, 2007, http://www.fastcompany.com/magazine/114/open_features-made-in-china.html, Accessed April 9, 2011.

27. Kent German, "Top 10 Dot-Com Flops," *CNET.com*, http://www.cnet.com/1990-11136_1-6278387-1.html, Accessed April 11, 2011.

28. Chris Connolly and Peter van Dijk, "What Is E-Commerce Legal Infrastructure?" *Galexia.com*, http://www.galexia.com/public/research/articles/research_articles-pa04.html#Heading296, Accessed June 20, 2008.

29. Consumer Measures Committee, *Canadian Code of Practice for Consumer Protection in Electronic Commerce*, http://www.ic.gc.ca/eic/site/cmc-cmc.nsf/eng/fe00064.html, Accessed November 14, 2011.

30. Canada/Manitoba Business Service Centre, "Online Legal Issues," http://www.canadabusiness.mb.ca/home_page/business___start_it/online_legal_issues/, Accessed November 14, 2011.

31. Franklin Pierce Law Center, *Intellectual Property in E-Commerce*, World Intellectual Property Organization's Worldwide Academy, http://ipmall.info/hosted_resources/pubspapers/WIPO.pdf, Accessed November 14, 2011.

32. Charles C. Mann, "How Click Fraud Could Swallow the Internet," *Wired* (online), January 2006, no. 14.01, http://www.wired.com/wired/archive/14.01/fraud.html, Accessed April 11, 2011.

33. Ellen Neuborne, "Viral Marketing Alert!" *Businessweek* (online), March 19, 2001, http://www.businessweek.com/magazine/content/01_12/b3724628.htm, Accessed April 11, 2011.

34. "Subservient Chicken," *Snopes.com*, 2004, http://www.snopes.com/business/viral/chicken.asp, Accessed April 11, 2011.

35. Frank Rose, "Secret Websites, Coded Messages: The New World of Immersive Games, "Wired (online), December 20, 2007, no. 16.01, http://www.wired.com/entertainment/music/magazine/16-01/ff_args, Accessed April 11, 2011.

36. Chris Lee, "Bat Infiltration," *Los Angeles Times* (online), March 24, 2008, http://articles.latimes.com/2008/mar/24/entertainment/et-batmanviral24, Accessed April 4, 2011.

37. 42Entertainment, "What We Do," http://www.42entertainment.com/do.html, Accessed April 11, 2011.

38. Public Safety Canada, "Canada's Cyber Security Strategy," http://www.publicsafety.gc.ca/prg/ns/cbr/ccss-scc-eng.aspx, Accessed November 14, 2011.

39. Ibid.

40. PayPal, "Who We Are," https://www.paypal-media.com/who, Accessed April 11, 2011.

41. TD Canada Trust, "Online Security Guarantee," http://www.td.com/privacy-and-security/privacy-and-security/how-we-protect-you/online-security-guarantee/guarantee.jsp, Accessed November 14, 2011.

42. "Spyware," *SearchSecurity.com*, http://searchsecurity.techtarget.com/definition/spyware, Accessed April 11, 2011.

43. Rebecca Porter, "Who's Watching Your PC?" *Trial* (online), August 1, 2004, vol. 40, no. 8, http://goliath.ecnext.com/coms2/gi_0199-107385/Who-s-watching-your-PC.html, Accessed April 11, 2011.

44. OnGuardOnline.gov, "Phishing," February 2008, http://onguardonline.gov/phishing.html.

45. SAS, "Mark's Work Wearhouse Selects SAS," *SAS.com*, http://www.sas.com/news/feature/21aug06/marks.html, Accessed July 2, 2011, and Shane Schick, "Mark's Work Wearhouse Tries BI on for Size," *itbusiness.ca,* http://www.itbusiness.ca/it/client/en/home/News.asp?id=40335, Accessed July 2, 2011.

Chapter 10

1. McDonald's Corporation, "Farm to Front Counter," http://www.aboutmcdonalds.com/mcd/sustainability/signature_programs/farm_to_front_counter.html, Accessed May 17, 2011.
2. Ibid.
3. "How McDonald's Fries Are Made," http://www.associatedcontent.com/article/1386768/how_mcdonalds_fries_are_made_pg3.html?cat=22, Accessed May 19, 2011.
4. McDonald's Corporation, *Worldwide Corporate Social Re sponsibility 2010 Report,* http://www.slideshare.net/McDonaldsUSA/mcd063-201020-pdfreportv9, Accessed May 19, 2011.
5. PBS, "Ford Installs First Moving Assembly Line 1913," *A Science Odyssey:* People and Discoveries Databank, http://www.pbs.org/wgbh/aso/databank/entries/dt13as.html, Accessed May 11, 2011.
6. Inter IKEA Systems B.V., "The IKEA Range," http://franchisor.ikea.com/showContent.asp?swfId=range3, Accessed May 12, 2011.
7. Dell, "Laptop Deals," http://www.dell.com/ca/business/p/laptop-deals?~ck=anav, Accessed May 11, 2011.
8. Walmart Canada, "Walmart Photo Centre," http://www.walmartphotocentre.ca/album/default.aspx, Accessed May 11, 2011.
9. Mars, "Personalize M&M's," http://www.mymms.com/, Accessed May 11, 2011.
10. "What Is Flexible Manufacturing System (FMS)?" *SeopromoLINKS.com*, http://www.seopromolinks.com/fms-advantages-disadvantages.asp, Accessed May 11, 2011.
11. Christopher W. Hart, "Creating Competitive Advantages through Mass Customization," http://www.spiregroup.biz/pdfs/06-04-07%20Creating%20Competitive%20Advantage%20through%20Mass%20Customization.pdf, Accessed May 11, 2011.
12. "Intro to Lean," *LeanProduction.com*, http://www.leanproduction.com/intro-to-lean.html, Accessed November 17, 2011.
13. "Robot," *Merriam-Webster Dictionary* (online), http://www.merriam-webster.com/dictionary/robot?show=0&t=1305166216, Accessed May 11, 2011.
14. David Kucera, "Computer-Aided Design (CAD) and Computer-Aided Manufacturing (CAM)," *Encyclopedia of Business*, 2nd ed. (online) http://www.referenceforbusiness.com/encyclopedia/Clo-Con/Computer-Aided-Design-CAD-and-Computer-Aided-Manufacturing-CAM.html, Accessed May 11, 2011.
15. Ibid.
16. "Customer-Made," *Trendwatching.com*, http://trendwatching.com/trends/CUSTOMER-MADE.htm, Accessed May 11, 2011.
17. mi adidas, "Getting Started," http://www.miadidas.com/CustomizeShoe.action?ident=I1271855297882_ST; and adidas Group,"Blog," http://blog.adidas-group.com/, Both accessed November 18, 2011.
18. Best Buy Canada website, http://www.bestbuy.ca/en-CA/home.aspx; and Twitter, "Twelpforce Best Buy," http://twitter.com/#!/twelpforce, both accessed November 18, 2011.
19. Starbucks, "My Starbucks Idea," http://mystarbucksidea.force.com/; and Dell, "IdeaStorm," http://www.ideastorm.com/ideaAbout?pt=About+IdeaStorm, Both accessed November 18, 2011.

20. Engadget, "Tag Results for: How Would You Change," http://www
    .engadget.com/tag/how+would+you+change/, Accessed
    November 18, 2011.
21. Tim Feemster, "A Step-by-Step Guide to Choosing the Right Site," *AreaDevelopment.com,* November 2007, http://www.areadevelopment.com/
    siteSelection/nov07/stepByStep.shtml, Accessed May 12, 2011.
22. Oracle, Press Release:"CNH Global Selects Oracle Transportation Management to Transform Worldwide Logistics Operations, " October 16, 2006,
    http://www.oracle.com/us/corporate/press/017200_EN, Accessed May
    12, 2011.
23. N. Shivapriya, "India Remains World's Top Outsourcing Destination," *Businessweek* (online), July 10, 2009, http://www.businessweek.com/globalbiz/
    content/jul2009/gb20090710_974200.htm, Accessed May 12, 2011.
24. City of Toronto, "Household Hazardous Waste: We Want It!"http://www
    .toronto.ca/garbage/hhw.htm, Accessed May 12, 2011.
25. U.S. Consumer Product Safety Commission, Press Release: "Mattel, Fisher-
    Price to Pay $2.3 Million Civil Penalty for Violating Federal Lead Paint Ban,"
    June 5, 2009, http://www.cpsc.gov/cpscpub/prerel/prhtml09/09237.html,
    Accessed May 15, 2011.
26. Canada Post, "eProcurement," http://www.canadapost.ca/cpo/mc/
    aboutus/suppliers/eprocurement.jsf, Accessed May 16, 2011.
27. Walmart, "Standards for Suppliers," October 2009, walmartstores.com/
    download/2727.pdf, Accessed November 21, 2011.
28. The Home Depot, Supplier Reference Manual, September 21, 2010, https://
    corporate.homedepot.com/en_US/Supplier_Center/Functional/SBA/
    Supplier_Reference_Manual.pdf, Accessed November 21, 2011.
29. SCORE (Counselors to America's Small Business), "Inventory Control,"
    http://www.ct-clic.com/Newsletters/customer-files/inventory0602.pdf,
    Accessed May 15, 2011.
30. Jonathan Byrnes, "Dell Manages Profitability, Not Inventory," Harvard
    Business School *Working Knowledge* (online forum), June 2, 2003, http://
    hbswk.hbs.edu/archive/3497.html, Accessed May 15, 2011.
31. American Society for Quality, "The History of Quality–Total Quality," http://asq.org/learn-about-quality/history-of-quality/overview/
    total-quality.html, Accessed November 18, 2011.
32. American Society for Quality, "Continuous Improvement," http://asq.org/
    learn-about-quality/continuous-improvement/overview/overview.html,
    Accessed May 16, 2011.
33. Tony Van Alphen, "Toyota Recalls More Vehicles," thestar.com, January
    26, 2011, http://www.thestar.com/business/auto/article/928719—toyota-
    recalls-more-vehicles, Accessed May 17, 2011.
34. CBC News, "More than 18 Million Mattel Toys on Recall Globally," cbc-
    news.ca, August 14, 2007, http://www.cbc.ca/news/story/2007/08/14/
    mattel-recall.html, Accessed May 17, 2011, and Louise Story, "Lead Paint
    Prompts Mattel to Recall 967,000 Toys," The New York Times (online),
    http://www.nytimes.com/2007/08/02/business/02toy.html, Accessed
    May 17, 2011.
35. Associated Press, "Bridgestone and Ford Settle Dispute Over Defective
    Tires," October 13, 2005, The New York Times (online), http://www.
    nytimes.com/2005/10/13/business/13ford.html, Accessed May 17, 2011.
36. International Organization for Standardization, "ISO Standards," http://
    www.iso.org/iso/iso_catalogue.htm, Accessed May 16, 2011.
37. Bizmanualz, "ISO Standards," http://www.bizmanualz.com/
    iso-9000-qms/ISO_Standards.html, Accessed May 16, 2011.
38. Toyota Motor Manufacturing Kentucky, Inc., "Toyota Production System
    Terms," http://www.toyotageorgetown.com/terms.asp, Accessed
    June 25, 2008.

39. Toyota Motor Manufacturing Kentucky, Inc., "History," http://www .toyotageorgetown.com/history.asp, Accessed June 25, 2008.

40. Toyota Motor Corporation, "Toyota Production System," http://www .toyota.co.jp/en/vision/production_system/, Accessed June 25, 2008.

41. Toyota Motor Manufacturing Kentucky, Inc., "The Toyota Production System," http://www.toyotageorgetown.com/tps.asp, Accessed June 25, 2008.

Chapter 11

1. Facebook, "Sponsored Stories," http://www.facebook.com/ads/stories/, Accessed July 2, 2011.

2. Cynthia Boris, "Facebook Adds Social Endorsement Stats," *MarketingPilgrim. com,* September 10, 2010, http://www.marketingpilgrim.com/2010/09/ facebook-adds-social-endorsement-stats.html, Accessed November 19, 2011.

3. Rob Pegoraro, "Facebook 'Sponsored Stories' Turn You into the Ad," *The Washington Post* (online), January 27, 2011, thttp://voices.washington-post.com/fasterforward/2011/01/facebook_sponsored_stories_tur.html, Accessed November 11, 2011.

4. Josh Costine, "Facebook's Sponsored Stories Turns News Feed Posts Into Home Page Ads," *InsideFacebook.com,* January 24, 2011, http://www. insidefacebook.com/2011/01/24/sponsored-stories-feed-ads/, Accessed July 2, 2011.

5. Ben Parr, "Facebook Turns Friend Activity Into New Ad Format," *Mashable.com,* January 25, 2011, http://mashable.com/2011/01/25/ facebook-sponsored-stories/, Accessed July 2, 2011.

6. Irina Slutsky, "Facebook Turns the 'Like' Into Its Newest Ad," *AdAge.com*, January 25, 2011, http://adage.com/article/digital/ facebook-turns-newest-ad/148452/, Accessed June 30, 2011.

7. Josh Constine, "Facebook Sponsored Stories Ads Have 46% Higher CTR, 18% Lower Cost Per Fan Says TBG Digital Test," *InsideFacebook. com*, May 3, 2011, http://www.insidefacebook.com/2011/05/03/ sponsored-stories-ctr-cost-per-fa/, Accessed July 2, 2011.

8. Canadian Marketing Association, *Code of Ethics and Standards of Practice,* http://www.the-cma.org/?WCE=C=47|K=225849#2, Accessed May 20, 2011.

9. Canadian Marketing Association, "Regulatory Affairs," http://www .the-cma.org/?WCE=C=32|K=s223391, and "Code of Ethics and Standards of Practice," http://www.the-cma.org/?WCE=C=47|K=225849, Accessed May 27, 2011.

10. Alex Cheng and Mark Evans, "Inside Twitter," *Sysomos.com*, June 2009, http://www.sysomos.com/insidetwitter/, Accessed May 29, 2011.

11. Charles W. Lamb, Jr., Joseph F. Hair, and Carl McDaniel, *Marketing,* 7th ed. (Stamford, CT: Thomson Publishing Company, 2004), p. 33.

12. Internet Center for Management and Business Administration, "Situational Analysis," *NetMBA.com,* http://www.netmba.com/marketing/situation/ ; and Matt Winn, "Situation Analysis Continued—The 5 C's," Volusion's Ecommerce Blog, February 2, 2010, http://onlinebusiness.volusion.com/ articles/situation-analysis-the-5-cs, Both accessed May 24, 2011.

13. Michael Malone, "A Dot-Com Pantomime," *Forbes.com*, http://www.forbes. com/2000/11/16/1116malone.html, Accessed May 26, 2011.

14. Statistics Canada, "Study: Canada's Visible Minority Population in 2017," *The Daily*, March 22, 2005, http://www.statcan.gc.ca/daily-quotidien/ 050322/dq050322b-eng.htm, Accessed November 12, 2011.

15. Philip Kotler and Gary Armstrong, *Principles of Marketing,* 12th ed. (Upper Saddle River, NJ: Pearson/Prentice Hall, 2008), pp. 131–147.

16. Philip Kotler and Kevin Lane Keller, *Marketing Management,* 12th ed. (Upper Saddle River, NJ: Pearson/Prentice Hall, 2006), pp. 211–212; and Kotler and Armstrong, *Principles of Marketing,* 12th ed., pp. 161–162.

17. Andy Reinhardt, "Steve Jobs: 'There's Sanity in Returning,'" *BusinessWeek. com*, May 25, 1998, http://www.businessweek.com/1998/21/b3579165. htm; Sohrab Vossoughi, "Apple: More than a Pretty Face," *BusinessWeek. com*, January 4, 2008, http://www.businessweek.com/innovate/content/ jan2008/id2008014_858681.htm; and Ina Fried, "Celebrating Three Decades of Apple," *CNET News.com*, March 28, 2006, http://news.cnet.com/ 2009-1041-6054524.html, Accessed June 30, 2011.

18. Rehan Choudhary, "An Introduction to Apple Computer, Inc.," suite101.com, March 30, 2010, http://www.suite101.com/content/ an-introduction-to-apple-computer-inc-a219539, Accessed June 30, 2011.

19. Sherilynn Macale, "Apple Has Sold 300M iPods, Currently Holds 78% of the Music Player Market," *thenextweb.com*, http://thenextweb.com/ apple/2011/10/04/apple-has-sold-300m-ipods-currently-holds-78- of-the-music-player-market/, Accessed November 19, 2011.

Chapter 12

1. Kraft Foods, *2010 Annual Report*, February 28, 2011, http:// www.kraftfoodscompany.com/SiteCollectionDocuments/pdf/ KraftFoods_10K_20110228.pdf, Accessed June 1, 2011.

2. Kraft Foods, Press Release:"Do You Like to Do It in Public or Keep It Private?" February 2, 2011, http://www.kraftfoodscompany.com/ SiteCollectionDocuments/ca/en/pdf/Press_Releases/2011/ca_pr_ en_02022011.pdf, Accessed June 1, 2011.

3. Kraft Foods, *Creating a More Delicious World: Our 2010 World Report*, May 2011, http://www.kraftfoodscompany.com/SiteCollectionDocuments/pdf/ kraftfoods_deliciousworld.pdf, Accessed June 1, 2011; and Kraft Foods, *2010 Annual Report*.

4. Kraft Foods, *2010 Annual Report*.

5. Adbrands.net, "Kraft Foods (US)," http://www.adbrands.net/us/ kraftfoods_us.htm, Accessed June 1, 2011.

6. Kraft Foods, "Find a Job With Us," http://www.kraftfoodscompany. com/Careers/Find_a_Job_With_Us/index.aspx; and Kraft Foods, "Kraft Kitchens Experts," http://www.kraftcanada.com/en/about/experts/ KraftKitchensExperts.aspx, Both accessed November 20, 2011.

7. Giselle Tsirulnik, "Kraft Sets Bar for Food Marketing with New iPad," *MobileMarketer.com*, July 12, 2010, http://www.mobilemarketer.com/cms/ news/advertising/6775.html, Accessed June 3, 2011.

8. Sarah Kessler, "5 Invaluable Marketing Lessons from an Epic Campaign for...Cream Cheese?" *Mashable.com*, November 17, 2010, http://mashable. com/2010/11/17/cream-cheese-social-network/, Accessed June 3, 2011.

9. Briana Southward, "Diamond Shreddies," TorqueCustomerStrategy.com, May 7, 2008, http://www.torquecustomerstrategy.com/gallery_comments. php?gallery_id=42, Accessed June 3, 2011.

10. Jeromy Lloyd, "More Diamonds from Shreddies," *Marketing Magazine* (online), September 17, 2008, http://www.marketingmag.ca/news/marketer-news/ more-diamonds-from-shreddies-17677, Accessed June 3, 2011.

11. Duane D. Standford, "Kraft's Tang Makeover Led to 30% Sales Jump Abroad Last Year," *Bloomberg.com*, March 6, 2010, http://www.bloomberg.com/ apps/news?pid=newsarchive&sid=aRrQGB8IvwaM, Accessed June 3, 2011.

12. Chris Powell, "Kraft Brings Back Hockeyville to Showcase Canadian Passion for Hockey," *Marketing Magazine* (online), November 8, 2010, http:// www.marketingmag.ca/news/marketer-news/kraft-brings-back- hockeyville-to-showcase-canadian-passion-for-hockey-5869, Accessed November 17, 2010.

13. Stuart Elliott, "Kraft Hopes to Encourage Adults to Revert to a Childhood Favorite," *The New York Times (online)*, May 26, 2010, http://www.nytimes.com/2010/05/27/business/media/27adco.html, Accessed June 1, 2011.

14. Theresa Howard, "Coke Finally Scores Another Winner," *USAToday.com*, October 28, 2007, http://www.usatoday.com/money/advertising/adtrack/2007-10-28-coke-zero_N.htm, Accessed May 27, 2011.

15. Michael E. Ross, "It Seemed Like a Good Idea at the Time," *msnbc.com*, April 22, 2005, http://www.msnbc.msn.com/id/7209828, Accessed May 29, 2011.

16. Robert E. Cannon, "A Tutorial on Product Life Cycle," *MRO Today* (online), 2003, www.trainingpeople.biz/DevBus/CommonResources/productlifecycletutorial.doc, Accessed May 29, 2011.

17. "Toyota Motor Corporation," *Reuters.com*, http://www.reuters.com/finance/stocks/companyProfile?symbol=TM, Accessed May 27, 2011.

18. The Coca-Cola Company, "Growth, Leadership, Sustainability," http://www.thecoca-colacompany.com/ourcompany/index.html, Accessed May 27, 2011.

19. The Coca-Cola Company, "Product List," http://www.thecoca-colacompany.com/brands/brandlist.html, Accessed May 27, 2011.

20. General Electric Company, "Products and Services," http://www.ge.com/, Accessed May 27, 2011.

21. The Coca-Cola Company, "Products," http://www.thecoca-colacompany.com/brands/index.html, Accessed May 27, 2011.

22. Ad Council, "About," http://www.adcouncil.org/About-Us, Accessed May 28, 2011.

23. Advertising Standards Canada, "The Canadian Code of Advertising Standards," http://www.adstandards.com/en/Standards/theCode.aspx, Accessed May 28, 2011.

24. Consumers Council of Canada, "About Us," http://www.consumerscouncil.com/, Accessed May 28, 2011.

25. Association for Dressings & Sauces, "Package of the Year," October 2007, http://www.dressings-sauces.org/pressroom_poty_2007.html, Accessed May 28, 2011.

26. Campbell Company of Canada, "Soup at Hand," http://campbellsoup.ca/en/products/family.asp?fam=7, Accessed November 20, 2011.

27. Wikinvest, "Campbell Soup Company (NYSE: CPB)," http://www.wikinvest.com/stock/Campbell_Soup_Company_%28CPB%29, Accessed November 20, 2011.

28. Straight Dope, "Is there a term for 'trade names that become generic'?" http://www.straightdope.com/columns/read/1464/is-there-a-term-for-trade-names-that-become-generic, Accessed August 12, 2011.

29. Ibid.

30. Department of Justice, *Consumer Packaging and Labelling Act*, http://laws.justice.gc.ca/eng/acts/C-38/page-3.html#h-5, Accessed November 20, 2011.

31. Dan Swenson, Shahid Ansari, Jan Bell, and Il-Woon Kim, "A Field Study of Best Practices in Target Costing," *Management Accounting Quarterly*, Winter 2003, pp. 12–17.

32. Interactive Advertising Bureau and PricewaterhouseCoopers, Press Release:"Internet Advertising Revenues Again Reach New Highs, Estimated to Pass $21 Billion in 2007 and Hit Nearly $6 Billion in Q4 2007," February 25, 2008. http://www.iab.net/about_th_iab/recent_press_releases/press_release_archive/press_release/195115, Accessed June 4, 2011.

33. John Zarwan, "Direct Mail Delivers," *American Printer*, August 2006, http://www.johnzarwan.com/pubs/608APdir.pdf, Accessed June 4, 2011.

34. "2011 Superbowl Commercials Cost," http://superbowlcommercials.tv/1071.html, Accessed June 30, 2011.

35. "'Iron Man' and Audi: R8 Takes Leading Role in New Summer Blockbuster Movie 'Iron Man' from Marvel Studios and Paramount Pictures," *PRNewswire.com,* April 8, 2008, http://www.prnewswire.com/news-releases/iron-man-and-audi-r8-takes-leading-role-in-new-summer-blockbuster-movie-iron-man-from-marvel-studios-and-paramount-pictures-57301927.html, Accessed June 4, 2011.

36. Davide Dukcevich, "TV's Most Successful Products," *Forbes.com,* November 13, 2002, http://www.forbes.com/2002/11/13/cx_dd_1113products.html, Accessed June 4, 2011.

37. Scott M. Cutlip, Allen H. Center, and Glen M. Broom, *Effective Public Relations,* 9th ed. (Upper Saddle River, NJ: Pearson Prentice Hall, 2009), pp. 517–526.

38. Ibid.

39. Sandra Moriarty, Nancy Mitchell, and William Wells, *Advertising, Principles and Practices,* 8th ed. (Upper Saddle River, NJ: Pearson Prentice Hall, 2009), p. 528.

40. Neal Santelmann, "Companies That Care," *Forbes.com,* http://www.forbes.com/2004/09/29/cx_ns_0929feat.html, Accessed June 4, 2011.

41. Lisa Z. Eccles, "Point of Purchase Advertising," *Advertising Age* Supplement, September 1994, pp. 1–6.

42. Philip Kotler and Gary Armstrong, *Principles of Marketing,* 12th ed. (Upper Saddle River, NJ: Pearson Prentice Hall, 2008), p. 386.

43. Ibid.

44. Peter Cohen, "Jobs Introduces iPhone, Apple TV," *InfoWorld.com*, January 9, 2007, http://www.infoworld.com/article/07/01/09/HNiphoneappletv_1.html, Accessed June 30, 2011.

45. Associated Press, "Apple Unveils Cell Phone, Apple TV," *msnbc.com*, http://www.msnbc.msn.com/id/16542805, Accessed June 30, 2011.

46. Chris Barylick and Mathew Honan, "iPhone Release Brings Out the Crowds," *Macworld.com*, June 30, 2007, http://www.macworld.com/article/58682/2007/06/iphone_crowds.html, Accessed June 30, 2011.

47. Jim Dalrymple and Jason Snell, "Apple Sets iPhone Sights on the Long Long Haul," *PCWorld.com*, July 26, 2007, http://www.pcworld.com/article/id,135095-page,1/article.html, Accessed June 30, 2011.

48. Anna Lagerkvist, Anna, "Apple Sells One Millionth iPhone," *techradar.com*, September 9, 2007, http://www.techradar.com/news/phone-and-communications/mobile-phones/apple-sells-one-millionth-iphone-153982, Accessed June 30, 2011.

49. Steve Jobs, "Letter to All iPhone Customers," *Apple.com*, http://www.apple.com/hotnews/openiphoneletter, Accessed June 30, 2011.

Chapter 13

1. Investopedia, "Generally Accepted Accounting Principles (GAAP)," http://www.investopedia.com/terms/g/gaap.asp#axzz1eJBd9eAO, Accessed November 20, 2011.

2. Chartered Accountants of Canada, "Definition of Publicly Accountable Enterprises," http://www.cica.ca/ifrs/item2722.aspx, Accessed June 26, 2011.

3. American Institute of Certified Public Accountants, "International Financial Reporting Standards FAQs," http://www.ifrs.com/ifrs_faqs.html#q3, Accessed June 26, 2011.

4. Thomas H. Beechy et al., *Advanced Financial Accounting*, 6th ed. (Toronto: Pearson Canada, 2012), pp. 21–22.

5. Ibid., p. 4.

6. Chartered Accountants of Canada, "New Accounting Standards for Not-for-Profit Organizations – Questions for Directors to Ask," March 2011, http://www.rogb.ca/npo/npo-directors-series/director-alerts/item49752.pdf, Accessed November 21, 2011.

7. Beechy et al., *Advanced Financial Accounting*, p. 16

8. "6 Sources of Bootstrap Financing, " *Entrepreneur.com,* http://www.entrepreneur.com/money/financing/selffinancingandbootstrapping/article80204.html, Accessed June 22, 2011.

9. Cynthia E. Griffin, "Breaking the Bank: Non-bank Lenders Are Pulling Ahead in Small-Business Financing.Here's What the Playing Field Looks Like," *Entrepreneur.com,* December 4, 2011, http://findarticles.com/p/articles/mi_m0DTI/is_n3_v26/ai_20484710/pg_4/?tag=content;col1, Accessed June 22, 2011.

10. Google, "Google History," http://www.google.com/intl/en/about/corporate/company/history.html#2004, Accessed June 22, 2011.

11. "Difference Between CA and CGA," *DifferenceBetween.net,* http://www.differencebetween.net/business/finance-business-2/difference-between-ca-and-cga/, Accessed November 21, 2011.

12. "Managerial Accounting," *Encyclopedia of Business*, 2nd ed. (online), http://www.referenceforbusiness.com/encyclopedia/Man-Mix/Managerial-Accounting.html, Accessed November 21, 2011.

13. Chartered Accountants of Canada, "What Do CAs Do?" http://www.cica.ca/about-the-profession/what-do-cas-do/index.aspx, Accessed November 21, 2011.

14. Travel PLC, "About Us," http://www.tuitravelplc.com/tui/pages/aboutus/corporateprofile, Accessed November 13, 2011; Jamie Barnett, "TUI Travel Drops KPMG after Accounting Error," *Asap.com,* December 31, 2010, http://www.asap.co.uk/news/tui-travel-drops-kpmg-after-accounting-error-5635754.html; Simon Bowers, "Tui Travel Finance Director Steps Down After £117m Accounting Error," *The Guardian* (online), October 21, 2010, http://www.guardian.co.uk/business/2010/oct/21/tui-travel-finance-director-accounting-error; and Sean Farrell, "TUI Finance Director Stands Down After £117m Accounting Mistake," *The Independent* (online), http://www.independent.co.uk/news/business/news/tui-finance-director-stands-down-after-117m-accounting-mistake-2113292.html, Accessed June 24, 2011.

15. Automatic Data Processing Canada, "What Is the Sarbanes-Oxley Act and How Does It Affect Your Business?" *TheJournalofFranchise.com,* http://www.thejournaloffranchise.com/art/article.cfm?id=3, Accessed June 24, 2011.

16. "What Is Forensic Accounting and What Does a Forensic Accountant Do?" *ForensicAccountingDemystified.com*, http://forensicaccountingdemystified.com/, Accessed November 21, 2011.

17. Press, "Wyatt Pleads Guilty at U.N. Oil-For-Food Trial," *FoxNews.com,* October 10, 2007, http://www.foxnews.com/story/0,2933,298744,00.html, Accessed June 24, 2011.

18. "Toyota Motor Corporation (NYSE:TM)," *Forbes.com,* http://finapps.forbes.com/finapps/jsp/finance/compinfo/Ratios.jsp?tkr=TM, Accessed June 25, 2011.

19. Starbucks Corporation, *2010 Annual Report*, http://phx.corporate-ir.net/External.File?item=UGFyZW50SUQ9NzkzODl8Q2hpbGRJRD0tMXxUeXBlPTM=&t=1, Accessed June 25, 2011.

20. Amey Stone, "SOX: Not So Bad After All?" *Businessweek.com,* August 1, 2005, http://www.businessweek.com/bwdaily/dnflash/aug2005/nf2005081_7739_db016.htm?chan=search, Accessed June 26, 2011.

21. Google Inc., "Google History," *Google.com*, http://www.google.com/corporate/history.html, Accessed June 30, 2011.

22. Google Inc., Google 2010 Annual Report, http://investor.google.com/pdf/2010_google_annual_report.pdf, Accessed November 21, 2011.

23. Google Inc., "Our Philosophy," *Google.com*, http://www.google.com/corporate/tenthings.html, Accessed June 30, 2011.

24. Google Inc., *Google 2010 Annual Report*, http://investor.google.com/pdf/2010_google_annual_report.pdf, Accessed November 21, 2011.

Credits

Chapter 1; 3 © Kaphoto | Getstock.com; 7 Reprinted with permission from the Canadian Diabetes Association; 10t & 22t © Yuri Arcurs/Shutterstock; 10cl & 22cl © Stephen VanHorn/Shutterstock; 10cr & 22cr © Sergey150770/ Shutterstock; 10bl & 22bl © iDesign/Shutterstock; 10br & 10br © Fotokostic/ Shutterstock; 12 ASSOCIATED PRESS; 13 & 22 © Kheng Guan Toh/Shutterstock; 16 Lang shuchen – Imaginechina; 17t Reprinted with permission of the Council of Better Business Bureaus, Inc. Copyright 2009; 17b The BBB logo is owned by the Council of Better Business Bureaus, Inc. Reprinted with permission of the Council of Better Business Bureaus, Inc. Copyright 2009; 19 © Darren Baker | Getstock.com; 21 Goodshoot/Thinkstock; Chapter 2; 27 Source: Euromonitor International; 29 © Andy Dean Photography /Shutterstock; 32 istockphoto/Thinkstock; 35 Jupiterimages/© Getty Images; 38 © Pcruciatti | Getstock.com; 41 © Michael Newman/PhotoEdit; 49 Used with permission of the Bank of Canada; Chapter 3; 59 © Samrat35 | Getstock.com; 65 ASSOCIATED PRESS; 66 ASSOCIATED PRESS; 73 © Naashon Zalk/Corbis; 81 Gao lin hk – Imaginechina; 83 Courtesy of GreenStop, © GreenStop; 85 © David Young-Wolff/ PhotoEdit; Chapter 4; 93 Mark Pearson | Getstock.com; 97 © Sherwin Crasto/ Reuters/Corbis; 99 © Jbk_photography | Getstock.com; 106 © Gallo Images/ Alamy; 108 AFP/Getty Images; 114 © Christine Schneider/Corbis; Chapter 5; 121t&b Compliments of WhyHire.me Corp; 123 © Spflaum | Getstock.com; 124 © Odua | Getstock.com; 126 © Allstar Picture Library/Alamy; 129 © Svanblar/Shutterstock; 130 © Amy Walters/Shutterstock; 133 © Benjamin Gelman | Getstock.com; 135 © Denys Kuvaiev | Getstock.com; 141 © Stephen Coburn/Shutterstock; 142 © Elena Elisseeva/Shutterstock; Chapter 6; 153 ASSOCIATED PRESS; 168 ASSOCIATED PRESS; Chapter 7; 177 ASSOCIATED PRESS; 178 JupiterImages/Thinkstock; 184 © Gary Cookson/Shutterstock; 189 © Najlah Feanny/Corbis; 195t Ross Mantle/AP Images for MasterCard; 195b Bananastock/Thinkstock; 199 © Andresr | Getstock.com; Chapter 8; 207 © Yuri Arcurs/Shutterstock; 208 © Andres Rodriguez | Getstock.com; 216 ASSOCIATED PRESS; 217 ASSOCIATED PRESS; 221 © Charles Knox Photo/Shutterstock; 223 © Yuri Arcurs | Getstock.com; 224l&r Courtesy of The Home Depot Canada Foundation; 228 Ablestock.com/© Getty Images; 229 Thinkstock; 230 Wissman Design/Shutterstock; 233 David Cooper/Getstock.com; Chapter 9; 243 © Pressureua | Getstock.com; 244 Ryan McVay/ Getty Images; 247t © Choreograph (Konstantin Yuganov) | Getstock.com; 247bl & br © Andreyuu | Getstock.com; 248; Comstock/Thinkstock; 249 © Pressmaster | Getstock.com; 251 Used with Permission of Pearson Canada Inc.; 256 © Lunamarina | Getstock.com; 257 Courtesy of Charles Schwab & Co Inc.; 259tl&tc Algis Balezentis/Shutterstock 259tr Jason Stitt/Shutterstock; 259bl javarman/Shutterstock; 259bc Ken Brown/ Shutterstock; 259br mm-images/Alamy images; 261 Screenshot courtesy of Google; 263 Lee Morris/Shutterstock.com; 264 Reprinted with permission from Harley Schwadron; Chapter 10; 271 © Retska | Getstock.com; 276 Getty Images; 277t © Dikiiy | Getstock.com; 277b © Ragsac19 | Getstock.com; 279 Comstock; 282 © Nataliya Hora | Getstock.com; 284 © Robert Puglia/epa/Corbis; 288 © Photobac | Getstock.com; 290 ASSOCIATED PRESS; 292 © Lingcity | Getstock.com; Chapter 11; 299 Screenshot used with permission of Facebook. Facebook is a trademark of Facebook, Inc.; 301 © Ruaridh Stewart/ZUMA; 305t © Mim Friday/Alamy; 305btl Ingvald Kaldhussater/Shutterstock; 305btr Morgan Lane Photography/Shutterstock; 305bc Stephen Coburn/Shutterstock; 305bl Kaspars Grinvalds/Shutterstock; 305br Yanik Chauvin/Shutterstock; 306t © Jeff Greenberg/PhotoEdit; 306b IFCAR; 308 olly/Shutterstock; 313 Jacob Bøtter from Copenhagen, Denmark; 315 David Sacks/ Getty Images; 317 Losevsky Pavel/

Index